JUDAIC RELIGION
IN THE SECOND TEMPLE PERIOD

What was the Jewish religion like in the time of Jesus and the early church?

The developments in Judaism which occurred during the Second Temple period (*c*.550 BC to 100 AD) were of great importance for the nature of Jewish religion in later centuries, yet few studies have examined the era in full. Now Lester L. Grabbe's lucid and accessible volume provides a much-needed encyclopaedic study and holistic interpretation of the period. Topics examined include:

- views about God and the spirit world
- the temple and priesthood
- scripture and synagogue
- the main religious sects and revolutionary movements
- eschatology and messianism
- magic and predicting the future
- religion in the Jewish diaspora
- converts and "God-fearers"

With an extensive, up-to-date bibliography, plus numerous helpful cross-references, summaries and syntheses, this book is essential reading for scholars and students of the history of Jewish religion. It will also be of great value as a reference tool.

Lester L. Grabbe is Professor of Hebrew Bible and Early Judaism at the University of Hull. He has written extensively on the history, society and literature of ancient Israel and early Judaism. His previous publications include *Judaism from Cyrus to Hadrian* (1992) and *Priests, Prophets, Diviners, Sages* (1995).

JUDAIC RELIGION IN THE SECOND TEMPLE PERIOD

Belief and practice from the Exile to Yavneh

Lester L. Grabbe

London and New York

First published 2000
by Routledge
11 New Fetter Lane, London EC4P 4EE

Simultaneously published in the USA and Canada
by Routledge
29 West 35th Street, New York, NY 10001

Routledge is an imprint of the Taylor & Francis Group

Typeset in Baskerville by
BC Typesetting, Bristol
Printed and bound in Great Britain by
St. Edmundsbury Press, Bury St. Edmunds, Suffolk

British Library Cataloguing in Publication Data
A catalogue record for this book is available from the British Library

Library of Congress Cataloging in Publication Data
Grabbe, Lester L.
Judaic religion in the Second Temple period: belief and practice from the
Exile to Yavneh/Lester L. Grabbe.
p. cm.
Includes bibliographical references and index.
1. Judaism–History–Post-exilic period, 586 B.C.–210 A.D.
2. Bible. O.T.–Criticism, interpretation, etc. I. Title.
BM176.G68 2000
296′.09′014–dc21 00-023228

ISBN 0–415–21250–2

To
Professor Jacob Neusner
and
Professor Philip Davies

CONTENTS

Preface   xiii
List of abbreviations   xvi

1 Introduction   **1**

Aims of this study 1
Definitions 3
   Religion 3
   Judaic 5
   Second Temple period 5
Apologia pro historia mea 6
Some technical matters 9

PART I
Chronological survey   **11**

2 Persian period (539–333 BCE)   **13**
Major sources 13
   Books of Ezra and Nehemiah 13
   Haggai, Zechariah, Malachi 15
   Joel 17
   Jonah 17
   Isaiah 56–66 18
   Books of Chronicles 19
   Proverbs 21
   Job 22
   Esther 23
   Ruth 25
   Song of Songs 25
   The P Document 26

Archaeology, papyri, and coins 28
Synthesis 29

3 Early Greek period (333–200 BCE)   **37**

Major sources 37
   Hecateus of Abdera 37
   Zenon papyri 39
   The story of the Tobiads 40
   Ethiopic Enoch (*1 Enoch*) and the *Book of Giants* 41
   Qohelet (Ecclesiastes) 42
   Tobit 44
   The edicts of Antiochus III 46
   Demetrius the Chronographer 48
   The Septuagint translation of the Bible 49
   Ben Sira (Ecclesiasticus) 50
Synthesis 52

4 Later Greek period and Hasmoneans (200–63 BCE)   **59**

Major sources 59
   1 and 2 Maccabees 59
   Daniel 60
   1 Enoch 83–105 62
   Book of *Jubilees* 63
   Sibylline Oracles 3–5 64
   Judith 65
   1 Baruch 66
   Qumran scrolls 67
   Fragmentary Jewish Writers in Greek 70
   Pseudo-Hecateus 73
   Testament of Moses (Assumption of Moses) 74
   Letter of (Pseudo-)Aristeas 75
Synthesis 76

5 Under Roman rule (63 BCE–70 CE)   **84**

Major sources 84
   Psalms of Solomon 84
   3 Maccabees 86
   Wisdom of Solomon 86
   Pseudo-Phocylides 88
   Philo of Alexandria 89
   Josephus 92
   Liber Antiquitatum Biblicarum (Pseudo-Philo) 94

Adam and Eve literature 95
Similitudes (Parables) of Enoch (1 Enoch 37–71) 97
Sibylline Oracles 97
Slavonic Enoch (*2 Enoch*) 98
4 Maccabees 99
Testament of Moses 100
Testament of Abraham 100
Testaments of the Twelve Patriarchs 101
Testament of Job 104
Joseph and Asenath 105
Judean Desert manuscripts, inscriptions, and archaeology 106
Synthesis 108

6 Transition to rabbinic Judaism: Yavneh   **116**
Major sources 116
Rabbinic literature 116
Apocalypses of Ezra, Baruch, Abraham, and John 117
Sibylline Oracles 120
The reconstruction at Yavneh 120
Synthesis 124

PART II
Special topics   **127**

7 Temple and priesthood   **129**
Theological basis of the cult 129
Temple and cult 132
The physical temple 134
The cultic personnel 135
Financial support for the temple 137
The cultic rituals 138
Women and the cult 140
The cultic year: sabbath and annual festivals 141
Music and singing 143
The high priest and "the Sanhedrin" 144
Synthesis 147

8 Scripture, prayer, and synagogue   **150**
Scribes and literacy 150
Scripture and canon 152

Main texts 153
Conclusions about canonization 156
Development of the text 158
Summary about textual developments 164
Scriptural interpretation 165
Conclusions about scriptural interpretation 169
Prayer and the rise of the synagogue 170
"Popular religion" 175
Synthesis 178

9 Sects and movements   **183**
Beginnings of sectarianism 183
Sadducees and Pharisees 185
Josephus 187
New Testament 192
Rabbinic literature 194
4QMMT and the *Temple Scroll* (11QT) 196
Summary and conclusions 196
Essenes 199
Sources 200
The question of Qumran 201
Some tentative conclusions 205
Other sects and groups 206
Synthesis 206

10 Concepts of the Deity and the spirit world   **210**
Developing views about God 210
Ancient Israel 212
Innovations during the Second Temple period 215
The question of monotheism 216
The spirit world 219
Main texts 220
Summary on angelic beings 224
The figure of Wisdom and the Logos 225
Main texts 225
Summary of the figure of Wisdom 227
The Logos tradition 228
Synthesis 230

**11 Prophecy, apocalypticism, the esoteric arts, and
predicting the future**   **232**
Problems of definition 232

Did prophecy cease in the Second Temple period? 236
  Main texts 237
  Conclusions 239
The esoteric arts and their use 241
  Astrology 241
  Dreams 243
  Textual interpretation 245
  Chronography 246
  Magic, mysticism, and controlling the spirits 248
Prophetic and charismatic individuals 251
Synthesis 254

12 Eschatologies and ideas of salvation   **257**
Main texts 257
Synthesis 266
  Personal eschatology: ideas about life after death 267
  Heavens and hells 268
  Cosmic eschatology: expectations about the end of the world 269

13 Messiahs   **271**
Main texts 271
  Hebrew Bible 271
  Ben Sira 273
  Qumran scrolls 273
  Psalms of Solomon 276
  Similitudes of Enoch (1 Enoch 37–71) 276
  Philo 276
  Josephus 278
  4 Ezra/*2 Baruch* 279
  Sibylline Oracles 280
  New Testament 280
  Rabbinic literature 281
The "Son of Man" 282
Sicarii, Zealots, and other "revolutionary" groups 283
  General comments 284
  The "Fourth Philosophy" and the Sicarii 285
  Zealots 287
Synthesis 288

14 Jews and Judaism in the Hellenistic world   **292**
How they saw themselves 292
  Jewish identity and conversion 292

Ideology of the land and the concept of exile 297
Gender and sexuality 300
How others saw them 305
Philo-Judaism and anti-Judaism 305
Religious tolerance 308
Synthesis 310

PART III
Conclusion   **313**

**15 Judaism in the Second Temple period: a holistic
    perspective**   **315**

Bibliography   335
Indexes   387
    Index of modern authors   387
    Index of names and subjects   396
    Index of citations   407

PREFACE

As will be explained in Chapter 1, this is a companion to my book *Judaism from Cyrus to Hadrian* (*JCH*). That 1992 work had as its primary aim to be a history of Second Temple Judaism. To cover such a large entity, even in two volumes, required that much be treated only in concise form, but the work was intended to be a contribution of synthesis and to take its place alongside parallel one-volume histories of ancient Israel. Unfortunately, in describing my aims, I took for granted the main aim and only explicitly mentioned the subsidiary aim of providing a handbook for students and scholars. The result is that a number of reviewers, perhaps not wishing to wade through nearly 800 pages, assumed the work was meant to be only a textbook and dealt with it accordingly. Some further comments and a list of the main reviews are given below.

The present work has had to be written under some constraints. Given the ideal conditions of time and space, I would have written a much more stand-alone volume, or perhaps even have incorporated the contents of this book into a enlarged version of the earlier history since I do not believe that Judaic religion can ultimately be isolated from the rest of Jewish history. We never work under ideal conditions, however; this book has been written with too many other distractions, not least the pressures of university administration. Also, despite the generosity of the publisher, some restrictions had to be placed on the length of the book. In other circumstances, the length here might be considered more than adequate, but not for such a large topic as Second Temple religion. Thus, I have had to omit planned chapters on the Samaritans (but see *JCH*:502–7, and Grabbe 1993b), Gnostic and mystical trends (but see *JCH*:507–11, 514–19, and Grabbe 1996a: 94–110), and gender and sexuality (though some of this is included in the text at various points). In a number of cases, I would have included a treatment of some relevant subjects here that I had also discussed elsewhere, but in order to keep to the prescribed length I have had to refer the reader to my other studies for details. Thus, there are more cross-references to *JCH* (and other studies) than I would have liked.

The reviews of *JCH* that have come to my attention are the following:

Alexander, P. S. (1993) *Society for Old Testament Study Book List*: 135–36
Holladay, Carl R. (1995) *SPA* 7: 231–36
Mason, S. (1994) "Method in the Study of Early Judaism: A Dialogue with Lester Grabbe", *JAOS* 115: 463–72
Price, J. J. (January 1994) *IOUDAIOS Review* 4.003: 1–6
Rajak, T. (1995) *Society for Old Testament Study Book List*: 149–50
Saldarini, A. J. (1993) *CBQ* 55: 580–81
VanderKam, J. C. (1994) *Interpretation* 48: 291–93
Wright, J. W. (1993) *AUSS* 31: 245–46

Of course, authors are never happy with anything but complete adulation, and there is a temptation to reply to any points in reviews that are not overwhelmingly positive. I shall resist this temptation for the most part but will comment briefly on a few points. Most of the reviews limited themselves to one or two aspects of the work, because of lack of either time and space, or expertise, but this can leave a misleading impression. For example, my chapter on the post-70 period was not intended to be as full as the other chapters, yet one review focused almost entirely on this section. Another chided me – after I had covered almost seven centuries, which few such histories have done – for not continuing on into the rabbinic period. I was strangely faulted for not taking account of publications which did not in fact appear until after I sent my manuscript to press in late 1990. On specific reviews, I have replied to some of Steve Mason's comments in a separate contribution (Grabbe 2000e). The most comprehensive – and helpful review – was that of Jonathan Price on the electronic journal *IOUDAIOS Review* (whose excellent book on the siege of Jerusalem unfortunately appeared too late for me to use); however, he queried whether my title might indicate some sort of ideology because it used "Cyrus" and "Hadrian", both non-Jews, as chronological markers. I find this a bit humorous since my original title was quite different, and I evolved the title that eventually appeared in conjunction with the suggestions and requirements of the publishers. Lest I sound complaining, I hasten to add that almost all of these reviews (apart from one short one that dismissed the book apparently without reading it) have been helpful, and I thank the reviewers.

We now come to the dedication of this book. In my work on Judaism, I have been influenced by many people. Like all of us, I am beholden to the giants of nineteenth- and twentieth-century scholarship such as Bickerman and Tcherikover. Of living scholars I could mention many contemporaries, quite a few of whom I have worked with personally, whose specialties range from the biblical text to the Scrolls, to Josephus and the Greco-Roman world. To list any can be invidious because I am bound to omit someone who should be included, but with apologies for anyone overlooked I mention Robert Carroll, Amélie Kuhrt, Pierre Briant, Sebastian Brock, Michael Knibb, Philip Alexander, George Brooke, Martin Goodman, Tessa Rajak, Stefan

Reif, Shaye Cohen, John Collins, Burton Mack, John Bartlett, Hans Barstad, Joseph Blenkinsopp, and Eugene Ulrich. However, two individuals have stamped my work on early Judaism more than any others, in quite different ways.

I read Jacob Neusner's *From Politics to Piety* in the spring of 1994 at a time when I was trying to break free from biblical fundamentalism. It was like a revelation, not only articulating many of the thoughts I had been having about religious authority but also showing the critical and analytical approach necessary to come to grips with religious texts from a historical perspective. I went on to *Development of a Legend, Rabbinic Traditions about the Pharisees before 70, Eliezer ben Hyrcanus*, and many more (no doubt Jack would now regard these as among his juvenilia!). Although I can claim to have read only a fraction of his output, those writings relating to Second Temple Judaism have continued to be a fount of scholarly wisdom which I seek out with an avid thirst. Much of Jack's work is on rabbinic and later Judaism, areas for which I claim no specialist competence nor feel in a position to take sides in the many debates. But when it comes to historical arguments, I do claim to know something, and whatever weaknesses there are in those pioneering works they ask the right questions, they show how to analyze sources, and they point toward possible answers. I have often spoken of the "Neusnerian revolution", orally and in print. Sometimes this term has been objected to by editors and others, but to me it is still the only way to describe a phenomenon which has changed the field so dramatically.

I cannot begin to count the number of discussions and debates I have had with Philip Davies (though those in a sober state are probably in the minority), but I have never found him less than thought-provoking, and he seems to be an inexhaustible source of new ideas. I often disagree, but that doesn't matter; the intellectual stimulation is exhilarating. I have seen him argue positions quite at odds with those only just taken in another context, but this is typical of his questing mind. He has written some classic articles, such as "*Hasidim* in the Maccabean Period" (*JJS* 28 [1977] 127–40, and it irritates me to see how often it gets overlooked). However, it is with his controversialist writings that he has probably made the most impact, such as his *In Search of "Ancient Israel"*. I am still not sure how far I am willing to follow him in his conclusions, but it was one of the reasons I founded the European Seminar on Methodology in Israel's History (of which Philip is an enthusiastic member and supporter). This is an occasion to wish him well in his (very early!) retirement from the Sheffield Department of Biblical Studies but also to hope that it will mean only a greater amount of time devoted to scholarship.

Lester L. Grabbe
Kingston-upon-Hull
5 November 1999

ABBREVIATIONS

NB: Standard abbreviations are used for the biblical books. For the writings of Philo and classical authors, see the editions of their writings where the abbreviations will be obvious. A few abbreviations of Pseudepigrapha are given here because they might cause problems to non-specialists.

AB	Anchor Bible
ABD	D. N. Freedman (ed.) (1992) *Anchor Bible Dictionary*
AfO	*Archiv für Orientforschung*
Ag. Apion	Josephus, *Against Apion*
AGAJU	Arbeiten zur Geschichte des antiken Judentums und des Urchristentums
ALGHJ	Arbeiten zur Literatur und Geschichte des hellenistischen Judentums
A.M.	*anno mundi*, a dating system which begins with the supposed date of the world's creation
AnBib	Analecta biblica
ANET	J. B. Pritchard (ed.) *Ancient Near Eastern Texts*
ANRW	*Aufstieg und Niedergang der römischen Welt*
Ant.	Josephus, *Antiquities of the Jews*
AP	A. Cowley (1923) *Aramaic Papyri of the Fifth Century B.C.*
APOT	R. H. Charles (ed.) (1913a) *Apocrypha and Pseudepigrapha of the Old Testament*
AUSS	*Andrews University Seminary Studies*
BA	*Biblical Archeologist*
BAR	*Biblical Archaeology Review*
BASOR	*Bulletin of the American Schools of Oriental Research*
BCE	Before the Common Era (= BC)
BETL	Bibliotheca Ephemeridum Theologicarum Lovaniensium
BHS	*Biblia Hebraica Stuttgartensis*
BiOr	Biblica et Orientalia
BJS	Brown Judaic Studies
BZAW	Beihefte zur *ZAW*

BZNW	Beihefte zur *ZNW*
CBQ	*Catholic Biblical Quarterly*
CBQMS	*Catholic Biblical Quarterly* Monograph Series
CE	Common Era (= AD)
ConB	Conjectanea biblica
CPJ	V. A. Tcherikover, *et al.* (1957–64) *Corpus Papyrorum Judaicarum*
CRINT	Compendia rerum iudaicarum ad Novum Testamentum
CR: BS	*Currents in Research: Biblical Studies*
CSCT	Columbia Studies in Classical Texts
*DDD/DDD*²	K. van der Toorn, B. Becking, and P. W. van der Horst (eds) *Dictionary of Deities and Demons in the Bible*: 1st edn 1995 (= *DDD*); 2nd edn 1999 (= *DDD*²)
DJD	Discoveries in the Judaean Desert
DSD	*Dead Sea Discoveries*
ESHM	European Seminar in Historical Methodology
ET	English translation
FAT	Forschungen zum Alten Testament
FRLANT	Forschungen zur Religion und Literatur des Alten und Neuen Testaments
FS	Festschrift
GLAJJ	M. Stern (1974–84) *Greek and Latin Authors on Jews and Judaism*
HdO	Handbuch der Orientalistik
HSCP	*Harvard Studies in Classical Philology*
HSM	Harvard Semitic Monographs
HSS	Harvard Semitic Studies
HTR	*Harvard Theological Review*
HUCA	*Hebrew Union College Annual*
ICC	International Critical Commentary
IDB	G. A. Buttrick (ed.) (1962) *Interpreter's Dictionary of the Bible*
IDBSup	Supplementary volume to *IDB* (1976)
IEJ	*Israel Exploration Journal*
JANES	*Journal of the Ancient Near Eastern Society of Columbia University*
JAOS	*Journal of the American Oriental Society*
JBL	*Journal of Biblical Literature*
JCH	L. L. Grabbe (1992) *Judaism from Cyrus to Hadrian*, 2 vols but with continuous pagination
JCS	*Journal of Cuneiform Studies*
JEA	*Journal of Egyptian Archaeology*
JHS	*Journal of Hellenic Studies*
JJS	*Journal of Jewish Studies*
JLBM	G. W. E. Nickelsburg (1981) *Jewish Literature between the Bible and the Mishnah*
JNES	*Journal of Near Eastern Studies*
JQR	*Jewish Quarterly Review*

JR	*Journal of Religion*
JRS	*Journal of Roman Studies*
JSHRZ	Jüdische Schriften aus hellenistisch-römischer Zeit
JSJ	*Journal for the Study of Judaism*
JSJSup	Supplements to *Journal for the Study of Judaism*
JSNT	*Journal for the Study of the New Testament*
JSOT	*Journal for the Study of the Old Testament*
JSOTSup	Journal for the Study of the Old Testament – Supplementary Series
JSP	*Journal for the Study of the Pseudepigrapha*
JSPSup	Journal for the Study of the Pseudepigrapha – Supplementary Series
JSS	*Journal of Semitic Studies*
JTS	*Journal of Theological Studies*
JWSTP	M. E. Stone (ed.) (1984) *Jewish Writings of the Second Temple Period*
KAI	H. Donner and W. Röllig (1962–64) *Kanaanäische und aramäische Inschriften*
KAT	Kommentar zum Alten Testament
KTU	Dietrich, M., O. Loretz, and J. Sanmartín (eds) (1995) *The Cuneiform Alphabetic Texts from Ugarit, Ras Ibn Hani and Other Places*, 2nd, enlarged edn
LAB	*Liber Antiquitatum Biblicarum* (*Book of Biblical Antiquities* or Pseudo-Philo)
LCL	Loeb Classical Library
Life	Josephus, *Life*
LXX	Septuagint translation of the OT
NJPS	New Jewish Publication Society translation of the Hebrew Bible
NovT	*Novum Testamentum*
NovTSup	Novum Testamentum, Supplements
NRSV	New Revised Standard Version
NT	New Testament
NTS	*New Testament Studies*
OBO	Orbis Biblicus et Orientalis
OT	Old Testament/Hebrew Bible
OTL	Old Testament Library
OTP	J. H. Charlesworth (ed.) (1983–85) *Old Testament Pseudepigrapha*
OTS	Oudtestamentische Studiën
PVTG	Pseudepigrapha Veteris Testamenti graece
RB	*Revue biblique*
REB	Revised English Bible
REJ	*Revue des études juives*
RevQ	*Revue de Qumran*

RSR	*Religious Studies Review*
RSV	Revised Standard Version
SBL	Society of Biblical Literature
SBLASP	SBL Abstracts and Seminar Papers
SBLBMI	SBL Bible and its Modern Interpreters
SBLDS	SBL Dissertation Series
SBLEJL	SBL Early Judaism and its Literature
SBLMS	SBL Monograph Series
SBLSCS	SBL Septuagint and Cognate Studies
SBLSPS	SBL Seminar Papers Series
SBLTT	SBL Texts and Translations
Schürer	E. Schürer (1973–87), *The Jewish People in the Age of Jesus Christ* (revised G. Vermes, *et al.*)
SCI	*Scripta Classica Israelica*
SFSHJ	South Florida Studies in the History of Judaism
SJLA	Studies in Judaism in Late Antiquity
SJOT	*Scandinavian Journal of the Old Testament*
SNTSMS	Society for New Testament Studies Monograph Series
SPA	*Studia Philonica Annual*
SPB	Studia postbiblica
SR	*Studies in Religion/Sciences religieuses*
STDJ	Studies on the Texts of the Desert of Judah
SVTP	Studia in Veteris Testamenti pseudepigrapha
TAD	B. Porten and A. Yardeni (1986–) *Textbook of Aramaic Documents from Ancient Egypt: 1–*
TDNT	G. Kittel and G. Friedrich (eds) (1964–76) *Theological Dictionary of the New Testament*
TSAJ	Texte und Studien zum antiken Judentum
TSSI	J. C. L. Gibson (1975–82) *Textbook of Syrian Semitic Inscriptions*
VAE	*Vita Adae et Euae (Life of Adam and Eve)*
VT	*Vetus Testamentum*
VTSup	Vetus Testamentum, Supplements
War	Josephus, *War of the Jews*
WBC	Word Bible Commentary
WMANT	Wissenschaftliche Monographien zum Alten und Neuen Testament
WUNT	Wissenschaftliche Untersuchungen zum Neuen Testament
ZAW	*Zeitschrift für die Alttestamentlichen Wissenschaft*
ZNW	*Zeitschrift für die Neutestamentlichen Wissenschaft*
ZPE	*Zeitschrift für Papyrologie und Epigraphik*

1

INTRODUCTION

AIMS OF THIS STUDY

Albertz, R. (1994) *A History of Israelite Religion in the Old Testament Period.*

Barclay, J. M. G. (1996) *Jews in the Mediterranean Diaspora from Alexander to Trajan (323 BCE–117 CE).*

Boccaccini, G. (1991) *Middle Judaism: Jewish Thought, 300 B.C.E. to 200 C.E.*

Cohen, S. J. D. (1987) *From the Maccabees to the Mishnah.*

—— (1999) *The Beginnings of Jewishness: Boundaries, Varieties, Uncertainties.*

Grabbe, L. L. (1992a) *Judaism from Cyrus to Hadrian: Vol. I: Persian and Greek Periods; Vol. II: Roman Period* (pagination continuous through both volumes).

Maccoby, Hyam (1989) *Judaism in the First Century.*

Maier, J. (1990) *Zwischen den Testamenten: Geschichte und Religion in der Zeit des zweiten Tempels.*

Neusner, J. (1996) Review of G. Boccaccini, *Middle Judaism*, *JSJ* 27: 334–38.

Neusner, J., A. J. Avery-Peck, and W. S. Green (eds) (2000) *The Encyclopaedia of Judaism.*

Niehr, H. (1998) *Religionen in Israels Umwelt.*

Sanders, E. P. (1992) *Judaism: Practice and Belief 63 BCE–66 CE.*

Schiffman, L. H. (1991) *From Text to Tradition: A History of Second Temple and Rabbinic Judaism.*

This book is first and foremost a synthetic history of religion among the Jewish people during a significant period in their history. In format and content it is designed to be a companion to my *Judaism from Cyrus to Hadrian*, a two-volume history which covered all aspects of Jewish life including religion (see the Preface to this volume, p. xiii). The purpose of the present volume is to focus purely on the religious side of Judaism and leave the details of political, social, and economic history to the larger work. This will allow a greater concentration on original sources, a more detailed look at the religious belief and practice, and a chance to update in areas where the earlier work is already becoming dated. Like my *Judaism from Cyrus to Hadrian*, the present book has as its primary aim to contribute to the field by presenting an overall synthesis and interpretation, though I hope also to make original contributions in some individual areas as well.

Although this study is a synthesis – with working scholars as a prime target – every effort has been expended to make it accessible to scholars in other areas, to students, and to others who are not specialists. For this reason, I quote original sources in English translation and try to cite English translations of secondary sources where available. I have also tried to be as complete as practicable in secondary studies, though the sheer volume in some areas means that only the most important or recent works are listed. However, because this supplements *JCH*, much of the bibliography in that work is not repeated. Approximately half the thousand or so bibliographical items in this book were published in 1990 or later, a sign of the astonishing scholarly activity in the field of Second Temple studies at the moment.

Several other recent volumes overlap in their aims or in the ground covered, and a word should be said about where and why I differ from them. Sanders (1992) aims to convey to the reader what it would have been like to live in Jewish society in the late Second Temple period. This is a very laudable – even brave – attempt and to some extent succeeds. My main criticism (even though there are many areas where we agree) is a methodological one: in order to gain enough data to give the picture he wants, Sanders often draws indiscriminately on sources separated by hundreds and even thousands of years in date (the OT, Josephus, the NT, rabbinic literature) with questions of reliability, credibility, development, and interpretation left unaddressed. My approach in the present study is to delineate the extent and limits of our knowledge by carefully indicating what the data are and the problems with interpreting them. As will become clear, it is often impossible to know how Judaism worked in actual daily life because such data have not been preserved. There is nothing wrong with taking the little information we have and producing an imaginative reconstruction, as long as it is carefully labeled for what it is, but such reconstructions too often take on a reality of their own and become treated as "facts" themselves.

In a very small compass, Cohen (1987) surveys some of the main areas of belief and practice. He is normally careful to distinguish between data taken from Second Temple sources and those from rabbinic literature. Maccoby's little book (1989) unfortunately sees everything through the eyes of traditional rabbinic Judaism and shows little knowledge of developments in Jewish studies for the past twenty years. Maier (1990) gives an intelligent overview, though his book could have benefited from more sections of synthesis. Schiffman (1991) is very good on the Dead Sea Scrolls and rabbinic literature, but he gives few references to primary data and only a general reading guide rather than exact references to secondary studies. Boccaccini's volume (1991) has some useful information on aspects of the topic but is somewhat unfocused, covers an odd period of time, and is hardly a complete treatment of belief, much less practice (see the review by Neusner 1996). Also, his attempt to clarify matters by new terminology, done with the best of intent, has in turn created its own problems, and his designation "Middle Judaism" has not caught on. Barclay (1996) gives a good account of the Diaspora.

The present study has much in common with Albertz's (1994) two-volume work which appeared in the German original at about the same time as my *Judaism from Cyrus to Hadrian* and had certain similarities in size and format. They naturally overlap because Albertz is interested in including the "post-exilic" period, bringing his account down to the Maccabean period. As will be clear in those areas where our studies overlap, I have found Albertz's work stimulating and have learned much from it, but I also differ from it in a number of aspects of approach and also in many individual interpretations. Niehr (1998) has provided a useful model of how to write about the religions in this region and, although his work overlaps with mine only briefly, it provides an important example of how such works should be done.

A further characterization of my work is given below (pp. 6–9) when I discuss how I approach the writing of history.

DEFINITIONS

Barstad, H. M. (1996) *The Myth of the Empty Land: A Study in the History and Archaeology of Judah During the "Exilic" Period.*

Grabbe, L. L. (ed.) (1998b) *Leading Captivity Captive: The "Exile" as History and Ideology.*

——— (1999a) "Israel's Historical Reality after the Exile", in B. Becking and M. Korpel (eds) *The Crisis of Israelite Religion: Transformation of Religious Tradition in Exilic and Post-Exilic Times*: 9–32.

Idinopulos, T. A. and B. C. Wilson (eds) (1998) *What Is Religion? Origins, Definitions, and Explanations.*

Neusner, J. (1991) *Judaism as Philosophy.*

——— (1992) *The Transformation of Judaism: From Philosophy to Religion.*

Scott, J. M. (ed.) (1997) *Exile: Old Testament, Jewish, and Christian Conceptions.*

The purpose of definitions is to clarify and aid understanding, not to obfuscate, and certainly not to become a focus in themselves and distract discussion. The following discussion is meant only to clarify to the reader what I am trying to do in this book.

Religion

"Religion" is very difficult to define. The languages of the ancient Near East and Mediterranean world had no word that corresponds to "religion" as used in most modern European languages (the Latin word *religio*, from which we get "religion", indicated scrupulousness or conscientiousness but included more than just the religious sphere). We all have a basic core of meaning in mind when we use the word; the problem is to set its boundaries. For example, how does one distinguish "religion" and "magic"? What definition of religion can be sufficiently broad to take in what we all agree are religious belief and practices without also including ideologies such as Communism or leisure pursuits such as football fanaticism or ardent trainspotting? A common definition is to relate religion to activities concerning the divine, but even this falls down in the case of Buddhism. There is also the perennial problem of Confucianism and even the ancient Greek philosophies. Can these, including Stoicism and Pythagoreanism, justifiably be called religions as well as philosophies? Indeed, Neusner has recently argued that rabbinic Judaism began in a philosophical mode and then developed to religion and then theology (Neusner 1991, 1992). Some recent studies (e.g. Idinopulos and Wilson 1998) have illustrated the problem and shown the variety of approaches used in the past, unfortunately without producing a more workable one. Without taking further space to discuss this knotty question, I propose to include the following sorts of mental and physical activity under the discussion of Judaic religion:

- beliefs about the deity and a spirit world
- Temple and altar cult and regulations relating to them (tithes, priestly dues and regulations)
- purity observances
- prayer
- scriptures and their study
- veneration of holy places and persons
- the "esoteric arts" (magic, divination, and mysticism)
- sects and movements (though whether some of these are religious can be debated)
- eschatology (including beliefs about salvation, reward and punishment, an afterlife, and messianism)

It is often asserted that the ancients did not distinguish between religion and other aspects of culture in the way that moderns do. This is correct up to a point, with some caveats: it actually ignores the fact that many modern people in the Western world regard religion as an integral part of their way of life and thus do not make a distinction between religion and society, either; on the other hand, the ancients were clearly able to differentiate between cultural aspects which relate to what we call religion (the gods, temples, sacred entities, piety, sacrilege) and other aspects of their culture. One of the most obvious examples was marking off the activities of the temple from those of the mundane world. Activities which might be acts of worship (e.g. sacrifice and prayer) produced a different mental set from those used to gain food, clothing, and shelter. Those deeds that might attract the wrath of God or those claiming to act on his behalf (violation of purity or sanctity, and even many crimes) were distinguished from other deeds. In that sense, one could speak of a conscious separation between the religious and the secular spheres by pre-moderns. It was also recognized by the Persians, Greeks, and Romans that the Jews were different. Some of these peculiarities were seen simply as ethnic customs, but it was widely recognized that the Jews did certain things because this was considered necessary by their God.

Judaic

The terms "Judaism", "Jewish", and "Judaic" have become matters of considerable debate in recent years (cf. Cohen 1999). Are the terms religious or ethnic? At what historical point should the terms begin to be used? Are they to be used interchangeably with "Israel", "Israelite", and the like? The question of who is a Jew and Jewish identity are discussed on pp. 292–97 below. For present purposes, I include under Judaic those individuals and communities labeled "Jewish" in the sources (e.g. *Yehudi/Yehudim, Iouda/Ioudaios/Ioudaioi, Judaea/Judaeus/Judaei/Judaicus*). In the few cases where such terminology is not used, I include communities and individuals worshiping Yhwh or the God of the Jews or observing practices associated only with Jews according to present information. There are still occasionally questions, especially about the identity of particular writings and whether they are Jewish in origin (e.g. the *Testaments of the Twelve Patriarchs*; these are discussed and their use as sources delineated in each case).

Second Temple period

The term "Second Temple", referring to Judaism and to a specific historical period, has become established in recent years. The term "Early Judaism" is often used as a synonym, though there is a certain ambiguity to it since some want to include rabbinic Judaism in the term. (Boccaccini's "Middle Judaism" has not become widely accepted and, in my opinion, creates confusion rather than the clarity it was intended to bring.) The strict dates of 539 BCE to 70 CE might be given for this period, but it is more useful to think of it as defined by the exilic period at the beginning and the Yavnean period at the end. This recognizes that both these periods were transitions to something else which represents an entity with its own characteristics and dynamics, even though there were many continuities. The Second Temple period began in the trauma of the "exile" and ended in the trauma of the 66–70 war with Rome.

Some scholars have recently questioned the accuracy and even usefulness of the term "exile" (see the essays and discussion in Grabbe 1998b; cf. Scott

1997). True, recent scholarship has emphasized that only a minority of the population of Judah was removed from the land after Nebuchadnezzar's conquest of Jerusalem about 587/586 BCE (Barstad 1996); nevertheless, this loss of statehood and monarchy created a physical and ideological crisis that left its mark in many ways, regardless of whether "exile and return" is a historical fact as opposed to a theological one. The broad period of the fall of Jerusalem, the destruction of the temple, the loss of statehood, and the incorporation of Judah formally as a province into a series of Near Eastern empires marked an important watershed in the history of the region and its peoples. Similarly, the consequences of a disastrous war, the permanent loss of the temple, and the end of apocalyptic hopes created a new situation both traumatic and fruitful after 70 CE, even if exactly what happened in the following decades cannot yet be reconstructed in great detail.

The Judaic communities and religion after 587/586 BCE incorporated much from an earlier period (Grabbe 1999a), and much continued in one form or another after 70. The Second Temple period had its own defining characteristics for Judaic religion, however, and the dynamics through this period require that it be treated as a whole. Many treatments begin "Judaism" with the coming of Greek rule to the Near East, and Alexander's conquests are quite important. Yet the sharp changes so often assumed to coincide with the coming of Greek rule are exaggerated: the real break had come two hundred years earlier at the time of the Neo-Babylonian and Persian empires. Data from both the First Temple period and from the rabbinic period can be used with profit for understanding Second Temple Judaism, but the Second Temple period is a self-contained entity that needs to be studied and understood in its own right.

APOLOGIA PRO HISTORIA MEA

Barstad, H. M. (1997) "History and the Hebrew Bible", in L. L. Grabbe (ed.) *Can a "History of Israel" Be Written?*: 37–64.

Evans, R. J. (1997) *In Defence of History*.

Grabbe, L. L. (1997g) "Are Historians of Ancient Palestine Fellow Creatures – Or Different Animals?" in L. L. Grabbe (ed.) *Can a "History of Israel" Be Written?*: 19–36.

—— (ed.) (1998b) *Leading Captivity Captive: The "Exile" as History and Ideology*.

—— (1998c) "'The Exile' under the Theodolite: Historiography as Triangulation", in L. L. Grabbe (ed.) *Leading Captivity Captive: "The Exile" as History and Ideology*: 80–100.

—— (2000h) "Hat die Bibel doch recht? A Review of T. L. Thompson's *The Bible in History*", *SJOT*, 14: 114–38.

Jenkins, K. (1991) *Re-Thinking History*.

—— (ed.) (1997) *The Postmodern History Reader*.

McCullagh, C. B. (1998) *The Truth of History*.

Scott, J. M. (ed.) (1997) *Exile: Old Testament, Jewish, and Christian Conceptions*.

Thompson, T. L. (1999) *The Bible in History: How Writers Create a Past* (UK title); *The Mythic Past: Biblical Archaeology and the Myth of Israel* (American title).

It is appropriate that I make explicit my approach to writing history and also why my history of Judaic religion will differ from that of others. There is currently a debate among historians about how to write history, in part a response to post-modernism (cf. Barstad 1997; Evans 1997; Jenkins 1991). It seems to me that there are insights to be gained from the post-modernist challenge (cf. Evans 1997: 243–49), and yet those claiming to be post-modernists do not seem necessarily to have escaped the normal requirements of evaluating data and arguing their case (cf. Evans 1997; McCullagh 1998). Those who claim that writing a history of the past is impossible are not usually professional historians – for obvious reasons! For all his pretensions to challenge the way history has been done for centuries, a scholar such as Jenkins (1991) seems only to adumbrate in a somewhat radical guise a lot of what historians do as a matter of routine. The idea that history can be "objective" or "scientific" in an absolute sense has long been given up; nevertheless, there are still many who feel that a limited form of objectivity is possible (cf. McCullagh 1998: 129–33). Historians are constrained by their data and most judgments, however subjective they may be, are made within certain limits and are far from being purely arbitrary.

Lest we become too obsessed with theory in how to write history, historians by and large seem to be getting on with their job without concerning themselves too much with the great debate – certainly those known to me seem to do so. The medieval and modern historians of my acquaintance are concerned about access to archives, computerized primary data (e.g. the Domesday Book), databanks of secondary studies, and the arguments of those in their specialized fields. Classical historians want to know about new discoveries to supplement their meager fund of primary material and new interpretations of the well-known sources. The debates that so exercise some in biblical studies affect them little, by all appearances. I have discussed my own approach in general several times (Grabbe 1997g, 1998c). My method can be characterized as follows, including where and why I perhaps differ from some other writers on this period:

1. My basic approach is the classical one of focusing on original sources and then working outward from the detailed study of these sources to broader conclusions. This is why most chapters (or major chapter sections) in this book first survey the original sources and their main contribution to our knowledge of Judaic religion. The approach is essentially inductive, with the broader picture developed empirically rather than beginning with a grand scheme which is then imposed on the data.

2. I try to make explicit the reasons for my judgments. Every stage of historical work involves judgment, and there are no uninterpreted data. Subjective evaluation is made at every stage, at both micro- and macro-levels; other historians may take the same data and come to different judgments. This to be expected, but scholars should always make clear what their arguments are. Although objectivity in the proper scientific sense is not possible, I do believe that a limited form of objectivity is still not only desirable but essential. There are limits imposed by the sources and proper method, and some interpetations are better than others. For this reason, scholars should also be willing to say when they do not know. There is nothing wrong with speculation, but speculation should always be plainly identified and remain that; how often has speculation at one stage suddenly become the solid basis for the next stage in the argument! The state of our ignorance must always be kept in mind and acknowledged.

3. To the best of my knowledge I do not have an agenda beyond a scholarly one. That is, I do not see my history as serving some political or religious aim. Of course, all of us as scholars have the desire to be recognized, gain a good reputation, and be promoted to a post that pays a decent salary (whatever amount that should be), and our scholarly writings are an aid to that and thus not completely disinterested. But my study is not aimed at interests beyond the academy, and judgments in it are based on academic criteria – however subjective these may be. It is meant to be a description of a bygone age and has no agenda for modern times, whether for modern politics of the Middle East or disputes within the present-day synagogue (or the Christian church, for that matter). It certainly has no intention of denigrating ancient Judaism but it also has no desire to idealize it, either. It eschews, as far as possible, heroes and villains; on the other hand, in seeking to redress the balance with regard to some who have been regarded as heroes (e.g. Nehemiah) or villains (e.g. Herod) it may emphasize certain negative or positive aspects in a way to achieve this balance.

4. While recognizing the importance and value of social and economic drivers to history, I am also convinced that ideas can also be powerful forces of change and that individuals can make a difference. Recognizing the importance of ideology in history is perhaps one of the insights of post-modernism over modernism (cf. Evans 1997: 248), though this is hardly new (Weber knew how important ideas could be).

5. Few other works have attempted to cover the whole of the Second Temple period. This attempt to interpret the entire period holistically has distinct advantages over other works which are narrowly focused, but it also has the dangers of breadth. In trying to cover seven centuries, I have been very conscious that there is hardly an area where there is not someone more expert than I. For that reason, although the emphasis is always on original sources, this study tries to be up to date with current debate and take account of it. Hence, the length of the secondary bibliography.

SOME TECHNICAL MATTERS

This book is very much a companion and supplement to *JCH*. Limitations of space have meant that matters treated fully in *JCH* are not repeated here, except in certain areas where the subject was quite important for religion (e.g. the various sects). In that case, an updated version of the section of *JCH* is included here. Where relevant information is found in *JCH*, cross-references are often made to it. Some may feel that the name "Grabbe" occurs too frequently in the bibliographies, but I plead necessity: I have written elsewhere on quite a few of the topics related to the present study. Ideally, I would have repeated that treatment here, along with full bibliography, but limitations of space have meant that only an outline of the argument could be given, or perhaps not even that; therefore, references to a fuller or related discussion of mine are given where required.

The transliteration of Hebrew should be clear to those who know the language. I have used *v* and *f* for the non-*dagesh*ed forms of *bet* and *pe*, while *w* is always used for *waw* (even though now pronounced *v* by most modern users of Hebrew). Unless otherwise indicated, English translations of the Hebrew Bible are taken from the NJPS (New Jewish Publication Society) version; of the Apocrypha, from the REB (Revised English Bible); of the Pseudepigrapha, from *OTP* (Charlesworth); of the Dead Sea Scrolls, from García Martínez/Tigchelaar 1997–98; of classical texts (including Philo and Josephus), from the LCL (Loeb Classical Library).

I use a number of words purely as descriptive terms without any political or sectarian motivation: Old Testament (OT) and Hebrew Bible are normally used interchangeably to mean the collection of writings found in the present Hebrew canon. However, if I am referring to the Septuagint version or any other which includes the Deutero-canonical books, I shall use "OT" (or "Septuagint"); it has no sectarian or theological significance. "Palestine" is purely a geographical term, used because it has been widely accepted for many years and because it is difficult to find a suitable substitute. Whenever the term "the exile" is mentioned, it is both a convenient chronological term to refer to the watershed between the monarchy/First Temple period and the Second Temple period and also a means of referring to the deportations from Judah that took place in the early sixth century BCE (cf. the discussion and essays in Grabbe 1998b). The terms "apocalyptic" and "apocalypticism" are used interchangeably here; some North American scholars object to "apocalyptic" as a noun, but it has a long and respectable history of such usage and is still so used on the European side of the Atlantic. The divine name for the God of Israel is written as "Yhwh"; although often vocalized as "Yahweh", the pronunciation is in fact unknown.

I

CHRONOLOGICAL
SURVEY

2

PERSIAN PERIOD (539–333 BCE)

By any reckoning the Persian period was a seminal episode in Jewish history. Despite the fact that great sections of it are largely blank, we have some direct evidence of the changes that were going on and a good deal of indirect evidence of what began in this period but for which the actual attestation is documented only later. The accumulation of evidence – direct and indirect – makes us view this period as extremely significant for the character taken on by Second Temple religion and the directions in which it was to move during the subsequent centuries.

MAJOR SOURCES

Books of Ezra and Nehemiah

Ackroyd, P. R. (1970) *The Age of the Chronicler* (1970).

Barstad, H. M. (1996) *The Myth of the Empty Land: A Study in the History and Archaeology of Judah During the "Exilic" Period.*

Becking, B. (1998) "Ezra's Re-enactment of the Exile", in L. L. Grabbe (ed.) *"The Exile" as History and Ideology*: 40–61.

Böhler, D. (1997) *Die heilige Stadt in Esdras α und Esra-Nehemia: Zwei Konzeptionen der Wiederherstellung Israels.*

Clines, D. J. A. (1990) "The Nehemiah Memoir: The Perils of Autobiography", *What Does Eve Do to Help?*: 124–64.

Grabbe, L. L. (1991b) "Reconstructing History from the Book of Ezra", in P. R. Davies (ed.) *Second Temple Studies: The Persian Period*: 98–107.

—— (1992c) "The Authenticity of the Persian 'Documents' in Ezra".

—— (1998a) *Ezra and Nehemiah.*

—— (1998d) "Triumph of the Pious or Failure of the Xenophobes? The Ezra/Nehemiah Reforms and their *Nachgeschichte*", in S. Jones and S. Pearce (eds) *Studies in Jewish Local Patriotism and Self-Identification in the Graeco-Roman Period*: 50–65.

Gunneweg, A. H. J. (1987) *Nehemiah.*

Japhet, S. (1982) "Sheshbazzar and Zerubbabel – Against the Background of the Historical and Religious Tendencies of Ezra–Nehemiah, Part I", *ZAW* 94: 66–98.

—— (1983) "Sheshbazzar and Zerubbabel – Against the Background of the Historical and Religious Tendencies of Ezra–Nehemiah, Part II", *ZAW* 95: 218–30.

Steins, G. (1995) *Die Chronik als kanonisches Abschlussphänomen: Studien zur Entstehung und Theologie von 1/2 Chronik*.

Talshir, Z. (1999) *I Esdras: From Origin to Translation*.

The books of Ezra and Nehemiah are no doubt extremely important for any history of the Jews during the Persian period, but their use is far more complicated than is often appreciated. For one thing we have not just the books as found in the Hebrew Bible but also versions and traditions found in Greek and other sources which must be taken into account in trying to evaluate the Hebrew versions. For example, it has been frequently argued that 1 Esdras (or a version of it) is prior to the Hebrew Ezra–Nehemiah (most recently Grabbe 1998a: 109–15; Böhler 1997). The final work of Hebrew Ezra–Nehemiah is likely to have been completed after the coming of Alexander. See *JCH* (30–42, 126–29, 131–38) and Grabbe (1998a; 1998d) for a full analysis of the Ezra and Nehemiah traditions and my conclusions about them. Points about religion that arise from the Ezra and Nehemiah traditions are the following:

1. The stories of Joshua and Zerubbabel, Ezra, and Nehemiah occur in a variety of forms and contexts, showing a complex development. It looks as if there were at one point three "foundation legends" of Jerusalem after the exile: a founding by Joshua and Zerubbabel, a founding by Ezra, and a founding by Nehemiah (Grabbe 1998a: 119–21, 187–89). This has resulted in a stereotyping of some of the presently available accounts and also the suppression of some traditions that did not fit the particular foundation-legend pattern in question. There is no reason to give the Hebrew Ezra–Nehemiah precedence over the other traditions.

2. The existence of three foundation legends does not negate the historical value of the material available, but it severely complicates it. The most reliable data are probably to be found in the remains of the Nehemiah Memorial and in one or two of the Aramaic documents. There is general agreement that a significant portion of the book of Nehemiah is made up of an account written by Nehemiah himself (even Gunneweg [1987: 176–80] agrees with this, despite his skepticism about much of the material in Ezra). It is usual to find this source in 1:1–7:4 (Eng. 1:1–7:5); 11:1–2; 12:27–43. Neh. 13:4–31 is also often assigned to the Nehemiah Memorial, though this is also disputed (Ackroyd 1970: 28, 41; Steins 1995: 198-207). Recognizing that we have at least some of Nehemiah's own words available to us does not, however, mean that his account can always be taken at face value (cf. Clines 1990; Grabbe

1998a: 159–77). The Joshua and Zerubbabel story can be supplemented from other sources. Sheshbazzar is likely to have been a key figure in the very early period under Persian rule. The Ezra story (Ezra 7–10; Neh. 7:72 [Eng. 7:73]–8:12) is very problematic for a number of reasons and deconstructs itself (Grabbe 1991b; 1998a: 138–52; Becking 1998).

3. A central theme is the attempt of the early returnees to establish an entity which kept itself aloof from the native inhabitants. This is odd because these native peoples were mostly the descendants of those Jews left in the land at the time of Nebuchadnezzer's conquest (Barstad 1996). Indeed, a family such as that of Tobiah may have had some of its members deported after the fall of Jerusalem (Ezra 2:60; Neh. 7:62). The avoidance of the "peoples of the land" is almost an obsession in some portions of the tradition. This is manifested in a strong "theology of the land" (cf. pp. 297–300 below).

4. The apartheid attitude toward the native inhabitants is paralleled in Nehemiah's measures to isolate Jerusalem and the Jewish community from the surrounding world. The community is not just split between Nehemiah and his opponents, but the ruling priesthood and the nobility as a whole attempt to occupy a mediating position, not just to cooperate with Nehemiah (up to a point) but also to keep communicative and other links with his opponents such as Tobiah (cf. Grabbe 1998d).

5. The centrality of the temple and priesthood, and in particular the high priest, is very much in evidence. Even under Nehemiah, who was evidently able to override the decisions of the high priest (no doubt due to his control of the military), the priesthood was still a key institution of power.

6. The importance of the written law in parts of the tradition must be considered seriously (see Chapter 8 below), though interpreting the traditions is complex.

Haggai, Zechariah, Malachi

Butterworth, M. (1992) *Structure and the Book of Zechariah*.

Hill, A. E. (1998) *Malachi: A New Translation with Introduction and Commentary*.

Larkin, K. J. A. (1994) *The Eschatology of Second Zechariah: A Study of the Formation of a Mantological Wisdom Anthology*.

Meyers, C. L., and E. M. (1987) *Haggai, Zechariah 1–8*.

—— (1993) *Zechariah 9–14*.

O'Brien, J. M. (1995) "Malachi in Recent Research", *CR: BS* 3:81–94.

Person, R. F. (1993) *Second Zechariah and the Deuteronomic School*.

Petersen, D. L. (1984) *Haggai and Zechariah 1–8*.

—— (1995) *Zechariah 9–14 and Malachi: A Commentary*.

Redditt, P. L. (1992) "Zerubbabel, Joshua, and the Night Visions of Zechariah", *CBQ* 54: 249–59.

—— (1994a) "The Book of Malachi in its Social Setting", *CBQ* 56: 240–55.

—— (1994b) "Nehemiah's First Mission and the Date of Zechariah 9–14", *CBQ* 56: 664–78.
—— (1995) *Haggai, Zechariah and Malachi*.

An overview and earlier bibliography to these three books was given in *JCH* (43–45). Our concern here is to look at some of the religious implications; the following points relating to Judaic religion can be found in these three Minor Prophets:

1. The picture of the so-called restoration of the Palestinian community differs at significant points from the Ezra tradition in both 1 Esdras and Hebrew Ezra–Nehemiah. The "people of the land" seem to be included in the community and not demonized as in Ezra and Nehemiah (cf. Hag. 2:4). The temple is to be built from local resources, not expensive imports from abroad (Hag. 1:8).

2. According to both Haggai and Zechariah, leadership is invested in a diarchy, with Zechariah as the governor of the province (evidently appointed by the Persians) and Joshua as high priest (e.g. Mal. 1:12; Zech. 4). The few indications we have are that this sharing of political and religious leadership continued throughout the Persian period. Although there was an officially appointed governor most or all of the time, the high priest was still the main religious representative of the people.

3. The temple is important. Haggai emphasizes how the people have worried too much about their own welfare and have neglected to rebuild the temple (Hag. 1:2–11). The people begin the work, though when and whether it was completed lies outside the purview of these books, and we have to go elsewhere to confirm what happened once the work began. The purity of the high priest and the sanctuary are the subject of Zech. 3 and 5.

4. The place of the priesthood is an issue. Most of the concern in Haggai and Zechariah is about the high priesthood; however, in Malachi we have discussion of the priesthood as a whole, including criticism of it. The assumption that Malachi was therefore anti-priest or anti-cult has sometimes been made, but this fails to recognize that strong critique can come internally. The writer seems to see the covenant with Levi as important and accords the priesthood a central role in teaching as well as the cult (Mal. 2:4–7).

5. Haggai and Zechariah are significant stages in the development of messianism. Both books put the governor and the high priest on the same plane. Haggai emphasizes the role of Zerubbabel (a member of the royal family) as God's "signet ring" (Hag. 2:4–9, 20–23). Zechariah recognizes both Joshua and Zerubbabel as anointed (Zech. 4). Both Joshua and Zerubbabel are crowned and sit on thrones, but it is expected that Zerubbabel (called "the Branch") will be enthroned as ruler (Zech. 6).

6. Eschatology is important to all three books. Haggai seems to focus most of its energies on the present, though present events will inaugurate a new beginning. Zechariah has a number of passages relating to the future (seen as

imminent), including 2:11–17; 6:9–13; 8; 9–14. Zech. 8 ends the first part of the book with a prophecy of prosperity and idyllic existence in Jerusalem now that God's presence is again there. The "Day of Yhwh" is a theme of Zech. 14. Malachi ends with a message about the future (3:1–5, 19–24 [Eng. 3:1–5; 4:1–6]).

7. Zechariah especially is central for the development of apocalyptic. In my opinion, the book is an apocalypse, including chapters 1–8, though not everyone would agree (cf. pp. 232–36 below).

Joel

Mason, R. (1994) *Zephaniah, Habakkuk, Joel*.

See Mason (1994; also *JCH*: 42, 45–46) for introduction and bibliography. The book makes two main contributions to the study of Judaic religion:

1. The priesthood and cult. The effects of famine and locust plagues on the temple are noted (1:9, 13, 16; 2:17). The future place and holiness of Zion are part of the culmination of the book (2:14; 3:5 [Eng. 2:32]; 4:16–18, 21 [Eng. 3:16–18, 21]).

2. Eschatology. In common with Zechariah 9–14, Joel concentrates on the "Day of Yahweh" and supernatural intervention of God (see pp. 257–59 below). The suffering of the people is described but little is said about their sins (but see 2:13–14), unlike some other prophetic books; instead, it is the nations and not Judah who will be punished (4:2–14, 19 [Eng. 3:2–14, 19]). Zion will be restored, God's people exalted, and a new order brought about (2:14, 18–27; 3:5 [Eng. 2:32]; 4:1, 16–18, 21 [Eng. 3:1, 16–18, 21]). A number of motifs found here recur in other prophetic and apocalyptic books, such as judgment in the valley of Jehoshaphat (4:2, 12–14 [Eng. 3:2, 12–14]).

Jonah

Bolin, T. M. (1997) *Freedom Beyond Forgiveness: The Book of Jonah Re-Examined*.
Craig, K. M., Jr (1999) "Jonah in Recent Research", *CR: BS* 7:97–118.
Grabbe, L. L. (1998d) "Triumph of the Pious or Failure of the Xenophobes? The Ezra/Nehemiah Reforms and their *Nachgeschichte*", in Siân Jones and Sarah Pearce (eds) *Studies in Jewish Local Patriotism and Self-Identification in the Graeco-Roman Period*: 50–65.
Limburg, J. (1993) *Jonah: A Commentary*.
Person, R. F., Jr (1996) *In Conversation with Jonah: Conversation Analysis, Literary Criticism, and the Book of Jonah*.
Salters, R. B. (1994) *Jonah & Lamentations*.
Sasson, J. (1990) *Jonah: A New Translation with Introduction, Commentary, and Interpretations*.

The book of Jonah has been of considerable interest in recent years. See Salters (1994; also *JCH*: 42, 46) for an introduction and earlier bibliography. Several recent commentators have suggested or discussed the idea of Jonah as satire or parody. The book has two main themes:

1. Failure of prophecy. The theme is not new (assuming the book belongs to the Persian period) but is already addressed in such passages as Ezekiel 33 and Jeremiah 18 (though when these are to be dated is a moot point; Joel 2:12–14 also leaves open the possibility that God will relent). In spite of his initial reluctance, Jonah carries out his prophetic mission, yet God does not destroy Nineveh as prophesied because it repented. Thus, one point of the book is the contingency of prophecy on the actions of the people against whom it is directed.

2. Universalism and the place of Gentiles within God's plan (see the discussion in Sasson 1990: 24–26). One of its messages still seems to be that non-Israelites can have access to the God of Israel. A similar idea is found in writings which probably also date to the same general period of time (Isa. 56 and perhaps the book of Ruth and Mal. 1:11); these indicate a tendency in some circles toward universalism of worship and salvation. This does not mean that Gentiles would be accepted just as they are because conversion to Yahwism is presupposed, but it goes against the narrow genealogical and exclusivist view in some circles (e.g. Ezra–Nehemiah; cf. Grabbe 1998d). Gentiles can repent of their sins; God will listen to them in such cases; God is concerned for their welfare and not just Israel's.

Isaiah 56–66

Emmerson, G. I. (1992) *Isaiah 56–66.*
Grabbe, L. L. (1995a) *Priests, Prophets, Diviners, Sages: A Socio-historical Study of Religious Specialists in Ancient Israel.*
Schramm, B. (1995) *The Opponenets of Third Isaiah: Reconstructing the Cultic History of the Restoration.*

On the one hand, Third Isaiah or Trito-Isaiah as a whole has commonly been dated to the Persian period; on the other hand, it is also agreed that various sorts of material, from various periods, has found its way into the collection (see *JCH* [46–49] and Emmerson [1992] for a further discussion). Without hoping to resolve the question, the following points can be noted: the themes of the book generally fit the Persian period, there is little to demand a post-Persian dating, and the collection of prophetic books in the present Hebrew canon was probably complete by the Greek period (pp. 152–54 below). A complication is that there is little in the book to relate directly to Ezra–Nehemiah, but the complicated nature of Ezra–Nehemiah's relationship to contemporary history has already been discussed (see pp. 13–15 above).

Here are some of the main points that emerge from Third Isaiah that have implications for religion:

1. The return has taken place and the temple has been rebuilt (60:7, 13; 62:6–9, though a few verses might suggest otherwise: 57:13–19; 58:12; 64:9–10). Part of the problem is that the apparent expectations, perhaps based on the promises of Deutero-Isaiah (e.g. 41:8–20), have not been fulfilled: life is hard, crop failure frequent, and the returnees seem to be having a difficult time making a living (60:17; 62:8–9). Indeed, much of the book could be interpreted as an attempt to cope with a situation in which the expectations of the community are far different from the reality.

2. A universalist view is found in some passages (especially 56:3–7), a rare perspective though not unknown in other passages (cf. Jonah above). The idea that non-Israelites could hope for salvation and God's blessings as long as they were obedient to God's law is something found in only a few other contemporary sources.

3. Several passages seem to discuss cultic practices condemned in the book and also elsewhere, such as Deut. 18:9–14 (Isa. 57:3–13; 65:1–7, 11–12; 66:3–4, 17). These may relate to a cult of the dead or necromancy (cf. Grabbe 1995a: 141–45).

4. A number of recent studies have argued that Trito-Isaiah shows evidence of sectarian developments (along with a number of other passages); see pp. 183–85 below.

5. A number of passages discuss a future which seems not just a hyperbolic description of the present or the immediate future, but eschatological in nature (cf. Isa. 60). The new heavens and new earth (Isa. 65:17–25) are the most striking, but see also the coming of Yhwh in wrath, reminding one of the day of Yhwh (63:1–6; 66:15–16), and the pilgrimage of all nations to Jerusalem and the judgment on the wicked (66:18–24).

Books of Chronicles

Albertz, R. (1994) *A History of Israelite Religion in the Old Testament Period*.

Auld, A. G. (1994) *Kings Without Privilege: David and Moses in the Story of the Bible's Kings*.

Dyck, J. E. (1998) *The Theocratic Ideology of the Chronicler*.

Grabbe, L. L. (1995) *Priests, Prophets, Diviners, Sages: A Socio-historical Study of Religious Specialists in Ancient Israel*.

Graham, M. P., and S. L. McKenzie (eds) (1999) *The Chronicler as Author: Studies in Text and Texture*.

Gunneweg, A. H. J. (1965) *Leviten und Priester: Hauptlinien der Traditionsbildung und Geschichte des israelitisch-jüdischen Kultpersonals*.

Japhet, S. (1993) *I & II Chronicles: A Commentary*.

—— (1997) *The Ideology of the Book of Chronicles and Its Place in Biblical Thought*.

Johnstone, W. (1997) *1 and 2 Chronicles: Vol. 1 1 Chronicles 1–2 Chronicles 9: Israel's Place among the Nations; Vol. 2 2 Chronicles 10–36: Guilt and Atonement*.

Jones, G. H. (1993) *1 & 2 Chronicles*.

Kalimi, I. (1995) *Zur Geschichtsschreibung des Chronisten: Literarisch-historiographische Abweichungen der Chronik von ihren Paralleltexten in den Samuel- und Königsbüchern*.

Kelly, B. E. (1996) *Retribution and Eschatology in Chronicles*.

Peltonen, Kai (1996) *History Debated: The Historical Reliability of Chronicles in Pre-Critical and Critical Research*.

—— (2000) "A Jigsaw without a Model?: The Dating of Chronicles", in L. L. Grabbe (ed.) *Did Moses Speak Attic? Jewish Historiography and Scripture in the Hellenistic Period*.

Steins, G. (1995) *Die Chronik als kanonisches Abschlussphänomen: Studien zur Entstehung und Theologie von 1/2 Chronik*.

Willi, T. (1995) *Juda–Jehud–Israel: Studien zum Selbstverständnis des Judentums in persischer Zeit*.

Williamson, H. G. M. (1979) "The Origins of the Twenty-Four Priestly Courses: A Study of 1 Chronicles xxiii–xxvii", VTSup 30: 251–68.

A great deal of work has been done on 1 and 2 Chronicles in recent years, with areas of strong debate. Some of these were already discussed at length, such as the question of whether the Chronicler's authorship should also encompass Ezra–Nehemiah (see *JCH*: 49–51), but see now Jones (1993) and especially Peltonen (1996; 2000). Although some want to date the books to the Maccabean period (Steins 1995: 491–99), a consensus for the dating of Chronicles is tending toward the Greek period, probably the early third century BCE (Japhet 1993: 27–28; Albertz 1994: 545; Peltonen 2000). One of the most interesting debates developing in recent years is whether Chronicles uses Samuel–Kings as a source, as has been almost universally agreed to the present, or whether both sets of writings go back to a common post-exilic source (Auld 1994). If the latter, this has consequences for interpreting the differences between Chronicles and Samuel–Kings and for the dating of both collections. Some of the implications relating to religion are the following:

1. The genealogies seem to provide clues to the structure and settlement patterns of the post-exilic community (Willi 1995: 110–68).

2. The question of Israel's identity is raised by the text. Recent study suggests that "Israel" to the Chronicler includes the northern tribes as well, so that the sustained anti-Samaritan polemic identified by an earlier scholarship must be abandoned (e.g. Japhet 1997: 325–34). However, Albertz argues, contrary to these recent trends, that the cultic split with the Samaritan community forms the background to the books (1994: 544–56). He dates this split to the early Greek period.

3. Especially important for historical purposes is the view that 1 and 2 Chronicles reflect the structure of the priesthood and the functioning of the

temple cult in the Persian or early Greek period (cf. Japhet 1997: 222–65; Williamson 1979), though some mutual contradictions suggest the juxtaposition of material from different sources (cf. Gunnneweg 1965; Japhet 1993: 411–66).

4. There is some indication that cultic prophets in the temple were being absorbed into the levitical ranks of temple singers (cf. Grabbe 1995a: 112–13). The book is an crucial indicator of the importance of singing and music in the cult (cf. pp. 143–44 below).

Proverbs

Clifford, R. J. (1999) *Proverbs*.

Golka, F. W. (1993) *The Leopard's Spots: Biblical and African Wisdom in Proverbs*.

Kayatz, C. (1966) *Studien zu Proverbien 1–9: Eine form- und motivgeschichtliche Untersuchung unter Einbeziehung ägyptischen Vergleichsmaterials*.

Lyons, E. L. (1987) "A Note on Proverbs 31.10–31", in K. G. Hoglund, *et al.* (eds) *The Listening Heart: Essays in Wisdom and the Psalms in Honor of Roland E. Murphy, O. Carm.*: 237–45.

McCreesh, T. P. (1985) "Wisdom as Wife: Proverbs 31:10–31", *RB* 92: 25–46.

Maier, C. (1995) *Die "fremde Frau" in Proverbien 1–9: Eine exegetische und sozialgeschichtliche Studie*.

Murphy, R. E., and E. Huwiler (1999) *Proverbs, Ecclesiastes, Song of Songs*.

Washington, H. C. (1994) *Wealth and Poverty in the Instruction of Amenemope and the Hebrew Proverbs*.

Weeks, S. (1994) *Early Israelite Wisdom*.

Westermann, C. (1995) *Roots of Wisdom: The Oldest Proverbs of Israel and Other Peoples*.

Whybray, R. N. (1994a) *The Composition of the Book of Proverbs*.

—— (1994b) *Proverbs*.

—— (1995a) *The Book of Proverbs: A Survey of Modern Study*.

Wolters, A. (1985) "*Ṣôpiyyâ* (Proverbs 31:27) as Hymnic Participle and Play on *Sophia*", *JBL* 104: 577–87.

The book of Proverbs has a long history of growth (cf. Whybray 1994a), going back to the period of the monarchy, if not even to the folk tradition of early Israel. Whether the book as it stands is primarily a scribal work or one rooted in folk culture is very much debated at the moment (cf. Golka 1993; Westermann 1995). Whatever its origins, many would accept that much of the book originated in the pre-exilic period; however, it has long been argued that some sections, especially Proverbs 1–9, are post-exilic in origin. This is not a simple matter since a good case can be made that much of the material even in these chapters is paralleled in the early Egyptian wisdom tradition, creating the possibility that they could also be pre-exilic (Kayatz

1966; cf. Weeks 1994). But the consensus is probably that they are post-exilic, and there are other sections, such as Proverbs 30–31, which are also often dated to post-587 and may possibly show evidence of Greek influence (cf. Wolters 1985, though I am not convinced). What is clear is that much of the book of Proverbs was available in the Persian period, and the book may well have been given its final form then. Some of the issues affecting Second Temple religion are the following:

1. Traditional Israelite wisdom was very influential on the developing religious tradition. It recurs in later books such as Ben Sira. Proverbs is an important summary of some aspects, even though the phenomenon was rather wider than just what we find in Proverbs.

2. The figure of wisdom first attested in Prov. 1–9 has a long history in Judaism and makes an important theological contribution (see pp. 225–28 below).

3. Some passages of Proverbs show a more prominent place for women than many other sections of the OT. For example, the teaching of the mother is stressed (1:8; 6:20; 31:1–9). Although not all feminist interpreters are convinced, Prov. 31:10–31 gives a positive picture of a woman as an independent entity who makes an equal contribution to the household. It is has been suggested that the woman is in fact Lady Wisdom (McCreesh 1985), but this seems less persuasive. Lyons (1987) has shown how the passage fits into conditions of the Persian period as she reconstructs them.

Job

Clines, D. J. A. (1989) *Job 1–20*.

Dell, K. J. (1991) *The Book of Job as Sceptical Literature*.

Gordis, R. (1978) *The Book of Job: Commentary, New Translation, and Special Studies*.

Grabbe, L. L. (1977) *Comparative Philology and the Text of Job: A Study in Methodology*.

Gray, J. (1970) "The Book of Job in the Context of Near Eastern Literature", *ZAW* 82: 251–69.

Habel, N. C. (1985) *The Book of Job: A Commentary*.

Hurvitz, Avi (1974) "The Date of the Prose-Tale of Job Linguistically Reconsidered", *HTR* 67: 17–34.

Pope, M. H. (1973) *Job*.

Robertson, D. A. (1972) *Linguistic Evidence in Dating Early Hebrew Poetry*.

Soden, W. von (1965) "Das Fragen nach der Gerechtigkeit Gottes im Alten Orient", *MDOG* 96: 41–59 (= *Bibel und Alter Orient*, 1985: 57–75).

Whedbee, J. W. (1977) "The Comedy of Job", in R. Polzin and D. Robertson (eds) *Studies in the Book of Job*: 1–39.

Zuckerman, B. (1991) *Job the Silent: A Study in Historical Counterpoint*.

The book of Job is no doubt one of the most intriguing books in the Bible. As well as being a great piece of literature, it (along with Qohelet) stands out from traditional theology in the questions it raises and the answers it gives. Although many would date it late, Pope (1973: xxxii–xl) is surely right that the poetic part is early for the most part, not least because of the archaic language and many *hapax legomena* (cf. Robertson 1972; Grabbe 1977). The form of the folktale that makes up the prologue and epilogue is late, however, and it is likely that the final book was completed during the Persian period (cf. Hurvitz 1974). The book takes its place within what is sometimes called the "skeptical literature" (cf. Dell 1991), a section of wisdom and related literature known not only from the OT but from Egypt and Mesopotamia. Job is the pinnacle of such literature which asks questions about theodicy and about God in general, but such questioning has a long history in the ancient Near East. Accepting Job as skeptical literature does not preclude other genres; a good case has been made that the final form of the book is a comedy in the classical sense of the word (Whedbee 1977). Some of its contributions to Judaic religion are the following:

1. Job (along with Qohelet) raises the important question of theodicy, of God's actions and why the assumptions found elsewhere in the OT do not hold true in real life. Like all great literature, Job gives no simple answer but explores the question with depth and sophistication. The contrast between it and a work like the *Testament of Job* (pp. 104–5 below), which returns to the traditional simple answers, makes clear the superior nature of Job. This is an oft-neglected branch of the wisdom tradition but one well established.

2. It counters the messages of obedience with the important corrective of independent thought and skepticism. This includes calling into question the frequent OT admonition that if obedient, one will receive good, or if disobedient, bad (the *Tun–Ergehen-Zusammenhang*, or act–consequence relationship).

3. The book contains a good deal of traditional wisdom content and forms. The poem on wisdom in Job 28 develops the idea of wisdom as hidden and available only through God. Job's "friends" often present the side of traditional wisdom, but the interaction between Job and his friends in the dialogues is a complex exploration and not limited to a simplistic exchange.

4. The present form of the book is Yahwistic; however, the poem does not use the name Yhwh (except for the framework) but Eloah and some other names (e.g. Shaddai).

Esther

Brenner, A. (ed.) (1995) *A Feminist Companion to Esther, Judith and Susanna.*
Bush, F. (1996) *Ruth/Esther.*
Clines, D. J. A. (1984a) *Ezra, Nehemiah, Esther.*
—— (1984b) *The Esther Scroll: The Story of the Story.*

Day, L. (1995) *Three Faces of a Queen: Characterization in the Books of Esther.*

De Troyer, K. (1997) *Het einde van de Alpha-tekst van Ester: Vertaal- en verhaaltech-niek van MT 8,1–17, LXX 8,1–17 en AT 7,14–41.*

Dorothy, C. V. (1997) *The Books of Esther: Structure, Genre and Textual Integrity.*

Grabbe, L. L. (1999e) Review of K. De Troyer, *Het einde van de Alpha-tekst van Ester, CBQ* 61: 331–32.

Jobes, K. H. (1996) *The Alpha-Text of Esther: Its Character and Relationship to the Masoretic Text.*

Klein, L. R. (1997) "Esther's Lot", *CR: BS* 5:111–45.

Kossmann, R. (2000) *Die Esthernovelle – Vom Erzählten zur Erzählung: Studien zur Traditions- und Redaktionsgeschichte des Estherbuches.*

Lacocque, A. (1999) "The Different Versions of Esther", *Biblical Interpretation* 7: 301–22.

Laniak, T. S. (1998) *Shame and Honor in the Book of Esther.*

Larkin, K. J. A. (1995) *Ruth and Esther.*

Levenson, J. D. (1997) *Esther: A Commentary.*

Esther has been a popular subject of commentary and monographic study in recent years and many new studies have appeared since 1990 (see *JCH* [51–52] and Larkin [1995] for earlier studies and an introduction). The book makes a number of contributions to Jewish religion:

1. It provides the basis for the festival of Purim, not one of the original OT festivals nor considered a holy day, but an important traditional celebration nonetheless.

2. The book is an example of what many would call the *Diasporanovelle*. Like Tobit and Ahiqar (this latter perhaps not originally Jewish but adopted), it is a story which represents Jewish aspirations in the Diaspora, as well as an example of how Jews were to conduct themselves in relation to their neighbors. The story suggests that it was possible for Jews to attain high office (cf. also Tobit and Ahiqar). Like other novels of the period (e.g. Xenophon's *Cyropaedia*) it makes use of historical information, but its aim is not historical and some of its data are actually unhistorical.

3. Esther gives another example of a heroine, alongside people such as Ruth, Jael, and Judith. It is perhaps this feminist aspect that has spawned the great interest in the book recently, along with its textual complexity.

4. The various versions of the Esther text have been the basis of a good deal of study in recent years. There is the Hebrew version (MT), the Septuagint version, and the Alpha or A-Text (also called the Lucian or L-Text) of the Greek. The question of their relationship has received several answers. De Troyer (1997) has recently argued that the Alpha Text is a deliberate redactional creation from the Greek and not a translation from a particular Hebrew original (see the summary in Grabbe 1999e).

Ruth

Brenner, A. (ed.) (1993c) *A Feminist Companion to Ruth*.
Bush, F. (1996) *Ruth/Esther*.
Larkin, Katrina J. A. (1995) *Ruth and Esther*.
Zakovitch, Y. (1999) *Das Buch Rut: Ein jüdischer Kommentar*.

The book of Ruth has had a revival of interest in recent years, with a number of new studies and commentaries (see Larkin [1995]; also *JCH* [51–52] for earlier studies). The book has a number of themes relating to early Judaism:

1. One theme of the book is the favorable picture it gives of a non-Israelite, even to the extent of making her a close ancestor of David. This is not the only message, of course, but if the book arose in the Persian period, it would go along with other passages having universalistic tendencies about the same time, such as Jonah and Third Isaiah.

2. The book presents not only a female protagonist but one who is an outsider. The figure of another woman (Naomi) is also prominent in the book.

3. It illustrates the complexity of trying to use legal sections of the OT (such as the "Covenant Code" [Exod. 20–23] and Deuteronomy) as evidence of actual practice, since the book of Ruth differs on several issues from the Pentateuch. For example, the ceremony relating to inheritance where a widow is concerned has some interesting differences from Deut. 25:5–10.

Song of Songs

Brenner, A. (1989) *The Song of Songs*.
—— (ed.) (1993a) *A Feminist Companion to Song of Songs*.
Keel, O. (1994) *The Song of Songs*.
Kramer, S. N. (1969) *The Sacred Marriage Rite: Aspects of Faith, Myth, and Ritual in Ancient Sumer*.
Murphy, R. E., and E. Huwiler (1999) *Proverbs, Ecclesiastes, Song of Songs*.

The Song of Songs or Song of Solomon has received a good deal of attention in the past two decades, with a number of commentaries (see Brenner 1989 and *JCH* [51–52] for earlier studies). The book is not easy to date but was probably compiled in the Persian or early Greek period. The religious contribution it makes includes the following:

1. The book illustrates the complex development of the canon. Many researchers have had problems because by their criteria the Song of Songs should not have been canonical. So they propose that it was accepted only because it was given an allegorical interpretation, or they come up with other justifications. The fact is that we have no idea how the book got into the canon, nor do we know how the canon was formed; we need to accept the possibility that its overt sexuality may not have been a problem to the canonizers.

2. The prominent place of the female lover has attracted a good deal of feminist interpretation. It has even been proposed that the book was the product of a woman writer.

3. Although the book can be applied to married lovers, there is no indication in the text that they are married; on the contrary, in common with love poetry elsewhere in the ancient Near East they are presented as young unmarried lovers.

4. The proposal that the book originated as a collection of poetry from a fertility cult (a favorite interpretation of an earlier generation) is now widely rejected. Although sacred marriage poetry from Mesopotamia provides some parallels and can be helpful for understanding certain aspects of the Song (cf. Kramer 1969), it is not the origin of other known love poetry and also probably not the basis for the Hebrew book.

The P Document

Blenkinsopp, Joseph (1991) *The Pentateuch: An Introduction to the First Five Books of the Bible.*
—— (1996) "An Assessment of the Alleged Pre-Exilic Date of the Priestly Material in the Pentateuch", *ZAW* 108: 495–578.
Budd, P. J. (1996) *Leviticus.*
Gerstenberger, E. S. (1996) *Leviticus: A Commentary.*
Grabbe, L. L. (1993a) *Leviticus.*
—— (1995a) *Priests, Prophets, Diviners, Sages: A Socio-historical Study of Religious Specialists in Ancient Israel.*
—— (1997d) "The Book of Leviticus", *Currents in Research: Biblical Studies* 5: 91–110.
Grünwaldt, K. (1999) *Das Heiligkeitsgesetz Leviticus 17–26: Ursprüngliche Gestalt, Tradition und Theologie.*
Haran, M. (1978) *Temples and Temple-Service in Ancient Israel.*
Jamieson-Drake, D. W. (1991) *Scribes and Schools in Monarchic Judah: A Socio-Archeological Approach.*
Knohl, I. (1987) "The Priestly Torah Versus the Holiness School: Sabbath and the Festivals", *HUCA* 58: 65–117.
—— (1995) *The Sanctuary of Silence: The Priestly Torah and the Holiness School.*
Milgrom, J. (1991) *Leviticus 1–16.*
—— (1993) "Response to Rolf Rendtorff", *JSOT* 60: 83–85.
Nicholson, E. (1998) *The Pentateuch in the Twentieth Century: The Legacy of Julius Wellhausen.*
Poorthuis, M. J. H. M., and J. Schwartz (eds) (2000) *Purity and Holiness: The Heritage of Leviticus.*
Rendtorff, R. (1993) "Two Kinds of P? Some Reflections on the Occasion of the Publishing of Jacob Milgrom's Commentary on Leviticus 1–16", *JSOT* 60: 75–81.

Rofé, Alexander (1999) *Introduction to the Composition of the Pentateuch*.

Sawyer, J. F. A. (ed.) (1996) *Reading Leviticus: A Conversation with Mary Douglas*.

Wegner, Judith Romney (1992) "Leviticus", in Carol A. Newsom and Sharon H. Ringe (eds) *The Women's Bible Commentary*: 36–44.

Whybray, R. N. (1995b) *Introduction to the Pentateuch*.

The past few years have seen challenges to the classic Graf–Wellhausen or Documentary Hypothesis from several angles (see the summary in Grabbe 1993a: 12–18; 1997d). The first of these relates to whether the various sources exist at all. A second challenge is somewhat different. It accepts the various sources but the dating of them is called into question; however, there is not a consistent attack, for some tend to date some or all the sources later than was once done, while others date the P document very early. The entire subject of the Documentary Hypothesis is too lengthy to cover here (cf. Blenkinsopp 1991; Whybray 1995b; Rofé 1999). For purposes of the present study, I shall not deal with the J, E, and D sources (although I recognize that the debate is far from over) but shall confine my remarks to the P document.

In the classic form of the hypothesis, the post-exilic dating of P has been a cornerstone, and it is here that one of the main objections to the consensus has emerged. The key study arguing for an a pre-exilic date of P was Haran's (1978). His argument has since been bolstered by a series of individual studies (see Grabbe 1997d), as well as by the massive commentary of Milgrom (1991); however, we are a long way from seeing the traditional late dating of P abandoned (cf. Blenkinsopp 1996; Rendtorff 1993). A further complication to the discussion is the question of the Holiness Code (H) which was usually seen as separate from P and to be dated as earlier. Several scholars have doubted the existence of H as a separate document (e.g. Gerstenberger 1996). Knohl, although accepting the existence of H, came to the conclusion that it was later than Leviticus 1–16 (1987; 1995), arguing that there were two priestly schools, one of which produced the earlier P document and the other which not only wrote H (the later document) but also did the final editing of the Pentateuch (cf. also Milgrom). Whether P is a Persian-period composition or whether it only became widely known in the Persian period, the effect on religion is much the same:

1. The P document summarizes a good deal of the traditional cult practices. The cult is likely to have changed only slowly over time, and even a pre-exilic cultic description was probably still current in early post-exilic times.

2. It was not a "manual" for the temple service, however. Apart from its lack of completeness (much that the priests would need to know is omitted), it is probably to some extent stylized. Part of the reason is that it is set in a hypothetical tabernacle shrine made by Moses in the wilderness. Therefore, the cult in a fixed temple, with a king and something like a national structure,

would have had some differences. For example, there is no place for the king or the cult prophets (cf. Grabbe 1995a: 10–40, 112–13).

3. Much of the legislation fits a small, self-contained community such as one might find in Persian Yehud. The only alternative setting would be in another similar small community such as pre-monarchic Israel, which is the setting given by Haran (1978) and Milgrom (1991); however, the recent debates on the development of monarchy suggest that monarchic Judah was also rather small until the late eighth century (cf. Jamieson-Drake 1991). A good case can be made for how P fits quite well into the context of Persian Yehud (Gerstenberger 1996).

Archaeology, papyri, and coins

Leith, M. J. W. (ed.) (1997) *Discoveries in the Judaean Desert XXIV: Wadi Daliyeh I The Wadi Daliyeh Seal Impressions.*

Mildenberg, L. (1996) "*yĕhūd* and *šmryn*: Über das Geld der persischen Provinzen Juda und Samaria im 4. Jahrhundert", in H. Cancik, H. Lichtenberger, and P. Schäfer (eds) *Geschichte–Tradition–Reflexion: Festschrift für Martin Hengel zum 70. Geburtstag: Band I Judentum*: 119–46.

Porten, Bezalel (ed.) (1968) *Archives from Elephantine: The Life of an Ancient Jewish Military Colony.*

—— (1996) *The Elephantine Papyri in English: Three Millennia of Cross-Cultural Continuity and Change.*

Porten, B., and A. Yardeni (1986–) *Textbook of Aramaic Documents from Ancient Egypt: 1– = TAD.*

—— (1993) "Ostracon Clermont-Ganneau 125(?): A Case of Ritual Purity", *JAOS* 113: 451–56.

An introduction to the Elephantine papyri, with full bibliography, was given in *JCH* (53–55). The new edition of Porten/Yarden with three volumes (*TAD* 1–3) is still not complete, while the new English translation by Porten (1996) is unfortunately not a complete collection of the Aramaic papyri, though it includes a good deal of Egyptian material not otherwise easily available. So far (since 1990) there are no further publications of the Wadi ed-Daliyeh papyri, though the seal impressions without any writing have now been published (Leith 1997). Some of the main points about religious worship arising from the papyri are the following:

1. The community in Elephantine looked to Jerusalem as its first religious ally, writing for support for the rebuilding of their temple (*AP* ##30–32; *TAD* A4.7–9).

2. The authority in the Jerusalem community consisted of the high priest, with his fellow priests, and the nobility who were probably non-priests (*AP* 30:18–19; *TAD* A4.7:18–19, corrected by the parallels in *AP* 31; *TAD* A4.8):

We sent a letter to our lord [Bagohi the governor] and to Yehohanan the high priest and his companions the priests who are in Jerusalem and to Ostan the brother of Anan and the nobles of the Jews. They did not send a single letter to us.

3. The community was also in touch with Samaria and the Tobiad family of governors, when they received no response from Jerusalem (*AP* ##30–32; *TAD* A4.7–9; see the quotation in point #2).

4. One of the most interesting and curious of the papyri is the so-called "Passover Papyrus" (*AP* #21; *TAD* A4.1). It is often stated that this is an example of an order to regulate a local cult or religion by the Persian government; however, it is not at all clear that this is the case (Porten 1968: 130–33). Although the text is not completely preserved, it seems most likely that it is a response by the official administration to a request from the Jewish community, which had asked for approval of its normal Passover celebrations. Several ostraca indicate that Passover was a regular observance (Porten 1968: 131; Porten/Yardeni 1993). It would not be surprising if the annual celebration of the Passover caused offense to some of the local Egyptians, both because of the Exodus story and also because of the lambs involved (the local god Chnum was a ram-headed god). Therefore, this looks simply like an official permit to the Jews for their worship. All older reconstructions of the text must now be corrected in light of recent study (*TAD* A4.1).

5. The marriage documents indicate that women were able to initiate divorce against their husbands (*AP* 15 = *TAD* B2.6; *TAD* B3.8).

SYNTHESIS

Avigad, N. (1976) *Bullae and Seals from a Post-Exilic Judean Archive.*

Barstad, H. M. (1996) *The Myth of the Empty Land: A Study in the History and Archaeology of Judah During the "Exilic" Period.*

Berquist, J. L. (1995) *Judaism in Persia's Shadow: A Social and Historical Approach.*

Carroll, R. P. (1992) "The Myth of the Empty Land", in David Jobling and T. Pippin (eds) *Ideological Criticism of Biblical Texts*: 79–93.

Carter, Charles E. (1999) *The Emergence of Yehud in the Persian Period: A Social and Demographic Study.*

Grabbe, L. L. (1991b) "Reconstructing History from the Book of Ezra", in P. R. Davies (ed.) *Second Temple Studies: The Persian Period*: 98–107.

—— (1995a) *Priests, Prophets, Diviners, Sages: A Socio-historical Study of Religious Specialists in Ancient Israel.*

—— (1997g) "Are Historians of Ancient Palestine Fellow Creatures – Or Different Animals?" in L. L. Grabbe (ed.) *Can a "History of Israel" Be Written?*: 19–36.

—— (1998a) *Ezra and Nehemiah*.

—— (ed.) (1998b) *Leading Captivity Captive: "The Exile" as History and Ideology*.

—— (1998c) 'Triumph of the Pious or Failure of the Xenophobes? The Ezra/ Nehemiah Reforms and their *Nachgeschichte*', in S. Jones and S. Pearce (eds) *Studies in Jewish Local Patriotism and Self-Identification in the Graeco-Roman Period*: 50–65.

Hoglund, K. G. (1992) *Achaemenid Imperial Administration in Syria-Palestine and the Missions of Ezra and Nehemiah*.

Kuhrt, A. (1983) "The Cyrus Cylinder and Achaemenid Imperial Policy", *JSOT* 25: 83–97.

Roberts, J. J. M. (1973) "The Davidic Origin of the Zion Tradition", *JBL* 92: 329–44.

Schaper, J. (1995) "The Jerusalem Temple as an Instrument of the Achaemenid Fiscal Administration", *VT* 45: 428–39.

It is primarily in retrospect that the Persian period was seen as marking a new departure in this history of Jewish religion. Although the traumas of the destruction of Jerusalem and the temple and the various deportations taking place in 597, 586, and perhaps other times were great, the bulk of the population was left in the land. It was apparently still possible to worship at the site of the temple (Jer. 41:4–5). The majority of the people were mainly concerned with making a living, but this had always been the case since the overwhelming mass of the population lived by agrarian work of some sort. No doubt many looked forward to a rebuilding of the temple, while others perhaps were not so concerned as long as they had enough to eat. On the surface, though, there was no reason why major changes should take place in the religion.

Yet the evidence we have indicates that the Persian period was seminal in the development of Judaism, with major innovations which set the scene for the entire Second Temple period. It was here that the transition was made from a monarchic system, with the king as the chief religious and cultic figure, to one in which the high priest was the main religious leader. This change from a monarchy, as well as other changes in the status of Judah, unavoidably led to other changes in the religion. It is thought by many that the crystalization of the biblical literature came about primarily in the Persian period, as the Jews began to feel the loss of their monarchic past and the need to interpret it and explain the new situation.

In order to assess what happened under Persian rule, we need to know the situation in the last century or so of the Judean monarchy. This is difficult to evaluate. The Israelite religion had been one of many Northwest Semitic religions, with cult places and a pantheon, though the ruling dynasty evidently had a favourite deity and a royal cult in Jerusalem (see pp. 212–15 below). Both the biblical tradition and analogies from other peoples show that the Jerusalem temple was patronized by the Davidic royal family. This family claimed to be descended from an eponymous ancestor called David who was said to have been the first king over a united monarchy (though this was slightly complicated by the fact that in the tradition he had been preceded by a king Saul who was also theoretically ruler over the entirety of Israel).

There were those who held to the "Zion tradition" (even the prophet Isaiah, in the opinion of many), the view that because Yhwh's throne was on Mount Zion he would never allow it to be conquered by foreigners (cf. Roberts 1973). Nevertheless, Zion fell, first in 597 when the king and some of the population of Jerusalem were deported, then especially in 587/586 when the city and Temple were destroyed. Many of the elite – at least those in Jerusalem – were removed. Yet according to all indications the vast bulk of the population remained in the land (Carroll 1992; Barstad 1996).

At this point, the question of Jewish history becomes acute because there are major problems with the sources. If the bulk of the people remained in the land, can we speak of an "exile"? Some argue that the concept – and the term – "exile" should be abandoned, but others feel it is a conventional term and therefore useful for discussion (see the debate in Grabbe 1998b). Also, the ideological symbolism of the exile–restoration concept becomes quite important to some Jewish writers later on, which can stereotype the interpretation of the history of this period. We know little or nothing about what was happening in Judah during this period, nor do we have any accounts by deportees about their experiences. Although the temple site and perhaps even Jerusalem itself were desolate for at least half a century, the change of rule from the Neo-Babylonians to the Persians marked a change of fortune.

The new regime evidently allowed some of the descendants of the deportees in the Babylonian region to return and resettle the old area of Judah – now the Persian province of Yehud. Cyrus makes an issue of restoring the captive gods and peoples to their homelands in the Cyrus Cylinder (*ANET*: 315–16). Although the propagandistic nature of this claim must be recognized (Kuhrt 1983), allowing the return of some of the deportees from various sites evidently had a basis in fact. On the surface, Ezra 1–6 seems to present a straightforward picture of return and restoration, albeit in the face of a certain amount of opposition; however, the further we probe beneath the textual facade, the more difficulties arise in accepting the text at face value (Grabbe 1991b, 1998a). In the mass of traditions about the reestablishment of Judah we find three separate, independent, and perhaps competing "foundation legends" which describe how the restoration took place (Grabbe 1998a: 119–21, 187–89). In one, it is Joshua and Zerubbabel who bring new settlers and attempt to get the temple rebuilt; in another, it is Ezra who restores the temple and cult and establishes the law; a third makes Nehemiah the founder of the new Jewish entity in the land. This is not to say that actual history does not lie behind all three stories, but the way the historical events were first assimilated to a stereotyped pattern and then recombined in at least one version of the tradition (viz., Ezra–Nehemiah) makes getting at the actual events more difficult. Also, these traditions have to be evaluated in the light of other, different traditions about the founding of the temple such as are given in Haggai and Zechariah.

What is clear is that the Hebrew books of Ezra and Nehemiah attempt to suppress two historical facts: first, that the "people of the land" were not foreigners but were by and large the descendants of those Jews left behind in the deportations in the early sixth century, to whom the returnees must have seemed like interlopers and colonists attempting unwarranted interference with their property rights, religious practices, and lives in general; secondly, that a clear effort has been made to minimize or cut out some individuals important to the story. A prime example of this latter is Sheshbazzar in Ezra 1 who has a brief mission to bring back temple vessels and then disappears; yet a quoted document indicates that he was actually the first governor of the new province of Yehud and even ascribes to him the laying of the foundations of a new temple (Ezra 5:14–16). Nothing of this is found in the edited text of Ezra 1–6, showing how partial, distorted, and incomplete is its version of the early years of Yehud.

Although the high priest had important authority in the temple and cult during the First Temple period, as envisaged by a number of biblical passages (pp. 144–45 below), the king was still the chief cultic official (Grabbe 1995a: 38–39, 60–62). This situation changed considerably in the Second Temple period because of the loss of the monarchy. The priesthood, especially in the person of the high priest, was in a position to fill that vacuum, at least in part. We must accept that the power of the high priest is likely to have varied from time to time, and a lot may have depended on the personality and strength of character of the individual holding the office. Nevertheless, the high priest was the leading political as well as religious figure through much of the Second Temple period. There is also evidence that he was advised by a ruling council (the forerunner of the later "Sanhedrin") whose power and influence probably waxed and waned, depending on the strength of character of the high priest.

In the Persian period, however, the high priest was subordinate to a Persian-appointed governor at least part of the time and perhaps all the time. This is indicated already in the sources about the early part of the "restoration" by a diarchy of Zerubbabel, appointed as governor of Judah by the Persians, and the high priest Joshua (Haggai 1:1; 2:2, 21; Ezra 1; 3). As the official Persian appointee Zerubbabel would have had the pre-eminence, but Joshua is clearly seen as a partner and active player in the restoration of the cult (Zech. 3; 4; 6:9–15) since he was now the chief cultic official in the absence of a king. We have evidence of other Persian governors of Judah, including Sheshbazzar (Ezra 1:8–11; 5:14), Nehemiah (Neh. 5:15–18), and Bagohi (*AP* 30–31; *TAD* A4.7–8). A collection of seal impressions seems to list other governors, though these were unfortunately not found *in situ* (Avigad 1976). It is possible that they were mostly or all Jewish, though we cannot be certain. It seems likely that the Persians would have continued to appoint an official governor of the province throughout their period of rule, but the last part of the Persian period is largely a blank.

The biblical tradition (Haggai, Zechariah, Ezra–Nehemiah, some passages in Isaiah 56–66) puts a good deal of emphasis on the temple. According to it, one of the first concerns with the coming of Persian rule was to rebuild the holy place which had been destroyed by the Neo-Babylonians. Although there are hints that not everyone was quite as enthusiastic as the implied narrators of these writings (e.g. Hag. 1:4–11), and even active resistance is alleged (though supposedly from "foreigners" [Ezra 4–6]), the temple was probably rebuilt in the early Persian period, even if the completion date as early as 516 BCE (Ezra 6:15) is suspect. The resources needed would have been considerable for a small community, even if it was begun in the days of Cyrus (Ezra 5:13–16) and even if Zerubbabel was pressed to complete the job in the early days of Darius I (Haggai; Zech. 3–4; 6:9–8:17). The disappearance of Zerubbabel from the tradition of its completion (Ezra 6:13–22) makes one wonder whether this is because it was completed long after his governorship (though some have suspected that the Persians removed him for various nefarious reasons [*JCH*: 79]).

The temple would have been a natural focus of the rather small community around Jerusalem that made up the province of Yehud. Some have argued that the Persians had a special interest in the temple because it was responsible for collecting taxes (Schaper 1995). The Persians may well have used existing structures, including temples, to collect taxes. However, many of the recent arguments that the Persians interfered in or even directed the internal religious affairs of the community do not fit well with what we know of Persian administration, which was not as directive or pervasive as rule became under the Greeks (pp. 52–54 below). The Persian system of government was that more suited to a large, enormously diverse, and rather rambling empire. Satraps had a great deal of autonomy (which was one of the weaknesses of the government, because powerful satraps periodically rebelled against the Persian monarch); likewise, governors seem also to have had a good deal of leeway in how they governed as long as they collected the necessary tribute. This receives confirmation from the rivalry between Nehemiah and Sanballat, governors of two separate provinces. Their clash was hardly in the best interests of the Persian government, and no doubt the satrap would have intervened if it had become too heated, but the loose structure of the administration allowed it.

The Persians would have been interested in Judah as a part of the frontier area in general (Hoglund 1992), though it must be remembered that Jerusalem was always out of the main strategic areas because of its relative inaccessibility. The argument that the Persians would have had a hand in the regulations about marriage between the returnees and the people of the land is doubtful, however. This would imply an intervention policy not found anywhere else in ancient Near Eastern history (apart from the actions of Antiochus IV, which present a special case [*JCH*: 281–85]).

In the case of Nehemiah, we find a governor with great local powers and also strong views about what sort of society Jerusalem should be. The extent to which Jews were allowed to conform to the lifestyle and ways of the peoples around them was already debated at an earlier time. There were those who argued that the worship of Yhwh did not allow the worship of other gods (Exod. 20:3), that Israel was a holy nation which should be different from other nations (Exod. 19:6), and that association with Gentiles would only corrupt and lead Israelites astray from the true religion (Deut. 7:1–5). How much this debate was really carried on while Israel was a nation can only be speculated on; it became a reality, however, as the community sought religious reconstruction in the early Persian period.

We know from the books of Ezra and Nehemiah that the question of relations with the other peoples living in the Palestinian region became acute. Apparently many of the returnees by the second or third generation had married wives from the surrounding peoples. This was opposed by Nehemiah when he came as governor in 445 (Neh. 9–10; Ezra 9–10 gives a similar picture, though its relationship to the Nehemiah episode is debated), and many Jews were compelled to send away their wives and the children of the marriages. The odd thing is that these "peoples of the land" were, as already noted, probably in many cases the descendants of those from the Northern and Southern Kingdoms who had not been taken captive and were thus as much Israelite as those who returned from Babylon. A land theology and belief in a "holy remnant" may have been operating by this time and may have affected the situation (pp. 297–300 below).

The question of when monotheism developed in Israel has been much debated in the past decades, though the recent trend is to put it later rather than earlier (see pp. 216–19 below). Deuteronomy has statements which might be taken as monotheistic, but perhaps the first clear declaration of the non-existence of other gods is found in Deutero-Isaiah (Isaiah 40–55) which is normally dated to the exilic period. We cannot assume, however, that all Jews accepted the viewpoint of Second Isaiah, and the spread of monotheism (however the term might be understood) might have continued well into the Second Temple period. Zoroastrianism, which became the official religion of the Persian rulers, may have helped in the spread of monotheism, though there is no evidence that the Persians imposed particular religious practices on anyone as some have alleged (*JCH*: 130).

The Persian period saw considerable changes in the concept of the spirit world, though this was mainly the development of themes already begun in pre-exilic times. Other heavenly beings were acknowledged in the form of angels and demons. Angelology has its roots in the old Israelite religion (some have suggested they were simply the old gods demoted to an inferior status), though some have also detected Persian influence here. The development of a complex angelology and demonology is a characteristic of Second Temple Judaism as a whole but with strong roots in the Persian period.

In the past couple of decades, more and more people would put the final editing – and perhaps even the major composition – of many or all the biblical books in the post-exilic period. There is no consensus, however, and it would be unwise to make confident statements. What one can say is that many would see the Persian period as the time for the main editorial work of collecting and crystallizing the traditions into the present biblical books (see pp. 152–57 below). The destruction of Jerusalem and the temple and the loss of the monarchy and a semi-autonomous state was quite traumatic. Although the city and temple were rebuilt, it became clearer and clearer that the monarchy and a Jewish state were unlikely to be restored in the near future. The loss of traditions and records, such as there were, would have made the scribal classes (mainly the priests) aware of the need to collect and crystalize what was left.

What already existed in written form is difficult to say. Certain information about the succession of kings and some of their deeds was available, either in the form of state or temple records or perhaps even a narrative of some sort. We can tell this because the names, order, and approximate chronological placing of the kings is accurate wherever it can be checked from external sources (Grabbe 1997g: 24–26; 1998b: 84–90). On the other hand, there is evidence that the Pentateuch, Deuteronomistic History, and most of the prophetic corpus were in much their present shape by the end of the Persian period. Unless we assume that all of this happened in pre-exilic times, which few would be willing to do, we must place the bulk of the literary and redactional activity in the Persian period.

The fact that much of the Persian period is a blank, as far as our knowledge of the Jewish community is concerned, has led some to be uneasy about placing so much activity in what is presently a "black hole". But the provincial resources and general situation were no better in the Ptolemaic period, which also has large gaps. Judging from later data, the number of priests available was larger than required for the regular temple service. Those priests with education and leisure would have been well placed to take on this literary activity. Also, the idea that the "Deuteronomic School" (assuming it was active at this time) was somehow completely separate and isolated from the "priestly school" ignores the realities of the pool of literate and leisured individuals able to undertake such a task (cf. Grabbe 1995a: 198–99); a "Deuteronomic School" would almost certainly have included priests.

The size of the community would have encouraged a certain unity, but sectarian movements may have already begun during this period (cf. pp. 183–85 below). There were certainly internal divisions within the community, if nothing else. Nehemiah seems to have caused a good deal of disruption in the community and even looks like a sectarian leader in certain ways; however, it looks as if his views were by and large rejected in the next two centuries, only to be revived at a much later time (Grabbe 1998c).

The question of Persian influence is a difficult one (see *JCH* [100–102] for a discussion and bibliography). There was undoubtedly Persian influence; the problem is quantifying it. A number of later Jewish beliefs have remarkable parallels in Zoroastrianism (e.g. resurrection and judgment, other aspects of eschatology and apocalypticism, angelology), but each also has roots in earlier native tradition. In some cases, Persian religion probably encouraged developments in certain directions rather than providing something entirely new.

The Persian period was already pregnant with many of the features we associate with Second Temple Judaism, and the next several centuries were to see them born and grow. What emerged at the end was rather different in certain ways than what began it, because new trends and developments not foreseen were also to ensue, but the Persian period set the stage for the entire span of almost seven centuries. This is why any characterization of the Second Temple period must include the time of Persian rule.

3

EARLY GREEK PERIOD
(333–200 BCE)

The Greek conquest has often been seen as having far-reaching consequences for Judaism. As so often with such over-arching generalities, there is a certain truth in this view but there is also a danger of grave distortion. The process of Hellenization affected the Jews as it did all peoples of the ancient Near East, bringing benefits as well as disadvantages, but it was a very complex and lengthy process. Some of the developments in this period were quite important for Judaism, but they were not always of the spectacular sort. For example, the translation of the Pentateuch into Greek was one of the most momentous events in its subsequent effects on Judaic religion, yet its significance is often overlooked.

MAJOR SOURCES

Hecateus of Abdera

Bar-Kochva, B. (1996) *Pseudo-Hecataeus,* On the Jews: *Legitimizing the Jewish Diaspora.*

Pucci Ben Zeev, M. (1993) "The Reliability of Josephus Flavius: The Case of Hecataeus' and Manetho's Accounts of Jews and Judaism: Fifteen Years of Contemporary Research (1974–1990)", *JSJ* 24: 215–34.

Writing about 300 BCE, Hecateus has one of the few descriptions of the Jewish people in Palestine and one of the earliest in Greek. A survey of the most recent scholarship on the work is given by Bar-Kochva (7–43; see also *JCH* [173] for a discussion and earlier literature). The excerpts in Diodorus have been almost universally accepted as authentic, but there has been much more controversy over further quotations in Josephus. Bar-Kochva's study has now concluded that they are not from Hecateus (pp. 73–74 below). The relevant section is worth quoting at length (Diodorus 40.3.1–7):

[1] When in ancient times a pestilence arose in Egypt, the common people ascribed their troubles to the workings of a divine agency. . . .
[2] Hence the natives of the land surmised that unless they removed the foreigners, their troubles would never be resolved. At once, therefore, the aliens were driven from the country, and the most outstanding and active among them banded together and, as some say, were cast ashore in Greece. . . . But the greater number were driven into what is now called Judea, which is not far distant from Egypt and was at that time utterly uninhabited.

[3] The colony was headed by a man called Moses, outstanding both for his wisdom and for his courage. On taking possession of the land he founded, besides other cities, one that is now the most renowned of all, called Jerusalem. In addition he established the temple that they hold in chief veneration, instituted their forms of worship and ritual, drew up their laws and ordered their politcal institutions. He also divided them into twelve tribes, since this is regarded as the most perfect number and corresponds to the number of months that make up a year.

[4] But he had no images whatsoever of the gods made for them, being of the opinion that God is not in human form; rather the Heaven that surrounds the earth is alone divine, and rules the universe. The sacrifices that he established differ from those of other nations, as does their way of living, for as a result of their own expulsion from Egypt he introduced an unsocial and intolerant mode of life. He picked out the men of most refinement and with the greatest ability to head the entire nation, and appointed them priests; and he ordained that they should occupy themselves with the temple and the honours and sacrifices offered to their god.

[5] These same men he appointed to be judges in all major disputes, and entrusted to them the guardianship of the laws and customs. For this reason the Jews never have a king, and authority over the people is regularly vested in whichever priest is regarded as superior to his colleagues in wisdom and virtue. They call this man the high priest [archierea], and believe that he acts as a messenger to them of God's commandments. [6] It is he, we are told, who in their assemblies and other gatherings announces what is ordained, and the Jews are so docile in such matters that straightway they fall to the ground and do reverence to the high priest when he expounds the commandments to them. And at the end of their laws there is even appended the statement: "These are the words that Moses heard from God and declares unto the Jews".

[7] He [Moses] led out military expeditions against the neighbouring tribes, and after annexing much land apportioned it out, assigning equal allotments to private citizens and greater ones to the priests,

in order that they, by virtue of receiving more ample revenues, might be undistracted and apply themselves continually to the worship of God.

The following insights are suggested by Hecateus's account:

1. In addition to discussing the supposed origin of the Jews (expelled from Egypt under the leadership of Moses), Hecateus describes a Jewish ethnic and national community centering on Jerusalem.

2. The priests provide leadership and act as judges, as well as running the cult and teaching the law. One rather interesting statement is that the priests possess land, at least collectively, and this differs from the explicit statements of the OT (Num. 18:24; Deut. 10:9; 12:12; 28:1). Coincidentally, this statement is more likely to match the reality of the Hellenistic period than the idealized portrait of the Pentateuch.

3. Chief authority is invested in the high priest who is chosen for his wisdom. This does not suggest a hereditary office. How seriously to take this inplication is difficult to say: most other sources indicate that the office was passed from father to son, but it may be that this was no more than the usual custom rather than a hard and fast rule; on the other hand, this may be a detail on which Hecateus was not fully informed.

4. Hecateus presents an aniconic and most likely a monotheistic temple-based religion.

5. He states that they have a law and gives a quotation which closely parallels Lev. 27:34 and Num. 36:13.

Zenon papyri

Durand, X. (1997) *Des Grecs en Palestine au III$_e$ siècle avant Jésus-Christ: Le dossier syrien des archives de Zénon de Caunos (261–252)*.
CPJ: 1.115–30.

Probably the most important source for the Jews in this period is the Zenon papyri (see *JCH* [172, 189–92, 202–3] for the more important historical implications and especially the administrative and economic data). Only six papyri are really directly important for Jewish affairs (*CPJ* 1.118–30, texts ##1–6). Some of the points arising from the Zenon papyri can be summarized as follows:

1. Local figures such as Tobias (*CPJ* ##1, 4) and Jeddous (*CPJ* #6) seem to have exercised considerable power and autonomy, whether in relation to the Ptolemaic government or to whatever provincial administration was exercised from Jerusalem.

2. Information on Tobias can be fitted with other sources to reconstruct some of the history of what seems to be an important Jewish family dynasty in the Transjordanian region.

3. The importance of Greek language and the need for those in power to work in the Greek medium is indicated by these letters. Tobias clearly had a Greek secretary, and if he did not already possess a Hellenistic education himself, the pressure to give such to his sons would have been very strong.

4. There is no indication that Tobias was anything but a loyal Jew, but the letters suggest a person who was not bothered by a polytheistic greeting to the king (cf. *CPJ* #4).

The story of the Tobiads

Gera, D. (1998) *Judaea and Mediterranean Politics 219 to 161 B.C.E.*

Grabbe, L. L. (2000g) "Jewish Historiography and Scripture in the Hellenistic Period", in L. L. Grabbe (ed.) *Did Moses Speak Attic? Jewish Historiography and Scripture in the Hellenistic Period.*

Will, E. (1991) '*Iraq el-Amir: Le Chateau du Tobiade Hyrcan.*

A significant section of Josephus's treatment of the Ptolemaic period is taken up with the story of Joseph Tobiad and his sons (*Ant.* 12.4.1–11 §§154–236; for details and discussion, see *JCH*: 174–75, 192–98, 217–18). This story has often been called a "romance" because it clearly contains novelistic elements. Exactly how much of it to believe has been a major question. The details are all to be treated with extreme caution, and Gera (1998: 36–58) has recently argued that, although the story of Joseph Tobiad and his sons is based on actual people and events, a number of the important elements in Josephus's account are fiction. Nevertheless, the story is supported in its essential features by information from other sources (cf. Grabbe 2000g), which Gera does not seem to dispute. The main points of the story as they have implications for religion are the following:

1. A powerful local family with a long history emerges in both the Tobiad romance and other early sources.

2. The high priest of the Oniad family was the chief representative of the Jews to the Ptolemaic government, as well as being the head of the temple and cult. This apparently included responsibility for tax collection (*Ant.* 12.4.1 §§158–59, though whether he had the formal office of *prostatēs* "leader, patron" is debated).

3. The Tobiad family evidently spoke Greek and was very much at home in the Greek world. Although they were wealthy and required to deal with the Greeks, the account illustrates the extent to which Greek culture had become a part of the ancient Near Eastern scene (though not displacing what was there beforehand).

4. The Tobiads were intermarried with the high priestly Oniads. A binary opposition of Tobiads versus Oniads is, therefore, likely to be simplistic.

5. The Tobiad family was itself split, probably between pro-Ptolemies and pro-Seleucids.

Ethiopic Enoch (*1 Enoch*) and the *Book of Giants*

Argall, R. A. (1995) *1 Enoch and Sirach: A Comparative Literary and Conceputal Analysis of the Themes of Revelation, Creation and Judgment.*

Milik, J. T. (1976) *The Books of Enoch: Aramaic Fragments of Qumran Cave 4.*

Reeves, J. C. (1992) *Jewish Lore in Manichaean Cosmogony: Studies in the* Book of Giants *Traditions.*

Stuckenbruck, L. T. (1997) *The Book of Giants from Qumran.*

Stone, M. E. (1978) "The Book of Enoch and Judaism in the Third Century B.C.E.", *CBQ* 40: 479–92.

An introduction with bibliography was given to the whole of the *1 Enoch* in *JCH* (180–81), and this is only supplemented here. Only a portion of the book is likely to have been written as early as the Ptolemaic period, namely the *Book of Watchers* (1–36) and the *Astronomical Book* (72–82). Despite the differences between the sections, there are several themes that cut through the different parts of the book: the fall of the Watchers; the fate of the righteous and the wicked; the place of angels; a concern for the movements of the cosmos and the calendar and the cosmic secrets in general. This could be an editorial consequence of combining the various sections, but it may be that the themes were already there and actually served to suggest bringing the individual writings together. Several points about Jewish religion emerge from *1 Enoch* 1–36 and 72–82 and the *Book of Giants*:

1. These chapters from *1 Enoch*, and the book as a whole, form one of the best examples of the development of apocalyptic (see pp. 232–36 below).

2. The myth of the fall of the Watchers, evidently a widespread myth in early Judaism, has its fullest exposition here. It is very important theologically because it presents an explanation of the present evil state of the world, and why humans sin, that differs from all other Jewish and Christian theologies (e.g. the fall of Adam and Eve or the existence of the the two *yeṣer*s "tendencies" in each individual).

3. Eschatology is a significant theme, including interest in the future and the endtime and attempts to calculate it. The fate of all who live, whether good or evil, and the question of an afterlife are dealt with explicitly. The book is one of the first Jewish writings to exhibit the concept of a soul that survives death (see pp. 267–68 below).

4. *1 Enoch* 72–82 demonstrates the importance of the calendar and the fact that more than one version seems to have been in use (see pp. 141–43 below). The astronomical book apparently once contained a comparative table that reconciled the solar and the lunar cycles (Milik 1976: 274–77). The Ethiopic version shows the use of a solar calendar which seems to coincide with that known from the Qumran texts (see p. 143 below).

5. Cosmic secrets, revealed through Enoch's visions and heavenly journeys, are a feature of the book, especially in 17–36 and 72–82. Enoch has visions

of, or takes journeys to, various exotic places: the dwelling of God in heaven (14:8–25), the workings of the earth and the underworld (17–19), the place of punishment for the fallen angels (21), the storehouses of the souls of the dead (22), the western extremes of the earth (23–25), the environs of (the later) Jerusalem and the "accursed valley" (26–27), and the other extremities of the earth with their exotic sights (28–36). The *Astronomical Book* is entirely taken up with the workings of the cosmos.

6. The extent to which angelology and demonology at this time had evolved is well indicated. No other early Jewish writing gives such details about the spirit world (see pp. 219–25 below).

7. The growth of authoritative scripture seems to have included the book, since *1 Enoch* had the status of scripture in some Jewish circles (Jude 14–15 quotes 1:9; the number of copies at Qumran suggests the book's authority there).

Qohelet (Ecclesiastes)

Bartholomew, C. G. (1998) *Reading Ecclesiastes: Old Testament Exegesis and Hermeneutical Theory*.

Bickerman, E. J. (1967) "Koheleth (Ecclesiastes) or The Philosophy of an Acquisitive Society", *Four Strange Books of the Bible*: 139–67.

Burkes, S. (1999) *Death in Qoheleth and Egyptian Biographies of the Late Period*.

Crenshaw, J. (1988) *Ecclesiastes*.

Fischer, A. A. (1997) *Skepsis oder Furcht Gottes? Studien zur Komposition und Theologie des Buches Kohelet*.

Fox, M. V. (1999) *A Time to Tear Down and a Time to Build Up: A Rereading of Ecclesiastes*.

Loader, J. A. (1979) *Polar Structures in the Book of Kohelet*.

Lohfink, N. (1998) *Studien zu Kohelet*.

Murphy, R. E., and E. Huwiler (1999) *Proverbs, Ecclesiastes, Song of Songs*.

Schwienhorst-Schönberger, L. (ed.) (1997) *Das Buch Kohelet: Studien zur Struktur, Geschichte, Rezeption und Theologie*.

Seow, C.-L. (1997) *Ecclesiastes*.

—— (1999) "Qohelet's Eschatological Poem", *JBL*: 209–34.

Schoors, A. (1992) *The Preacher Sought to Find Pleasing Words: A Study of the Language of Qoheleth*.

—— (ed.) (1998) *Qohelet in the Context of Wisdom*.

Whybray, R. N. (1981) "The Identification and Use of Quotations in Ecclesiastes", *Congress Volume: Vienna 1980*: 435–51.

—— (1989) *Ecclesiastes*.

A brief introduction and earlier studies were given in *JCH* (175–76). There has been an overwhelming consensus that Qohelet dates from the Ptolemaic period, based on the lateness of its Hebrew and also the view of some scholars about the influence from Greek thought on the book. Very recently Seow has argued for the Persian period (1997: 20), based partly on linguistic grounds and partly on the parallels of thought with literature from the Persian period. I do not find Seow's arguments ultimately convincing. The lack of borrowings of Greek words is not unusual because few Greek words can be found in any of the Hebrew or Aramaic writings of the Greek period, while the alleged parallels with Persian period literature are no more convincing than those from Greek. But what Seow has shown is the difficulty of dating the book precisely.

This book is unique in early Jewish literature in the way it challenges conventional thought. This seems true even despite the widely differing interpretations of the book. One of the problems of interpretation is the existence of a number of apparently contradictory statements in the book, some of which appear extremely radical, whereas others express a more conventional piety. An older solution was to assume that the more traditional statements were made by a later editor trying to tone down the skeptical message. One can ask why a reader scandalized by the message would try to edit it rather than simply rejecting it – and why so many extreme statements were allowed to stand. Most recent studies have attempted to explain the book as all by one author (except Qoh. 12:9–14). The various attempts to reconcile some of the content have included an appeal to quotations (Whybray 1981), "polar structures" (the writer deliberately explores both extremes by means of thesis and antithesis: Loader 1979), or the special meaning of *hevel* (often translated "vanity" but the meaning is very much debated; see, e.g. Fox 1999) which occurs at key passages in the book (1:2, 14; 2:17, 19, 21, 23, 26; 4:4, 8, 16; 6:9; 11:8; 12:8).

How to understand the book as a whole depends to some extent on what one thinks its background is. Bickerman (1967: 139–67) has given an interesting interpretation of Qohelet on the assumption that it was written in the Ptolemaic period and was influenced by Greek thought, but regardless of whether Qohelet's scepticism arose from his Near Eastern background (cf. Seow 1997) or from Hellenistic thought, he says things found nowhere else in Jewish literature until many centuries later. Qohelet may thus tell us more about the thought of one writer than about Judaism in general; nevertheless, the work is still useful and contributes to our knowledge of religious development. Here are points important for Judaic religion:

1. Qohelet (along with Job) is practically unique in early Jewish literature in expressing a skeptical position in reference to knowledge, including knowledge of the deity. This book is probably the closest of any Jewish writing to the inquiring mind first exhibited in the "Ionic Enlightenment" of the Greeks.

2. The book carries forward the earlier wisdom tradition but also questions it; it is an example of what is sometimes called the "crisis in wisdom". It affirms the importance of wisdom (2:13–14) but also emphasizes its severe limitations (7:23–24; 8:16–17). Instead of the wise being in the know, their

wisdom can go only so far and it has no ultimate advantage because all die (2:14–16; 8:5–8).

3. The exact message of the book is debated by specialists. For example, Crenshaw sees it as ultimately negative (1988), whereas Whybray has seen a much more positive message (1989).

4. The book is very much preoccupied with death but does not appear to see anything beyond it (2:16; 3:18–21). In that sense it is in the old tradition about death being the end of the individual.

5. The language of the book is an important stage in trying to determine the history of the Hebrew language. Although clearly still Classical Hebrew, it already has many features known from later Mishnaic Hebrew. One can debate the origins of these features (e.g. natural language change or influence of Aramaic), but they suggest that linguistic features can help in dating various Hebrew writings of early Judaism.

Tobit

Fitzmyer, J. A. (1995a) "The Aramaic and Hebrew Fragments of Tobit from Cave 4", *CBQ* 57: 655–75.

— (1995b) "Tobit", in J. VanderKam (ed.) *Qumran Cave 4: XIV Parabiblical Texts, Part 2*: 1–84.

Gamberoni, J. (1997) "Das 'Gesetz des Mose' im Buch Tobias", in G. Braulik (ed.) *Studien zu Pentateuch: Walter Kornfeld zum 60 Geburtstag*: 227–42.

Grabbe, L. L. (forthcoming) "Tobit", in J. D. G. Dunn and J. W. Rogerson (eds) *Commentary 2000*.

Hanhart, R. (1983) *Tobit*, Septuaginta 8/5.

Moore, C. A. (1992) "Tobit, Book of", *ABD* 6.585–94.

—— (1996) *Tobit: A New Translation with Introduction and Commentary*.

Rabenau, M. (1994) *Studien zum Buch Tobit*.

Soll, W. (1988) "Tobit and Folklore Studies, with Emphasis on Propp's Morphology", in D. J. Lull (ed.) *Society of Biblical Literature 1988 Seminar Papers*: 39–53.

Spencer, R. A. (1999) "The Book of Tobit in Recent Research", *CR: BS* 7: 147–80.

Thomas, J. D. (1972) "The Greek Text of Tobit", *JBL* 91: 463–71.

Wills, L. M. (1995) *The Jewish Novel in the Ancient World*.

This is one of the earliest Jewish writings to deal with Jews in the Diaspora (see *JCH* [176–77] for a brief introduction and bibliography). The text of Tobit exists in two main major forms (see Hanhart for critical editions of both texts). It had been thought that the book was originally written in a Semitic language, and that the Greek text was only a translation. Most scholars have tended to see the longer Sinaiticus manuscript as more original (Fitzmyer 1995a). The shorter text of the Vaticanus is also in more elegant Greek and seems therefore to be a revision of a longer, Semiticized text similar to Sinaiticus (Thomas 1972). Among the Qumran scrolls are four manuscripts of Tobit in Aramaic and one in Hebrew (Fitzmyer 1995b). It is not absolutely clear whether the original language was Hebrew or Aramaic, but scholars tend to favor Aramaic.

The book is an example of what has been called a "Jewish novel" (Soll 1988; Wills 1995: 68–92); it has some characteristics of the folk tale but has been developed by the incorporation of didactic, hymnic, and prophetic elements which are not usually found in a folk tale. It also has characteristics in common with the Greco-Roman novel or romance but differs in some respects (e.g. being shorter and de-emphasizing the erotic element). The book gives a number of insights into Judaism and its concerns for the period in which it was written:

1. Tobit is one of the few books set in the Diaspora, with one of its aims that of illustrating how Jews were to live in a hostile Gentile environment.

2. The question of theodicy (or why God allows innocent suffering) is an important theme, one also addressed by the books of Job and Qohelet.

3. The family is seen both as a refuge from the outside world and an entity to which one owes various duties, such as help to relatives in times of trouble. Above all is the need to marry those related (though it is not entirely clear whether this is with fellow Israelites generally or within one's own tribe specifically). Although the family is a social matter, it cannot be separated from the practice of religion.

4. The importance of proper burial not only for one's parents (4:3–4; 6:15; 14:11–13) but also for the anonymous Jews whose bodies are left in the streets (1:17–19; 2:3–8) has a significant place. One might think this was in some way related to an expectation of a resurrection or an afterlife, but neither of these is hinted at anywhere in the book.

5. There is quite a bit of what many would call moral teaching. Almsgiving is a major theme (1:16–17; 2:14; 4:8–11; 12:8–9; 14:10–11). The "negative Golden Rule" first occurs here, centuries before Jesus or Hillel (4:15). There may be also be one of the first indications of an ascetic view of sex as being only for procreative purposes (cf. 8:7).

6. What are often referred to as cultic or ritual instructions include the proper observance of the festivals (2:1–5), temple worship (1:4–6), the necessity for observing the food laws (1:11), and tithing (1:6–8).

7. The authority of the Scriptures is invoked: the "book of Moses" and the prophets are specifically mentioned [1:8; 2:6; 6:13; 7:11–13; 14:3]. Tobit seems to presuppose knowledge of the contents of our present Pentateuch (Gamberoni 1997).

8. Angelology and demonology are recurring themes (3:7–9, 17; 5:4–5; 12:6–21).

9. Magical practices are mentioned (8:1–3).

The edicts of Antiochus III

Bertrand, J. M. (1982) "Sur l'inscription d'Hefzibah", *ZPE* 46: 167–74.

Bickerman, E. J. (1980a) "Une question d'authenticité: les privilèges juifs", *Studies in Jewish and Christian History*: 2.24–43.

—— (1980b) "La charte séleucide de Jérusalem", *Studies in Jewish and Christian History*: 2.44–85.

—— (1980c) "Une proclamation séleucide relative au temple de Jérusalem", *Studies in Jewish and Christian History*: 2.86–104.

Fischer, T. (1979) "Zur Seleukideninschrift von Hefzibah", *ZPE* 33: 131–38.

Gauger, Jörg-Dieter (1977) *Beiträge zur jüdischen Apologetik: Untersuchungen zur Authentizität von Urkunden bei Flavius Josephus und im I. Makkabäerbuch.*

Grabbe, L. L. (1998a) *Ezra and Nehemiah.*

—— (2000g) "Jewish Historiography and Scripture in the Hellenistic Period", in L. L. Grabbe (ed.) *Did Moses Speak Attic? Jewish Historiography and Scripture in the Hellenistic Period.*

Landau, Y. H. (1966) "A Greek Inscription Found Near Hefzibah", *IEJ* 16: 54–70.

Lenger, M.-T. (1964) *Corpus des Ordonnances des Ptolémées.*

Liebesny, H. (1936) "Ein Erlass des Königs Ptolemaios II Philadelphos über die Deklaration von Vieh und Sklaven in Syrien und Phonikien (PER Inv. Nr. 24.552 gr.)", *Aegyptus* 16: 257–91.

Marcus, R. (1943) "Appendix D. Antiochus III and the Jews (*Ant.* xii. 129–153)", in H. S. J. Thackery (ed.) *Josephus* (LCL; London: Heinemann; Cambridge, MA: Harvard, 1943) 7.743–66.

Antiochus III defeated Scopas, the general of Ptolemy V, about 200 BCE. According to Josephus (*Ant.* 12.3.3–4 §§138–46), Antiochus III issued a decree which listed the temple personnel and relieved some of their taxes temporarily so that the temple could be repaired of war damage. The decree is as follows (the sections in italics being further discussed below):

> King Antiochus to Ptolemy, greeting. Inasmuch as the Jews, from the very moment when we entered their country, showed their eagerness to serve us and, when we came to their city, gave us a splendid reception and met us with their senate and furnished an abundance of provisions to our soldiers and elephants, and also helped us to expel the Egyptian garrison in the citadel, we have seen fit on our part to requite them for these acts and to restore their city which has been destroyed by the hazards of war, and to repeople it by bringing back to it those who have been dispersed abroad. In the first place we have decided, on account of their piety, to furnish them for their sacrifices an allowance of sacrificial animals, wine, oil and frankincense to the value of twenty thousand pieces of silver, and sacred

artabae of fine flour in accordance with their native law, and one thousand four hundred and sixty *medimni* of wheat and three hundred and seventy-five *medimni* of salt. *And it is my will that these things be made over to them as I have ordered, and that the work on the temple be completed, including the porticoes and any other part that it may be necessary to build.*

The timber, moreover, shall be brought from Judea itself and from other nations and Lebanon without the imposition of a toll-charge. The like shall be done with the other materials needed for making the restoration of the temple more splendid. And all the members of the nation shall have a form of government in accordance with the laws of their country, and the senate, the priests, the scribes of the temple and the temple-singers shall be relieved from the poll-tax and the crown-tax and the salt-tax which they pay. *And, in order that the city may be the more quickly be inhabited, I grant both to the present inhabit-ants and to those who may return before the month of Hyperberetaios exemption from taxes for three years.*

We shall also relieve them in future from the third part of their tribute, so that their losses may be made good. And as for those who were carried off from the city and are slaves, we herewith set them free, both them and the children born to them, and order their property to be restored to them.

This document has generally been taken as authentic, even if those in §§145–46 and §§148–153 are rejected (Gauger 1977: 19, 23–24, 61–63, 136–39; Bickerman 1980: 2.24–104; Marcus 1943; Grabbe 2000g). We should expect such a decree from a conqueror, and a number of considerations argue for its existence. First, there is the statement in 2 Maccabees about "the royal concessions to the Jews, secured through John the father of Eupolemus" (4:11), the only logical context being the time of Antiochus III's conquest. Second, it fits the general situation in Syro-Palestine at the time. A subordinate people are often ready for a change, in hope of bettering their condition, if ruled by a particular power for a long period of time. Third, the last section of the decree fits the general approach of Ptolemy II's decree in the Rainer papyrus (Lenger 1964: 21–22; Liebesny 1936; *JCH*: 185–87), suggesting not only a common administrative approach and style but also a common administrative policy toward those being governed. The basic agreement in style and content (even by one so exacting as Gauger) with other Seleucid documents, such as the Rainer papyrus and the Hefzibah inscription (Landau 1966; Fischer 1979; Bertrand 1982; *JCH*: 240–41), has been well demonstrated, and the contents are not intrinsically unlikely. Antiochus also interacts with his minister Ptolemy, just as he does in the Hefzibah stela. Fourth, there is little that looks like Jewish propaganda here, such as one finds in other documents (e.g. the Ezra decrees [cf. Grabbe 1998a: 128–32]). Antiochus remits certain taxes temporarily to help in rebuilding the damaged city, as one might expect. He does not deliver fantastic sums of money nor treat the Jews in any special way, as one might expect in falsified letters (cf. Ezra 8:26–27).

These positive points do not remove all the problems. There are two problems which remain, despite the positive arguments: the first is that in contrast to the normal style of royal Seleucid documents, two sections (§§141 and 143) are in the first person singular, making them the most suspect (Gauger 1977: 19, 23–24, 61–63, 136–39). These are set off in italics above. The second is the failure to mention the high priest. There are several possible explanations for this: Antiochus may have wanted to concentrate on the institutions (the "senate" [gerousia]) or groups rather than individuals; Simon may have opposed Antiochus (but then why was he allowed to continue in office?); there was no high priest at the time of the invasion, or perhaps the high priest was killed in the fighting over Jerusalem, and Simon came to the office only after Antiochus had entered the city. These are only suggestions, but lack of mention of Simon is not fatal to the decree's authenticity.

Although some of these points are more indirectly relevant for religion, the decree suggests the following:

1. The bulk of the Jews seem to have been pro-Seleucid at the time of Antiochus's invasion.

2. The king provides a modest allowance for sacrifices, though it is not clear whether this is on a temporary basis or for a longer period.

3. The temple personnel (including members of the gerousia) are relieved from certain taxes; however, the statement that all Jews are granted a tax exemption for three years is in a suspect part of the decree. In any case, this would be only a temporary exemption.

4. Taxes for the entire population are reduced by one-third for an indefinite future.

5. Those enslaved in the war are to be freed and have their property returned.

Demetrius the Chronographer

DiTommaso, L. (1998) "A Note on Demetrius the Chronographer, Fr. 2.11 (= Eusebius, PrEv 9.21.11)", JSJ 29: 81–91.

Grabbe, L. L. (1979b) "Chronography in Hellenistic Jewish Historiography", in P. J. Achtemeier (ed.) Society of Biblical Literature 1979 Seminar Papers: 2.43–68.

Holladay, C. R. (1983) Fragments from Hellenistic Jewish Authors, Volume I: Historians.

For general information on the Fragmentary Jewish Writings in Greek, including Demetrius, see JCH (236–38) and pp. 70–73 below. The following points about religion can be taken from the preserved text:

1. The only version of the Bible that Demetrius seems to know is that of the LXX (Septuagint). Thus, he is an important witness not only to the text of the LXX but also to the fact that it had already been translated before he wrote. There is good reason to date his writing before 200 BCE, which also puts the LXX about the mid-third century (Holladay 1983: 51–2).

2. The few bits of Demetrius's work which survive show a rationalistic approach which attempts to sort out difficulties, especially as they relate to chronology. For example, he explains why it was no problem for Moses and Zipporah to be of two different generations (*apud* Eusebius, *Praep. Evang.* 9.29.1–3) and how the Israelites leaving Egypt got their weapons (*Praep. Evang.* 9.29.16). His work fits the spirit of Hellenistic historiography in which traditions and legends were subjected to scrutiny and remolded into history.

3. The core of his work is trying to develop a rational chronology of biblical events (cf. Grabbe 1979b). Most of it is internal to the Bible, but there are some attempts to relate to external chronology.

The Septuagint translation of the Bible

Barr, J. (1979) "The Typology of Literalism in Ancient Biblical Trans-lations", *Mitteilungen des Septuaginta-Unternehmens* 15: 275–325.

Brock, S. P. (1979) "Aspects of Translation Technique in Antiquity", *Greek, Roman, and Byzantine Studies* 20: 69–87.

Lee, J. A. L. (1983) *A Lexical Study of the Septuagint Version of the Pentateuch.*

Orlinsky, H. M. (1975) "The Septuagint as Holy Writ and the Philosophy of the Translators", *HUCA* 46: 89–114.

For information and discussion on translations of the Bible, see pp. 158–65 below. According to the legendary *Letter of Aristeas* (pp. 75–76 below) the Pentateuch was first translated into Greek in the reign of Ptolemy II. This account of how the Torah came to be translated is generally rejected by modern scholars, though the time may be correct (Orlinsky 1975). A need was probably being felt for a Greek version of the Bible fairly early in the Greek period. To see the initial translation of portions of the Bible into Greek as early as the middle of the third century BCE is not unreasonable: Demetrius the Chronographer (above) seems already to have used the LXX as the basis for his exegesis, which would put it in existence already before 200 BCE. However, it seems clear that the first translation involved only the Pentateuch since this shows a coherence in language not found elsewhere in the text (Lee 1983).

The translation of the Pentateuch into Greek (to be followed over time with translation of the other books) marked a significant step in the development of Judaism as a religion. The religious value of the LXX translation can be summarized as follows:

1. The need to translate the Bible emphasizes the important part that the written scriptures were now starting to play in the Jewish religion, especially for those worshipers too far from the temple to visit it regularly. As noted above, the Pentateuch seems to have been translated about the mid-third century BCE. This translation into Greek represented a significant innovation since there was little precedent for the translation of sacred literature, and the model used has been debated (cf. Brock 1979; Barr 1979).

2. The LXX made the biblical material available to the increasing number of Jews whose first language was Greek and who knew little or no Hebrew. The LXX became *the* Bible of the Greek-speaking Jews to the extent that its very letter was considered inspired and was used for detailed exegesis by such writers as Philo of Alexandria (pp. 89–92 below).

3. The LXX is testimony to the variety of biblical text circulating during the centuries before the fall of Jerusalem and to the continuing growth and development of the text, perhaps even to the very end of the Second Temple period. In some sections the LXX is quite different from the Masoretic text which became the standard Hebrew text of the OT. Discoveries at Qumran now support what had often been argued by scholars: that the LXX, where different, often attests a different Hebrew *Vorlage*.

4. Here and there in the LXX is found evidence of interpretative traditions that circulated among the Jews during this period. A good example is the counting of Pentecost, with the LXX probably giving an interpretation that differed from the actual practice in the temple (pp. 141, 199 below).

Ben Sira (Ecclesiasticus)

Argall, R. A. (1995) *1 Enoch and Sirach: A Comparative Literary and Conceptual Analysis of the Themes of Revelation, Creation and Judgment.*

Beentjes, P. C. (1997a) *The Book of Ben Sira in Hebrew: A Text Edition of all Extant Hebrew Manuscrits and a Synopsis of all Parallel Hebrew Ben Sira Texts.*

—— (ed.) (1997b) *The Book of Ben Sira in Modern Research.*

Calduch-Benages, N., and J. Vermeylen (eds) (1999) *Treasures of Wisdom: Studies in Ben Sira and the Book of Wisdom: Festschrift M. Gilbert.*

Coggins, R. J. (1998a) *Sirach.*

DiLella, A. (1996) "The Wisdom of Ben Sira: Resources and Recent Research", *CR: BS* 4: 161–81.

Hayward, C. T. Robert (1992) "The New Jerusalem in the Wisdom of Jesus ben Sira", *SJOT* 6: 123–38.

Liesen, J. (2000) *Full of Praise: An Exegetical Study of Sir 39, 12–35.*

Mack, B. L. (1985) *Wisdom and the Hebrew Epic: Ben Sira's Hymn in Praise of the Fathers.*

Muraoka, T., and J. F. Elwolde (eds) (1997) *The Hebrew of the Dead Sea Scrolls and Ben Sira: Proceedings of a Symposium Held at Leiden University, 11–14 December 1995.*

Stadelmann, H. (1980) *Ben Sira also Schriftgelehrter: einer Untersuchung zum Berufsbild des vor-makkabäischen Sofer unter Berücksichtigung seines Verhältnisses zu Priester-, Propheten- und Weisheitslehrertum.*

Talmon, S., and Y. Yadin (eds) (1999) *Masada VI: Yigael Yadin Excavations 1963–1965, Final Reports: Hebrew Fragments; The Ben Sira Scroll.*

Wright, B. G. (1989) *No Small Difference: Sirach's Relationship to its Hebrew Parent Text.*

Ziegler, J. (1980b) *Sapientia Iesu Filii Sirach.*

The book of Jesus ben Sira is one of the first books for which we have some explicit information about its author and when it was written (see *JCH* [176] for a brief introduction and earlier bibliography). The book is important also because we have about two-thirds of it in its Hebrew original (Beentjes 1997a), as well as in the Greek translation (Ziegler 1980b). The question of how faithful the Greek is to the Hebrew is an important one since large sections of the text are extant only in Greek. The most recent studies suggest that the translation is faithful in conveying the thought but is not slavishly literal (Wright 1989: 249). Although the book itself was composed, or at least completed, in the Seleucid period, the overall situation which one gleans from it would seem to be that current during Ptolemaic rule. Some of the main points relating to religion can be summarized here:

1. Ben Sira is quite important for its insight into the priesthood of his time. Although evidently drawing on the biblical text for many of his comments, such passages as 7:29–31 (honor and support of the priests), 34:18–35:16 (offerings), 38:9–11 (cult and physicians), and 50:1–29 seem to reflect the priesthood known to him. It has even been suggested that he himself was a priest (Stadelmann 1980), though this is problematic because one cannot imagine his not mentioning what would to him have been a great honor; nevertheless, he shows close connections with the priesthood and certainly great sympathy with it.

2. The book shows the continuity of the wisdom tradition, having much in common with Proverbs and the old wisdom tradition; however, it also exhibits many of the theological characteristics of other traditions such as the book of Deuteronomy. It is often asserted (with good reason) that Ben Sira brings together the wisdom and the deuteronomic traditions. On the other hand, the originality of Job and Qohelet have been left behind.

3. Scribalism as an entity is first expounded in his book, especially at 38:24–39:11.

4. The relationship of the book with eschatology and apocalypticism has been much debated. It seems to have no concept of an afterlife. Many think that it rejects the apocalyptic tradition such as exemplified in *1 Enoch*, a view supported by such passages as 34:1–7 that polemicize against dreams and divination; yet passages such as 36:20–21 and 39:1–3 on prophecy suggest some interest in the esoteric traditions, and Ben Sira even accepts that some

visions can come from God (34:6). There is also the possibility that the book contains an allusion to messianic expectations (p. 273 below).

SYNTHESIS

Baumgarten, A. I. (1997) *The Flourishing of Jewish Sects in the Maccabean Era: An Interpretation.*

Funck, B. (ed.) (1996) *Hellenismus: Beiträge zur Erforschung von Akkulturation und politischer Ordnung in den Staaten des hellenistischen Zeitalters, Akten des Internationalen Hellenismus-Kolloquiums 9.–14. März 1994 in Berlin.*

Grabbe, L. L. (1995a) *Priests, Prophets, Diviners, Sages: A Socio-historical Study of Religious Specialists in Ancient Israel.*

—— (1999d) Review article: A. I. Baumgarten, *The Flourishing of Jewish Sects in the Maccabean Era, JSJ* 30: 89–94.

Schwartz, S. (1994) "On the Autonomy of Judaea in the Fourth and Third Centuries B.C.E.", *JJS* 45: 157–68.

There is no doubt that from the conquest of Alexander to the end of Ptolemaic rule – a period of less than one and a half centuries – enormous developments took place in Judaism. These were not all new in that the seeds of many of them were evidently already well sown and even growing during Persian rule. Yet when we look at what is likely to have reached a significant level of progression during this time, we see monumental changes to the Jewish religion – changes in many ways in contrast to the little-altered lifestyle of the bulk of Jewish people. The trunk of Judaism had not changed, but these new developments presaged much greater changes for a later time, and new buds sprouted in new and unfamiliar directions.

What becomes especially evident in the Ptolemaic period is the importance of the high priest as the leader of the nation in the political sphere as well as the religious (pp. 144–47 below). This may well have been the case in the later Persian period as well, but the lack of proper documentation makes us uncertain. But Hecateus of Abdera (pp. 37–39 above) testifies to the priesthood in general and the high priest in particular as the governors of the people, under the Hellenistic ruler, of course. The high priest may have been given the specific Ptolemaic office of *prostasis* "governance, patronage" (though this is disputed: p. 40 above). A "sanhedrin" of some sort, probably made up of both priests and lay aristocracy, also assisted or advised him (pp. 144–47 below). There was possibly a Ptolemaic governor over the region, though the evidence is against it (cf. *JCH:* 190), but in essence the Jewish province was a theocracy (or hierocracy) under control of the priestly establishment in Jerusalem. Although the province was subject to the government in Alexandria, this was mainly for taxation purposes. The high priest did not always have his own way, as the story of Joseph Tobiad suggests

(p. 40 above), and the Jewish community in Palestine was probably not all that large or powerful. Nevertheless, the temple had a strong control over the people, and existence in a context of foreign rule would have made the people look up to the priestly leadership even more.

What this suggests is that religion would have been mostly in the hands of the priests. The situation was not monolithic since we have indications that some groups may have opposed the priestly establishment. It is difficult to know much in detail, yet there are reasons for suggesting the existence of groups who may have been alienated from the dominant temple establishment. For example, the group mentioned in the *Damascus Document* (CD 1:4–9) may have been in existence already by this time. Similarly, sections of *1 Enoch* which had already been written by 200 BCE suggest a group that used a solar calendar (*1 Enoch* 72–82), even though the calendar in use by the temple at this time was likely to have been a solar–lunar calendar (p. 143 below). This may suggest a group who had actually broken away from the temple.

None of these points is uncontroversial, and our evidence is indirect; still, what we might call sectarianism probably already existed during the Ptolematic period. The situation of the Jewish community under foreign rule (cf. Baumgarten 1997: 188–92) and the simple instinct of self-preservation probably helped to dampen such developments without, however, suppressing them entirely. We should be careful about assuming a lay/priestly dichotomy as has too often been done, however, because it is likely that some movements of defection were led by members of priestly families. The literature we have indicates a good education on the part of the authors, and the general indication is that much intellectual knowledge was a priestly preserve (Grabbe 1995a: 170). But there were many priests, more than were needed to service the temple; not all priests would have been equally educated or adept in intellectual matters, but the opportunity to study, write, and engage in theological speculation was mainly a priestly one (pp. 150–52 below). Any sectarian movements during this period had a good chance of being priestly led (see below on *1 Enoch*).

Similarly, the lay opposition to the high priest was led by the aristocratic family of the Tobiads. Yet one must keep in mind that this was not a simple "priest versus lay" or even an Oniad versus Tobiad opposition, for the Tobiad and Oniad families were intermarried: Joseph Tobiad was indeed a "layman", but he was an aristocrat and actually the nephew of the high priest. The importance of these two families in this period is made very clear in Josephus's narrative, as well as other sources (e.g. 2 Macc. 3:10–11).

One of the most interesting phenomena, but also one of the hardest to come to grips with, is that of Hellenization. (A full discussion with bibliography is found in *JCH* [ch. 3, pp. 147–70] with only a brief survey here; cf. also the essays in Funck 1996.) Despite the fact that this is a complex entity and not easily summarized in a sentence or two, much unnecessary nonsense has been written about it, partly because so many writers treat it only in relationship to the Jews and not in its complete context. Hellenization is in many ways analogous to the Anglicization of India or the spread of American popular culture to much of the world. When Alexander's armies marched across the Persian empire, beginning in 334 BCE, Greek culture was not new to Asia. Many cities under Persian rule in Anatolia were Greek, and Greek culture had long since made an inroad into other coastal areas such as Phoenicia. Greek mercenary armies had been fighting in the Near East for a long time, possibly centuries. As Alexander and his successors settled veterans in newly founded *poleis* (cities set up on the Greek model), there was little desire on the part of the Greeks to share their privileges with the natives – there was no mission to Hellenize. However, many of the upper class and local aristocracy were useful in administration, and some saw that a Greek education would be useful to their heirs in gaining the best advantage with the Greek rulers. A man like Tobias of the Zenon papyri had a Greek secretary and may have spoken Greek. Certainly, the Tobiad romance depicts Joseph and Hyrcanus as being fully at home in the Ptolemaic court, including its language and culture.

What began as a move on the part of native peoples to better themselves continued on for centuries to the point that "Greek" became a matter of education and language rather than ethnic origin, but it was a gradual process. Greek institutions and cultural elements took their place alongside those of Egypt and Mesopotamia but did not displace them. Rather than driving out the native cultures, Greek simply became another element in the multifarious mixture already indigenous to the region. Many of the features that we think of as characteristic of the Hellenistic empires were not known in the Greek homeland but were simply continued from the Oriental empires which had preceded Alexander, not least the institution of the Hellenistic king and court.

The Jews were not particularly different from other native peoples in their reaction to Hellenization. Certain overt cultural elements were probably rejected as conspicuous symbols of the conquerors, but most became so much a part of their world that they would not have been recognized as having a foreign origin. There is no evidence of rejection of general Greek culture; on the other hand, the lives of most Jews who were simple agrarian workers was not particularly changed by the coming of the Greeks. The lives of peasants all over the ancient Near East seem to have gone on with little alteration from the days of Sumer to the Ottoman empire. The inhabitants of Judah would have noticed the most changes in the collection of taxes and the fact that Ptolemaic officials were present even in the individual villages to oversee such matters, though such officials were often local people. Greek was used for official communication, but local languages continued in widespread use, especially at the lower levels of administration (Aramaic was still the *lingua franca* for much of the ancient Near East).

The ones most immediately affected by Greek institutions and culture were the upper classes. They were also the ones most likely to see the advantages of embracing some of these or, as time went on, even to regard them as desirable in their own right. Being able to communicate on terms of some equality with the Greek administration could be useful, but a Greek education could supply more than that. Greek theatre and literature provided entertainment. The daily exercises in the gymnasia would have furnished a spectacle to divert those with time on their hands. Some individuals became literati with a considerable reputation, though most Jews who set their hand to composing literature in Greek seem not to have been known much outside Jewish circles (e.g. Ezekiel the tragedian). But there is no question that some Jews found Greek culture very seductive.

However, ordinary Jews would also have come into contact with Greek to a lesser or greater extent as time went on. Not a few Jews followed military occupations, from the brief references we find in the literature, either as mercenaries or perhaps as a part of certain official units. Josephus claims that Ptolemy I used Jewish soldiers (*Ant.* 12.1.1 §8), and various anecdotes put Jews in Hellenistic armies (*Ag. Apion* 1.22 §§192, 201–4). Tobias's military settlement included Jews, though there were other ethnic groups as well (*CPJ* 1.118–21). The papyri also show a number of Jewish military settlers in Ptolemaic Egypt (*CPJ* 1.11–15, 147–78). The result was a slow but steady acculturation to the new civilization, the Hellenistic civilization, which was neither Hellenic nor Oriental but a dynamic synthesis of the two, forming a *sui generis*.

The question of how far the Hebrew Bible had developed before the Greek period has become an area of controversy in recent years. The position taken here is that some of the main documents had already reached more or less their present form by the end of the Persian period (pp. 152–57 below) and were also seen as a collection. The term "canonical" may be too strong a word to use at this point, but it seems clear that certain writings had become in some sense authoritative or sacred. This applies to Genesis, to 2 Kings, the Major Prophets, all the Minor Prophets, Proverbs, Job, Lamentations, and the Song of Songs. Granted this assessment, a good deal of scriptural activity still took place during the Greek period, including Qohelet, Daniel (completed under Seleucid rule), and the finalizing of a number of other works (probably Chronicles, Ezra–Nehemiah, Esther). The text also continued to develop for another century or so, with many of these works extant in more than one version, sometimes in versions considerably different from one another.

With the acceptance of certain writings as authoritative, biblical interpretation took its place as a religious activity (pp. 165–70 below). It was probably also during the Greek period that this began in earnest, even if its roots may lie earlier. As long as the text remained fluid, which it evidently did for several centuries, the process of interpreting and updating the tradition could be done simply by alteration of the text. Not much different from this, however, was the creation of new writings out of old traditions which then took their place alongside the sacred writing that incorporated the old tradition. "Rewritten Bible" and para-biblical writing were much like updating the text except that they took the perhaps more radical step of creating a new, parallel writing. A work like the *Exagoge* of Ezekiel the tragedian (p. 72 below) not only gave another version of the Exodus story but did so in a Greek literary form. But other forms of interpretation that gave greater weight to the authority of the text also developed, notably that of commentary. Demetrius's desire to reconcile potential contradictions and problems is evidence that the tradition has been crystalized into written form, and problems cannot be solved just by rewriting it. It was also important to resolve anything that might seem to call the validity of the "scriptures" into question.

What is often not realized is how radical the idea of translation was. Probably no other event was as significant in Second Temple Judaism as that of the translation of the Bible into Greek. The idea that the scriptural writings could be translated into a foreign tongue was significant enough in itself, but the practical effects of the Greek translation on knowledge of the Bible and especially on the history of intepretation are enormous. If it had been preserved only in Hebrew (and some passages in Aramaic), it would have been primarily the preserve of a small core of Jews in Palestine who possessed the requisite knowledge to read it and the leisure to discuss and debate it. Now the vast population of Greek-speaking Jews had direct access to their biblical tradition, and they began to develop other institutions to exploit it, in particular the synagogue.

The whole question of how the Pentateuch first came to be translated, the precedents for it, and whether the LXX was the first translation has exercised scholars a great deal. So far there is no evidence of any Greek translations before LXX. Although generally rejecting the account in the *Letter of Aristeas*, scholarship generally accepts the mid-third century as the date for the Greek Pentateuch. The LXX and other textual finds, such as the Qumran scrolls, indicate that the text was far from fixed or uniform. A number of diverse texts of some or all the extant biblical books circulated at this time; indeed, there seems to have been no hard and fast division between what we call textual development and continued literary development.

The first evidence of synagogues is found in Egypt about the same time as the LXX was created (pp. 170–75 below). The name of *proseuchē* "prayer house" suggests that one of the main initial activities was public prayer, but the biblical text must have had a place at an early time, though we have no direct evidence. Because of the proximity of the temple, the Jews of Palestine felt no need for such an institution this early, and we have no indication of synagogues in Palestine for another couple of centuries.

The wisdom tradition continued to thrive during the Ptolemaic period. Two of the major Hebrew wisdom books probably originated under Ptolemaic rule, Qohelet and Ben Sira. Qohelet is such an unusual book that it is hard to know how to relate it to the development of Jewish religious thought. No other Jewish writing apart from Job comes close to the "skeptical thought" expressed in this work. Comparing Qohelet with Proverbs, Job, and Ben Sira suggests that some – though not all – wisdom circles were experiencing a "crisis in wisdom", perhaps already as early as the Persian period (cf. pp. 42–44 above). Yet this crisis was evidently not universal because there is no sign of it in Proverbs, some of which may be as late as the Persian period, nor in Ben Sira. Qohelet, like Job, shows the radical questioning of the wisdom tradition itself. Wisdom is ultimately reaffirmed as good – as definitely preferable to folly (Qoh. 2:13–14) – but it does not provide the certainties and security of existence that many wisdom writers seemed to find in it (Qoh. 7:23–24; 8:16–17). Whether Qohelet is influenced by Greek thought is very much a moot point: there are parallels, but he does not use the language of Greek philosophy (though this could be because Hebrew had not yet been adapted to express philosophical thought in his time).

Ben Sira describes a new phenomenon: scribalism. Scribes are of course known from an early period in the ancient Near East. In Egypt, Mesopotamia, and a number of other centers of civilization the scribes formed a closed profession; they were essential to the operation of the government and commerce, but the complications of the writing system meant that few outside the scribal profession could read, much less write (only three kings in the entire history of Assyria are known to have been able to read). Literacy in those peoples with an alphabetic script, such as Israel, was probably greater, but knowledge of more recent societies shows that a simple script does not necessarily lead to widespread literacy (pp. 150–52 below).

Scribes were thus essential to government and the administrative bureaucracy, even in a small country or province. They would naturally be the ones who studied and preserved the national literature, even if they had no official mandate to do so; however, the assumption that many scribes were priests or Levites (pp. 150–52 below) would suggest that there was an interest in the religious literature and also an official duty to be in charge of its preservation. Ben Sira is the first indication that the concept of the scribe might be not just one who wrote but one who studied and interpreted sacred literature. There seems little doubt that in 38:24–39:11 Ben Sira was describing an ideal that included himself. Keeping in mind that many scribes were clergy of some sort (either priests or Levites), it is wrong to assume that sacred scriptures were being wrestled away from the priesthood by the laity; after all, the Ezra story – however problematic in some respects – puts the possession, teaching, and exposition of the Law in the hands of the priesthood. On the other hand, if Ben Sira was not a priest, he is suggesting that interpretation of the Law is not confined to the priesthood; even non-priests could become experts in the Jewish sacred texts.

Our sources do not mention prophetic figures in society, but this does not mean that they had ceased to exist. Prophecy had not ceased in this period, but written prophecy now took on the form of one of its sub-genres, that of apocalypses (see pp. 232–41 below). Apocalyptic had its roots in the Persian period, but it flourished in the Greek period, with many extant examples of it. The earliest of these is certain sections of *1 Enoch*, most likely the *Astronomical Book* and the *Book of Watchers*. Even though priests may have cultivated the knowledge that feeds apocalyptic, *1 Enoch* is likely to have been the product of a group which was actually at odds with the temple establishment. The main reason for saying this is that the solar calendar which is the basis for *1 Enoch* 72–82 was at odds with the solar–lunar calendar used in the temple at this time (p. 143 below). The book may well be the product of a dissident priestly group, though given the smallness of the community at this time and the threat of Ptolemaic intervention, the group producing *1 Enoch* may not actually have made any public break with the temple.

1 Enoch also provides considerable information to show how far angelology had developed by this time. The fallen angels myth, the lists of both obedient angels and fallen angels, and the evil spirits that came from the dead giants, all show a lengthy period of speculation about the spirit world. By this time all our texts are monotheistic (at least in some sense of the word; see pp. 216–19 below). We also find non-Jewish writers who comment on the monotheistic and aniconic nature of Jewish worship, such as Hecateus of Abdera (pp. 37–39 above).

Although the focus of worship in Palestine was the temple and its cult, there is some evidence of para-temple religious activities among the people, so-called "popular religion". Some of these would have been widely acceptable, but others would have been officially proscribed. There is evidence that divination (including even necromancy) and the esoteric arts were cultivated in some circles (pp. 241–51 below). Many of these activities would not have been written down by their proponents nor have other remains been left for scholars to find; it is only through references by their enemies and some other hints that we have an inkling of their existence.

The first evidence that the Jews had begun to think about history writing in a critical sense appears in the Greek period. Demetrius's discussions about problems in the tradition and how to resolve these, and his chronological frameworks worked out with considerable care, show that he was trying to rationalize biblical history. It is not critical history of the sophistication already developed by some Greek writers a century and more earlier, but it shows a historical consciousness not evident in Jewish writings up to this time.

4

LATER GREEK PERIOD AND HASMONEANS (200–63 BCE)

The period of about 150 years dealt with in this chapter saw the rise of two institutions which must have seemed (to some Jews, at least) to herald a golden age for the Jewish people. Yet these institutions pulled in quite different directions, were controversial and even dangerous in the eyes of some Jews, and in both cases led to strife, bloodshed, and civil war. The first was Jason's "Hellenistic reform"; the other was the Hasmonean kingdom of Judah under the leadership of priest–kings. Both of these had far-reaching consequences – potentially, at least – and yet each was cut off in midstream before running the course dictated by its own internal logic. In many ways, this period is the fulcrum on which Second Temple history pivots.

MAJOR SOURCES

1 and 2 Maccabees

Bergren, T. A. (1997) "Nehemiah in 2 Maccabees 1:10–2:18", *JSJ* 28: 249–70.

Henten, J. W. van (1997) *The Maccabean Martyrs as Saviours of the Jewish People: A Study of 2 and 4 Maccabees.*

Williams, D. S. (1999) *The Structure of 1 Maccabees.*

The two books of Maccabees are our main sources for what happened to Judea under Antiochus IV and for the next quarter of a century, until the founding of the Hasmonean state. Without them we would know extremely little. A basic introduction, with relevant literature, has been given to each of these books in *JCH* (222–25); see also van Henten 1997 (17–57) on 2 Maccabees. Our concern here is to look at their importance for religion, with the following points some of the main ones:

1. Both works represent a pro-Hasmonean bias, exaggerating the achievements of the Maccabees, ignoring the other elements of the anti-Seleucid resistance, and vilifying the "Hellenists" who are all lumped together without distinction between them.

2. Both works center on a dispute within the priesthood over religious leadership of the nation; because religious leadership also entailed political leadership at this time, victory in one also led to victory in the other. It is not quite this neat, of course, because the Maccabees did not originally take action to pursue either of these goals, at least as mentioned by the sources, but religious and political leadership was always at stake in the revolt against the Seleucids.

3. Both books make the temple and its service the center of Jewish religion and give no hint of any shift away from this. No hint is given of the existence of synagogues and the like. However, mention is made of scrolls of the law (1 Macc. 1:56–57), and some sort of collection of official writings (ascribed to Nehemiah) is assumed (2 Macc. 2:13–15).

4. Both books attest directly and indirectly the extent to which Jews within Palestine were a broader part of the Hellenistic world. Neither book speaks of a resistance to cultural Hellenization; indeed, both books circulated widely in Greek and also present the Hasmoneans as fully at home in the Hellenistic world.

5. A somewhat enigmatic group called the *Hasidim* (Greek *Asidaioi*) is mentioned in both books. Whether they are as important as some have alleged is a moot point, but they are likely to continue to be discussed (see further pp. 183–85 below).

6. A feature of both books, but especially of 2 Maccabees, is that of martyrdom. This seems to be a new concept in Jewish theological thinking (pp. 177–78 below).

7. The letters in 2 Maccabees 1–2 have a complicated tradition history, though one or more authentic letters may lie at the base of this section (van Henten 37–50). This section attests to the new festival celebrating the purification of the temple (later called Hanukkah, though not here) and also promotes its celebration among Jewish communities outside Palestine. The Nehemiah story may have been a way of legitimating both the Second Temple cult and also Judas Maccabeus (cf. Bergren 1997).

Daniel

Brenner, A. (ed.) (1995) *A Feminist Companion to Esther, Judith and Susanna*.

Collins, J. J. (1993) *A Commentary on the Book of Daniel*.

Collins, J. J., and P. W. Flint (eds) (2000) *The Book of Daniel: Composition and Reception*.

Grabbe, L. L. (2000f) "A Dan(iel) for All Seasons: For Whom Was Daniel Important?", in J. J. Collins and P. W. Flint (eds) *The Book of Daniel: Composition and Reception*.

Koch, K. (1995) *Die Reiche der Welt und der kommende Menschensohn: Studien zum Danielbuch*.

—— (1997) *Europa, Rom und der Kaiser vor dem Hintergrund von zwei Jahrtausenden Rezeption des Buches Daniel.*

Redditt, P. L. (1999) *Daniel, Based on the New Revised Standard Version.*

Steck, O. H., R. G. Kratz, and I. Kottsieper (eds) (1998) *Das Buch Baruch; Der Brief des Jeremia; Zusätze zu Ester und Daniel.*

Ziegler, J. (1999) *Susanna, Daniel, Bel et Draco* (2nd edn).

The introduction and basic bibliography in *JCH* (225–27) can be supplemented by the more recent studies listed here, especially the commentary by Collins (1993). Daniel is a very important book with regard to developments in the area of religion:

1. The book is a significant source for certain events during the Maccabean revolt. It is, in fact, the only real contemporary source since even the books of Maccabees were written some decades later.

2. Although not the earliest apocalypse, Daniel 7–12 is one of the best examples of the genre. The book forms a vital link in the development of apocalyptic in general, as well as serving as a source for later apocalyptic speculation.

3. The book well illustrates the practice of *ex eventu* prophecy which serves to interpret the significance of the Maccabean period for at least one segment of the Jewish community. These prophecies also became a vehicle for reinterpretation and further attempts to discern the future in both subsequent Judaism and in Christianity. Attempting to present history as a series of kingdoms leading up to a final empire (the Greek, in this case) is one that became common in apocalyptic writings.

4. Other eschatological aspects of the book include new developments, especially the idea of a resurrection (12:1–3).

5. Martyrdom is one theological theme, expressed as a means of resistance to the Greek oppression. This idea of passive resistance is different from the military stance taken in other books (such as 1 and 2 Maccabees) but parallel to that in the *Testament of Moses* (pp. 74–75 below).

6. Daniel 1–6 provides a model of Jewish apologetic and self-identity. It even gives a model of how Jews in the Diaspora were meant to conduct themselves among their Gentile neighbors: not that most Jews would have moved in royal circles, but it shows the proper attitude toward putting the Jewish law first, even to the point of risking one's life.

7. Wisdom is a key concept in the book, representing both wisdom which comes from study and learning and wisdom which is revealed by God, thus uniting what might be called "proverbial wisdom" and "mantic wisdom". There is evidence that the author was an educated member of the upper classes in Jerusalem, probably someone much like Eupolemus son of John, rather than a member of a disaffected sect (Grabbe 2000d).

1 Enoch 83–105

Dexinger, F. (1977) *Henochs Zehnwochenapokalypse und offene Probleme der Apokalyptikforschung*.

Tiller, P. A. (1993) *A Commentary on the Animal Apocalypse of* 1 Enoch.

A general introduction and bibliography to *1 Enoch* as a whole is given on pp. 41–42 above and in *JCH* (180–81). The various sections of *1 Enoch* 83–105 are likely to have been composed between the Maccabean revolt and the Roman conquest (*c*.168–63 BCE). This section of *1 Enoch* is probably made up of two separate writings: first, the *Dream Visions of Enoch* (83–90) which contain two visions of Enoch about the future: the first vision predicting the great flood to come on the earth (83–85); the second containing a review of history beginning with Adam and Eve and extending to the time of Judas Maccabeus in the form of the *Animal Apocalypse* (86–89); and second, the *Epistle of Enoch* (90–105) which contains a diversity of material, including the *Apocalypse of Weeks* (93; 91:12–17) and material from a *Book of Noah* (105–7), with "another Book of Enoch" at the very end (108). The main points about Judaic religion include the following:

1. The apocalyptic vision of history is very much in evidence. The *Animal Apocalypse* and the *Apocalypse of Weeks* both contain *ex eventu* prophecies which lead into genuine predictions about the near future. The two writings suggest that the authors expected the endtime to come in their lifetimes, both of which were about the time of the Maccabean revolt.

2. This is further evidence of a lost "Book of Noah" which also appears to be drawn on in the *Similitudes of Enoch* (*1 Enoch* 37–71).

3. The *Animal Apocalypse* views the temple and cult set up in the Persian period as polluted and the post-exilic period as a time of religious blindness and poor leadership (89:73–90:5).

4. There is a positive attitude to the Maccabean revolt and to Judas in particular (90:6–15). There is no indication that the author formed part of a group that supported the revolt actively, but he regarded Judas as God's instrument. Because the revolt ends with the direct intervention of God, we find no indication of how the group represented by the author might have related to the new leadership after 165 BCE.

5. One of the Qumran manuscripts (4QEn^c) shows that the *Apocalypse of Weeks* has suffered textual displacement in the Ethiopic tradition and confirms the emendation long made by scholars to correct this. Apparently, the *Apocalypse of Weeks* envisioned that the present age was to end with the seventh week, and so weeks eight to ten refer to a time of judgment and to a new age.

6. A good deal of the *Epistle* is taken up with paranetic material either condemning certain activities or encouraging others. Much of this is worded in very general terms, though some of the things condemned are those familiar from the prophets and other early Jewish writings, such as the rich and those

who oppress the poor, and pagan worship. Other points are that men will wear more bodily decoration than women (98:2), abortion and abandonment of children (99:5).

7. A major theme is judgment. The spirits of the dead, whether righteous or wicked, are apparently already undergoing some sort of reward or punishment (102:5–11), but there would be a resurrection for a final judgment of all the dead (103–104). The final reward of the righteous is to "shine like the lights of heaven", sometimes referred to as "astral immortality" (104:2), and to sit on thrones of honor (108:11–12).

8. There is a hint of disputes about scripture, with the charge that the wicked have altered or invented words in the scriptures, but the righteous will be given proper books (104:10–12).

Book of *Jubilees*

Halpern-Amaru, B. (1999) *The Empowerment of Women in the* Book of Jubilees.
Kugel, J. (1994) "The Jubilees Apocalypse", *DSD* 1: 322–37.
VanderKam, J. C. (1994b) "Genesis 1 in Jubilees 2", *DSD* 1: 300–21.

A basic introduction and bibliography to the book were given in *JCH* (234–35). The book of *Jubilees* tells us a number of things about Jewish religion during the period of what was probably the second century BCE:

1. The book is a prime example of "rewritten Bible" (p. 168 below), a means of interpreting the biblical text by paraphrasing and rewriting it. It seems almost certain that the writer has drawn on the canonical version of Genesis 1 through Exodus 12 (though it has been speculated that he was trying to write a book to replace the present books of Genesis and Exodus).

2. The author has a schematic view of history in which all major events happen according to a jubilee cycle of 49 years (versus the 50 years of Lev. 25). All the events of the patriarchs' lives are marked according to these cycles, and one is left with the impression that all history fits this same scheme.

3. The book proclaims the observance of a 364-day solar calendar and polemicizes against use of a lunar calendar (6:32–38).

4. A good deal of emphasis is placed on proper observance of the law, which did not come about only with the mission of Moses. On the contrary, many Jewish beliefs and practices normally associated with Moses and later were already in effect or presaged in the lives of the patriarchs according to *Jubilees*. For example, the main annual festivals (Feast of Firstfruits = Pentecost: 6:17–31; 15:1–4; 22:1–9; Feast of Booths: 17:20–31; 32:27–29; 44:1–4; Day of Atonement: 34:17–19) arose in commemoration of events in the lives of Abraham, Isaac, and Jacob (even though the Pentateuch strongly indicates their origins at or after the exodus). Also, Levi was already appointed priest through a vision from God during his own lifetime (30:18–20; 31:11–17).

5. One of the earliest detailed descriptions of the Passover observance is given in *Jub.* 49. There are also detailed regulations relating to sabbath observance (2:25–33; 50).

6. Belief in the resurrection of the spirit is evidently a concept found in the book (23:31); if so, this is important evidence of the diversity of eschatological views.

Sibylline Oracles 3–5

A general discussion and bibliography of the Jewish *Sibylline Oracles* were given in *JCH* (562–64). Because the material in the *Sibylline Oracles* 3, 4, and 5 is so diverse, and from different time periods, the relevant material will be isolated and related to the particular chapter in question in each case. Several sections seem to relate to the period of our present chapter and have relevance for Jewish religion:

1. The *Sibylline Oracles* can be seen as a prime example of how the nations of the east attempted to resist their conquerors, in particular the Greeks and Romans. This resistance could take a literary form, as in this case, as well as physical resistance in the form of a revolt. The three Jewish *Sibylline Oracles* (3, 4, 5) are particularly anti-Roman in their present form.

2. *Sib. Or.* 4:40–114 seems to contain an old Hellenistic oracle (from early in the Greek period?) which presented both a schema of four successive world kingdoms and also one of ten generations into which the time of their rule could be placed:

> First kingdom: Assyria, 6 generations
> Second kingdom: Media, 2 generations
> Third kingdom: Persia, 1 generation
> Fourth kingdom: Greece, 1 generation
> —   : Rome, no generations

This illustrates how an original schema which ended with the Greeks was reinterpreted to apply to Rome. The fourfold, ten-generation model had Rome added to it; but, since the ten generations have all been used up, Rome has no generations assigned to it (4:102–14). Also, the fourfold scheme of kingdoms ends with the Macedonians, and no attempt is made to fit Rome into it.

3. A messianic figure in the form of the Egyptian king was expected in the second century BCE. *Sib. Or.* 3:97–349 and 3:489–829 (the original core of the book?) seem to refer to events of the second century BCE, with possible allusons to Antiochus IV (3:601–18). More important are references to the "king from the sun" (3:652) who is also said to be the "seventh" (3:193, 3:318, 3:608). It is generally agreed that the reference is to one of the

Ptolemaic rulers, though Ptolemy VI (180–145 BCE), Ptolemy VII (co-ruler with Ptolemy VIII about 145–144 BCE), and Ptolemy VIII (145–116 BCE) are all possible candidates. Perhaps the most likely one is Ptolemy VI Philometor, who had good relations with the Jews.

3. *Sib. Or.* 3:489–829, as well as envisioning a messiah, also has various other eschatological passages. *Sib. Or.* 3:741–95 pictures a renewed form of life on earth, a type of golden age or millennium.

4. *Sib. Or.* 3 is very supportive of the temple (286–94, 564–67, 715–19, 772–73). There may also be a positive reference to the temple at Leontopolis in Egypt (3:319–20; 5:501–3).

5. Various sins are denounced, as one would expect, but special emphasis is placed on sexual sins, homosexuality in particular (3:185–86, 595–607, 762–66). Of particular interest is the section on the Jews as a model of proper observance, including the avoidance of astrology and divination (3:213–64).

Judith

Brenner, A. (ed.) (1995) *A Feminist Companion to Esther, Judith and Susanna.*
Shedl, C. (1965) "Nabuchodonosor, Arpaksad und Darius: Untersuchungen zum Buch Judit", *ZDMG* 115: 242–54.
Stocker, M. (1998) *Judith: Sexual Warrior, Women and Power in Western Culture.*

As the brief introduction and bibliography in *JCH* (178) indicate, the exact date of Judith is uncertain. Some of the main points in it about Judaism as a religion are the following:

1. Judith demonstrates without a doubt that historical "facts" can be used quite inaccurately to bolster theological narratives. The historical setting, with Nebuchadnezzar as king of the Assyrians, bears no resemblance to history, though there is some evidence that some historical remembrances of the Babylonian rebel Artaxerxes III in early Persian period may be found in the book (Shedl 1965).

2. The book has been quite popular for feminist interpreters because it features a heroine, which is somewhat rare in Jewish literature, especially her direct action in slaying Holophernes, a deed not normally associated with a woman. This episode has been of much interest to artists through the ages (cf. Brenner 1995).

3. One of the main messages is that, when threatened, the Jewish people must trust in God. This does not exclude militant means, however, as Judith's own attack on Holophernes shows. There are indications that the story is to be understood symbolically: the eponymous name of the heroine Judith (= "Jewess"); the name of the town Bethulia (= *bĕtulāh* "virgin"?).

4. The book places a great deal of emphasis on prayer (9; 12:6–8). This is one of the chief means for Judith to express her piety.

5. Judith's strict observance of dietary laws, including her argument that violation of them would cause the city to fall, is an important theme in the book (11:12–15; 12:1–4, 17–19).

6. A new attitude to fasting is attested here, perhaps for the first time: regular fasting as an act of piety. In the OT fasting was primarily a thing to do in a crisis, though a late passage such as Isaiah 56 makes fasting a means of expressing humility. Fasting and wearing sackcloth also occur in Judith in the old sense when Jerusalem is threatened (4:11–15); however, before this crisis arose Judith fasted every day – apart from sabbaths, holidays, and the preparation day ("eve") before each festival (8:6) – as a normal part of her lifestyle. Another possible ascetic act is her remaining unmarried, despite many opportunities to remarry (16:22). This might be simply out of loyalty to her first husband, but it may also be another element of her ascetic lifestyle.

7. The book does not seem to represent a "democratization" of Jewish worship as such, however, since the temple, cult, and priesthood are taken for granted and in no way slighted (4:2–3, 12, 14–15; 8:21, 24; 9:8, 13; 11:13; 16:16–20). The high priest also acts as the leader of the nation (4:6–8), though a reference is also made to the *gerousia* "council of elders" in Jerusalem which is able to make important decisions (11:14).

1 Baruch

JLBM: 109–14.
JWSTP: 140–46.
Kabasele Mukenge, A. (1998) *L'unité littéraire du livre de Baruch.*
Moore, C. A. (1977) *Daniel, Esther and Jeremiah: The Additions.*
Schürer: 734–43.
Steck, O. H. (1993) *Das apokryphe Baruchbuch: Studien zu Rezeption und Konzentration "kanonischer" Überlieferung.*
Steck, O. H., R. G. Kratz, and I. Kottsieper (eds) (1998) *Das Buch Baruch; Der Brief des Jeremia; Zusätze su Ester und Daniel.*
Tov, E. (1976) *The Septuagint Translation of Jeremiah and Baruch: A Discussion of an Early Revision of the LXX of Jeremiah 29–52 and Baruch 1:1–38.*

This takes the form of a letter, written by Jeremiah's scribe Baruch in exile, to those remaining in Jerusalem. The exact purpose of the book is unclear since it seems to be made up of disparate sections on the situation of the exile (1:1–14), a prayer of confession over sins (1:15–3:8), the figure of wisdom (3:9–4:4), and a poem on Zion (4:5–5:9). The precise dating is also uncertain. A number of scholars have seen Antiochus IV and the high priest Alcimus behind the images of Nebuchadnezzar and the high priest Jehoiakim (e.g. Kabasele Mukenge 1998); if so, that dates the book fairly precisely to about 150 BCE. However, this interpretation is by no means certain, and the dating of the book still remains unclear. Tov (1976) connnects the book with the translation of the LXX Jeremiah which, he argues, was done about 116 BCE. Among points to be gleaned from the book are the following:

1. The theme of exile and return is strong in the book. The "letter" of Baruch should be compared with Jer. 24 (which compares the exiles to good figs and those remaining in the land to bad) and Jer. 29 (which contains a letter in the name of Jeremiah encouraging the exiles to settle and make the best of it). The focus of 1 Baruch is on the return from exile as a sort of second exodus (cf. Isa. 51: 10–11).

2. A good portion of the book is a prayer (1:15–3:8), apparently based on (or having much in common with) Dan. 9:4–19. Although a literary prayer, it may well tell us something of prayer of the time (pp. 170–75 below).

3. The image of wisdom (3:9–4:4) is an indication of how the figure was being developed at the time (see pp. 225–28 below). Like Ben Sira 24, wisdom is equated with the Torah (4:1), though much of the poem seems to draw on Job 28:12–28 about the inaccessibility of wisdom.

Qumran scrolls

Abegg, M., P. Flint, and E. Ulrich (eds) (1999) *The Dead Sea Scrolls Bible*.

Baumgarten, J. M., E. G. Chazon, and A. Pinnick (eds) (2000) *The Damascus Document: A Centennial of Discovery*.

Bernstein, M., F. García Martínez, and J. Kampen (eds) (1997) *Legal Texts and Legal Issues: Proceedings of the Second Meeting of the International Organization for Qumran Studies, Cambridge 1995, Published in Honour of Joseph M. Baumgarten*.

Boccaccini, G. (1998) *Beyond the Essene Hypothesis: The Parting of the Ways between Qumran and Enochic Judaism*.

Brooke, G. J., L. H. Schiffman, and J. C. VanderKam (eds) (1994–) *Dead Sea Discoveries* 1– .

Brooke, G. J., with F. García Martínez (eds) (1994) *New Qumran Texts and Studies: Proceedings of the First Meeting of the International Organization for Qumran Studies, Paris 1992*.

Charlesworth, J. H., *et al.* (eds) (1994–) *The Dead Sea Scrolls: Hebrew, Aramaic, and Greek Texts with English Translations*. I– .

Chazon, E. G. and M. E. Stone (eds) (1999) *Pseudepigraphic Perspectives: The Apocrypha and Pseudepigrapha in Light of the Dead Sea Scrolls: Proceedings of the International Symposium of the Orion Center for the Study of the Dead Sea Scrolls and Associated Literature, 12–14 January, 1997*.

Collins, J. J. (1997) *Apocalypticism in the Dead Sea Scrolls*.

Cross, Frank M., and Esther Eshel (1997) "Ostraca from Khirbet Qumran", *IEJ* 47: 17–29.

Cryer, F. H. (1997) "The Qumran Conveyance: A Reply to F. M. Cross and E. Eshel", *SJOT* 11: 232–40.

Cryer, F. H., and T. L. Thompson (eds) (1998) *Qumran between the Old and New Testaments*.

Chyutin, M. (1997) *The New Jerusalem Scroll from Qumran: A Comprehensive Reconstruction*.

Davies, P. R. (1995a) "Was There Really a Qumran Community?" *CR: BS* 3: 9–36.

Dimant, D., and U. Rappaport (eds) (1992) *The Dead Sea Scrolls: Forty Years of Research*.

Falk, D. K. (1998) *Daily, Sabbath, and Festival Prayers in the Dead Sea Scrolls*.

Flint, P. W., and J. C. VanderKam (eds) (1998) *The Dead Sea Scrolls after Fifty Years: A Comprehensive Assessment, vol. 1.*

—— (1999) *The Dead Sea Scrolls after Fifty Years: A Comprehensive Assessment, vol. 2.*

García Martínez, F. (1988) "Qumran Origins and Early History: A Groningen Hypothesis", *Folio Orientalia* 25: 113–36.

—— (1992) *Qumran and Apocalyptic: Studies on the Aramaic Texts from Qumran*.

—— (1996) *The Dead Sea Scrolls Translated: The Qumran Texts in English*.

García Martínez, F., and E. J. C. Tigchelaar (eds and trans.) (1997–98) *The Dead Sea Scrolls Study Edition: Volume One 1Q1–4Q273; Volume Two 4Q274–11Q31.*

Golb, N. (1995) *Who Wrote the Dead Sea Scrolls?*

Grabbe, L. L. (1997b) "The Current State of the Dead Sea Scrolls: Are There More Answers than Questions?" in S. E. Porter and C. A. Evans (eds) *The Scrolls and the Scriptures: Qumran Fifty Years After*: 54–67.

—— (1997h) Book review: N. Golb, *Who Wrote the Dead Sea Scrolls?*, *DSD* 4: 124–28.

Harrington, D. J. (1997) *Wisdom Texts from Qumran*.

Kapera, Z. J. (ed.) (1990–) *The Qumran Chronicle* 1– .

—— (ed.) (1996) *Mogilany 1993: Papers on the Dead Sea Scrolls Offered in Memory of Hans Burgmann*.

—— (ed.) (1998) *Mogilany 1995: Papers on the Dead Sea Scrolls Offered in Memory of Aleksy Klawek*.

Kugler, R. A., and E. M. Schuller (eds) (1999) *The Dead Sea Scrolls at Fifty: Proceedings of the 1997 Society of Biblical Literature Qumran Section Meetings*.

Lefkovits, J. K. (2000) *The Copper Scroll (3Q15): A Reevaluation*.

Lim, T. H. (1993) "The Wicked Priests of the Groningen Hypothesis", *JBL* 112: 415–25.

Lim, T. H., and P. S. Alexander (1997) *The Dead Sea Scrolls Electronic Reference Library*, vol.1.

[no ed.] (1999) *The Dead Sea Scrolls Electronic Library, 2, including the Dead Sea Scrolls Database (Non-Biblical Texts) Edited by Emanuel Tov*.

Magness, J. (1995) "The Chronology of the Settlement at Qumran in the Herodian Period", *DSD* 2: 58–65.

Metso, S. (1997) *The Textual Development of the Qumran Community Rule*.

Parry, D. W. and E. Ulrich (eds) (1999) *The Provo International Conference on the Dead Sea Scrolls: Technological Innovations, New Texts, and Reformulated Issues.*

Stegemann, H. (1998) *The Library of Qumran: On the Essenes, Qumran, John the Baptist, and Jesus.*

Steudel, A. (1994) *Der Midrasch zur Eschatologie aus der Qumrangemeinde (4QMidrEschat*[a,b]*): Materielle Rekonstruktion, Textbestand, Gattung und traditionsgeschichtliche Einordnung des durch 4Q174 ("Florilegium") und 4Q177 ("Catena A") repräsentierten Werkes aus den Qumranfunden.*

Stone, M. E. and E. G. Chazon (eds) (1998) *Biblical Perspectives: Early Use and Interpretation of the Bible in Light of the Dead Sea Scrolls: Proceedings of the First International Symposium of the Orion Center for the Study of the Dead Sea Scrolls and Associated Literature, 12–14 May, 1996.*

Swanson, D. D. (1995) *The Temple Scroll and the Bible: The Methodology of 11QT.*

VanderKam, J. C. (1994) *The Dead Sea Scrolls Today.*

—— (1998) *Calendars in the Dead Sea Scrolls: Measuring Time.*

Woude, A. S. van der (1990) "A 'Groningen' Hypothesis of Qumran Origins and Early History", *RevQ* 14: 521–42.

The older secondary literature on the Qumran scrolls was surveyed in *JCH* (229–84). Since that work went to press, a great many of the Scrolls have now been published in preliminary form or definitive editions (cf. García Martínez/Tigchelaar 1997–98). Two journals are now flourishing: *Dead Sea Discoveries* (Brooke/Schiffman/VanderKam and *The Qumran Chronicle* (Kapera). A flurry of studies in the Scrolls is also taking place. Because many of these studies have been published in collected editions, a number of these are listed here for convenience. Most of the original material is appearing in the DJD series (not listed here). A considerable amount of this material involves the remains of various biblical books in a variety of text-types, important for understanding the development of the text (pp. 158–65 below). There are also textual fragments of other Jewish literature in the apocrypha and pseudepigrapha. A number of other works are important for religion, including 4QMMT, which has been of considerable interest (cf. p. 196 below).

New debates have arisen and new suggestions for solutions proposed. The dominant "Essene hypothesis" has rightly been questioned; however, questioning it does not mean that it is wrong, only that it should receive proper scholarly scrutiny. A modified form of the Essene thesis has been advanced in the "Groningen Hypothesis" (García Martínez 1988; van der Woude 1990; criticized by Lim 1993), as well as by Boccaccini (1998). One of the significant debates concerns the provenance of the Scrolls. More important perhaps is the origin of the physical Scrolls themselves. Long accepted as basically the product of the Qumran community, that has now been challenged, especially by Golb in a series of articles, with most of his arguments now summarized in a recent book (1995). He has argued that the Scrolls are from a Jerusalem library or libraries brought to the caves during the 66–70 revolt. His thesis draws attention to what many had already concluded: a considerable portion of the Scrolls would not have been the product of any community at the site of Khirbet Qumran but had diverse origins, their presence at Qumran being only as part of a community library. Golb's thesis explains certain features about the Scrolls, especially the number of different copyist hands, but ultimately it has greater problems than the theory it is meant to replace (see Grabbe 1997b: 60–63; 1997h):

1. His dismissal of the location of the Scrolls around the the Khirbet Qumran site is a weakness. At least the Scrolls were found physically near Qumran, whereas there is nothing specifically to tie the Scrolls to Jerusalem. If one is looking for another site, why not Damascus? (This would undermine Golb's thesis, of course.)

2. If the Scrolls were originally in Jerusalem, it would have made more sense to store them there, where many potential hiding places existed. The idea that they could have been transported to Qumran during the siege of Jerusalem is unrealistic when the situation is considered. The city was surrounded by the Romans, and getting in and out very difficult. A vehicle would have been required, and the Romans would have noticed any such activity, whether getting the Scrolls out of Jerusalem, transporting them over the roads to Qumran, or carrying them up or down to the various caves. Before the Romans invested Jerusalem, some of the various Jewish factions guarded the gates to prevent anyone going out without their permission (*War* 4.4.3 §236). A few managed to escape with their lives, but they were hardly carrying wagonloads of manuscripts. A careful reading of Josephus shows that this aspect of the theory is fatally flawed.

3. He takes too lightly the statement of Pliny the Elder that the Essenes lived on the northwest shores of the Dead Sea (*Natural History* 5.73). Golb is quite right that this account is not without its problems, but it must be dealt with adequately, not simply dismissed. (For further information on the Essene hypothesis, see pp. 199–206 below.)

One defence of the Essene hypothesis has been the find of the so-called "*Yaḥad* ostracon" (Cross/Eshel 1997). This was read as the record of a donation to the community (*yaḥad*) living at Qumran. That interpretation was immediately challenged by Cryer (1997) who gave a different reading of the line in question (line 8). The debate is likely to continue for some time.

Fragmentary Jewish Writers in Greek

Collins, J. J. (1980) "The Epic of Theodotus and the Hellenism of the Hasmoneans", *HTR* 73: 91–104.

Collins, N. L. (1991) "Ezekiel, the Author of the *Exagoge*: His Calendar and Home", *JSJ* 22: 201–11.

Holladay, C. R. (1983) *Fragments from Hellenistic Jewish Authors, Volume I: Historians*.

—— (1989) *Volume II: Poets: The Epic Poets Theodotus and Philo and Ezekiel the Tragedian.*

—— (1995) *Volume III: Aristobulus.*

—— (1996) *Volume IV: Orphica.*

For general bibliography and introduction, see *JCH* (236–38); Holladay's invaluable edition is still in progress. Several of the writers in this collection probably belong to the present period, 200–63 BCE, though the dating is often difficult. Each writer is rather different, and tells us something different about Judaism as a religion.

Eupolemus seems likely to be the same as the son of the John who negotiated with Antiochus III about allowing the Jews to observe their traditional laws (2 Macc. 4:11), while Eupolemus himself served as a Hasmonean ambassador to Rome (1 Macc. 8:17):

1. Eupolemus's name and background indicate a knowledge of Greek culture and language. One would expect him to have been a part of Jason's new Hellenistic Jerusalem (though we do not know this for certain). In any case, his prominence in the new Hasmonean regime shows the extent to which Hellenistic culture was as much a part of the new order as it had been of the Hellenistic reform.

2. The preserved excerpts of Eupolemus are all on the period of OT history and thus give no direct evidence about the history of his own times. On the other hand, they show that the OT account of Israel's early history was interpreted, cherished, and used as a model for the ideals of many Jews during the rise of the Hasmonean state. For example, Moses is made the inventor of the alphabet. Eupolemus also attempts to integrate the information from both 1 Kings and 2 Chronicles, showing a conscious desire to interpret and rationalize (Holladay 1983: 102 n. 20).

3. Eupolemus provides a good example of "rewritten Bible". The author seems to be following the outline of the biblical text, but he adds many details not in the Bible, such as the correspondence between Solomon and the kings of Egypt and Tyre. The physical description of the temple differs as well.

4. His work is another example of the use of the LXX form of the text, though he seems also to have known the Hebrew text (Holladay 1983: 100–101 nn. 14–15).

5. As argued elsewhere (p. 61 above), it is possible that Eupolemus was even the final author of Daniel. There are a number of arguments suggesting that a person like him compiled the final book. This would require Eupolemus to have been a member of a group calling themselves the *maskilim*. We have no evidence that he was, but there is also nothing to rule it out.

Artapanus could date anywhere from the third to the first century BCE. Although we know nothing about him, Artapanus seems to be an intriguing writer, judging by the contents of his work:

1. The biblical personages are magnified and turned into heroes by literary embellishments of biblical events. Thus, Abraham taught the Egyptians astrology, while Moses became an Egyptian general who conquered the Ethiopians and married the daughter of the Ethiopian king (incidentally providing an explanation for Moses's "Ethiopian" wife in Num. 12:1). One might label Artapanus's account as "rewritten Bible", but it almost goes beyond that and could perhaps be called "parabiblical".

2. Israel's history is accommodated to pagan customs and practices in a surprising way. For example, Moses is alleged to have appointed the particular gods to be worshiped by each nome in Egypt. This has led some scholars to argue that Artapanus was a pagan rather than a Jew, but this interpretation is generally rejected today. What his writings do show is the extent to which some Jews were ready to take a "broad-minded" view of the surrounding Greek culture.

3. An interesting point is the power of God's name, which Moses only whispers into the king's ear and which kills an Egyptian priest who sees it written down.

Ezekiel the Dramatist is very difficult to date but may be from the second century BCE:

1. His drama on the exodus, in Greek verse, demonstrates how educated some Jews were in Greek culture and literature.

2. Ezekiel's willingness to use a Greek literary form with a Jewish theme shows not only his integration into the surrounding Hellenistic culture but also willingness to be identified as a Jewish writer. There is no hint that Ezekiel was trying to hide his identity or pretend to be a non-Jewish writer.

3. The text drawn on is the LXX, though whether he wrote in Alexandria or elsewhere is uncertain.

4. He – along with Demetrius (pp. 48–49 above) – is one of the earliest biblical interpreters to show an awareness of difficulties in the text and to attempt to resolve them.

Aristobulus is most likely dated to the second century BCE:

1. He is said to have been an Aristotelian, and one long fragment explains how anthropomorphisms applied to the deity are only figurative. God could not have descended on to Mount Sinai because he is everywhere.

2. In his opinion the Greek philosophers, including Socrates, Plato, and Pythagoras, took many of their views from the Hebrews, via the Greek translation of the Bible.

3. He is the first Jewish interpreter to use allegory to any major extent and forms a clear predecessor of Philo; he also seems to be from Alexandria, like Philo, suggesting there is an organic link with the giant of Jewish biblical interpretation.

4. The sabbath is explained and defended as not being a day of idleness (as Greco-Roman writers often alleged), and certain poetic passages are quoted to support his views (see next point).

5. A number of alleged passages from Greek writers are quoted, but these are clearly Jewish forgeries (see below). Like the *Sibylline Oracles*, these illustrate how Jews with a good Hellenistic education nevertheless drew on their knowledge to create pseudepigraphic works in the defence of Judaism.

There are also a number of verses and poetic fragments, found in Jewish sources (or quoted in Christian writings) and ascribed to known Greek poets, but probably examples of Jewish pseudepigrapha. Only the *Orphica* have appeared in Holladay's editon, but see *OTP* (2.821–30) for an English translation of the main ones.

Philo the Epic Poet apparently wrote a book, *Concerning Jerusalem*. The exact nature of this book is difficult to be sure about, though the surviving fragments talk of Abraham and also describe the Jerusalem water system. The following points arise from them:

1. Although the quality of his Greek is debated, it is generally accepted that this Philo had a reasonable command of the language – possibly a good command. The problem is that his language is very difficult, which could be because he draws on obscure words and expressions but could as well be because of lack of full command of the literary language. Recent studies have tended to evaluate his language positively. Philo the Epic Poet is another example of a Jew educated in Greek.

2. He apparently wrote of Abraham's aborted sacrifice of Isaac. This may be an example of "rewritten Bible", though it is so brief and oblique that one cannot be sure.

3. His description of the Jerusalem water works (whether accurate or not) shows an interest in Jerusalem that goes so far as to make it a worthy subject of epic poetry.

It has long been argued that **Theodotus** was written by a Samaritan, mainly because of the focus on Shechem; recent studies have favored Jewish authorship, however (e.g. Collins 1980). Dating and provenance are difficult (cf. Holladay 1989: 68–72), but sometime in the second century BCE is a reasonable guess. If the work is by a Jewish author, it tells us the following:

1. The writer is clearly at home in Greek literature and language, since he makes use of Homeric poetic language.

2. Yet the writer also opposed any sort of intermarriage between the "Hebrews" and other peoples.

3. Because the fragments are all confined to the story of the rape of Dinah and the subsequent destruction of the Shechemites (Gen. 34), it is hard to say what else (if anything) was included in his original story. Nevertheless, as it stands Theodotus gives us a good example of "rewritten Bible".

Pseudo-Hecateus

Bar-Kochva, B. (1996) *Pseudo-Hecataeus,* On the Jews*: Legitimizing the Jewish Diaspora.*

Pucci Ben Zeev, M. (1993) "The Reliability of Josephus Flavius: The Case of Hecataeus' and Manetho's Accounts of Jews and Judaism: Fifteen Years of Contemporary Research (1974–1990)", *JSJ* 24: 215–34.
OTP: 2.905–19.

It has long been debated whether the quotations ascribed to Hecateus of Abdera in the *Contra Apionem* by Josephus are genuine or not. Whether the recent study by Bar-Kochva will settle the matter remains to be seen (cf. Pucci Ben Zeev 1993), but if nothing else it considerably strengthens the case for considering them the work of a Jewish forger. Bar-Kochva dates the book to about 100 BCE, by a moderately conservative Jew living in Egypt who wrote to justify Jewish residence in Egypt. Bar-Kochva also argues that the Ezechias who supposedly led the Jews to Egypt is not to be identified with "Hezekiah the governor" (cf. *JCH*: 192) as has often been argued. There was no such high priest; rather, the writer changed the governor into a high priest, and a forced deportation of Jews to Egypt by Ptolemy I was transformed into a voluntary immigration. A number of the studies on Hecateus (pp. 37–39 above) also discuss these alleged quotations. The following points about Judaism of the time arise from the quotations.

1. The Jewish population in Egypt is said to date from the time of Ptolemy I and to have been a voluntary immigration led by Ezechias, a high priest.

2. Jews were supposed to have fought in Alexander's army.

3. The Jewish adherence to the law and the willingness to defend it to the death are emphasized.

4. The Jewish population, both in and outside Palestine, is quite large, and their land, city, and temple are beautiful and admirable.

5. Divination (or at least pagan divination) is rejected.

6. About 1500 priests were supposed to be serving at the time of writing.

Testament of Moses (Assumption of Moses)

Collins, J. J. (1977) *The Apocalyptic Vision of the Book of Daniel.*
Nickelsburg, G. W. E. (ed.) (1973) *Studies on the Testament of Moses.*
Tromp, J. (1993) *The Assumption of Moses: A Critical Edition with Commentary.*

This work (see *JCH* [238–39] for brief introduction and bibliography) is placed in this chapter because it appears that a substantial portion (or a first edition) was written not long after the Maccabean revolt, although this book was probably completed between 4 BCE and about 30 CE (because it mentions the death of Herod but does not know of that of his sons Archelaus, Philip, or Herod Antipas [6:2–9]). The recent edition and commentary by Tromp is an important tool for study, especially since the book survives only in a single manuscript in Latin translation (probably translated from a Hebrew original). The book is significant for a number of reasons:

1. It is a good example of a testament but also has all the features of an apocalypse (though some would see these as mutually exclusive, mistakenly in my view [pp. 234–36 below]).

2. The book contains (or apparently contained in its original form) some significant interpretative traditions about Moses. Unfortunately, both the beginning and ending are lost, but the ending once evidently included a dispute between Michael and Satan over Moses's body and the ascension of Moses's soul to heaven (Jude 9; cf. Origen, *De Princ.* 3.2.1, and see the discussion in Tromp 1993: 270–85).

3. A good portion of the book is taken up with a review of history, much of which relates to biblical history, though its section on the Maccabean revolt is a quite valuable historical source (suggesting to some [e.g. Nickelsburg 1973: 34–37] that an original work was produced about that time and only subsequently updated in the first century).

4. The book seems to calculate the world as ending about 4000 A.M. and is a good example of the works for which chronography was an important issue (pp. 246–48 below).

5. *T. Moses* 9 exhibits a variant attitude toward the Antiochean persecution, that of passive resistance and martyrdom rather than active military measures against the oppression. In this it shows clear affinities with the book of Daniel and may well have originated in similar circles (Collins 1977: 198–210); these circles were not necessarily those which supported the Maccabean cause.

6. The book contains some negative references to the temple and its sacrifices (5:1–6:1). These are difficult to interpret since the author is not anti-temple as such. Whether it is a critique of the past or current priesthood, whether it merely notes that the second temple was inferior to the first temple, or whether it has another purpose is unclear.

Letter of (Pseudo-)Aristeas

Orlinsky, H. M. (1975) "The Septuagint as Holy Writ and the Philosophy of the Translators", *HUCA* 46: 89–114.
Tilly, M. (1997) "Geographie und Weltordnung im Aristeasbrief", *JSJ* 28: 131–53.

See *JCH* (179–80) for an introduction and bibliography. Some of the points about Jewish religion are the following:

1. The whole story of LXX origins is meant to strengthen the support and validate the accuracy of the translation (pp. 158–65 below). Not only its alleged royal origins but also the fact that the Jewish community publicly accepted it when it was read out (cf. Orlinsky 1975) indicate an impressive attempt to give authority to the text, which was evidently becoming widely

used among Greek-speaking Jews but was perhaps also being criticized or questioned by some.

2. Judah is presented as a utopian state, with ideal geography, climate, organization, and buildings (83–120; cf. Tilly 1997).

3. The description of the sages who come to translate the Pentateuch emphasizes not only their knowledge of both Jewish and Greek culture but also their astuteness, cleverness, and other attributes of the Hellenistic and Jewish sage. The representation of these 72 Jews from Palestine fits very well into both the oriental and the Hellenistic wisdom traditions, reminding one of both Ahiqar and some of the traditions in Artapanus (p. 72 above). The claim that six came from each of the twelve tribes is symbolic of the connection seen with ancient Israel.

4. One of the most interesting parts of the book is the apologetic for the Jewish law, including why certain animals were not eaten by the Jews (128–71). It is defended not just on the grounds of being a command of God but as being rational according to normal Greek thinking. On the other hand, the author is in no way embarrassed about Jewish beliefs, including belief in one God and rejection of images, and the general refusal of the Jews to mix freely with others (134–43).

5. Presented as a letter from a Greek official, the book is another example of a pseudepigraphic writing designed to gain respect and admiration for the Jews in the Greek world. The fact that Ptolemy II is pictured as seeing his library as incomplete without a copy of the Jewish law, and the other references, are designed to boost support for the Jewish law (9–40), though whether in the Jewish community or among non-Jews might be debated.

6. The emphasis on a translation of the law, so that any Jews literate in Greek would have access to it, is a sign of the growing importance of the written law at least among Diaspora Jews, probably sometime during the second century BCE.

SYNTHESIS

Bohak, G. (1995) "CPJ III, 520: The Egyptian Reaction to Onias' Temple", *JSJ* 26: 32–41.

—— (1996) *Joseph and Aseneth and the Jewish Temple in Heliopolis.*

Cohen, S. J. D. (1999) *The Beginnings of Jewishness: Boundaries, Varieties, Uncertainties.*

Grabbe, L. L. (1998c) "Triumph of the Pious or Failure of the Xenophobes? The Ezra/Nehemiah Reforms and their *Nachgeschichte*", in S. Jones and Sarah P. (eds) *Studies in Jewish Local Patriotism and Self-Identification in the Graeco-Roman Period*: 50–65.

—— (2000b) "The Hellenistic City of Jerusalem", in J. Bartlett and S. Freyne (eds) *Jews in the Hellenistic and Roman Cities.*

Hayes, J. H., and S. R. Mandell (1998) *The Jewish People in Classical Antiquity: From Alexander to Bar Kochba.*

Kerkeslager, A. (1997) "Maintaining Jewish Identity in the Greek Gymnasium: A 'Jewish Load' in *CPJ* 3.519 (= P. Schub. 37 = P. Berol. 13406)", *JSJ* 28: 12–33.

Mandell, S. R. (1991) "Did the Maccabees Believe that They Had a Valid Treaty with Rome?" *CBQ* 53: 202–20.

Taylor, J. E. (1998) "A Second Temple in Egypt: The Evidence for the Zadokite Temple of Onias", *JSJ* 29: 297–321.

In the long history of Second Temple Judaism, this period is in many ways the most exciting. The Jewish community and religion reached one of its lowest points in history, with the attempted suppression of Judaism by Antiochus IV, but perhaps also its highest point in antiquity from the point of view of independence and freedom, with the expanded territory and control under John Hyrcanus I and Alexander Janneus. The actions by the community leaders during this period were controversial, however, with opposition as well as support. This applies not only to Antiochus and his actions but also the rule of the Hasmonean priest–kings.

With the coming of Seleucid rule in 200 BCE, nothing much seemed to change at first, and those modern scholars who have seen Seleucid rule as negative can point to nothing in the sources for the first quarter of a century. The only incident reported is that Seleucus IV (187–175 BCE) sent his finance minister to confiscate the temple treasury, but that the money was not in fact taken (2 Macc. 3). The exact historical event is difficult to determine because of a number of unanswered questions: Why did Seleucus suddenly decide on this course of action? Once decided, why did he allow it to remain unfulfilled? Otherwise, the Seleucid rulers do not seem to have taken a lot of interest in the Jews, which was also initially the case with Antiochus IV (175–164 BCE).

But shortly after Antiochus IV took the throne, one of the most debated events of Jewish history took place: the Hellenistic reform of Jason. It must first be recognized that the initiative for this came from the Jewish side: Antiochus only acquiesced to Jason's request. The Hellenistic reform is often misunderstood and caricatured. It must be clearly recognized that the Hellenistic *polis* set up by Jason was a civic and politic entity (2 Macc. 4; *JCH*: 277–81; Grabbe 2000b). There is little or no evidence that temple worship, the cult, or other aspects of the religion were adversely affected. All extant sources are hostile to Jason, yet not one suggests any opposition to his reforms at the time, nor do they point to any specific breaking of the traditional Jewish law on his part. What we see is the triumph of one aspect of Jewish thinking during this period: the school of thought that the Jews could and should be open to the outside world as long as their religion was not compromised (cf. Grabbe 1998c).

This view of accommodating Hellenistic culture can be seen in a number of Jewish writings from this general period, especially the Fragmentary Writers in Greek. Some of these probably wrote in such major Hellenistic centers as Alexandria where a greater assimilation to the local culture might be expected. However, a figure such as Eupolemus demonstrates that even natives of Jerusalem had a Greek education and were quite willing to make use of a Greek vehicle for their works. Although we cannot be certain, Eupolemus is a good candidate for a member of Jason's *polis*; if so, he would show that many of Jason's followers supported the resistance to Antiochus once the king tried to suppress Judaism.

All later sources, writing in the aftermath of the suppression of Judaism and the Maccabean revolt, naturally saw Jason's reforms as symbolic of all that went wrong, but they failed to recognize the actual situation when Jason first turned Jerusalem into a Greek *polis*. His measures were widely welcomed by the inhabitants of Jerusalem at the time and were a natural development of trends that had been taking place over the previous century and more. Yet the vilification of Jason shows grasp of one important fact: Judah's troubles began with the rivalry over the high priesthood, and it was Jason who started it. The suppression of Judaism took place under Jason's successor Menelaus (indeed, some argue that he was the prime instigator of the persecution), but if Jason had not displaced his own brother in the first place, would Menelaus have ever been in a position to wrest the priesthood from Jason?

The exact reason for the measures taken against Judaism by Antiochus remains puzzling (*JCH*: 247–56, 281–85), but whatever the reason for them they were devastating to all Palestinian Jews. The members of Jason's Hellenistic Jerusalem were as opposed to what Antiochus did as anyone else; in fact, they had been the first to contest Menelaus's desecration of the holy place when he sold off the temple vessels (2 Macc. 4:39–50; *JCH*: 280–81). Only Menelaus and his followers accepted (promoted?) the suppression of traditional worship, while Jason and his followers opposed it. It is difficult for moderns – generally without the experience of temple worship – to appreciate how traumatic the pollution of the temple was. The author of Daniel 7–12, however, saw this "abomination of desolation" as heralding the eschaton (Dan. 7:24–27; 8:23–26; 9:24–27; 11:25–12:3). Similarly, the *Animal Apocalypse* considered Judas Maccabee's actions as leading up to a restoration of a golden age for the Jews (*1 En.* 90:6–39). For some Jews, what Antiochus did to the temple in halting the daily *tamid* offering threatened the very foundations of the cosmos.

What is only hinted at in our sources is the diverse nature of the opposition to the Seleucid actions. The main sources (1 and 2 Maccabees) have a Hasmonean bias and give the Maccabees all the credit for resisting Antiochus's decrees and retaking the temple from Seleucid control. For example, Daniel (11:33–35) and a passage in 1 Maccabees (2:29–38) suggest that there was a strong passive resistance, but it is also likely that others took up arms even before the Maccabean family became involved (*JCH*: 285). Most resistance movements seem to spend as much energy fighting among themselves as fighting the enemy, and what we now call the "Maccabean" revolt was not likely to have been different.

In the event, the Maccabees took over the revolt and received credit for it. In the process, their vision seems to have changed: from one of only restoring the temple and Jewish worship to one of political independence from foreign rule. Most Jews were evidently happy with restoration of the old rights, and support for further military resistance was not great; they were also content with Alcimus, chosen to be high priest in place of Menelaus, whom the Seleucids had eventually executed. The sources extol the continued resistance of the Maccabees and revile Alcimus, but a careful reading shows that support for the Maccabees' new vision of an independent Judah took a long time to develop. As so often, support came with success, so that after another 25 years of fighting, an independent Judah was declared about 142 BCE (1 Macc 13:41–42). This declaration was more symbolic than real, for the Seleucids continued to press their claim to rule the country and all five of the Maccabean brothers died violently, but under John Hyrcanus (135–104 BCE) the symbolic became a reality. His successors even took the old title of "king" which had not been used since the Neo-Babylonian period.

It has recently been argued that the Maccabean state became a vassal of Rome (Mandell 1991; cf. Hayes/Mandell 1998: 76–78, 102, etc.). The case is a circumstantial one at best because no source makes such a statement. From the point of view of the Romans, this may well have been true, but reality has to be considered as well as theory. The fact is that Rome had had little to do with Judah and was not involved in that part of the Mediterranean for most of the century from Antiochus's invasion of Egypt in 168 BCE until Pompey's expedition there in 67 BCE. In 63 BCE Judea became a Roman province, but whatever the Romans thought before this, there is little evidence that they interfered practically in the activities of the Hasmonean state.

Hasmonean rule was a mixed blessing, both internally and externally. Most of what we know of the Hasmoneans from John Hyrcanus on is from Nicolaus of Damascus (*JCH*: 228–29), though filtered through Josephus who used Nicolaus as a source. Whatever the original perspective of Nicolaus, the account in Josephus is given from a Jewish point of view. John Hyrcanus and Alexander Janneus both extended the boundaries of Jewish territory to God's glory – and their own. The ill-treatment of the Jews by the Seleucids and by the Gentiles in the various areas was reversed. Many were expelled from areas such as Galilee, and the Idumeans and Itureans were converted to Judaism (by force according to Josephus). The question of forcible conversion may not be so simple as that pictured by Josephus, since the Idumeans retained their Judaic religion (*JCH*: 329–31; Cohen 1999: 110–19); however, whatever the Jewish population had suffered from their Gentile neighbors in

Galilee and elsewhere, from our perspective the policies of the Hasmoneans were ones of religious and ethnic intolerance and bigotry, and their religious and ethnic persecutions were no more acceptable than those originally against the Jews. Where Antiochus had attempted to suppress Judaism, the Hasmoneans sought to suppress non-Jewish religions. Thus, the picture we get is that a certain amount of anti-Jewish feeling built up in the surrounding region during the Hasmonean period (see pp. 305–8 below).

Internally, many Jews opposed the Hasmonean kingdom. Far from restoring the original high priesthood subverted under Antiochus, the Maccabees had usurped it. Little of this opposition is suggested in 1 and 2 Maccabees, but some of the Qumran scrolls refer regularly to the "wicked priest" (*hakkôhēn hārāšāʿ*), which is almost certainly a play on the title "high priest" (*hakkôhēn hārōʾš*), and this figure has been widely identified with one or more of the Hasmonean rulers. The *Psalms of Solomon* apparently criticize the Hasmoneans shortly after their reign had come to an end (1:4–8; 2:2–5; 8:11–22; 17:5–15, 22). According to Josephus, Hyrcanus himself turned against the Pharisees (though this is alleged only in the *Antiquities* [13.10.6 §§293–300] and nothing is said of it in the *War*). In any case, there was apparently some opposition to him during his reign, but the real antagonism from the Jewish people came during the reign of Alexander Janneus. (Again, only in the *Antiquities* does Josephus make an issue of Pharisaic opposition, but at no point does he suggest that it was limited to the Pharisees.) At one point, those Jews against Janneus actually hired one of the rivals to the Seleucid throne, Demetrius III, to come against the Jewish king. Janneus was saved only when some of the Jews fighting with Demetrius switched sides.

The changing relations between the Hasmonean priest-kings and the people may be reflected in the coinage (*JCH*: 242–45). Some of them have the Hebrew inscription "high priest and the *ḥever* (congregation) of the Jews" (*ḥbr yhwdym*), preceded by a name. The names include Jonathan and Johanan, though "*ḥever* of the Jews" is sometimes used by itself. The name Johanan could refer to either John Hyrcanus or Hyrcanus II, and Jonathan could refer to either Aristobulus I or II. Without getting into the debate about which Hyrcanus or Aristobulus is in question, we can accept the possibility that these titles reflect the shifting relationship between the ruler and the Jewish people as a whole; however, it should be kept in mind that these coins also contain Greek inscriptions with the title "king" (*basileus*).

By this time, a body of sacred writers appears to be firmly established, and there are a number of examples of biblical interpretation (cf. pp. 165–70 below). The most easily apparent are the biblical commentaries from Qumran, though these are generally from the Roman period. Several of the Fragmentary Writers in Greek seem to be from the second century, however, and exemplify several forms of biblical interpretation, including "rewritten Bible" (Eupolemus, perhaps Ezekiel the Dramatist), "parabiblical writing" (Artapanus), and allegory (Aristobulus). There was also a cottage industry in using the Greek literary tradition for apologetic purposes to defend the Jews. This includes pseudepigraphic items such as the *Sibylline Oracles*, the *Letter of Aristeas*, and various verse compositions pretending to be Homer, the Orphic writers, and others (p. 73 above).

Eschatology became quite important during the Maccabean revolt, as one might expect, and a number of writings (Daniel 7–12; *1 En.* 90; *Sibylline Oracle 3*, an early version of the *Testament of Moses*) indicate that many Jews expected divine intervention at the time. The martyrdom of various individuals for their faith is celebrated in the rise of martyrdom literature (e.g. 2 Macc. 7). This also led to expectations that the martyrs who had suffered without deliverance or evident reward would be vindicated, which may be one of the reasons for a developing belief in a resurrection of the dead (e.g. Dan. 12:1–3). Martyrdom as a topic forms a significant feature of Jewish thinking from this point on (pp. 77–78 below).

We hear very little about Jewish women as such (just as we hear little about most men beyond the priesthood and aristocracy). Among the martyrs were women who had their children circumcised in defiance of Seleucid orders (1 Macc. 1:60–61; 2 Macc. 6:10), and 2 Macc. 7 is the story of a mother and her seven sons who die for their religion (fictitious in its present form but perhaps based on an actual episode). Two women are especially important for this period, one probably fictitious and one a queen (significantly, both are women of the upper stratum of society). Judith is the heroine of a tale of threat and deliverance (pp. 65–66 above). She appears to be a woman of some substance, perhaps a member of the aristocracy, and exhibits the traditional feminine virtues of loyalty to her husband, chastity, and piety. She is also very beautiful, and when the occasion requires it, exerts masterful leadership and takes the initiative to deliver Israel.

Alexandra Salome is unusual in being only the second queen in Israel's history and the only one worthy of praise (the other being the notorious Athalia [2 Kings 11]). Almost all we know of her comes from Josephus, and he exhibits an ambivalent attitude toward her. In the *War* (1.5.1–4 §§107–19) he pictures her as a sympathetic figure and good administrator but one somewhat weak (being a woman) who lets the Pharisees take over the country. His attitude in the *Antiquities* is rather different (13.6.1–6 §§407–32), making her not only a despot but also one who lacks the sensitivities of a woman and who lets hostile forces take over. The change in perspective is difficult to fathom, but it illustrates the quite different attitudes to her rule – even by the same person, if on different occasions. She was remembered positively in rabbinic literature (*b. Taʿanit* 23a), perhaps because of her concessions to the Pharisees. A more disinterested evaluation suggests that she was a good administrator and made the best of what was not always an ideal situation, either with her own sons or with forces both within and without the Jewish state (*JCH*: 305).

In addition to martyrdom and eschatology, certain particular beliefs arose or were further developed during this period. The story of Judith indicates a continuing trend (in some circles, at least) in the development of ascetic practices as part of worship and piety that was already in evidence at least as early as the Ptolemaic period (pp. 45, 66 above). The independence of the Jewish state stimulated greater awareness of the importance of their theology of the land and exile, especially leading to further theological reflection when Judah came under foreign domination again (pp. 297–300 below).

Perhaps one of the most obvious innovations in religion in this period was the development of various sects. Sects were probably already developing in the Persian period (p. 184 below), but the sects which came to be most important (Sadducees, Pharisees, and Essenes) seem to have originated sometime in the aftermath of the Maccabean revolt. This is uncertain, of course, and some think the Essenes or even the Pharisees had a much longer history. The Hasidim have been a favorite candidate for the progenitors of various movements, but this has been based more on hypothesis and wishful thinking than evidence (pp. 183–85 below). What does seem evident is that the Sadducees, Pharisees, and Essenes were all functioning by the early first century BCE. Although it would be a mistake to see the subsequent history of Judaism as a history of these sects, they were important and influenced many Jews. The Sadducees seem to have a particular stronghold among the upperclass, though it would be foolish to assume an identity of the two, but both they and the Pharisees were vying for political power during this period. The Pharisees finally succeeded during the reign of Alexandra Salome and were even able to enforce some of their halakic beliefs as royal law (though precisely what these laws were is never clear). There is no evidence that this position of power continued after Alexandra's death, a period which indeed was almost immediately dominated by civil war.

A curious episode in Jewish history is the temple built at Leontopolis in Egypt (*JCH*: 266–67; Bohak 1995; 1996). Josephus gives two accounts, one of which (*Ant.* 12.9.7 §387) alleges it was built by Onias IV, son of the high priest Onias III who was deposed by his brother Jason; however, another account (*War* 7.10.2 §423) claims that it was Onias III himself who built it. There are a number of problems with accepting either account, and it is far from clear that either represents the truth of what happened (cf. Taylor 1998). What the incident tells us is how complex the religious situation was: although Judaic religion had now accepted for several centuries the centrality of the one true temple, a member of the high priestly family – or even the high priest himself – was willing to set up a second, rival temple outside the promised land. No doubt it was justified on exegetical grounds, but that is beside the point. If we had no evidence and someone were to present this as a hypothesis, few scholars would accept the proposition! Once again it illustrates how incomplete our knowledge of Judaism of the time still is.

The Hasmonean period ended in many respects the way it had begun: with Judah under foreign rule and the high priest as the main representative of the people to their overlord. But the internal conflicts and the brief period of independence left great resentments, and the rest of the Second Temple period was marked by internal divisions and by continual attempts to express or alleviate the frustrations arising from the Seleucid and Hasmonean periods.

5

UNDER ROMAN RULE
(63 BCE–70 CE)

The Roman period was in many ways the most eventful and also the most traumatic period in Jewish history. It opened up opportunities for many Jews in the Diaspora. Despite the consistent bias of both ancient primary sources and much modern scholarship, Herod's rule was probably the high point of Judea's prestige in the world, and his championship of Jews and Judaism abroad and his magnificent building program at home could only be good for the religion as a whole. His undoubted oppressive treatment of some Judean inhabitants has made historians overlook the fact that most Jews benefited from his rule, and that some of the things subsequently suffered at Roman hands would not have taken place under his rule. The contrast with the position of Jews under his rule and the rapid deterioration afterward is striking. Thus, we have the paradoxical situation that at a time when Judaism was officially tolerated and certain Jewish leaders and families had access to the Roman emperor himself, the Jewish religion suffered some of its greatest perils.

MAJOR SOURCES

Some writings placed in this period by some scholars are considered too problematic with regard to dating and redaction to be included here, e.g. *Testament of Solomon* (pp. 250–51 below). As will be obvious, the NT is an important source for understanding Judaism in the first century; however, the scholarship is simply too large and unwieldy to attempt to deal with here. Secondary studies relating to Judaism and the NT will be cited at the relevant places.

Psalms of Solomon

Atkinson, K. (1998) "Towards a Redating of the Psalms of Solomon: Implications for Understanding the *Sitz im Leben* of an Unknown Jewish Sect", *JSP* 17: 95–112.

Brock, S. P. (1984) "The Psalms of Solomon", in H. F. D. Sparks (ed.) *The Apocryphal Old Testament*: 649–82.

Hann, R. R. (1982) *The Manuscript History of the Psalms of Solomon*.

—— (1988) "The Community of the Pious: The Social Setting of the Psalms of Solomon", *SR* 17: 169–89.

JLBM: 203–12.

JWSTP: 573–74.

OTP: 2.639–70.

Schüpphaus, J. (1977) *Die Psalmen Salomos: Ein Zeugnis jerusalemer Theologie und Frömmigkeit in der Mitte des vorchristlichen Jahrhunderts*.

Schürer: 3.192–97.

Trafton, J. L. (1985) *The Syriac Version of the Psalms of Solomon: A Critical Evaluation*.

—— (1986) "The Psalms of Solomon: New Light from the Syriac Version?" *JBL* 105: 227–37.

—— (1992) "Solomon, Psalms of", *ABD*: 6.115–17.

—— (1994) "The *Psalms of Solomon* in Recent Research", *JSP* 12: 3–19.

A group of eighteen psalmic writings has come down to us in Greek and Syriac, though the original language is generally agreed to be Hebrew (now lost). Arguments have now been made that both the Greek and the Syriac versions were translated directly from the original (Hann 1982; Trafton 1985, 1986). The language is often general, covering themes familiar from the canonical Psalms. However, there are historical allusions which put the general date for the collection as a whole in the period following Pompey's conquest of Jerusalem in 63 BCE, probably about the middle of the first century BCE. The *Psalms* have a number of points relating to Judaism of the time:

1. The attitude to Rome, and especially the subordination of Judea by the Romans, is clear. The destruction of Jerusalem is seen as a punishment for the sins of the Jews (2:1–14; 8:1–22; 17:5–18), but God in turn punished the arrogant Pompey with death at the hands of Caesar (*Pss. Sol.* 2:15–31).

2. The *Psalms* are critical of what was being done in the temple and by the leadership in Jerusalem (1:4–8; 2:2–5; 8:11–22; 17:5–15, 22). This seems to be anti-Hasmonean criticism. A criticism of "profane" Jews is found in *Psalm* 4.

3. *Psalms* 17–18 describe an idealized king like David who is a larger-than-life character but still very much on the human plane. These chapters are obviously important for the question of messianic expectations during this general period of time (see further p. 276 below).

4. The righteous will be resurrected, apparently to an ideal form of existence on the earth, in contrast to the wicked who are destroyed (2:31; 3:11–12; 14:3–5, 9–10). Nothing is said of an immortal soul.

3 Maccabees

As noted in *JCH* (177–78), 3 Maccabees is difficult to date, part of it being perhaps as early as Ptolemaic times, but the final form of the book was perhaps as late as the Augustan period. Its main value is as an example of persecution-and-deliverance literature, in company with Daniel 3 and 6.

Wisdom of Solomon

Calduch-Benages, N., and J. Vermeylen (eds) (1999) *Treasures of Wisdom: Studies in Ben Sira and the Book of Wisdom: Festschrift M. Gilbert.*
Cheon, S. (1997) *The Exodus Story in the Wisdom of Solomon.*
Collins, J. J. (2000) *Between Athens and Jerusalem: Jewish Identity in the Hellenistic Diaspora*: 195–202.
Engel, H. (1998) *Das Buch der Weisheit.*
Focke, F. (1913) *Die Entstehung der Weisheit Salomos: Ein Beitrag zur Geschichte des jüdischen Hellenismus.*
Georgi, D. (1980) *Weisheit Salomos*: 391–478.
Gilbert, M., S.J. (1973) *La critique des dieux dans le Livre de la Sagesse (Sg 13–15).*
—— (1984) "Wisdom of Solomon", in *JWSTP*: 301–13.
—— (1986) "Sagesse de Salomon (ou Livre de la Sagesse)", in J. Briend and E. Cothenet (ed) *Supplément au Dictionnaire de la Bible*: 11.58–119.
Grabbe, L. L. (1997a) *Wisdom of Solomon.*
Hogan, K. M. (1999) "The Exegetical Background of the 'Ambiguity of Death' in the Wisdom of Solomon", *JSJ* 30: 1–24.
Hübner, H. (1999) *Die Weisheit Salomons.*
Kolarcik, M. (1991) *The Ambiguity of Death in the Book of Wisdom 1–6.*
JLBM: 175–85.
Larcher, C., O.P. (1969) *Études sur le Livre de la Sagesse.*
—— (1983–85) *Le Livre de la Sagesse ou la Sagesse de Salomon.*
Mack, B. L. (1973) *Logos und Sophia: Untersuchungen zur Weisheitstheologie im hellenistischen Judentum.*
Reese, J. M. (1970) *Hellenistic Influence on the Book of Wisdom and Its Consequences.*
Reider, J. (1957) *The Book of Wisdom.*
Schürer: 568–79.
Schwenk-Bressler, U. (1993) *Sapientia Salomonis als ein Beispiel frühjüdischer Textauslegung: Die Auslegung des Buches Genesis, Exodus 1–15 und Teilen der Wüstentradition in Sap 10–19.*
Winston, D. (1979) *The Wisdom of Solomon: A New Translation with Introduction and Commentary.*
Ziegler, J. (1980a) *Sapientia Salomonis.*

The Wisdom of Solomon is one of the main representatives (along with Philo) of what is often referred to as "Hellenistic Judaism"; it is certainly one of the most important writings that can be said with a great deal of assurance to have an origin outside Palestine. The book was almost certainly written in Alexandria in the early Roman empire (for a further discussion of many points in this brief introduction, see Grabbe 1997a). Although it has recently been argued by some important interpreters that the book was written during the crisis under Caligula (Winston 1979: 20–25; Cheon 1997), it seems more likely to stem from some decades earlier in the reign of Augustus (Gilbert 1986: 91–93; Grabbe 1997a: 102–5). There is a strong consensus among modern scholars that the book is a literary unity and thus probably the product of a single author who, nevertheless, drew strongly on the Jewish wisdom and biblical traditions. He is likely to have had a good education in the Greek language and was knowledgeable in Hellenistic literary culture.

The book itself falls well into one of the main Hellenistic genres, being probably either an *encomium* or a *logos protrepiticus* (Latin, from the Greek *logos protreptikos*). The encomium is a well-known genre in which the writer or orator praises a particular thing, often a person but sometimes something more abstract such as a particular course of action or way of life. As for the protreptic discourse, this was not primarily aimed at persuasion on a course of action but at encouraging listeners to admire someone or something. On the other hand, if the admired thing was a value of some sort, the praise would have the ultimate aim of convincing one to adopt it. It is evident that the encomium and the protreptic are closely related in many ways, and both fit Wisdom to a large degree.

The prime audience most likely in the mind of the author was those educated Jewish youth of Alexandria who found the surrounding Hellenistic culture attractive, including the various Hellenistic religious cults (e.g. Isis worship), and might be tempted to abandon Judaism altogether. That such might happen can be exemplified from even the very family of the upper-class Philo whose nephew Tiberius Alexander had abandoned his ancestral religion (at least, according to Josephus, *Ant.* 20.5.2 §100). Except for the matter of religion, there was little to prevent educated young Jewish men from partaking of the delights of Greek culture glittering all round them. The book was also likely to have been intended as encouragement to the Jewish community in opposing not only the attractions of the larger Greco-Roman society but also the antagonism and sometimes even oppression from that same society. (The problem of oppression would have been a particularly important factor if the book was written during the rule of Caligula, though the book does not dwell on oppression.)

It cannot be ruled out that the author also wanted to reach a Greco-Roman readership, as some have suggested, but this would have been a secondary aim at best. Non-Jews would have had a difficult time understanding some aspects of the book, which drew heavily on Jewish tradition. The book touches on a number of issues about Judaic religion, especially as manifested in the Diaspora:

1. The figure of wisdom is significant in the book, culminating a long tradition beginning with Proverbs 1–9 (pp. 225–28 below). The importance of seeking and gaining wisdom is emphasized.

2. The writer combines a good Greek education (evidenced in the rhetoric and literary forms) with Jewish tradition, almost half the book being a midrash on the exodus from Egypt (Wisd. 11–19).

3. The writer devotes a good deal of space contrasting the righteous and wicked, with a clear moral aim. Although these are not explicitly identified with the Jews and Gentiles respectively, this seems to be implied for the most part. Presumably some Jews could be considered wicked (primarily those seen as apostates), but whether some Gentiles could be seen as righteous is unclear. However, in the last part of the book, the righteous are represented by the Israelites, and the wicked by the Egyptians.

4. The book is an important witness to a Jewish eschatology which focused on the soul and its fate after death, with no hint of a resurrection. The text is deliberately ambiguous about the sort of death meant in some passages, referred by some modern scholars as the "ambiguity of death" in the book (Kolarcik 1991). The soul is not seen as naturally immortal, however, with only the souls of the righteous having immortality bestowed upon them. The reward of the righteous is to become like the stars, what is sometimes called "astral immortality" (3:7–9; cf. chapter 12 below). Whether the author believed in transmigration of souls is unclear, though 8:19–20 might imply that.

5. An important theme is opposition to polytheism and, especially, to the use of images in worship (12:24–13:19); however, worship of animals (ascribed to the Egyptians) was considered even lower than idol worship (15:18–19).

Pseudo-Phocylides

Collins, J. J. (2000) *Between Athens and Jerusalem: Jewish Identity in the Hellenistic Diaspora*: 168–74.

Horst, P. W. van der (1978) *The Sentences of Pseudo-Phocylides: Introduction, Translation and Commentary*.

—— (1988) "Pseudo-Phocylides Revisited", *JSP* 3:3–30.

JWSTP: 313–16.

OTP: 2.565–82.

Schürer: 3.687–92.

Wilson, W. T. (1994) *The Mysteries of Righteousness: The Literary Composition and Genre of the Sentences of Pseudo-Phocylides*.

Although there was a genuine Greek poet Phocylides of the sixth century BCE, it is generally agreed that the present text is a Jewish one. A large part of the content is parallel with the OT or compatible with what we know of Judaism;

on the other hand, there is little that could be specifically Christian and little to show a non-Jewish authorship unless possibly written by a "God-fearer". A study of the Greek vocabulary and the lack of clashes between Jew and Gentile suggests the early Roman empire (the reign of Augustus or perhaps of Tiberius), making it roughly contemporary with the Wisdom of Solomon and Philo. The prohibition against dissection of corpses (102) suggests Alexandria as its place of origin. It tells us the following about Jewish beliefs:

1. The "universalism" in its teaching is very strong. There is not the hostility toward the wider Greco-Roman world that one finds even in the Wisdom of Solomon. Although there is no agreement about its precise audience, it shows a knowledge of Hellenistic literature and culture, and seems to see no conflict between those and Judaism.

2. Its content is mainly ethical. Many of its teachings can be matched more or less with OT passages (e.g. not taking the young of a bird and also the mother [84–85//Deut. 22:6–7]; not eating meat torn by animals [147–48//Exod. 23:3]), but most are also compatible with contemporary Greco-Roman thought and even paralleled by Greco-Roman maxims. Overt Jewish practices (e.g. the sabbath) are not mentioned, though there is an emphasis on monotheism (8, 54).

3. There are certain eschatological points made, including the soul as the person, immortal, created in God's image; the residence of the soul in Hades after death; the idea of the resurrection; and the goal of humans to become gods (102–15).

4. A long section on sexual morality (175–206) seems to speak against any sort of sex without procreation as its goal. It also appears to condemn lesbianism, which is not mentioned in the OT (192).

Philo of Alexandria

Alexandre, M., Jr (1999) *Rhetorical Argumentation in Philo of Alexandria*.

Bamberger, B. J. (1977) "Philo and the Aggadah", *HUCA* 48: 153–85.

Birnbaum, E. (1996) *The Place of Judaism in Philo's Thought. Israel, Jews, and Proselytes*.

Borgen, P. (1997) *Philo of Alexandria: An Exegete for his Time*.

Borgen, P., K. Fuglseth, and R. Skarsten (2000) *The Philo Index: A Complete Greek Word Index to the Writings of Philo of Alexandria*.

Calabi, F. (1998) *The Language and the Law of God: Interpretation and Politics in Philo of Alexandria*.

Dillon, J. (1977) *The Middle Platonists*.

Grabbe, L. L. (1988) *Etymology in Early Jewish Interpretation*.

—— (1991c) "Philo and Aggada: A Response to B. J. Bamberger", in D.T. Runia, *et al.* (ed) *Heirs of the Septuagint: Philo, Hellenistic Judaism and Early Christianity: Festschrift for Earle Hilgert*: 153–66.

—— (2000a) "Eschatology in Philo and Josephus", in A. Avery-Peck and J. Neusner (ed) *Judaism in Late Antiquity: Part 4 Death, Life-after-Death, Resurrection and the World-to-Come in the Judaisms of Antiquity*: 163–85.

Hay, D. M. (1979–80) "Philo's References to Other Allegorists", *Studia Philonica* 6: 41–75.

—— (ed.) (1991b) *Both Literal and Allegorical: Studies in Philo of Alexandria's* Questions and Answers on Genesis and Exodus.

Kenney, J. P. (ed.) (1995) *The School of Moses: Studies in Philo and Hellenistic Religions in Memory of Horst R. Moehring*.

LaPorte, J. (1983) Eucharistia *in Philo*.

Mack, B. L. (1974–75) "Exegetical Traditions in Alexandrian Judaism: A Program for the Analysis of the Philonic Corpus", *Studia Philonica* 3: 71–112.

Mendelson, A. (1988) *Philo's Jewish Identity*.

Nikiprowetzky, V. (1996) *Œtudes philoniennes*.

Royse, J. R. (1991) *The Spurious Texts of Philo of Alexandria: A Study of Textual Transmission and Corruption with Indexes to the Major Collections of Greek Fragments*.

Runia, D. T. (1986) *Philo of Alexandria and the* Timaeus *of Plato*.

—— (1993) *Philo in Early Christian Literature: A Survey*.

—— (1995) *Philo and the Church Fathers: A Collection of Papers*.

Seland, T. (1995) *Establishment Violence in Philo and Luke. A Study of Non-Conformity to the Torah and Jewish Vigilante Reactions*.

Sly, D. I. (1996) *Philo's Alexandria*.

Terian, A. (ed.) (1992) *Quaestiones et solutiones in Exodum I et II, e versione armeniaca et fragmenta graeca: Introduction, traduction et notes*.

Winter, B. W. (1997) *Philo and Paul among the Sophists*.

The brief introduction and bibliography of editions and relevant studies of Philo up to about 1990 given in *JCH* (372–74) is only supplemented here, attesting to the current interest in this important Jewish writer. There is no doubt that of all the Hellenistic Jewish writers preserved, Philo of Alexandria (*c*.20 BCE–50 CE) is the main representative of "Hellenistic Judaism", the Judaism of those communities living in the Greco-Roman world outside Palestine. He is one of our main sources about Jews in the Greek-speaking Diaspora and also a prime source about biblical interpretation. Most of his writings are commentaries on the Pentateuch in one form or another. A summary of Philo's contribution to our understanding of Judaic religion is difficult to give, for two reasons: first, the extent of his writings rules out a simple précis; secondly, there is always the question of how typical he was of Hellenistic Judaism. That is, did he represent a particular school or interpretative tradition in Alexandria, or was his exegetical system and comment uniquely his own, differing widely from other interpreters of the time? His contribution to our knowledge of Judaic religion includes the following points:

1. The debate about Philo's place in Judaism is in line with general developments in Jewish studies that recognize the complexity of Second Temple Judaism and the unhelpfulness of neat oppositions such as Jewish/Hellenist. Recent treatments have argued correctly that the "Hellenistic" and the "Jewish" were both integral parts of Philo's persona (e.g. Mendelson 1988).

2. His theology is a version of Middle Platonism (Dillon 1977: 139-83; although recognizing that Philo borrowed much from Plato, Runia [1986: 505–19] argues that he is not a Middle Platonist as such). He admires the intellectual side of Greek culture and is fully at home in it. It is this interplay between, and synthesis of, Greek philosophy and Jewish tradition that makes up one important strand of Judaism during this period. How widespread his version of Jewish thinking was at the time is a moot point since we have little other information (but see next point); however, books such as the Wisdom of Solomon show how indebted writers could be to Greek rhetoric and literature.

3. He attests to a variety of viewpoints, perhaps schools of interpretation or even sects, in Alexandria (cf. Hay 1979–80). These are presented primarily in terms of their exegesis, which makes it difficult to pin down other characteristics and to know whether they formed definite sects; however, one group (opposed by Philo) is often labeled the "extreme allegorists" because it argued that one did not necessarily have to keep the traditional laws once true allegorical meaning was understood. The few references given by Philo show no particular influence from Palestinian sects of the time (cf. Grabbe 1991c).

4. Philo seldom refers to other sections of the Bible apart from the Pentateuch, though a few citations show that he was familiar with at least some of the books now making up the Hebrew canon (see p. 154 below). On the other hand, it is not clear to what extent they had equal authority with the Pentateuch for him nor whether he knew all the twenty-four books of the later Hebrew canon (see pp. 156–57 below).

5. Philo exhibits a variety of biblical interpretation in his writings (Mack 1974–75), and this list is probably not exhaustive. His use of Hebrew etymologies for biblical names is extremely interesting because it was exploited in a productive sense mainly outside the Hebrew/Aramaic-speaking Jewish communities (Grabbe 1988), the only other Jewish writer making significant use of etymological exegesis being Aristobulus (pp. 72–73 above). It is likely that the real influence on Philo in this particular area came from Greek exegesis of Homer (Grabbe 1988: 49–87).

6. His relation to rabbinic exegesis and tradition has been much debated but, unfortunately, even some recent works on Philo's exegesis (e.g. Calabi 1998) are not up to date with the present debate on rabbinic literature. The

current trend is to be cautious (Bamberger 1977) and to recognize the large difference between most of Philo's exegesis and its essential characteristics and that found in rabbinic commentaries (Grabbe 1991c). This does not mean that some comparisons cannot be made with profit, but a good deal of methodological care is in order. By and large, the spirit and content of Philo's treatment of the biblical text is in a different world from that of the rabbis.

Josephus

Feldman, L. H. (1998a) *Studies in Josephus' Rewritten Bible*.

—— (1998b) *Josephus's Interpretation of the Bible*.

Feldman, L. H., and J. R. Levison (eds) (1996) *Josephus'* Contra Apionem*: Studies in its Character and Context with a Latin Concordance to the Portion Missing in Greek*.

Grabbe, L. L. (1999b) "Sadducees and Pharisees", in J. Neusner and A. J. Avery-Peck (ed) *Judaism in Late Antiquity: Part Three. Where We Stand: Issues and Debates in Ancient Judaism: Volume 1*: 35–62.

—— (2000a) "Eschatology in Philo and Josephus", in A. Avery-Peck and J. Neusner (eds) *Judaism in Late Antiquity: Part 4 Death, Life-after-Death, Resurrection and the World-to-Come in the Judaisms of Antiquity*: 163–85.

—— (2000e) "The Pharisees – A Response to Steve Mason", in J. Neusner and A. Avery-Peck (eds) *Where We Stand, Vol. 3*: 35–47.

Kottek, Samuel S. (1995) *Medicine and Hygiene in the Works of Flavius Josephus*.

Lindsay, D R. (1993) *Josephus and Faith*: Pistis *and* Pisteuein *as Faith Terminology in the Writings of Flavius Josephus and in the New Testament*.

McClaren, J. S. (1998) *Turbulent Times? Josephus and Scholarship on Judaea in the First Century* CE,

Mason, Steve (1991) *Flavius Josephus on the Pharisees: A Composition-Critical Study*.

—— (1992) *Josephus and the New Testament*.

—— (ed.) (1998) *Understanding Josephus: Seven Perspectives*.

—— (1999) "Revisiting Josephus's Pharisees", in J. Neusner and A. Avery-Peck (eds) *Where We Stand, Vol. 2*: 23–56.

Parente, F. and J. Sievers (eds) (1994) *Josephus and the History of the Greco-Roman Period*.

Pucci Ben Zeev, Miriam (1993) "The Reliability of Josephus Flavius: The Case of Hecataeus' and Manetho's Accounts of Jews and Judaism: Fifteen Years of Contemporary Research (1974–1990)", *JSJ* 24: 215–34.

—— (1998) *Jewish Rights in the Roman World: The Greek and Roman Documents Quoted by Josephus Flavius*.

Rajak, T. (1984) "Was There a Roman Charter for the Jews?" *JRS* 74: 107–23.

Schröder, B. (1996) *Die "väterlichen Gesetze": Flavius Josephus als Vermittler von Halachah an Griechen und Römer*.

Spilsbury, P. (1998) *The Image of the Jew in Flavius Josephus' Paraphrase of the Bible*.

For a general introduction to Josephus and his writings (with an extensive bibliographical guide), and his value as a historian, see *JCH* (pp. 4–13). Unfortunately, such is the interest in Josephus at the present that that treatment is already well out of date in certain aspects (though I still stand by the methodological principles and cautions). For example, Mason (2000) has come forward with a new proposal for the context in which Josephus produced his works; whether he is right is beside the point here, which is only that new theories and insights are being produced on a regular basis. The brief bibliography here is likely to need supplementing even by the time it appears in print.

Josephus is of course our main historical source for the history of the Jews during Hasmonean and Roman times to about 75 CE. His importance for religion is of a different order. Although he writes mainly as a historian, he still says a good deal about Jewish religion. Also, his book *Against Apion (Contra Apionem)* contains a variety of material of relevance to religious issues. Since Josephus is cited continually throughout this book, it would be both difficult and superfluous to try to describe his contribution in detail, but some of the main areas where he makes a contribution can be summarized as follows:

1. He claims to be a priest and consequently to have special knowledge of the religious laws. Judging from *Life* (2 §9) where he alleges to have been consulted as an expert already by age 14, some of his claims are certainly exaggerated. Nevertheless, he would have had some training, whether formal or just from contact with family members, while growing up, and he would certainly have been familiar with the temple and its cult before the destruction in 70. There are many passages that mention the temple and cult in passing.

2. A section on the Jewish law (*Ant.* 4.8.1–46 §§176–314) gives an insight into how some of the OT laws were interpreted and applied. This does not mean that we can always accept Josephus's presentation as evidence of actual practice since he also has an apologetic aim in his description. At times his interpretation is at variance with other sources, but his writings at least give one particular view of the time.

3. His information on Judean society, including its religious aspects, is very valuable. For example, he is one of the main sources on the various sects and groups which moved briefly across the field of historical vision before being lost to view forever. Whether he claimed to have been a Pharisee or not (*Life* 2 §12; cf. Grabbe 1999b: 43–44), there is no evidence that he ever was. Nevertheless, he knew prominent Pharisees and members of other Jewish sects of the time.

4. Two of his writings (*Antiquities* and *Against Apion*) are particularly important for showing us the sort of attacks made on Jews by some Greco-Roman writers and the type of defences used in return by Jewish writers (see Rajak 1984, Pucci Ben Zeev 1998, and pp. 305–8 below). Josephus is very important for illustrating the complexities of outlook on the Jews and their laws held among the educated members of Greek and Roman society during the Second Temple period.

5. Josephus gives information on the biblical canon, especially in the important passage in *Ag. Apion* (1.8 §§37–43), but also in the biblical books used as the basis of some of his own writings. See further the next point and pp. 152–57 below.

6. He also provides information on the state of the biblical text. This is mainly through the various texts used as the basis for parts of his own writings which are by and large paraphrases of the biblical text (see further at pp. 158–65 below). He alleges that the text had been fixed since Persian times (*Ag. Apion* 1.8 §42), but this is belied by his own use of texts other than the Hebrew, and by the different versions of the Greek text which served as the basis of his discussion.

Liber Antiquitatum Biblicarum (Pseudo-Philo)

Harrington, D. J. (1971) "The Biblical Text of Pseudo-Philo's *Liber Antiquitatum Biblicarum*", *CBQ* 33: 1–17.

—— (1974) *The Hebrew Fragments of Pseudo-Philo's* Liber Antiquitatum Biblicarum *Preserved in the* Chronicles of Jerahmeel.

—— (1992) "Philo, Pseudo-", *ABD* 5:344–45.

Harrington, D. J., J. Cazeaux, C. Perrot, and P. Bogaert (eds) (1976) *Pseudo-Philon, Les Antiquités Bibliques*.

Jacobson, H. (1996) *A Commentary on Pseudo-Philo's* Liber Antiquitatum Biblicarum, *with Latin Text and English Translation*.

James, M. R. (1917) *The Biblical Antiquities of Philo*.

JLBM: 265–68.

JWSTP: 107–10.

Murphy, F. J. (1993) *Pseudo-Philo: Rewriting the Bible*.

OTP: 2.297–377.

Schürer: 3.325–31.

The attribution of the *Liber Antiquitatum Biblicarum* to Philo is late, and scholarship is agreed that it had nothing to do with Philo of Alexandria. The book parallels the biblical text from Genesis 1 to the reign of Saul (2 Samuel 28) and is usually taken to be an example of "rewritten Bible" (see p. 168 below). In some cases, it is simply a paraphrase of the biblical text, but at times it incorporates extra-biblical traditions and interpretations, often being brief where the biblical text gives much detail (e.g. the creation story of Genesis 1–3 and most of Leviticus are omitted), but sometimes expansive where the biblical text is brief (e.g. the judge Kenaz: 25–28). The text is preserved in Latin (Harrington, *et al.* 1976) and a late Hebrew translation made from the Latin text (Harrington 1974); however, it is now generally agreed that the original text was Hebrew. The recent commentary by Jacobson (1996) is a major aid to study. Because of Pseudo-Philo's enlightened views on women, one recent study has suggested that the author could have been a woman (Murphy 1993: 267). There is a strong consensus that the book is first century CE, though whether before or after 70 is debated. Aspects of the message important for religion include the following:

1. *LAB* is an example of one important form of biblical interpretation in late Second Temple Judaism, viz., rewritten Bible.

2. A key theme is the pattern of sin–punishment–repentance–salvation, a theme well known from the biblical text. Some have seen this as a message of hope after the destruction of the 66–70 war.

3. The temple and cult are accepted as normal for atonement of sin (32:3), and the temple seems to be presupposed (22:8–9), which is why some date the book before 70.

4. The book's teachings on eschatology are important. Life after death (which is defined as separation of the body and soul: 44:10), immediate punishment or reward for deeds (32:13; 33:3–5; 62:9), resurrection, and final judgment are all accepted (3:10; 16:3). However, no special emphasis is placed on eschatology; rather the author seems more concerned to stress the correct way of living in this life.

5. It has been argued that the text depends on a variant text, differing from the MT (sometimes labeled the "Old Palestinian"; see Harrington 1971).

6. Despite the frequent past assertion that the writer was a Pharisee, there is no evidence that the author belonged to one of the major sects, but the book expresses views that were likely to have been accepted by many Jews of the time (Murphy 1993: 267).

Adam and Eve literature

Anderson, G. A., and M. E. Stone (eds) (1999) *A Synopsis of the Books of Adam and Eve.*

Collins, J. J. (2000) *Between Athens and Jerusalem: Jewish Identity in the Hellenistic Diaspora*: 246–48.

Hedrick, C. W. (1980) *The Apocalypse of Adam: A Literary and Source Analysis.*

JLBM: 253–57.

JWSTP: 110–18.

Levison, J. R. (1988) *Portraits of Adam in Early Judaism, from Sirach to 2 Baruch.*

Lipscomb, W. L. (1990) *The Armenian Apocryphal Adam Literature.*

Mahé, J.-P. (1981) "Le livre d'Adam georgien", in R. van den Broek and M. J. Vermaseren (eds) *Studies in Gnosticism and Hellenistic Religons Presented to Gilles Quispel on the Occasion of his 65th Birthday*: 227–60.

Nickelsburg, G. W. E. (1981) "Some Related Traditions in the Apocalypse of Adam, the Books of Adam and Eve, and 1 Enoch", in B. Layton (ed.) *Rediscovery of Gnosticism, vol. 2: Sethian Gnosticism*: 515–39.

OTP: 2.249–95.

Perkins, P. (1977) "Apocalypse of Adam: The Genre and Function of a Gnostic Apocalypse", *CBQ* 39: 382–95.

Schürer: 3.757–61.

Stone, M. E. (1992) *A History of the Literature of Adam and Eve*.

—— (1996a) *Texts and Concordances of the Armenian Adam Literature: Volume I: Genesis 1–4, Penitence of Adam, Book of Adam*.

—— (1996b) *Armenian Apocrypha Relating to Adam and Eve*.

Turdeanu, E. (1981) *Apocryphes slaves et roumains de l'Ancien Testament*: 75–144.

Older introductions to Jewish literature mention two books dealing with Adam and Eve, the *Apocalypse of Moses* (in Greek) and the *Vita Adae et Euae* (*Life of Adam and Eve*) in Latin. Now the study of the rich Armenian and other traditions has turned up other Adam-and-Eve works that may have their roots in Second Temple Judaism in some cases (Mahé 1981; Lipscombe 1990; Stone 1992; 1996a; 1996b; cf. Turdeanu 1981: 75–144). The Gnostic *Apocalypse of Adam* has certain traditions in common with the *Vita*, which has suggested that they both depend on a common "Testament of Adam" (Perkins 1977; Nickelsburg 1981; cf. Hedrick 1980). Some of the main texts are now collected into a synoptic edition (Anderson/Stone 1999). Despite the different titles, the two main books, *Apocalypse of Moses* and *Life of Adam and Eve*, are parallel in many respects with a similar general content, but with the latter having some sections (*Vita* 1:1–22:2; 25–29; 49:1–50:2) not found in the former, and vice versa (*Ap. Mos.* 15–30); the parallel sections are also sometimes of unequal length or different in other ways. It is not easy to date the two works, but many scholars would put the original compositions around the first century CE. Some points arising from them are the following:

1. They reveal the continued interest of many Jews in the origin myths and traditions known from the first few chapters of Genesis. For example, Philo of Alexandria concentrates on the early chapters of Genesis, and these chapters are also very important to quite a few Gnostic writings.

2. There is information on the concept of death (*Ap. Mos.* 13:3–6; 32:4) and afterlife in various passages, including the ascent of the soul to paradise (*Ap. Mos.* 37:5; 40:1–2) and the resurrection of all who have died (*Ap. Mos.* 13:3–5).

3. Angelology and demonology are important. Michael has a prominent place in dealing with Adam and Eve. Various ranks of angels are listed or

described (*Ap. Mos.* 22:3; 33; 37:3; 40:2). The fall of Satan from heaven, with overtones of Isaiah 14, is presented in *Vita* 12–16.

4. The time that Adam and Eve spend in the Jordan and the Tigris rivers (*Ap. Mos.* 29//*Vita* 6–10) has suggested to some scholars that a group believing in ritual bathing lay behind these works.

Similitudes (Parables) of Enoch (1 Enoch 37–71)

Milik, J. T. (1976) *The Books of Enoch: Aramaic Fragments of Qumran Cave 4.*
Suter, David W. (1979) *Tradition and Composition in the Parables of Enoch.*

See *JCH* (180–81) and pp. 41–42 above for a short introduction and bibliography to *1 Enoch*. As noted there, there is a good deal of debate about *1 Enoch* 37–71 at the moment. Milik's argument (1976: 89–107) for the late third century CE is not generally accepted, and something of a consensus has developed around the first century CE, though whether before or after 70 is still disputed. There is nothing that must be Christian within the book (*pace* Milik), and most scholars accept that it is a Jewish work. It continues a number of the themes found in other sections of the book and seems to give us an insight into one form of Judaism, probably before 70 CE (no indication of the fall of the temple or the post-70 situation is found in the book).

1. God is often referred to as the "Lord of spirits". There are also other titles, such as the "Head of Days".

2. The writing illustrates the rich angelology and demonology of the time. The fallen angels myth is repeated here (54; 56), with a list of participants (69); also listed are the four archangels (40; 54:6).

3. Daniel 7 has been taken up as one theme, with the "Head of Days" (equivalent to the "Ancient of Days" of Daniel) and the figure of the "Son of Man" who is identified with both the heavenly Elect One and with the messiah (see pp. 282–83 below).

4. Several chapters seem to be extracted from a lost "Book of Noah" (65–68), also known from other sections of *1 Enoch* (e.g. 106–07).

5. Enoch himself has a prominent role, even to the point of being identified with the "Son of Man" in what is probably a later development of the book (71). One can compare his exaltation here with his role as scribe in the judgment scene of one version of the *Testament of Abraham* (B 11:3–10).

Sibylline Oracles

For an introduction to the *Sibylline Oracles*, see *JCH* (562–64). A portion of *Sibylline Oracle* 3 seems to relate to the Roman period before 70 CE:

1. A reference to the "mistress" (*despoina*) appears to have Cleopatra VII in mind and to associate her with the subjugation of Rome to Asia (verses

350–80), suggesting that this section was written before her defeat at Actium and death shortly afterward in 31 BCE.

2. A number of prophecies relate to the endtime: verses 46–63 and 75–92 indicate a period after the disappointment of Actium when hope in Cleopatra had failed. 3:46–63 predicts the destruction of Rome, while 3:75–92 speaks more generally of a universal conflagration (*ekpyrosis*).

3. For passages relating to the fall of Jerusalem and Nero *redivivus*, see p. 120 below.

Slavonic Enoch (*2 Enoch*)

Böttrich, C. (1991) "Recent Studies in the *Slavonic Book of Enoch*", *JSP* 9: 35–42.

——— (1992) *Weltweisheit, Menschheitsethik, Urkult: Studien zum slavischen Henochbuch.*

——— (1996) *Das slavische Henochbuch.*

Charles, R. H., and W. R. Morfill (1896) *The Book of the Secrets of Enoch.*

Collins, J. J. (2000) *Between Athens and Jerusalem: Jewish Identity in the Hellenistic Diaspora*: 252–55.

Fischer, U. (1978) *Eschatologie und Jenseitserwartung im hellenistischen Diaspora-judentum.*

Grabbe, L. L. (1996) *An Introduction to First Century Judaism: Jewish Religion and History in the Second Temple Period.*

JLBM: 185–88.

JWSTP: 406–8.

Milik, J. T. (1976) *The Books of Enoch: Aramaic Fragments of Qumran Cave 4*: 107–16.

Orlov, A. A. (1998) "Titles of Enoch-Metatron in *2 Enoch*", *JSP* 18: 71–86.

OTP 1.91–221.

Schürer: 3.746–50.

Turdeanu, E. (1981) *Apocryphes slaves et roumains de l'Ancien Testament*: 37–43.

Vaillant, A. (1952) *Le livre des secrets d'Hénoch: Texte slave et traduction française.*

There are many questions about *2 Enoch*, partly because it has a shorter history of study than some of the other apocalyptic writings and partly because fewer scholars are Slavonic specialists. There is not yet a consensus about the text which occurs in several versions, and eminent specialists have preferred different ones. Even the trend to reduce the various manuscripts and sources to two versions, a long one and a short one, only partially alleviates the problem. There is agreement that the translations of Charles/Morfill 1896 and of *APOT* are based on inferior manuscripts. Both versions are given in translation by F. I. Anderson (in *OTP*). Vaillant has preferred the shorter version, though readings from manuscripts of the longer version are included there, in what is the only edition with the Slavonic text. Böttrich (1992: 59–107) argues that the best form of the text is the long version (especially as found in manuscripts J and R) which is the basis of his translation (1996).

A second problem is the dating and provenance of the book. Charles/Morfill (1896) dated it to the first half of the first century CE. Vaillant argued that it was Christian. More recently J. T. Milik has claimed that it was a Christian work, no earlier than about the ninth or tenth centuries AD (1976: 107–12). Neither this late dating nor the attempt to make it Christian have gained a following, but both questions are difficult. There is little to suggest a Christian work, especially in the short recension. The suggestion that it is from a "fringe sect" of Judaism or that it is syncretistic (*OTP*: 1.96) presupposes that we know enough about the Judaism of the time to speak in those terms. The view that it was adapted to fit Bogomil doctrine is also improbable (cf. Böttrich 1992: 28–31, 54–55). The book is mainly important for it teachings on eschatology and the heavenly world:

1. A large section of the book (1–38) is taken up with a heavenly journey through either seven (shorter version) or ten heavens (longer version).

2. The cosmological interests of the *Astronomical Book of Enoch* (*1 En.* 72–82) are also found in *2 Enoch* (11–17), including a detailed account of creation (24–32).

3. There is much paranetic material in the book, especially in the part in which Enoch speaks with his children (38–67).

4. There is a definite cultic interest. A priesthood is established even before Noah's flood, with Methusalah as the first priest, passing the office down to his second son (69–70). The command to tie sacrificial animals by all four legs is otherwise unknown (59:3; 69:12).

5. The book contains a unique Melchizedek tradition (71–72), though it confirms the speculation about the mysterious figure of Genesis 14 already known from 11QMelchizedek and and the book of Hebrews. This story does not seem to have any Christian influence, at least in the shorter recension.

6. There are certain resemblances to some of the Gnostic texts, and *2 Enoch* has been used to support the thesis of a Jewish Gnosticism (*JCH*: 514–19; Grabbe 1996: 94–110, especially 106).

4 Maccabees

Bickerman, E. J. (1976) "The Date of Fourth Maccabees", *Studies in Jewish and Christian History*: 1.275–81.

Breitenstein, U. (1976) *Beobachtungen zu Sprache, Stil und Gedankengut des Vierten Maccabäerbuchs*.

Collins, J. J. (2000) *Between Athens and Jerusalem: Jewish Identity in the Hellenistic Diaspora*: 202–9.

deSilva, David A. (1998) *4 Maccabees*.

Henten, J. W. van (1986) "Datierung und Herkunft des Vierten Makkabäerbuches", in J. W. van Henten, *et al.* (ed) *Tradition and Re-interpretation in
Jewish and Early Christian Literature*: 136–49.

—— (1997) *The Maccabean Martyrs as Saviours of the Jewish People: A Study of
2 and 4 Maccabees*.

JLBM: 223–27.
JWSTP: 316–19.
OTP: 2.531–64
Schürer: 3.588–93

This is a philosophical treatise on the topic of control of the passions by reason,
written in diatribe form. The name "Maccabees" has become attached to it
because it uses the Maccabees as examples, probably taken from a copy of
2 Maccabees. The work is written in a good Greek, which was probably
its original language. Based on the language and some possible historical
references, it has been dated from the mid-first century CE to about the time
of the Bar Kokhba revolt. An argument has been made for a composition in
Syria or Asia Minor rather than Egypt (van Henten 1986).

1. The work illustrates how a Jewish writer might use fully Hellenistic forms
and ideals to write a very Jewish work. The work takes its place alongside
those of Philo, the Wisdom of Solomon, and several of the Fragmentary
Writers in Greek (pp. 70–73 above); however, if van Henten is correct, this
Hellenistic context may be in Syria or even Palestine and not just in
Alexandria.

2. The book is essentially Jewish in its interests and emphases. For example,
the "reason" promoted is the reason of piety or religion (1:1: *ho eusebēs
logismos*).

3. The author believes in the immortality of the soul and reward and
punishment immediately after death (13:17; 15:3; 17:5, 18; 18:23). There is
no evidence of a belief in a resurrection, despite the occurrence of this belief
in 2 Maccabees.

4. Like its source 2 Maccabees, the work stresses the value of martyrdom as
a way of atoning for the sins of the people (1:11; 6:29; 17:21).

Testament of Moses

See pp. 74–75 above for a general introduction. Although much of the book
may have been written during the Maccabean period, it was not completed
until the early first century CE.

Testament of Abraham

Collins, J. J. (2000) *Between Athens and Jerusalem: Jewish Identity in the Hellenistic
Diaspora*: 248–51.

Delcor, M. (1973) *Le Testament d'Abraham: Introduction, traduction du texte grec et commentaire de la recension greque longue.*

JLBM: 248–53.

JWSTP: 60–64.

Munoa, P. B. (1998) *Four Powers in Heaven: The Interpretation of Daniel 7 in the Testament of Abraham.*

Nickelsburg, G. W. E. (ed.) (1976) *Studies in the Testament of Abaham.*

OTP: 1.871–902.

Schürer: 3.761–67.

Stone, M. E. (1972) *The Testament of Abraham: The Greek Recensions.*

The work is found in two different Greek versions which are sometimes fairly different from one another (Stone 1972), though generally parallel and often similar in content. It is not clear that there was a Semitic original of either or both the versions, though the type of language used may be a form of "Jewish Greek" which included a number of Semitisms. It is now common to date the work to the first century CE. There are some Christian passages, especially in the longer version, but these do not seem to be essential to the text and are generally taken as interpolations. The book is an important source for eschatological beliefs about the turn of the era:

1. The judgment scene is at the core of both versions (A 11–13; B 8–11) and is an important witness to one view of what happened at death: the soul was judged immediately, the righteous going to paradise and the wicked to torture and destruction. There is a hint of a general resurrection (of the bodies of the dead) and a judgment at the end of the age (see #3 below).

2. The first appearance of the later Jewish belief in the "merits of the fathers" as a means of doing away with sin is found in one version (A 12:16–18; 14:1–11).

3. Both versions seem to presuppose some sort of fixed chronological scheme for history, apparently the idea that history lasted 6,000 years (or possibly 7,000 years) before the bodies of the dead were resurrected for a final judgment (A 19:7; B 7:15–16; cf. further pp. 246–48 below).

Testaments of the Twelve Patriarchs

Charles, R. H. (1908) *The Testaments of the Twelve Patriarchs, Translated . . . with Notes.*

Collins, J. J. (2000) *Between Athens and Jerusalem: Jewish Identity in the Hellenistic Diaspora*: 174–83.

JLBM: 231–41.

Jonge, M. de (1978) *The Testaments of the Twelve Patriarchs: A Critical Edition of the Greek Text.*

—— (1992) "Patriarchs, Testaments of the Twelve", *ABD*: 5.181–86.

JWSTP: 331–44.

Kugler, R. A. (1996) *From Patriarch to Priest: The Levi-Priestly Tradition from Aramaic Levi to* Testament of Levi.

OTP: 1.775–828.

Schürer: 3.767–81.

Slingerland, H. D. (1977) *The Testaments of the Twelve Patriarchs: A Critical History of Research*.

Stone, M. E. (1996) "B. Testament of Naphtali", in *Qumran Cave 4: XVII Parabiblical Texts, Part 3*: 73–82.

Stone, M. E., and J. C. Greenfield (1979) "Remarks on the Aramaic Testament of Levi from the Geniza", *RevB* 86: 214–30.

—— (1988) "Enoch, Aramaic Levi and Sectarian Origins", *JSJ* 19: 159–70.

—— (1996) "A. Aramaic Levi Document", in *Qumran Cave 4: XVII Parabiblical Texts, Part 3*: 1–72.

This is a collection of writings which may have come together in its present form rather late. Although there is a certain unity of language and theme, this may be a redactional unity; certainly most studies have found evidence of extensive redactional activity over a considerable period of time. In its present form the *Testaments* is a Christian work, with many undoubted Christian passages; the question is whether a Jewish work has been taken over by Christian scribes who made some Christian interpolations that can be removed to leave the original more or less intact or whether a Christian composition has made extensive use of Jewish sources (cf. Charles versus de Jonge). This debate about the final form of the *Testaments* in Greek has not really been resolved, but finds from the Qumran scrolls and the Cairo Genizah have complicated matters. Fragments of an Aramaic work related to the *Testament of Levi* appear among the the texts from the Cairo Genizah (Stone/Greenfield 1979); similarly, fragments of works about Levi and Naphthali found among the Qumran scrolls have some connections with the *Testament of Levi* and the *Testament of Naphthali*.

Although the Aramaic texts have some relationship to the Greek texts, they also show many differences (cf. Kugler 1996). In the case of these two works, the present Greek text probably incorporates material from, or a reworking of, something like the known Aramaic versions, but whether we can speak of an earlier and a later version of the two *Testaments* in question is another matter. Further, it is not at all clear that the testaments of the other patriarchs had any relationship to Semitic originals. A later Jewish or Christian author, knowing the *Testaments of Levi* and *Naphthali*, could have then written works in the names of the other patriarchs to fill out the number. These new testaments could have been composed in Greek from the start (though language does not necessarily settle the issue, since it is not always possible to distinguish translation Greek from a work composed originally in "Jewish Greek"). Alternatively, a Christian or Jewish writer could have composed the additional testaments in Aramaic, and these were subsequently translated or incorporated into Greek versions, whether by Jews or Christians. In sum, the existence of the *Testaments of Levi* and *Naphthali* does not prove either the Jewish or early origin of the testaments of the other patriarchs.

Two aspects of the *Testaments* as a whole stand out: the ethical/paranetic content, focusing on specific virtues and vices, and the passages dealing with eschatology. The ethical and instructional material is often compatible with other Jewish works in Greek and is not necessarily Christian in character; however, the specific elements of Jewish law and practice one might find in such a work (e.g. sabbath-keeping and circumcision) are missing, while the eschatological passages show a good deal of Christian content. Yet there is much in the contents that shows primarily Jewish interests and does not fit a Christian context, even a Jewish-Christian one.

These considerations make use of the Greek *Testaments* as Jewish sources difficult to control. This is not to deny that much Jewish material may be there, but at this stage of study, separating out Jewish material from the Second Temple period is too problematic. Comments will therefore be limited to the Levi material from Qumran (1Q21; 4QLevi^{a-f} ar [4Q213–214b]; 4QTNaph [4Q215]) and the Cairo Genizah *Testament of Levi* which have the following content useful for Jewish religion of the time:

1. The importance and place of the priesthood are a particular emphasis in the Levi material, with Levi chosen to be priest through a vision even in his own lifetime. The work may have been written by a member of the priesthood. If so, and if the eschatological section in the Greek version is original, it would show what has been argued extensively elsewhere: that, far from being opposed to eschatology and apocalyptic, some priests at least cultivated these traditions (see p. 58 below). Fragment 5 of 4QLevi^{a} ar (4Q213) has been interpreted as criticizing the priesthood, and there is also a mention of Enoch. The text is very fragmentary, however, and we do not know whether the reference to Enoch has anything to do with the fallen angels myth, nor whether the criticism of the priesthood, if it is such, is by an outsider.

2. The writer was quite concerned about the correct execution of the cult. Detailed regulations are laid down in the surviving fragments, including even the sorts of wood to be used and the need to reject that which has worms in it (4Q214b, frags 2–6, 1:2–6 // Cairo *T. Levi*, Bodleian col. c, 9–21).

3. Like the book of *Jubilees*, the author gives chronological details of the lives of the patriarchs and the precise time when particular things happened to them. This suggests belief in a predetermined chronological scheme to history, or at least a desire to calculate the various events of history with a view to understanding the future (cf. the Greek *T. Levi* 16–18).

4. It has been proposed that the Cairo Genizah *Aramaic Levi* shows evidence of use of the solar calendar (Stone/Greenfield 1979), though this seems rather uncertain to me. The 364-day calendar as such is not actually mentioned; instead, use of the solar calendar is inferred from the births of Levi's children: the first is born in the tenth month; the second, on the first day of

the first month; the third, in the third month; the fourth, on the first day of the seventh month. Since the first day of the first and the seventh months is a Wednesday in the solar calendar known from other sources, this might be significant, but the inference is rather precarious. The first, fourth, seventh, and tenth months are all the same in the solar calendar, but the months in *Aramaic Levi* are the first, third, seventh, and tenth. To be born on the first day of the 1st month would be significant in any calendar. Similarly, the seventh month is an important one in the Jewish calendar, with the Festival of Trumpets, Yom ha-Kippurim, and Sukkot, and to be born on the first day of the seventh month could be symbolic in any version of the calendar. So the 364-day calendar *may* be implied by these dates in the *Aramaic Levi*, but they are perfectly capable of being explained in other ways.

5. The question of apocalyptic and eschatology is an intriguing one. The Aramaic fragments mention visions but nothing clearly eschatological; however, the Greek *Testament of Levi* has a section with what some have seen as belief in an eschatological high priest (16–18; others see this as a Christian passage).

Testament of Job

Brock, S. P. (1974) *Testamentum Iobi*.
Collins, J. J. (2000) *Between Athens and Jerusalem: Jewish Identity in the Hellenistic Diaspora*: 240–46.
JLBM: 241–48.
JWSTP: 349–55.
Knibb, M. A., and P. W. van der Horst (eds) (1990) *Studies on the Testament of Job*.
Kraft, R. A. (1974) *The Testament of Job according to the SV Text*.
OTP: 1.829–68.

This is a form of "rewritten Bible", using the LXX version of the book of Job. There are many midrashic details added to the original story, and the whole has been recast from the innovative, challenging biblical book, which questioned the very actions of God, to form a story of traditional piety. The book was likely to have been written in Egypt since Job is king of this country, but the dating is difficult. It could be first century, but a later date is not excluded. Although several suggestions have been made (e.g. missionary literature, martyrdom literature), the purpose of the book is still unclear. A favorite origin has been the Egyptian group called the Therapeutae, described by Philo, but the actual existence of such a group has recently been questioned (p. 206 below). Some of the points of interest are the following:

1. Job is a model of the pious man, exhibiting the quality of patience (*hupo-monē*). Instead of denouncing God's unfairness and calling for a confrontation, Job meekly accepts his fate and even makes sure that he suffers to the full

extent allowed by God (e.g. by putting back the worms on his flesh when they fall off! [20:9]). Clearly, the wisdom tradition has veered away from following the lead of Job and Qohelet and back toward the piety exemplified in Ben Sira.

2. Women have a prominent place. Job's (first) wife is given sympathetic treatment and even has a name. Her suffering as a result of Job's situation is made much clearer than in the Hebrew Job. Job's daughters speak in ecstasy (48:3, though some think this is part of a later Montanist addition to the text).

3. In the original book Satan is still a member of the heavenly court, a sort of divine prosecutor, but here he has become the devil (see pp. 219–25 below).

4. There are some connections with merkavah mysticism (the version of Jewish mysticism dealing with the divine chariot [52:6–10]; see pp. 248–51 below).

5. Idolatry is strongly denounced (2–5); indeed, Satan's attack on Job is said to be the direct consequence of Job's destroying an idol.

6. Job has been more tightly brought into the biblical tradition by identifying him with Jobab, one of the Edomite kings (Gen. 36:33–34; *T. Job* 1:6; 2:2) and making his second wife Dinah, the daughter of Jacob (Gen. 34; *T. Job* 1:6; cf. *LAB* 8:7–8).

Joseph and Asenath

Bohak, G. (1996) *Joseph and Aseneth and the Jewish Temple in Heliopolis.*
Chesnutt, R. D. (1995) *From Death to Life: Conversion in Joseph and Aseneth.*
Collins, J. J. (2000) *Between Athens and Jerusalem: Jewish Identity in the Hellenistic Diaspora*: 103–10.
JLBM: 258–63.
JWSTP: 65–71.
Kraemer, R. S. (1998) *When Aseneth Met Joseph: A Late Antique Tale of the Biblical Patriarch and his Egyptian Wife, Reconsidered.*
OTP: 177–47.
Schürer: 3.546–52.

This book is problematic because arguments about its origin and dating have ranged widely in recent scholarship. The central story of the book is about how Asenath, the daughter of an Egyptian priest, renounces idolatry and converts to Judaism so she can marry Joseph (the section of the story that makes her a daughter of Joseph's half-sister Dinah seems to be a separate tradition). Thus, the main message of the book has been taken to be in what it says about proselytes and conversion to Judaism and about marriage of Jews to Gentiles. It has often been dated to the first or second centuries CE, though whether it is Jewish or Christian has been disputed. There is also the problem that the text exists in two versions, a shorter and a longer. The recent study by Kraemer (1998) argues that the book is from the third or fourth centuries CE and may well be Christian. She also believes that the shorter version of the text is more original. On the other hand, concentrating on *Jos. Asen.* 14–17 Bohak (1996) argues that the book was written as justification of the Leontopolis temple and is to be dated to the second century BCE. Unfortunately, the difficulties about provenance, date, and setting make it difficult to use with confidence for Jewish beliefs at a particular time.

Judean Desert manuscripts, inscriptions, and archaeology

Applebaum, S. (1979) *Jews and Greeks in Ancient Cyrene.*

Barag, D., *et al.* (eds) (1994) *Masada IV: The Yigael Yadin Excavations 1963–1965, Final Reports.*

Benoit, P., *et al.* (1961) *Les grottes de Murabba'ât.*

Cotton, H. M. (1995) "The Archive of Salome Komaïse Daughter of Levi: Another Archive from the 'Cave of Letters'", *ZPE* 105: 171–208.

Cotton, H. M., and J. Geiger (1989) *Masada II: The Yigael Yadin Excavations 1963–1965, Final Reports: The Latin and Greek Documents.*

Cotton, H., and A. Yardeni (eds) (1997) *Aramaic, Hebrew and Greek Documentary Texts from Naḥal Ḥever and Other Sites, with an Appendix Containing Alleged Qumran Texts (The Seiyâl Collection II).*

Edwards, D. R., and C. T. McCollough (eds) (1997) *Archaeology and the Galilee: Texts and Contexts in the Graeco-Roman and Byzantine Periods.*

Fittschen, K., and G. Foerster (eds) (1996) *Judaea and the Greco-Roman World in the Time of Herod in the Light of Archaeological Evidence: Acts of a Symposium Organized by the Institute of Archaeology, the Hebrew University of Jerusalem and the Archaeological Institute, Georg-August-University of Göttingen at Jerusalem, November 3rd–4th 1988.*

Foerster, G. (1995) *Masada V: The Yigael Yadin Excavations 1963–1965, Final Reports: Art and Architecture.*

Horbury, W., and D. Noy (eds) (1992) *Jewish Inscriptions of Graeco-Roman Egypt, with an Index of the Jewish Inscriptions of Egypt and Cyrenaica.*

Kuhnen, H.-P. (1990) *Palästina in griechisch-römischer Zeit.*

Leon, H. J. (1995) *The Jews of Ancient Rome.*

Lewis, N. (ed.) (1989) *The Documents from the Bar Kokhba Period in the Cave of Letters: Greek Papyri,* with Y. Yadin and J. C. Greenfield (eds) *Aramaic and Nabatean Signatures and Subscriptions.*

Meyers, Eric M., Adam Lynd-Porter, Melissa Aubin, and Mark Chancey (1995) "Second Temple Studies in the Light of Recent Archaeology: Part II: The Roman Period, A Bibliography", *CR: BS* 3: 129–154.

Mildenberg, L. (1998) *Vestigia Leonis: Studien zur antiken Numismatik Israels, Palästinas und der östlichen Mittelmeerwelt.*

Netzer, E. (ed.) (1991) *Masada III: The Yigael Yadin Excavations 1963–1965, Final Reports: The Buildings: Stratigraphy and Architecture.*

Noy, D. (ed.) (1993) *Jewish Inscriptions: Volume 1 Italy (excluding the City of Rome), Spain and Gaul.*

—— (1995) *Jewish Inscriptions of Western Europe: Volume 2 The City of Rome.*

Overman, J. A. (1993) "Recent Advances in the Archaeology of the Galilee in the Roman Period", *CR: BS* 1: 35–58.

Rutgers, L. V. (1995) *The Jews in Late Ancient Rome: Evidence of Cultural Interaction in the Roman Diaspora.*

Talmon, S., and Y. Yadin (eds) (1999) *Masada VI: Yigael Yadin Excavations 1963–1965, Final Reports: The Hebrew Fragments; The Ben Sira Scroll.*

Tov, E. (1999b) "The Papyrus Fragments Found in the Judean Desert", in J.-M. Auwers and A. Wénin (eds) *Lectures et relectures de la Bible*: 247–55.

Tov, E., et al. (1990) *The Greek Minor Prophets Scroll from Nahal Hever (8HevXIIgr).*

Trebilco, P. (1991) *Jewish Communities in Asia Minor.*

Williams, M. H. (1994) "The Jews of Corycus – A Neglected Diasporan Community from Roman Times", *JSJ* 25: 274–86.

—— (1998) *The Jews among the Greeks and Romans: A Diaspora Handbook.*

Yadin, Y., and Y. Meshorer (1989) *Masada I: The Yigael Yadin Excavations 1963–1965, Final Reports: The Aramaic and Hebrew Ostraca and Jar Inscriptions; The Coins of Masada.*

This section includes some material from the period 70–135 CE since it is not always easy or convenient to separate it into neat periods. *JCH* (318–20; 379–83; 564–65) surveyed the published material (including preliminary publications) of the the non-Qumran scrolls from the Judean Desert. The last few years have seen the publication of many of these in official form. Most of the Wadi Murabba'at documents (from the period before the First Revolt and from the time of Bar Kokhba) were already published (Benoit, *et al.* 1961). The scroll of the Minor Prophets in Greek, often discussed in textual critical contexts, is now edited (Tov, *et al.* 1990). The written material from Masada is unfortunately limited, but it and much of the archaeological data have now been published officially (Yadin/Meshorer 1989; Cotton/Geiger 1989; Netzer 1991; Barag, *et al.* 1994; Foerster 1995; Talmon/Yadin 1999). Some of the Naḥal Ḥever and related material (already known in preliminary form from Yadin's popular publications) has now appeared in final form (Lewis 1989; Cotton/Yardeni 1997). Of particular interest are the archives of Babatha and Salome Komaïse, two ordinary women of the early second century CE. These are one of the closest encounters we have with ordinary people during this period since so much of what we know of individuals is about the upper classes or leaders of movements or those who were famous (notorious) in other ways.

New editions of inscriptions have provided new tools for studying Jewish communities, especially in the Diaspora. In addition to actual editions and collections (Horbury/Noy 1992; Noy 1993, 1995; *GLAJJ*; Williams 1998), one should also be aware of several recent studies that both publish and study various inscriptions and also relate them to specific local Jewish communities (Applebaum 1979; Leon 1995; Rutgers 1995; Trebilco 1991; Williams 1994). The archaeology of Palestine too has been well surveyed (Kuhnen 1990; Overman 1993; Meyers/Lynd-Porter/Aubin/Chancey 1995). In addition to the works on coins listed in *JCH* (318–20; 380–83; 564) see now Mildenberg (1998).

Many of the Qumran scrolls are relevant to the Roman period (pp. 67–70 above) and will be discussed at the appropriate places.

SYNTHESIS

Baumgarten, A. I. (1997) *The Flourishing of Jewish Sects in the Maccabean Era: An Interpretation.*

Goodman, M. (1997) *The Roman World 44 BC–AD 180.*

Grabbe, L. L. (1996a) *An Introduction to First Century Judaism: Jewish Religion and History in the Second Temple Period.*

McClaren, J. S. (1998) *Turbulent Times? Josephus and Scholarship on Judaea in the First Century CE.*

Neusner, J. (1965–70) *A History of the Jews in Babylonia.*

Price, J. J. (1992) *Jerusalem Under Siege: The Collapse of the Jewish State 66–70 CE.*

Richardson, P. (1996) *Herod: King of the Jews and Friend of the Romans.*

Rutgers, L. V. (1998) *The Hidden Heritage of Diaspora Judaism.*

Schwartz, S. (1990) *Josephus and Judaean Politics.*

The Roman period of Jewish history did not strictly come to an end until the Muslim conquest, but for our purposes it covers a period of about a century and a half. This period cannot help being dominated by the disastrous 66–70 war with Rome. We now see that much that happened can be linked forward to that revolt. McClaren (1998) has made the case that the "spiral of violence" is Josephus's own literary creation and interpretation. He is quite correct about Josephus's part in this interpretation and his cautions are in order; nevertheless, it still seems that the war with Rome became more likely after the death of Agrippa I and the continuing problems with Roman administrators. Herod was very unlikely to let a revolt get out of hand. There was certainly potential for revolt during the first period of Roman administration (6–41 CE), but the Romans would have been most alert at the beginning, especially considering that the transition to direct Roman rule was itself marked by a revolt (*JCH*: 422–23). The important factor was the build-up of Jewish frustration with Roman rule. After Judea had experienced the return to a native monarchy under Agrippa I, whose reign was short enough not to have developed any major difficulties, the unsatisfactory nature of direct Roman rule would have been felt more strongly than immediately after the end of Herod the Great's and Archelaus's administration. In other words, a consideration of Judean history through the first century CE finds a Jewish revolt about where one would be expected, even if one places less emphasis on Josephus's "spiral of violence" than is sometimes done (see also pp. 283–86 below).

For practical purposes we can divide the period into Herodian rule and Roman rule. With the apparent exception of Archelaus, Herodian rule benefited the people and helped to dampen down frustrations with the Romans. Herod's rule was complex, and the term "benevolent" is not the first one that springs to mind about his rule; on the other hand, the demonization of Herod in ancient and modern literature is unjustified and has made many historians and others miss the important positive aspects of his rule that had significant effects on the history of the time (*JCH*: 362–66; Richardson 1996). Direct opposition – and anything interpreted as opposition – would not have been allowed: Herod's security system seems to have been quite efficient (cf. *Ant.* 15.10.4 §§365–71). This meant that most Jews under his rule lived in a condition of relative peace and public order. Economically the country seems to have been in good shape, and there is no evidence that the tax burden was worse than under the Hasmoneans or his grandson Agrippa I for that matter (*JCH*: 336). He also did a good deal for the Jews in the Diaspora, interceding with the Romans when necessary (e.g. *Ant.* 16.2.3–5 §§27–65). We have no way of knowing to what extent Herod was liked or disliked (the prejudices of the sources do not help us here), but that is beside the point. The main consequence is that the peaceful practice of religion was allowed to flourish.

The public religious structures were seriously affected by Herod's rule, however, with two important innovations: he first suppressed the Sanhedrin (either abolishing it or completely emasculating it – see pp. 144–47 below) and, secondly, began the practice of frequent change of the high priest. Herod did not interfere in the temple or cult as such; on the contrary, his renovation of the temple was a great enhancement of its prestige in many ways. Nor was any unqualified person appointed to be high priest, but the office of high priest lost much of the political power it had gained through the previous centuries, as well as some of its moral authority, since the state was seen as interfering with the appointment to the post. This began with Herod's dominance of Hyrcanus II who had retained some political power alongside Herod's father Antipater under direct Roman rule. But the Parthian crisis, during which Herod became king, also saw Hyrcanus's disqualification as high priest (because of being physically mutilated at the time of the Parthian invasion [*War* 1.13.9 §270]), and Herod eventually had him executed (*War* 1.22.1 §433–34). Even the high priestly garments, necessary for certain cultic ceremonies, were kept under Herod's control (*Ant.* 18.4.3 §§92–95). This is why a delegation of Jews went to Augustus after Herod's death to ask for direct Roman rule (*War* 2.6.1–2 §§80–91), though they had opportunity to rue their words when this became a reality a decade later!

Ironically, the restoration of direct Roman rule in 6 CE brought certain religious benefits. Some political power was restored to the high priesthood, and the high priest became a significant representative of the Jews to the Roman rulers, unlike under Herod. Unfortunately, the Romans continued Herod's habit of making frequent changes of person in the high priestly office, and there was certainly no restoration of the power exercised by Hyrcanus II under early Roman rule. The robes of the high priest were also kept under Roman control until Vitellius allowed their return to the priests (*Ant.* 18.4.3 §§92–95; but cf. 20.1.1–2 §6–13). From then until the 66–70 war, the main native government was in the hands of the high priestly families and the Herodian family. Agrippa I was of course king for a brief period of time (41–44 CE), but although Agrippa II was not king over Judea, he spent a good deal of time in Jerusalem and had a great deal of influence. Under direct Roman rule, they were the main mediators on behalf of the Jewish people. No doubt many Jews considered them collaborators, not without some reason, but they were also able to ameliorate some of the worst Roman excesses. On the other hand, some members of these families were also the leaders during the 66–70 revolt (Price 1992). The war was to remove their power base, but not immediately: they continued to have influence for some decades after the revolt, though this gradually declined (Schwartz 1990).

Roman domination and the relationship with the Romans left their mark on the religion. Not all resistance to Rome was necessarily religious in nature, and we would be mistaken to think every Jew had an apocalyptic view of the future; yet a number of apocalyptic and related writings were produced during this period, showing the beliefs and concerns of some segments of the population. To some extent we can probably draw a distinction between Judea (and the other Jewish areas of Palestine) and the Diaspora. A number of Diaspora writings of this period show no evidence of apocalyptic expectations, even after some major incidents with the Romans such as Caligula's attempt to place his statue in the Jerusalem temple. For example, Philo's view of eschatology is personal rather than national or cosmic (see pp. 261–62 below), as is the Wisdom of Solomon's (though it is probably to be dated before Caligula [p. 87 above]).

All Jews were affected by Caligula's plans to place his statue in the temple in 40 CE. The threat carried strong parallels with what had happened two hundred years before under Antiochus Epiphanes and, if it had gone ahead, might have precipitated a war in the first part of the first century. As it was, it may have stimulated apocalyptic speculation as well as whipping up anti-Roman feeling.

There is still a tendency to see the religion of this period in terms of sects, with special emphasis on the Pharisees, but there is no reason to see such minority movements as anything more than just a part of the picture. According to our sources, such groups formed only small numbers, whatever influence they had beyond their actual adherents (cf. Baumgarten 1997). The sects varied greatly, not only in their history but also in their aims. The three main sects had already originated in the Hasmonean period (or possibly earlier), but they were also prominent during Roman rule. What we especially see during the Roman period is the rise of various revolutionary movements. Some of these may have been primarily religious movements, whereas others were possibly more political and nationalistic in origin. Drawing lines between these two categories would not be easy, however, even if we had a great deal of information; as it is, the dearth of facts means that in many cases we have no way of knowing and can only make suggestions.

To what extent the "revolutionary" movements (e.g. the Sicarii) saw their goals in religious terms is not always easy to say, but the sources suggest that some were messianic or apocalyptic movements. It was dangerous to be part of such movements, and most Jews were not members. The sources also suggest that most were not Pharisees and, whatever prestige the Pharisees may have had in the eyes of the common person, he or she did not generally live by Pharisaic laws or strictures. The Essenes had withdrawn from society in part, even if they lived to a lesser or greater extent in society, perhaps in conventicles of some sort. The Sadducees were small in number as well, though having close links with the aristocracy and high priests.

A number of these groups sought power and influence, of course. The Pharisees had sought to form links with the Hasmonean king but on their own terms, and were evidently seen as a threat until the reign of Alexandra Salome who let them have their way. But they then disappear from view in the extant sources until some tried to gain a toehold in Herod's household, unsuccessfully as it turns out. Whether all Pharisees sought political power might be questioned. The movement was complex, and a few Pharisees seem to have been in public office (e.g. Gamaliel I [p. 194 below]. Also, considering the traditions about the Houses of Hillel and Shammai in rabbinic literature, these groups may have focused on internal matters and rivalry among themselves rather than the more dangerous route of maneuvering for position vis-a-vis the government.

Other movements also came into conflict with the ruling authorities because of their goals. Some had the specific aim of opposing and contesting the powers that be, whether Herodian or Roman, and the authorities took every opportunity to suppress them. A few groups such as the Sicarii (pp. 285–86 below) were quite successful, but most were short-lived (cf. *Ant.* 20.5.1 §§97–99; 20.8.6 §§167–72; Acts 5:36; 21:38). The "Zealots" evidently did not come into existence until after the war with Rome had begun in 66 CE (pp. 287–88 below).

One cannot help feeling that a war between the Jews of Judea and the Romans was bound to happen (*pace* McClaren 1998) because of the continued build-up of tensions under Roman rule. The most interesting aspect of this war is the extent to which it was led by the upper classes who had the most to gain from cooperation with the Romans, though in some cases these were younger members of the leading priestly and Herodian families. Although Josephus strives to give the impression that a few low-born gangsters caused it all, a careful study of his own data shows the true leadership (Price 1992). As a member of the aristocracy Josephus himself was one of these very people and – once again, despite his efforts to divert the issue – seemed to be an enthusiastic supporter of the war until captured by the Romans.

The war itself still presents many puzzles, not least why so many intelligent people thought it would be possible to defeat the Romans, especially without better preparation and coordination of efforts. The various groups who fought one another in Jerusalem through much of this time would be characters in a farce if it were not so tragic. Josephus does not explain this. One has an inkling that apocalyptic speculations fueled the hopes of some, if not all, of the fighters (pp. 283–88 below); if so, Josephus wanted to downplay that aspect of the situation.

New sources, especially the Dead Sea Scrolls, and new studies of previously known sources have demonstrated the complexity of Judaism during this epoch which is probably the best documented of the entire Second Temple period, not only between Palestine and the Diaspora but within the various areas. We have some small inkling about the lives of ordinary Jewish men and even women (e.g. marriage contracts; bills of sale; burial customs; the Babatha and Salome Komaïse archives [pp. 106–8 above]). They marry, they have children, they buy and sell property, they divorce, they die and are buried. The catacombs of Rome and the papyri of Egypt have been valuable sources on the communities living outside Palestine during this period.

Life for most people was not easy, being mainly a struggle for enough to eat and to provide reasonable clothing and shelter. Religion was important, as was religious and ethnic identity, but we have little indication that this personal piety was very extreme. As so often, local people adapted their religion to their needs and eschewed those aspects requiring major inconvenience. This is why Pharisaic practices, with the minute emphasis on ritual purity in daily life (pp. 196–99 below), would not have been adopted by most people, however much some of them may have looked up to Pharisees as models of piety. The same would apply to an even greater degree to exclusivistic groups like the Essenes who were apparently seen as examples of piety and special favor from God. Most people did not join sects; they did not have the luxury of leisure and money; however, if Baumgarten (1997: 64) is correct, some destitute people may have been attracted to sects because they provided food for all members. This is unlikely to have been a major factor in recruitment, however, since the group ultimately had to find the resources to support themselves.

Our surviving sources report on a number of charismatic preachers and traveling holy men (see pp. 251–54 below). We should not underestimate their value to the people as entertainment. To listen to them would have been a diversion, a social event, and would cost little or nothing. This was no doubt a factor in gaining a hearing, but there is evidence that such individuals were often looked on with some awe and respect by some people, though others clearly thought them charlatans. Indeed, the picture gradually emerging from scattered sources and hints within sources long-known is the extent to which there was lack of an "orthodoxy" or uniformity within religious practice. There are indications that mysticism was important to some Jews, though by nature this was kept secret by devotees. Magic, astrology, and other forms of divination were clearly practiced, but being esoteric arts not much information has been left about them (pp. 241–51 below). Even Gnostic ideas seem to have informed some Jewish groups or circles, though to what extent the ideas circulated and how far they had first developed is a matter of speculation (*JCH*: 514–19; Grabbe 1996a: 94–110). The hints we have about this diversity and complexity unfortunately do not allow us to quantify these trends.

It was mainly during the Roman period that developments within Diaspora Jewish communities started to have a significant influence on religion in the homeland. By this time, the indication is that the population of Jews in Palestine (about a million is a reasonable guess) was far exceeded by the number scattered across the Mediterranean world and elsewhere. There seems to have been considerable communication between many far-flung communities and Judea itself, not only those in the Mediterranean region (which are best documented) but also the Mesopotamian cities where a very large population now lived (known to us mainly from later rabbinic literature; cf. Neusner 1965–70, especially vol. 1). Such famous rabbis – at least, famous in rabbinic writings – as Hillel were born in Babylonia and immigrated to Palestine as adults (e.g. *T. Nega'im* 1:16 = Zuckermandel: 619).

Many Diaspora Jews came up each year to worship at the temple to the extent that "tourism" was one of the main occupations for those living in and around Jerusalem. The temple was still the spiritual center of Judaism. This does not mean, however, that the Diaspora communities did not have a lively religious life of their own, and with the increase in numbers and the maintenance of communications with Judea, practices in the Diaspora began to have an effect on what people did closer to home. It is still not absolutely established that synagogues existed in Judea proper before 70 CE, though the circumstantial case is reasonable, but they arrived late in any case. Josephus mentions synagogues in Caesarea (*sunagogē*) and Tiberias (*proseuchē*), neither of these in Judea itself. There were possibly synagogues in Jerusalem and Herodium by the turn of the era (see pp. 170–75 below);

however, the institution had developed where the need was really felt (viz., in those areas away from the temple) and crept in only gradually.

Temple worship did not require written scripture since the priests could instruct the people on the proper cultic procedures and decorum, and the religious meaning of the cult. Away from the temple, though, the written word was a vital link and pillar of worship, along with public and private prayer. The exact form of worship undertaken in the Diaspora is uncertain, though Agatharchides mentions the Jewish "temples" (*ta hiera*) where the worshipers pray with outstretched hands until evening on the seventh day (*Ag. Apion* 1.22 §§208–9, though he inserts this in a reference to the Jerusalem temple). The text of various holy books was still developing, and no standard collection seems to have become established until the first century, if then, but the Pentateuch, the Prophets, and some of the Writings of the later Hebrew canon seem to have been widely accepted long before Pompey threatened Jerusalem (pp. 152–57 below). Even groups in the region of Palestine are attested as basing themselves on the written word by this time, notably the Qumran group (accepting that the scrolls found in the Qumran caves are by and large to be associated with the settlement at Khirbet Qumran [pp. 201–5 below]). Temple worship was being simultaneously enriched, supplemented, and diluted by other forms of worship coming from the Diaspora. Biblical interpretation in its widest sense had become well developed by the Roman period and took its place alongside cultic worship (though many of the interpreters evidently had priestly associations of some sort [pp. 165–70 below]). If the temple had not been destroyed, it would have been interesting to see how temple worship evolved in the light of these new practices.

There are reports of interest in Judaism on the part of Greco-Romans, as well as examples of anti-Jewish feeling. Proselytizing may have caused a disturbance in Rome in 19 CE (*JCH*: 398; cf. Rutgers 1998: 176–81). Josephus reports the conversion of the royal of house of Adiabene, and Queen Helena was a benefactor to the people of Judea (*Ant.* 20.2.1–5 §§17–53). It is doubtful that there was a Jewish "mission" of conversion as such, but Judaism outside Palestine had many points in common with other Hellenistic "religions of conversion" (*JCH*: 533). The main obstacle to conversion was circumcision, and our evidence is that this was a requirement for full conversion of males; as a result women were more likely to join the Jewish community as such. On the other hand, there was a evidently an active number of "God-fearers" (a term sometimes used of those who had not taken the step of full conversion) associated with many communities (see pp. 292–97 below).

The 66–70 war caused a significant breach in some but not all trends: some were completely chopped off, some were stifled for a time only to flourish later, but some were actually enhanced because rivals were removed, like saplings responding when old trees of the forest are cut down. The temple and nation, along with those whose power base lay there, were gone. Groups like the Pharisees apparently found a new meaning in a changed situation, and the Jewish sect that later became Christianity found a fertile ground in which to grow. However, what especially survived and sustained Judaism were those developments that had first expressed themselves in the Diaspora away from the homeland and temple. It was not immediately apparent, but Judaism had changed forever.

6

TRANSITION TO RABBINIC
JUDAISM: YAVNEH

The fall of the temple in 70 brought the Second Temple period formally to an end. In retrospect, we see that destruction of the temple as symbolic of the end of an era, from whose ashes a new entity grew up and became the Judaism that survives to the present time. Yet the Jewish people of the time did not have the benefit of such hindsight. Some mourned the ruined temple but also expected God to intervene supernaturally in the near future to set things right. Others saw an opportunity to establish their own ideas in the religious power vacuum that suddenly emerged. Unfortunately, we do not have the vision of Yohanan ben Zakkai left for us in his own handwriting. What he expected to accomplish at Yavneh can only be guessed at, yet what happened in that small coastal town had repercussions for the entire history of Judaism.

MAJOR SOURCES

Rabbinic literature

Neusner, J. (1988) *Invitation to the Talmud: A Teaching Book.*
—— (1988) *Invitation to Midrash: The Workings of Rabbinic Bible Interpretation: A Teaching Book.*
—— (1994) *Introduction to Rabbinic Literature.*
—— (ed.) (1995a) *Judaism in Late Antiquity: Part 1 The Literary and Archaeological Sources; Part 2 Historical Syntheses.*
—— (1995b) "Evaluating the Attributions of Sayings to Named Sages in the Rabbinic Literature", *JSJ* 26: 93–111.
Neusner, J., A. J. Avery-Peck, and W. S. Green (eds) (2000) *The Encyclopaedia of Judaism.*
Stemberger, G. (1996) *Introduction to the Talmud and Midrash.*

Rabbinic literature is one of our main sources for some aspects of the post-70 period. It is to the Mishnah and other Tannaitic sources that we must go to gain information on the most important religious development of this period:

the rise of rabbinic Judaism. Scholarship on rabbinic literature is too extensive to be summarized here, but there are very good guides to both the textual sources and the scholarly study of the literature (Neusner 1994; Stemberger 1996; the various essays in Neusner 1995). References to Yavneh are found throughout rabbinic literature, but it is first and foremost to the Mishnah, followed by the Tosefta and other Tannaitic sourcs, that we must look for the transformation that began with the reconstruction at Yavneh. Some studies on the question have attempted to use the later literature in a careful and critical fashion (see below pp. 120–24), but many of the older studies are completely uncritical in this regard, whatever their value in other respects (for a discussion and some older bibliography, see *JCH*: 13–16).

The question of whether and to what extent we can reconstruct historical events from rabbinic literature is a difficult one (cf. Neusner 1995b), yet if we know anything about what happened between the 66–70 war and the Bar-Kokhba revolt, it is because of data from the Mishnah and other Tannaitic writings. The struggle for power and leadership at Yavneh and the disruptions of the Bar-Kokhba revolt are likely to have meant only a partial and biased version of events has reached us, even in the earliest documents. Nevertheless, if the Mishnah was completed and edited by the circle of Rabbi Judah ha-Nasi sometime about 200 CE, as is widely accepted, it is likely that the outlines of what happened at Yavneh can be reconstructed. There is, furthermore, another approach which can be used as as an aid to and a check on this reconstruction. This is a "triangulation method" in which the situation before 70 and the better attested events of the third century and following are used as anchor points to fit Yavneh into the attested changes and development between the two time periods.

Apocalypses of Ezra, Baruch, Abraham, and John

Bauckham, R. (1993) *The Climax of Prophecy: Studies on the Book of Revelation.*

Charles, R. H. (1920) *A Critical and Exegetical Commentary on the Revelation of St. John.*

Chyutin, M. (1997) *The New Jerusalem Scroll from Qumran: A Comprehensive Reconstruction.*

Grabbe, L. L. (1981) "Chronography in 4 Ezra and 2 Baruch", *Society of Biblical Literature 1981 Seminar Papers*: 49–63.

—— (1987c) "The Scapegoat Ritual: A Study in Early Jewish Interpretation", *JSJ* 18: 152–67.

Hall, R. G. (1988) "The 'Christian Interpolation' in the *Apocalypse of Abraham*", *JBL* 107: 107–11.

Hayman, A. P. (1998) "The 'Man from the Sea' in 4 Ezra 13", *JJS* 49: 1–16.

Longenecker, B. W. (1997) "Locating 4 Ezra: A Consideraton of its Social Setting and Functions", *JSJ* 28: 271–93.

Rubinkiewicz, R. (1992) "Abraham, Apocalypse of", *ABD*: 1.41–43.

Schmid, K. (1998) "Esras Begegnung mit Zion: Die Deutung der Zerstörung Jerusalems im 4. Esrabuch und das Problem des 'bösen Herzens'", *JSJ* 29: 261–77.

Wright, J. E. (1997) "The Social Setting of the Syriac Apocalypse of Baruch", *JSP* 16: 81–96.

Yarbro Collins, A. (1976) *The Combat Myth in the Book of Revelation*.

The *Apocalypse of Ezra*, the *Apocalypse of Baruch*, the *Apocalypse of Abraham*, and the NT book of Revelation all seem to arise from approximately the same time: about 100 CE. Although Revelation is very much Christian in its present form, a good deal of Jewish material seems to be drawn on, and it represents the same spirit as the Jewish apocalypses of the same time. All four have much in common in spite of different (fictional) settings and a different patriarchal figure as the main actor, while 4 Ezra and *2 Baruch* are probably related organically in some way. See further *JCH* (561–62) for introduction and bibliography on 4 Ezra and *2 Baruch*. The Revelation (or Apocalypse) of John is probably the most familiar work to many readers. Because of his unprecedented knowledge of Jewish apocalyptic literature, the commentary by R. H. Charles is still very important despite its age.

The *Apocalypse of Abraham* is known only in a Slavonic version, and scholarly study of the book is less advanced than with the other works (see *JLBM*: 294–99; *JWSTP*: 415–18; *OTP*: 1.681–705; Schürer: 3.288–92; Rubinkiewicz 1992). This writing exists in several versions, and there is no agreement on which is the most original (though the original language was probably Hebrew). The first part of the book (1–8) is how Abraham destroyed his fathers' idols; the second half (9–32), a description of a heavenly journey and the things Abraham saw there, including the original Adam and Eve in Eden. It was thought that ch. 7 was a Christian interpolation, but this now seems doubtful (Hall 1988). The author has priestly interests and may have been a priest (cf. Rubinkiewicz 1992: 1.42). The demon Azazel has a prominent part to play as the tempter and opponent of God (13; 14:5; 22:5–23:13; 29:5–7; 31:2–7), while the angel Iaoel is equally important (10:3). The temple has been destroyed (25; 27:1–5) but will be rebuilt (29:17–18).

Although there are many differences in content and approach between the four books, they have much in common, even given that Revelation is a Christian work with an outlook not found in any of the Jewish apocalypses. The following points about Judaism arise from these books:

1. A preoccupation with Roman rule and an expectation of its imminent end are common themes. In 4 Ezra and *2 Baruch* the destruction of the temple and its continuing ruinous state is a problem, raising questions about theodicy which are answered by appeal to the fall of Rome. The eagle vision of 4 Ezra 11-12, the beast from the sea (Rev. 13:1–8) as well as the beast ridden by the scarlet women (Rev. 17) of Revelation, and the fourth kingdom

of *2 Baruch* (39–40) are all symbols of Rome's expected destruction. In each case the Roman empire as it existed about 100 CE is pictured, but heavenly intervention (by Jesus in Rev. 18, though announced by an angel; by a messianic figure in 4 Ezra 12:31–34) will bring about the destruction of Rome. The *Apocalypse of Abraham* speaks more generally of punishment of the heathen (31:2), but it predicts the restoration of the temple and cult which suggests that their destruction was seen as a problem.

2. They expect the rise or coming of a messianic figure which is naturally, in Revelation, the heavenly Jesus who returns for judgment of the wicked, but the messiah of *2 Baruch* (29–30; 39:7–40:3; 70:9; 72–74) is also apparently a heavenly figure, though hardly divine. 4 Ezra 7:26–32 posits an earthly messiah who will rule for 400 years, after which he and all mankind will die, but then the resurrection and judgment will follow after seven days. In 4 Ezra 13, however, the "man from the sea" appears to be a heavenly messianic figure. The *Apocalypse of Abraham* speaks more generally of the coming of a "chosen one" who will gather God's chosen people (31:1).

3. The "messianic woes" (the various problems, plagues, and unnatural events preceding the endtime) have a prominent place in all the apocalypses (4 Ezra 5:1–13; 6:18–28; *2 Bar.* 70; *Apoc. Abr.* 29:15; 30:2–8; Rev. 6, 8–9, 15–16). The "four horsemen" of Revelation 6:1–8 are based on a traditional list of plagues of war, famine, and pestilence (e.g. Ezek. 6:11).

4. The fate of the individual after death is also a major concern. The soul has some sort of existence continuing immediately after death, perhaps kept in some sort of storage place or "treasury" (4 Ezra 7:78–101; *2 Bar.* 21:23; 30:2; 49–51; Rev. 6:9–11). At the time of the end, there will be a resurrection and judgment, followed by reward for the righteous and punishment for the wicked (4 Ezra 7:28–44; *2 Bar.* 50–51; Rev. 20:4–15). The *Apocalypse of Abraham* has no resurrection (though some see hints of it [cf. Rubinkiewicz 1992: 1.42]), but God has prepared rewards and punishments for the righteous and wicked (31:1–4).

5. Periodization of history is typical: *2 Baruch* 53–74 divides history into periods of alternating light and dark waters. *Apoc. Abr.* 29:2 divides the final age into twelve parts, as do 4 Ezra 14:10–12 and *2 Bar.* 27; 53:6, while 4 Ezra apparently calculates history according to a 7,000-year period or millennial week (Grabbe 1981; pp. 246–48 below).

6. History culminates in new heavens and a new earth (Rev. 21; 4 Ezra 7:31–44; *2 Bar.* 72–74; cf. Isa. 65:17–25) and a new stylized Jerusalem (cf. Ezek. 40–44; Qumran *New Jerusalem* texts [1Q32; 2Q24; 4Q554–55; 5Q15; 11Q18]; Chyutin 1997), to be preceded by a messianic age (4 Ezra 7:26–30) or millennium (Rev. 20:1–6).

7. Good and evil angelic beings have a major role to play. The leading righteous angels are Michael in Revelation, Iaoel in the *Apocalypse of Abraham*, Uriel who reveals things to Ezra in 4 Ezra, Ramael the angel of visions in *2 Baruch* (55:3). The picture of Satan and his battle with the archangel

Michael (Rev. 12) draws on the old *Chaoskampf* mythology in which God defeated the monsters of chaos (p. 215 below; also Yarbro Collins 1976). Old mythology lies behind the figures of Behemoth and Leviathan (4 Ezra 6:49–52; *2 Bar.* 29:4; Job 40–41; cf. *KTU* 1.5.1.1-3) and Azazel in the *Apocalypse of Abraham* (cf. Grabbe 1987c).

Sibylline Oracles

For a basic introduction and bibliography, see *JCH* (562–64) and pp. 64–65 above. A number of points in all three Jewish oracles relate to the period after 70 CE:

1. All three of the Jewish oracles (*Sib. Or.* 3, 4, 5) are very anti-Roman and predict its destruction. *Sib. Or.* 5 also shows anti-Egyptian sentiment.

2. *Sib. Or.* 3:1–96 contains a reference to Nero *redivivus* (the assumption that Nero was not dead but would soon gather an army and invade Judea) as does *Sib. Or.* 5 (93–110, 137–154, 214–27, 361–80). According to *Sib. Or.* 3:63–74, Nero is to be identified with the demonic figure of Belial (pp. 219–25 below).

3. *Sib. Or.* 3 and 5 are very supportive of the temple and sacrificial system, bemoaning its destruction (e.g. 3:624–34; 5:397–413). However, an unusual feature of *Sib. Or.* 4:4–30 is its anti-temple polemic, perhaps unique in Jewish literature up to this time. This is true even though the eruption of Vesuvius in 79 CE was said to be punishment for the conquest of Jerusalem (4:115–36).

4. *Sib. Or.* 4 places a good deal of store in the efficacy of washing in rivers (4:165), suggesting its origin in a Jewish baptismal sect (cf. *JCH*: 507–11), most likely in the Palestinian area.

5. The imminent expectation of the end seems to be part of the message of all three *Sib. Or.* 3, 4, 5, with some common themes and some differences. *Sib. Or.* 4 gives an eschatology that includes an ekpyrosis or universal conflagration because of wickedness (4:159–61, 171–78), followed by a resurrection and judgment of all, with the wicked assigned to Tartarus and Gehenna but the righteous living again on earth (4:179–92). *Sib. Or.* 5 also includes destruction by fire (5:155–61, 527–31).

6. *Sib. Or.* 5 shows a different sort of messianism (vv. 108–9, 155–61, 414–28). The attitude is openly hostile to Egypt (5: 179–99), and hope is now placed in a messianic figure who comes from heaven. Even after the revolts under Trajan and Hadrian, at least in Egypt some Jews still hoped for deliverance from God in the not-too-distant future.

THE RECONSTRUCTION AT YAVNEH

Aleksandrov, G. S. (1973) "The Role of Aqiba in the Bar Kokhba Rebellion", in J. Neusner, *Eliezar ben Hyrcanus*: 2.428–42.

Cohen, S. J. D. (1984) "The Significance of Yavneh: Pharisees, Rabbis, and the End of Jewish Sectarianism", *HUCA* 55: 27–53.

Finkelstein, L. (1936) *Akiba: Scholar, Saint and Martyr*.

Gereboff, J. (1979) *Rabbi Tarfon*.

Goodblatt, D. (1980) "Towards the Rehabilitation of Talmudic History", in B. Bokser (ed.) *History of Judaism: The Next Ten Years*: 31–44.

—— (1994) *The Monarchic Principle: Studies in Jewish Self-Government in Antiquity*.

Goodman, M. (1983) *State and Society in Roman Galilee, A.D. 132–212*.

Green, W. S. (ed.) (1977) *Persons and Institutions in Early Rabbinic Judaism*.

—— (1978) "What's in a Name? – The Problematic of Rabbinic 'Biography'", in W. S. Green (ed.) *Approaches to Ancient Judaism: Theory and Practice*: 77–96.

—— (1980) "Context and Meaning in Rabbinic 'Biography'", in W. S. Green (ed.) *Approaches to Ancient Judaism, Volume II*: 97–111.

Habas, E. (Rubin) (1999) "Rabban Gamaliel of Yavneh and his Sons: The Patriarchate before and after the Bar Kokhva Revolt", *JJS* 50: 21–37.

Hezser, C. (1998) *The Social Structure of the Rabbinic Movement in Roman Palestine*.

Jacobs, M. (1995) *Die Institution des jüdischen Patriarchen: Eine quellen- und traditionskritische Studie zur Geschichte der Juden in der Spätantike*.

Kanter, S. (1979) *Rabban Gamaliel II*.

Lapin, H. (1995) *Early Rabbinic Civil Law and the Social History of Roman Galilee. A Study of Mishnah Tractate* Baba' Meṣi'a'.

Longenecker, B. W. (1997) "Locating 4 Ezra: A Consideraton of its Social Setting and Functions", *JSJ* 28: 271–93.

Neusner, J. (1970) *Development of a Legend*.

—— (1971) *The Rabbinic Traditions about the Pharisees before 70*.

—— (1972) "Emergent Rabbinic Judaism in a Time of Crisis: Four Responses to the Destruction of the Second Temple", *Judaism* 21: 313–27.

—— (1973a) *From Politics to Piety: The Making of Pharisaic Religion*.

—— (1973c) *Eliezer ben Hyrcanus*.

—— (1979) "The Formation of Rabbinic Judaism: Yavneh (Jamnia) from A.D. 70 to 100", *ANRW II*: 19.2.3–42.

—— (1980) "The Present State of Rabbinic Biography", in G. Nahon and C. Touati (eds) *Hommage à Georges Vajda*: 85–91.

—— (1981) *Judaism: The Evidence of the Mishnah*.

—— (1983) "Varieties of Judaism in the Formative Age", *Formative Judaism II: Religious, Historical, and Literary Studies*: 59–89.

—— (1984) *Messiah in Context: Israel's History and Destiny in Formative Judaism*.

—— (1995b) "Evaluating the Attributions of Sayings to Named Sages in the Rabbinic Literature", *JSJ* 26: 93–111.

Porton, G. G. (1976–82) *The Traditions of Rabbi Ishmael*.

Saldarini, A. J. (1975) "Johanan ben Zakkai's Escape from Jerusalem: Origin and Development of a Rabbinic Story", *JSJ* 6:189–204.

Schäfer, P. (1978) "R. Aqiva und Bar Kokhba", *Studien zur Geschichte und Theologie des rabbinischen Judentums*: 65–121.

—— (1980) "Aqiva and Bar Kokhba", in W. S. Green (ed.) *Approaches to Ancient Judaism II*: 113–30.

Schwartz, S. (1999) "The Patriarchs and the Diaspora", *JSJ* 50: 208–222.

Zahavy, T. (1977) *The Traditions of Eleazar Ben Azariah*.

It can be said with certainty that what happened at Yavneh had great consequences for the development of Judaism after 70, yet the precise interactions at Yavneh have been obscured by the later editing and interpretation of the period in rabbinic literature. The intervention of the Bar Kokhba revolt, the executions or deaths of some important rabbinic leaders, and the re-evaluation of some of the Yavnean leaders by a later generation, all led to the heavy censorship and recontextualization of the Yavnean traditions.

Although neither biography nor narrative history is possible because of the nature of the traditions (Green 1978; 1980; Neusner 1980; 1995b), there is still material of value to the historian in the rabbinic literature (Goodblatt 1980). Most importantly, source analysis shows the development of religious ideas in the major periods of the growth of the Mishnah (Neusner 1981). Before 70 the areas of most interest were those of purity, agriculture, festivals, and women, i.e., the areas of importance for a table fellowship sect which had control of its internal affairs but not of society as a whole. The Yavnean layer shows an interesting transitional phase toward the final outlook of the Mishnah in its final form. There is little development in the order dealing with civil law (*Neziqin*), indicating the group is not administering society at large. The considerable discussion about the cult does not seem rooted in the experience of cultic personnel but in the biblical text alone; that is, the interest is in creating a new, idealized cult according to the sect's principles, not in extending or developing the old Second Temple practices.

The preserved tradition seems to be unanimous that the reconstruction of Judaism after the fall of Jerusalem was due to Yohanan ben Zakkai, an intriguing figure about whom much is still a puzzle (Neusner 1970). According to legend Yohanan was given permission to establish an academy in the city of Yavneh (Jamnia) by the emperor Vespasian himself (*Avot de Rabbi Natan* 4; cf. Neusner 1970: 114–19; Saldarini 1975). Since the story of his prediction that Vespasian would become emperor is late and looks suspiciously like that of Josephus, it is likely to be legend. (Although Josephus's own accounts often invite skepticism, in this case subsequent events seem hard to explain unless he indeed made such a prediction that turned out to be correct.) Whatever the origins of the academy, it goes down as an extremely important episode in Jewish history.

It is usually thought that Yohanan was a Pharisee, but his characteristics according to the earliest traditions do not fit well what we know of pre-70 Pharisaism (cf. Neusner 1979: 30–32, 36–37). He looks more like a scribal figure whose religion centered on scripture, and since this is an important feature of rabbinic Judaism, it was probably Yohanan who pushed matters in this direction in the religious reorientation. Perhaps more important was his apparent ability to work with a variety of groups. According to one statement (*M. Avot* 2:8), a number of groups were represented at Yavneh; if so, a variety of viewpoints may have fed into what became a Yavnean synthesis. As an area which had come into Roman possession, Yavneh represented an important concession to Judaism by the Romans: it means that the reconstruction which began under Yohanan had, if not Roman sanction, at least Roman tolerance. Yavneh is often misrepresented as a "synod", as if it were something analogous to a church council; on the contrary, it was more like an academy, and the number of participants seems to have been quite small at first, nor were the members necessarily recognized as representatives of Jews of the country. The group behind the Mishnah came to be influential for Jewish society, but this took well over a century or more.

Whatever Yohanan's sectarian affiliation (if any), there is evidence that the dominent influence was Pharisaic (Neusner 1971; 1979; Cohen 1984), unless one wants to disassociate the schools of Hillel and Shammai from Pharisaism. Much of the content of debates appears to be based on tradition or interests that have been identified with the pre-70 Pharisees (Neusner 1971; 1973; cf. 1981). From this distance we cannot say why this was; on the other hand, it is especially interesting that Pharisaism had the means to exist without the temple, which was not the case with a number of other strands of Judaism (cf. Neusner 1972; 1983). This survivability may be part of the answer, if not the entire reason, why Pharisaism dominated discussion at Yavneh. Yohanan himself seems to have outlived the destruction of the temple by only a few years, but in addition to the schools of Hillel and Shammai, there was the family of Gamaliel, whose grandson Gamaliel II was an important figure at Yavneh, according to the tradition (Kanter 1979). Later tradition makes the Gamaliel faction a part of the Hillel family, but this is not the case in the earliest layer of traditions. We seem to have a jockeying for power in which the school of Hillel eventually wins, though the family of Gamaliel maintained a significant influence, with the school of Shammai losing out.

The major concern of pre-70 Pharisaism, at least in the first century, was with religious law. Therefore, most of the pre-70 tradition seems to have centered on legal discussions and disputes. Each school had its own rulings, some or many of which may have differed from those of other schools. These traditions also represented the interests and sphere of authority of the Pharisees, namely, their own homes and inter-sectarian concerns. At Yavneh the differences had to be threshed out between the various schools and whatever non-Pharisaic parties were represented there. The exact maneuverings which went on can only be guessed at, but at some point agreement was reached that the opinions of both the school of Hillel and the school of Shammai would be preserved. As already noted, the school of Hillel eventually became the dominant one, though this seems to have taken time since the school of Shammai was apparently more influential in pre-70 Pharisaism.

Developing Judaism at Yavneh appears to owe a great deal to the pre-70 Pharisaic tradition, yet it is also a synthesis of a variety of elements. The important factor toward the religious development was the injection of a perspective from another source. This was the concept of Torah-centeredness and the religious efficacy of study. The early rabbinic traditions about the Pharisees do not indicate that they were a group whose focus was on the study of the Torah. Rather, they were a table fellowship sect for whom legal concerns and debate were important but not study as a religious act. In the developing rabbinic Judaism the center shifted to Torah study. There were also clearly some priestly traditions and likely other traditions as well.

In many ways the most intriguing figure is Aqiva. Unfortunately, older studies are uncritical and simply conflate the various early and later traditions (e.g. Finkelstein 1936). More recent critical studies have recognized the problem (Aleksandrov 1973; Schäfer 1978; 1980), though whether we are close to the historical Aqiva is difficult to say. The aspect that is most intriguing is Aqiva's relationship to Bar Kokhba. Did Aqiva declare Bar Kokhba the messiah? There is even some question of whether Bar Kokhba thought of himself as the messiah, though the matter is complicated (*JCH*: 603–5), and Aleksandrov thinks not. On the other hand, there is some evidence that Aqiva held a nationalistic-messianic view (Schäfer 1978: 119–21; 1980: 124–25), which would put him at odds with the general outlook of the Mishnah which has a completely different world view from the apocalyptic-messianic (cf. Neusner 1984; also pp. 232–41, 281 below).

Despite our ignorance of the detailed events and inability to reconstruct a narrative history, we know enough to appreciate how vital the Yavnean period was in the history of Judaism. It was here that the roots of modern Judaism first put down; a period of about 60 years saw the reconstruction of Judaism after the disaster of 70 and the birth of a new phenomenon previously unknown to history: rabbinic Judaism.

SYNTHESIS

Goodman, M. (1983) *State and Society in Roman Galilee, A.D. 132–212.*

Hezser, C. (1998) *The Social Structure of the Rabbinic Movement in Roman Palestine.*

Lapin, H. (1995) *Early Rabbinic Civil Law and the Social History of Roman Galilee. A Study of Mishnah Tractate* Baba' Meṣi'a'.

Neusner, J. (1972) "Emergent Rabbinic Judaism in a Time of Crisis: Four Responses to the Destruction of the Second Temple", *Judaism* 21: 313–27.

—— (1983) "Varieties of Judaism in the Formative Age", *Formative Judaism II: Religious, Historical, and Literary Studies* (1983) 59–89.

—— (1984) *Messiah in Context: Israel's History and Destiny in Formative Judaism.*

Schwartz, S. (1990) *Josephus and Judaean Politics.*
—— (1999) "The Patriarchs and the Diaspora", *JSJ* 50: 208–222.
Stone, M. E. (1982) "Reactions to the Destructions of the Second Temple",
    JSJ 13: 195–204.

One of the major problems with writing a history of the Jews after 70 CE is that Josephus's narrative – an invaluable survival from antiquity despite all its problems – ceases, and the history has to be pieced together from scattered bits and pieces. Most of what we know of specific events revolves around two periods of revolt in 115–17 and 132–35, yet despite recent important discoveries, even today only a few data are known regarding the extremely important rebellion under Bar Kokhba (*JCH*: 601-5). We have a good deal of what might be called prosopographic material about rabbis for the entire period, but the nature of the rabbinic literature which preserves it is problematic: in spite of the amount of material regarding certain individuals, it is doubtful whether we could write a biography of them in a rigorously historical sense (see previous section).

The period following the fall of Jerusalem in 70 is one of the most enigmatic in the history of Judaism. We know of a few events in the next few years (such as the siege of Masada) because Josephus tells us of them (*War*, book 7), but on the really crucial developments, we must fall back on inference from scattered data. Even if the material about Yavneh in rabbinic literature is felt to be reliable – at least in outline – this gives us the formation of only one strand of Judaism at this time. Rabbinic Judaism eventually became dominant and ousted or absorbed most of the other strands of post-70 religion; however, this took much longer than was once thought, and the rabbis probably did not achieve a leading position until well into the third century or later (Goodman 1983; Lapin 1995; Hezser 1998; Schwartz 1999).

During the late first and the second centuries, we get brief glimpses of other forms of Judaism that do not find expression in the Mishnah, especially in apocalyptic and related works such as 4 Ezra, *2 Baruch*, the *Apocalypse of Abraham*, and the *Sibylline Oracles*. These forms of Judaism focused much of their energy on the imminent eschaton and the expectation of some sort of savior figure or messiah. The Mishnah, on the other hand, eschews eschatology and messianic expectations (Neusner 1984). How is this to be explained? One way of understanding it is that the conceptual world of the Mishnah simply excludes eschatology; the lessons of the failed messianic and resistant movements of the pre-70 period had been learned, and a new world view was developed in which eternity consisted of a focus on the timeless observance of the Torah. There seems no question that this is the outlook of the Mishnah as it stands, while the messianic views developed subsequently have a different character. Does this represent the view of the Yavnean figures?

Complicating the picture are the traditions which ascribe eschatological beliefs to such prominent Yavnean rabbis as Aqiva (p. 124 above). Were these a part of the original tradition or were they subsequent additions? The obscurity of the Yavnean period may hide much of the debate and the power-plays in which various groups sought to impose their own views on the others. If so, it would not be surprising if some of those at Yavneh had eschato-logical views that others had given up. Such views would have been especially embarrassing in the Ushan period (c.140–200 CE) when the pre-Bar-Kokhba traditions were reshaped and had to be either explained as simply wrong or ignored and quietly forgotten. We may have some evidence of both processes in the tradition of Aqiva who was probably such a dominant figure as to elicit various reactions on the part of his successors. Those who thought he led them into a disastrous situation with Bar Kokhba may have been quite happy to see his name blackened, whereas those who gave him patriarchal status would have wanted to edit out awkward parts of the tradition. Unfortu-nately, the nature of the tradition makes it difficult to know whether we have a grasp on his actual views.

The picture that emerges is a complex one. The temple was destroyed, but the pre-70 high priestly families continued to have a good deal of power for some decades (Schwartz 1990). The Herodian family was weakened after 70, but Herodians continued to have a good deal of influence, as well. Agrippa II lived until the early 90s CE. Although he had never been king of Judea, he had had a good of power to intervene in Jerusalem affairs. It was probably in the 90s that the old power structures had become so weakened that they were ousted by new forces. We know little of the politics or even the details of the general situation in Palestine at the time. The Judean Desert manuscripts do give us a brief glimpse into the lives of ordinary Jews during this period (pp. 106–8 above), such as through the archives of Babatha and Salome Komaïse, but this is not enough to answer many of our major questions. What does emerge is the amount of religious change and redirection going on, the results of which become apparent in the post-135 period.

Many of the strands of pre-70 religion continued in post-70 Palestine (such as messianism and the imminent expectation of the eschaton) but new entities began to form. The influence of Diaspora innovations had started to have an effect before 70, and some of these proved quite productive in the new situa-tion (e.g. synagogues and the place of scripture). At the beginning of the period, there was probably still a widespread hope that the temple might be rebuilt in time; by the end of the Bar Kokhba revolt that hope had been decisively dashed. It is difficult to find apocalyptic and other Jewish works with a strong apocalyptic-messianic world view after 135 CE. From all we can tell, apocalyptic expectations ceased in their old form, having dis-appointed once and for all. Priests existed but they had nowhere to exercise their priesthood, and any continuation of the temple tradition had to take on new forms. It is the nascent rabbinic movement (as well as the breakaway sect of Christianity) that had the dynamics to fit the new situation (Neusner 1972; 1983; Stone 1982).

II

SPECIAL TOPICS

7

TEMPLE AND PRIESTHOOD

As a typical Northwest Semitic religion, the Israelite worship was centered on the sacrificial cult. In the ancient Near East, as also elsewhere in many of the ancient religions (e.g. Hinduism and Zoroastrianism), the cult place and the attendant rituals were the primary expression of the national or ethnic religion. The cult was thus at the heart of Jewish worship in both the First and Second Temple periods. The question of temple and cultic worship are complex issues, and this chapter will look at a number of related themes. Relevant sources will be given as appropriate during the discussion rather than surveyed, though most sources have been dealt with individually in Chapter 2 above.

THEOLOGICAL BASIS OF THE CULT

Anderson, G. A. (1987) *Sacrifices and Offerings in Ancient Israel: Studies in their Social and Political Importance*.

Anderson, G. A., and S. M. Olyan (eds) (1991) *Priesthood and Cult in Ancient Israel*.

Bourdillon, M. F. C., and M. Fortes (ed.) (1980) *Sacrifice*.

Douglas, M. (1966) *Purity and Danger: An Analysis of the Concepts of Pollution and Taboo*.

—— (1999) *Leviticus as Literature*.

Evans-Pritchard, E. (1956) *Nuer Religion*.

Gennep, A. van (1960) *The Rites of Passage*.

Gorman, F. H., Jr. (1990) *The Ideology of Ritual: Space, Time and Status in the Priestly Theology*.

Grabbe, L. L. (1993a) *Leviticus*.

Hamerton-Kelly, R. G. (ed.) (1987) *Violent Origins: Ritual Killing and Cultural Formation*.

Heger, P. (1999) *The Three Biblical Altar Laws: Developments in the Sacrificial Cult in Practice and Theology, Political and Economic Background*.

Heusch, L. de (1985) *Sacrifice in Africa: A Structuralist Approach*.

Houston, W. (1993) *Purity and Monotheism: Clean and Unclean Animals in Biblical Law.*

Jenson, P. P. (1992) *Graded Holiness: A Key to the Priestly Conception of the World.*

Kiuchi, N. (1987) *The Purification Offering in the Priestly Literature: Its Meaning and Function.*

Knierim, R. P. (1992) *Text and Concept in Leviticus 1:1–9: A Case in Exegetical Method.*

Kunin, S. D. (1998) *God's Place in the World: Sacred Space and Sacred Place in Judaism.*

Levine, B. A. (1974) *In the Presence of the Lord: A Study of Cult and Some Cultic Terms in Ancient Israel.*

Marx, A. (1989) "Sacrifice pour les péchés ou rites de passage? Quelques réflexions sur la fonction du *ḥaṭṭā't*", *RB* 96: 27–48.

—— (1994) *Les offrandes végétales dans l'Ancien Testament: Du tribut d'hommage au repas eschatologique.*

Meigs, A. S. (1978) "A Papuan Perspective on Pollution", *Man* 13: 304–18.

Milgrom, J. (1976) *Cult and Conscience: The ASHAM and the Priestly Doctrine of Repentance.*

Neusner, J. (1973b) *The Idea of Purity in Ancient Judaism: The Haskell Lectures, 1972–1973.*

Poorthuis, M. J. H. M., and J. Schwartz (eds) (2000) *Purity and Holiness: The Heritage of Leviticus.*

Sawyer, J. F. A. (ed.) (1996) *Reading Leviticus: A Conversation with Mary Douglas.*

It is easy for moderns to dismiss the sacrificial cult as outdated, irrelevant, or even barbaric; for that reason, the cult is often slighted or even ignored when Israel's religion is discussed. However much we may agree or disagree with an ancient practice, it is our duty to describe it in any history of religion. Yet the sacrificial system was evidently based on some important religious and theological principles that too frequently get overlooked. Fortunately, the work of anthropologists has helped to elucidate the ideology behind such cultic and ritual systems.

Three basic concepts underlie the sacrificial system. The first is the concept of sin and guilt and relates to human beings; the second is the principle of sacred and profane, and the third is ritual purity and impurity, both of which pertain to the deity. The first concept is a very pragmatic one: in a theological system in which the concept of sin and guilt played a prominent part, there had to be a means of removing sin. The sacrificial system did just that. The well-known Christian dogma that the "blood of bulls and goats" could not take away sin (Heb. 10:4) is true only within the Christian mythical system; the temple sacrificial system was underpinned by a different mythical system. The text makes it clear that the blood of the sacrifices *did* take away sin (Lev. 4:20, 26, 31, 35; 5:10, 13, 16, 18, 26 [Eng. 6:7]; 19:22; Num. 15:25,

26, 28). One of the main rituals of expiation was the ritual with the two goats on the Day of Atonement (Lev. 16).

The reason sin could be forgiven or removed was, of course, because the deity was thought to be present in some way in the temple and to be affected by the sacrifice. Some passages make the temple his dwelling place, though there is often a reluctance to be too categorical (cf. Deuteronomy which has the "name of Yhwh" dwelling at the cult site [e.g. 12:11], rather than Yhwh directly). The presence of God meant that humans had to be very careful and approach him only according to strict rules relating to what was sacred and profane; these rules included rigorous requirements of cultic purity for all worshipers.

Perhaps one of the most misunderstood concepts is that of ritual purity (see especially Neusner 1973b; also Houston 1993). It has little or nothing to do with hygiene or with the clean/dirty distinction in a physical sense. For example, in the Israelite system, excrement was not usually included in the category of unclean, even though ancient Israelites had much the same view toward it that we do today. One of the major attempts to work out the meaning of the biblical purity system in detail was by Douglas (1966; for an account of this book and criticisms of it, see Grabbe 1993a: 56–59). Despite some criticisms against Douglas (e.g. Meigs 1978), some of her points about the meaning of the system in Israelite society have not been affected and still seem valid, especially the notion that the system of permitted and forbidden animals was a microcosm of the world according to the Israelite view.

The rules of pollution and purity also drew strict boundaries around the altar and sanctuary. No pollution and no polluted persons were allowed to penetrate into the sacred area. This clear and rigid boundary drawing suggests a concern with political boundaries as well as social ones. If so, the message of the rules which, on the surface, might seem arcane ritual turn out to be a rich symbolic system with significant meaning for understanding the concerns of ancient Israel. For example, Gorman (1990) argues that a complex creation theology is presupposed and represented by the cult, and Jenson (1992) has made similar points. The priestly view had a cosmological and sociological dimension, as well as a cultic. In order to express this, it made distinctions between holy and profane, clean and unclean, life and death, order and chaos. This is one of significant insights given by the application of anthropology to the OT cultic texts.

Attempts have also been made to understand the significance of blood sacrifice, including the origins of the concept (cf. Hammerton-Kelly 1987). A number of theories have been advanced over the past century or more (summarized in Grabbe 1993a: 43–48), of which some of the more helpful are the following:

1 a gift, which might serve to appease the wrath of a god or to evoke his good will toward the offerer or both

2 communion with God, which fits such sacrifices as the offering of well-being
3 substitution, which is controversial for Israelite sacrifice (see below), but for which a good case can nonetheless be made
4 a rite of passage, including a rite of separation (van Gennep 1960; de Heusch 1985; Marx 1989)

But central to most sacrifices are the notions of expiation, cleansing, and re-establishment of cosmic – or at least microcosmic – harmony.

One area of considerable debate concerns the function of the blood. For example, Levine (1974) argues that it has two functions: (1) an apotropaic function for the deity; that is, the blood was placed on the altar to protect God from the malignancy of impurity which was regarded as an external force; (2) purificatory or expiatory, in which the blood served as a ransom substituting for the life owed by the offerer. According to Milgrom (1976), the blood acted as a ritual detergent, washing off the impurities which had attached themselves to the sacred things. Milgrom has also dismissed the idea of the sacrificial victim being a substitute for the sinner. That this is really a type of substitute or surrogate for the sinner, however, is a point made by Kiuchi (1987) who argues that the sin offering is envisaged as a substitute for the sinner, and that it purges the sin of the individual, not just purging the effect on the sanctuary. Knierim (1992: 34–40) opposes the idea of substitution and considers the gesture (which he translates as 'firm pressing down of the hand') a means of denoting transfer of ownership, i.e., from the one offering to God. Heger (1999) has recently argued that a change in concept took place in the time of Ahaz, from the concept of sacrifice as food for God to sacrifice on behalf of the worshipers, for their spiritual exaltation (since God has need of nothing).

Perhaps part of the problem is being too literal in interpretation. The sacrificial system was a symbolic system, filled with metaphor, allegory, and analogy. It would be a mistake to assume that only one symbol or metaphor was used for removing sin (e.g. ritual detergent). In the same way, the cultic terminology may have had a more general meaning and should not be defined in terms of the specific metaphor used. The individual's sins were removed, whatever the precise symbolic conceptualization used. It is the fact that the cult expresses important theological and religious truth via a complex symbolic system that needs to be recognized and appreciated.

TEMPLE AND CULT

Albertz, R. (1994) *A History of Israelite Religion in the Old Testament Period.*
Andreasen, N.-E. A. (1972) *The Old Testament Sabbath.*
Ben-Dov, M. (1985) *In the Shadow of the Temple: The Discovery of Ancient Jerusalem.*

—— (1986) "Herod's Mighty Temple Mount", *BAR* 12/6: 40–49.

Blenkinsopp, J. (1998) "The Judaean Priesthood during the Neo-Babylonian and Achaemenid Periods: A Hypothetical Reconstruction", *CBQ* 60: 25–43.

Bokser, B. M. (1992) "Unleavened Bread and Passover, Feasts of", *ABD*: 6.755–65.

Braun, J. (1999) *Die Musikkultur Altisraels/Palästinas: Studien zu archäologischen, schriftlichen und vergleichenden Quellen.*

Busink, T. A. (1980) *Der Tempel von Jerusalem von Salomo bis Herodes: Eine archäologisch-historische Studie unter Berücksichtigung des westsemitischen Tempelbaus: 2. Von Ezechiel bis Middot.*

Clines, D. J. A. (1974) "The Evidence for an Autumnal New Year in Pre-exilic Israel Reconsidered", *JBL* 93: 22–40.

—— (1976) "New Year", *IDBSup*: 625–29.

Cody, A. (1969) *A History of Old Testament Priesthood.*

Cryer, F. H. (1987) "The 360-Day Calendar Year and Early Judaic Sectarianism", *SJOT* 1: 116–22.

Douglas, M. (1966) *Purity and Danger: An Analysis of the Concepts of Pollution and Taboo.*

—— (1975) *Implicit Meanings: Essays in Anthropology.*

Eissfeldt, O. (1917) *Erstlinge und Zehnten im Alten Testament: Ein Beitrag zur Geschichte des israelitisch-jüdischen Kultus.*

Finkelstein, J. J. (1961) "Amisaduqa's Edict and the Babylonian 'Law Codes'", *JCS* 15: 91–104.

Goodman, M. (1998b) "Jews, Greeks, and Romans", in M. Goodman (ed.) (1998a) *Jews in a Graeco-Roman World*: 3–14.

Goudoever, J. van (1961) *Biblical Calendars.*

Grabbe, L.L. (1987c) "The Scapegoat Ritual: A Study in Early Jewish Interpretation", *JSJ* 18: 152–67.

—— (1991a) "Maccabean Chronology: 167–164 or 168–165 BCE?" *JBL* 110: 59–74.

—— (1993a) *Leviticus.*

—— (1995a) *Priests, Prophets, Diviners, Sages: A Socio-historical Study of Religious Specialists in Ancient Israel.*

—— (1998a) *Ezra and Nehemiah.*

Gunneweg, A. H. J. (1965) *Leviten und Priester: Hauptlinien der Traditionsbildung und Geschichte des israelitisch-jüdischen Kultpersonals.*

Haran, M. (1978) *Temples and Temple-Service in Ancient Israel.*

Hayward, C. T. R. (1996) *The Jewish Temple: A Non-Biblical Sourcebook.*

Kleinig, J. W. (1993) *The Lord's Song: The Basis, Function and Significance of Choral Music in Chronicles.*

Knoppers, G. N. (1999) "Hierodules, Priests, or Janitors? The Levites in Chronicles and the History of the Israelite Priesthood", *JBL* 118: 49–72.

Körting, C. (1999) *Der Schall des Schofar: Israels Feste im Herbst.*

Kraus, H.-J. (1966) *Worship in Israel: A Cultic History of the Old Testament*.
—— (1988) *Psalms 1–59: A Commentary*.
Lemche, N. P. (1976) "The Manumission of Slaves–the Fallow Year–the Sabbatical Year–the Jobel Year", *VT* 26: 38–59.
—— (1979) "*Andurārum* and *Mīšarum*: Comments on the Problem of Social Edicts and their Application in the Ancient Near East", *JNES* 38: 11–22.
Lewy, H. (1958) "The Biblical Institution of *Derôr* in the Light of Akkadian Documents", *EI* 5: 21*–31*.
Lim, T. H. (1992) "The Chronology of the Flood Story in a Qumran Text (4Q252)", *JJS* 43: 288–98.
Netzer, E. (1982) "Ancient Ritual Baths (*Miqvaot*) in Jericho", *Jerusalem Cathedra* 2: 106–19.
Nurmela, R. (1998) *The Levites: Their Emergence as a Second-Class Priesthood*.
O'Brien, J. M. (1990) *Priest and Levite in Malachi*.
Porten, B., and A. Yardeni (1993) "Ostracon Clermont-Ganneau 125(?): A Case of Ritual Purity", *JAOS* 113: 451–56.
Prosic, T. (1999) "Origin of Passover", *SJOT* 13: 78–94.
Ritmyer, L., and K. Ritmyer (1998) *Secrets of Jerusalem's Temple Mount*.
Rubenstein, J. L. (1995) *The History of Sukkot in the Second Temple and Rabbinic Periods*.
Schams, C. (1998) *Jewish Scribes in the Second-Temple Period*.
Schwartz, D. R. (1992) *Studies in the Jewish Background of Christianity*.
Segal, J. (1963) *The Hebrew Passover*.
Talmon, S. (1958) "The Calendar Reckoning of the Sect from the Judaean Desert", in C. Rabin and Y. Yadin (eds) *Aspects of the Dead Sea Scrolls*: 162–99.
Ulfgard, H. (1998) *The Story of Sukkot: The Setting, Shaping, and Sequel of the Biblical Feast of Tabernacles*.
VanderKam, J. C. (1998) *Calendars in the Dead Sea Scrolls: Measuring Time*.
Wegner, J. R. (1992) "Leviticus", in C. A. Newsom and S. H. Ringe (eds) *The Women's Bible Commentary*: 36–44.
Werman, C. (1997) "Levi and Levites in the Second Temple Period", *DSD* 4: 211–25.
Williamson, H. M. G. (1979) "The Origins of the Twenty-Four Priestly Courses: A Study of 1 Chronicles xxiii–xxvii", *Studies in the Historical Books of the Old Testament*: 251–68.
Yadin, Y. (ed.) (1983) *The Temple Scroll*.
Zipor, M. A. (1997) "The Flood Chronology: Too Many an Accident", *DSD* 4: 207–10.

The physical temple

The temple for which we have most information is the so-called Herod's temple, destroyed in 70 CE. Archaeology, iconographic representations, and literary descriptions have allowed a substantial reconstruction of the temple buildings and court (Ritmyer/Ritmyer 1998; Ben-Dov 1985; Busink 1980; cf. *Ant.* 15.11.3–5 §§391–20; *Ag. Apion* 2.8 §§102–9). Beyond that our knowledge becomes much vaguer. Whatever existed during the time of the Judean monarchy, the basis of Herod's temple was probably the temple constructed during the Persian period, though we know nothing with any certainty about it at the present (cf. p. 33 above). A study of the remains of the Herodian temple indicates some of the pre-Herodian structures. For example, the Herodian temple precinct seems to have been extended beyond the earlier area to take more of the temple mount within the walls. With the present political and religious situation in Jerusalem, it remains difficult to explore the issue beyond a certain point.

The tabernacle described in the books of Exodus and Leviticus may have been based in part on one of the actual temples, perhaps that rebuilt in the early Persian period. Also, the *Temple Scroll* (11QT; Yadin 1983) may accurately portray features of the actual temple, though its overall description seems to have been an idealized one. One of the most intriguing questions relates to the courts of the Gentiles and of women, which we know existed in the Herodian temple (cf. *Ag. Apion* 2.8 §§102–4). No biblical passage indicates that women were kept away from the sacrificial area that was open to the ordinary Israelite (see further, pp. 140–41 below).

The cultic personnel

The indications of the biblical text are that the temple priesthood reached a certain configuration early in the Second Temple period after a long period of struggle between rival factions (Grabbe 1995a: 52, 57–62; Albertz 1994: 219–22, 427–36; Gunneweg 1965; Nurmela 1998). That struggle may have continued into the Second Temple (cf. Ezek. 44:10–15); however, the only indications of rivalry are those relating to the high priesthood and are between members of the same family (*Ant.* 11.7.1 §§297–301; 2 Macc. 4) until the Hasmoneans assumed the priesthood after a period when the office was apparently vacant (*JCH*: 294). Regardless of the earlier history of the priesthood, most of the Second Temple texts present a reasonably uniform picture and, although the OT itself does not present a unified picture, much of what is found there is also compatible with that found in Second Temple texts.

The temple personnel were divided into priests proper and the lower clergy, often referred collectively as "the Levites" (Num. 3–4, 8). This distinction does not appear in Deuteronomy but is found widely in other OT texts. O'Brien (1990: 47–48, 111–12) has argued that Malachi also makes no such distinction, but this seems unlikely (cf. Grabbe 1995a: 49). The priests were the only ones allowed to preside at the altar (Num. 17:5; 18; Ezek. 40:45–46; 44:15–16). Their main function was to carry out the sacrificial cult (as described especially in Lev. 1–16), but they had other duties as well. They were the custodians of the written law with responsibility to teach it to the people and make cultic rulings where needed (Deut. 31:9–13, 24–26; 33:10; Ezek. 44:23–24; Hag. 2:11–13; 2 Chron. 15:3; 19:11). They had to pronounce on all matters of ritual purity, including certain diseases (Deut. 24:8; Lev. 11–15). According to some texts, they also functioned in a wider civic context in such things as judging lawsuits and acting as appeal judges for lower courts (Deut. 17:8–13; 19:17; 21:5; Ezek. 44:24; 2 Chron. 19:5–11). They also had custody over the sacred objects of priestly divination called the Urim and Thumim (Deut. 33:8; Num. 17:18–21), though these are said to have ceased to function or were perhaps lost by Second Temple times (Ezra 2:63). It appears from the biblical data that a high priest existed even under the monarchy, when the king was officially the head of the cult (pp. 144–47 below).

The duties of the "Levites" included a variety of functions. Their most important task was to assist the priests in carrying out the sacrificial cult, though they were not to carry out the ceremonies at the altar itself (Ezek. 44:13; Num. 16). They also had other duties such as maintaining security and evidently a variety of menial duties (2 Chron. 19:11; Ezek. 44:10–14; cf. 1 Chron. 23:4). The text refers to gatekeepers, singers, Netinim, and temple servants alongside the Levites (Ezra 2:36–63; Neh. 7:39–60, 72). There are indications within the text itself that certain of these cultic servants originally seen as separate became assimilated into the Levites (cf. Grabbe 1998a: 14; Nurmela 1998). On the question of music and singing in the temple, see pp. 143–44 below.

The temple personnel held an important position in society. During the periods in which there was no king, the priesthood in general and the high priest in particular were in positions of political as well as religious power. There is evidence that the Levites were especially drawn on for the scribal skills necessary to run the nation as well as the temple (Grabbe 1995a: 160–61; Schwartz 1992: 89–101). The temple personnel were the ones who had the education and leisure for intellectual pursuits and thus constituted the bulk of the educated and those who read, wrote, and commented on religious literature. They were also the primary teachers in religious matters. Thus, not only the cult but also a large portion of the religious activity of other sorts, including teaching and development of the tradition, took place in the temple context.

There are indications that toward the end of the Second Temple period, the number of hereditary priests far exceeded the needs of the temple. The writer now called Pseudo-Hecateus (pp. 73–74 above), writing perhaps about 100 BCE, says that there were 1500 priests (*Ag. Apion* 1.22 §188), though we have no way of knowing the basis of this statement (Bar-Kochva suggests it is the number of priests in the Hasmonean administration [1996: 160]). Josephus suggests that in his own time, there were upwards of 20,000 priests (this number sounds exaggerated) who served on a system of rotation (*Ant.* 7.14.7 §§365–67; *Ag. Apion* 2:8 §108). As early as the Persian period the priests were apparently divided into twenty-four courses to serve on a rota basis (1 Chron. 24; *Life* 1 §2; cf. Williamson 1979; Talmon 1958).

Financial support for the temple

The priestly texts of the OT state that the priests and Levites were to have no inheritance (i.e., no land, except for the Levitical cities and a small amount around them [Num. 35:1–8]) but were to live from the tithes and offerings of the people (Deut. 18:1–2). There is some question as to accuracy of the statement that the priesthood could own no property since other texts suggest differently (cf. Jer. 32:6–15; Neh. 13:10; Hecateus of Abdera [pp. 38–39 above]; Josephus, *Life* 76 §422). But many different texts indicate that the temple personnel by and large lived from the priestly dues exacted from the people. These dues took a number of forms, though as will become clear some aspects of this system remain elusive even now (cf. Grabbe 1993a: 66–72; Eissfeldt 1917). The priestly dues were:

1 Portions of various sacrifices, referred to as the *tĕnûfāh* and the *tĕrûmāh* (Lev. 7:29–36), traditionally translated as "wave offering" and "heave offering" respectively, but this understanding seems to be based in part on the much later Mishnah (*M. Menahot* 5:6), and the precise meaning of the terms is still debated (cf. Grabbe 1993a: 66–68)
2 Certain one-off payments of agricultural produce such as firstlings and first-fruits (Exod. 13:11–15; 34:19–20; Lev. 2:14–16; 27:26–27; Num. 18:12–18; Deut. 18:4; 26:1–11)
3 Gifts (including land), vows, and dedications (Lev. 27)
4 Apparently the main source of revenue, the annual tithes of all agricultural produce and (supposedly) livestock.

The whole question of tithing in ancient Israel is one fraught with difficulties. Numbers 18:21–32 states that all the tithes were to go to the Levites who were in turn to tithe this tithe and give it to the priests. Neh. 10:37–39 seems to give a similar picture. Deut. 13:17–19 and 14:22–29, on the other hand, speak of eating the tithe in the "place that the Lord your God will choose". If the way was too far, the tithe could be converted to money and brought to the sanctuary to be exchanged for food for a feast. All the members of the household were to take part in the feast, and the Levite was to be included (Deut. 13:18). In the third year, however, the tithe was to be brought into the settlements and given to the Levites, the stranger, the fatherless, and the widow.

These instructions appear to be irreconcilable and may have originated as two separate systems. Another possibility is that some of the differences belong to an idealized cult which some groups wanted to impose but which was in fact never practiced. Whatever the origin of these differences, Second Temple literature gives some indication as to how the system worked during the final centuries while the temple was still functioning, though even here there appear to be differences between the sources. The main tradition seems to envisage two tithes: a first tithe to the priests and a second tithe to be used to come up to Jerusalem at the annual festivals (Tobit 1:6–8 [according to Codex Sinaiticus]; *Jub.* 31:8-15; *M. Ma'aserot* and *M. Ma'aser Sheni*). There was also a poor man's tithe (from Deut. 14:28–29). This seems to have been regarded as a different use of the second tithe in the third and sixth years of a seven-year cycle (see also *M. Pe'ah* 8:2). For various reasons (including economic), this is likely to have been the actual practice; however, some sources appear to envisage that three full tithes were paid in the third and sixth years (Tobit 1:6–8 [Codex Vaticanus]; *Ant.* 4.8.22 §240). One suspects that Josephus's picture is an idealized one, since for a farmer to pay 30 per cent of his income (not to mention firstlings, etc.) in some years would be an intolerable burden. From what little indication we have, the tithes were paid directly to the priests rather than to the Levites who then tithed to the priests (Judith 11:13; *Ant.* 20.8.8 §181; 20.9.2 §206; *Life* 12 §63; 15 §80), but there is some unclarity (cf. *Ant.* 4.4.3 §68; 4.8.8 §205; Philo, *Virt.* 95; *Spec. Leg.* 1.156; Tobit 1:6–8).

A further puzzle is the tithe of cattle, mentioned in only one biblical passage (Lev. 27:32–33; see Grabbe 1993a: 70). The only other reference to this tithe is 2 Chron. 31:6 which suggests that this tithe was to go to the priests as a part of their income. Why is not the tithe of animals referred to elsewhere in the biblical text? How such tithing would be carried out is not discussed and is itself a puzzle. Is it because this was only a theoretical law which was never put into practise? The one comment of the Mishnah on the tithe of cattle indicates that it was used as second or festival tithe (*M. Bekorot* 9:1–8).

It is evident that there is still a lot not known about the details of how the system worked; on the other hand, it evidently followed the general outline of the Pentateuchal instructions. The importance of the tithe for support of the cultic personnel is indicated by a late Second Temple reference. Josephus states that shortly before the 66–70 war with Rome, the high priest's men were taking the tithes directly at the threshing floor, by force if necessary, with the result that some priests starved (*Ant.* 20.9.2 §206-7). This is almost certainly exaggerated, but the tithe as the basic support for the temple is well illustrated.

The cultic rituals

The backbone of temple worship was animal sacrifice (though there were also lesser offerings of cereal, wine, and the like). The various sacrifices are described in detail in Leviticus 1–7 (for a summary, see Grabbe 1993a: 29–43;

a number of relevant bibliographical items are found on pp. 129–30 above). There are still some puzzles about it (e.g. the difference between the "sin offering" [*ḥaṭṭā't*] and the "guilt offering" ['*āšām*]), and other biblical and Jewish texts show differences of detail. On the other hand, Leviticus does not describe the daily or *tāmîd* animal offering known from a variety of texts (Exod. 29:38–42; Num. 28:3–8), though Leviticus does have a daily meal offering (6:12–16). Yet even on the important *tāmîd* offering the texts differ over details of its content (cf. 1 Sam. 18:29; 2 Kings 16:15; Ezek. 46:13–15; Dan. 8:11–14). Some of these texts may reflect historical changes, which would not be surprising as the cult was carried out over many centuries and in a changing context in the ancient Near East.

Very much tied up with temple worship was the system of purity (*ṭhr*) and impurity (*ṭm'*). Only those members of the congregation of Israel considered "pure" were allowed to enter the sacred area and to worship at the temple (Lev. 7:19–21; Num. 9:6–7). The basic regulations for cultic purity are found primarily in Leviticus 11–15. The system is quite extensive (summarized in Grabbe 1993a: 49–54), covering various aspects of life and affecting both genders (though in different ways), but the focus tends to be on food entering the body and various discharges from the body: animal foods, diseases, genital discharges (seminal and menstrual), and childbirth. Impurity could be corrected through a combination of (a) the passage of time, (b) washing, and (c) offering certain sacrifices, depending on the particular impurity incurred. Some of the simpler forms of impurity (e.g. that incurred by sexual intercourse or menstruation) were eliminated by the first two, but the more serious forms required sacrifice as well for their full cleansing.

Although sacrifice was the main activity in the temple, it was by no means the only one. Prayer is often mentioned in the context of the temple (see pp. 170–75 below), and there are indications of various "liturgies of the word". Precisely what went on is nowhere described as a system, though there are many passing references that indicate liturgical practices beyond animal sacrifice. Some of these have been systematized into major theories about the cult, such as associating various of the Psalms with a particular temple celebration (e.g. an annual new year celebration). Although each of these theories can be criticized (cf. Grabbe 1995a: 35–38), they recognize what was probably the case: that some or even a good deal of the poetry within the Hebrew Bible originated in the temple service.

Many of the regulations and much of the ritual in the Second Temple probably coincided in broad terms with the data of Leviticus and the P source; however, apart from areas of contradiction within the biblical text itself (as noted above), there is one important area where actual practice seems to have gone in a quite different direction from the biblical instructions: this is the area of purification by washing. The biblical text envisioned either the use of running water (Lev. 14:50–51; Num. 19:17) or seems not to have been

concerned with the sort of water in which one bathed or washed for purification; also, purification was specifically for attendance at the temple and not
other gatherings. Yet archaeology indicates the extensive development of the
ritual bath (*miqve*) during this period (Netzer 1982), including its presence
apparently even in the synagogue, if the identification of *miqvā'ôt* at
Jerusalem, Gamla, Jericho, and elsewhere is correct (but see the criticism of
Goodman 1998: 9).

Women and the cult

The regulations about purity affected both genders, yet there is no question
but that they would have been particularly felt by women. The interpretation
of some feminist writers has been negative, though Wegner's recent commentary on Leviticus (1992) gives a generally positive assessment, recognizing its general context in the ancient world. Women are mentioned
specifically in only two sections of the cultic regulations:

One context is childbirth which made a woman impure for ritual purposes
(Lev. 12). In order to be allowed to re-enter the sanctuary, she had to undergo
a period of cleansing which culminated in sacrifices. The other occasion of
impurity with women was menstruation (15:19–24). Although the regulations about bodily issues in Leviticus 12–15 do not make a particular
point about menstruation, most of the other regulations concern unusual
occurrences, unlike the monthly period. However, it should be noted that
menstruation, like the impurity contracted from normal sexual intercourse,
did not require a sacrifice for cleansing and was thus in a different category
from "abnormal" discharges.

Anthropological studies have suggested that regulations about menstruation often mirror the relationship between the sexes and the place of each
sex within the society (Douglas 1975: 60–72; cf. Grabbe 1993a: 59–61). It
seems clear that in Israelite society, women had a particular sphere and
place in which they were confined. They were not generally allowed to participate in activities which were associated with the male Israelite (despite
some stories of exceptional women who broke through the traditional
boundaries). Any woman who carefully observed the rules about menstrual
pollution would have found her activities severely restricted in certain ways.
A similar purpose seems to be associated with the rules surrounding childbirth.

One puzzling area relates to women and participation in the sacrificial cult.
With regard to purification after childbirth, the woman herself is envisioned
as participating in the sacrificial cult (Lev. 12:6). Although the general
directions relating to sacrifice are addressed in the masculine form of the
verb (whether singular or plural), this could be thought to include women
under normal circumstances. Women are not specifically excluded in the P
legislation. This apparently changed at some unknown point during the

Second Temple period. Our main information relates to Herod's temple. If Josephus's description is correct, women were not allowed to go beyond the Court of Women nor the non-priestly men to go beyond the Court of the Israelites (*Ag. Apion* 2 §§102–4).

The cultic year: sabbath and annual festivals

Cultic activity took place on a daily basis, but the focus tended to be on certain regular festivals (Grabbe 1993a: 85–100): the weekly sabbath and the seven annual festivals. The annual festivals grew out of the agricultural year and celebrated significant points within it (beginning of the barley harvest; end of the wheat harvest; grape harvest; cf. Körting 1999). Special sacrifices were designated for the weekly sabbath, the monthly new moon, and especially for the main festivals.

Although the origin of the **weekly sabbath** is debated, it was well established at least by the early Second Temple period (Isa. 56:2–6; Neh. 13:15–22) and becomes one of the main characteristics of the Jews commented on by non-Jews (Agatharchides of Cnidus [*GLAJJ*: ##301a]; Meleager [*GLAJJ*: #43]; Ovid [*GLAJJ*: ##141–43]; Frontinus [*GLAJJ*: #229]). One of the earliest descriptions in extra-biblical Jewish literature is *Jubilees* 50.

It has long been thought that **Passover and Unleavened Bread** had a separate origin, but where our sources for the Second Temple period are explicit, they show them to be combined into a unit (Bokser 1992; Haran 1978: 317–48; Segal 1963; Prosic 1999). The celebration is first attested in extra-biblical sources in the Passover papyrus from Elephantine (*AP* #21 = *TAD* A4.1; cf. *JCH* 54–55; Porten-Yardeni 1993). Interestingly, this mentions both a prohibition against drinking beer during this period and also the practice of sealing up leaven rather than destroying it. The first real description of the Passover in extra-biblical literature is in *Jubilees* (49), which also witnesses to the custom of drinking wine at the meal (49:6), apparently a general practice by the end of the Second Temple period (cf. Mark 14:12–25), and eating the Passover only in the temple (49:17–21).

The time of the festival **Feast of Weeks (Pentecost or Shavuot)** was determined by counting from the wave sheaf day, the day during Unleavened Bread on which the first sheaf of the barley was ceremonially cut and offered up (Lev. 23:9–14). The different sects apparently disagreed on when this day was, with four different methods of reckoning (cf. Goudoever 1961: 15–29). The key was the "day after the sabbath" (*mimmoḥŏrat haššabbāt*), but was this the weekly sabbath or the annual sabbath of either the first or last holy day of the festival (day one or day seven)? Also, did one count seven weeks or seven sabbaths (Lev. 23:15)? The most natural interpretation (the weekly sabbath in both cases) is the one allegedly followed by the Boethusians (*M. Menaḥ.* 10:3; *M. Ḥag.* 2:4; see pp. 194–99 below). If so, the Feast of Weeks would have occured always on a Sunday seven weeks after Passover.

The **Day of Trumpets** was a festival on the first day of the seventh month (Tishri). For many centuries, that day has been considered the Jewish new year, but there is no indication that this is how the celebration originated. On the contrary, the new year began at various points, depending on how one viewed it (cf. *M. Rosh ha-Sh.* 1:1). The indication in the present form of the biblical text is that the new year began in the spring, on the first of Nisan (Aviv is the old Hebrew name of the month), and this may have been the case in reality (cf. Clines 1974, 1976).

The **Day of Atonement** became the most solemn day in the Jewish calendar, but it is difficult to know precisely how it was celebrated in antiquity. The only thing we do know is that the high priest went into the Holy of Holies on this day only, and the ceremony with the two goats was enacted (cf. Grabbe 1987; 1993a: 92–93). Surprisingly, the day does not appear to have a place among the events of the seventh month in Neh. 8–9.

The **Festival of Booths or Tabernacles (Sukkot)** is mentioned in a number of sources and was evidently one of the major Jerusalem festivals (Rubenstein 1995; Ulfard 1998). This actually lasted eight days, beginning with a holy day and concluding with a closing or last great day (cf. Lev. 23:36; Neh. 8:18; John 7:37). The Israelites built temporary shelters or booths to live in during the festival. The text of Leviticus mentions the use of "four kinds" of vegetation to build the booths (Lev. 23:40; Neh. 8:14–17), but later interpretation envisions the people parading with them (*Jub.* 16:30–31; cf. *M. Sukk.* 4:1–6; 5/6HevEp15).

These are the only festivals known from the biblical text. There is some indication that the new moon was once a festival, but it had apparently ceased to be so by the Second Temple period (Grabbe 1993a: 86). We know of Purim from the book of Esther, though the lack of this book at Qumran suggests that it was not universally celebrated by Jews. The *Temple Scroll* mentions three more festivals: Festival of the First Fruits of Oil, Festival of the First Fruits of Wine, and Festival of Wood Offering (11QT 19–25). The only one of these attested in other sources is the Festival of Woodgathering, with the indication that, while not one of the annual holy days, this was an observance connected with the temple from perhaps as early as the Persian period (*War* 2.17.6 §425; cf. Neh. 10:35). Two other observances are mentioned in the biblical text:

Every seventh year was a **sabbatical year** (*šĕmiṭṭāh*) when, according to Leviticus 25:19–22 (cf. Exod. 23:10–11), the land was to be left fallow; other passages indicate a remission of debt and release of indentured slaves as well (Deut. 15:1–3, 12–15; Jer. 34:8–16). From indications in a variety of Second Temple sources, this was not just a theoretical command but was actually observed (Grabbe 1991a: 60–63).

The **Jubilee year** is described in Leviticus (25:8–17, 23–34) though, confusingly, it has some of the characteristics of the sabbatical year by also being a year of release from debt (cf. also Lev. 27:16–24; Num. 36:4). It appears to be the fiftieth year (Lev. 25:10–11), though some later sources (e.g. *Jubilees*) make it the forty-ninth. None of our sources indicates that it was actually observed as such (even if we find its use in chronology). Indeed, it may be a reflex of the Mesopotamian custom for a new king to declare a debt amnesty in his first year of reign and even occasionally at other times (cf. Lewy 1958; Finkelstein 1961; Lemche 1976, 1979).

The question of which calendar was used is a difficult one (cf. VanderKam 1998; Talmon 1958; Goudoever 1961). All indications are that the calendar used officially in the temple was a solar–lunar one; i.e., months were marked by the phases of the moon, with a new month beginning with each new moon. (The Hebrew word for month is *ḥodeš* "new (moon)".) The priests met on the thirtieth day of the month to hear witnesses who claimed to have sighted the new moon. If there were credible witnesses, that day was counted as the first day of the new month; if not, the next day was declared as such (*M. Rosh ha-Sh.* 1:7, which mentions the priests even though rabbinic literature usually ascribes it to a rabbinic court). The year was periodically reconciled with the solar year by the addition of a thirteenth lunar month. However, some groups (the Qumran group, *Jubilees*) apparently used a solar calendar which may have been an old one (cf. the dates in Gen. 6–9; cf. Cryer 1987; Lim 1992; Zipor 1997), though this calendar would have become more and more out of line with the seasons as time went on, which was probably why it was abandoned if it was ever used officially. If it was used, it had been abandoned at an early date since no texts indicate its use in the temple, nor do they suggest a dispute about the calendar (*JCH*: 309).

Music and singing

The *Letter of (Pseudo-)Aristeas* makes the surprising statement that during the cult activity, "complete silence prevailed" (95: *hē te pasa sigē kathestēken*). The exact basis for such a statement is difficult to understand. Perhaps the sacrificial ritual itself was conducted in silence (though it would hardly have been quiet, with animals bleating and bellowing, fire crackling, and priests bustling about), but there is abundant textual evidence for singing and music in the temple (cf. Braun 1999; Kleinig 1993). Temple singers are mentioned in many passages which probably relate to the Second Temple (1 Chron. 25; 2 Chron. 20:14–17; Ezra 2:41; Neh. 7:44; 11:22–23; 12:24; *Ant.* 20.9.6 §§216–18). There is some evidence that the singers grew out of cultic prophets, though the matter is complicated (Grabbe 1995a: 112–13). According to Ezra 3, the founding of the new temple was celebrated with instrumental music by priests and Levites (3:10–13). Similarly, the dedication of the wall in the time of Nehemiah includes a band of Levites playing instruments and singing (Neh. 12:27–47).

It has been argued since the nineteenth century that psalms were originally connected with the cult, though the question of whether the present-day collection of the book of Psalms owes it origins to the pre-exilic cult is more controversial. Despite the supposed cultic connections, priests are hardly mentioned in the book; nevertheless, the Psalms provide important insight into temple worship. They show that the central cultic act of blood sacrifice was enriched by accompanying rites of thanksgiving, singing, praise of God, and instrumental music. The headings of many psalms are thought to refer to musical instruments or musicians (see the summary in Kraus 1988: 21–32). The terms are not always easy to figure out, and many of them are subject to debate, but it is hardly likely that we can dismiss all interpretations to do with music. The "Psalms of Asaph" (50, 73–83) are probably to be connected with the Levites and singers of the same name (1 Chron. 25).

THE HIGH PRIEST AND "THE SANHEDRIN"

Goodblatt, David (1994) *The Monarchic Principle: Studies in Jewish Self-Government in Antiquity.*

Grabbe, L. L. (1995a) *Priests, Prophets, Diviners, Sages: A Socio-historical Study of Religious Specialists in Ancient Israel.*

Mantel, H. (1961) *Studies in the History of the Sanhedrin.*

—— (1976) "Sanhedrin", *IDBSup*: 784–86.

According to the biblical text, the most important priestly figure was the chief priest (*hakkōhēn haggādōl*) or high priest (*hakkōhēn hārō'š*) whose existence is envisioned even in texts which are possibly pre-exilic (e.g. the two chief priests Zadok and Abiathar in the time of David [2 Sam. 17:15; 19:12; 20:25]; Jehoida [2 Kings 11–12]). Because the king was seen as the head of the cult during the time of the monarchy (Grabbe 1995a: 20–40), the place of the high priest seems not to have been as important as later, but the number of passing references suggests a continuing office with an important function even while a native king reigned in Jerusalem (Grabbe 1995a: 60–62).

With the loss of the monarchy and the incorporation of Judah into the Persian empire as a province, the office of high priest expanded in importance to fill the gap of local leadership (*JCH*: 73–83). This was true even though there was a provincial governor appointed by the Persians, as is clear in the books of Haggai and Zechariah where the two figures are mentioned together as a sort of diarchical leadership. The harmonious relationship between the high priest and the Persian governor suggested by Haggai and Zechariah was not necessarily a given, however. For one thing, we do not know that the Persian governor was always Jewish (*JCH*: 75), and a non-native governor would probably not be so inclined to work closely with the high priest. We also know from the book of Nehemiah that even a Jewish governor might not feel compelled to establish a good working relationship with the high priest (Neh. 13:4–9, 28; cf. Grabbe 1998a: 161–67).

In later biblical texts – not only Haggai–Zechariah and Ezra–Nehemiah but also Chronicles (e.g. 2 Chron. 23–24; 26:16–20; 34:9–18) – the office of high priest is routinely mentioned and is clearly the most important figure of the cult in subsequent texts. The classic reference is Ben Sira's description of Simon II (Sir. 50:1–21).The high priest acted as spokesman for the Jewish community, in most of the references we have from the period of Greek rule. His power no doubt waxed and waned, depending on the political circumstances. For example, because of the high priest Onias II's refusal to pay a tribute to the Ptolemaic court, some of his authority may have been taken by Joseph Tobiad (*Ant.* 12.4.2 §§160–66; but see p. 40 above on doubts about this and also the details of the Joseph story). One question is what family held the high priesthood, since it is often asserted that the high priest had to be a Zadokite in pre-Maccabean times. Although Ezekiel (e.g. 43:15–16) confines the priesthood to the Zadokites, most of our sources say nothing on this question (though compare the expression "sons of Zadok" for priests in some of the Qumran scrolls), and it is not at all clear that the Oniad family claimed to be of Zadokite descent.

Somewhat less clear is the status – or even existence – of "the Sanhedrin". References to such a body are often found in secondary literature, though a variety of terms is found in the original sources: *gerousia* "council of elders, senate", *boulē* "advisory council", or Sanhedrin, from Greek *sunedrion* "assembly". Some recent scholars have doubted that such an institution even existed (Goodblatt 1994). Part of the problem is that many treatments of this subject have begun with the Mishnaic tractate *Sanhedrin* and later rabbinic texts, which is very problematic (Goodblatt 1994: 105–8). These may well be describing an idealized concept centuries after the temple had fallen and the office of high priest had disappeared. The unsatisfactory nature of trying to reconcile Second Temple sources with later rabbinic literature is demonstrated by a number of older treatments, some of which even end up hypothesizing two Sanhedrins, a "religious" and a "political" one (e.g. Mantel 1961, 1976).

The main problem with thinking of a permanent institution, however, is that some of the Greek words are clearly used of *ad hoc* assemblies called to try cases of conspiracy (e.g. *War* 1.27.1 §537;1.28.3 §559; *Ant.* 16.11.1–3 §§357–67 [*sunedrion*]) and to give advice (*Life* 66 §368 [*sunedrion*]), of regional councils (*War* 1.8.5 §170; *Ant.* 14.5.4 §91 [*sunedrion*]), and of city councils (*Life* 12 §64; 13 §69; 34 §169 [*boulē*]). The question is whether the references to a "Sanhedrin" of the Jews are really just references to such *ad hoc* councils to decide on issues as the occasion warranted.

Yet a series of texts suggest that some sort of body assisted in the governance of Judah through much of the Second Temple period, though its function and even its designation may well have varied over the centuries. The following points summarize the main sources of information:

1. Where the high priest is mentioned in the OT, he is often presented as acting in conjunction with other priests – a natural sitution if he was seen as the head of the priests (2 Kings 23:4; 2 Chron. 26:16–20). Yet the high priest also often brought in others under his leadership to help carry out necessary tasks or worked with others outside the priesthood (2 Kings 11; 12:8–11; 22:8–14; 2 Chron. 23; 24:4–11; 34:14–22).

2. One of the Elephantine papyri (*AP* 30:18–19 = *TAD* A4.7:18–19) states, "We sent a letter to our lord [Bagohi the governor] and to Yehohanan the high priest and his companions the priests who are in Jerusalem and to Ostan the brother of Anan and the nobles of the Jews". Here the leadership includes not only the governor and the high priest but also the other priests and the nobility.

3. The alleged decree of Antiochus III (*Ant.* 12.3.3–4 §§138–46: thought to be mostly authentic [p. 47 above]) mentions "the senate [*gerousia*], the priests, the scribes of the temple and the temple-singers", stating that the *gerousia* met the king when he entered the city. The one puzzling thing about this document is that the high priest is not mentioned.

4. The books of Maccabees attest a "senate" (*gerousia*). This definitely functioned for the Hellenistic city established by Jason (2 Macc. 4:43–50), but this body was likely to have been in existence already because a *gerousia* was not the traditional governing body for Greek cities. Thus, Jason seems to have continued a pre-existing body, even if he reconstituted it. The letter at the beginning of 2 Maccabees claims to be from Judas Maccabee and the *gerousia* (1:10); even if this letter is fictitious, as many feel, the writer is not likely to have invented the council alongside Judas. A letter thought to be authentic is addressed to the "senate" (*gerousia*) of the Jews during the Maccabean conflict (2 Macc. 11:27). Later on Jonathan Maccabee is supposed to have written a letter on behalf of himself the high priest and "the *gerousia* and the community of priests" (*Ant.* 13.5.8 §166). Judith 11:14 assumes that the Jerusalem senate would make decisions on cultic matters.

5. A formal body appears definitely to have existed during the early period of Roman rule. When some complained of Herod's actions as governor of Galilee, because he had executed a "brigand" without permission of "the assembly" (*to sunedrion* [*Ant.* 14.9.3 §167), he was called to answer before that assembly under the chairmanship of Hyrcanus II the high priest (*Ant.* 14.9.4–5 §§168–80). Later on Herod is alleged to have executed many members of that body (*Ant.* 14.9.4 §175).

6. When there was trouble during the office of the Roman governor Florus, he called "the chief priests and the council" (*hoi archiereis kai hē boulē*) who were clearly responsible for civic order in Jerusalem (*War* 2.15.6 §331; 2.16.2 §336).

It is likely that any ruler would have had his advisers, whether they were "official" or not, and the existence of an advisory council is suggested by various sources noted above (cf. also Acts 5:21-41). The power of this body would probably have varied, being completely subservient to strong high priests but perhaps dominating the decision-making process under weaker leaders (under Herod it seems almost to have disappeared, only to be revived after his death). There is nothing to argue against such a regular body throughout much of the Second Temple period, though its status – both *de jure* and *de facto* – may have varied considerably from period to period. This seems a simpler explanation than that all the references are merely to *ad hoc* assemblies. However, it is difficult to know how early such a body developed since the earliest references are to the Greek period. Although an advisory Sanhedrin can easily be postulated for the Persian period, we have too little information to be certain.

SYNTHESIS

Grabbe, L. L. (1993a) *Leviticus*.
Sanders, E. P. (1992) *Judaism: Practice and Belief 63 BCE–66 CE*.

This chapter has covered the highly complex core of ancient Judaism. A thorough treatment of each aspect requires a good deal of detail, and only a quick survey was possible, with the danger of oversimplification. The temple, priesthood, and cult formed a coherent system, and an understanding of Second Temple Judaism (in Palestine, at least) requires one to grasp the structure of temple worship. One cannot get away from the fact that the sacrificial cult, especially blood sacrifice, lay at the heart of worship in Israel. On the other hand, the Israelite cult, like all religious ritual – and all religions have their ritual – was extremely meaningful to the participants even if we do not always understand it from our time and culture millennia later. A number of recent studies have focused on the symbolism of the cult and attempted to decipher the priestly world view which lay behind it (see Grabbe 1993a for a detailed discussion). The priestly view had a cosmological and sociological dimension, as well as a cultic.

A major question is whether we can describe how this all functioned at the time. There have been attempts to reconstruct the temple activities; for instance, Sanders (1992) has made a bold attempt to do so. One can only admire the effort, but in the end it is only speculative. The main problem is that Sanders mixes data from a variety of sources (biblical, Josephus, rabbinic, and so on) and does so without first analyzing each source to determine whether it is relevant or reliable: biblical data are not necessarily a description of what actually happened in society, Josephus sometimes idealizes, and rabbinic literature often recreates pre-70 times according to its own image. Sanders's description (1992: 112–14) of an ordinary Jew bringing an animal for sacrifice is interesting as long as it is recognized that this can be no more than an educated guess. Archaeology has given us some control over the literary texts, but much remains uncertain, and we must recognize the limits of our knowledge.

The biblical text asserts that there were multiple shrines before the time of Josiah. Most of these seem to have vanished by the early Second Temple period, and for most of the time after that, the main shrine was the Jerusalem temple, though we know that there were also temples at Gerizim, at Leonto-polis after 175 BCE and, some have suggested, even at Araq el-Emir (though present knowledge is against it: *JCH*: 188–89). Even the Jews in the Diaspora looked to the temple as the symbol of their Jewish and religious identity, even if their form of worship had of necessity ceased to have the temple cult at its center (pp. 170–75 below), as Philo shows (e.g. *Spec. Leg.* 67–70).

The center of worship in Palestine was the temple cult, and the focus of this was the sacrifices on the altar. To ignore this is to miss the essence of Jewish worship during this time and to misunderstand its main concerns and pre-occupations. However, sacrifice was not the sum total of Judaism, nor was it all that happened in the temple: the regular service also seems to have included singing and perhaps even public prayer (private prayer was appar-ently always possible). Essential to the temple cult was the system of ritual purity since all worshipers had to appear pure before God, and the sanctuary had to be protected from all pollution. These regulations had to be taken seriously and necessarily affected the lives of all worshipers in various ways (especially women). But these were not just "meaningless ritual" and in fact had deep symbolic meaning that must be understood and appreciated to comprehend Judaism of the time.

The priesthood was divided into the priests proper, who could preside at the altar, and the lower clergy or Levites, whose duty was to assist the priests as well as to undertake a variety of tasks relating to the running of the temple (e.g. security and cleaning). There are also indications that some of the Levites were temple singers. All the temple personnel were supported by the tithes and various other gifts to the temple. This regular income was vital to enable them to have the time and energy to carry out the temple functions without the distraction of having to live by another occupation.

The priesthood provided religious leadership, including the duty of teach-ing and making rulings about the application of the law. Although toward the end of the Second Temple period non-priests gained access to the written scriptures and set themselves up as teachers in some cases, there is no indica-tion that the priests ever gave up their right to decide and teach the law. Different sects had legal and other interpretations and traditions, and there was nothing to prevent their teaching them to others, but in a number of cases it is clear that they also included bona fide priests among their member-ship (e.g. the Pharisees, the Sadducees, the Qumran group; see Chapter 9 below).

The priesthood also provided the main intellectual and political leadership of Judah. The priests were the ones with the support for education and the leisure to pursue intellectual activities. Although wisdom and literature were no doubt cultivated in various circles, especially among some of the lay aristocrats, the primary group who had the time and education to study and write literature, carry out scribal activities, keep records, and cultivate esoteric knowledge were members of the clergy (including the Levites). The priests also seem to have acted as judges at certain times and/or in certain capacities, though the details of this are somewhat unclear.

We also find that through much of the Second Temple period, the high priest was the chief representative of the community to the ruling empire. He was assisted through most of this time by an advisory body called variously (in Greek) the *gerousia* (senate), *boulē* (council), or *sunedrion* (from which comes the Hebrew Sanhedrin). The only religious issues likely to be brought before the Sanhedrin, however, were such serious matters as blasphemy or perhaps desecration of the temple (cf. Josephus, *Ant.* 20.9.1 §§199–200). The Sanhedrin or other priestly body also determined the calendar, which was essential for religious observance and reckoned by the observation of the new moon each month.

In sum, the religious life of pre-70 Jews in Palestine was dominated by the priesthood and the cult. Apart from the Romans and the Herodian dynasty (when Herodian rulers were actually over Judea proper) the chief civil – as well as religious – authority was the priesthood. This does not mean that all those of priestly descent exercised this authority, but the civil institutions below emperor and king were dominated by the priesthood, especially the "chief priests" (*archiereis*). Otherwise, the people were basically free to choose their religious observances, and the opportunities for the development of sects were readily available.

8

SCRIPTURE, PRAYER, AND SYNAGOGUE

This chapter brings together what may seem to be a number of disparate topics, but they all relate to the growing importance of the written word through the Second Temple period. Several institutions first served as a way of substituting for the temple because of inaccessibility but then began to be the vehicle for effecting changes, even in the Jewish heartland around Jerusalem. These changes were:

- the growth of an authoritative set of writings which can be designated Scripture
- a strong emphasis on the interpretation of that Scripture in diverse and changing contexts
- the origin and spread of the synagogue as a place of study and worship
- the increasing importance of prayer as a means of individual and collective worship away from the temple.

The disparate nature of the sources and indeed the subjects themselves makes it difficult to preface discussion by a survey of the sources. Instead, in this chapter the sources are dealt with in each section.

SCRIBES AND LITERACY

Baumgarten, A. I. (1997) *The Flourishing of Jewish Sects in the Maccabean Era: An Interpretation.*

Blenkinsopp, Joseph (1995) *Sage, Priest, Prophet: Religious and Intellectual Leadership in Ancient Israel.*

Bowman, A. K., and G. Woolf (eds) (1994) *Literacy and Power in the Ancient World.*

Crenshaw, J. L. (1998) *Education in Ancient Israel: Across the Deadening Silence.*

Cribiore, R. (1996) *Writing, Teachers, and Students in Graeco-Roman Egypt.*

Finnegan, R. (1988) *Literacy and Orality: Studies in the Technology of Communication.*

Goodman, M. (1994b) "Texts, Scribes and Power in Roman Judaea", in A. K. Bowman and G. Woolf (eds) *Literacy and Power in the Ancient World*: 99–108.

Grabbe, L. L.(1995a) *Priests, Prophets, Diviners, Sages: A Socio-historical Study of Religious Specialists in Ancient Israel*.

Harris, W. V. (1989) *Ancient Literacy*.

Kalmin, R. (1999) *The Sage in Jewish Society of Late Antiquity*.

Mackay, E. A. (ed.) (1999) *Signs of Orality: The Oral Tradition and its Influence in the Greek and Roman World*.

Ong, W. J. (1982) *Orality and Literacy: The Technologizing of the Word*.

Schams, C. (1998) *Jewish Scribes in the Second-Temple Period*.

Schwartz, D. R. (1992) *Studies in the Jewish Background of Christianity*.

Small, J. P. (1997) *Wax Tablets of the Mind: Cognitive Studies of Memory and Literacy in Classical Antiquity*.

Street, B. V. (1984) *Literacy in Theory and Practice*.

In order to understand ancient Judaism fully, we must keep in mind that it was mainly an oral society. The extent of literacy has often been discussed, but most people in the ancient world were not literate, even in cultures with an alphabetic script rather than the more complicated cuneiform or hiero-glyphic writing systems, and we have no indication that the Jews were any different from their Greek or Near Eastern neighbors (Harris 1989). The question of schools has been much debated (Grabbe 1995a: 171–74; Crenshaw 1998). There are two issues: Did schools exist that taught scribes? Did schools exist that offered education to the general public? The answer to the first question is, possibly, but the case is not proved; the answer to the second is definitely negative. Although scribes were trained in schools in ancient Egypt and Mesopotamia, the scribal needs for a small entity such as Judah could probably be met by a form of apprenticeship. If there were schools for others than scribes, they would have been for the wealthy and aristocratic, though these could probably afford to hire tutors.

Thus, a few people in most Jewish communities could read and write, some could read with various levels of proficiency, most could do neither; in any case, the services of the professional scribe were much in demand since he often had duties similar to a modern civil servant and lawyer as well. Scribes were an important part of the intellectual scene during the Second Temple period. However, one of the main employers of scribes through much of the Second Temple period was likely to have been the temple, and these scribes were probably priests or Levites. Levites as scribes are mentioned in a number of biblical passages (1 Chron. 2:55; 24:6; 2 Chron. 34:13). Temple scribes are referred to in the decree of Antiochus III about 200 BCE (*Ant.* 12.3.3 §§142). Perhaps the most famous passage on the scribe is that of Ben Sira (38:24–39:11) who makes the scribe responsible for knowledge and study of God's law. It should be kept in mind, however, Ben Sira's close association with the temple (some have argued that he was himself a priest). It is not clear that Ben Sira was suggesting that everyone with scribal training was to be an expert in the law. (For a thorough study of scribes, see Schams 1998.)

The differences between the society of the ancient world and today – and the greater amount of oral culture then – have been exaggerated, a distortion which more recent studies have criticized (cf. Bowman/Woolf 1994: 1–16; Street 1984; Harris 1989). All societies, including contemporary Western ones, are a mixture of the oral and the literate, and oral tradition plays a remarkable role even today. The argument that the development of literacy changed the way people thought in antiquity (e.g. Ong 1982) has been widely criticized as simplistic (cf. Finnegan 1988; Street 1984). Although the wider horizon of this debate is beyond our purposes here, it will nevertheless help us to consider the implications of the change from the teaching authority of the priests to a set of sacred writings collected into a canon and with a fixed text.

We need to keep in mind two aspects of the question in the Second Temple period: first, there was the far-reaching change from a mainly oral law and tradition to written scriptures; secondly, most people knew the sacred writings in an oral context, perhaps via hearsay, exposition and paraphrase, and perhaps public readings. Whether literacy increased in the Hellenistic period is possible (Baumgarten 1997: 114–36) but not certain. It is also a moot point whether written scriptures reached the hands of ordinary Jews more, since the number of ordinary people who had access to them and could read was likely to have been small (the main implications of Harris 1989). Scriptural interpretation was (from the indications of surviving sources) still in the hands of an elite; however, this elite ceased to be confined to the temple priesthood. It may have included priests who had broken with the temple (including some of the people of the Qumran scrolls?), scribes who were not priests or Levites, and others for whom the tradition was an avocation (the Pharisees?). In that somewhat qualified sense, then, the scriptures became democratized (this nuance seems to be missed by Baumgarten 1997: 114–36).

SCRIPTURE AND CANON

Barton, J. (1997) *The Spirit and the Letter: Studies in the Biblical Canon = Holy Writings, Sacred Text: The Canon in Early Christianity.*
—— (1997) *Making the Christian Bible = How the Bible Came to Be.*
Bauer, W. (1971) *Orthodoxy and Heresy in Earliest Christianity.*
Beckwith, R. (1985) *The Old Testament Canon of the New Testament Church and its Background in Early Judaism.*

Bolin, T. M. (1996) "When the End Is the Beginning: The Persian Period and the Origins of the Biblical Tradition", *SJOT* 10: 3–15.

Davies, P. R. (1998) *Scribes and Schools: The Canonization of the Hebrew Scriptures.*

Grabbe, L. L. (1997g) "Are Historians of Ancient Palestine Fellow Creatures – Or Different Animals?" in L. L. Grabbe (ed.) *Can a "History of Israel" Be Written?*: 19–36.

—— (1998a) *Ezra and Nehemiah.*

—— (1998c) "'The Exile' under the Theodolite: Historiography as Triangulation", in L. L. Grabbe (ed.) *Leading Captivity Captive: "The Exile" as History and Ideology*: 80–100.

—— (2000g) "Jewish Historiography and Scripture in the Hellenistic Period", in L. L. Grabbe (ed.) *Did Moses Speak Attic?*

Kooij, A. van der, and K. van der Toorn (eds) (1998) *Canonization and Decanonization: Papers Presented to the International Conference of the Leiden Institute for the Study of Religions (Lisor) Held at Leiden 9–10 January 1997.*

Lemche, N. P. (1993) "The Old Testament – a Hellenistic Book?" *SJOT* 7: 163–93.

Lewis, J. P. (1964) "What Do We Mean by Jabneh?" *Journal of the Bible and Religion* 32: 125–32.

Orlinsky, H. A. (1991) "Some Terms in the Prologue to Ben Sira and the Hebrew Canon", *JBL* 110: 483–90.

Main texts

There is probably no subject in the history of Judaism about which more is said and less known than that of canon. The actual references, in both Jewish and Christian literature, are only a handful and can be surveyed quickly. The real problem is how to interpret them. The earliest evidence relating to a canon of any sort involves the LXX translation of the Pentateuch which was probably done about the middle of the third century BCE (see pp. 49–50 above).

Ben Sira is perhaps the first writer to indicate a specific collection of books with religious authority. Writing about 132 BCE the grandson of Ben Sira and his translator speaks several times of "the law and the prophets and the other (or the rest of the) books", in the Prologue to his grandfather's work. He nowhere lists these books, but his threefold division is significant. It looks as if there was a definite category called "the Law" and one called "the Prophets", the third being probably not a category so much as a miscellaneous collection of "the other books" or the "rest of the books". However, the existence of a miscellaneous category suggests that the first two were probably more or less fixed. Ben Sira himself may give some firm indications of what books went into the "Bible" of his time in his "Praise of the Fathers" (44–50; Grabbe 2000g). Here he indicates that essentially the present biblical text of the Pentateuch, Joshua to 2 Kings, 1–2 Chronicles, and the Prophets were in front of him; one can only say "essentially" the present biblical text since it is clear that slightly different versions of some parts of the OT circulated in Hebrew until at least the 1st century CE (see pp. 158–65 below for the development of the text).

2 Maccabees 2:13–15 states that Nehemiah collected a "library" (*bibliothēkē*) containing a collection of "the books concerning kings and prophets and of David and the letters of kings about the devoted things (*anathēmata*)". This passage is often cited as evidence that the canonization process had begun already in the Persian period. However, if we accept this statement about Nehemiah, we then encounter problems, because this is clearly a tradition which omits the work of Ezra and thus differs from the present Hebrew canon (cf. Grabbe 1998a: 88–9). The statement that Judas Maccabeus similarly collected books dispersed because of the Maccabean crisis is more credible because of being closer to the actual time of the alleged event, though whether that has anything to do with canonization is debatable.

The situation at **Qumran** is instructive for any theory of canonization. Every book of the present Hebrew canon, except Esther, is found there. On the other hand, it is also evident that many books not in the traditional Hebrew canon were treated as authoritative. There is also the problem that some books look like possible "substitutes" for existing biblical books. For example, it has been suggested that the *Temple Scroll* (11QT) might be conceived as a substitute for Deuteronomy or even the entire Pentateuch. We also have to take account of scrolls like the Psalms Scroll (11QPsalms^a), which by and large agrees with the present canonical Hebrew book of Psalms but has an additional five psalms. On the other hand, the recently published 4QMMT (*circa* mid-second century BCE) speaks of heeding or understanding "the book of Moses, the books of the prophets, and David" (4Q397 frags 14–21:10 = 4Q398 frags 14–17:2–3), suggesting the three divisions known from Ben Sira.

Philo nowhere discusses the concept of canonization, or which books might be authoritative for Jews. Much of his work is commentary, and almost all of it relates to the Pentateuch. He does not talk about other books of the Hebrew Bible or suggest that books other than the Pentateuch are authoritative, yet he does have some quotations from other books: 1 Samuel (1:28 in *Quod Deus* 6 and *Somn.* 1.254; 2:5 in *Quod Deus* 10 and *Mut.* 143; 9:9 in *Quod Deus* 139, *Migr. Abr.* 38, *Quis Heres* 78), Psalms (23:1 in *Agric.* 50 and *Mut.* 115; 37:4 in *Plant.* 39 and *Somn.* 2.242), Proverbs (8:22 in *Ebriet.* 31 and *Virt.* 62), and Hosea (14:9, 10 in *Plant.* 138 and *Mut.* 139). Much has been made of a supposed "Alexandrian canon", which supposedly contained the books of the Apocrypha as well as the contents of the Hebrew Bible. This is problematic, however, since there is no evidence that Alexandrian Jews such as Philo had such books as a part of their canon. The Apocrypha as a part of the Greek Bible can be clearly attested only for Christians.

Josephus gives one of the most important passages about canonization (*Ag. Apion* 1.8 §§37–43), which states:

> Our books, those which are justly accredited, are but two and twenty, and contain the record of all time. Of these five are the books of Moses, comprising the laws and the traditional history from the birth of man down to the death of the lawgiver. . . . From the death of Moses until Artaxerxes . . . the prophets subsequent to Moses wrote the history of the events of their own times in thirteen books. The remaining four books contain hymns to God and precepts for the conduct of human life.

We should be careful to notice what he says and what he does not say. It is obvious that he describes much of the traditional Hebrew canon; however, a exact delineation is not found, and the number of 22 books should not mislead us into saying that it coincides with the present Hebrew canon. The Hebrew canon now has 24 books, and it is difficult to get it to fit into 22. The suggestion that Lamentations was combined with Jeremiah or Ruth with Judges, for example, ignores the fact that Lamentations and Ruth are in different divisions of the Hebrew canon. Although it may have been that Josephus's list was exactly the same as the present Hebrew canon, it more likely differed slightly.

In **4 Ezra** 14:44–46 is a curious story about Ezra's having restored the law by divine inspiration after it had been lost. Nothing along this line is found in any of the extant books of Ezra in the Hebrew or Greek Bibles. To what extent it is a traditional story and to what extent it is invented by the writer of 4 Ezra is a moot point (cf. Grabbe 1998a: 90–91). However, it refers to 94 books, 24 of which are exoteric and 70 esoteric. The 24 seem to coincide with the canonical books, since the number agrees with the contents of the traditional Hebrew canon. We cannot be sure that the content was the same, but there is a good chance that it was.

One of the myths of modern scholarship, often adumbrated in the context of canonization, is that of the **"Synod of Jamnia"**. With the work done on rabbinic literature in the past several decades, this should have long been expunged from discussion, but it still rears its head. Yavneh was of course not a synod, along the analogy of the synods known from church history (see pp. 120–24 above). Although in the Yavnean traditions there are a few references to a discussion of whether certain books "make the hands unclean" (*M. Yad.* 3:5, over Qohelet and Song of Songs) plus some other late traditions of debate (*B. Meg.* 7a over Esther; even over Ezekiel: *B. Shab.* 13b; *B. Hag.* 13a; *B. Men.* 45a), there is no discussion of canonization as such nor any suggestion that canonization was on the agenda (cf. Lewis 1964). Indeed, in each case the canonical status of the books in question is affirmed. Within rabbinic literature, the present books of the Hebrew canon – and only they – are treated as canonical.

The Christian sources give a similar picture to the Jewish ones. **Luke 24:44** refers to "the law of Moses, the prophets, and the psalms" (which look like the same division designations as 4QMMT). This is often taken to be a reference to the threefold division of the present Hebrew Bible; however, even if this is correct, it is not clear what the contents of "the psalms" section was. **Jude 14–16** quotes *1 Enoch* 1:9 and clearly accepts it as authoritative. To argue, as some do, that the book of Jude was only on the margins of early Christianity depends on a monolithic view of the development of Christianity which has been unacceptable since Bauer's *Rechtgläubigkeit und Ketzerei* appeared in 1934 (ET Bauer 1971). The earliest Christian biblical manuscripts show a variety of content and include a number of the Apocrypha. When we turn to the various patristic writers, we find a large variation in the contents list of the OT. **Melito of Sardis** in the mid-second century was the first Christian writer to show any consciousness of a canon of scripture as such. According to Eusebius (*His. Eccl.* 4.26.13–14) he gave a list of sacred books that included the Wisdom of Solomon but omitted Esther and Lamentations. Even today, a number of different canons are accepted by different Christian churches. Most people will be aware that the Protestant churches tend to follow the traditional Hebrew canon, while the Roman Catholic and Greek Orthodox churches also give a place to the deutero-canonical books (even though the great church father Jerome himself favored the Hebrew canon). What is often not realized is that the Ethiopic church accepts both *1 Enoch* and *Jubilees* into its canon.

Conclusions about canonization

Canonization was a complex process which continued for several centuries and cannot be separated from particular communities or institutions (e.g. the priesthood). Neither can it be easily separated from textual standardization: although the two processes were somewhat different, they ran side by side and affected each other. Evidence that a particular book was "canonical" at a particular time does not immediately tell us whether it had the exact same text as the book in the traditional Hebrew canon. To summarize the main points about canon, I would note the following (on which I comment further in Grabbe 2000g):

1. The need for a set of written scriptures was probably felt at least by the Persian period. The Judean deportations in the early sixth century and the destruction of Jerusalem about 587 BCE were traumatic events. People often become aware of their traditions when there are major disruptions, when their heritage and even their identity might be lost. It seems unlikely, prima facie, that no attempt to gather the traditions or create a national or

ethnic "history" would have been made after the fall of Jerusalem. The fact that some sections of the Deuteronomistic History show a rather accurate outline of the kings of Israel and Judah, as attested by external sources, suggests that the distance between the writing of these (or at least their sources) and the actual events was not great (cf. Grabbe 1997g: 24–26; 1998c: 84–90).

2. The concept of canon in our modern sense may have taken a long time to develop. Some books evidently took on authoritative status earlier than others, beginning probably with the Pentateuch since these books occur in all known Jewish (including Samaritan) and Christian collections. Other books may have been associated with them, but with lesser authority, for quite some time. The fact that the LXX "canon" seems larger than the traditional Hebrew canon may be because the Pentateuch was given primary status in Alexandria (cf. Philo), and the associated books formed a looser, more flexible collection.

3. A good portion of the Pentateuch and the Former and Latter Prophets seem to have been in existence and accepted as authoritative in some circles by the end of the Persian period. The evidence for this is Ben Sira 44–50 and also the translation of the Pentateuch into Greek in Alexandria. We cannot be sure to what extent the books continued to develop after that, but it was probably mainly on the textual plane (though different textual versions of some books circulated side by side, as the next section shows). The bulk of the Hebrew Bible is therefore not a "Hellenistic book" (cf. Lemche 1993); whether it is a "Persian book" or whether portions of it can be pushed back to the time of the monarchy is a question which cannot be answered at the moment.

4. Some books are, of course, from the Hellenistic period, as critical scholarship has long recognized, such as Qohelet (though see pp. 42–44 above) and Daniel. Some recent works put the completion of the books of Chronicles after the time of Alexander (see pp. 19–21 above). Books which might be from either the Persian or the Hellenistic period are Ezra and Nehemiah, Esther, Ruth, and the Song of Songs. If one includes Jewish writings which entered other canons (albeit in Greek or other translations), we could perhaps add as post-Alexander the books of 1 Esdras, *1 Enoch* (except 37–71), Tobit, Ben Sira, *Jubilees*, Judith, and 1 and 2 Maccabees. In that sense, a substantial percentage of the OT text is Hellenistic in origin.

5. The contents of the "canon" continued to remain fluid at least to the end of Second Temple times. The Qumran scrolls give no indication of a closed canon in the later sense of the term, and the LXX collection also seems to have had books not found in the later Hebrew canon. It may well be that there were different grades of authority which continued to operate in some or even all Jewish circles (cf. Philo).

DEVELOPMENT OF THE TEXT

Barthélemy, D. (1963) *Les devanciers d'Aquila.*

Brock, S. P. (1996) *The Recensions of the Septuagint Version of I Samuel.*

Brock, S. P., *et al.* (1973) *A Classified Bibliography of the Septuagint.*

Clines, D. J. A. (1984b) *The Esther Scroll: The Story of the Story.*

Cook, J. (1997) *The Septuagint of Proverbs: Jewish and/or Hellenistic Proverbs?*

Cross, F. M. and S. Talmon (eds) (1975) *Qumran and the History of the Biblical Text.*

De Troyer, K. (1997) *Het einde van de Alpha-tekst van Ester: Vertaal- en verhaaltechniek van MT 8,1–17, LXX 8,1–17 en AT 7,14–41.*

Díez Macho, A. (1960) "The Recently Discovered Palestinian Targum: Its Antiquity and Relationship with the Other Targums", in *Congress Volume Oxford 1959*: 222–45.

Dogniez, Cécile (1995) *Bibliography of the Septuagint/Bibliographie de la Septante (1970–1993).*

Dorothy, C. V. (1997) *The Books of Esther: Structure, Genre and Textual Integrity.*

Grabbe, L. L. (1977) *Comparative Philology and the Text of Job: A Study in Methodology.*

—— (1979) "The Jannes/Jambres Tradition in Targum Pseudo-Jonathan and its Date", *JBL* 98: 393–401.

—— (1982) "Aquila's Translation and Rabbinic Exegesis", *JJS* 33: 527–36.

—— (1992b) "The Translation Technique of the Greek Minor Versions: Translations or Revisions?" in G. J. Brooke and B. Lindars (eds) *Septuagint, Scrolls and Cognate Writings*: 505–56.

—— (1999e) Review of K. De Troyer, *Het einde van de Alpha-tekst van Ester: Vertaal- en verhaaltechniek van MT 8,1–17, LXX 8,1–17 en AT 7,14–41, CBQ* 61: 331–32.

Greenspoon, L. (1997) "'It's All Greek to Me': Septuagint Studies Since 1968", *CR: BS* 5: 147–74.

Hanhart, R. (1999) *Studien zur Septuaginta und zum hellenistischen Judentum.*

Jeansonne, S. P. (1988) *The Old Greek Translation of Daniel 7–12.*

Jellicoe, S. (1968) *The Septuagint and Modern Study.*

Jobes, K. H. (1996) *The Alpha-Text of Esther: Its Character and Relationship to the Masoretic Text.*

Lacocque, A. (1999) "The Different Versions of Esther", *Biblical Interpretation* 7: 301–22.

McLay, Tim (1996) *The OG and Th Versions of Daniel.*

McNamara, M. (1966) *The New Testament and the Palestinian Targum to the Pentateuch.*

Meadowcroft, T. J. (1995) *Aramaic Daniel and Greek Daniel: A Literary Comparision.*

Schürer: 3:474–93.

Swete, H. (1914) *An Introduction to the Old Testament in Greek.*

Talmon, S. and Y. Yadin (eds) (1999) *Masada VI: Yigael Yadin Excavations 1963–1965, Final Reports*.

Tov, E. (1988) "The Septuagint", in *Mikra*: 161–88.

—— (1992) *Textual Criticism of the Hebrew Bible*.

—— (1997a) *Der Text der Hebräischen Bibel: Handbuch der Textkritik*.

—— (1997b) *The Text-Critical Use of the Septuagint in Biblical Research*.

—— (1999a) *The Greek and Hebrew Bible: Collected Essays on the Septuagint*.

Ulrich, E. C. (1978) *The Qumran Text of Samuel and Josephus*.

—— (1999) *The Dead Sea Scrolls and the Origins of the Bible*.

Waltke, B. K. (1965) *Prolegomena to the Samaritan Pentateuch*.

—— (1970) "The Samaritan Pentateuch and the Text of the Old Testament", in J. B. Payne (ed.) *New Perspectives on the Old Testament*: 212–39.

Weitzman, M. P. (1999) *The Syriac Version of the Old Testament: An Introduction*.

Wernberg-Møller, P. (1961) "Some Observations on the Relationship of the Peshitta Version of the Book of Genesis to the Palestinian Targum Fragments", *Studia Theologica* 15: 128–80.

—— (1962) "Prolegomena to a Re-examination of the Palestinian Targum Fragments of the Book of Genesis Published by P. Kahle, and their Relationship to the Peshitta", *JSS* 7: 253–66.

York, A. D. (1974–75) "The Dating of Targumic Literature", *JSJ* 5: 49–62.

The growth and development of the biblical text has been a major area of discussion in the past half-century since the Qumran scrolls were first discovered. For a couple of centuries previously, the data had not changed. There was the traditional Hebrew text, called the **Masoretic text (MT)**, consisting of a consonantal text plus vowels, accents, and other markers giving a good deal of information on how the text was read. Although some had proposed that the vocalization was an artificial creation by medieval Jewish scholars, the evidence was mostly against this (cf. Grabbe 1977: 179–97). Although the vowels and accents had been added sometime in the seventh to the ninth centuries CE, they generally represented an old reading tradition. Nevertheless, the earliest Masoretic manuscripts were not known to be any older than the ninth century. Otherwise, the text was attested only in quotations in rabbinic literature (without vowels and accents), though these quotations almost always agreed with the Masoretic consonantal text.

The **Samaritan Pentateuch (SP)** did not become known to European scholars until the seventeenth century. The long debate as to whether it represented a separate tradition or only a corrupted version of the MT is long over as far as most textual scholars are concerned (though it still continues to some extent; see below). One of the advantages of this version is that it is in Hebrew; unfortunately, good editions of the SP have not been available, and textual judgments have frequently been made on inadequate editions of the text. Finally, there were the Greek versions, primarily the **Old Greek or Septuagint (LXX)**. This had the advantage of being preserved independently of the MT, and some of its manuscripts were several centuries older than any MT manuscript. The disadvantage was that it was not in Hebrew, and any assumed underlying Hebrew text was always a scholarly reconstruction and thus hypothetical, and will not be further discussed here (see Tov 1992 for details).

In addition, there were a number of late versions. From the rabbinic period Aramaic translations of portions of the Hebrew text were known and used, the **Targums**. Some books (e.g. Daniel, Ezra, Nehemiah, 1 and 2 Chronicles) did not have targumic versions, but the Pentateuch had three targums: a somewhat literal translation called the *Targum Onqelos*, a version discovered only in the 1950s called *Targum Neofiti*, and a rather midrashic version called *Targum Pseudo-Jonathan* (because it was wrongly associated with the *Targum Jonathan to the Prophets*). Targum Onqelos was once connected with Aquila, a translator of the Hebrew Bible into Greek ("Onqelos" is one way of rendering "Aquila" into Hebrew), but it is now accepted that there was probably not a single translator of the targums but that they represent community literature in some sense. A translation was made into Syriac sometime about the third or fourth century CE, called the **Peshitta** (Weitzman 1999). This is usually assumed to have been done by Syriac Christians, though some have argued for a Jewish translation or at least Jewish influence (cf. Wernberg-Møller 1961; 1962; Tov 1992: 152; 1997a: 126–27). Also known were the so-called **Greek Minor Versions**, known only in fragments, under the names of Aquila, Symmachus, and Theodotion. The Old Latin was a translation of the LXX, but about 400 CE the well-known patristic figure Jerome translated a Latin version directly from the Hebrew, called the **Vulgate**.

Beginning in 1947 the manuscripts found in various sites in the Judean Desert changed the situation dramatically, with manuscripts centuries older than any biblical manuscript known heretofore, going back to 200 BCE or so in some cases (according to some paleographers). It soon became clear that representatives of all three of the text-types previously known in Jewish history were in use by those producing the Scrolls. Good examples of the Masoretic-type consonantal text established that that tradition was not a late invention by the Masoretes as some had argued. In a number of cases, even the main textual divisions were shown to have a history going back at least a millennium before the earliest dated MT manuscripts (see the survey of studies in Grabbe 1977: 179–97). Even the famous long Isaiah scroll from Cave 1 (1QIs^a) is basically a MT text-type, despite the impression sometimes given in early studies, while its fellow Isaiah scroll (1QIs^b) is even closer to the known MT.

The biblical manuscripts found in the Judean desert outside Qumran all exhibit the MT-type of text. Perhaps the best-preserved example is the scroll of the Minor Prophets (Mur 88). Although it has no vowels or accents, it is otherwise indistinguishable from a Masoretic manuscript a thousand years later. Its differences from the *BHS* are very much like the minor variations among Masoretic manuscripts. The biblical texts from Masada are quite fragmentary, but they also fall into the MT-type of text (Talmon/Yadin 1999: 24–26).

The LXX text-type is also well represented at Qumran. There are a few fragments of the LXX in Greek (4Q119–122 = 4QLXXLev^{a,b}, 4QLXXNum, 4QDeut). Other manuscripts, although in Hebrew, show a text in line with that known from the LXX. The different order and text of the LXX Jeremiah, for example, are attested in 4QJer^a (4Q70). In other cases, readings known from the LXX have been found in texts that otherwise belong to another text-type. Thus, the Scrolls have well established that readings unique to the LXX are in many cases due to the use of a different underlying Hebrew reading and not the product of the translator.

Examples of the SP text-type are also attested among the Qumran scrolls (4Q22 = 4QpaleoExod^m; Sanderson 1986). These are not specifically Samaritan because the unique sectarian readings (e.g. the extra addition to the Decalogue referring to Mount Gerizim) are not present (where these passages survive), suggesting that we have a stage of the SP before it was taken over and adapted by the Samaritan community. This leads to the conclusion that most of the peculiarities of the SP were not developed by the Samaritans themselves but had already originated in another (Jewish?) context and were then taken over by the Samaritan community for whatever reason. It is now agreed that the SP has a long history, going back to Second Temple times. More difficult is its relationship to the MT and the LXX. Its oft agreement with the LXX has led some to suggest that it was the original on which the LXX was based, but this is a superficial judgment since the SP is actually closer to the MT than the LXX in its primary readings (Waltke 1965; Waltke 1970). Many SP passages indicate expansion from other sections of the text, which gives it greater bulk without increasing the amount of primary material (e.g. Exod. 32:10–11, expanded by an addition from Deut. 9:20). The SP resemblance to the LXX is caused by the secondary expansions that they share.

The exact relationship of the LXX to the MT was long debated since there are many differences between the two. In most books of the Bible the differences affect mainly individual words or phases; however, in some books the LXX can be said to represent not just a different text-type but almost a different version of the book. For example, the LXX text is one-eighth shorter in Job and one-sixth shorter in Jeremiah, while the LXX in Proverbs is often different from the MT (cf. Cook 1997). The text of Qohelet appears to be one of the Minor Versions, that of Aquila (see below). Recent finds from Qumran and comparative textual study indicate that many of these differences between the LXX and the MT are due to a different Hebrew text having been used by the LXX translators (as noted above). Yet this is not the full story, for many differences can also be attributed to the translation techniques being used and the attempts to render a Semitic text into an Indo-European language. At any given point, either explanation for apparent textual differences is theoretically possible, and only careful study can show which is likely to be the correct explanation.

As time went on, attempts were made to revise the LXX text, apparently to bring it more in line with the developing Hebrew text. This led first of all to more than one version of the LXX itself. One revision which was probably pre-70 is the **"Lucian revision"**, named for the patristic figure around AD 400 once thought to have created the revision. However, the basic Lucian revision is attested in texts from Jewish circles long before the historical Lucian: for example, it seems clear that Josephus used the Lucianic text in Greek as the basis of his account paralleling Samuel and Kings (Ulrich 1978; Brock 1996). This suggests that the patristic figure may have had something to do with the final revision but did not initiate the first revision, which was probably Jewish in origin.

There is also evidence of another revision now called the **kaige** (Barthélemy 1963), named from the Greek particle used to translate the Hebrew particle *wĕgam* "and also" and which is one of the characteristics of this version. The *kaige* version used to be associated with the patristic writer Theodotion of the second century CE; however, it is clear that the basic "Theodotion" text was in existence long before the historical figure, and the Greek Minor Prophets scroll from the Judean desert (8ḤevXIIgr) confirmed the basic text in the first century CE. Again, modern scholarship is more or less unanimous that the *kaige* represents a Jewish revision of the LXX to bring it more into line with the Hebrew text (cf. Grabbe 1992b). This text may later have been revised by the historical Theodotion to improve the Greek (Brock 1996).

In addition to the Theodotion version there were two other Greek Minor Versions. The translation of **Aquila** was supposed to have been made by a convert to Judaism who produced a very literal translation into Greek, literal to the point that very small elements of the Hebrew text were rendered even when they would have made little sense to a Greek speaker (e.g. the Hebrew particle *'et* as the sign of the direct object was sometimes translated by the Greek preposition *sun* "with"). By this time the LXX was widely used by Christians, and Jews were thus less comfortable with it; Aquila's translation, despite its woodenness, apparently became quite popular among Greek-speaking Jews. **Symmachus** was said to have been an Ebionite (a Jewish–Christian sect) who produced a fluent translation in good Greek. Since the Ebionites do not appear to have long survived the early period of the Christian church, this was probably some time in the second century CE.

With his theory of a *kaige* recension, Barthélemy (1963) challenged the idea of separate translators. Instead he proposed that each of these was merely a revision of the basic *kaige* text. This thesis has been widely accepted; however, although the Theodotion version seems to be clearly a revision of the *kaige*

text, a case can be made for Aquila and Symmachus to be new and independent translations (Grabbe 1992b, though Aquila may have followed a school
of translation that had developed further the *kaige* principles). In any case,
Aquila and Symmachus (as well as the historical Theodotion) are probably
to be dated after 70 and are therefore not so relevant for pre-70 Judaism.
The picture that emerges is of a series of revisions of the LXX text because of
perceived differences between it and various forms of the Hebrew text, which
itself was developing and circulating in more than one version.

The scrolls from Qumran and other sites in the Judean desert have both
clarified many points and also made it patent that the history of the text is
more complicated than previously thought. It is not always easy to delineate
a particular text-type, but it could be misleading to assume that all the
various biblical manuscripts found at Qumran could be shoehorned into one
of the three main text-types previously known. This has been attempted (e.g.
Cross in Cross/Talmon 1975: 177–95, 278–92, 306–20), but there are good
arguments to accept that there is greater diversity than this among the
Qumran manuscripts (cf. Tov 1992: 114–17, 185–87; 1997a: 95–97, 152–
53). We cannot put this great diversity at Qumran down to the unofficial
eccentricities of a breakaway sect. On the contrary, it is clear that a priestly
writer such as Josephus was quite willing to use the LXX text (sometimes in
its Lucianic version) as the basis of his history even when it differed considerably from the MT. For example, his Esther story is based on the LXX version
with its variations and extra content, and his story of the initial return after
the exile is based on 1 Esdras (cf. Grabbe 1998a: 81–86).

One of the causes of some of the debate is the sharp line traditionally drawn
between lower (textual) and higher (traditio-historical) criticism. Rather
than simply the existence of several textual variations among the Qumran
scrolls, we may actually be observing a text still growing organically. As
Talmon has noted, the textual and the traditio-historical are closely inter-
connected at this point (in Cross/Talmon 1975: 327–32). The fluidity of the
text, at least for certain books, is well illustrated from some recent studies. As
is well known, the Greek Daniel is known in two versions, the older LXX
version preserved in only a few manuscripts and the later "Theodotion" version which is found in most manuscripts. Although the differences are often
explained on the basis of a differing Hebrew or Aramaic text (e.g. Jeansonne
1988; contrast McLay 1996), others have argued that there is at least a
strong theological basis for the differences in many passages (Meadowcroft
1996). Another example is Esther which also has two Greek versions, the
LXX and the alpha-text (sometimes known as the L- or Lucianic text),
which has been explained on the basis of differing Hebrew texts (Clines
1984b; Jobes 1996; Dorothy 1997). De Troyer, however, has recently argued
that the alpha-text is a revision to interpret the book in the light of events in
the time of Agrippa I (De Troyer 1997; cf. Grabbe 1999e: 331–32); see also
Lacocque 1999.

In recent years, a good deal of work has been done on the **Aramaic targums**. The rabbinic targums have played an important role alongside the Bible itself from the rabbinic period to the present. The question is when targumizing began and whether any of the rabbinic targums are as early as the Second Temple period. Since the 1950s there has been a considerable debate over whether there was once a "pre-Christian Palestinian targum", widely used by the Jews and containing many interpretative traditions that may also have influenced Christianity (see especially McNamara 1966; also Díez Macho 1960). Although the issue is too complicated to go into in detail here and is in any case not fully settled, it seems that the case of a single pre-Christian Palestine targum has not been made, for several reasons. First, we know that the Aramaic translations of some books were available, because remains have been found at Qumran (4QtgJob = 4Q157; 4QtgLev = 4Q156; 11QtgJob = 11Q10), but since the finds are so far limited to Leviticus and Job, this does not suggest that a targum of the whole Bible had been made. Second, the targumic material from Qumran represents a fairly literal translation and gives no support for the idea that a paraphrastic, midrashic targum analogous to Targum Pseudo-Jonathan (and to a lesser extent to Neofiti) was in circulation. Third, the argument of Díez Macho that such targums were non-rabbinic does not mean that they were necessarily pre-rabbinic (York 1974–75). Fourth, some of the alleged early traditions in the Targum Pseudo-Jonathan do not stand up to investigation (Grabbe 1979).

Part of the argument about the targums has to do with their supposed origin in the synagogue services (see pp. 170–75 below). This is a complicated question, but so far there is no evidence that the targums originated in spontaneous oral translation in synagogue services. On the contrary, the targums from Qumran and the Targum Onqelos look like learned translations, the product of a scribe or an academy of some sort, not the mere collection of a popular oral tradition. The later midrashic targums such as Pseudo-Jonathan could be the product of a popular synagogue tradition (though this is not necessary), but they could nevertheless have built on what was originally a written tradition. It seems that the most persuasive case is of a targumic tradition which began as written fairly literal translations of the Hebrew text and that their use in the synagogue developed from the existence of written targums (even if written targums were not allowed in the service itself).

Summary about textual developments

1. The existence and use of a number of text-types among the Jews at least until the first century CE is clearly demonstrated.

2. There is a still a question of how many text-types there were. The argument that all the variants can be reduced to three is not convincing, on the other hand.

3. A sharp line between textual and redactional criticism cannot necessarily be drawn since it is clear that some biblical books circulated in more than version which differed in more than just the normal variants associated with textual development.

4. There is a preference for the MT-text-type in areas outside Qumran, but none of these predates the first century.

SCRIPTURAL INTERPRETATION

Auld, A. G. (1994) *Kings Without Privilege: David and Moses in the Story of the Bible's Kings*.

Brewer, D. I. (1992) *Techniques and Assumptions in Jewish Exegesis before 70 CE*.

Brooke, G. J. (1985) *Exegesis at Qumran: 4Q Florilegium in its Jewish Context*.

Feldman, L. H. (1998a) *Studies in Josephus' Rewritten Bible*.

—— (1998b) *Josephus's Interpretation of the Bible*.

Fishbane, M. (1985) *Biblical Interpretation in Ancient Israel*.

Grabbe, L. L. (1982b) "Aquila's Translation and Rabbinic Exegesis", *JJS* 33: 527–36.

—— (1988a) *Etymology in Early Jewish Interpretation: The Hebrew Names in Philo*.

—— (1997a) *Wisdom of Solomon*.

—— (1998a) *Ezra and Nehemiah*.

Harrington, D. J. (1986) "The Bible Rewritten (Narratives)", in R. A. Kraft and G. W. E. Nickelsburg (eds) *Early Judaism and its Modern Interpreters*: 239–47.

Hay, D. M. (1979–80) "Philo's References to Other Allegorists", *SPA* 6: 41–75.

—— (ed.) (1991) *Both Literal and Allegorical: Studies in Philo of Alexandria's Questions and Answers on Genesis and Exodus*.

Horgan, M. P. (1979) *Pesharim: Qumran Interpretations of Biblical Books*.

Horst, P. W. van der (1998) "Sortes: Sacred Books as Instant Oracles in Late Antiquity", in L. V. Rutgers, *et al.*, *The Use of Sacred Books in the Ancient World*: 143–73.

Longenecker, R. N. (1999) *Biblical Exegesis in the Apostolic Period*.

Mulder, M. J., and H. Sysling (eds) (1990) *Mikra: Text, Translation, Reading and Interpretation of the Hebrew Bible in Ancient Judaism and Early Christianity*.

Neusner, J. (1981) *Judaism: The Evidence of the Mishnah*.

Porton, G. G. (1976–82) *The Traditions of Rabbi Ishmael*.

—— (1981) "Defining Midrash", in J. Neusner (ed.) *The Ancient Study of Judaism*: 1.55–92.

—— (1992) "Midrash", *ABD*: 4.818–22.

Pulikottil, P. U. (2000) *Transmission of the Biblical Text in the Qumran Scrolls: The Case of the Large Isaiah Scroll (1QIs^a)*.

Sæbø, M. (ed.) (1996) *Hebrew Bible/Old Testament: The History of its Interpretation, Volume I: From the Beginnings to the Middle Ages (Until 1300), Part 1: Antiquity*.

Schultz, R. L. (1999) *The Search for Quotation: Verbal Parallels in the Prophets*.

Snaith, John G. (1967) "Biblical Quotations in the Hebrew of Ecclesiasticus", *JTS* 18: 1–12.

Trebolle Barrera, J. (1998) *The Jewish Bible and the Christian Bible: An Introduction to the History of the Bible*.

Willi, T. (1995) *Juda–Jehud–Israel: Studien zum Selbstverständnis des Judentums in persischer Zeit*.

The subject of scriptural interpretation is a huge one since it takes into account all the various means by which writings with the status of scripture are given meaning and also serve as a source of meaning in the contemporary situation. This includes everything from commentary to translation, and only a brief survey can be given here. For further discussion, see especially the essays in Sæbø (1996), Trebolle Barrera (1998: 423–89), Mulder/Sysling (1990); unfortunately the brief discussion of Jewish exegesis in Longenecker (1999: 6–35) does not take account of recent scholarship on rabbinic literature (despite the discussion in xix–xxvi). A number of individual studies will be noted below.

As will be obvious, scriptural interpretation could not begin until there was a body of writings conceived of as scripture. When this situation first obtained is a moot point. Fishbane (1985) has provided a valuable service in pointing out the way tradition may have developed to include intertextual allusions and interpretation in the biblical text itself. While much of what he says has been a source for further study, many scholars would say that the question of when the tradition became sufficiently authoritative to be the object of interpretation is still too uncertain to be so dogmatic about it (see pp. 152–57 above). It seems unlikely that "intra-scriptural exegesis" had begun before the exile, whatever the state of written portions of what became the Bible, and stories often related to biblical interpretation such as Nehemiah 8 are probably anachronistic (cf. Grabbe 1998a: 143–50). The reason is that the tradition was still fluid enough to be changed and altered so that there was no need for an interpretative process; rewriting and revising the tradition, rather than scriptural interpretation, was more likely to have been the process (cf. Pulikottil 2000).

Since an oral tradition can be subtly revised and reformulated as it is passed on, it is likely that interpretation as we know it came into play only when the tradition had both been written down and also come to be seen as authoritative enough not to be easily altered at will. As noted above (pp. 153–54), this was likely to have been no later than the Persian period for the Pentateuch, the Deuteronomistic History, the Major and Minor Prophets, and some of the Writings. In the minds of many, one of the first major acts of interpretation was the production of the books of Chronicles as a retelling of the story in Samuel–Kings (and also in some sense the story of Genesis to Judges by means of the genealogies in 1 Chron. 1–9). It has recently been suggested that perhaps rather than Chronicles using Samuel–Kings, they both revised a common source (Auld 1994). If so, Chronicles is not really an example of scriptural interpretation, and we must look elsewhere for the first example.

It has been suggested (using Chronicles as a major example) that the Jewish writings of the post-exilic period were mainly interpretations of scripture rather than original writings (e.g. Willi 1995: 35–36). This does not stand up to investigation. There are many Second Temple works that have little or nothing to do with the Hebrew Bible we know (e.g. Ben Sira, Tobit, Judith, *1 Enoch*, the books of Maccabees). Yet it is true that literature from Ben Sira on becomes permeated with a knowledge of portions of the Hebrew Bible in a form similar to, or the same as, that we now use. Ben Sira himself does not normally give explicit quotations (Snaith 1967; Schultz 1999: 146–59), and he can in many ways be considered a continuation of an old wisdom tradition, but there are many passages with parallels to the current OT, not least in Sir. 44–49.

One of the most ubiquitous forms of biblical interpretation through history has been **commentary**, though this is not as widespread in early Judaism as it becomes in later Judaism and Christianity. The term "midrash" is widely used as a synonym, though there are problems with calling any sort of commentary by this title (cf. Porton 1981). Midrash is a specific form of commentary, to be defined as follows (Porton 1981: 62; 1992: 819):

> a type of literature, oral or written, which has its starting point in a fixed, canonical text, considered the revealed word of God by the midrashist and his audience, and in which the original verse is explicitly cited or clearly alluded to.

By this definition there is very little pre-rabbinic midrash (Porton 1981: 67). One type of interpretation known solely from Qumran is **pesher** exegesis (some have wanted to label it "midrash"); indeed, it seems to fit Porton's definition. In some ways, it is more a form-critical category than a type of exegesis, identified by its quotation of a biblical passage and then an explication beginning with the phrase, "its meaning concerns" (*pišrô 'al*) or "its meaning is that" (*pešer 'ăšer*). However, the special characteristic of pesher exegesis is often thought to be the interpretation of biblical passages as the contemporary history of the community in coded form (see below). The best example of this sort of exegesis is of course the Qumran Habakkuk commentary (1QpHab), but other examples include other commentaries from Qumran (cf. Horgan 1979). An example in a Hellenistic context is the midrash on the plagues of the exodus in the Wisdom of Solomon (cf. Grabbe 1997a: 39–46).

A form of interpretation is known from early Jewish texts and became quite popular in early Christian circles: **allegory**. Allegory already occurs in the Bible in such passages as Ezekiel 16 and 23. Some have alleged that the Song of Songs is allegorical, though most modern scholars would see any allegorical interpretation as a later imposition rather than one present in the book from its final composition. The first post-biblical writer to use allegory extensively was Aristobulus (pp. 72–73 above), but the best-known example is that of Philo (pp. 89–92 above). Judging from Philo's statements, we can surmise that allegory was especially characteristic of interpreters in Alexandria of the first century or so BCE and CE (cf. Hay 1979–80; 1991).

If Chronicles is a rewriting of Samuel–Kings, however, it is a good example of one of the main means of interpretation: the retelling of the biblical account, now often known as **"rewritten Bible"** (Harrington 1986). We have many examples of this among the Second Temple Jewish writings. In some cases, the writer accepted the authority of Scripture and was only trying to make the meaning clear. This would apply to Josephus's *Antiquities*, the first ten books of which are more or less a paraphrase of biblical texts (cf. Feldman 1998a, 1998b). (Similarly, the Targum Pseudo-Jonathan is essentially a form of rewritten Bible, often going beyond mere translation, though it is likely to be post-70 [see p. 164 above].) This is a bit of a problematic category because it could include so much. For example, a number of the Fragmentary Jewish Writers in Greek (pp. 70–73 above) seem to be addressing themselves to biblical themes and interpretation (e.g. trying to resolve "difficulties" in the text), yet their approach varies greatly (from the Exodus drama of Ezekiel to the chronography of Demetrius).

It is clear that we quickly come up against the problem of a number of writings which seem related to the Bible in some way but are not clearly interpretations of it in any normal sense of the word. In some cases, they may continue and develop old traditions or religious interpretations that did not make it into the canonical collection, though they still addressed issues important to the Jewish people. Perhaps we might call this process **"parabiblical"**. Some of the texts in this category have been considered examples of "rewritten Bible", yet have a content quite different from the Bible. For example, much of the Enoch tradition might fall into this category (though some see the *Book of Watchers* as an interpretation of Genesis 6:1–4 whereas others see the Genesis passage as only a reflex of an old tradition more fully given in *1 Enoch*). Whether other texts whose contents are by and large different from the biblical text might bear this designation (instead of "rewritten Bible") is a moot point (e.g. 4 Ezra, the Adam and Eve literature, *Testament of Abraham*, *Testament of Moses*). A number of "para-biblical" texts from Qumran have been published in volumes from Cave 4 (see the volumes of DJD 13, 19, 22). We also have many halakic traditions whose relationship to the Pentateuch is unlikely to be one of simple interpretation (cf. examples in Neusner 1981).

The fact that some important Jewish religious writings have only a loose relationship to the biblical text should alert us to the dangers of focusing on the various techniques or the exegetical wrappings in which interpretation is presented. The main reason is that much "biblical interpretation" was rather a different activity from that with which we are familiar. It might well involve developing para-biblical material rather than being an actual attempt to understand a particular biblical passage. Also, even when we can identify the connection with a specific biblical passage with reasonable confidence, we must recognize both that ancient exegesis was was not primarily concerned with the original literal meaning of the text (*pace* Brewer 1992), and also that it was almost always atomistic in nature. Thus, what we are inclined to label "exegesis" or "interpretation" may be nothing more than building bridges between the biblical text and some other set of intellectual information that the writer wants to legitimate. For example, a writer such as Philo is clearly interested in finding his theologico-philosophical system (a form of Platonism) in the text of the LXX (cf. Grabbe 1988a: 115–19). This system did not arise primarily from study of the Bible, but Philo still wants to find it in the text. Allegory helps him do it, including the use of various devices such as the etymologies of Hebrew names. Similarly, the Qumran writers were able to find contemporary references to their community and history in some biblical texts, again by focusing on minute details of the text. When writers rewrite sections of the biblical text or produce stories that run alongside the biblical text, they may also simply be discovering in the text what they want to discover.

This does not suggest that the biblical text was not used to find new information. On the contrary, it was often the vehicle to develop a new ruling, especially in matters about personal conduct (halakha) or law. There was also a strong belief in many circles that the text was a code with secret information, especially information about the future. The writers of the Qumran *pesharim* not only find their own past history encrypted in the text, but they also think their future is there as well, just waiting to be deciphered (cf also van der Horst 1998). Philo also seems to treat the text in the same way. The last thing we should be doing in such cases is trying to find "rules of interpretation" because they do not exist in the conventional sense of the expression.

Conclusions about scriptural interpretation

The following are some of the points that arise when ancient biblical interpretation is studied:

1. Scriptural interpretation became an important activity in the latter part of the Second Temple period, but how early it began is debatable. Many would see little if any before the Greek period, and many Jewish writings which have something in common with biblical characters or passages seem to be something other than just interpretation in the strict sense of the word.

2. A canon in the later sense may have taken a long time to develop, perhaps not until the end of the Second Temple period. Nevertheless, the rather fluid tradition could still be enormously productive in generating new traditions, insights, and views without involving strict biblical interpretation in the later canonical sense of the word.

3. One reason for biblical interpretation was to seek information on various subjects: the cult, festival observance, purity regulations, theological concepts and ideals. It would be expected that God's revelation generally included such vital information. However, although it is often assumed that this was the primary function of scripture – as a source of information – other purposes were in fact often more important to the individual person or group.

4. Scriptural interpretation was often a way of justifying or legitimating a particular belief or idea. That is, the writer came to certain views by another route (perhaps even subconsciously) but then wanted to justify them by appeal to sacred writings. Philo is a good example of one who uses exegesis to find in scripture what is in fact a Platonic-based theologico-philosophical system, but he is only one of many. Much of what has been called "Jewish exegesis" seems actually to be in this category, rather than a straightforward attempt to understand the text in its literal form.

PRAYER AND THE RISE OF THE SYNAGOGUE

Binder, D. D. (1999) *Into the Temple Courts: The Place of the Synagogues in the Second Temple Period*.

Chazon, E. G. (1992) "Is *Divrei ha-Me'orot* a Sectarian Prayer?" in D. Dimant and U. Rappaport (eds) *The Dead Sea Scrolls: Forty Years of Research*: 3–17.

—— (1994) "Prayers from Qumran and Their Historical Implications", *DSD* 1: 265–84.

Charlesworth, J. H. (ed.) (1994) *The Lord's Prayer and Other Prayer Texts from the Greco-Roman Era*.

Chiat, M. J. S. (1981) "First-Century Synagogue Architecture: Methodological Problems", in L. I. Levine (ed.) *Ancient Synagogues Revealed*: 49–60.

—— (1982) *Handbook of Synagogue Architecture*, BJS 29; Atlanta: Scholars.

Falk, D. K. (1998) *Daily, Sabbath, and Festival Prayers in the Dead Sea Scrolls*.

Fine, S. (ed.) (1996) *Sacred Realm: The Emergence of the Synagogue in the Ancient World*.

—— (1997) *This Holy Place: On the Sanctity of the Synagogue during the Greco-Roman Period*.

—— (ed.) (1999) *Jews, Christians, and Polytheists in the Ancient Synagogue: Cultural Interaction during the Greco-Roman Period*.

Flesher, P. V. M. (1989) "Palestinian Synagogues before 70 CE: A Review of the Evidence", in J. Neusner (ed.) *Approaches to Ancient Judaism VI: Studies in the Ethnography and Literature of Judaism*: 68–81.

Foerster, G. (1981) "The Synagogues at Masada and Herodium", in L. I. Levine (ed.) *Ancient Synagogues Revealed*: 24–29.

Grabbe, L. L. (1988b) "Synagogues in Pre-70 Palestine: A Re-assessment", *JTS* 39: 401–10.

Griffiths, J. G. (1987) "Egypt and the Rise of the Synagogue", *JTS* 38: 1–15.

Hachlili, R. (1997) "The Origin of the Synagogue: A Re-assessment", *JSJ* 28: 34–47.

Heinemann, J. (1968) "The Triennial Lectionary Cycle", *JJS* 19: 41–48.

—— (1977) *Prayer in the Talmud: Forms and Patterns*.

Hoffman, L. A. (1995) "Jewish Liturgy and Jewish Scholarship", in J. Neusner (ed.) *Judaism in Late Antiquity: Part 1 The Literary and Archaeological Sources*: 239–66.

Horbury, W. (1982) "The Benediction of the *Minim* and Early Jewish-Christian Controversy", *JTS* 33: 19–61.

Horst, P. W. van der (1994a) "The Birkat ha-minim in Recent Research", *Hellenism–Judaism–Christianity: Essays on Their Interaction*: 99–111.

—— (1994b) "Silent Prayer", *Hellenism–Judaism–Christianity: Essays on Their Interaction*: 252–77.

—— (1998b) "Neglected Greek Evidence for Early Jewish Liturgical Prayer", *JSJ* 29: 278–96.

—— (1999) "Was the Synagogue a Place of Sabbath Worship before 70 CE?" in S. Fine (ed.) *Jews, Christians, and Polytheists in the Ancient Synagogue: Cultural Interaction during the Greco-Roman Period*: 18–43.

Horst, P. W. van der, and G. E. Sterling (2000) *Prayers from the Ancient World: Greco-Roman, Jewish and Christian Prayers*.

Hüttenmeister, F., and G. Reeg (1977) *Die antiken Synagogen in Israel*.

JWSTP: 551–77.

Kee, H. C. (1990) "The Transformation of the Synagogue after 70 CE: Its Import for Early Christianity", *NTS* 36: 1–24.

Kiley, M., *et al.* (1997) *Prayer from Alexander to Constantine: A Critical Anthology*.

Levine, L. I. (ed.) (1981) *Ancient Synagogues Revealed*.

—— (1996) "The Nature and Origin of the Palestinian Synagogue Reconsidered", *JBL* 115: 425–48.

—— (2000) *The Ancient Synogogue*.

McKay, H. A. (1994) *Sabbath and Synagogue: The Question of Sabbath Worship in Ancient Judaism*.

—— (1998) "Ancient Synagogues: The Continuing Dialectic Betwen Two Major Views", *CR: BS* 6: 103–42.

Newman, J. H. (1999) *Praying by the Book: The Scripturalization of Prayer in Second Temple Judaism*.

Newsom, C. A. (1985) *Songs of the Sabbath Sacrifice: A Critical Edition*.

Rajak, T., and D. Noy (1993) "*Archisynagogoi*: Office, Title and Social Status in the Greco-Jewish Synagogue", *JRS* 83: 75–93.

Reif, S. C. (1993) *Judaism and Hebrew Prayer*.

Urman, D., and P. V. M. Flesher (eds) (1995) *Ancient Synagogues: Historical Analysis and Archaeological Discovery.*

Werline, R. A. (1998) *Penitential Prayer in Second Temple Judaism: The Development of a Religious Institution.*

Prayer is so ubiquitous in religious literature that it seems almost superfluous to speak about it. Yet the place of prayer in Judaism seems to have varied over time, and the presence of a functioning temple and cult were an important factor in this equation. Whether there was prayer in the cult, as well as in special prayer houses such as synagogues, is an important historical question.

The texts known to us suggest that certain broad groupings of prayers were in existence as far back as we can go in our history of the subject. The OT is filled with prayers or references to praying. There were both public prayers and private prayers, with public prayers divided between those uttered at a sanctuary and those made elsewhere. Prayer in public places is usually represented as being given on behalf of a larger group, though the setting varies: in the sanctuary (1 Kings 8), in the street (Ezra 9). It should also not be forgotten that private prayers could often be made at sanctuaries. Many prayers, both public and private, are uttered in times of distress.

Many texts place prayers in a private setting, often in the home of the one praying. Daniel prays on his knees three times a day before an open window turned toward Jerusalem (Dan. 6:11). Tobit prays in the courtyard of his house, and his niece Sarah prays toward the window of a roofchamber (Tobit 3; however, it should be noted in Sarah's case that she originally went to the roofchamber to commit suicide). Prayer forms an important theme in Judith (8:4–6; 9; 12:6–8), with different settings. Jesus's famous prayer on the night of his arrest was in the private garden of Gethsemane (Mark 14:32//Matthew 26:35//Luke 22:39). There are also examples of private prayer being said in a sanctuary. When Hannah prayed for a child, this was in the temple at Shiloh during one of the annual festivals (1 Sam. 1:9–13). David prayed at the "House of Yhwh" after his child by Bathsheba had died (2 Sam. 12:20). The post-resurrection followers of Jesus went regularly to the temple "at the hour of prayer", though it is not entirely clear whether this was to pray, nor whether any prayers were public or private (Acts 2:46; 3:1; 5:42).

When we ask about the content of prayers, we have an *embarras de richesse* of examples in literary sources. The Greek version of Daniel has the "Prayer of Azariah", the "Song of the Three Young Men" in the fiery furnace, and the "Prayer of Manasseh". A large portion of 1 Baruch is a prayer (1:15–3:8). Among the Qumran texts are many prayers (cf. Falk 1998), such as the *Thanksgiving Hymns* (1QH), the daily prayers (4Q507–9; 1Q34; 1Q34[bis]), the festival prayers (4Q503), the *Songs of the Sabbath Sacrifice* (4QShirShabb[a–h] = 4Q400–407, 11Q17; cf. Newsom 1985), *Divrei ha-Me'orot*

(4QDibHam^{a-c} = 4Q504–6; cf. Chazon 1992). Many other prayers are scattered throughout the literature of the period.

The question, however, is the relationship between these literary texts labeled prayers and the frequent statement that someone prayed. We have the same problem as with prayers associated with the temple (such as many of the Psalms): are these literary prayers artificial creations or were they actually uttered as real prayers? It is difficult to know how to settle the matter. On the other hand, it is hard to believe that these prayers were completely divorced from the worshiping and praying religious context.

There is also a considerable debate about when the standard daily prayer, the *Amidah* or *Eighteen Benedictions* (*Shimoneh Esreh*), became established. A scholar such as Heinemann (1977: 224) is willing to assert that it was pre-70, pointing to parallels for a number of the benedictions in early literature. These parallels seem to be relevant, but the general consensus seems to be against their having crystallized into the precise Eighteen Benedictions known from post-70 times (Reif 1993: 60–61). As for the famous clause of benediction twelve cursing the heretics, called the *birkat ha-minim*, this is probably a late addition (van der Horst 1994 versus Horbury 1982).

In the past it has been widely assumed that the need for public prayer was always present in Judaism. When the temple was destroyed and the Jews taken captive to Babylon in 587, it was argued, they would have felt the need to establish some institution for public prayer. Therefore, the concept of the synagogue as a house of prayer first arose during the exile, according to this logic. Indeed, some have wanted to go further and put synagogues earlier, even in the period of the monarchy, citing certain biblical verses (e.g. Ps. 74:8). Most of this is wishful thinking. To evaluate the situation, the following points need to be kept in mind:

1. Judaism in pre-70 times was temple-centered. The growth of a large Diaspora population complicated this position, but this took time.

2. The early Diaspora literature presupposes religious celebration and worship in private, usually in the home (e.g. Dan. 6:11; Tobit 2:1–3); even literature set in Palestine puts prayer in the home (Judith 8:36–10:2; Acts 1:13–14) or the temple (2 Sam. 12:20; Isa. 56:7; 2 Chr. 6:40; 7:15; Acts 2:46–3:1).

3. The earliest references in extant literature to anything like synagogues are in Philo (*proseuchē*: *Flaccus* 47–49, 53; *Leg. ad Gaium* 132–34, etc.). Both Josephus and the NT make reference to synagogues in various parts of the Roman empire. Josephus mentions synagogues in Caesarea (*sunagogē*: *War* 2.14.4 §285), Dora (*sunagogē*: *Ant.* 19.6.3 §§300–05), as well as in Tiberias (*proseuchē*: *Life* 54 §277), though not elsewhere in Palestine. The NT is the earliest set of writings that specifically locates synagogues in the center of Palestine, including Jerusalem.

4. The earliest inscriptions mentioning synagogues are from Egypt, dating to the reign of Ptolemy II in the mid-3rd century BCE (Griffiths 1987; Hachlili

1997). The Theodotus inscription is a Greek text, on a dislocated building stone, about the establishment of a synagogue for purposes of learning the law and providing hospitality to travelers (Hüttenmeister/Reeg 1977: 192–94; Binder 1999: 104). Although it was not discovered in its original architectural context, it has been widely accepted as coming from the synagogue itself and being pre-70 in origin, though the early dating has also been questioned (Kee 1990, but see the criticisms in van der Horst 1999: 18–23; Binder 1999: 104–09).

5. Archaeology has so far not turned up anything earlier than the first century BCE in Palestine, and even the interpretation of these finds is controversial. Although it has been accepted by many that pre-70 synagogues have been found during the excavations of Herodium, Gamla, Masada, and perhaps one or two other places (Foerster 1981), this has also been queried (Chiat 1981; 1982: 116–18, 204–07, 248–51, 282–84).

What seems clear is that the synagogue was a late development – probably no earlier than the Greek period – and did not reach Palestine until not long before the destruction of the Jerusalem temple in 70. The fact that the books of Maccabees and the narrative of Josephus say nothing about synagogues being attacked or affected by the Maccabean revolt or the subsequent events in Palestine until the first century CE is a good indication that they were not present until post-Maccabean times. Exactly when they became established in Judea is difficult to say at the present. A lot depends on one's estimate of the credibility of the NT, especially the gospels and Acts. The Theodotus inscription indicates that some at least were private foundations (cf. also Luke 7:1–5).

A further question is the function of the synagogue and what went on in it. This is very important because some far-reaching conclusions have been made on assumptions about the synagogue liturgy, such as that the law was read according to a fixed lectionary cycle or that the reading of the law was regularly accompanied by an Aramaic translation. The Theodotus inscription speaks only of reading and study of scriptures (as well as hospitality). On the other hand, the argument that the synagogue had nothing originally to do with prayer or worship (McKay 1994) seems misplaced for several reasons, in particular, that the earliest name in inscriptions is *proseuchē* "(place of) prayer, prayer (house)", which seems an odd name to give a building which had nothing to do with prayer; and Agatharchides of Cnidus states that the Jews "pray with outstretched hands in the temples (*hiera*) until the evening" (quoted in *Ag. Apion* 1.22 §209). Although speaking of Jerusalem, he is likely drawing on his experience of synagogues in Alexandria and elsewhere in the Diaspora. (See further the criticisms of McKay in van der Horst 1999: 23–37; Binder 1999: 404–15.)

Some attempt at describing the activities can be made (cf. Binder (1999: 389–450), but the data are insufficient to give a full picture. Reading scripture, prayer, and teaching and homiletic activity seem to have been a part, but it is difficult to go beyond that. Despite the occasional argument that a biblical reading was done according to a fixed lectionary cycle (e.g. Perrot in Mulder/Sysling 1990: 149–59), this seems unlikely; the arguments advanced generally depend heavily on rabbinic literature and a lot of wishful thinking, but even rabbinic literature does not attest a fixed cycle until quite late (Heinemann 1968; Grabbe 1988b: 408–09). The same applies to the translation of the biblical readings into Aramaic. Although this apparently had a place in synagogue services during the rabbinic period, there is no evidence that targums or targumizing had a place in the pre-70 synagogues (cf. p. 164 above).

''POPULAR RELIGION''

Albertz, R. (1978) *Persönliche Frömmigkeit und offizielle Religion: Religionsinterner Pluralismus in Israel und Babylon.*

—— (1994) *A History of Israelite Religion in the Old Testament Period.*

Berlinerblau, J. (1996) *The Vow and the "Popular Religious Groups" of Ancient Israel: A Philological and Sociological Inquiry.*

Frerichs, E. S., and J. Neusner (eds) (1986) *Goodenough on the History of Religion and on Judaism.*

Goodenough, E. R. (1935) *By Light, Light.*

—— (1953–65) *Jewish Symbols in the Greco-Roman Period.*

—— (1988) (ed. J. Neusner) *Jewish Symbols in the Greco-Roman Period.*

Grabbe, L. L. (1995) *Priests, Prophets, Diviners, Sages: A Socio-historical Study of Religious Specialists in Ancient Israel.*

—— (1996) *An Introduction to First Century Judaism: Jewish Religion and History in the Second Temple Period.*

Henten, J. W. van (ed.) (1989) *Die Entstehung der jüdischen Martyrologie.*

—— (1997) *The Maccabean Martyrs as Saviours of the Jewish People: A Study of 2 and 4 Maccabees.*

Lease, G. (1987) "Jewish Mystery Cults since Goodenough", *ANRW II*: 20.2.858–80.

Meyers, E. M. *Jewish Ossuaries: Reburial and Rebirth* (1971).

—— (1976) "Galilean Regionalism as a Factor in Historical Reconstruction", *BASOR* 221: 93–101.

—— (1985) "Galilean Regionalism: A Reappraisal", *Approaches to Ancient Judaism, Volume V*: 115–31.

Meyers, E. M., and J. F. Strange (1981) *Archaeology, the Rabbis and Early Christianity.*

Neusner, J. (1986) "Preface", in E. S. Frerichs and J. Neusner (eds) *Goodenough on the History of Religion and on Judaism*: ix–xix.

—— (1988) "Introduction" to E. R. Goodenough, *Jewish Symbols in the Greco-Roman Period* (abridged edn).

Smith, Morton (1967) "Goodenough's *Jewish Symbols* in Retrospect", *JBL* 86: 53–68.

Strange, J. F. (1979) "Archaeology and the Religion of Judaism in Palestine", *ANRW II Principiat*: 19.1.646–85.

Toorn, K. van der (1996) *Family Religion in Babylonia, Syria and Israel: Continuity and Change in the Forms of Religious Life.*

In recent years the concept of "popular religion" or "family religion" has been investigated in a number of works (Albertz 1978; 1994: 94–103, 186–95, 399–411; van der Toorn 1996; Berlinerblau 1996). This is not to suggest that there is another sort of religion which can be called "popular religion" nor that there is necessarily a sharp divide between "popular" and "official" religion. What these studies recognize, however, is that the piety, rites, and beliefs carried on in the family and home sometimes have significant variants or additional elements not normally attested for the "official" or "dominant" religion. The term "official religion" has its problems, of course. It can mean the religion of the ruler or ruling class; it can mean the religion of a dominant ethnic group; it can mean the religion of a conqueror; it can mean the most popular religion of a people. In every case, there will be minority forms of the religion or minority separate religions.

In the case of Second Temple Judaism, the "official religion" was that perpetuated by the Jerusalem temple and its priesthood. This religion was official in the sense that the ruling power (the Persians, the Ptolemies, the Seleucids, the Hasmoneans, the Herodians, the Romans) approved it or at least recognized it and permitted it to function. Although a few groups may have withdrawn from the temple as polluted or at least regarded the current priesthood as disqualified, the indication is that the vast majority of people accepted and recognized them. In the Diaspora, where the temple was not available, the counterpart to official religion (if there was one) was probably the community synagogue (at least from the third century BCE on); on the other hand, the synagogue may have had little if any status in Palestine before the fall of the temple (to the extent that synagogues existed, as discussed on pp. 270–75 below).

Therefore, in this brief discussion of "popular religion", I have in mind those aspects of Judaism that do not seem to be attested for the temple or the main manifestations of religion before 70. Whether a neat line can be drawn between the "sects" (Chapter 9 below), "esoteric" practices (pp. 241–45 below), Gnostic trends (*JCH*: 514–19; Grabbe 1996a: 94–110), and "popular religion" is difficult to say. Perhaps the only real distinction is that most of the information cited here comes from archaeology rather than literary sources (Strange 1979; cf. Meyers 1976; 1985; Meyers/Strange 1981). One of the main sources is the work of Goodenough (1953–65) whose monumental thirteen-volume work attempted to assemble the bulk of early Jewish art and interpret it on its own terms (cf. Neusner 1986; 1988; Smith 1967). Although much of this material is post-70, it helps to illustrate the problems and benefits in studying popular religion.

What Goodenough demonstrated was how important Jewish art was in helping to round out the religious picture of the times. Not only are literary sources too sparse and episodic to give a full picture of the religious situation, but they also often represent a partisan point of view and even an attempt to palm off an entirely spurious *status quo* on the reader. Goodenough was able to show from the art and artifacts that there was another side to religion among the Jews in the first few centuries of the Common Era. His name is often associated with a particular theory, that of "mystical Hellenistic Judaism" (cf. Goodenough 1935). The fact that this has been widely rejected (cf. Lease 1987) has meant that Goodenough's greater and more basic contribution is often overlooked. One does not have to accept his thesis about "mystical Hellenistic Judaism" to recognize the fundamental way in which his study has shown a pluralistic and even fragmented Judaism in which many different currents still flowed at a time when it was thought that the rabbis were fully in charge (see the evaluation in Neusner 1988).

Other aspects of popular religion are not so easily discovered. Since popular religion is often frowned on by the established religious authorities, it may be ignored or quietly swept under the carpet in the preserved sources. We may have only hints of the practice of magic, astrology, divination, or analogous rites in the literature (pp. 241–51 below). For example, the evidence that astrology was widespread consists largely of synagogue motifs of the later Roman period, but this picture does not emerge from the literary sources. Ossuaries and other burial customs may show some sort of views about an afterlife (Meyers 1971). There is also some evidence of the veneration of holy sites such as Mamre (Strange 1979: 671–72) which may well have its origins in pre-Israelite times. Tombs of holy men were also made the object of veneration and perhaps even pilgrimage (Strange 1979: 667–70), a fact well known from Christianity but not usually associated with Judaism of this period. These may well have grown out of, or even have been a part of, the cult of the dead whose existence has been demonstrated by recent study (see the summary in Grabbe 1995: 141–45).

Incorporation of martyrs and martyrdom into the religious picture seems to have taken place at least from Maccabean times (van Henten 1989; 1997). Although martyrdom does not have the prominent place in Judaism that it does in Christianity, we have a number of Jewish writings about persecutions (e.g. 3 Maccabees). These writings often end with the vindication of the innocent sufferers. However, the first time Jews were executed for their religious practices appears to be at the time of the Antiochan persecutions about 168 BCE. The fact that apparently righteous individuals died for their beliefs (rather than being delivered by God) may have led to the doctrine of the resurrection (cf. Dan. 12:2; p. 280 below). The later accounts in 2 and 4 Maccabees describe the deaths of a number of individuals from a martyr perspective, with their blood seen as a factor in defeating the Seleucids and cleansing the land. Similarly, the willing deaths of Taxo and his seven sons in *T. Moses* 9 will cause God to avenge their blood.

SYNTHESIS

Goodman, M. (1983) *State and Society in Roman Galilee, A.D. 132–212.*

Grabbe, L. L. (ed.) (2000d) *Did Moses Speak Attic? Jewish Historiography and Scripture in the Hellenistic Period,*

Lightstone, J. N. (1984) *The Commerce of the Sacred: Mediation of the Divine among Jews in the Graeco-Roman Diaspora.*

—— (1988) *Society, the Sacred, and Scripture in Ancient Judaism.*

Neusner, J. (1981) *Judaism: The Evidence of the Mishnah.*

—— (1987a) *The Wonder-Working Lawyers of Talmudic Babylonia: The Theory and Practice of Judaism in its Formative Age.*

Smith, J. Z. (1978) "Sacred Persistence: Towards a Redescription of Canon", in W. S. Green (ed.) *Approaches to Ancient Judaism: Theory and Practice*: 11–28.

Although until 70 CE the temple and cult repesented the main form of religious worship among the Jews, private prayer was no doubt also present from earliest times. With the deportation of some Jews to Babylonia after the destruction of the First Temple and the subsequent events during the next two or three centuries, a large Jewish population in various areas outside Palestine grew up. These communities did not have ready access to the temple, even if some individuals had the time and finance to travel to Jerusalem on occasion to worship. Thus, during the Second Temple period we find another stream of worship gaining importance alongside temple worship, that focusing on scripture and prayer.

Approaching the divine through various intermediaries was widespread in antiquity, including priests and the cult, prophetic figures (pp. 236–41 below), diviners and other mantic figures (pp. 241–54 below). Yet we have many examples of people praying directly or even receiving revelations without any sort of professional intermediary present. We have no evidence that private and personal prayer was ever forbidden or discouraged, however important the temple and cult were.

Little is known for certain about the development of the Bible, and the subject is currently being intensely debated (see the essays in Grabbe 2000d). The first positive evidence for writings being treated in some way as scripture and canon is found in the book of Ben Sira, probably written soon after 200 BCE, especially in a section known as the "Praise of the Fathers" (Ben Sira 44–50). The Greek version of Ben Sira's book is even more informative. Produced about 132 BCE by the author's grandson, it has a prologue which talks several times about "the law, the prophets, and the other writings".

This suggests that for the grandson, there was already a somewhat authoritative list of books (canon?) which consisted of our Pentateuch, a collection of "prophets" which probably did not differ significantly from our present Former and Latter Prophets (since it included the Minor Prophets as a unit), and a number of other writings, some of which are probably part of our present-day canon but not necessarily all.

This impression is confirmed, but also complicated, by information from other sources. The books among the Dead Sea Scrolls contain every book of the Hebrew canon but Esther; however, many other books are also in the collection and cited as authoritative, suggesting that canonical boundaries were seen as much wider (embracing a much larger number of books) or possibly much narrower (a small core with special status, such as the Pentateuch, with a much wider collection of non-canonical but nevertheless significant books). The last view fits well some other communities, such as the Samaritan in which only the Pentateuch and a version of Joshua are canonical but other books are known and used in a semi-authoritative way. Similarly, Philo cites a number of the books of the canon at one time or another, but he focuses his main activity on the Pentateuch, and his text is the Septuagint (he apparently knew little if any Hebrew). A closed canon before 70 CE is unlikely, and the text remained fluid through most of this period. It is not unusual to find books of the present Hebrew canon in substantially different forms even late in the Second Temple period (e.g. 1 Samuel; Jeremiah).

A Diaspora began as early as the deportation of people from the Northern Kingdom by the Assyrians in 722 BCE. With the coming of the Greeks, Jewish communities sprang up in various cities around the Hellenistic Near East until the inhabitants of Judah were a minority of all Jews. Perhaps best documented is the Jewish community in Alexandria and others in Egypt, but we also know of Jewish populations in various cities in Syria and Asia Minor and even as far away as Rome, as well as in the Palestinian area outside Judah proper.

This development of a major Diaspora eventually had a significant effect on Judaism as a religion. Many of the particular features of Judaism which became characteristic after the fall of the Second Temple were those which we find already developing in the Diaspora religious practices. Yhwh the God of Israel became the God of a people rather than just of a nation. The Jerusalem temple was still the focus of religious worship, but in many ways it became a distant ideal, especially the further away from it one lived. Many Diaspora Jews desired to visit the temple and, in late Second Temple times certainly, pilgrimage to worship in Jerusalem expanded greatly.

Nevertheless, the reality was that visits to the temple were very infrequent and, for many of the Diaspora population, probably non-existent. This meant that the traditional worship centering on the cult was simply not possible. The home and family replaced the temple and community as the focus of worship. Prayer, acts of piety, and faithful observance of some aspects of the law (sabbath, circumcision, food laws) replaced the sacrificial cult. None of these was incompatible with the temple cult; indeed, they were part of the traditional practice of religion. The difference in the Diaspora was that they were given greater emphasis because that was all that could be done.

To what extent synagogues played a part in weekly sabbath worship away from the temple remains a question to be resolved. The reason is that synagogues, though an institution of Diaspora Judaism from at least the middle of the 3rd century BCE, were a late development in Palestine itself – post-Maccabean from the data currently available. Although no conclusion can be certain, these data all suggest that the number of synagogues in Palestine before 70 was rather limited, and the size of those that existed was insufficient to take more than a fraction of the local population. Thus, the synagogue may have served as the religious center for some, but whether for any more than a small minority seems doubtful. Any sort of central hierarchy over synagogues as a whole is even more unlikely for this period. The ruler(s) of individual synagogues could probably keep out individuals whom they did not like, but the picture of excommunication from all the synagogues as given by John 9:13–34 is probably anachronistic. Also, the idea that synagogues were usually controlled by the Pharisees is a modern scholarly myth in no way supported by the sources.

Thus, long before the destruction of the temple, the Jews had also become a "people of the book", and a sort of cult centered on scripture had developed alongside temple worship, especially in the Diaspora. To what extent the actual text was read by the average Jew is uncertain, but only a rather small minority were likely to have read the text for themselves; nevertheless, even the illiterate can gain familiarity from public readings, teachings, and other word-of-mouth activities. Synagogue public reading (to the extent that it existed) would have been one such means. Some individuals and groups made study of the text a religious duty, of course, and this resulted in the production of commentaries and other works which heavily depended on or reworked the biblical text (cf. 1QS 6:6–8 and the Qumran *pĕšārîm*). But it would be a mistake to take the later rabbinic ideal of the Torah scholar as characteristic of Judaism before 70. It was not even a correct description of Judaism in the Talmudic period, much less earlier (Neusner 1987a: 39–138; Goodman 1983: 93–118).

Yet even though the canon (and text) for most groups seems to have been still somewhat fluid, by the first century certain books appear to have been in practically all canons while others were widely accepted, even if not by everyone. This has crucial implications for the use of scripture. It seems a feature of being human is to restrict oneself in a particular area of concern, then to create great diversity within this restriction by ingenuity (Smith 1978). So it is with a canonized or semi-canonized sacred literature, and the holy books had a diversity of functions within the different forms of Judaism:

1. The simplest function was as a source of information: for the cult, festival observance, purity regulations, theological concepts, and religious ideals. It would be expected that God's revelation generally included such vital information. However, it is often assumed that this was the primary function of scripture – as a source of information – whereas other purposes were often more important to the individual person or group.

2. The holy books could be used as a justification or authorization for beliefs and practices which arose from quite other sources. To take the example of the Mishnah, much of its contents did not arise from the OT, even though often parallel, or was related to Pentateuchal regulations only tangentially (Neusner 1981). Yet the authors of the Tannaitic Midrashim were concerned that these teachings be seen as exegeses of scripture, and they arranged the material as commentary rather than as an autonomous legal collection as in the Mishnah. Another example is that of the Christian apostle Paul. The book of 1 Corinthians represents a case of how personal rulings about a particular situation (that in the Corinthian church) are justified by appeal to the OT writings; however, Paul's exegesis is plainly *post hoc*. He was seeking biblical authority for decisions which he thought were right for quite other reasons. It is in this light that many of the so-called "exegetical rules" and other forms of interpretation are to be seen. That is, much of ancient exegesis was not an attempt to understand the text in its own right. On the contrary, the "rules" served to bridge the gap between teachings which were considered (or desired to be) authoritative and the sacred text. Thus, Philo would hardly accept that his views about the soul and the Logos were merely borrowing from Greek philosophy; instead, he exercised great ingenuity in finding all the various elements in the text of the LXX (pp. 89–92 above). Various rules or devices can be extrapolated from his activity, but it would be erroneous to take these as a neutral attempt to understand the text. He already understood the text before he started.

3. In the minds of many, the ultimate source for understanding scripture was evidently thought to have been direct inspiration from God. This idea is found at Qumran, one of the best examples being 1QpHab (7:1–5) where "God made known all the mysteries of the words of his servants the prophets" to the Teacher of Righteousness. God who inspired the prophets to write now inspired the Teacher with the correct understanding of the prophecies. Philo makes similar claims about his interpretation (p. 238 below).

4. Holy books might also have a "magical" function (Neusner 1987: 62–70; Lightstone 1984; 1988). The words of the Bible were not just a means of communication but of effication. They would "do" things if properly employed. They could be used as amulets or the like. There was something mysterious about the word of God in written form which went beyond the mere message of the text.

The preoccupation with the written word represents a change of focus in religious activity and orientation. This does not mean that Jews ceased to be concerned about temple worship, ritual purity, and the festival year, but when holy books became widely available (and this may not have been until comparatively late), the temple became less essential to instruction, while reading and interpretation could become a religious activity in themselves. For those Jewish communities far removed from the temple, worship would have embraced reading and interpreting scripture. While prayer would no doubt also have been very important, the written word would have become a major element in the various activities of worship. Many Jews found their own particular identities primarily by reading and interpreting the biblical text, whatever their relationship to the temple. Others could use written scripture as a way of developing beliefs and practices apart from the temple and its official priesthood; the welcome increase in their own independence may then have encouraged further weakening of the ties with temple worship well before its destruction in 70 CE.

The main difference between pre-70 and post-70 Judaism was the centrality of the temple to worship. From the earliest times, Jews had considered the primary form of worship to be tied up with the temple and its cult. Any other form was secondary and perhaps the result of circumstances beyond one's control, such as living outside the land of Israel. Yet just as the loss of the temple in 70 forced a revamping of the religion to one which did not require a physical temple, so the lack of access to a temple among an increasing number of Jews living outside Palestine resulted in some important new developments. Some of these innovations also anticipated developments in post-70 Judaism in Palestine.

9

SECTS AND MOVEMENTS

A long chapter in *JCH* (ch. 8) examined the various sects and movements. Probably no other section of the book has dated as quickly. In a few cases, there is nothing really new to add (e.g. with the Herodians), and the reader is referred to the appropriate section of *JCH* for discussion; the scribes are discussed at pp. 150–52 above. For a number of groups, however, the debate has moved on considerably, and the discussion here supersedes my earlier one. Primarily examined are the beginnings of sectarianism (including the Hasidim), the Sadducees and Pharisees, and the Essenes. Certain "revolutionary movements" are discussed in Chapter 13 below.

BEGINNINGS OF SECTARIANISM

Blenkinsopp, J. (1981) "Interpretation and the Tendency to Sectarianism: An Aspect of Second Temple History", in E. P. Sanders *et al.* (eds) *Jewish and Christian Self-Definition 2*: 2.1–26.

—— (1990) "A Jewish Sect of the Persian Period", *CBQ* 52: 5–20.

Collins, J. J. (1977) *The Apocalyptic Vision of the Book of Daniel*: 201–6.

Davies, P. R. (1977) "*Hasîdîm* in the Maccabean Period", *JJS* 28: 127–40.

Kampen, J. (1988) *The Hasideans and the Origins of Pharisaism.*

Lightstone, J. N. (1983) "Judaism of the Second Commonwealth: Toward a Reform of the Scholarly Tradition", in H. Joseph *et al.* (eds) *Truth and Compassion: Essays on Judaism and Religion in Memory of Rabbi Dr. Solomon Frank*: 31–40.

Redditt, P. L. (1986a) "The Book of Joel and Peripheral Prophecy", *CBQ* 48: 225–40.

—— (1986b) "Once Again, the City in Isaiah 24–27", *HAR* 10: 317–35.

—— (1989) "Israel's Shepherds: Hope and Pessimism in Zechariah 9–14", *CBQ* 51: 632–42.

Rofé, A. (1985) "Isaiah 66:1–4: Judean Sects in the Persian Period as Viewed by Trito-Isaiah", in A. Kort and S. Morschauser (eds) *Biblical and Related Studies Presented to Samuel Iwry*: 205–17.

Smith, Morton (1971a) *Palestinian Parties and Politics That Shaped the Old Testament*.

Stone, M. E. (1988) "Enoch, Aramaic Levi and Sectarian Origins", *JSJ* 19: 159–70.

Talmon. S. (1986) "The Emergence of Jewish Sectarianism in the Early Second Temple Period", *King, Cult and Calendar in Ancient Israel*: 165–201.

In a society such as ancient Israel, we would not be surprised to find various cults centering on particular deities. We probably have too little evidence to determine whether such existed, though Morton Smith (1971a) postulated a "Yahweh-alone" movement which began as a minority movement and eventually became dominant. When we reach the Persian period, however, a number of scholars have felt that they could find evidence of sectarian movements (*JCH*: 103–12). Both Talmon (1986) and Blenkinsopp (1981: 24) thought that the post-exilic situation would be naturally conducive to the development of sects because of the lack of a central authority, and Blenkinsopp (1990) has seen evidence of sectarian development in various passages, including those that mention the *ḥărēdîm*, those who "tremble" at God's word. Rofé (1985) came to similar conclusions. Redditt argued for more than one group, represented in different texts (1986a, 1986b, 1989). These and other suggestions are discussed and evaluated in *JCH* (107–11). When we come to the Greek period, books such as *1 Enoch* may suggest groups which had broken with the Jerusalem temple.

No doubt work will continue to be done on biblical and other texts to find evidence of sectarianism. However, the one early group most often seized upon in the past is that of the Hasidim (Greek *Asidaioi*). They have been seen as the source of the later sects such as the Pharisees and Essenes, as the movers behind the Maccabean revolt, the authors of the book of Daniel, and much else. The evidence for this has been very skimpy, however; as Collins (1977: 201) noted,

> The party of the Hasideans has grown in recent scholarship from an extremely poorly attested entity to the great Jewish alternative to the Maccabees at the time of the revolt. There has been no corresponding growth in the evidence.

Most of the relevant passages have been critically studied in the seminal article by Davies (1977; cf. also Collins 1977: 201–6; Lightstone 1983: 36–40; Saldarini 1988: 251–54; and see the discussion in *JCH*: 465–67). About all we are told is that they were a group of "mighty warriors" who joined the Maccabees (1 Macc. 2:39–42), that they were the first to seek peace after Alcimus was made priest (1 Macc. 7:12–16), and that they were a group led by Judas Maccabeus (2 Macc. 14:6). These few facts already contradict some assumptions (e.g. that they were pacifists), but they tell us next to nothing about the group. Attempts to make them the ancestors of the Essenes or the Pharisees (e.g. Kampen 1988) go beyond the evidence. We do not even know if they were a united group, since the term Hasidim ("merciful, pious") may be a general term for various "pious" groups or individuals who bore no connection with one another.

What we do know is that sometime around 100 BCE, the three groups of Sadducees, Pharisees, and Essenes are said by our sources to be in existence, but we know nothing of their origins. The fact that the Sadducees and Pharisees are first mentioned when Josephus is talking about the reign of Jonathan Maccabee is hardly evidence that they already existed at that time; on the contrary, he first connects their activities with John Hyrcanus (135–104 BCE) some decades later. If this is correct (and there are some problems), they *might* have originated in the post-Maccabean-revolt situation, but they could be earlier or even later. The Essenes are first connected with the reign of Aristobulus I (104–103 BCE). At the moment, their origins are a matter of speculation.

SADDUCEES AND PHARISEES

Baumgarten, A. I. (1984–85) "*Korban* and the Pharisaic *Paradosis*", *JANES* 16–17: 5–17.

—— (1987) "The Pharisaic *Paradosis*", *HTR* 80: 63–77.

—— (1997) *The Flourishing of Jewish Sects in the Maccabean Era: An Interpretation*.

Cohen, S. J. D. (1984) "The Significance of Yavneh: Pharisees, Rabbis, and the End of Jewish Sectarianism", *HUCA* 55: 27–53.

Daube, D. (1990) "On Acts 23: Sadducees and Angels", *JBL* 109: 493–97.

Deines, R. (1997) *Die Pharisäer: Ihr Verständnis im Spiegel der christlichen und jüdischen Forschung seit Wellhausen und Graetz*.

Fitzmyer, J. A. (1998) *The Acts of the Apostles: A New Translation with Introduction and Commentary*.

Goodman, M. (1999) "A Note on Josephus, the Pharisees and Ancestral Tradition", *JJS* 50: 17–20.

Grabbe, L. L. (1994b) review of S. Mason, *Flavius Josephus on the Pharisees*, *JJS* 45: 134–36.

—— (1997b) "The Current State of the Dead Sea Scrolls: Are There More Answers than Questions?" in S. E. Porter and C. A. Evans (eds) *The Scrolls and the Scriptures: Qumran Fifty Years After*: 54–67.

—— (1997c) "4QMMT and Second Temple Jewish Society", in M. Bernstein, F. García Martínez, and J. Kampen (eds) *Legal Texts and Legal Issues: Proceedings of the Second Meeting of the International Organization for Qumran Studies*: 89–108.

—— (1999b) "Sadducees and Pharisees", in J. Neusner and A. J. Avery-Peck (eds) *Judaism in Late Antiquity: Part Three. Where We Stand: Issues and Debates in Ancient Judaism: Volume 1*: 35–62.

—— (1999d) Review article: A. I. Baumgarten, *The Flourishing of Jewish Sects in the Maccabean Era, JSJ* 30: 89–94.

—— (2000e) "The Pharisees – A Response to Steve Mason", in J. Neusner and A. Avery-Peck (eds) *Where We Stand, Vol. 3*: 35–47.

Harrington, H. K. (1995) "Did the Pharisees Eat Ordinary Food in a State of Ritual Purity?" *JSJ* 26: 42–54.

Hemer, Colin J. (1989) *The Book of Acts in the Setting of Hellenistic History.*

LeMoyne, J. (1972) *Les Sadducéens.*

Main, E. (1990) "Les Sadducéens vus par Flavius Josèphe", *RevB* 97: 161–206.

Mason, S. (1989) "Was Josephus a Pharisee? A Re-Examination of *Life* 10–12", *JJS* 40: 31–45.

—— (1991) *Flavius Josephus on the Pharisees: A Composition-Critical Study.*

—— (1994) "Method in the Study of Early Judaism: A Dialogue with Lester Grabbe", *JAOS* 115: 463–72.

—— (1999) "Revisiting Josephus's Pharisees", in J. Neusner and A. Avery-Peck (eds) *Where We Stand, Vol. 2*: 23–56.

Mattill, A. J., Jr. (1978) "The Value of Acts as a Source for the Study of Paul", in C. H. Talbert (ed.) *Perspectives on Luke–Acts*: 76–98.

Neusner, J. (1971) *The Rabbinic Traditions about the Pharisees before 70.*

—— (1973a) *From Politics to Piety.*

—— (1981) *Judaism: The Evidence of the Mishnah.*

Neusner, J., and C. Thoma (1995) "Die Pharisäer vor und nach der Tempel-zerstörung des Jahres 70 n. Chr.", in S. Lauer and H. Ernst (ed.) *Tempelkult und Tempelzerstörung (70 n. Chr.): Festschrift für Clemens Thoma zum 60. Geburtstag*: 189–230.

Poehlmann, W. (1992) "The Sadducees as Josephus Presents Them, or The Curious Case of Ananus", in A. J. Hultgren, *et al.* (eds) *All Things New: Essays in Honor of Roy A. Harrisville*: 87–100.

Poirier, John C. (1996) "Why Did the Pharisees Wash their Hands?" *JJS* 47: 217–33.

Rivkin, E. (1972) "Defining the Pharisees: The Tannaitic Sources", *HUCA* 43: 205–40.

Saldarini, A. J. (1988) *Pharisees, Scribes and Sadducees in Palestinian Society: A Sociological Approach.*

Schremer, A. (1997) "The Name of the Boethusians: A Reconsideration of Suggested Explanations and Another One", *JJS* 48: 290–99.

Stemberger, G. (1995) *Jewish Contemporaries of Jesus: Pharisees, Sadducees, Essenes.*

Sussmann, Y. (1989–90) "The History of *Halakha* and the Dead Sea Scrolls: A Preliminary to the Publication of 4QMMT", *Tarbiz* 59: 11–76 (Heb.).

Viviano, B. T., and Justin Taylor (1992) "Sadducees, Angels, and Resurrection (Acts 23:8–9)", *JBL* 111: 496–98.

Waubke, H.–G. (1998) *Die Pharisäer in der protestantischen Bibelwissenschaft des 19. Jahrhunderts*,

A major discussion and extensive bibliography up to about 1990 was given in *JCH* (467–87), but in less than a decade the field has moved on considerably. Even selecting which sources to use is not an easy task. One might think that at least the sources for the Pharisees and Sadducees were generally agreed on, but even this is not the case, and choosing which sources to use already sets the agenda to some extent. Because of limits of space, I look only at the major sources and summarize the relevant information; the full data with discussion are found in Grabbe 1999b which should be consulted for the full argument. For the earlier literature, most of which is not repeated here, see *JCH* (467–68, 484).

The sources are contained essentially in three collections: the writings of Josephus, the New Testament, and rabbinic literature. It has also recently been suggested that some Qumran writings represent Sadducean viewpoints and, by implication, give an insight into the development of the Pharisaic movement.

Josephus

The writings on Josephus are extremely important because he lived at a time when the Pharisaic and Sadducean movements were active, and he had personal knowledge of some prominent Pharisees and Sadducees. In the *War* he seldom mentions either the Sadducees or the Pharisees. The Pharisees are first mentioned in the context of Alexandra Salome's reign when, Josephus says, they dominated her administration (1.5.2–3 §§110–14). He next suggests that they opposed Herod in some undefined way (1.29.2 §§571). His only real discussion of the two groups is in 2.8.14 §§162–66:

> Of the two first-named schools, the Pharisees, who are considered the most accurate interpreters of the laws, and hold the position of the leading sect, attribute everything to Fate and to God; they hold that to act rightly or otherwise rests, indeed, for the most part with men, but that in each action Fate co-operates. Every soul, they maintain, is imperishable, but the soul of the good alone passes into another body, while the souls of the wicked suffer eternal punishment.
>
> The Sadducees, the second of the orders, do away with Fate altogether, and remove God beyond, not merely the commission, but the very sight, of evil. They maintain that man has the free choice of good or evil, and that it rests with each man's will whether he follows the one or the other. As for the persistence of the soul after

death, penalties in the underworld, and rewards, they will have none of them.

The Pharisees are affectionate to each other and cultivate harmonious relations with the community. The Sadducees, on the contrary, are, even among themselves, rather boorish in their behaviour, and in their intercourse with their peers are as rude as to aliens.

Finally, he mentions that at the beginning of the 66–70 revolt, "the principal citizens assembled with the chief priests and the most notable Pharisees" to try to determine what to do about their predicament with regard to the Romans (2.17.2–3 §§410–11).

In the ***Antiquities*** there is much more frequent mention of both sects, especially the Pharisees who suddenly appear in episodes where the *War* was completely silent about them. Is this because Josephus knew more, or has he inserted them for rhetorical or other reasons? He first gives a general description of the three main sects, but most of the space is devoted to the Essenes; he actually says little about the Sadducees and Pharisees, repeating their views on fate (*Ant.* 13.5.9 §171–72).

Unlike the *War*, he makes the Sadduces and Pharisees active already under John Hyrcanus, describing an episode in which Hyrcanus supposedly changed from supporting the latter to backing the former (*Ant.* 13.10.5–7 §§288–99). Interestingly, in one of the few references to Hasmonean history in rabbinic literature, this episode seems to be referred to but is assigned to the reign of Alexander Janneus (*B. Qidd.* 66a), a dating supported by Main (1990: 190–202). As a result, according to the *Antiquities*, Hyrcanus was faced with a revolt. The *War* (1.2.8 §§67–69) had said nothing about the Pharisees but ascribed the revolt to the "successes" (*eupragia*) of Hyrcanus and his sons, which is also how the *Antiquities* actually begins the passage. Despite supposedly not having the people behind him, Hyrcanus put down the revolt, and the rest of his reign was peaceable (both the *War* and the *Antiquities* give the same picture).

The next mention in the *Antiquities* is puzzling because it concerns the death of Alexander Janneus and assumes strong Pharisaic opposition to him, yet no such opposition is recorded in the life of Janneus up to this point. Josephus had described considerable opposition to the Hasmonean ruler, including an incident in which some Jews brought the Seleucid pretender Demetrius III against him, but at no point has Josephus suggested that this opposition was Pharisaic nor even that Pharisees were among its number. But then *Ant.* 13.15.5–16.1 §§401–8 has Alexander Janneus on his deathbed instruct his wife Alexandra to yield some power to the Pharisees because they have the confidence of the masses. Alexandra did as he advised and, "while she had the title of sovereign, the Pharisees had the power". Because of concern over Pharisaic power and fear that the Pharisees might take over completely, her son Aristobulus (II) tried to seize power when Alexandra became ill

(*Ant.* 13.16.1–5 §§408–23). His coup did not succeed, but it led to a contest between him and Hyrcanus II after Alexandra's death; however, the Pharisees are no longer mentioned in the account, and there is no suggestion that they were enlisted in support of either side in the following battle. They disappear from the account for the next forty years or so.

The Pharisees surface again during Herod's reign. Herod honored two individual Pharisees, Pollion and his disciple Samais, because of advice they had given with regard to Herod at an earlier stage in his career (*Ant.* 15.1.1 §3). When Herod required an oath of loyalty, he did not punish Pollion and Samais and most of their disciples who did not take the oath (*Ant.* 15.10.4 368–71). However, Josephus then states that the Pharisees opposed Herod and refused to take the oath of loyalty and were fined by him, while some who were implicated in a plot with members of Herod's household to assassinate the king were executed (*Ant.* 17.2.4–3.1 §§41–47). That Herod would punish particular Pharisees who opposed him is not surprising, but how to relate the non-punishment of Pollion and Samais for not taking the loyalty oath with the fine on the Pharisees in general is more difficult. Is this just another example of Josephus's many internal contradictions, perhaps due to the use of different sources? Did Herod impose the loyalty oath on more than one occasion? Were most Pharisees fined but only Pollion, Samais and their followers exempted? The last option is certainly a reasonable one, but Josephus is less than clear.

Having mentioned the Sadducees and Pharisees on a number of occasions in the *Antiquities*, Josephus suddenly devotes a section to a general discussion of them (18.1.3 §§4–23). Three things should be noted about this passage: first, Josephus seems to give a general description of the sects at this point because he now includes the "fourth philosophy", but this shows that the point at which he discusses the sects is not when they necessarily originated; second, he actually says very little about them and hardly gives their main characteristics or beliefs; third, he makes statements about the Pharisees' control of the government and cult which he makes nowhere else nor does he give any example of such power *except* during the reign of Alexandra Salome.

The Sadducees had been only occasionally mentioned in the *Antiquities*, but Josephus then recounts that the Ananus who became high priest in 62 CE was a Sadducee, with the Sadducees supposedly being harsher in their legal judgments than any of the other Jews (*Ant.* 20.9.1 §§199–200). The negative picture of Ananus in this passage is exceptional since elsewhere Josephus speaks more positively of the high priest (cf. Poehlmann 1992).

The Pharisees appear several times in Josephus's **Life**. He first of all mentions them in connection with his youth (*Life* 2 §§10–12):

At about the age of sixteen I determined to gain personal experience of the several sects into which our nation is divided. These . . . are three in number – the first that of the Pharisees, the second that of the Sadducees, and the third that of the Essenes. I thought that, after a thorough investigation, I should be in a position to select the best. So I submitted myself to hard training and laborious exercises and passed through [*diēlthon*] the three courses. Not content, however, with the experience thus gained, on hearing of one named Bannus.... With him I lived for three years and, having accomplished my purpose, returned to the city. Being now in my nineteenth year I began to govern my life [*politeuesthai*] by the rules of [*katakolouthōn*] the Pharisees, a sect having points of resemblance to that which the Greeks call the Stoic school.

Mason (1989; 1991: 242–56) has recently argued, that contrary to widespread interpretation, this passage does not mean that Josephus himself became a Pharisee. Mason states that those who say Josephus became a Pharisee are dependent on a particular understanding of the last phrase of the quote, but if so, "he has chosen an excruciatingly circuituous way of saying it" (Mason 1991: 355–56). Mason thinks it has a different meaning and translates it more or less as "engage in public affairs following the school of the Pharisees". He is right about the roundabout way of speaking, but Hellenistic historians were often more interested in rhetoric and literary style than in being straightforward and clear; however, the predominant judgment does not depend on just that phrase but also on the entire context: the most natural way of understanding Josephus's statement in the passage overall is that at age 19 he became a Pharisee. Mason's argument – that Josephus simply means to say that he followed the Pharisees in his public activities because they dominated public life – is not convincing. If everyone followed them, as he implies, would there be any point in Josephus making the statement? Mason rightly points out that there is no evidence elsewhere that Josephus was a Pharisee (cf. also *JCH*: 5), but that is beside the point – Josephus often makes claims according to the circumstances, not necessarily according to the truth.

Next, Josephus mentions that after Menahem had been killed, "I ventured out of the Temple and once more consorted with the chief priests and the leading Pharisees" (*Life* 5 §§21). His final comments involve Simon, son of Gamaliel, who was a Pharisee. As part of the provisional government in the early part of the 66–70 revolt, Simon supposedly wanted to remove Josephus from his post of commander in Galilee and sent a delegation to carry this out. The delegation was composed of two men of the lower social order who were Pharisees, another Pharisee from a priestly family, and a young man from the high priests (*Life* 39 §197).

Josephus's statements about the Sadducees and Pharisees can be summarized as follows:

1. Josephus himself had personal acquaintance with the Pharisaic and Sadducean movements and knew or had knowledge of prominent figures in

the movements. However, there is no evidence that he was himself ever a member of either movement.

2. His attitude toward both movements is ambivalent. Toward the Pharisees he is sometimes favorable, sometimes neutral, and occasionally negative. Toward the Sadducees there are positive points in his descriptions, but he often has an edge to his presentation and never seems completely favorable or even neutral. To what extent he follows his sources in individual passages is debatable. Although in typical Hellenistic manner he usually rewrote his sources, this does not mean that he imposed a consistent view on them: in some cases he may have (or has) allowed the viewpoint of the original source to stand.

3. One has to be careful to distinguish Josephus's claims about the Pharisees from the actual events he describes. His claims are more likely to represent interpretation and even propaganda. Although he says that the Pharisees were able to gain credence when they spoke up against even a king or high priest, his narrative demonstrates no such thing. Only during the reign of Alexandra Salome did they seem to have power to enforce their will to any major extent. During the war with Rome, certain Pharisees gained prominence (e.g. Simon son of Gamaliel), but they did so as individuals since the Pharisees as a group do not appear to have been important in the revolt. Nowhere are the Pharisees as an undifferentiated group shown to control or dominate, either in the civil or the religious sphere. The Hasmoneans, Romans, and Herodians rule the country; only under Alexandra do the Pharisees have sufficient influence to get their way. The Pharisees are kept under control by John Hyrcanus, Alexander Janneus, and Herod, and not even mentioned for other rulers. The priests are in charge of the temple.

4. In the later *Antiquities* Josephus has the Pharisees in some passages where they do not appear in the earlier *War*, especially with regard to John Hyrcanus and Alexander Janneus. Why this is so is not completely clear. It could be that he abbreviated his sources in the earlier work or perhaps used sources which did not have them. Equally, he could have had different sources in the later work or even have introduced the Pharisees artificially or at least given them greater prominence than the sources did.

5. According to his presentation, both the Pharisees and Sadducees have political aspirations much of the time. Although so little is said about the Sadducees that it is difficult to draw any certain conclusions, one has the impression that the Sadducees – or at least some individual Sadducees – were significantly involved in government. They number the wealthy and prominent among their number or their sympathizers. The Pharisees are often pictured as seeking political power, sometimes exercising it as a group (as under Alexandra Salome), and sometimes having individuals with a prominent position. The only time Josephus depicts them as actually in power as a group, however, is under Alexandra Salome.

6. Both groups are portrayed as having religious beliefs, but very little is actually said as to what these are. Apart from the somewhat irrelevant question of fate, the Pharisees are characterized by having "traditions from the fathers" not written in the books of Moses (though what these were is never spelled out in detail); this is the one consistent thread throughout Josephus's references to them (cf. Baumgarten 1984–85; 1987). Goodman (1999) has recently argued that the "ancestral traditions" were not special Pharisaic teachings but conservative teachings of the populace as a whole, which helps to explain their popularity; however, this explanation does not seem to me to fit well the context of the statements. The Pharisees respect the teachings of the elders and also believe in reward and punishment after death. They have a reputation for accurate interpretation of the scriptures and are influential among the common people. The Sadducees do not accept anything not written in the scriptures and allow younger members to argue with elders. They reject reward and punishment after death. In several passages the Pharisees have a reputation for being able to predict the future.

New Testament

The one individual claiming to be a Pharisee whose actual words we seem to have is the **Apostle Paul**. Information about his Pharisaic background is given in two sources: the genuine letters of Paul (Phil. 3:4–6) and the Acts of the Apostles (discussed below). There is a further problem in that Paul's Christian teachings in some cases may represent a reaction against his Jewish background. It is difficult, therefore, to determine which (if any) of Paul's views or beliefs or teachings show a Pharisaic influence. His being a Pharisee is associated with observance of the law; beyond that it is difficult to go.

The gospels mention the Pharisees a good deal but also the Sadducees to some extent. Here is a summary of the major statements about the various groups (see Grabbe 1999b for further details; cf. also Saldarini: 134–98; Neusner 1973a: 57–80):

1. The gospel traditions are difficult because of their tradition history and the question of their interrelationships. The two earliest sources of the gospel tradition are, by a strong consensus, Mark and Q. There is very little Q information on the question, the main parallel being Q (Luke) 11:39–52. The most valuable source of information is therefore Mark (usually considered the earliest gospel, written around 70 or not long afterward) with its synoptic parallels.

2. There is also the problem that certain groups and individuals seem only to be ciphers set up as Jesus's opponents simply for the sake of being knocked down, yet despite this some patterns do emerge. The opponents of Jesus most frequently cited in Mark are the Pharisees, but they appear in only slightly more than half the pericopae; on the other hand, they often appear accompanied by others (scribes, Herodians, John's disciples), and there are quite a

few others (e.g. scribes) cited alone. Thus, the Pharisees are associated with a variety of groups, including scribes (Mark 7:1–23), Herodians (Mark 3:1–6; 12:13), Sadducees (Mat. 3:7–10), and even the chief priests (Mat. 21:45). Sometimes they oppose each other, but at other times they seem to be in an alliance against Jesus; however, there is good reason to see the bulk of these as secondary ascriptions. Where Mark (2:6; 12:38) has only "scribes", Matthew (23:2) and Luke (5:21) have "scribes and Pharisees". In what is generally assumed to be a Q–pericope, Matthew's "Pharisees and Sadducees" (Mat. 3:7–10) is probably less original than Luke's "crowds" (3:7–9). Similarly, the Pharisees of Mark 8:11 become "the Pharisees and Sadducees" (Mat. 16:1) or "scribes and Pharisees" (Mat. 12:38). In sum, there seems a tendency to increase the opponents of Jesus in any episode, with the later sources more likely to add names. Interestingly, the Herodians found three times in Mark disappear except for Matthew 22:15–16.

3. By and large, there is little attempt to give detailed information about the Sadducees, Pharisees, and others; rather, they serve simply as a foil to Jesus. They come to question him but then the focus is on his reply; they usually have no comeback.

4. The teachings of the Pharisees include agricultural law, washing, and ritual purity in general. Much is made of eating and ritual purity ("eating with unwashed hands": Mark 2:15–17//Mat. 9:10–13//Luke 5:29–32; Mark 7:1–23//Mat. 15:1–20//Luke 11:37–41). There are also some other questions, such as about the sabbath (Mark 2:23–28//Mat. 12:1–8//Luke 6:1–5; Mark 3:1–6//Mat. 12:9–14//Luke 6:6–11), marriage (Mark 10:2–12//Mat. 19:3–12//Luke 16:18), how to recognize the messiah (Mark 12:35–37// Mat. 22:41–46//Luke 20:41–44), and obedience to the Roman authorities (Mark 12:13–17//Mat. 22:15–22; Luke 20:20–26). They have "traditions from the elders" (Mark 7:5), though it is not stated that this is in the form of an "oral Torah".

5. There are several ways of relating the gospel evidence to history. One is to conclude that most of the statements about the Pharisees, especially those indicating Pharisaic dominance, are post-70 additions to the tradition and may well represent later controversies (cf. Neusner 1973a: 67–80). It has also been suggested that they may represent intra-Pharisaic disputes between those who had become Christians and those who had not, or even intra-Christian debates to some extent; however, most NT scholars would agree that there is some manifestation of the pre-70 situation even if not always reaching back to the time of Jesus (Saldarini 1988: 144–98). For example, Mark's traditions may reflect the mid-first century, while the role of the Pharisees in society as described by him is intrinsically probable (Saldarini 1988: 145, 156–57).

6. The pericopae which imply special religious authority for the Pharisees are in the later sources (Mat. 23:2; John 9:22–35; 12:42).

There is considerable disagreement among NT scholars on the extent to which the **Book of Acts** is a credible historical source (cf. Fitzmyer 1998; Mattill 1978; versus Hemer 1989). The book associates the Sadducees with the leading priests. According to Acts 4:1–2, the Sadducees come with the temple authorities to arrest Peter and John for teaching in the temple. When Peter and John are then brought before the Sanhedrin, the "sect of the Sadducees" are with the high priest (5:17–39). But the Pharisee Gamaliel, "a teacher of the law respected by all the people", is also a member of the Sanhedrin, and his advice is accepted. Paul is said to have been a disciple of this Gamaliel (22:3). These events are dated to the early 30s CE. Some three decades later, about 60 CE, Paul is arrested and brought before the Sanhedrin (22–23). He observes that the council is split between the Pharisees and Sadducees, and causes a dissension by claiming to be a Pharisee and by saying that he is on trial for believing in the resurrection of the dead, for "the Sadducees say that there is no resurrection, or angel, or spirit; but the Pharisees acknowledge all three" (23:8). However, the Sadducees are represented as dominant since their point of view prevails.

Rabbinic literature

Two sorts of information in rabbinic literature are of potential value for information on the Pharisees. First, we have a number of pericopae that mention the *Pĕrûšîm* and *Ṣaddûqîm*, which have usually been identified with the Pharisees and Sadducees of the Greek sources. This is not as straightforward as it may seem, as will be discussed below. Secondly, we have the traditions about the named pre-70 sages and the houses of Hillel and Shammai which have often been drawn on for evidence about the Pharisees. The problem is that these figures are not labeled Pharisees. The Tannaitic pericopae which talk about the *Pĕrûšîm* never associate them with the named sages or their schools. This might lead one to conclude that there was no connection. Yet this does not settle the matter because we have the additional complication that two of the pre-70 sages *are* called Pharisees in other sources: Gamliel the Elder looks very much like the individual called Gamaliel in Acts 5:34; similarly, Šimʿon son of Gamliel of the rabbinic traditions seems to be the Simon son of Gamaliel known from Josephus (*Life* 38 §§190–91).

It would be impossible even to survey here all the statements in rabbinic literature which could be relevant. For a consideration of the pericopae about the *Pĕrûšîm* and *Ṣaddûqîm* in Tannaitic literature, see Rivkin (1972; the main ones are also listed in Grabbe 1999b); all of the material relating to the pre-70 named figures has been assembled and analyzed in Neusner (1971; cf. also Saldarini 1988: 199–237). Some of the major points to notice are the following:

1. The terminology of *Pĕrûšîm* and *Ṣaddûqîm* is already problematic. *Pĕrûšîm* could be used in the sense of "separatists" or "abstainers/ascetics" as well as

Pharisees. *Ṣaddûqîm* was sometimes inserted in manuscripts in place of an original *minîm* or similar expression. It is difficult to take all references to the *Pĕrûšîm* as a reference to the same entity (whether Pharisees or something else). Although the teachings of the *Pĕrûšîm* seem to agree with those of the sages most of the time, it is interesting to see that none of the pre-70 figures is designated as one of the *Pĕrûšîm*.

2. The dating of the pericopae about the *Pĕrûšîm* and *Ṣaddûqîm* is very difficult. Only two of those with both the *Pĕrûšîm* and *Ṣaddûqîm* concern matters relevant only to the pre-70 situation (*T. Hag.* 3:35 on the immersion of the menorah; cf. also *M. Parah* 3:7 on the *Ṣaddûqîm* and "the elders"). Another with the *Ṣaddûqîm* alone concerns matters which relate to a time when the temple still stood (*T. Parah* 3:8); the same applies to the pericope about the Boethusians who seem especially to be associated with the temple. Most of the others give no indication that they are supposed to be related to Second Temple times. There are several possibilities with regard to the historical reality about the debates between the *Pĕrûšîm* and *Ṣaddûqîm*. They could be, first, a memory of actual pre-70 debates; or a memory of debates between post-70 groups; or perhaps an artificial construct to reflect a contemporary debate by using old or traditional names. There may also be other possibilities, and determining which is the correct evaluation is not easy.

3. The content of the Mishnah, the foundational rabbinic document, focuses on certain topics: laws of purity, eating, festivals, and agriculture; and laws relating to the exchange of women, such as betrothal, marriage, and divorce. The vast bulk of the traditions relate to these subjects. An analysis of the early traditions about pre-70 figures and the Houses of Shammai and Hillel also shows a preoccupation with the same topics which form the bulk of the traditions in the Mishnah. The pre-70 traditions of the Mishnah, as well as the early traditions about pre-70 figures, do not indicate a concern with civil law, governance of the country, or the oversight of the temple cult. Rather, they relate to matters which would be under the control of an individual, the head of a family, or a small community: household affairs, family affairs, daily life, the exchange of women. Exceptions are Gamaliel I and his son Simeon (Simon) son of Gamaliel, both of whom seem to have had some sort of civil office (Neusner 1971: 3.291). Although a minority section of the Mishnah deals with civil law (*Neziqin* "Damages"), there is no evidence of any part of it arising before 70 (Neusner 1981: 62, 198–204). Similarly, the Mishnaic order relating to the temple (*Qodasim* "Holy Things") lacks one of the main components found in similar documents (e.g. Leviticus 1–15 and the Epistle to the Hebrews): a discussion of priestly law. That is, the expected contents of sacrifice, sources of cultic purity, and the temple are all there, but the priesthood as such is ignored, a surprising omission if it arose in a group which allegedly controlled the priesthood.

4. A number of the important figures of pre-70 times seem to have had nothing to do with Hillel (or Shammai). The Gamaliel family (Gamaliel I,

Simeon son of Gamaliel, Gamaliel II) is not associated with Hillel and not said to be descended from him (though later tradition makes Gamaliel I his grandson). Simon does agree with the House of Shammai on one or two points and is likely to have been a Shammaite, as was his son Gamaliel II (Neusner 1971: 1.380, 387; 3.274). Similarly, Yohanan ben Zakkai is not associated with Hillel even though later tradition attempts to make him so; rather, he seems independent of the Houses (Neusner 1970: 289–90; 1971: 3.275–77).

5. The size of the Houses of Hillel and Shammai seems to have been quite small (Neusner 1971: 3.267). Their elders could all meet in one room (cf. *M. Suk.* 2.7). Even a sufficient quorum of the two Houses to make decisions affecting their entire membership could meet in an "upper room" (*'aliyyāh* [*M. Shab.* 1:4]). Evidently all the ritual immersions of cooking utensils by the Pharisees in Jerusalem could be done at one trough (*M. Miq.* 4.5). In the talmuds, Hillel is alleged to have had only eighty disciples (or pairs of disciples: *Y. Ned.* 5.6; *B. Suk.* 28a; *B. B. Batra* 134a). None of these accounts may be historical, but what needs explaining is why the second-century compilers would present the Houses as small if they remembered them as being quite large. This suggests that the traditions available to them knew only of small groups around Hillel and Shammai.

6. Whether the Boethusians (*Baitôsîm*) are to be equated with the *Ṣaddûqîm* is a moot point. No explicit equation is made in rabbinic literature, yet there are indications that the Boethusians may be closely related to the *Ṣaddûqîm*. Neither seems to believe in the *ṭĕvûl yôm*, and the debates between the *Pĕrûšîm* and *Ṣaddûqîm* in *M. Yad.* 4:6–8 are said to be between the *Pĕrûšîm* and the Boethusians in *T. Yad.* 2:20. Sometimes the high priest is identified with the the *Ṣaddûqîm* and sometimes with the Boethusians.

4QMMT and the *Temple Scroll* (11QT)

It has recently been argued that some of the regulations in 4QMMT and also the *Temple Scroll* represent Saducean *halakha* and specifically oppose Pharisaic rulings. I have dealt with the question in detail elsewhere (Grabbe 1997c). Out of the seventeen separate *halakot* in 4QMMT, only four have been suggested as agreeing with the Sadducees. Of these four I argue that only two are possibilities. If one or two of these regulations coincide with the views of the *Ṣaddûqîm* alleged by rabbinic literature, this is a long way from saying that the author(s) of 4QMMT were Sadducees and opposed the Pharisees.

Summary and conclusions

We have essentially three sources, each one with problems of dating, *Tendenz*, and reliability. In many cases, the sources are so problematic, one wonders whether we can know anything about the Pharisees and Sadducees. Yet the main sources all seem to be independent of each other, which makes coincidences between their different pictures of potential significance. Whatever our conclusions, though, they can only be tentative at best; we simply do not know a great deal about these groups.

Josephus is the most valuable source: he knew certain individual Pharisees and had access to information on the group before 70; he wrote while they were in existence or during the time that they were transforming themselves; his biases are probably the easiest to analyze and to take into account. The NT writings cover a considerable span of time and are characterized by a general hostile attitude to the various Jewish groups. Although post-70, both Mark and Q seem to have had some pre-70 traditions and show a more nuanced description than the synoptic parallels and the Fourth Gospel. Acts is very difficult to evaluate. Rabbinic literature is the latest and most problematic to use. Even the Tannaitic writings were redacted long after 70 CE, and the extent to which genuine pre-70 data is preserved is not easy to determine. References to the *Pĕrûšîm* and *Ṣaddûqîm* may or may not have the historical pre-70 Pharisees and Sadducees in mind; on the other hand, those figures most often designated as Pharisee in modern treatments are not so identified in rabbinic literature.

Keeping in mind these major difficulties with using and evaluating the sources, some tentative concluding observations can be made:

1. The Greek sources (and possibly rabbinic literature) make both the Pharisees and the Sadducees important at least some of the time, beginning about the reign of John Hyrcanus (135–104 BCE). They also make the Sadducees and Pharisees rivals, both seeking political power at the expense of the other.

2. There may have been certain socio–economic differences between the groups, in that the Sadducees are said to have the support of the wealthy and prominent persons, whereas the Pharisees have the support of the masses (Josephus); on the other hand, popular leaders do not necessarily come from the lower social strata, and some priests are said to be Pharisees.

3. The Sadducees and Pharisees are also alleged to differ on a number of religious beliefs. The Pharisees are especially characterized by the traditions of the fathers, whereas the Sadducees do not accept as authoritative anything not in the written scripture (Josephus). The Pharisees believe in the survival of the soul and rewards and punishments in the afterlife; the Sadducees reject this. If the Boethusians are to be associated with the Sadducees, the two groups also differ at other points: the counting of the wave sheaf day and the celebration of the Feast of Weeks (see #7 below), the concept of the *ʿêrûv* which was a means of extending the limits of a sabbath day's journey (LeMoyne 1972: 201–4), the popular customs of pouring water and beating with willow branches at the Feast of Tabernacles (LeMoyne 1972: 192–95, 283–89). It is often asserted that the Sadducees accepted only the Pentateuch as canonical, but this is only a deduction from their supposed rejection of

beliefs in angels and spirits (on this, see Daube 1990; Viviano/Taylor 1992). It may be that a late book such as Daniel, with an elaborate angelology and the resurrection, was not accepted, but it is not clear that the OT canon was closed at this time in any case. The Sadducees may well have accepted the Pentateuch, Prophets, and some of the Writings just as apparently many other Jews did (cf. LeMoyne 1972: 357–79). According to Josephus, the Pharisees (like the Essenes) have a reputation for knowing the future.

4. The rabbinic traditions about named pre-70 figures do not identify them as members of any group, including the the *Pĕrûšîm* or *Şaddûqîm*. Yet two individuals in the Greek sources identified as Pharisees look very much like pre-70 sages of rabbinic literature: Gamaliel (the Elder) and Simon son of Gamaliel. There seems to be justification in accepting Hillel and Shammai and their subsequent "houses" as Pharisaic. (An important figure such as Yohanan ben Zakkai does not have Pharisaic characteristics, however.) On the other hand, the house of Hillel, which became dominant in the Yavnean period, seems to have been subordinate to Shammai before 70, and the house of Gamaliel appears to have been separate from either Hillel or Shammai. The family of Gamaliel may have been an important link between the Pharisees and the later rabbinic movement (cf. Neusner/Thoma 1995: 198–99). These differences between Pharisaic groups might explain the different statements about whether Pharisees were seeking political power or not, since some groups may have been more active in this than others, at least at certain times.

5. Two of our sources seem to make the Pharisees especially concerned about halakic matters. The gospels have them particularly exercised about tithing, ritual purity (washings), sabbath observance, and the like. According to rabbinic literature, the *Pĕrûšîm* and *Şaddûqîm* also have certain halakic differences. The Pharisaic agenda according to the gospels – as far as one can determine it from the few brief references – accords well with the contents of the Mishnah/Tosefta (with the exception of the gospel debates about the messiah and the question of the government of Judea). This is not to suggest that all the pre-70 traditions of the Mishnah necessarily go back to Pharisees (Neusner 1981: 70–71; cf. Saldarini 1988: 201–02); some of the laws and legal themes may have been created by groups other than the Pharisees. Although the legal agenda of the Mishnah probably tells us a good deal about the pre-70 Pharisees, it may not tell us their complete interests. That is, there may have been concerns which were not preserved for one reason or another by the framers of the Mishnah (Saldarini 1988: 212–16).

6. Those sources which give the Pharisees a general dominance of religious belief and practice are those which come later in relation to parallel sources. Thus, it is only two later passages in the *Antiquities* which state that public worship is carried out according to Pharisaic regulations and that the Sadducees are required to follow them even when they hold office. This is not stated in the *War* and is not borne out in Josephus's other passages on the

Pharisees. The one exception is the reign of Alexandra; indeed, the statement of Josephus about the Pharisees controlling the king and high priest fits well with her reign. Similarly, although the gospels give considerable prominence to the Pharisees as opponents of Jesus, it is only the late Fourth Gospel which suggests that they can cast people out of the synagogues. It is also the later passages in the book of Acts which suggest that the Pharisees make up a significant part of the Sanhedrin (though they are still not dominant). It is the Ushan stratum of Tannaitic literature which begins to assert that Hillel controlled the temple (Neusner 1971: 3.255–59).

7. An important question is whether the Boethusians of rabbinic literature represent another group, or are identical with (or a sub-division of) the Sadducees. There is no clear answer on this, but the Boethusians are associated with the priesthood and their teachings seem to be closer to those of the Sadducees. The argument that the term is derived from the high priestly family of Boethus is plausible and seems more likely than the theory that they are the Essenes (Sussmann 1989–90: 40–60; cf. Schremer 1997); if so, this fits with the classic argument that "Sadducee" comes from the priestly name "Zadok". Their reckoning of Pentecost as falling always on a Sunday and the day of the wave sheaf is likely to have been the priestly tradition in the temple (see p. 141 above).

ESSENES

Davies, P. R. (1982a) *Qumran*.

—— (1982b) "The Ideology of the Temple in the Damascus Document", *JJS* 33: 287–301.

—— (1983) *The Damascus Covenant: An Interpretation of the "Damascus Document"*.

—— (1987) *Behind the Essenes: History and Ideology in the Dead Sea Scrolls*.

Golb, N. (1995) *Who Wrote the Dead Sea Scrolls?*

Goodman, M. (1995) "A Note on the Qumran Sectarians, the Essenes and Josephus", *JJS* 46: 161–66.

Grabbe, L. L. (1997b) "The Current State of the Dead Sea Scrolls: Are There More Answers than Questions?" in S. E. Porter and C. A. Evans (eds) *The Scrolls and the Scriptures: Qumran Fifty Years After*: 54–67.

—— (1997h) Book review: N. Golb, *Who Wrote the Dead Sea Scrolls?*, *DSD* 4: 124–28.

Kampen, J. (1986) "A Reconsideration of the Name 'Essene' in Greco-Jewish Literature in Light of Recent Perceptions of the Qumran Sect", *HUCA* 57: 61–81.

Murphy-O'Connor, J. (1974) "The Essenes and their History", *RB* 81: 215–44.

—— (1985) "The *Damascus Document* Revisited", *RB* 92: 223–46 (= *SBL 1986 Seminar Papers*, 369–83).

Vermes, G. "The Etymology of 'Essenes'", *RevQ* 2 (1960) 427–43.

The Essenes were discussed at length in *JCH* (491–99), with bibliography (most of which is not repeated here). Much of that section as it deals with with original sources is repeated here for the sake of completeness; however, there are some issues of debate that have arisen in the meantime, and these are dealt with here (or in my discussion of the scrolls [pp. 67–70 above]). Only current relevant secondary studies are given here.

Sources

There are several ancient descriptions of the Essenes. One of the most important comes from the Roman writer, **Pliny the Elder** (*c*.24–79 CE), who makes the following statement in his *Natural History* (5.73):

> On the west side of the Dead Sea, but out of range of the noxious exhalations of the coast, is the solitary tribe of the Essenes, which is remarkable beyond all the other tribes in the whole world, as it has no women and has renounced all sexual desire, has no money, and has only palm-trees for company. . . . Lying below [*infra*] the Essenes was formerly the town of Engedi . . . Next comes Masada.

The approximate location of the Essenes' habitation is made clear by Pliny's geographical description. While the term "below" may be ambiguous, the sequence of listing is from north to south. Thus, the Essenes evidently lived on the northern part of the west coast of the Dead Sea north of Engedi. The exact spot is not clarified, though the description potentially includes the area where Khirbet Qumran is found.

The accounts which **Philo** gives in *Quod omnis probus* (75–87) and *Hypothetica* (as quoted by Eusebius, *Praep. evang.* 8 [LCL 9.437–43]) are both very close to those in **Josephus** (*War* 2.8.2–13 §§120–61; *Ant.* 18.1.5 §§18–22). This leads to the supposition that the two used a common earlier source, at least in part, rather than having personal knowledge in their description of the Essenes (despite Josephus's claim to have been initiated into the sect [*Life* 2 §§10–11]). Both Josephus and Philo (one or more accounts) agree that the Essene community:

1 number about 4,000 males (*Ant.* 18.1.5 §20; *Probus* 75)
2 live in many towns and villages (*War* 2.8.4 §124; *Probus* 76; *Hyp.* 11.1)
3 have no wives, women, or marriage (*War* 2.8.2 §§120–21; *Ant.* 18.1.5 §21; *Hyp.* 11.14–17)
4 have community of goods and communal meals (*War* 2.8.3 §122; *Ant.* 18.1.5 §20; *Probus* 85–86; *Hyp.* 11.4–5)

5 work at agriculture and crafts (*Ant.* 18.1.5 §19; *Probus* 76; *Hyp.* 11.6, 8–9)
6 do not swear oaths (*War* 2.8.6 §135; *Probus* 84)
7 do not change clothes (*War* 2.8.4 §126; *Hyp.* 11.12)
8 keep no slaves (*Ant.* 18.1.5 §21; *Probus* 79)

In addition, the *War* and the *Antiquities* (but not either of Philo's accounts) mention that the Essenes:

9 elect their overseers and officials (*War* 2.8.3 §123; *Ant.* 18.1.5 §22)
10 believe in the immortality of the soul (*War* 2.8.11 §§154–58; *Ant.* 18.1.5 §18)

The *War* makes a number of points about the Essenes which do not occur in the *Antiquities* or in Philo:

11 oil defiling (*War* 2.8.3 §123)
12 prayers to the sun (*War* 2.8.5 §128)
13 daily schedule of work (*War* 2.8.5 §§128–32)
14 bathing before eating (*War* 2.8.5 §129) and if touched by an outsider (*War.* 2.8.10 §150)
15 speaking in turn (*War* 2.8.5 §132)
16 study of the writings of the ancients and medicines (*War* 2.8.6 §136)
17 regulations for admission to (*War* 2.8.7 §§137–42) and expulsion from the order (*War* 2.8.8 §§143–44)
18 preservation of angels' names (*War* 2.8.7 §142)
19 no spitting in company or to the right (*War* 2.8.8 §147)
20 strictness in observing the sabbath (*War* 2.8.8 §147)
21 foretelling the future (*War* 2.8.12 §159)
22 include a group which marries (*War* 2.8.13 §160)

Philo's two accounts are very moralizing, and most of what he gives is paralleled in Josephus and thus has already been listed.

Josephus also mentions a few individual Essenes: Judas who was noted for his successful foretelling of events in the time of Aristobulus I (*Ant.* 13.11.2 §311); Manaemus who predicted Herod's rise to rule and was rewarded by him (*Ant.* 15.10.5 §373); Simon who interpreted a dream of Archelaus (*Ant.* 17.13.3 §§347–48); John who was one of the commanders during the war against Rome (*War.* 2.20.4 §567; 3.2.1 §11).

The question of Qumran

Although in the early days after the discovery of the Scrolls, the group producing them was identified with one or the other of most of the ancient sects, the suggestion of the Essenes (apparently first proposed by E. Sukenik) became widely accepted. Some still refer to the "Essenes at Qumran" as an established fact, but a number of substantial objections have been made to this identification. The question of whether the Scrolls themselves are to be associated with the ancient habitation at Qumran is discussed elsewhere (pp. 69–70 above), but this question is also relevant for the identity of the group in the Scrolls, since it is generally agreed that some of the Scrolls have sufficient points in common (characteristic vocabulary, peculiar terminology, and theological outlook) to be considered as related. These include the *Damascus Document* (CD; 4Q266–273; 5Q12; 6Q15), the *Community Rule* (1QS), the *Rule of the Congregation* (1QS^a), the *Habakkuk Commentary* (4QpHab), the *Hodayot* (1QH), and the *War Scroll* (1QM).

Golb has recently argued for diverse origins of the Scrolls (e.g. 1995; see the review of Grabbe 1997h), but it must be said that this argument is not new or unique to him. The real question is not whether many of the Scrolls originated in another context and were simply taken over by the Qumran community but whether the clearly identified core of "sectarian" writings have any connection with what we know of the Essenes. To discuss this question, the evidence of Philo and Josephus is compared with evidence from just two of the Scrolls: the *Damascus Document* and the *Community Rule*. The reason is that both of these contain regulations about the organization of a community and are generally agreed to be related to each other.

1. On the settlements of the Essenes, Philo (*Probus* 76; *Hyp.* 11.1) and Josephus (*War* 2.8.4 §124) indicate communities in a variety of towns and villages; this also seems to be the view of the *Damascus Document* about its own communities (CD 7:6; 12:19–14:16; 19:2). The statement of Pliny the Elder, on the other hand, indicates only one settlement: on the northwest shore of the Dead Sea, though the exact spot is not indicated.

2. On the community of goods, Philo (*Probus* 85–86; *Hyp.* 11.4), Josephus (*War* 2.8.3 §122; *Ant.* 18.1.5 §20), and 1QS (1:11–12; 5:1–22; 6:16–23) all agree that property was held in common. All new entrants turned over their property to the community on attaining full membership. However, certain passages in the *Damascus Document* can be interpreted as allowing at least some private ownership (CD 9:10–16; 14:12–16).

3. There were common meals, preceded by bathing (*Probus* 86; *Hyp.* 11.5, 11; *War* 2.8.5 §129; CD 10:10–13; 1QS 3:4–5; 5:13–14; 6:2, 25; 7:2–3).

4. In the regulations for assemblies, the members were to sit according to a particular order (*Probus* 81; 1QS 6:8–10), to speak in turn (*War* 2.8.5 §132; 1QS 6:10–13), and not to spit (*War* 2.8.8 §147; 1QS 7:13).

5. In the procedures for entry, the sources agree that a period of probation was required. Josephus (*War* 2.8.7 §137–42) describes it in three stages, each lasting a year. 1QS 6:13–23 mentions two stages, each of a year, though a further, less formal stage preceding these is not incompatible with Josephus's data.

6. Rigor in keeping the sabbath was shown by the Essenes. Josephus (*War* 2.8.9 §147) states that they were more particular in their sabbath observances than any other group. This seems to be confirmed by such regulations as those found in CD 10:14–11:18.

More controversial are some other points, though many would see them as also showing a connection:

7. On the question of worship at the temple, overall, the Qumran documents seem to oppose the Jerusalem cult as polluted (e. g., CD 6:11–20). Also, Philo indicates that Essenes had no interest in physical sacrifice (*Probus* 75); however, Josephus (*Ant.* 18.1.5 §19) says that the Essenes would send votive offerings to the temple, though he then immediately adds that they had their own cultic rites. Certain passages would appear to support the view that some offerings were allowed (CD 11:18–21; 12:1–2; 16:13). One explanation is that the Essenes as a whole (including the pre-Qumran community) allowed a minimal amount of participation in the temple cult, but that the Qumran group forbade even that (cf. Davies 1982b; 1983: 134–40; Murphy-O'Connor 1985).

8. Women and marriage. The ancient sources agree that the Essenes were celibate, except that Josephus asserts there was one group who married for purposes of procreation. The Scrolls present a diverse picture: the *Community Rule* is silent on the subject. However, the *Damascus Document* (CD 7:6–7; 12:1–2; 15:5; 16:10–12; 7:6–7//19:2–3), the *War Scroll* (1QM 7:3) and 1QS^a 1:4, 9–11 all indicate the presence of women; the *Damascus Document* also seems to have in mind the intention of procreation (CD 4:10–5:2; cf. Davies 1987: 73–85). On this particular question, the archaeology is also relevant. The burial excavations so far carried out at the Qumran cemetery have complicated matters: on the one hand, in what was only a sampling of the graves, skeletons of women and children were found; on the other hand, these were few and on the outskirts of the cemetery rather than in the main part of it, which might suggest women were not generally present (DeVaux 1973: 47–48). Various suggestions have been made to explain this: one is that the women and children were visitors who died on the site; another is that a few women worked at the site but were not a part of the Qumran community. The important thing is that future excavations may change the picture so far obtained.

How valid are these arguments? It is clear that there are some important disagreements between the sources, especially with regard to the location of the place where the Essenes lived and whether they were celibate. It is for this reason that the Essene hypothesis needs careful scrutiny at this time (cf. the cautions of Goodman 1995 and pp. 69–70 above). If identity requires exact correspondence, then this is clearly not found; nevertheless, there are some striking correspondences that go beyond common Jewish practices. It is also methodologically unsound to require such identity in every detail. There are various reasons why some discrepancy might occur:

- the natural differences between the perceptions of observers who are describing the same thing, especially an entity outside their normal experience
- the differing amount of completeness in the description, with one source emphasizing certain aspects, and another source giving most weight to other details
- sources that describe the same entity but at different points in its development
- the amount of variety or division within the movement, so that a description fits only one particular faction or perhaps excludes the differences nursed in certain factions

All of these points may be involved in our sources on the Essenes. A Greco-Roman writer such as Pliny would have interpreted his source (even if it was Jewish) from his own perspective; also his source may have been quite an old one. Although both Philo and Josephus were probably using detailed Jewish sources, they still interpret them. Philo in particular is making a theological point in his description, while Josephus wants to make the Essenes a philosophical school whose character will be admired by a Greco-Roman audience. On the other hand, there is no reason to assume that the Essenes were a rigidly organized group with no internal factions or developments over time. Both the questions of celibacy and place of settlement could be explained at least in part on this basis.

Whether one wishes to invoke such explanations depends on how likely one thinks the evidence is of a connection. In this case, most scholars find it difficult to believe that the agreements between Pliny, Philo, Josephus, and a certain group of the Scrolls can be mere coincidence. These agreements are on peculiar points, not on customs and practices likely to have been common to a wide range of Jewish groups. The view is that either we must postulate another unattested group at Qumran that had certain unique characteristics in common with the Essenes or we must assume that Qumran is somehow related to the Essenes. The first alternative goes against the natural principle of parsimony in argument; however, the latter would still leave open the possibilities that Qumran:

1 served as a sort of headquarters for a larger movement
2 was a celibate community where Essenes could go if they chose to adopt a more monastic style of life (temporarily or permanently), as opposed to other communities that lived more directly in Jewish society
3 was simply one of the many Essene groups which happened to live in the desert rather than in towns or villages
4 was a breakaway group, founded by the Teacher of Righteousness

This last case would suggest that Qumran renounced the parent movement and, despite still having much in common with it, cultivated some different beliefs and practices which it focused on as evidence of the corruption of the parent group. Present evidence seems to favor this last alternative.

Some tentative conclusions

Although the Essenes are in many ways the best attested of the ancient Jewish sects, many questions remain unanswered. Even the name "Essene" has not been satisfactorily explained. It has often been explained as from the Aramaic *ḥăsayyā'/ḥāsîn*, "pious", related to the Hebrew *ḥăsîdîm*, but this has been strongly influenced by various assumptions about the Hasidim (pp. 184–85 above). Also, the root *ḥsy* is known from Syriac but is not attested in Jewish Aramaic. Vermes (1960; Schürer: 2.559–60) suggested that the name was from *'āsyā'*, an Aramaic word for "healer", connecting the name with that of the Therapeutae (*JCH*: 499) which means "healers" in Greek; however, this explanation does not seem to have attracted many adherents. These and other suggestions have usually assumed a Semitic etymology of some sort, but Kampen (1986) has argued for a Greek origin, from *essēn*, the name for a cultic official of Artemis.

In spite of some recent doubts, the balance of the evidence still favors some sort of relationship between a group of "sectarian" documents among the scrolls and the Essenes, though this relationship may not be a simple one. Also, the most likely explanation is that the settlement at Khirbet Qumran used and hid many of the scrolls found in the surrounding caves, even if this connection is not without some problems. One initial point seems clear from the archaeology: the Qumran settlement took place in the late second (or early first) century BCE. The original community was only about fifty individuals, though later it seems to have expanded to about two hundred (cf. Davies 1982a: 42). Whatever the group was, it was very small and certainly not the 4,000 Essenes given by Philo and Josephus. It was evidently founded by an individual called the "Teacher of Righteousness": despite many suggestions, no consensus about his identity has emerged. The group was opposed by the "wicked priest" (*hakkôhēn hārāsā'*), usually equated with the high priest in the Jerusalem temple; most have identified him with one of the Hasmonean priest–kings, but the range of suggestions has been wide: Jonathan, Simon, Hyrcanus, Janneus, or even a succession of Hasmonean figures. Other opponents were the "Seekers after Smooth Things", who are often confidently asserted to be the Pharisees, but this is not at all certain (Grabbe 1997b: 58–60).

The most likely explanation is that the Qumran group began within the Essene movement but broke away. Several references to the "Man of Lies" look like an internal reference to the leader of the parent group, but we must keep in mind that a sect's bitterest attacks may be against those closest to it ideologically. No history of the larger movement can be traced (unless some hints of it are given in CD 1:1–11//4Q266 2:1–11; cf. Murphy-O'Connor 1974; Davies 1982a). The "390 years" (CD 1:5–6) has sometimes been used to calculate the beginnings of the group, but this is likely to be a stylized number borrowed from Ezekiel (4:5) and not historically useful (cf. pp. 246–48 below on such calculations). The Qumran group survived the (real or imagined) attacks of the "Wicked Priest" and the death of the Teacher, continued to flourish until the destruction of the settlement (probably by the earthquake of 31 BCE), later rebuilt it (how long it was abandoned is debated), and finally fell to the Romans who overran the area of Qumran about 68 CE. The group is not likely to have survived these events.

OTHER SECTS AND GROUPS

Engbert-Pedersen, T. (1999) "Philo's *De Vita Contemplativa* as a Philosopher's Dream", *JSJ* 30: 40–64.

Besides the groups discussed above, we have the names of a number of other groups, as well as individual leaders of movements. Some of these, such as the Sicarii and Zealots, are discussed under messianic movements (pp. 283–88 below). The Therapeutae were discussed in *JCH* (499); however, it has recently been suggested that rather than describing an actual group, Philo has invented a utopian picture which had no actual reality (Engbert-Pedersen 1999). This argument no doubt needs a good deal of discussion, but it is well founded and requires a careful rethink of how this particular group has been used in filling out the picture of early Judaism.

SYNTHESIS

Baumgarten, A. I. (1997) *The Flourishing of Jewish Sects in the Maccabean Era: An Interpretation.*
Grabbe, L. L. (1989) "The Social Setting of Early Jewish Apocalypticism", *JSP* 4: 27–47.
—— (1999b) "Sadducees and Pharisees", in J. Neusner and A. J. Avery-Peck (eds) *Judaism in Late Antiquity: Part Three. Where We Stand: Issues and Debates in Ancient Judaism: Volume 1*: 35–62.
—— (1999d) Review article: A. I. Baumgarten, *The Flourishing of Jewish Sects in the Maccabean Era*, *JSJ* 30: 89–94.
Stemberger, G. (1995) *Jewish Contemporaries of Jesus: Pharisees, Sadducees, Essenes.*

Factionalism is inherent in religion. Polytheistic religions are structured by the fact that multiple gods are worshiped, but even those who honor a variety of gods often focus on one particular god some or much of the time. There are also often special cults for different groups such as professions or women, and certain gods tend to attract cults, perhaps because they are seen as personal gods rather than national or high gods. However, this is not a trait only of polytheism, for all the monotheistic and monistic religions have developed factions, sects, or schools of thought of one sort or another even though they ostensibly worship only a single deity.

Religion among the Jewish people in the late Second Temple period has often been seen in terms of the "sects", especially the Pharisees and Sadducees. Writers on the subject have tended to give a somewhat more nuanced picture in recent years, but the old emphasis on the Pharisees and Sadducees has by no means gone away. Although I feel that focusing on the sects is likely to distort our understanding of Second Temple Judaism(s), there is no question that these two groups are important. They are also extremely difficult to come to grips with, despite the frequent statements made with great confidence about them. One problem with a number of recent treatments is their concentration on the Pharisees rather than recognizing that the Sadducees are as prominent in the sources as the former. This leads to a skewed discussion because of concentrating on the Pharisees in isolation.

We cannot afford to take anything for granted. Any study of the different sects has to go back to the basics, looking first of all at the sources and the problems with using them, with as few preconceptions as possible. This is what I have attempted to do in my fuller article on the Sadducees and Pharisees (Grabbe 1999b) and my summaries of the different groups here (though the discussion here has of necessity been abbreviated because of space). What I hope I have made clear is the basis of any positive statement made about the different groups, as well as the uncertainties in our knowledge.

The question of the different groups in Jewish society of the Second Temple period is an important one and well addressed in the recent study by Baumgarten (1997; cf. the review in Grabbe 1999d). Some interesting proposals about how groups originate (e.g. an attempt to return to an idealized past, a product of the growth of literacy, a consequence of urbanization) must be considered hypothetical, if sometimes plausible. On the other hand, the conventional mentality of assigning all sectarian origins to some sort of crisis situation ignores the fact that one cannot necessarily draw a sharp distinction between a sect and other forms of the religion. Sects are not just "crisis cults", and ideology and theology can also be significant social drivers (cf. Grabbe 1989; 1999d: 91; Baumgarten 1997: 152–66).

The following are some overall conclusions:

1. Sects and movements have a long history in Judaic religion, perhaps going back to pre-exilic times but most likely being present already in the Persian period. They become well attested in post-Maccabean times, though

some of the "schools of thought" known or postulated from earlier writings could well be in the nature of sects (e.g. the "Deuteronomistic School", the "wise" of Daniel).

2. Although much has been ascribed to the Hasidim, we actually know little about them. It is unclear that they are a unified movement, and a number of recent scholars have argued that the term is applied to a diversity of groups in the books of Maccabees. *A fortiori*, we do not know that they have any connection with the later sects.

3. The Sadducees seem to have been in existence by the end of the second century BCE. We first encounter them as a group seeking political power with the Hasmonean ruler. There is only sporadic evidence after this, though some prominent individuals are said to have been Sadducees. They are associated with the upper classes and the priesthood, and certain religious beliefs are ascribed to them, some of which also point to a priestly or temple group.

4. The Pharisees also seem to have been around by about 100 BCE and first appear as seeking political power, with the Sadducees as their rivals. They gain actual power under Alexandra Salome but then appear only sporadically in history to 70. A few prominent Pharisees are known, and some Pharisees seem to have been priests. They are supposed to have been interested in their own particular "traditions of the fathers" not written in the law of Moses, though exactly what these traditions are is never described. The family of Gamaliel seems to have been an important Pharisaic "school" which bridged the gap between the Second Temple and rabbinic periods, with some members of the family in prominent civic positions. If Hillel and Shammai were Pharisees, as often alleged, they seem to have been concerned mainly with basic laws relating to agricultural matters, purity, and the sabbath and festivals; there is little evidence that they held positions in civic society or the temple administration. On the other hand, they were probably the core making up the religious reconstruction at Yavneh after 70 (see Chapter 6 above).

5. The Essenes are also attested as early as 100 BCE. In contrast to the Sadducees and Pharisees, they seem to have withdrawn – at least to some extent – from ordinary society and developed a communal life based on religious ideals of common property and careful observance of the law (as they interpreted it). Some of the communities appear to have been celibate, though not all. Despite some recent doubts, the Essenes evidently are to be connected in some way with a core group of "sectarian" writings among the Scrolls which were probably, in turn, to be associated with the settlement at Qumran; however, the Qumran community may have been a breakaway group with some differences from other Essenes, as well as much in common.

6. Other groups are known, mainly with revolutionary overtones, though there is evidence that at least some of these were probably messianic movements of some sort: the "Fourth Philosophy", the Sicarii, and the Zealots (pp. 283–88 below). The fact that our sources focus on their revolutionary

aims and generally say little about their other beliefs, as well as their rather shorter existence, may distort the overall picture. It may be that their aims and goals were not necessarily different from those of the Pharisees or Sadducees who, at least sometimes, included political power among their objectives.

7. From all we can tell, the numbers of Jews belonging to a sect were few. Each individual sect was small, and even if their membership was totaled all together, they still constituted very much a minority. In some cases their influence may have significantly exceeded their size, but it is one thing to influence and another to control. Sometimes a sect would seize a position of power (the Pharisees under Alexandra Salome; the Zealots in the 66–70 revolt), but this did not last. The place of sects in the religous picture of the times must be kept in proportion.

10

CONCEPTS OF THE DEITY AND
THE SPIRIT WORLD

According to the accounts in both Jewish and Greco–Roman literature, the
Jews had a unique concept of the deity. Jewish people were seen as being different in many ways from their neighbors, but one of the main distinctions
lay in the way the Jews depicted their God. In case the issue seems to be a
simple one of monotheism versus polytheism, however, it should be said that
the picture is considerably complicated by current ideas on how Israelite
religious thought developed, eventually leading to the view that there was a
complex spirit world which included angels, demons, and souls, as well as
God. This chapter is organized around the topics of the deity, the spirit
world (including angels and demons), and the figure of Wisdom and the
Logos. To avoid repetition, the sources are treated under each heading
rather than separately. For this chapter, the Hebrew Bible is rather more
central than for most other topics treated in this book.

DEVELOPING VIEWS ABOUT GOD

Aharoni, Y. (1981) *Arad Inscriptions*.
Athanassiadi, P. and M. Frede (eds) (1999) *Pagan Monotheism in Late Antiquity*.
Barker, M. (1992) *The Great Angel: A Study of Israel's Second God*.
Becking, B., and M. Dijkstra (eds) (1998) *Één God aleen . . .? Over monotheïsme in
    Oud-Israël en de verering van de godin Asjera*.
Davies, G. I. (1991) *Ancient Hebrew Inscriptions: Corpus and Concordance*.
Day, J. (1985) *God's Conflict with the Dragon and the Sea*.
*DDD*².
Dietrich, W., and M. A. Klopfenstein (eds) (1994) *Ein Gott allein? JHWH–
    Verehrung und biblischer Monotheismus im Kontext der israelitischen und altorienta-
    lischen Religionsgeschichte*.
Dillon, J. (1977) *The Middle Platonists: A Study of Platonism 80 B.C. to A.D. 220*.
Edelman, D. V. (ed.) (1995) *The Triumph of Elohim: From Yahwisms to
    Judaisms*.

Fossum, Jarl E. (1985) *The Name of God and the Angel of the Lord: Samaritan and Jewish Concepts of Intermediation and the Origin of Gnosticism.*

Gnuse, R. K. (1997) *No Other Gods: Emergent Monotheism in Israel.*

Hamilton, G. J. (1998) "New Evidence for the Authenticity of *bšt* in Hebrew Personal Names and for Its Use as a Divine Epithet in Biblical Texts", *CBQ* 60: 228–50.

Hayman, A. P. (1991) "Monotheism – A Misused Word in Jewish Studies?" *JJS* 42: 1–15.

—— (1999) "The Survival of Mythology in the Wisdom of Solomon", *JSJ* 30: 125–39.

Hurtado, L. W. (1993) "What Do We Mean by 'First-Century Jewish Monotheism'?", in E. H. Lovering, Jr (ed.), *Society of Biblical Literature 1993 Seminar Papers*: 348–68.

—— (1998a) *One God, One Lord: Early Christian Devotion and Ancient Jewish Monotheism.*

—— (1998b) "First-Century Jewish Monotheism", *JSNT* 7: 3–26.

Jellicoe, S. (1968) *The Septuagint and Modern Study.*

Keel, O., and C. Uehlinger (1998) *Gods, Goddesses, and Images of God in Ancient Israel.*

Mettinger, T. N. D. (1995) *No Graven Image? Israelite Aniconism in Its Ancient Near Eastern Context.*

Moor, J. C. de (1997) *The Rise of Yahwism: The Roots of Israelite Monotheism.*

Niehr, H. (1990) *Der höchste Gott: Alttestamentlicher JHWH–Glaube im Kontext syrisch-kanaanäischer Religion des 1. Jahrtausends v. Chr.*

Pietersma, A. (1984) "Kyrios or Tetragram", in A. Pietersma and C. Cox (eds) *De Septuaginta*: 85–101.

Porten, B. (1968) *Archives from Elephantine: The Life of an Ancient Jewish Military Colony.*

Royse, J. R. (1991b) "Philo, Κύριος, and the Tetragrammaton", in D. T. Runia, D. M. Hay, and D. Winston (eds) *Heirs of the Septuagint: Philo, Hellenistic Judaism and Early Christianity: Festschrift for Earle Hilgert = SPA* 3: 167–83.

Segal, A. F. (1977) *Two Powers in Heaven.*

Smith, M. S. (1990) *The Early History of God: Yahweh and the Other Deities in Ancient Israel.*

Smith, Morton (1971) *Palestinian Parties and Politics That Shaped the Old Testament.*

Stuckenbruck, L. T. (1995) *Angel Veneration and Christology: A Study in Early Judaism and in the Christology of the Apocalypse of John.*

Toorn, K. van der (1990) "The Nature of the Biblical Teraphim in the Light of the Cuneiform Evidence", *CBQ* 52: 203–22.

—— (1992) "Anat-Yahu, Some Other Deities, and the Jews of Elephantine", *Numen* 39: 80–101.

—— (ed.) (1997) *The Image and the Book: Iconic Cults, Aniconism, and the Rise of Book Religion in Israel and the Ancient Near East.*

Wyatt, N. (1996) *Myths of Power: A Study of Royal Myth and Ideology in Ugaritic and Biblical Traditions.*

Ancient Israel

The classic picture of Judaism is that of a monotheistic religion in which the one God is essentially different from creation. All other objects in the universe are part of creation, even those beings of the spirit world who surround God's throne. He alone is without beginning or end, uniquely divine and God alone, the creator of the cosmos, and there is nothing like him (Isa. 46:9; 48:12–13). Unfortunately, this picture – which is indeed found in some texts (such as Second Isaiah) – only developed from polytheistic beginnings and was not a universal one. There are many indications that the original beliefs of ancient Israel were polytheistic, and even some of the biblical texts show a polytheistic origin. This topic is too large to treat fully here, though a number of recent studies go into the matter in detail (Morton Smith 1971; M. S. Smith 1990; Becking/Dijkstra 1998; Niehr 1990; many entries in DDD^2; various essays in Edelman 1995 and Dietrich/Klopfenstein 1994; cf. the survey in Gnuse 1997: 62–128). Here follows a brief survey of the evidence.

The main deity worshiped by the Israelites and Judeans was evidently Yhwh (exact form uncertain, though it is often reconstructed as *Yahweh*). The name is clearly attested first in the Mesha stela from the ninth century BC (*KAI* #181.14–18; *TSSI* #16.14–18). Among the Khirbet Beit Lei inscriptions (about 600 BC) is a reference to a Yhwh who is apparently the god of Jerusalem (Davies 1991: #15.005). The ostraca from Arad (Aharoni 1981) dated to about 600 BC contain a number of blessings and invocations in the name of Yhwh (16:3; 18:2; 21:2, 4; 40:3). There is also a reference to the "house of Yhwh" (*byt Yhwh*) which is probably the local temple (18:9). The Lachish ostraca, also evidently from the last days of the kingdom of Judah, contain a number of invocations using the name of Yhwh (e.g. *KAI* #192.2, 5; #193.3; #194.3, 9; #195.1, 7–8; #196.1, 12; #197.1; *TSSI* #12 ii.2, 5; iii.3, 9; iv.1; v.7–8; vi.1, 12; ix.1).

The surface picture of the biblical text is that God delivered a pure form of worship from the beginning, and revealed it again to Israel captive in Egypt. Yet it also acknowledges that Israel often did not actually practice this "true worship", for Israel supposedly had a tendency toward "falling away" into paganism, idolatry, and worship of other gods, suffering punishment, and being delivered when re-embracing the true faith (e.g. Joshua 24; 2 Kings 8:15–53; Jeremiah 2; Ezra 9:6–15). There are a number of references to *Asherim* (e.g. 1 Kings 14:15), usually conceived of as cult objects but ultimately standing for the goddess Asherah. Worship of the "host of heaven"

(2 Kings 17:16; 21:3; 23:4–5) is confirmed by solar symbols found on a number of Israelite seals (Keel/Uehlinger 1998: 282–309). Jeremiah (44:17–19, 25) mentions worship of the "Queen of Heaven" who is likely to have been Asherah or Anat or perhaps even an amalgam of the two goddesses. There are also the teraphim, associated with David himself (1 Sam. 15:22–23; 2 Kings 23:24; Ezek. 21:26–27; Hos. 3:4; Zech. 10:2; cf. van der Toorn 1990).

The Bible often polemicizes against Baal worship, which was seen as a major threat. What is surprising, then, is the indications of Baal worship in unexpected contexts. Saul's family had theophoric names with Baal: there was his son Eshbaal ("man of Baal": 1 Chron 8:33; 9:39), and Jonathan's son was Meribaal (1 Chron 8:34; 9:40). These names are often overlooked because the Samuel texts actually substitute surrogate names compounded with the word *bōšet* "shame" (Ishbosheth [2 Sam. 2:8]; Mephibosheth [2 Sam. 21:7]; though cf. Hamilton 1998). Yet even though the text presents these as acts of apostasy, there is no hint that such worship was criticized or opposed at the time. (The criticism in the biblical text is imposed by the final editors much later than the time pictured.) If there was criticism against worship of gods other than Yhwh, it was likely to have been from a minority movement, perhaps a "Yhwh-alone movement" (as argued by Morton Smith 1971). The Samaria ostraca (*ANET*: 321; *KAI* ##183–88; *TSSI* 1: text #2) show Yhwh and Baal names used side by side.

One might well point to the opposition to Baal worship in the time of Elijah (1 Kings 18–19). However, it is not entirely certain that this is what it appears to be, for the "Baal" of Jezebel was most likely a Phoenician god – and thus a foreign cult – introduced into Israel. It was symbolic of a foreign queen and would have been opposed by certain traditionalists. The fact that all the Baal worshipers could supposedly fit into the small Baal temple (2 Kings 10:18–28) is evidence that this was not a widespread alternative to Yhwh worship. Further indication is found in the names of Ahab's family and associates. His chief minister was named Obadiah ("servant of Yhwh": 1 Kings 18:3) and his two sons had Yhwh names (Ahaziah and Jehoram); the prophets he consulted were prophets of Yhwh (1 Kings 22:5–28). Although the text accuses him of Baal worship (1 Kings 16:31–32), we see no actual evidence that he promoted Baal worship beyond the royal cult specifically established for his wife. The opposition of Elijah and others was probably political opposition to Jezebel, even if disguised as religious piety. Ahab himself, by all accounts, was a Yhwh worshiper. On the other hand, the Elijah story pictures the prophet as building up an altar outside Jersualem (1 Kings 18:30–32), contrary to the commands of Deuteronomy (12:4–14). He also failed to condemn the cult places in Dan and Bethel which had been set up long before his time (1 Kings 12–13).

The biblical text also refers to "Asherah", though at times this seems to designate a cult object, especially when appearing in the masculine plural

("Asherim"). Yet a number of passages seem definitely to refer to a goddess: 1 Kings 15:13 mentions the cult object made for Asherah which was presumably in the temple; indeed, 2 Kings 23:4, 7 mentions vessels of Asherah (among others) and cult personnel dedicated to Asherah in the Jerusalem temple, and 2 Kings 21:7 also speaks of an image of Asherah in the temple. 1 Kings 18:19 speaks of "the prophets of Asherah", alongside the prophets of Baal, which can only be a reference to a goddess. Thus, the biblical text itself preserves evidence that Asherah was worshiped – even in the Jerusalem temple – most likely as a consort of Yhwh.

An inscription found in 1975–76 at Kuntillet Ajrud in the Negev (dated about the eighth century BC) reads: "I blessed you by Yhwh of Samaria and by his Asherah" (Davies 1991: #8.017, #8.021). A similar inscription was found at Khirbet el-Qom near Hebron and dated to the seventh century (Davies 1991: #25.003). These finds have created a great deal of debate because this is the first time that any direct evidence of goddess worship had turned up (even the Samaria ostraca had no goddess names). There was naturally some question as to whether the "Asherah" was a reference to a cult object or to a goddess. After considerable disagreement, the consensus is moving definitely in the direction of seeing a consort with Yhwh, a female divinity called Asherah (even if not everyone agrees, e.g. Keel/Uehlinger 1998: 281–82). If so, this would be quite parallel to Ugarit in which El the head of the pantheon has Athirat (cognate with Hebrew Asherah) as his consort.

Further support for a consort of Yhwh seems to be found in the Elephantine papyri (on these, see *JCH*: 54–55). The normal term for God among the Elephantine papyri is *Yhw* (perhaps pronounced Yahu, though we also find *Yhh* which may be only a graphic variant). However, a list of contributors to the cult indicates that other divinities also had a place. Specifically listed are Eshem–Bethel and Anat–Bethel (*TAD* C3.15:127–8 = *AP* 22:124–25), and Anat–Yahu (*TAD* B7.3:3 = *AP* 44:3). It has been suggested that these were actually only hypostases of Yhwh (cf. Porten 1968: 179), but this seems unlikely for several reasons (cf. van der Toorn 1992).

Other biblical texts also suggest a time when Yhwh was not only a deity alongside other deities but perhaps even a subordinate of El. Scholars had long wondered whether the reading of the Hebrew text of Deuteronomy 32:8 was not a later version created by later editing. The LXX text, the reading of a Qumran manuscript (4QDeut[j] = 4Q37), and other considerations have suggested that the original reading was that the god Elyon (= "Most High") "established the boundaries of the peoples according to the number of the sons of El". This suggests that Yhwh (as one of these sons of El) inherited Israel as his particular portion, much like Psalm 89:7–8 in which Yhwh is only one among the sons of El in the divine assembly. Here Yhwh is a son of El among other sons, even if he is said to be incomparable to his fellow sons of El. Similarly, Psalm 82:1 speaks of God judging among the gods.

There are a number of passages that give a mythical view of creation, as a defeat of various monsters of chaos, and quite at variance with Genesis 1 (Psa. 74:13–14; 89:9–10; Job 26:12–13; Isa. 27:1; 51:9–10). They remind one of myths about Baal known from the Ugaritic texts and even have overtones of Marduk's defeat of Tiamat, from whose body he created the heavens and the earth (as told in the "Babylonian Creation Myth", known as the *Enuma Elish*). They can be compared with Ugaritic texts which allege that Baal defeated such monsters. One prominent Baal myth describes Baal's defeat of the sea god Yamm (*KTU* 2). Other passages allude to battles which so far have not come to light in detailed texts (*KTU* 1.3.3.37–42; 1.5.1.1–3; cf. 1.5.1.27–30). The Hebrew and Ugaritic texts are not only similar in theme but even share some of the same basic vocabulary. (On this *Chaoskampf* or myth of a cosmic battle, see Day 1985; Wyatt 1996.)

These biblical passages, archaeological data, and the other evidence all suggest that during much or all of the period to the end of the Judean monarchy, Israel and Judah were polytheistic societies. This raises the question of when monotheism arose, a complex question which will be dealt with below (pp. 216–19) after looking at the non-biblical Jewish texts. Most of the non-biblical literature of the Second Temple period dates from the Greek period or later and is often in Greek or in a version translated from Greek. The question of how the deity was to be represented becomes an intra-Greek debate to some extent.

Innovations during the Second Temple period

In the Second Temple period, the name Yhwh came to be used less and less. It was replaced by more generic titles such as "God of Heaven" (mainly a Persian-period usage but probably not a Persian creation; see *DDD*[2]: 370–72) and Adonai, "Lord". A number of what were originally separate deities had become assimilated to Yhwh in pre-exilic times. With the translation of the Bible into Greek, these divine names were translated as if they were titles (e.g. Shaddai became *hikanos* "(all) sufficient", *pantokratōr* "almighty"; Elyon, *hupsēlos*, *hupsistos* "most high"). The name Yhwh and also the more generic term Elohim were also translated, as *kurios* "Lord" and *theos* "God" respectively. It has been argued, however, that the tetragrammaton was originally not translated but written out in paleo-Hebrew letters (cf. the summary of scholarship in Royse 1991: 167–73; Jellicoe 1968: 270–72). Certainly, some LXX manuscripts have the tetragrammaton written in such a way or with the Greek letters *pipi* (which has been explained as a misreading by Greek scribes of Yhwh in Aramaic letters). It is not as clear cut as one might think, though, and arguments have been made against this interpretation (Pietersma 1984; cf. *DDD*[2]: 494), though Royse (1991) has recently made a case that Philo did in some cases have a biblical manuscript with the tetragrammaton in Hebrew letters.

The question of use of these terms is complicated because usage varies from writing to writing, not to mention the fact that a number of writings were not originally written in Greek. The terms *kurios* and *theos* are widely and apparently interchangeably used in the Greek texts of *Jubilees*, *Psalms of Solomon*, *Testament of Moses*, *Vita Adae et Euae*, *Apocalypse of Moses*, Pseudo-Philo, and *2 Enoch*. Josephus favors *theos*, usually with the article (*ho theos*). The term "heaven" is occasionally used as a surrogate for the divine name (e.g. 1 Macc. 2:21; 3:18; Mat. 4:17; 5:3). A number of other titles appear in other writings. The *Similitudes of Enoch* (37–71) often use "the Lord of the Spirits" (37:4; 38:2, 4, 6; 3:2, etc.); also "the one to whom belongs time before time" or "Antecedent of Time" (46:1; 47:3; 48:2; 60:2; 71:10) seems to be a translation of "Ancient of Days" (Dan. 7:9). The *Apocalypse of Abraham* appears to have great variety of titles (e.g. Sole Ruler, Light, Unbegotten, Incorruptible, Lover of men, Sabaoth, Eli, El), though "Lord" is rare.

Philo has a wealth of material on his concept of God and the invisible world (see Dillon 1977: 155–66). One should also keep in mind that he has been heavily influenced by contemporary Platonic philosophy. For Philo, God is beyond being and beyond unity – ultimately unknowable – but he uses the expression *to ōn* "the one who is" for the deity (*Praem.* 40; *Leg. All.* 2.3). God is transcendent and has no direct dealings with the world. But an emanation comes from him like a stream of light which reaches toward the world and makes him immanent and accessible to humanity. The first stage of the emanation is referred to as the Logos. It then divides into two powers, the creative power and royal power. In some treatments there is a further bifurcation. Each of the stages is progressively less pure. Thus, God maintains his unity and purity, but the gap is bridged by the Logos (discussed further on pp. 228–30 below).

The NT seems to reflect the view of the deity found in the surrounding Jewish world for the most part. However, the question of Jesus's relationship to God and the status of the resurrected Christ is a major issue. It seems to be treated differently in different texts, though most texts agree that Jesus is in some sense divine, and God is his father. The idea of being a "son of God" was not new. In ancient Israel and the OT texts, the king (Psa. 2:7) and perhaps even an ordinary Israelite could be considered a "son of God" (Psa. 82:6). This did not in any way imply equality with God, and if the "son of God" was thought to share in divinity, it did not suggest being divine in the same way that God was. However, the question of the development of Christology is beyond the scope of this study (see Hurtaldo 1998, Stuckenbruck 1995, and the literature cited there for some of the debate on this topic).

The question of monotheism

This brings us to the much-debated topics of monotheism and its development. The book of Deuteronomy and the other work of the Deuteronomists in the OT give a strong focus on Yhwh as the only God. Yet Deuteronomy does not ultimately deny the existence of other gods (Deut. 5:7; cf. Exod. 20:3), and even the *Shema* (the traditional prayer quoted from Deut. 6:4) must be read in the context of the rest of the book. It has commonly been accepted that it is in Second Isaiah that we first find a monotheistic view in which other gods are not only denigrated but even have their existence denied (Isa. 41:21–29; 43:10–13; 44:6–8; 45). When the writer makes use of the old *Chaoskampf* mythology (Isa. 51:9–11), it is to demythologize it. Similarly, when it is proposed that this mythology is drawn on in the Wisdom of Solomon (Hayman 1999), this would not indicate compromise of a monotheistic view. However, some recent writers have even denied that "monotheism" is a correct term for pre-70 Jewish beliefs in God (Hayman 1991; cf. Barker 1992). Part of the problem is one of definition. "Monotheism" is, of course, our term and does not occur in early Jewish texts. The radical monotheism of some Islamic, Jewish, and even Christian theologians is one extreme whose philosophical basis would probably not have been understandable to the ancient writers.

On the other hand, it has long been argued that there were monotheistic and monistic trends in the Greco-Roman world, especially in philosophical circles (cf. Athanassiadi/Frede 1999), and this has also been hypothesized for the ancient Near East (cf. Gnuse 1997: 129–76; de Moor 1997). The monotheistic tendencies in Judaism are clear; the question is how far they had developed, since one part of the problem is getting at the precise views of the ancient writer who is often writing polemic or making isolated statements, not giving a philosophical exposition; another part is that we are in danger of imposing a thought world, with modern categories, onto the ancient theologian. Yet we do have a writer such as Philo who seems to have a strong view of God's unity, even if this is influenced by his Platonism (cf. Dillon 1977: 155–58). Some have been misled by Philo's references to the Logos and the "Powers" (e.g. Barker 1992) which might seem to suggest a divided Godhead; however, Philo's use of hypostases – which is what these are – is a way of safeguarding God's oneness, not an indication of watering down monotheism (see pp. 228–30 below).

Since a world of other heavenly beings or angels has been a part of Jewish thinking even to the present, any concept of monotheism must take this into account. We can draw the line perhaps with whether the angels were venerated or not. There is little or no evidence that angels were worshiped as a part of the cult in any part of Second Temple Judaism (Hurtado 1998; Stuckenbruck 1995); however, the question of veneration on a popular level or in some circles is more difficult and still a moot point. There is some evidence that in some circles angel veneration was practiced (Fossum 1985: 220–38). Segal (1977) examines the rabbinic attack on the "two powers in heaven" belief (though this is mainly post-70). At a later point the polemic became directed at any "heretical" group, including Christians, but the earlier discussions (early second century) were against beliefs which seemed to compromise God's unity by the acceptance of an angelic power alongside him. Full-blown Gnosticism, with its dualism between the inferior creator God and the good higher God, "was a product of the battle between the rabbis, the Christians and various other 'two powers' sectarians who inhabited the outskirts of Judaism" (Segal 1977: 265).

To outsiders the Jewish beliefs certainly looked different, and comment is often made on the Jewish divinity who is seen as singular and exclusive. Writing about 300 BCE, Hecateus of Abdera makes the following statement (*apud* Diodorus of Sicily 40.3.4):

> But he [Moses] had no images whatsoever of the gods made for them, being of the opinion that God is not in human form; rather the Heaven that surrounds the earth is alone divine, and rules the universe.

This indicates a monotheistic, aniconic religion in his day; however, his statement is brief and may not have included all the complications or qualifications necessary for a full understanding. On the other hand, it is probably indicative that at least the community around the Jerusalem temple, if not the wider Jewish community, was monotheistic and did not make use of images in worship any later than the beginning of the Greek period.

The Greek and Roman writers are universal in proclaiming Jewish worship of one God. Although this God is sometimes identified with Jove (Varro, *apud* Augustine, *De cons. Evang.* 1.22.30; 1.23.31; 1.27.42) or even Dionysus (Plutarch, *Ques. conviv.* 6.2; Tacitus, *Hist.* 5.5), the sources always emphasize how different the Jews are from other people, and they are especially astonished at the lack of imagery in Jewish worship (e.g. Varro, *apud* Augustine, *De civ. Dei* 4.31; Strabo 16.2.35; Livy, *apud Scholia in Lucanum* 2.593; Cassius Dio 37.17.2–3).

The question of whether the worship of the Israelite god was aniconic is also a topic in current debate. A number of the biblical texts forbid the use of images in worship, such as the Second Commandment (Exod. 20:4; Deut. 5:8) and images are often ridiculed (Isa. 40:18–20; 44:9–20; 46:1–2; Jer. 10:2–10). We know from later Jewish texts that the use of images or living forms of any kind was considered abhorrent and strongly rejected (Wisdom 13–15; *LAB* 44; *Test. Job* 2–5; *Apoc. Abraham* 1–8; see also the quote from Hecateus above). Some have argued that the worship of Yhwh was aniconic from the beginning; that is, that the non–use of images was a characteristic of Yhwh worship in the earlier period. Yet there are a number of indications that images were used in divine worship in Israel and Judah (cf. the essays in van der Toorn 1997). In an inscription relating to the fall of Samaria about 722 BCE (Nimrud Prism 4:29–33), Sargon II states that he counted as spoil the gods of Samaria. It was quite normal for the Assyrians to remove the divine images of the people they conquered, often melting them down for the metal. The most reasonable interpretation in the context is that these referred to images of the Samarian gods. That is, the temple(s) of the Samarians contained images of more than one god, and the Assyrians took these away as spoil as was their custom. A second indication of iconism is the many "Astarte" images found by archaeologists all over Palestine. These by themselves do not prove that idols were used to represent Yhwh since the passages just mentioned could be referring to other deities, but the possibility that an image of Yhwh was found in the Jerusalem temple at one stage is a reasonable inference from the data just presented. As noted above, the Greco-Roman writers most knowledgeable about the Jews tend to emphasize that no imagery was used in the cult. We have some writers who allege that a statue of an ass's head (Mnaseas of Patara [*GLAJJ*: 1.97–100]; Apion [*GLAJJ*: #170]; Damocritus [*GLAJJ*: #247]) or of Moses seated on an ass (Diodorus 34–35.1.3 [*GLAJJ*: #63]) was found in the temple. This is plainly a calumny to make the Jews look bad ("ass-worshipers"), and there is no evidence that it had any basis in reality.

Throughout the Second Temple period our sources indicate an exclusive worship of Yhwh and an aniconic cult. Whether one wants to use "monotheism" in its most radical sense might be debated, but there are certainly Jewish texts and Greco-Roman testimonies that the Jews deny the existence of other gods. By most people's definition, this is monotheism (a point well made by Hurtado [1993; 1998b]).

THE SPIRIT WORLD

Craigie, P. (1973) "Helel, Athtar and Phaethon (Jes 14₁₂₋₁₅)", *ZAW* 85: 223–25.

Davidson, M. J. (1992) *Angels at Qumran: A Comparative Study of 1 Enoch 1–36, 72–108 and Sectarian Writings from Qumran*.

*DDD*².

Day, P. L. (1988) *An Adversary in Heaven: Śāṭān in the Hebrew Bible*.

Deutsch, N. (1999) *Guardians of the Gate: Angelic Vice Regency in Late Antiquity*.

Fossum, J. E. (1985) *The Name of God and the Angel of the Lord: Samaritan and Jewish Concepts of Intermediation and the Origin of Gnosticism*.

Grabbe, L. L. (1987) "The Scapegoat Ritual: A Study in Early Jewish Interpretation", *JSJ* 18: 152–67.

Grelot, P. (1956) "Isaie xxiv 12–15 et son arrière-plan mythologique", *RHR* 149: 18–48.

Handy, L. K. (1994) *Among the Host of Heaven: The Syro-Palestinian Pantheon as Bureaucracy*.

Jackson, H. M. (1996) "Echoes and Demons in the Pseudo-Philonic *Liber Antiquitatum Biblicarum*", *JSJ* 27: 1–20.

Keel, O. (1977) *Jahwe–Visionen und Siegelkunst: Eine neue Deutung der Majestätsschilderungen in Jes 6, Ez 1 und 10 und Sach 4.*

Kobelski, P. J. (1981) *Melchizedek and Melchireša'.*

Mach, M. (1992) *Entwicklungsstadien des jüdischen Engelglaubens in vorrabbinischer Zeit.*

McKay, J. (1970) "Helel and the Dawn-Goddess", *VT* 20: 451–64.

McKenzie, J. L. (1956) "Mythological Allusions in Ezek 28₁₂₋₁₈", *JBL* 75: 322–27.

May, H. G. (1962) "The King in the Garden of Eden: A Study of Ezekiel 28:12–19", in B. W. Anderson and W. Harrelson (eds) *Israel's Prophetic Heritage: Essays in Honor of James Muilenburg*: 166–76.

Mullen, E. T., Jr (1980) *The Assembly of the Gods: The Divine Council in Canaanite and Early Hebrew Literature.*

Olyan, S. M. (1993) *A Thousand Thousands Served Him: Exegesis and the Naming of Angels in Ancient Judaism.*

Piñero, A. (1993) "Angels and Demons in the Greek *Life of Adam and Eve*", *JSJ* 24: 191–214.

Stuckenbruck, L. T. (1995) *Angel Veneration and Christology: A Study in Early Judaism and in the Christology of the Apocalypse of John.*

Tabor, J. D. (1986) *Things Unutterable: Paul's Ascent to Paradise in its Greco-Roman, Judaic, and Early Christian Contexts.*

Wyatt, N. (1973–74) "'Attar and the Devil", *Transactions of the Glasgow University Oriental Society* 25: (1976) 85–97.

—— (1996) *Myths of Power: A Study of Royal Myth and Ideology in Ugaritic and Biblical Traditions.*

Main texts

Heavenly beings other than God are a part of the divine arena, even in a monotheistic context. The concept of the divine assembly or divine council is one widespread among Semitic pantheons (Mullen 1980). Perhaps one of the clearest examples of Yhwh himself having a divine council is 1 Kings 22:19–22 in which he presides over the "host of heaven" (*ṣěvā' haššāmayim*). In later times this divine council was interpreted as consisting of angels who surrounded Yhwh, but angels have only a minor place in Israelite tradition until the post-exilic period. The Hebrew word for "angel" is *mal'ak*, meaning "messenger" and may be used of human messengers (cf. Ezek. 23:40; Neh. 6:3); however, some of these figures in the OT seem to have characteristics of heavenly beings (Gen. 32:23–33; Judges 6:11–22; 13:2–23; 2 Sam. 24:15–17//1 Chron. 21:16–20). Studies of the Northwest Semitic pantheons have found that the gods had various ranks, the lowest being the messenger gods who spoke for the gods sending them (Handy 1994). Similarly, angels in the Bible speak for Yhwh; for example, Exodus 3:2–5 mentions that "the *mal'ak Yhwh*" appeared to Moses, but then the rest of the passage goes on to say that

"Yhwh said". Thus, the messenger gods of the original Northwest Semitic pantheon (and perhaps other divinities as well) became reduced to angels in later Judaism, but the outlines of the original polytheistic divine council were still retained despite the monotheistic views of the final editors of the tradition.

Several heavenly beings may have been taken over from Israel's environment. The cherubim who act as guardians (Gen. 3; 1 Kings 6:29, 32, 35) and carry Yhwh's throne (1 Kings 6:23–28; 1 Sam. 4:4; 2 Sam. 6:2; 22:11 = Psa. 18:11; Ezek. 1, 10) bear a resemblance to winged bulls and other figures known from Mesopotamia (cf. Keel 1977). The seraphim (Isa. 6:1–2) have much in common with the *uraeus*, a cobra–like figure of Egypt which was a symbol of kingship. The *uraeus* is often pictured with hands and feet or wings; the winged figures normally have two or four wings, but there is at least one example with six (Keel 1977: 77).

The *Hêlēl ben Šaḥar* of Isaiah 14:12 is another intriguing heavenly being whose background probably lies in an old Canaanite myth (cf. KTU 1.6.1:39–63; 1.23; Craigie 1973; Wyatt 1973–74; 1996: 30–31) or possibly a myth also known from the Greek world (Grelot 1956; McKay 1970). The Hebrew name is often translated as "shining one, son of the dawn"; in the Vulgate Latin text, this was rendered as *Lucifer*, "lightbringer". This story has a number of features in common with Ezekiel 28 (cf. McKenzie 1956; May 1962; Wyatt 1996: 59–65). On the contribution of this fallen figure to the development of the devil, see below. Demonic figures are not well developed in the OT. The figure of *ha-Satan* ("the Adversary") of Job 1–2 seems to be a heavenly prosecutor who is an essential part of the heavenly court and a "son of God" (Job 1:6–12; 2:1–7). The same interpretation probably applies to 1 Chron. 21:1 (cf. 2 Sam. 24:1), though it is possible there has been further development.

Olyan (1993) has demonstrated how many of the names of angelic brigades and some names of individual angels are derived from exegesis of the biblical text; especially productive are Ezekiel 1 and 10, other sources being the divine attributes and cultic terms in various parts of the OT. Nevertheless, it seems that most of the individual names of angels known from non-biblical literature do not derive from biblical exegesis but originate in other ways (see below on *1 Enoch*).

One of the earliest non-biblical Jewish texts is the book of Tobit (from later Persian or Ptolemaic times). A central figure in the book is the angel (*ml'k'*) Raphael who carries out God's plans for Tobit and his family after Tobit prays for help or death. Raphael is brought in both to cure Tobit's blindness and to drive away a demon called Asmodaeus (3:8) who is killing all of Sarah's husbands on the wedding night (3:7–9). Raphael instructs Tobias to save the liver, gall, and heart of a fish they catch. Part of this is burned by Tobias and Sarah in the bridal chamber to drive away the demon who flees to Egypt, where Raphael pursues him and binds him (8:1–3).

The book of *1 Enoch* is one of the richest sources for views about the deity and the spirit world, though it must be kept in mind that the different sections do not necessarily reflect the same set of beliefs or constituency or time period. The *Book of Watchers* (1–36), probably from the third century BCE, is dominated by the myth of the fallen angels who leave their heavenly estate to have intercourse with human women and produce offspring. The present form of the story centers on two central angelic leaders called Asael and Shemihazah. The leaders of the 200 fallen angels are named, one of the first extensive lists of names of angelic beings (6, 8). The "evil spirits" are not the fallen angels themselves but the product of the giants who were the offspring of the unions between the fallen angels and human women. When the giants died, their spirits became the evil spirits who tempt humans (7; 9:7–10; 15:8–12). The book seems to pay less attention to the good angels, but a number of these appear and several are an essential part of the story. Most important are the (arch)angels, named as four initially (9:1; 10:1, 4, 9, 11: Michael, Gabriel, Raphael, Sariel) but later expanded to seven (19:1; 20), including Uriel who is important in the *Astronomical Book* (71:1, etc.). The *Astronomical Book* indicates that angels were associated with most or all the heavenly bodies (82:13–20).

The rest of the Enoch tradition is similar in theme, if not always in detail. The *Similitudes of Enoch* (probably first century) continue the themes of the earlier sections. The four archangels have Phanuel in place of Sariel (40:10). The fallen angels are named (69:1–15); mention is made of other angelic groups (61:10), as well as an angel of peace (56:1) and angels of punishment (56:1; 66:1). One of the most intriguing figures in the *Similitudes* is the "Son of Man"; this figure is discussed in detail elsewhere (pp. 282–83 below). *2 Enoch* (first or second century CE?) has much about the angelic world in the first part in which Enoch is given a tour of the heavens. He is guided by two huge angels (1:3–5). The first heaven has the (200) angels in charge of the stars and other natural phenomena (4–6); the fallen angels are imprisoned in the second heaven (7), though their leaders are in the fifth heaven (18); angels guard paradise in the third heaven (8:8), where punishing angels torment also the wicked (10); angels accompany the sun's chariot in the fourth heaven, bringing dew and heat (11–12, 14); the sixth heaven is filled with angels of all sorts (19), while the seventh heaven has the armies of the archangels and the cherubim and seraphim (20–21). Alongside the archangels Gabriel and Michael is another called Vrevoil (Uriel?: 22:10–11).

Ben Sira also seems to accept the existence of angels, even if he shows no great interest in them. Sir. 17:32 and 24:2 refer to the host of the heavens. Sir. 17:7 says that each nation has its ruler but that Israel's portion is Yhwh, perhaps indicating angelic rulers of each nation. Sir. 42:17 refers to the Holy Ones who are the hosts of heaven, and 45:2 uses *'ĕlōhîm* in a way which could mean "angel". *Jubilees* mentions the fallen angels myth (5:1–11), and has Noah utter a prayer against demons (10:1–14). The name Mastema for the wicked angelic leader is used several times (17:15–18; 48:9–19). *Vita Adae et Euae* has a reference to Satan's fall from heaven (12–16). The lost ending of the *Testament of Moses* apparently had a dispute between Michael and Satan.

The late book of Daniel not surprisingly shows a considerable development in its angelology. Two major angelic figures in the book are Michael (10:13, 21; 12:1) and Gabriel (8:16; 9:21), though it is implied that other angelic beings exist. Demonic figures also seem to occur: Gabriel mentions being opposed by the "prince of Persia" (10:13, 20–21) who was evidently an angelic figure with responsibility for or control over that nation. The picture is not entirely clear, but it appears that each nation has its own angelic guide, with Gabriel and Michael both assigned to the Jews. One might assume that the angels over the other nations are all a part of the heavenly court, but it looks more as if these are now being regarded in some sense as opponents of God.

The "sectarian" texts from Qumran, as might be expected, contain many references to angelic figures. The *Damascus Covenant* has several passages about the main demonic personage Belial, the first being the "three nets of Belial" passage (CD 4:12–21); this Belial is an opponent of the Prince of Lights (CD 5:17–19). The fallen angels myth known from *1 Enoch* is also alluded to (CD 2:18–21). The "two spirits" section of the *Community Rule* (1QS 3:13–4:26) speaks of the "Prince of Lights" who is opposed by the "Angel of Darkness"; both vie for the control of humanity. The wicked will be punished by "angels of destruction" (1QS 4:12). The *War Scroll* (1QM; 1Q33; 4Q491–496 = 4QM1–6) envisions an eschatological battle in which the forces of Belial (the "sons of darkness") are confronted by the "sons of light" (see especially 1QM 1), but the angels also participate in the battle (1QM 1:10–11). 4QVisions of Amram[b] (4Q544) has a dispute between angels for control over him. The *Melchizedek Scroll* (11Q13) has a heavenly figure Melchizedek ("king of righteousness"), identified with Michael, who is opposed by a Melchireša' ("king of wickedness"), if the reconstruction is correct (see Kobelsky 1981). Finally, the *Songs of the Sabbath Sacrifice* (4QShirShab = 4Q400–407; 11QShirShab = 11Q17; MasShirShabb) show the praise given to God by the heavenly "priests". Interestingly, the name Satan does not occur among the Qumran scrolls.

Philo differs in basic concept from the other Jewish writings. Although he may well have been aware of the various speculations about and elaborations on angelology, he ignores it all. Instead, he presents a very Platonic system in which angels are simply unembodied souls (*Plant.* 14; cf. *Gig.* 6–16). This passage suggests that there is more than one type of soul, those less pure souls that keep getting entangled in bodies and those purer souls which are the angels. One can infer that humans can become angels when they develop a soul that manages to break free from the body and leave it behind permanently. Philo thinks there are such things as punitive angels whose function is primarily to punish the wicked humans, but they are not themselves wicked as such (*Conf.* 177; *Fuga* 66); thus, there does not appear to be a Philonic equivalent of the demonic spirits.

The angel Michael is prominent in the *Testament of Abraham*, and Satan naturally has a prominent part in the *Testament of Job*. The *Apocalypse of Abraham* (about 100 CE?) makes much of the demonic Azazel (13; 14:5; 22:5– 23:13; 29:5–7; 31:2–7) who has a counterpart in the angel Iaoel, an equally important figure (10:3). The name Azazel comes from the "scapegoat" passage of Lev. 16 but, surprisingly, the *Apocalypse of Abraham* is one of the few writings to make much of this name (cf. Grabbe 1987).

Summary on angelic beings

The concept of heavenly messengers is already found in the OT, perhaps a reflex of the messenger gods of the old Semitic pantheon. With the developing monotheism, the angelic figures alongside God are probably derived from the original sons of God in the divine council. The angels are the helpers of the deity and responsible for the workings of the cosmos as well as for carrying out divine tasks relating to the human sphere. Most writers reflect the view that some angels unfortunately sinned, were cast out of heaven, became opponents of God, and are responsible for tempting and otherwise harrassing human beings.

Even though the world view is similar or even the same in many of the writings (where there are sufficient data to ascertain this), the details vary from one to another; for example, the names of the good and evil angels are not necessarily the same, and it would probably be a mistake to try to put them all together into one great synthesis. The names of four archangels are often uniform, and some of the names of the chief wicked angel are found in several writings. As one of the earliest writings on the subject, *1 Enoch* gives one of the most complex versions of angelology. The fallen angels myth, so important to several writings, probably has a long history in the ancient Near East; however, it is absent from a number of major writings, suggesting that it was not universally accepted.

One question is whether the development of the angelic world was a consequence of changes in the perception of God in the post-exilic period. It has been suggested that God began to be seen as more remote from mankind, and the angelic world came to bridge the gap between importunate humans and the increasingly inaccessible deity. Olyan has dismissed this as a "discredited" theory which even originated in "thinly veiled anti-Jewish bias" (1993: 5–6, 8–9, 11, 89–91). He is correct that usage of the term "hypostasis" can skew the discussion in a particular direction, but his interpretation is equally one-sided. The fact is that we find a variety of attitudes and approaches in the sources. Whether we can speak of a "development" in one direction is doubtful, but certainly some writers such as Philo do see a completely transcendent God. Thus, part of Philo's task was to make the deity immanent even though its very nature makes it normally inaccessible. His solution is, of course, the Logos concept (see below), and other writers seem to find the figure of Wisdom equally useful, though their conception of the Godhead is not necessarily the same as Philo's.

The "devil Gestalt" contains a variety of elements taken from different parts of the tradition. Opponents of God, though not referred to as "Satan" or the like, are found in Isaiah 14 and Ezekiel 28. These no doubt contributed to the tradition, but they were still separate components at the time they were written. Terms such as *beliar* and *belial*, implying general wickedness, become personified to the point that a demonic figure called Belial is frequent in the Qumran scrolls. The general term *mastema* "adversity" became the demonic name Mastema. The devil Gestalt, so well known in later Judaism and Christianity, is made up of several streams, including the heavenly prosecutor *ha-Satan* (Day 1988), the fallen heavenly being of Isaiah 14 and Ezekiel 28 (the Satan–Lucifer stream), and even the Day of Atonement ritual or Azazel stream (Grabbe 1987).

THE FIGURE OF WISDOM AND THE LOGOS

Grabbe, L. L. (1997a) *Wisdom of Solomon.*
Kayatz, C. (1966) *Studien zu Proverbien 1–9: Eine form- und motivgeschichtliche Untersuchung unter Einbeziehung ägyptischen Vergleichsmaterials.*
Kloppenborg, J. S. (1982) "Isis and Sophia in the Book of Wisdom", *HTR* 75: 57–84.
Lang, Bernhard (1986) *Wisdom and the Book of Proverbs: An Israelite Goddess Redefined.*
Mack, B. L. (1973) *Logos und Sophia: Untersuchungen zur Weisheitstheologie im hellenistischen Judentum.*
McNamara, M. (1972) *Targum and Testament.*
Maier, C. (1995) *Die "fremde Frau" in Proverbien 1–9: Eine exegetische und sozialgeschichtliche Studie.*
Sanders, J. A. (1967) *The Dead Sea Psalms Scroll.*
Whybray, R. N. (1994) *Proverbs.*

Main texts

The main texts have been surveyed in Grabbe 1997a (69–73), with a more abbreviated overview here. Proverbs 1–9 contains several passages that show a heavenly, even primal, figure called "Wisdom" or "Lady Wisdom" alongside Yhwh. How early these passages are is debated. Most consider Proverbs 1–9 post-exilic (cf. Maier 1995; Whybray 1994); however, it has been argued that there is nothing to prevent these chapters from being pre-exilic (Kayatz 1966). A lot turns on one's view of the development of theology and wisdom in Israel rather than specific indications in the chapters themselves. In any case, many of the later discussions about the figure of wisdom contain allusions to data in ch. 8 and other chapters in Proverbs 1–9. In Prov. 1:20–33, wisdom cries aloud in the streets, rebuking the scoffers and dunces for not heeding her call. Her speech in 8:1–11 is similar to that in ch. 1: she calls on all to hear – the dullards included – because her discipline is better than silver.

The next speech in 8:12–21 continues with this theme, pointing out the benefits to be had from love of wisdom. Prov. 8:22–34 is a passage of prime importance, because in it wisdom is closely identified with Yhwh. She was begotten at the beginning, even before the foundations of the earth were laid. She was an observer of God's work of creation, and even his *'āmôn*. The meaning of this Hebrew word in 8:30 has puzzled commentators for centuries (cf. Whybray 1994: 134–36). Some translate it as "technician" (perhaps in the sense of "architect"); others see it as "confidant" (NJPS) or even as "child". If the term means "architect", wisdom was not only present but even a part of the creation process. In any case, she is presented as an intimate of Yhwh with a privileged position. Proverbs 9 contrasts Lady Wisdom, who has prepared a feast with an open invitation for any to partake of, with the foolish woman – Dame Folly (presented in the image of a prostitute) – who invites the foolish into her house only to bring them down to Sheol (cf. Maier 1995). The imagery is intriguing here because, like Dame Folly, Lady Wisdom also appears as a seductress.

The beautiful poem in Job 28 gives a picture in marked contrast to that in Proverbs, at least in one aspect. Whereas Proverbs makes the point of how readily wisdom can be sought out and found, Job 28 emphasizes her inaccessibility. Only with great difficulty, and only with God's help, can wisdom be reached. Wisdom is within reach but only through God (28:20–24).

Ben Sira 24 has a good deal in common with Proverbs 8. Wisdom speaks in the assembly of the Most High, praising herself. She came forth from his mouth and abode in the highest heavens, then she moved over all the earth, looking for a dwelling place among mankind (24:6–12). Here she flourishes and grows, and calls those who desire her to come and eat their fill. She is then identified with God's law, the Torah (v. 23). The image of wisdom in Ben Sira is one in which she is accessible but only to Israel. It has been suggested that an erotic image of wisdom is found in Ben Sira 51:13–30. This poem is now known from the Psalms scroll from Qumran Cave 11 (11QPs^a), and a comparison of the Greek and Hebrew texts suggests that the translator toned down language which seems to be more explicitly erotic in the Hebrew text (see Sanders 1967 for a justification of this interpretation). 1 Baruch 3:15–4:4 (difficult to date but probably from the second century BCE) stresses the inaccessibility of wisdom and the fact that she was not available to the various nations who sought her (3:20–23). Only God knows how to find her (3:31–32), but he found her and gave her to Israel; indeed, she is identical to his law (3:36–4:1).

The main concept used in Philo is the Logos (pp. 228–30 below). There are, however, occasional references to wisdom (*sophia*). For example, the Logos is once said to be the offspring of God and wisdom (*Fug.* 109), which seems to make the Logos further down the chain of eminences than elsewhere. It is almost as if Philo has to make use of wisdom because she is a part of his tradition, but she does not actually fit his system (Dillon 1977: 164).

The figure of wisdom in the Wisdom of Solomon is found primarily in chs 6–12 but can be said to lie behind chs 13–19 as well, though these refer directly to God. She appears in both the guises of heavenly figure and of erotic image (6:12, 17–18; 8:2–3). The writer, in the guise of Solomon, extols the benefits from seeking wisdom (chs 6–7). Wisdom is closely associated with God, and the relationship is a fascinating one. That which is considered the activity of wisdom in Wisd. Sol. 10 gradually shifts to that of God in Wisd. Sol. 11 and following. Wisdom is the mother of all things (7:12); she is the fashioner (*technitis*) of all things (7:22). In 7:15–20 God is the guide of wisdom, and he also gives knowledge with regard to the cycles of nature and the world. Yet similar characteristics are ascribed to wisdom in 8:5–8.

The relationship is most clearly expressed in 7:25–26. This statement seems to fit the interpretation usually given, that wisdom in the Wisdom of Solomon is a *hypostasis*. That is, she is both product of God and also a manifestation of him. She represents him and she is him. Thus, many statements about God are interchangeable with statements about wisdom. The characteristics of wisdom are ultimately those we would also apply to God (7:22–23). More than this, these are also the characteristics which humans should strive for. This leads immediately to the central motif to which the author of the Wisdom of Solomon draws attention: the function of wisdom as a teacher.

Some have thought that the *Parables of Enoch* (first century CE?) preserve an old myth of wisdom as a goddess (*1 Enoch* 42:1–3). Although this is not clearly the case, we find here another version of wisdom's quest for a place among humans. In this version, wisdom maintains her place in the divine council after finding no resting place on earth, though presumably she is accessible to those who are worthy.

Summary of the figure of Wisdom

The figure of Lady Wisdom is an important theological motif in Second Temple Judaism. Some would argue that it had emerged already in the monarchic period; in any case, it was well developed by the Persian period. Wisdom is intimately connnected with God, and in later literature such as the Wisdom of Solomon the figure of Wisdom is a hypostasis of God himself. Some would already apply this to the Lady Wisdom of Proverbs 1–9, but most scholars would not go that far; however, it is accepted that already in Proverbs Wisdom has some goddess-like characteristics. The origin of these has been debated (cf. Grabbe 1997a: 73–76). One proposal is that a Hebrew goddess tradition existed and was the main influence (cf. Lang 1986). An old favorite is to see the main influence from the Egyptian *Maat* which is both a goddess and the abstract quality of "truth, order" (cf. Kayatz 1966), though this has recently been rejected (*DDD*[2]: 534–35). Regardless of the exact origin of the characteristics, it is widely agreed that Lady Wisdom already in Proverbs has some features of a goddess. The most developed form of the figure is probably in the Wisdom of Solomon. In this case, several recent studies have argued that the Egyptian goddess Isis has influenced the portrayal (Mack 1973; Kloppenborg 1982).

How are we to evaluate these different suggestions? None of the hypotheses mentioned above can be considered as demonstrated. Some are plausible, but plausibility is not proof. Lang (1986) has demonstrated that in its poly-theistic period, Israel *might* have had a goddess by the name of Wisdom or analogous to wisdom; on the other hand, although no direct connection with Egyptian *Maat* has been demonstated, the image of *Maat* has many close parallels with the passages on wisdom, especially Proverbs 8. No one has shown that the figure of wisdom must have been modeled on or influenced by *Maat*, yet it fits very well. This is as far as we can go in our present state of knowledge. The choice of one explanation over the other is very subjective.

The Logos tradition

Wisdom is the main personification or hypostasis found in many Jewish writings. However, in some writings the dominant concept used is that of *logos* "reason, mind" rather than wisdom. For example, in Philo the *logos* is a central element in his philosophical and theological system. Wisdom (*sophia*) certainly occurs, but it plays a less prominent role. The place of wisdom in other writings is taken by the Logos in Philo, even if there is inevitably a certain overlap between the two. Some have seen a connection between the Logos and the "word of the Lord" in the Old Testament. *Logos* of course means "discourse" as well as "mind, reason". In the theology of the OT itself the word does not play a central part. In Deuteronomy "the word of Yhwh" is a surrogate form for Yhwh himself, but there are the beginnings of a personification of "the word". Thus, there are times when God's word is slightly personified, but it is primarily in later Jewish literature that the word takes on features of personification or even hypostasization.

The Logos concept has a long history in Greco-Roman thought. Already in the fourth century BCE the Stoics used Logos to refer to the intelligence of the cosmos – in some ways equivalent to 'God'. The universe was co-extensive with God, but the Logos gave it guidance and intellect. It was the "reason" or "mind" of God. Middle Platonism has absorbed many elements from Stoicism and made them its own, including the Logos concept (Dillon 1977).

Philo uses the expression *to ōn/ho ōn* "the one that is/the one who is" for the deity (*Quod Deus* 11; *Quis Heres* 187). For him God is ultimately and utterly transcendent and distinct from the world (*Somn*. 1.67; *Vita Contemp*. 2; *Leg. Gaium* 6). The question, then, is how he can communicate and have care for the world and especially for human beings, which being the case Philo takes for granted. Here is where the Logos is central to Philo's theological system (*Cher*. 27–30; *Quaes. Gen*. 1.4). But an emanation comes from God like a stream of light which reaches toward the world and makes him immanent and accessible to humanity. The first stage of the emanation is referred to as the Logos (*Leg. Alleg*. 3.96). It then divides into two powers, the creative power and royal power (*Cher*. 27–30; *Quaes. Exod*. 2.68; *De Abr*. 120–31). In some treatments there is a further bifurcation (*Fuga* 94–118). Each of the stages is progressively less pure. Thus, God maintains his unity and purity, but the gap is bridged by the Logos.

The Logos can be referred to as a hypostasis. In some contexts, it is referred to as "God" (*Somn*. 1.229–30; *Leg. Alleg*. 3.207–8; *Quaes. Gen*. 2.62) and "son of God" (*Conf*. 146; *Agr*. 51; *Somn*. 1.215), but at other times it is treated as a separate being. There is no question, though, that the Logos is inferior and subordinate to God (*Somn*. 1.229–30). Although wisdom (*sophia*) occurs much less frequently, its relationship to the Logos is not completely clear. Sometimes wisdom is considered the parent of the Logos, but in the same context the Logos also generates wisdom (*Fuga* 97, 108–9). The overall impression is that Logos and wisdom are in some sense equivalent for Philo, but for some reason he prefers the term Logos.

With the boom in targumic studies in the past three decades, some have wanted to explain the Logos of Jewish tradition by means of targumic usage. The major rabbinic targums use the surrogate "word" (Aramaic *memrā'*) for the name of the deity. Thus, where the biblical text says "the Lord (Yhwh) said" or "God (Elohim) said", the targums have "the Word (*memrā'*) of the Lord/God said". The primary function of this usage is generally accepted as a way of distancing God from anthropomorphic action. Such usage makes God's doings more indirectly attributable to him; an agent is inserted between the reader and the divine, not only making it more remote but also shielding the reader and worshiper from any danger posed by too direct contact with the deity. It is argued that *memrā'* in the targums functions much as Logos does in the writings of Philo, and the targumic usage even parallels and explains the NT usage, such as in John 1:1–5 (e.g. McNamara 1972: 101–6). There are three problems with this argument:

1. The targumic usage is not really the same as Philo's. The use of *memrā'* is just a way of avoiding anthropomorphisms and goes no further that. The sophisticated hypostasis speculation of Philo, developed in part from his knowledge of Greek philosophy, is absent from targumic usage. In Philo, the Logos is an active agent (see above), not just a textual device.

2. The targums in question are the rabbinic targums and to be dated to the rabbinic period (i.e. post-200 CE); they are too late to be helpful in analyzing the development of thinking about the deity in the Second Temple period.

3. The earliest targums (those known from Qumran: 4QtgLev, 4QtgJob, 11QtgJob) do not have this device. The various names of God are translated directly (e.g. *'ĕlōhîm* by *'ĕlāhā'* "God" in 11QtgJob) rather than by a surrogate expression or circumlocution as in the later targums.

SYNTHESIS

The various books of the OT do not give a uniform view of the deity and the spirit world, but exhibit a long evolution. Further development is found in the non-biblical texts. The overall message of the OT is that true religion was delivered once to Israel by Moses (or even to mankind from Adam on), but the history of Israel is the history of continually turning away from this religion, suffering punishment, and being delivered when re-embracing the true faith. This picture is an editorial one, however, and many texts and other data from pre-exilic times show that Israel and Judah were polytheistic. Not only were gods other than Yhwh worshiped, but Yhwh himself evidently had a consort. It also appears that cultic images were found in the temples of Jerusalem and Samaria.

All this is not surprising since the religion of ancient Israel looks typical of Northwest Semitic religion. The real surprise is the development of monotheism. Some would argue that this development is not quite unique in that there were already trends toward monotheism in the classical world and even in the ancient Near East. Some others have recently affirmed that monotheism is an incorrect term to apply to Judaic religion before 70. This may depend partly on one's definition of monotheism, but if we define this as not only the belief in one deity as such but also the denial of the existence of other gods, then monotheism was found in Judaism or certain circles of Judaism from the Persian period. Second Isaiah already contains claims that no gods exist apart from Yhwh, and some of the earliest Greek writings about the Jews remark on their belief in one God and rejection of the Greek pantheon.

Monotheism in antiquity and the present has not denied the existence of other heavenly beings or a developed spirit world. What it denies is that these spirits are in any way equal to or comparable to God. In many of the early Jewish writings and even in the late OT books, a fairly uniform outline of the spirit world is to be found: God is assisted by various angelic figures (some are labeled "archangels"), and there seem to be other angels who form the celestial bodies or carry out different and often specialized tasks. Although heavenly beings, these angels are completely different from and subordinate to God himself. The complexity of this angelology varies from writing to writing, though we tend to see a growing elaboration as time goes on. It is doubtful that there was ever a common belief in angels except in basic concepts, though some details (e.g. the names of a few archangels) are fairly widely represented through the different writings.

Most writers also envisage angelic opponents of God. These are usually pictured as angels who were once part of God's entourage but had sinned and fallen at some point in the past. Leading these (evil) angels (also referred to as "demons" or evil/unclean spirits), according to many writings, is a chief evil angel (two in *1 En.* 1–36) who goes by various names (including Satan, Mastema, Belial, Lucifer, Azazel, the devil). Human beings are caught in the middle of this dualistic spirit world and must ultimately choose on which side to align themselves. Their choice is complicated by the fact that the evil spirits deceive and tempt them to do wrong and choose the side of evil. However, there is no question that in the end God will triumph, and Satan and his followers will be defeated and either destroyed or imprisoned in a place of punishment.

11

PROPHECY, APOCALYPTICISM, THE ESOTERIC ARTS, AND PREDICTING THE FUTURE

The juxtaposition of subjects in this chapter may seem strange to some, especially those taught a particular view of prophecy. As noted below and argued in detail elsewhere, I believe that many OT scholars operate with an artificial view of prophecy – even now. Many believe, for example, that prophecy "came to an end" in the post-exilic period, yet this is not what many Jewish texts indicate. The matter is complex, of course, but in the Second Temple context it becomes clear that prophecy, apocalypticism, and what might be called the "esoteric arts" (magic, divination, astrology, and the like) were all paths to a common goal: determining the future and finding a direct route to God's mind. This chapter brings together a number of these subjects, but because of its varied contents, there is no separate survey of sources. The main prophetic and apocalyptic writings of relevance to Second Temple religion are listed and discussed in the Chapters 2–6.

PROBLEMS OF DEFINITION

Blenkinsopp, J. (1996a) *A History of Prophecy in Israel*.

Collins, J. J. (1979) (ed.) *Apocalypse: The Morphology of a Genre*.

—— (1997) *Apocalypticism in the Dead Sea Scrolls*.

—— (1998) *The Apocalyptic Imagination: An Introduction to Jewish Apocalyptic Literature*.

—— (ed.) (1999) *The Encyclopedia of Apocalypticism: Volume 1, The Origins of Apocalypticism in Judaism and Christianity*.

Collins, J. J., and J. H. Charlesworth (eds) (1991) *Mysteries and Revelations: Apocalyptic Studies since the Uppsala Colloquium*.

Cook, S. L. (1995) *Prophecy and Apocalypticism: The Postexilic Social Setting*.

Grabbe, L. L. (1989) "The Social Setting of Early Jewish Apocalypticism", *JSP* 4: 27–47.

—— (1995a) *Priests, Prophets, Diviners, Sages: A Socio-historical Study of Religious Specialists in Ancient Israel*.

Sacchi, P. (1996) *Jewish Apocalyptic and its History*.

Tigchelaar, E. J. C. (1996) *Prophets of Old and the Day of the End: Zechariah, the Book of Watchers and Apocalyptic*.

VanderKam, J. C. (1986) "The Prophetic-Sapiential Origins of Apocalyptic Thought", in J. D. Martin and P. R. Davies (eds) *A Word in Season: Essays in Honour of William McKane*: 163–76.

—— (1997) "Mantic Wisdom in the Dead Sea Scrolls", *DSD* 4: 336–53.

The terms "prophecy", or "apocalyptic/apocalypticism" – the terms are used interchangeably in this discussion (p. 9 above) – and the like are too often defined as if they were unproblematic concepts, easily distinguished – and certainly to be separated from "divination" and similar practices. Scholars have wanted to distance prophecy from, on the one hand, the oracles and divination well known from the classical and Near Eastern world and, on the other, from apocalyptic which was alleged to have developed in Judaism when prophecy degenerated, and then replaced it. As I have argued elsewhere, though, theological prejudice and parochialism have created artificial distinctions and definitions that are not supported by the actual textual and social data (Grabbe 1989; 1995a: 66–84, 98–107). Only a brief discussion is possible here, for the sake of the present study, but see the works cited for a more detailed clarification and defense.

Although in one sense prophets and prophecy can be what we say they are, most definitions pay some lip service to the terminology of the biblical sources and the definitions given or assumed by the ancient authors. The Hebrew root *nb'/nāvî'* "prophesy/prophet" has usually lain at the core of the various definitions proposed. The problem we have for the Second Temple period is that few of our texts discussing prophecy and prophets are in Hebrew, which means that the characteristic Hebrew term is not present. Instead, we often have to do with the Greek word *prophētēs* or related words. Although they generally render *nāvî'* in the Septuagint and other Greek translations, this does not necessarily mean that they have the same connotation. Nevertheless, both concepts have fed into the English terms "prophet" and "prophecy".

A proper definition is one which covers not only Israel but prophecy and prophetic figures in the ancient Near East, in later Judaism, and in other pre-modern societies. In the past – and perhaps still unduly influencing the present – a variety of tendentious definitions have skewed the discussion by attempting to distance their idealized Israelite prophet from similar figures within and outside Israel. That is, they have started with the unproved assumption that prophecy in Israel was unique. Without claiming an unproblematic definition, I have suggested that

> a prophet is a mediator claiming to have messages direct from a divinity, by various means, and communicating these messages to recipients.

What that means is that most, if not all, prophecy is a subdivision of divination. Both prophets and diviners are mediators and both receive messages from the deity. The prophet receives these messages in the forms of auditions, visions, or perhaps direct inspiration. Thus, prophecy is basically a form of "spirit divination".

Furthermore, the oft-made distinctions between "pre-classical", "classical", and post-exilic prophecy cannot really be maintained and often carry an undercurrent of value judgment (Grabbe 1995a: 99–105). One of the main assumptions behind many discussions is that there was a common "prophetic movement" in ancient Israel. The belief seems to be that the "true, classical" prophets were almost a tightly knit group, all with the same outlook and characteristics. This owes more to theological preconception than to data from the OT. There are indeed great differences between the various prophets from Nathan to Malachi, but these do not fall into neat chronology distinctions, nor can we draw an artificial divide between the "true" and the "false" prophets, which represents only the bias of the OT text. From a sociological point of view the figures were all prophets and must be taken into account in any study. Prophets of all sorts were evidently a part of Israelite society from an early time, and they all had certain characteristics which were features of that culture, but this is normal in cultures the world over. There is little evidence of a unified "prophetic school" whose characteristics can be taken as normative in defining prophecy, nor was there a uniform evolution over time.

Defining "apocalyptic/apocalypticism" is equally difficult. The terms both come from the Greek words *apokaluptō* "to reveal" and *apokalupsis* "revelation", and have been especially influenced by the contents of such books as the NT book of Revelation (see especially Collins 1998: 1–42). A commendable attempt to define the genre of "apocalypse" is helpful (Collins 1979; 1998: 2–11):

> A genre of revelatory literature with a narrative framework, in which a revelation is mediated by an otherworldly being to a human recipient, disclosing a transcendent reality which is both temporal, insofar as it envisages eschatological salvation, and spatial insofar as it involves another supernatural world.

Nevertheless, there are still some problems with it (cf. Grabbe 1989): for example, how essential is the narrative framework, and how essential is the otherworldly mediator? Why does this definition fail to account for much that is found in acknowledged apocalypses? In any case, apocalypses are only a part of the phenomenon of apocalyptic, since the phenomenon of apocalyptic is known from literature other than apocalypses.

The assumption is generally that apocalyptic is different from prophecy, and the genre of apocalypse is different from a prophetic writing. However, a number of the alleged differences between prophetic and apocalyptic writings do not hold up to an actual study of the writings. Are the apocalypses pseudepigraphical? So are many prophetic texts. Do the apocalypses depend a lot on visions? So do many prophecies (cf. Grabbe 1995a: 83, 108–11, 116). Do many apocalypses describe an ideal world to come? So do many prophetic passages. One can of course come up with relatively neutral form-critical criteria to distinguish prophetic literary forms from apocalypses and their forms. From a form-critical perspective many of the old prophetic forms do tend to change or die out, and a new genre of apocalypse arises; however, apocalyptic is not by any means confined to formal apocalypses. In my opinion the sharp distinction between prophecy and apocalyptic is thus unjustified (cf. also Collins 1997: 4–8). For example, there is no reason why the prophetic book of Zechariah 1–8 cannot also be classified as an apocalypse (*contra* Collins 1998: 23–24). Indeed, I would rather see apocalyptic as a sub-genre of prophecy than as a separate entity. When there was no longer a king and court, and the country came under foreign domination, prophecies might well take the form of announcing a divine restoration of these or something even greater such as God's direct rule on a purified earth; alternatively, the idea of a personal afterlife might obviate particular concern for a restored monarchy. In either case, such prophecies might well take the form of an apocalypse or a related genre.

Prophecy and apocalyptic are further complicated in that both have social as well as literary dimensions; furthermore, we know of the social side primarily through the literature. Therefore, both the written prophets and the written apocalypses present many of the same problems with regard to relating them to a social context and to social reality. We can debate matters of genre and even definition, but the function of prophecies and apocalypses in society seems to have been similar. It is not just the prophetic figures who have a social function – the literature itself takes on a functional role in society.

Apocalypses are said to be pseudepigraphical, and most are. However, far too often overlooked is the fact that some or even a great deal of the prophetic writings did not originate with prophets. Whatever Amos, Isaiah, Jeremiah, and other prophets spoke as oracles from Yhwh, these were at least supplemented by a later generation of tradents who passed on the tradition. How much of this material is to be assigned to the later tradents is debated and probably varies from book to book, yet few would claim that the added material was itself primarily oracular material delivered by a fellow prophet: more likely it is poetic (or even prose) material purpose-written for its context. The prophetic books as we have them today are, therefore, pseudepigraphic writings with much material contributed by poets and scribes. The prophetic writings, and the apocalyptic and related writings, are all scribal works in their present form and thus present a similar problem when it comes to relating them to their social context.

Recent study has noted strong wisdom elements in apocalyptic (cf. Grabbe 1995a: 176–78). Some have taken this as evidence that apocalyptic has a separate origin from prophecy. These wisdom elements tend to be weighted toward what has been called "mantic wisdom", however, and mantic wisdom has much in common with prophecy (cf. VanderKam 1986). The development of apocalyptic is complex, with many different elements and influences enriching it as time went on, but this does not diminish its relationship to prophecy.

The term "esoteric arts" is not one I have seen used very much, but it is useful to delineate a group of phenomena with certain things in common, primarily a specialist, slightly mysterious knowledge, usually implying some peculiar acquaintance with the divine realm. This includes magic, astrology, divination, dream interpretation, and the like. These are closely related to prophecy and apocalyptic (indeed, if prophecy and apocalyptic are seen as forms of divination, they would naturally fall in this category). But there were special means of learning the future among the Jews: in particular, their possession of the Law and the Prophets. The written word had become a source of divine knowledge and was often thought to have all sorts of esoteric knowledge encoded within it, if one only knew the key to unlocking it.

DID PROPHECY CEASE IN THE SECOND TEMPLE PERIOD?

Aune, D. E. (1983) *Prophecy in Early Christianity and the Ancient Mediterranean World*.

Gnuse, R. K. (1996) *Dreams and Dream Reports in the Writings of Josephus: A Traditio-Historical Analysis*.

Grabbe, L. L. (1998e) "Poets, Scribes, or Preachers? The Reality of Prophecy in the Second Temple Period", in *Society of Biblical Literature 1998 Seminar Papers*: 2.524–45.

Gray, R. (1993) *Prophetic Figures in Late Second Temple Jewish Palestine: The Evidence from Josephus*.

Hay, D. M. (1991) "Philo's View of Himself as an Exegete: Inspired, but not Authoritative", *SPA* 3: 40–52.

Horsley, R. A. (1985) "'Like One of the Prophets of Old': Two Types of Popular Prophets at the Time of Jesus", *CBQ* 47: 435–63.

—— (1986) "Popular Prophetic Movements at the Time of Jesus: Their Principal Features and Social Origins", *JSNT* 26 (1986) 3–27.

Horsley, R. A., and J. S. Hanson (1999) *Bandits, Prophets, and Messiahs*.

Levison, J. R. (1994) "Two Types of Ecstatic Prophecy according to Philo", *SPA* 6: 83–89.

—— (1995) "Inspiration and the Divine Sprit in the Writings of Philo Judaeus", *JSJ* 26: 271–323.

Meeks, W. A. (1967) *The Prophet–King: Moses Traditions and the Johannine Christology.*

Sommer, B. D. (1996) "Did Prophecy Cease? Evaluating a Reevaluation", *JBL* 115: 31–47.

Teeple, H. M. (1957) *The Mosaic Eschatological Prophet.*

Wan, S. (1994) "Charismatic Exegesis: Philo and Paul Compared", *SPA* 6: 54–82.

Winston, David (1989) "Two Types of Mosaic Prophecy according to Philo", *JSP* 2: 49–67.

Wolfson, H. A. (1947) *Philo: Foundations of Religious Philosophy in Judaism, Christianity, and Islam.*

Main texts

The question of whether prophecy ceased sometime in the early post-exilic period has often been answered in the affirmative, yet seldom has the question been investigated seriously. I have done this in a recent article (Grabbe 1998e) which should be consulted for the full study and more details; only an abbreviated version is given here.

Although **Ben Sira** is often seen as an opponent of special revelations and all the various practices relating to the future, in describing the ideal sage he states: "He seeks out the wisdom of all the ancients, and is concerned with prophecies" (39:1–3). Continuing in the same vein is 36:20–21: "Bear witness to those whom you created in the beginning, and fulfill the prophecies spoken in your name. Reward those who wait for you and let your prophets be found trustworthy". Isaiah is said to have seen the future and "revealed what was to occur to the end of time, and the hidden things before they happened" (48:24–25). Joshua "was the successor of Moses in the prophetic office" (46:1), a statement also found in Josephus.

One of the main sources for the view that prophecy had ceased is **1 Maccabees**. The first passage is 4:44–46, which states that the stones of the polluted altar were stored away "until a prophet should come to tell what to do with them". The context does not suggest that prophets were only a phenomenon of the distant past; on the contrary, although there was no prophet currently available, it was still possible for one to come along in the future. The passage does not really argue for the cessation of prophecy but only that acceptable prophets were not necessarily common. A similar idea occurs a little later in the book (1 Macc. 14:41). The passage most explicitly stating the view that prophecy had ceased is 1 Maccabees 9:27: "So there was great distress in Israel, such as had not been since the time that prophets ceased to appear among them". According to this, prophets ceased sometime in the past and are no longer extant; however, it agrees with other passages in not ruling out a future prophet.

1 Macc

4

Some of the **Qumran texts** express belief in the appearance of a future prophet who is separate from the messiah(s) of Aaron and Israel (1QS 9:9–11). A good case can be made that the Teacher of Righteousness was seen by many as this eschatological prophet. For the people of the Scrolls, Daniel was also a prophet: "[a]s is written in the book of Daniel the prophet [*hnby'*]" (4QFlor frag. 1, ii, 3, 24, 5:3). The Scrolls also indicate an attitude toward the interpretation of prophetic literature which differs significantly from what we think of as biblical interpretation. With regard to one passage, the *Habakkuk Commentary* states, "Its interpretation concerns the Teacher of Righteousness to whom God has made known all the mysteries of the words of his servants, the prophets" (1QpHab 7:3–5). The Teacher was inspired to interpret prophecies of Habakkuk even though the original prophet himself did not understand them. The implication is that interpretation was not just a matter of interpretative rules or techniques; on the contrary, interpretation was a matter of inspiration by the same spirit which had inspired the original prophetic writer.

Philo of Alexandria is an important witness to Jewish views about the concept of prophecy at the turn of the era. He discusses the subject at some length, especially in *De Vita Mosis*. The first passage is 1.263–99 which recounts the story of Balaam. Philo makes the distinction between augury (which Balaam formerly practiced) and prophecy (1.264–68). But then Balaam "straightway became possessed, and there fell upon him the truly prophetic spirit which banished utterly from his soul his art of wizardry . . . he spake these oracles as one repeating the words which another had put into his mouth". For Philo, Moses is the prophet *par excellence* (2.187), and he distinguishes several sorts of prophecy (2.188–91):

> Of the divine utterances, some are spoken by God in His own Person with His prophet for interpreter, in some the revelation comes through question and answer, and others are spoken by Moses in his own person, when possessed by God and carried away out of himself.

The inspiration of prophets in general is described as a sort of possession in which God speaks through their mouth, using it simply as a channel (*Quis heres* 259–66; *Spec. leg.* 1.65).

Philo is quite important for another idea already noted with Qumran, the concept of inspired interpretation (*Vita Mosis* 2.264–65, 268–69). Interestingly, Philo sees himself as understanding scripture by means of inspiration: "But there is a higher thought than these. It comes from a voice in my own soul, which oftentimes is god-possessed and divines where it does not know" (*Cher.* 27; see also *Migr. Abr.* 34–35; *Somn.* 2.164–65).

Josephus speaks of "prophecy and the foreknowledge which it gives, for in this way God enables us to know what to guard against" (*Ant.* 8.15.6 §418), indicating his view that prophecy includes knowledge about the future. He is not afraid to use "prophecy" and "prophet" for figures other than the OT prophets; for example, Daniel is called a prophet (*Ant.* 10.11.4 §§245–49; 10.11.7 §§267–69, 280; 11.7.6 §322), as is Joshua (*Ant.* 4.7.2 §165) and John Hyrcanus had the gift of prophecy (*War* 1.2.8 §§68–69: *Ant.* 13.10.7 §299). Josephus refers to a number of individuals as "false prophets", indicating that they had the persona of a prophet (*War* 2.13.5 §§261–63; 6.5.2 §285–87; 7.11.1–3 §§437–50; *Ant.* 20.5.1 §97; 20.8.6 §169; 20.8.10 §188; *Life* 76 §§424–25). He also refers to the use of the ephod by the high priests to determine the future as prophecy or prophesying (*Ant.* 6.6.3 §115; 6.12.4–5 §§254, 257; 6.5.6 §359; 7.4.1 §76). Prophecy is also associated with the interpretation of scripture. For example, the Essenes have those who foretell the future because they are educated in the holy books and the sayings of the prophets from an early age (*War* 2.8.12 §159). Josephus also associates interpretation of the biblical books with prophecy and connects this with dream interpretation – and he claims these skills for himself (*War* 3.8.3 §§351–53).

A question of particular concern is how Josephus regarded himself, since he claimed to be able to foretell the future and predicted to Vespasian that he would become emperor. So why did he not refer to himself as a prophet? There are probably two reasons for this. The lesser is that he identified himself as a priest and claimed to obtain at least part of his skill through this fact. The other is more subtle but also more likely: a blatant claim to be a prophet might cause a reaction. Some people were suspicious of prophets, and it was also preferable that others acclaim him than that he did it himself. In this case he probably thought that "the wise would understand", and those who did not were probably not important, anyway.

The **Liber Antiquitatum Biblicarum** (or Pseudo-Philo) agrees with Philo in envisaging prophecy as the result of the spirit taking possession of the prophet and describing the future. It tells the story of a judge named Cenaz (not in the OT, unless he is to be identified with Othniel's father). The holy spirit came upon him, taking away his senses, and he began to prophesy; upon finishing, he woke up but did not know what he had spoken (28:6–10).

The writings of **the NT and other early Christian literature** give a number of examples of prophetic activity by living prophets, or in some way presuppose that such existed. These are collected in Grabbe (1998e).

Conclusions

We seem to have two separate evaluations of the social situation: passages such as 1 Macc. 9:27 appear to say that the prophets are in some sense in the past, yet other passages speak of "prophets" who are contemporary with the writer. Josephus exemplifies both attitudes. He mentions the gift of prophecy and the existence of prophets (or alleged prophets) long after the biblical period, yet he also states that the "exact succession of the prophets" had ceased after the time of Artaxerxes (*Ag. Apion* 1.8 §§40–41). Josephus's concern in this passage is to explain the status of certain writings when there was no further "exact succession" and sacred scripture was no longer written, however; he nowhere suggests that prophecy as such had completely ceased.

The model of the prophet which emerges from the Second Temple literature includes a number of characteristics. As in the OT, the prophet is someone who claims to have a message from God. He is likewise someone who gives information about the future, which is also the case with many OT prophets. This foreknowledge of the future is an important aspect of being a prophet according to a number of sources. We find three different sources for prophecy during the Second Temple period. First, prophets deliver oracles received from the deity in a variety of ways, including visions and dreams; secondly, prophetic material is written by scribes or sages who may or may not be in a state of "inspiration"; thirdly, prophetic and other material is interpreted via a special sort of inspiration which goes beyond mere intellect or training.

Once the utterance of a prophet has been reduced to writing, it does not differ in any significant way from a prophecy or apocalypse created by a scribe. It is not always possible to distinguish prophecy from apocalyptic by formal characteristics; however, even when it is, the impact on the reader and its general credibility may not be any different. The fact that one takes a form already known from the OT prophetic corpus while another belongs to the apocalypse genre or a related form may be of indifference to the reader who sees both as revelation from God, giving his will and perhaps hinting at what would come to pass hereafter. Therefore, the debate over the alleged differences is not particularly relevant at this point. They both function in society in much the same way.

From a social point of view, was there a difference between the writers of prophetic texts and the writers of apocalyptic texts? What was the experience of the writers who wrote them? It has been suggested that the apocalypticists were not mere scribes toiling at their desks but rather that they had visions or mantic experiences which were the source of the information in their writings. There seems to be no way to confirm this, but it is equally foolish to deny it, at least as a possibility. Thus, both prophetic and apocalyptic writings point to two potential social origins: first are the "inspired" individuals who receive messages in one form or another and proceed to teach or write their message for posterity; secondly, there are scribal individuals who compose prophetic or apocalyptic writings with the aim of influencing their co-religionists (or even the Greco-Romans in a few cases, such as perhaps the *Sibylline Oracles*).

Horsley (in criticism of Aune 1983: 121–29) has pointed out that literary descriptions of prophets (the "prophet like Moses", etc.) should not be lumped in with the social phenomena (1986: 25 n. 15). Although the attempt at a sociological analysis is commendable, it must not be forgotten that we do not have sociological field data. All we have are descriptions in ancient literature, and our sociological analyses represent an attempt to extract socio-logical data from literature. This suggests some methodological points that must be considered: the descriptions themselves may be influenced to a lesser or greater extent by literary-theological models; and the social phenomena may have been influenced by, or even inspired by, the literary-theological models extant at the time. A further problem is that the data in the ancient sources are far from complete. The fact that certain elements are lacking in the description (e. g., religious motives or messianic expectations) does not mean that they were not present in the actual historical situation. Of course, one has no right to read them in without evidence, but it certainly complicates any task of classification and makes one cautious about accepting any system which is overly schematic.

THE ESOTERIC ARTS AND THEIR USE

Berchman, R. M. (ed.) (1998) *Mediators of the Divine: Horizons of Prophecy, Divination, Dreams and Theurgy in Mediterranean Antiquity.*

Grabbe, L. L. (1995a) *Priests, Prophets, Diviners, Sages: A Socio-historical Study of Religious Specialists in Ancient Israel.*

Potter, D. (1994) *Prophets and Emperors: Human and Divine Authority from Augustus to Theodosius.*

It is sometimes thought that the Jews took a different view from others in the ancient Near East on things like divination and magic. One can think of the anecdote about the Jewish archer who shot the bird being observed by diviners to determine military strategy, with the comment that if the bird knew the future, he should have foreseen the archer's arrow (Josephus, *C. Apion.* 1.22 §§201–04). But many examples from history and social anthro-pology show that the rejection of one form of divination or esoteric art does not imply a wholesale rejection, and various forms of divination have a long history even among the priests (Grabbe 1995a: ch. 5). Many Jews seem to have found it useful to resort to divination and other forms of predicting the future, and we have hints even of magical practices in certain circles, though the data here are rather scarce.

Astrology

Alexander, P. S. (1996) "Physiognomy, Initiation, and Rank in the Qumran Community", in H. Cancik, H. Lichtenberger, and P. Schäfer (eds)

Geschichte–Tradition–Reflexion: Festschrift für Martin Hengel zum 70. Geburtstag: Band I Judentum: 385–94.

Charlesworth, J. H. (1987) "Jewish Interest in Astrology during the Hellenistic and Roman Period", *ANRW II: Principate*: 20.2.926–50.

Goldstein, Bernard R., and David Pingree (1977) "Horoscopes from the Cairo Geniza", *JNES* 36: 113–44.

Gruenwald, Ithamar (1970–71) "Further Jewish Physiognomic and Chiromantic Fragments", *Tarbiz* 40: 301–19 (Hebrew).

Kraus, F. R. (1939) *Texte zur babylonischen Physiognomatik*.

—— (1947) "Weitere texte zur babylonischen Physiognomatik", *Orientalia* 16: 172–206.

Strange, J. F. (1979) "Archaeology and the Religion of Judaism in Palestine", *ANRW II*: 19.1.646–85.

Waerden, B. L. van der (1952) "History of the Zodiac", *AfO* 16: 216–30.

Wise, Michael Owen (1994) "Thunder in Gemini: An Aramaic Brontologion (4Q318)", *Thunder in Gemini And Other Essays on the History, Language and Literature of Second Temple Palestine*: 13–50.

Astrology, as we think of it, is mainly a development of the Hellenistic period. Although it was referred to as the "Chaldean science", the Assyrians and Babylonians mainly looked at a broad range of celestial and even meteorological phenomena. The use of prognostication based on the zodiac, which we still associate with astrology today, developed mainly after the conquests of Alexander (van der Waerden 1952). The extant Jewish texts show an ambivalent attitude to the question. We can find statements of condemnation, such as *Sib. Or.* 3:213–64. Philo comments that Abraham had been an astrologer but left the practice, which is represented by means of allegory in his migration from Ur of the "Chaldeans" (*De Abrahamo* 62–84). On the other hand, Artapanus asserts that Abraham taught astrology to the Egyptians (Eusebius, *Prep. Evan.* 9.18.1). Similarly, the writer known as Pseudo-Eupolemus (a Samaritan?) says that Abraham taught astrology to the Phoenicians (Eusebius, *Prep. Evan.* 9.17.3–4). Josephus quotes with approval the statement ascribed to Berossus that Abraham was skilled in the "heavenly science" and taught it to the Egyptians (*Ant.* 1.7.2 §158; 1.8.2 §§166–68).

We know that astrology was used by Jews of the medieval period because we have a number of horoscopes (e.g. Goldstein/Pingree 1977), and astrological motifs are well known from the synagogue decorations of the Talmudic age (Strange 1979: 670–71). For the earlier period, we do not have much (cf. Charlesworth 1987), but there are some texts. The *Astronomical Book* of *1 Enoch* (72–82), including its Qumran fragments, seems to have nothing on astrology, at least in what has been preserved. Nevertheless, Qumran has some interesting examples. The first of these is the *Aramaic Brontologion* (4Q318, translation from Wise 1994):

[If] it thunders [on a day when the moon is in Taurus], (it signifies) [vain] changes in the wo[rld (?) . . .][7] [and] toil for the cities, and destru[ction in] the royal [co]urt and in the city of dest[ruction](?) [. . .][8] there will be, and among the Arabs [ ] . . . famine. Nations will plunder one ano[ther . . .].[9] [*vacat*] If it thunders (on a day when the moon is) in Gemini, (it signifies) fear and distress caused by foreigners and by [. . .].

Despite the fragmentary state, it seems to be a genuine astrological work making use of the zodiac for predictive purposes. It also includes physiognomy, the prediction of a person's character from physical features.

Another text which combines astrological and physiognomic features is 4Q186 (translation from DJD 5: 88–91):

[Frag. 1, col. II][5] and his thighs are long and thin, and his toes[6] are thin and long, and he is of the Second Vault.[7] He has six (parts) spirit in the House of Light, and three in the Pit of[8] Darkness. And this is the time of birth on which he is brought forth –[9] on the festival of Taurus. He will be poor; and this is his beast – Taurus.

The existence of several Mesopotamian physiognomic texts shows that physiognomy had a long history in the ancient Near East (Kraus 1939; 1947). Some later Jewish texts on the same subject from the Genizah may have some connection with Qumran (Gruenwald 1970–71).

Dreams

Gnuse, R. K. (1982) "A Reconsideration of the Form–Critical Structure in I Samuel 3: An Ancient Near Eastern Dream Theophany", *ZAW* 94: 379–90.

—— (1996) *Dreams and Dream Reports in the Writings of Josephus: A Traditio-Historical Analysis.*

Grabbe, L. L. (1995) *Priests, Prophets, Diviners, Sages: A Socio-historical Study of Religious Specialists in Ancient Israel.*

Gray, R. (1993) *Prophetic Figures in Late Second Temple Jewish Palestine: The Evidence from Josephus.*

Husser, J.-M. (1994) *Le songe et la parole: Étude sur le rêve et sa fonction dans l'ancien Israël.*

—— (1999) *Dreams and Dream Narratives in the Biblical World.*

Lewis, N. (1976) *The Interpretation of Dreams and Portents.*

Miller, J. E. (1990) "Dreams and Prophetic Visions", *Biblica* 71: 401–4.

Miller, P. C. (1994) *Dreams in Late Antiquity: Studies in the Imagination of a Culture.*

Niditch, S. (1980) *The Symbolic Vision in Biblical Tradition.*

Oppenheim, A. L. (1956) "The Interpretation of Dreams in the Ancient Near East, With a Translation of an Assyrian Dream-Book", *Transactions of the American Philosophical Society* 46: 179–354.

Sasson, J. (1982) "An Apocalyptic Vision from Mari?: Speculations on *ARM* X:9", *MARI* 1: 151–67.

—— (1983) "Mari Dreams", *JAOS* 103: 283–93.

Sasson, V. (1986) "The Book of Oracular Visions of Balaam from Deir 'Alla", *UF* 17: 283–309.

White, R. J. (ed.) (1975) *The Interpretation of Dreams:* Oneirocritica *by Artemidorus (Translation and Commentary).*

Dreams were seen as significant at an early point in Israelite tradition and were seen as one means of divine revelation as far back as we can go (cf. 1 Sam. 6:8; Husser 1994; Niditch 1980). Prophets might receive their messages from God by means of dreams as well as other modes (Grabbe 1995: 145–48), two well-known examples of dream interpretation being Joseph and Daniel. One question which immediately comes to mind is whether there is a distinction between "dream" and "vision". Husser (1994: 24–25) has attempted to distinguish them on the basis that dreams have a visual element whereas visions do not, but this is incorrect since visions often have a visual element. In some cases, the visual element is only of the deity and serves merely as the setting for an audition (cf. Gnuse 1982: 380–81). Several passages in Job make dream(s) (*ḥălôm[ôt]*) and "vision(s) of the night" (*ḥezyôn[ôt] lailāh*) parallel (Job 7:14; 20:8). Job 4:13 associates visions of the night with sleep, and 33:15 seems to make night vision equivalent to dream. Num. 24:4 connects seeing (*ḥzh*) and open eyes with a vision (*maḥăzeh*). Another word for vision (*mar'āh*) may have mainly words as its content (1 Sam. 3:1–15; Gen. 46:2); on the other hand, it may have a large visual element (Ezek. 1:1; 8:3; Dan. 10).

Furthermore, the descriptions of what are called "dreams" and what are called "visions" do not necessarily differ. The vision of Micaiah in which he eavesdrops on the divine council (1 Kings 22:13–28), Daniel's dream/vision (*ḥēlem/ḥezwā'*) in which he sees the Ancient of Days and the One Like a Son of Man (Dan. 7), the Mari dream or vision promising Zimri–Lim eternal sovereignty (Sasson 1983: 285), and another Mari dream (*ANET*: 623) have no formal distinguishing characteristics in the content of the actual message. One cannot label this one a vision and that one only a dream. Thus, despite terminologicial differences, any distinction is often merely academic.

Some ancient writers already postulated different sorts of dreams, such as the Greek writer Artemidorus (*c.*250 CE) who distinguished the prescient dreams (*oneiros*) from ordinary dreams (*Oneirocritica* 1.1–3; 4.1–2). He further divided the significant dreams between "direct" and "allegorical". A modern scholar (Oppenheim 1956) has made a distinction between "message" dreams, in which a direct message is conveyed, and "symbolic" dreams which require interpretation. Although many dreams do not fall neatly into one category or the other, the two categories illustrate the important connections between dreams and other forms of divine–human communication. Dreams are perhaps more often symbolic than visions, yet the categories of direct revelation (message) and symbolic do not necessarily separate dreams from visions. Some visions are symbolic, as Amos 7:7–9; 8:1–3; Jeremiah 24; and the visons of Zechariah (cf. Niditch 1980), while some dreams contain a direct message from the god(s). For example, the Mari dream in the temple of Dagan gave an immediate message and differed from a vision or even a prophecy only in the setting (*ANET*: 623).

Dreams as direct revelations are closely related to prophecy, whereas symbolic or allegorical dreams fit very well into the wisdom tradition with its accumulation and classification of traditional knowledge. It was accepted in antiquity that not all dreams were significant or, at least, that the dreams of a king or priest might have broader significance. The NT has a number of examples in which dreams give important divine communication (Matt. 1; cf. Acts 16:9–10; 18:9; 2 Cor. 12:1–4). Also, Juvenal (*Satires* 6.542–47) makes an intriguing statement which associates dream interpretation with the Jews.

Josephus's account of his own dreams has already been alluded to (p. 239 above; cf. Gnuse 1996; Gray 1993). These were especially associated with his prediction that Vespasian would become emperor (*War* 3.8.3 §§351–52). He tells how, when he made the prediction, Vespasian at first did not believe him but, on making further enquiries, found that Josephus supposedly foretold the day of the fall of Jotapata (*War* 3.8.9 §§399–407). Josephus does not say how this latter premonition came to him, but a dream is one possibility.

Textual interpretation

The use of texts was known to Greco-Romans as well as Jews if we think of such writings as the *Sibylline Oracles*, but the repository of religion primarily in a book was a special feature of Judaism. As noted in the previous section (pp. 238–39 above), Josephus stated that he himself used the Jewish sacred writings as a basis for predictions, though he does not give specific examples. Perhaps the clearest examples are found in the Qumran texts, especially the *pesharim*, where the recent history of the sect is found in minute detail in the first two chapters of Habakkuk. To be able to find information about the future in the pages of Holy Writ must have given special piquancy to the knowledge that one was among the Chosen, and that one's group was so plainly designated by God. Even the prophets themselves had not understood what they were writing, but God had revealed it to the Teacher of Righteousness (4QpHab 7:1–6).

Chronography

Grabbe, L. L. (1979b) "Chronography in Hellenistic Jewish Historiography", *Society of Biblical Literature 1979 Seminar Papers*: 2.43–68.

—— (1981) "Chronography in 4 Ezra and 2 Baruch", *Society of Biblical Literature 1981 Seminar Papers*: 49–63.

—— (1982a) "The End of the World in Early Jewish and Christian Calculations", *RevQ* 41: 107–108.

—— (1997d) "The 70-Weeks Prophecy (Daniel 9:24–27) in Early Jewish Interpretation", in C. A. Evans and S. Talmon (eds) *The Quest for Context and Meaning: Studies in Biblical Intertextuality in Honor of James A. Sanders*: 595–611.

Laato, A. (1998) "The Apocalypse of the Syriac Baruch and the Date of the End", *JSP* 18: 39–46.

Roddy, N. (1996) " 'Two Parts: Weeks of Seven Weeks': The End of the Age as *Terminus ad Quem* for *2 Baruch*", *JSP* 14: 3–14.

Wise, M. O. (1997) "To Know the Times and the Seasons: A Study of the Aramaic Chronograph 4Q559", *JSP* 15: 3–51.

Another mode of trying to work out the future was to use a combination of methods to try to calculate the age of the world. It was also taken for granted that certain patterns had been put into history by God himself and needed only to be calculated by the one to whom God's spirit had revealed such things. Two examples will illustrate this, one involving the supposed age of the world and the other the seventy weeks of Daniel 9.

The Age of the World could, it was thought, be calculated since, based on Psalm 90:4, the view had developed that human history followed the plan of a thousand-year week. That is, all human history would be packed into 6,000 years, followed by a millennial sabbath. Exactly how early this developed is not clear. One of the earliest plain references to it is from about 150 CE in the early Christian writing *Epistle of Barnabas* (15:4). However, the same idea seems to lie behind 2 Peter 3:8 and especially Revelation 20:4. This model for human history then became quite widespread in early Christian writers, though in time there was a reaction against what was seen as too much emphasis on the physical "indulgences" expected during the Millennium.

The question is how early the concept arose in Judaism. *Jubilees* 4:30 has a statement similar to Psalm 90:4 but does not go further. From the first century the *Testament of Abraham* seems to presuppose a 7,000-year programme of human history, though one version (B 7:15–16) is clearer than the other (A 19:7, though one manuscript has "6,000 years" instead of "seven thousand ages"). Josephus mentions that the earth was about 5,000 years old in his own time (*Ant.* Proem. 3 §13; *Ag. Apion* 1.1 §1). However, 4 Ezra has the puzzling figure of 5,042 years to the time of Ezra (14:48 Syriac version).

Although this has never been satisfactorily explained before, I believe that it is to be tied in with the messianic age of 400 years in 7:28 (Grabbe 1981). If we assume that the 5042 years is meant to refer to the Ezra of the OT, this would make the writing of the book (*c*.100 CE) close to the year 5600. If we add the 400 years of the Messiah, this gives an age of the world of 6,000 years before God then brings about the cosmic regeneration. If so, the writer seems to have believed that he was living near the time of the coming of the messiah. A number of Christian writers put the birth of Jesus in the year 5500 from the creation of the world, which also seems to fit in with the idea that human history would run for 6,000 years before "God's time" would be introduced (cf. Grabbe 1982a).

As discussed in more detail in Grabbe (1997d), Daniel 9 has one of the most startling prophecies with a specific time frame, **the seventy weeks prophecy**. This passage explicitly asks about the prophecy of seventy years mentioned by Jeremiah (25:11–12; 29:10). It then goes on to reinterpret Jeremiah's prophecy as a reference to seventy *weeks* of years (Dan. 9:24–27). What is surprising is that more explicit reference is not made to Daniel 9, especially to speculate on its meaning. It is normally taken to refer to the death of the high priest Onias III about 170 BCE just before the Maccabean revolt (2 Macc. 4:32–34), but it becomes important in later Christian writings as a way of calculating the coming of the messiah. There is also some evidence that speculation about it occurred among Jewish interpreters, but the evidence is more circumstantial.

Perhaps one of the clearer and more interesting examples is found in the Qumran scrolls. The *Damascus Document* 1:5–11 speaks of a figure of 390 years. This of course corresponds with the period of Israel's punishment as stipulated in the book of Ezekiel (Ezek. 4:4–5), but this would not prevent the writer from also thinking of Daniel 9. The 390 years in the *Damascus Document* are followed by the figure of twenty years of groping until the Teacher of Righteousness comes. There are statements to the effect that a period of forty years would elapse between the death of the Teacher until the end of the age (CD 20:14–15; 4QpPs^a 2:6–8). If one allows another figure of forty years (= one generation) for the life of the Teacher, we come to 490 years. The two figures of forty years are stereotyped, but stereotyping is typical of this sort of chronographical speculation.

Two further interpretations may have the seventy weeks of Daniel as their base. In his description of the siege of Jerusalem, Josephus states (*War* 6.5.4 §311):

> Thus the Jews, after the demolition of Antonia [the fortress near the temple], reduced the temple to a square, although they had it recorded in their oracles that the city and the sanctuary would be taken when the temple should become four-square.

A second oracle is mentioned in the same context (*War* 6.5.4 §§312–13):

> But what more than all else incited them to the war was an ambiguous oracle, likewise found in their sacred scriptures, to the effect that at that time one from their country would become ruler of the world. This they understood to mean someone of their own race, and many of their wise men went astray in their interpretation of it. The oracle, however, in reality signified the sovereignty of Vespasian, who was proclaimed emperor on Jewish soil.

Both these oracles are somewhat unclear as to which biblical passage they refer. It is difficult to find one which seems to fit better than Daniel 9, however, which is why many scholars have connected one or both these with the seventy-weeks prophecy. This suggests that it was used as a means of trying to work out the end of the age in some circles, though the failure of such prophecies may have been the reason that clearer examples have not survived (see Grabbe 1997d for a further discussion and examples).

Magic, mysticism, and controlling the spirits

Alexander, P. S. (1984) " Comparing Merkavah Mysticism and Gnosticism: An Essay in Method", *JJS* 35: 1–18.

—— (1986) "VII. Incantations and Books of Magic", in Emil Schürer, *The History of the Jewish People in the Age of Jesus Christ (175 B.C.–A.D. 135)*: 342–79.

Aune, D. E. (1980) "Magic in Early Christianity", *ANRW II*: 23.2:1507–57.

Cotter, W. (1999) *Miracles in Greco-Roman Antiquity: A Sourcebook.*

Cryer, F. H. (1994) *Divination in Ancient Israel and its Near Eastern Environment: A Socio-Historical Investigation.*

Davila, J. R. (1998) "4QMess ar (4Q534) and Merkavah Mysticism", *DSD* 5: 367–381.

Grabbe, L. L. (1995a) *Priests, Prophets, Diviners, Sages: A Socio-historical Study of Religious Specialists in Ancient Israel.*

—— (1996a) *An Introduction to First Century Judaism: Jewish Religion and History in the Second Temple Period.*

Graf, F. (1997) *Magic in the Ancient World.*

Gruenwald, I. (1980) *Apocalyptic and Merkavah Mysticism.*

—— (1995) "Major Issues in the Study and Understanding of Jewish Mysticism", in J. Neusner (ed.) *Judaism in Late Antiquity: Part Two. Historical Syntheses*: 2.1–49.

Halperin, D. J. (1988) *The Faces of the Chariot: Early Jewish Responses to Ezekiel's Vision.*

Jeffers, A. (1996) *Magic and Divination in Ancient Palestine and Syria.*

Loretz, O. (1993) "Nekromantie und Totenevokation in Mesopotamien, Ugarit und Israel", in B. Janowski, *et al.* (eds) *Religionsgeschichtliche*

Beziehungen zwischen Kleinasien, Nordsyrien und dem Alten Testament: Internationales Symposion Hamburg 17.–21.März 1990: 285–315.

Macmullen, R. (1967) *Enemies of the Roman Order: Treason, Unrest, and Alienation in the Empire.*

Margalioth, M. (1966) *Sepher Ha-Razim: A Newly Discovered Book of Magic from the Talmudic Period.*

Meyer, M., and P. Mirecki (eds) (1995) *Ancient Magic and Ritual Power.*

Morgan, M. A. (1983) *Sepher Ha-Razim: The Book of Mysteries.*

Naveh, J., and S. Shaked (1985) *Amulets and Magic Bowls: Aramaic Incantations of Late Antiquity.*

—— (1993) *Magic Spells and Formulae: Aramaic Incantations of Late Antiquity.*

Neusner, J. (1965–70) *A History of the Jews in Babylonia.*

—— (1987) *The Wonder-Working Lawyers of Talmudic Babylonia: The Theory and Practice of Judaism in its Formative Age.*

—— (1989) "Science and Magic, Miracle and Magic in Formative Judaism: The System and the Difference", in J. Neusner, E. S. Frerichs, and P. V. M. Flesher (eds) *Religion, Science, and Magic: In Concert and Conflict*: 61–81.

Potter, D. (1994) *Prophets and Emperors: Human and Divine Authority from Augustus to Theodosius.*

Schäfer, P. (1992) *The Hidden and Manifest God. Some Major Themes in Early Jewish Mysticism.*

Schäfer, P., and J. Dan (eds) (1993) *Gershom Scholem's* Major Trends in Jewish Mysticism *50 Years After: Proceedings of the Sixth International Conference on the History of Jewish Mysticism.*

Schäfer, P., and H. G. Kippenberg (eds) (1997) *Envisioning Magic: A Princeton Seminar and Symposium.*

Schäfer, P., and S. Shaked (eds) (1994–99) *Magische Texte aus der Kairoer Geniza I–III.*

Segal, A. F. (1981) "Hellenistic Magic: Some Questions of Definition", in R. van den Broek and M. J. Vermaseren (eds) *Studies in Gnosticism and Hellenistic Religions Presented to Gilles Quispel on the Occasion of his 65th Birthday*: 349–75.

Smith, Morton (1978) *Jesus the Magician.*

—— (1983) "On the Lack of a History of Greco-Roman Magic", in H. Heinen, *et al.* (eds) *Althistorische Studien: Hermann Bengtson zum 70. Geburtstag dargebracht von Kollegen und Schülern*: 251–57.

Swartz, M. D. (1996) *Scholastic Magic: Ritual and Revelation in Early Jewish Mysticism.*

Twelftree, G. H. (1993) *Jesus the Exorcist: A Contribution to the Study of the Historical Jesus.*

Veltri, G. (1997) *Magie und Halakha: Ansätze zu einem empirischen Wissenschaftsbegriff im spätantiken und frühmittelalterlichen Judentum.*

Wise, M. O. (1994) "By the Power of Beelzebub: An Aramaic Incantation Formula from Qumran (4Q560)", *JBL* 113: 627–50.

The term "magic" is quite evocative to many people. There is little point in giving a long discussion of what is and is not magic and how to distinguish it from religion (see Cryer 1994: 42–95; the discussion between Schäfer and Alexander in Schäfer/Dan 1993: 59–83; Segal 1981). Although the ancients did make distinctions, it was usually on the basis not of the alleged outcome but the source: what my group or side does is perform miracles; practising magic is what others get up to. The term "magic" was used in a pejorative sense to label what one did not like, while the same sort of practice might be given a respectable description if one approved of it (Aune 1980: 1510–23; Segal 1981; Macmullen 1967: 95–127). Thus, rabbinic Jewish sources recognized that Gentiles performed miracles – they just did it by demonic help rather than God's (Neusner 1989). One thinks of the Gospel example in which Jesus is accused of casting out demons by the power of Beelzebub but answers by asking by whose power their own exorcists cast them out (Matt. 12:27–28). Similarly, some would make a clear distinction between magic and mysticism; however justified this may be (though there is a danger that this is mainly because of value judgments), the two are still closely related (cf. Gruenwald 1995: 39–42; the discussion between Schäfer and Alexander in Schäfer/Dan 1993: 59–83). It has been argued that magic was a widespread feature of popular religion in antiquity (cf. Smith 1978: 68–80).

Unfortunately, because magic was a hidden art, either because one might be persecuted for practising it or to protect secret knowledge (or both), sources with explicit information are few and often rather late (most of the evidence is surveyed in Alexander 1986, but see now Naveh/Shaked 1985, 1993; Schäfer/Shaked 1994–99). A work like the medieval Latin *Clavicula Solomonis* may have drawn on Jewish magical tradition. The *Sepher Harazim*, recently discovered and published in a somewhat eclectic text (Margalioth 1966; Morgan 1983), had earlier sources, though the present text is no earlier than 350 CE and probably originated in the Byzantine era. The *Testament of Solomon* (Schürer: 372–75; *OTP*: 1.935–87) is a late work, most probably to be dated to the third or fourth century CE, and is identified by many as a Christian composition, yet most scholars agree that it made use of earlier Jewish material perhaps going back to Second Temple times.

The cult of the dead in ancient Israel, whose existence is becoming more evident with recent studies (see the survey in Grabbe 1995a: 141–45), apparently took different forms, but one was the consultation of the dead (or their spirits) for purposes of finding out about the future (Loretz 1993). A prime example of this is Saul and the woman of Endor (1 Sam. 28). There are further hints of cults and practices that made contact with the dead, either as necromancy or for other reasons (cf. Isa. 8:19–22; 57:3–13; 65:1–7). Although most of the OT presupposes no life after death, this may not have been a universal view in ancient Israel (see pp. 258–59 below). Later magical practice sometimes, though not always, took the form of harnessing spirits, either to drive them away or to use them to one's own purpose. A number of early Jewish sources allude to this practice even if they are not always very explicit (probably the most explicit is the *Testament of Solomon* but, as noted, it is problematic as a source).

Thus, practices that we today might label as magical represented a perfectly respectable craft, such as healing and exorcism. Exorcism and control of the spirit world were acceptable in Jewish society and even traced back to Solomon (Josephus, *Ant.* 8.2.5 §§45–49; cf. the *Testament of Solomon*); such skills were a common feature of the miracle worker. Healing and exorcism were closely associated since it was thought that many diseases were the result of demonic possession. Jews had a reputation as exorcists. The pre-Danielic tradition of Nabonidus (cf. 4QprNab) has his healing performed by a Jewish exorcist. Josephus traces exorcism of evil spirits back to Solomon himself (*Ant.* 8.2.5 §§45–49). The Babylonian Talmud is not particularly shy about reporting miracleworking, in contrast to the Tannaitic sources which tend to play it down (Neusner 1987). One should therefore be wary of transferring back to pre-70 times the beliefs and views of talmudic times, but in this case there is evidence that the society behind the Babylonian Talmud was only continuing what was an old tradition.

The problems with determining magical practice and thought, because of the nature of the sources, apply also to mysticism. Most of our information on mysticism comes from texts rather later than the Second Temple period, though a connection can be seen between them and the apocalyptic texts of an earlier time (Gruenwald 1980; Halperin 1988). The main sources are surveyed in Gruenwald (1980, 1995), Alexander (1986; cf. 1985), and Halperin (1988). The basis for the modern study of Jewish mysticism was laid by Gershom Scholem (for a summary of his contribution and main bibliography, see Gruenwald 1995; Schäfer/Dan 1993: 1–11).

One of the main purposes of mysticism was to obtain a vision or even a union with the divine. Certain of the mystical exercises and a good deal of the secret lore for achieving this were magical in nature, including incantation, knowledge and evocation of the names of angels and demons, speculations about the spirit world, and use of number and alphabet symbolism. There are also resemblances to and direct connection with knowledge cultivated in Gnostic circles. Again, this is a difficult area, but there is evidence of a Jewish form of Gnosticism, and some argue that Gnosticism arose originally in Jewish circles (see *JCH*: 514–19, and the survey in Grabbe 1996a, ch. 5).

PROPHETIC AND CHARISMATIC INDIVIDUALS

Aune, D. E. "Magic in Early Christianity", *ANRW II* (1980) 23.2. 1507–57.

—— (1983) *Prophecy in Early Christianity and the Ancient Mediterranean World.*

Barnett, P. W. (1980–81) "The Jewish Sign Prophets – A.D. 40–70: Their Intentions and Origin", *NTS* 27: 679–97.

Berman, D. (1979) "Hasidim in Rabbinic Traditions", *Society of Biblical Literature 1979 Seminar Papers*: 2.15–33.

Blackburn, B. L. (1991) *Theios Aner and the Markan Miracle Traditions: A Critique of the Theos Aner Concept as an Interpretative Background of the Miracle Traditions Used by Mark.*

Bokser, B. M. (1985) "Wonder-Working and the Rabbinic Tradition: The Case of Hanina ben Dosa", *JSJ* 16: 42–92.

Freyne, S. (1980) "The Charismatic", in G. W. E. Nickelsburg and J. J. Collins (eds) *Ideal Figures in Ancient Judaism*: 223–58.

Green, W. S. (1979) "Palestinian Holy Men: Charismatic Leadership and Rabbinic Tradition", *ANRW II*: 19.2:619–47.

Holladay, C. R. (1977) *Theios Aner in Hellenistic-Judaism: A Critique of the Use of this Category in New Testament Christology.*

Koester, H. (1985) "The Divine Human Being", *HTR* 78 (1985) 243–52.

Koskeniemi, E. (1994) *Apollonios von Tyana in der neutestamentlichen Exegese: Forschungsbericht und Weiterführung der Diskussion.*

Neusner, J. (1971) *The Rabbinic Traditions about the Pharisees before 70.*

—— (1987) *The Wonder-Working Lawyers of Talmudic Babylonia.*

Smith, M. (1978) *Jesus the Magician.*

Theissen, G. (1983) *The Miracle Stories of the Early Christian Tradition.*

Tiede, D. L. (1972) *The Charismatic Figure as Miracle Worker.*

Twelftree, G. H. (1993) *Jesus the Exorcist: A Contribution to the Study of the Historical Jesus.*

Vermes, G. (1972–73) "Hanina ben Dosa'. A Controversial Galilean Saint from the First Century of the Christian Era", *JJS* 23: 28–50; 24: 51–64.

—— (1973) *Jesus the Jew.*

We know of a number of teachers/sages whose adherence to a particular group or movement is not recorded, though in some cases they may have belonged to such. At other times the individual appears to be a loner, with perhaps only a disciple or two. The best known of these is, of course, Jesus. Josephus refers in passing to a number of figures whom he does not identify with any particular sect. One is Onias the Rainmaker (see below). Others are the "scribes" Judas and his disciple Matthias, who tore down the eagle which Herod had placed over the temple entrance (*War* 1.33.2–4 §§648–55; *Ant.* 17.6.2–4 §§149–67; contrary to frequent assertion, there is no evidence that these individuals were Pharisees). Both Josephus and the NT also mention various prophets who drew a following for a period of time, though generally not for long if their actions caught the Romans' attention (*War* 2.13.4–5 §§258–64; *Ant.* 20.8.6 §§167–72; Acts 21:37–38; cf. Barnett 1980–81). A number of individuals with the "miraculous" powers of healing, exorcism, and other charismatic gifts are sufficiently well attested from antiquity to demonstrate this was not an uncommon phenomenon.

Honi the Circle-drawer is known from rabbinic literature as an individual who could make rain by symbolic action (*m. Taan.* 3.8). Although the description of him is legendary, a development in the tradition can be discerned (Neusner 1971: 1.176–82; Green 1979). He does not fit the early rabbinic image of the sage and was thus evidently something of an embarrassment. The Tannaitic sources seem to downplay miracle working, unlike the Babylonian Talmud which shows no sign of suppressing such claims (cf. Neusner 1987: 46–70, 190–262). Green (1979) has shown that Honi has been "rabbinized" but his charismatic origins still shine through. The rabbinic tradition seems in some way related to Onias the Rainmaker mentioned by Josephus (*Ant.* 14.2.1 §§22–24).

Another individual is Hanina b. Dosa (Vermes 1971–72; to be corrected in light of Neusner 1971 [1.394–96]; Freyne 1980; Bokser 1985). Like Honi, he does not appear as a typical rabbinic sage but is noted for his miraculous powers. Probably a pre-70 figure, he too becomes rabbinized over a period of time. The figure of Jesus fits well with the general image of a traveling exorcist and miracle worker (Twelftree 1993; Aune 1980: 1523–44; Smith 1978; Vermes 1973: 58–82). The Gospels are unanimous that he healed, cast out demons, and did other marvelous works. These traits seem to have been ascribed to the historical Jesus and are not simply a later development of the tradition, but whether they are or not, the significant thing is that the early Christian tradition is happy to present him as an exorcist and miracle worker.

The basic question is not really one concerning the "historical" Honi or Hanina or Jesus, even if it is possible to find them underneath the tradition. The ascription of extraordinary powers seems to occur in the earliest layer of the tradition in each case, though this earliest layer naturally already represents interpretation. But even if this should be only a secondary development, it still demonstrates that the *concept* of the charismatic miracle worker was widely known and accepted. For the purposes here, that is all that is necessary to know, though whether there was a *model* of the charismatic is perhaps a moot question (cf. Freyne 1980: 247–49). The term *ḥāsîd* has sometimes been used of such figures (Vermes 1972–73; 1973), but this is probably inappropriate (Berman: 2.16–17; Freyne 1980: 224–27) since the rabbinic image of the *ḥāsîd* is rather different from the figures considered here.

This brings us to the controversy over the *theios anēr*. It has long been argued that Jesus is to be understand as modeled on this idea, with the argument that there is a *Gestalt* of the *theios anēr* which comes from the Greek philosophical tradition and consists of an individual who partakes of both the philosophical sage and the more popular image of the miracle worker (Tiede 1972; Holladay 1977). Recent studies have questioned whether there was such a model (Blackburn 1991; Koskeniemi 1994), and it has been suggested that it was mainly in the second century that the miracle worker became widespread, even though there are a few examples from the first century or earlier (Theissen 1983; Koskeniemi 1994). The appropriateness of the term in its application to Jesus is for NT scholars to debate, but that there were miracle workers of various sorts seems to be established (Koester 1985), even if the extent of their ubiquity is still to be determined.

It can be concluded that a variety of charismatic figures practiced (individually or in combination) magic, exorcism, healing, and other "miraculous" arts. Some of these – as well as others – also preached religious messages and even engaged in prophetism (as discussed on pp. 236–41 above). One could perhaps argue that such figures were only on the fringe or had only a marginal influence. The question is difficult to decide because of the episodic nature of our data, but no description of first-century Palestine can ignore them. Further, a comparison with various historical and contemporary traditional cultures argues that such beliefs were an integral part of society, a fundamental part of popular religion and culture. Magical practices and oracles are a way of life in many parts of the world, even among the well educated and the firm Christians. The data available to us suggest that such was no less the case in first-century Palestine and earlier.

SYNTHESIS

This chapter has been wide-ranging, covering a spectrum of topics that some would argue should be kept apart. Yet all the subjects discussed here have at least one point in common: they are all media for trying to find out about the future and even the mind of the deity. In most cases, they were associated in particular with individuals who claimed special knowledge or insight and are thus branches of mantic wisdom. Our sources have even produced the names of a few individuals from antiquity who are alleged to have been prophets, magicians, healers, exorcists, or wonder workers of various sorts. To what extent we can trust the tradition has to be examined critically in each individual case, but the existence of such individuals is taken for granted and unlikely to be just a literary construct, though the production of literature was itself an activity which must be part of any description of the social world. Some of the main points made in this chapter can be summarized as follows:

1. Despite the necessarily abbreviated nature of the survey given here, it strongly suggests that the Jews were not basically different from other peoples in the Greco-Roman world in their desire to see into the future. In some cases, they attributed certain special powers to the God of Israel while not differing from their non-Jewish neighbors in the outcome. For example, the Jews, like other peoples of the time, were certainly interested in the healing arts, yet the healing rites performed do not differ from what we would classify as magic. Granted, a certain ambiguity is found in Jewish sources, but the

Greco-Roman world as a whole was ambivalent about magic, or at least some aspects of it. Magic and the esoteric arts have an equivocal status in many societies, with what seem to an outsider to be arbitrary distinctions and borderlines. The data from Jewish sources do not show any major differences: a variety of views are held, and one sort may be frowned on while another – equally dubious from our point of view – is sanctioned. The Jewish views registered fit well with the general picture in the Greco-Roman period.

2. Most of our knowledge of prophecy, apocalyptic, the esoteric arts, and charismatic figures is literary. We have little from archaeology to give us data on the phenomena, and it is impossible to do anthropological fieldwork on Second Temple Judah. Therefore, any judgments about the social phenomena of prophetic and related figures have to be deduced from literary sources. The material is of different sorts, which aids us in making a historical determination, but we have to recognize the state of our information. The descriptions of society may be colored by literary and theological models, and the distinction between literary creations and social descriptions is not necessarily an easy one to make in many cases.

3. We get more than one message from the sources about whether prophecy had ceased. Some writers seem to have regarded prophecy as a thing of the past which had long since lapsed; others evidently accepted that prophets could exist in the present. The difference between the various writers is not necessarily all that great, however, since all sources seem to accept that a future prophet could arise, perhaps in an eschatological context. No writing explicitly rules out future prophets even when it seems to think that prophecy ceased at some time in the past. Additionally, those texts which accept the present reality of prophets do not usually see them as anything but an exception. Writers appear more willing to accept the presence of false prophets than of true ones. Our sources show that the concept of prophecy in Second Temple writers was rather broader than many OT scholars would allow. Prophecy could especially be used of predictions of the future or messages about what would come to pass hereafter, even though these predictions might take a variety of forms (e.g. oral message from a prophetic figure, vision, dream, or written oracle).

4. We do not know for sure how written prophecies and apocalypses came about. In most cases, they do not look like actual oracles received by a prophet and then written down; rather, they look like the work of scribes. It may well be that the writers were reporting actual visions and writing under what they would see as divine inspiration or possession, yet we cannot be sure.

5. Inspired interpretation is a concept which arises during the Second Temple period. It is a new concept, coming about when some writings had become authoritative. Once established it takes its place alongside other forms of determining the future. Not only the ancient prophetic literature but also other sections of the Bible, such as the Psalms and even the Torah, were seen as sources for God's plans and a key to the future if the right

interpretation could be found. This answer was found not in some sort of exegetical technique or "hermeneutical rules" but in the continued inspiration by the same spirit which had guided the prophets (whose numbers included Moses and David).

6. Whatever the actual differences between prophecy, apocalyptic, and some of the esoteric arts, they seem to have functioned in a very similar way. People read both both prophetic and apocalyptic texts for knowledge of the future.

7. The frequent assumption that this sort of literature arose mainly in a time of crisis is not well founded. The question of whether a "time of crisis" existed was always a very subjective one; further, there is no way to quantify how and when such literature was produced, making it impossible to demonstrate it as "crisis literature". An important consideration is that a tradition takes on a life of its own once it gets going. Apocalyptic and eschatology, once established, formed a self-perpetuating set of ideas that did not necessarily require particular external conditions to produce written expression.

12

ESCHATOLOGIES AND IDEAS OF SALVATION

The term "eschatology" encompasses a number of subjects relating in one way or another to the "last things". It incorporates personal eschatology, including questions of immortality of the soul, resurrection (whether of the body or the spirit), final judgment, and reward in paradise/heaven or punishment in hell. Cosmic eschatology is very important in some but not all texts, with the end of the world, the messianic age, a new heavens and earth. National eschatology is also a feature of the subject, though messianism which is often a feature of national eschatology (as well as cosmic eschatology) is treated separately in the next chapter.

MAIN TEXTS

Bauckham, R. (1998) *The Fate of the Dead: Studies on the Jewish and Christian Apocalypses.*

Cavallin, H. C. C. (1974) *Life after Death: Paul's Argument for the Resurrection of the Dead in I Cor 15, Part I: An Enquiry into the Jewish Background.*

Childs, B. S. (1959) "The Enemy from the North and the Chaos Tradition", *JBL* 78: 187–98.

Davies, P. R. (1985) "Eschatology at Qumran", *JBL* 104: 39–55.

Dihle, A. (1974) "ψυχή . . . A. ψυχή in the Greek World" and "C. Judaism: I. Hellenistic Judaism", in G. Friedrich (ed.) *TDNT* 9:608–17, 632–35.

Everson, A. J. (1974) "The Days of Yahweh", *JBL* 93: 329–37.

Fischer, U. (1978) *Eschatologie und Jenseitserwartung im hellenistischen Diaspora-judentum.*

Fohrer, G. (1982) "Der Tag Jhwhs", *Eretz-Israel* 16: 43*–50*.

Gowan, D. E. (1986) *Eschatology in the Old Testament.*

Grabbe, L. L. (1995a) *Priests, Prophets, Diviners, Sages: A Socio-historical Study of Religious Specialists in Ancient Israel.*

—— (1997a) *Wisdom of Solomon.*

—— (1999c) "Eschatology in Philo and Josephus", in A. Avery-Peck and J. Neusner (eds) *Judaism in Late Antiquity: Part 4 Death, Life-after-Death, Resurrection and the World-to-Come in the Judaisms of Antiquity*: 163–85.

Hoffmann, Y. (1981) "The Day of the Lord as a Concept and a Term in the Prophetic Literature", *ZAW* 93: 37–50.

Kolarcik, M. (1991) *The Ambiguity of Death in the Book of Wisdom 1–6: A Study of Literary Structure and Interpretation.*

Lewis, T. J. (1992) "Dead, Abode of the", *ABD* 2:101–5.

Mowinckel, S. (1956) *He That Cometh.*

Nickelsburg, G. W. E. (1972) *Resurrection, Immortality, and Eternal Life in Inter-testamental Judaism.*

Puech, E. (1993) *La croyance des Esséniens en la vie future: Immortalité, résurrection, vie éternelle? Histoire d'une croyance dans le Judaæsme Ancien*: vol. I: *La résurrection des morts et le contexte scripturaire*; vol. II: *Le données qumraniennes et classiques.*

Rad, G. von (1959) "The Origin of the Concept of the Day of Yahweh", *JSS* 4: 97–108.

Rutgers, L. V. (1998) "Jewish Ideas about Death and Afterlife: The Inscriptional Evidence", *The Hidden Heritage of Diaspora Judaism*: 157–68.

Sanders, J. T. (1979) "Ben Sira's Ethics of Caution", *HUCA* 50: 73–106.

Skehan, P. W., and A. A. Di Lella (1987) *The Wisdom of Ben Sira.*

Tromp, N. (1969) *Primitive Conceptions of Death and the Nether World in the Old Testament.*

Weiss, M. (1966) "The Origin of the 'Day of the Lord' – Reconsidered", *HUCA* 37: 29–60.

Apart from Daniel, which will be discussed separately below, most of the texts of the **Hebrew Bible** do not envisage an afterlife as such. The goal is a long life in which one dies in peace surrounded by one's family, including several succeeding generations (e.g. Ps. 128). A good example of this is Isaiah 65:17–26 which gives an idyllic picture of the future of God's people. Like much of the rest of the ancient Near East (with the notable exception of Egypt), the Israelites evidently had no concept of eternal life for human beings, at least as a general rule. The place of the dead is normally referred to as Sheol (Lewis 1992; Tromp 1969). It is pictured as under the ground and is often synonymous with the grave. Although some fragment of the person survived the disintegration of death and had a shadowy existence (cf. Isa. 14:9–15), one cannot speak of an afterlife since what survived in the underworld was not the whole person. The view seems to be similar to that in early Greek texts such as Homer where the "shades" of the dead were just that – like shadows and not the original persons themselves.

This picture is complicated by two further considerations. One of these is the cult of the dead, for which considerable evidence has been advanced in recent years (summary in Grabbe 1995a: 141–45). The other is the presence of some late texts which seem to envisage a resurrection of the dead: the

"Isaiah apocalypse" (Isaiah 24–27) and Daniel (pp. 267–68 below). The earliest reference to the resurrection is probably found in Isaiah 24–27, though the dating of this passage is controversial. Here the resurrection of the dead into their previous bodily form seems to be in the mind of the author (26:19–21). Other passages of the Old Testament have been interpreted as references to the resurrection but probably did not have that original meaning. For example, Ezekiel 37 talks of the dry bones which become living human beings; however, it is clear that this is an allegory for the restoration of Israel (37:11–14), not a return of dead Israelites to life when only skeletons remained.

A cosmic eschatology as such is not found in the OT (except perhaps in Daniel), but a number of texts indicate a developing concept of the "day of Yhwh" (sometimes just referred to as "that day"), a day of judgment on Israel and/or the nations, that in the Second Temple period eventually came to form a full-blown belief in a cosmic judgment and a catastrophic climax of history. The "day of Yhwh" may originally have been an expectation of help from Yhwh on behalf of Israel, implying a theophany and perhaps originally celebrated in a cultic context (cf. Mowinckel 1956: 143–54); however, it was turned by some of the prophets into a day of judgment on Israel/Judah (Amos 5:18–20) A number of passages mention an "enemy from the north" (cf. Childs 1959). This was originally a real threat since most invading armies (even those from the east) came down through Syria and approached Palestine from the north. This got transformed into an eschatological enemy (cf. Ezekiel 38–39; Rev. 20:7–9).

The earliest concept of a soul that survives death and serves as a basis for a future life is attested in *1 Enoch*. The *Book of the Watchers*, probably from Ptolemaic times, describes a tour of the underworld in which Enoch sees four "beautiful places" or chambers into which the souls or spirits of the dead are gathered until the day of judgment (*1 En.* 22). The souls of the dead are already experiencing reward and punishment in their intermediate state. In this case, the existence of the soul after death seems to be combined with the idea of a final judgment. This may imply a general resurrection, though this is not stated explicitly. *1 Enoch* 10:6 mentions a final judgment when the fate of the fallen angel Asael would be announced (even though he has been bound for the present). The *Epistle of Enoch* assumes that the spirits of the righteous will be rewarded at death and the spirits of the wicked punished in Sheol (102:3–104:6); a final judgment is also mentioned (104:5), with astral immortality for the righteous (104:2). In some sections of *1 Enoch*, a resurrection is also alluded to, such as the *Dream Visions* and the *Epistle of Enoch* (90:33; 91:10; 92:3–4). The *Similitudes of Enoch*, probably dating from the first century CE also mention a resurrection (46:6; 51:1; 61:5).

The view found in the "sectarian" scrolls from **Qumran** is not easy to interpret, nor can we be sure that there was a uniform belief. This group of the Scrolls seems to be shot through with the view that they were living in the endtime (e.g. CD 1:11–12; 1QSᵃ 1:1), and their escatological beliefs are determined by this context. There are passages that have been interpreted to refer to a resurrection (e.g. 1QH 14:29, 34; 19:12 [older 6:29, 34; 11:12]); unfortunately, these are not clear-cut. Puech (1993) argues for the concept of a resurrection but bases this only on two passages (4Q521 and 4Q385). Other passages, however, clearly envisage the community members as already dwelling with the angels and somehow partaking of eternal life even in this life (1QH 11:19–22; 19:3–14 [older 3:19–22; 11:3–14]). What exactly this intends is by no means clear, but it suggests that death is not a major break in the existence of the righteous. This can be taken to mean that the community of the Scrolls believed in a soul that continued to exist after the body died (cf. the beliefs alleged for the Essenes, p. 263 below; Nickelsburg 1972: 166–69). The fate of the wicked is described in various passages. 1QH 11:27–36 (older 3:27–36) describes fiery "streams of Belial" that rise up and overflow even into Abaddon. Angels of destruction torment them in the fire of the dark regions (1QS 4:11–14).

Ben Sira gives us a window on the beliefs of at least one Jew around 200 BCE. He seems to be much in line with the earlier views found in many OT passages. Although it has been argued that the resurrection can be found in his book (Skehan–Di Lella), this is very much a minority view. Most do not agree that any idea of an afterlife is found in the book. The goal of life is a long life without being implicated in "shame" (Sanders 1979).

Although **Daniel 7–12** may not contain the earliest reference to a resurrection, it is the earliest datable text (c.166–165 BCE) which clearly speaks of one (12:2–3). The wording of the passage suggests that not all the dead will be resurrected, only "some" for reward and "some" for punishment. The specific context is the period of the Maccabean revolt, and those resurrected may simply be the martyrs whose life had been cut short and the exceptionally wicked who were not punished in this life. On this view, the rest of the dead had their reward or punishment in this life and would not be resurrected; however, the book does not spell out the precise connotation. The "wise" or "knowledgeable" (*maśkîlîm*) are conceived of as attaining "astral immortality" by becoming like the stars of heaven. A number of passages in Daniel imply a cosmic eschatology, including the vision of the image (2:44), the vision of the four beasts (7:23–27), and the wars between the King of the North and the King of the South (11:40–12:3). God would establish his rule over all the kingdoms, with his people as the head of the nations.

The term "resurrection" is often assumed to be or to include resurrection of the body, and this is true in many cases. However, in **Jubilees** we appear to have resurrection of the spirit only (*Jub.* 23:22–31): "And their bones shall rest in the earth, and their spirits shall have much joy; and they shall know that the Lord is one who executes judgement (23:20–22). The book also mentions a new creation when heaven and earth will be renewed (1:29).

The book of **2 Maccabees** has several passages that suggest an afterlife. These mostly relate to a resurrection of the body (e.g. 7:9, 11, 14, 23; 14:46). It may be that only the pious dead can expect a resurrection, however (12:43–45).

The ***Psalms of Solomon*** apparently continue the view of death found in much of the OT. The wicked are destroyed forever (3:10–12; 13:11; 15:12–13) and inherit Sheol and darkness (14:6–9); contrary to most of the OT, however, the righteous have a chance to live forever (13:11; 14:1–5), perhaps through a resurrection (3:10–12), though nothing is said about a resurrection of the body. A day of judgment is mentioned but no specifics are given (15:12–13).

Philo has a lot to say on the subject but differs in a number of ways from many other Jewish sources (see Grabbe 1999c for a more detailed discussion of Philo's views); however, some other writings which may be from Alexandria have something in common with Philo's, suggesting perhaps an Egyptian Jewish tradition. For Philo the essential part of the person is the soul (*Leg. Alleg.* 3.161; *Somn.* 1.34; *Mut.* 223). Philo agrees with the Orphic slogan that "the body is a tomb" (*Leg. Alleg.* 2.108; *Spec. Leg.* 4.188), which makes a play on the similarity of the words for "body" (*sōma*) and "tomb" (*sēma*) in Greek. Death is the separation of body and soul (*Leg. Alleg.* 1.105; 2.77).

Philo sees rational souls as associated with the air, the heavens, and divinity (*Plant.* 14; *Gig.* 6–16). Human souls are of the same general substance as those who make up the ranks of angels and the stars. The difference is that in humans the souls are entangled with the body and the lower or irrational soul (cf. *Leg. Alleg.* 1.31–42; *Conf.* 176–82; *Quis Heres* 55–62; *Congr.* 97; *Quaes. Exod.* 2.13). The distinction between the rational and irrational soul is very important to Philo. He associates immortality with the soul but not with the irrational soul which is mortal and corruptible. Although a general assertion of immortality can be found (e.g. *Quaes. Gen.* 3.11), this really applies only to the rational part of the soul (*Fug.* 68–71; *Quod Det.* 81-8-5) which should control the passions (appetites, desires) produced by the lower part of the soul. The ultimate goal and end is alluded to in this passage: to escape the encumbrance of the body (*Gig.* 12–16).

What happens to the wicked is less clearly delineated. Philo thinks there are such things as punitive angels whose function is primarily to punish the wicked humans, but they are not themselves wicked as such (*Conf.* 177; *Fug.* 66). Philo's discussion of what happens to the wicked is given only in metaphorical terms. One passage suggests that just as the righteous go to heaven (or above the heavens), the wicked are sent down to Tartarus (Tartarus was originally the place where Zeus imprisoned the Titans after defeating them). Also, just as the righteous are said to look heavenward for their dwelling (*Quaes. Gen.* 4.74, 178) or to live on "Olympus" (*Somn.* 1.151), the wicked are associated with Hades (*Quis Heres* 45; *Congr.* 57; *Quaes. Exod.* 2.40). However, Hades and Tartarus are conventional expressions and represent conditions, not places. Philo can also refer to "eternal death" (*aidios thanatos*) for the impious (*Post.* 39), but again this looks very much like metaphorical language, for he makes nothing further of this statement. It is not clear that any soul is wicked of itself, apart from its entanglement with the body and the material world. Some souls are imprisoned in their own hell by refusing to exercise the wisdom to break free of the body and soar into the upper regions which are the soul's natural home. There is no reference to a resurrection in Philo. On the contrary, a resurrection does not fit at all well into his religious system. The whole point of the spiritual life is for the soul eventually to escape the encumbrance of the body. One cannot imagine Philo looking with favor on a general resurrection in which the souls of the righteous were again reunited with the body.

The **Wisdom of Solomon** has a good deal in common with Philo. The writer has two aims: negatively, to refute the false notion of death held by the wicked and, positively, to persuade the reader to love justice and God (Kolarcik: 160). In 1:13–15 it is stated that God did not create death and does not delight in it; on the contrary, he created life, and righteousness is itself immortal. The goal of life is immortality, and the soul at least has the potential for immortality in it (2:23; 3:4). Less clear is whether the soul is naturally immortal. The text seems to suggest that immortality is a gift to the righteous, not an inherent condition of the soul itself (3:4; 4:1; 8:13, 17; 15:3). Death is used in three different senses in the book: (a) mortality, (b) physical death as punishment, and (c) ultimate death, defined as separation from God and the cosmos (Kolarcik 1991: 156–58, 170).

One passage could imply *metempsychosis* or the transmigration of souls: "a good soul fell to my lot" (8:19–20; also said by Josephus to be a belief of the Pharisees [p. 187 above]). It would assume that Solomon's soul was good because of effort in a previous life. However, this is not explicitly stated, and it may just be that his soul was created by God to enter the body being prepared for him at the time of birth. This raises all sorts of questions about why he inherited a good soul, how he was chosen for the privilege, whether souls were predestined to be good or bad, and so on. Unfortunately, the author does not answer many of the questions he raises.

The book of **4 Maccabees** seems to agree with Philo and Wisdom in envisaging no resurrection (despite the presence of the resurrection in its source of 2 Maccabees). The soul is what has life (9:7–9; 10:4). Those who are martyred will be given immortality (13:17; 14:5–6; 18:23), but this seems to include all the righteous (7:18–19; 15:3; 16:25). They will be assumed into heaven (17:4–6), but the wicked will be punished in fire (9:9). Other books combine belief in a soul with the resurrection. **Pseudo-Phocylides** has both (102–15). The ***Testament of Job*** mentions the resurrection (4:1) but also talks about the soul (38:8–40:3; 52:10).

The **Testament of Abraham**, which is now generally dated to the first century CE, gives the clearest picture of how the souls are judged after death (Version A 11–14; Version B 9–11). Death is defined as separation of the soul from the body (A 1, 7; B 4, 13). The souls are brought before a throne on which Abel sits as judge. (According to Version B, the one who presents the souls for judgment is Enoch, the scribe of righteousness.) The judged souls go either through the strait gate which leads to life (for the righteous) or the broad gate to destruction (for the sinners). Although there is a brief indication of belief in a general resurrection (Version B 7:16), judgment of each individual seems to take place immediately after death, and the emphasis is on this immediate judgment of the soul while the body rests in the grave.

Josephus is an important source of views about eschatology (see Grabbe 1999c for a more detailed discussion). There are indications that he expected a cosmic end to the age, when Rome would be destroyed by divine intervention, but he is rather coy about being very explicit in a book which might be read by Roman friends (see pp. 278–79 below). On personal eschatology, two passages give some unambiguous views (*War* 3.8.1–7 §§340–91; *Ag. Apion* 2.30). The emphasis in both is on the soul: the soul is currently connected with the body, but it is the real person, even a small portion of the divine temporarily incarnated. Death is the separation of body and soul, and the soul lives on as an immortal entity; the good souls are rewarded, and the evil ones are punished. It also seems evident that Josephus believed in the transmigration of souls, stating that the soul released at death would eventually be reborn in a new body. This belief in *metempsychosis* seems to be a problem for some commentators, because they either ignore it or attempt to explain that this was not Josephus's view (e.g. Dihle 1974: 634 n. 104).

These two descriptions of Josephus's own views look remarkably similar to the views ascribed by Josephus himself to both the Pharisees and the Essenes (pp. 187 and 201 above). What does emerge from the various passages in Josephus is belief in a soul which survives death and is rewarded or punished for its deeds on earth. He also seems to think that at some point the soul, or at least the good soul, might well be reincarnated into a new body and reborn once more. Josephus also describes the Sadducees as rejecting any belief in an afterlife, a view that seems to be a continuation of the traditional OT view (see pp. 187–88 above). Surprisingly, Josephus gives no evidence of belief in a resurrection, even though this would not require him to bring the Romans into the picture. Yet we should not take this silence as proof that Josephus did not believe in the resurrection as such, since this was a concept alien to the Greeks and Romans (cf. Acts 17:32). It may well be that Josephus had no occasion on which to expound the belief and felt that because of his apologetic purposes, he should keep quiet about it. We do not know that this was the case, but if we had to guess at his views, it is more likely than not that the resurrection of the dead to judgment in the endtime was a part of his belief system.

The *Liber Antiquitatum Biblicarum* (**Pseudo-Philo**) exhibits the same ambiguity about how personal eschatology is conceived. Death is perceived as the separation of body and soul (44:10); the souls of the dead go to the underworld (*infernus*), to chambers (32:13; 33:3) where they can recognize each other (62:9), though the righteous will become like the stars (33:5). The person's fate is fixed at the time of death and cannot be changed afterward (33:3–5). All are resurrected for a judgment between the soul and the flesh, with the destruction of "hell" (*infernus*) and a new heaven and earth (3:10); however, some of the wicked apparently will not be resurrected but die forever (16:3). The *Apocalypse of Moses* seems to be similar, with death being the separation of body and soul (13:3–6; 32:4). The righteous soul goes to heaven on the seventh day (*Ap. Mos.* 43:1–3//*Vita Adae et Euae* 51:1–2), evidently to Paradise which is in the third heaven (*Ap. Mos.* 40:1–2). A final resurrection will be at the end of time, at which point there will no more sinners because the evil heart will be removed from them (*Ap. Mos.* 13:3–5; does this imply a universal salvation?).

According to **4 Ezra** 7:78–101, at death the spirit leaves the body and returns to its maker. Those that have been wicked will wander in torment, awaiting their fate at the final judgment. The righteous, on the other hand, will enter into rest in storehouses guarded by angels (cf. 4:40–42), knowing the reward to come to them which includes shining like the stars. The eschatological end of the age is prominent in 4 Ezra. Like the Olivet prophecy of the Gospels, a good deal of emphasis is placed on the signs preceding the end (5:1–13; 6:18–28). The main passages are found in 4 Ezra 11–13. The first is the eagle vision of 11–12, in which the eagle represents the Roman empire. The eagle is confronted by a lion from the forest and is eventually burnt (11:33–12:3). The lion represents the messiah who will call Rome before God's judgment seat for its wickedness, while the people of God will be freed and saved (12:31–34). After a messianic age of 400 years (7:28) there will be a resurrection and judgment of all (apparently lasting seven years), followed by reward in paradise or punishment in the furnace of "hell" (*Gehenna*: 7:31–36; 8:52–54; 14:35).

In the vision in 4 Ezra 13, the "man coming up out of the sea" is God's son revealed in the last time (13:32). Although the term "messiah" is not used of him, he seems to be a messianic figure (see pp. 279–80 below). The nations will gather against him but will be destroyed by his law which is like fire (13:38). He will also bring back the lost ten tribes from across the Euphrates (13:39–50). These passages seem to end with judgment on the nations, followed by the messianic age. What happens afterward is presumably that already described in 4 Ezra 7, as cited above.

While *2 Baruch* has a good deal on personal and cosmic eschatology, much of it is parallel with 4 Ezra. A significant portion of the book is taken up by the vision of the light and dark waters which lead up to the eschaton (53–74). The souls of the dead are kept in storehouses awaiting the final resurrection and judgment (30). They will be resurrected in the same bodily form as they died; the righteous will inherit paradise while the wicked will go into torment (49–51). The wicked are punished in fire (44:15; 59:2; 64:7).

If *2 Enoch* is as early as the first century, its elaborate set of heavens provides one of the most detailed looks "behind the scenes" for that time, though there are a number of differences between the two basic versions, with either seven (short recension) or ten (long recension) heavens (1–38). No underworld is described, but in both versions both paradise and the place of punishment are in the third heaven (8–10; 41–42). The place of punishment is described as a place of cold and of a dark fire. Although no explicit statement is made, the impression is that punishment and reward take place directly after death. Nothing is said about a resurrection, but neither are there any details of judgment, though a judgment day is certainly envisaged (52:15). Dwellings have been prepared for both the righteous and the wicked in the "great age" (61:2–5), which is a time when all things come to an end, including time itself, and all the righteous who have escaped God's judgment will be together in paradisial conditions (65:6–11).

The ***Apocalypse of Abraham*** has a large section of its text devoted to an ascension into heaven (15–29). Abraham sees God's throne with four living creatures that appear to be a combination of the cherubim and the seraphim (18). Eight heavens are enumerated (19), though a good portion of his vision is of the earth and events there (21–29), including the destruction of the temple (27). The last days seem to be calculated, though the exact result is not very clear (28–30). Ten plagues will come on the earth before some sort of golden "age of justice" in which the righteous triumph (29:14–21). This age appears to be ushered in by God's "chosen one" (31:1) and the wicked will be burned by the fire of Hades in the underworld (Azazel's belly?) where the fire of Azazel's tongue will torment them (31:2–8; cf. 21:3).

The ***Sibylline Oracles*** give ideas about eschatology over a lengthy period of time and from a variety of perspectives. A period of eschatological troubles will be followed by a messianic figure from Egypt, an idealized Egyptian king (3:635–56). The kings of the earth will attack the temple of God (3:657–68), but then God himself will intervene to punish the wicked (3:669–701) and the sons of God will dwell around a peaceful temple protected by the Creator and renewed earth of peace and plenty (3:702–95). The rise of Rome and the destruction of Jerusalem (4:102–29) will be followed by an attack on Rome of Nero *redivivus* (4:130–51). Wickedness and events will eventually culminate in a universal conflagration which destroys all human beings (4:152–78); this is followed by a resurrection and judgment in which the wicked are assigned to Tartarus and Gehenna but the righteous will live on the earth (4:179–92). *Sibylline Oracle* 5 refers a number of times to the myth of Nero *redivivus*, conceived of as an enemy of God (5:93–110, 137–54, 214–27, 361–85). He will be opposed by a savior figure from heaven (5:108-9, 155–61, 256–59, 414–25) who will beautify Jerusalem and rebuild the temple (5:420–24). A period of eschatological woes (5:447–83) will be followed by the conversion of Egypt to the true God, though the temple of God in Egypt will be destroyed by the Ethiopians (5:484–511). The book ends with a war in the heavens which burns the earth (5:512–31).

Within the various **New Testament** books, both a general resurrection of the dead at the end of the world and the immediate reward or punishment of the person at death are envisaged. Many passages talk of the resurrection, which often includes the concept of judgment in the same context, with the broader setting not infrequently the cosmic eschaton at the end of the world. Perhaps the clearest example is Revelation 20 which includes a first resurrection of saints alone and a second one of all the dead, with a millennial rule of God's people and a final judgment of all the dead. The catastrophic events leading up to God's intervention in world affairs is recounted in the "gospel apocalypse" (Mark 13//Matthew 24//Luke 21). Paul is said to agree with the Pharisees in believing in the resurrection, versus the Sadducees who do not (Acts 23:6–9). Perhaps the clearest passage indicating reward and punishment immediately after death is the parable of the beggar Lazarus (Luke 16:19–31). He and the rich man are pictured after death, with Lazarus in "the bosom of Abraham" while the rich man is tormented in the flames. There is no indication that they must wait until the resurrection before this reward/punishment takes place. In an episode when Jesus is on the cross, he says to one of the "thieves" crucified with him, "I say to you, today you will be with me in paradise" (Luke 23:43). This is probably the correct way of reading the text; however, it should be noted that the Greek is potentially ambiguous, and it is possible that the word "today" goes with "I say"; indeed, some early versions (e.g. the Old Syriac) interpret it in this way.

SYNTHESIS

Dupont-Sommer, A. (1949) "De l'immortalité astrale dans la 'Sagesse de Salomon' (III 7)", *Revue des Études Grecques* 62: 80–87.

Grabbe, L. L. (1995a) *Priests, Prophets, Diviners, Sages: A Socio-historical Study of Religious Specialists in Ancient Israel.*

Himmelfarb, M. (1983) *Tours of Hell.*

—— (1993) *Ascents into Heaven in Jewish and Christian Apocalypses.*

Nickelsburg, G. W. E. (1972) *Resurrection, Immortality, and Eternal Life in Intertestamental Judaism.*

Tabor, J. D. (1986) *Things Unutterable: Paul's Ascent to Paradise in its Greco-Roman, Judaic, and Early Christian Contexts.*

Tromp, N. (1969) *Primitive Conceptions of Death and the Nether World in the Old Testament.*

Some studies (especially those relating to the NT) emphasize the importance of eschatology in early Judaism. The eschatological interest can be exaggerated, especially since it is clear that many Jews had little concern for such views. What emerges from a study of the extant texts is the variety of views about what happened to the individual at death and eventually to the cosmos. To state that certain views were "characteristic" of Judaism (e.g. the resurrection of the body) is to mislead in most cases. Since the survey of the texts yields such a mixture of concepts, this section will give a more systematic picture of the different views that can be extracted from the sources.

Personal eschatology: ideas about life after death

Most of the books of the Hebrew Bible do not seem to envisage life after death as such. Life in its proper sense ends at death, even if there is some shadowy vestige which continues to exist in Sheol (it has many parallels with the realm of Hades as pictured in the Homeric poems). This also seems to be the view in Ben Sira, and the Sadducees are supposed to have maintained this belief if we can believe our sources.

When belief in some form of afterlife began to enter Israelite thinking is not known. Recent study on the cult of the dead suggests that the idea that the dead could communicate with and influence the living may have been around in some parts of Israelite society from an early time (Grabbe 1995a: 141–45). What is clear is that sometime in the Persian or early Greek period, ideas about an afterlife had entered Jewish thinking.

The frequent assertion that the resurrection of the body was the characteristic Jewish belief is not borne out by the data. Resurrection is apparently found in Isa. 27:19 and certainly in Dan. 12:1–3, but there is little reason to think that it was earlier or more characteristic of Jewish thinking than the immortality of the soul or resurrection of the spirit. And it is clear that some Jews still maintained the older belief in no afterlife. Therefore, it would be quite wrong to refer to any of these beliefs as "characteristically" Jewish or *the* Jewish belief on the subject.

After the book of Daniel, the resurrection appears regularly – though not universally – in Jewish writings, including 2 Maccabees, the later sections of *1 Enoch*, the *Apocalypse of Moses*, Pseudo-Philo, 4 Ezra, *2 Baruch*, and apparently the *Psalms of Solomon*. The exact form of the resurrection is not always specified. 2 Maccabees 7 seems to expect the resurrection of the body, because the parts cut off in torture would be restored. Another clear example is found in *2 Baruch* 50. However, we should not expect it always to entail resurrection of the body: sometimes only the resurrection of the spirit is in mind, as in *Jub.* 23:20–22.

Belief in the immortality of the soul is known at least as early as the beginning of the Greek period, as witnessed by the *Book of Watchers* (*1 Enoch* 1–36;

see especially 22). Other sources indicate belief that death is the separation of body and soul (a widespread definition of death in the Hellenistic period) and give no indication of a resurrection at all. Several of these are from Alexandria (or likely to be) such as Philo and the Wisdom of Solomon, but not all are. Other writings include the *Testament of Abraham* and 4 Maccabees.

On the other hand, the immortal souls and the resurrection may be combined, as in Pseudo-Philo, the *Apocalypse of Moses*, 2 *Baruch*, 4 Ezra, Pseudo-Phocylides, and the *Testament of Job* (and passages in the NT).

Heavens and hells

A number of early writings describe journeys to (the various) heaven(s) and through the underworld (cf. Tabor 1986; Himmelfarb 1983, though she is primarily concerned with Christian writings; 1993). An elaborate doctrine of heaven and hell as the reward of the righteous and the wicked is mainly a late development, however. In the different writings, the intermediate place of the dead is sometimes in the underworld, sometimes in one of the heavens, and sometimes not specified.

It is clear that the concept of hell developed from the old ancient Near Eastern view of *sheol* or the underworld as essentially the grave (cf. Tromp 1969). One of the earliest descriptions which shows a more developed concept of the underworld is found in the *Book of Watchers*. Enoch takes various journeys, including a visit to see the storehouses for the souls of both the righteous and the wicked which are apparently in the underworld (*1 En.* 22). The concept of a fiery hell does not come about until later. Punishment of the wicked by the "fire of the dark regions" is found in 1QS 4:11–14. Other texts mention a fiery punishment without specifying that this is in hell or the underworld (4 Macc. 9:9; 4 Ezra 13:38; 2 *Bar.* 44:15; 59:2; 64:7). In the *Testament of Abraham* sinners are punished in torment, but the location is not specified (e.g. A 13:12; B 9:9). In 2 *Enoch* (10:1–3) punishment includes darkness, ice, and "black fire", but since the place of torment is in the third heaven, no underworld emerges in this writing. In the *Apocalypse of Abraham* punishment of the wicked appears to be in a fiery abyss or underworld or Hades (conceived of as Azazel's belly?: 21:3; 31:2–3). The *Sibylline Oracles* several times talk about destruction of the earth by fire, but this is the Greek concept of *ekpyrosis* or universal conflagration and not really the same as hell (e.g. 3.84–92; 4.159–61, 171–78; 5.527–31).

The Enoch tradition has one of the earliest tours of heaven. In *1 Enoch* the patriarch is allowed to journey to heaven and have a vision of God's throne, but there are only angels attending; no human souls are there (14:8–25). One of the clearest visions of heaven is found in the *Testament of Abraham*. In both versions Abraham is taken up by angels and sees heaven and the judgment of the dead (which is apparently immediately *post mortem*). The reward of the saved is paradise, though its exact location is not given (A 14:8). The most detailed description of the heavens as such is *2 Enoch*. In the seven/ten heavens both paradise and the place of punishment for the wicked are in the third heaven; if there is an underworld, it is not referred to. The *Apocalypse of Abraham* describes an ascension to heaven by Abraham (15–29) where he sees God's throne, though much of the description is devoted to events on earth.

Several writings mention that the ultimate goal of the righteous is to become like the stars of the heavens (Dupont-Sommer 1949), which is sometimes referred to as "astral immortality" (e.g. Wisdom of Solomon 3:7–9, *1 Enoch* 104:2).

Cosmic eschatology: expectations about the end of the world

There was a widespread view that the age of the world was finite and that history was played out according to a predetermined divine plan (see further, pp. 246–48 above). This is indicated by the "review of history" found in many of the apocalypses and related writings. Reviews of history – *vaticinia ex eventu* (prophecies after the event) – are found in Daniel 11, the *Animal Apocalypse* (*1 En.* 85–90), the *Testament of Moses*, 2 Baruch 53–74, and the *Apocalypse of Weeks* (*1 En.* 93:2–9 + 91:12–17). One of the most characteristic elements of apocalyptic and related literature is the view that the eschaton has come, either for the individual or for the whole human race – in which case the world itself is in its last days.

The cosmic eschaton is often preceded by an oppressive world empire, with God intervening to destroy it. In Daniel this is Antiochus Epiphanes' Seleucid empire (7:19–27; 8:23–25; 11); other oracles against the Greeks are found in the *Sibylline Oracles* (e.g. 3.520–72). In most of the writings, however, the empire is Rome. The clearest example is probably the eagle vision of 4 Ezra 11–12 in which the Roman empire is symbolized by the eagle. A similar representation is found the NT book of Revelation which is roughly contemporary with 4 Ezra (Rev. 13; 17). In the *Sibylline Oracles*, a number of oracles predict the fall of Rome (e.g. 3.350–64; 4.130–48; 5.162–78). *Sib. Or.* 4 has an early Hellenistic oracle that also apparently once ended with the destruction of the Greek empires but was then updated to end with the Roman empire (4.40–114). Josephus also apparently believed that the fall of Rome was prophesied in Daniel, though he was careful not to be explicit. This belief probably also helped to fuel the 66–70 Jewish war against Rome (cf. pp. 278–79 below).

One view was that the approaching endtime would be heralded by a series of eschatological "troubles" or "woes" (sometimes referred to as the "Messianic woes" or "birthpangs of the Messiah"). These have a parallel in some of the classical writers (e.g. Herodotus) who report "prodigies" that herald important events. In Jewish literature a major feature of these "woes" is the reversal of normality: the world is turned upside down; the expected order of society has become its opposite; nothing is the way it

269

should be; chaos has reentered the cosmos. Yet even though these increase the suffering of mankind, they are welcome because God will soon intervene to bring an end to all human suffering. In some cases, the righteous escape the endtime woes, but this does not always seem to be the case.

A detailed description of these eschatological troubles tends to be found in the later literature, though the idea that God's people are being oppressed and will be delivered by divine intervention goes back to the biblical prophecies. The *Sibylline Oracles* are not always easy to make sense of because various sections may have been written independently and at different times; however, in some passages it seems that the warrings of the nations and a series of natural disasters will eventually culminate in a universal conflagration which destroys all human beings (4:130–78; 5:447–530). 4 Ezra gives details of a society in a topsy-turvy situation, along with nature in upheaval (5:1–13; 6:18–28). The vision of the light and dark waters in *2 Baruch* culminates in the final dark waters with the reversal of normality, as well as natural disasters (69–70). In the NT, the Olivet prophecy of the Gospels gives a similar picture (Mark 13; Matthew 24; Luke 21).

13

MESSIAHS

I use the terms "messiah" and "messianic" with some trepidation. The modern belief in the importance of "messianic expectations" in the first century is extremely strong and widespread, despite a number of warning voices raised by those specialists who best know the literature. The reason seems to be a distinctive understanding of the NT in general and Jesus in particular. The problem is not in assuming that messianism was an important concept during the Second Temple period but in recognizing the diversity of beliefs and the various developments that took place over time. Although messianic expectations were important to some groups, they seem to have been central to few, if any; others appear not to have had any sort of belief in a messianic figure.

MAIN TEXTS

Hebrew Bible

Becker, J. (1980) *Messianic Expectation in the Old Testament.*

Bellinger, W. H., Jr, and W. R. Farmer (eds) (1998) *Jesus and the Suffering Servant: Isaiah 53 and Christian Origins.*

Brownlee, William H. (1953) "The Servant of the Lord in the Qumran Scrolls I", *BASOR* 132: 8–15.

—— (1954) "The Servant of the Lord in the Qumran Scrolls II", *BASOR* 135: 33–38.

Collins, J. J. (1995) *The Scepter and the Star: The Messiahs of the Dead Sea Scrolls and Other Ancient Literature.*

Day, J. (1998) *King and Messiah in Israel and the Ancient Near East: Proceedings of the Oxford Old Testament Seminar.*

Hengel, M. (1996) "Zur Wirkungsgeschichte von Jes 53 in vorchristlicher Zeit", in Janowski, B., and P. Stuhlmacher (eds) (1996) *Der leidende Gottesknecht*: 49–91.

Janowski, B., and P. Stuhlmacher (eds) (1996) *Der leidende Gottesknecht: Jesaja 53 und seine Wirkungsgeschichte, mit einer Bibliographie zu Jes 53.*

Laato, A. (1997) *A Star Is Rising: The Historical Development of the Old Testament Royal Ideology and the Rise of the Jewish Messianic Expectations.*

Neubauer, A., and S. R. Driver (1876) *The Fifty-Third Chapter of Isaiah according to the Jewish Interpreters.*

Whybray, R. N. (1978) *Thanksgiving for a Liberated Prophet: An Interpretation of Isaiah Chapter 53.*

The term messiah comes from Hebrew *māšîaḥ*, a passive form meaning "anointed". In the OT it was used primarily of the king (Ps. 2:2) or the high priest (Lev. 8:10–12), though Cyrus the Persian king is also called God's anointed (Isa 45:1). The later development of the concept of messiah is influenced by this origin; in fact, it has been argued that two themes running through texts which feature a messiah are those of the king–priest and the warrior–judge. Both of these arise from the sacerdotal and royal traditions.

When the monarchy was lost (or at least threatened with loss, depending on when you date the texts), some writers began to think of a restoration of Israel/Judah – often in idealized terms. This restoration was frequently conceived of as being headed by a David *redivivus*, a king in the image of David with all his good attributes magnified (Isa. 9:5–6 [Eng. 9:6–7]; 16:5; Jer. 17:24–25; 23:5–6; 30:8–9; 33:12–26; Ezek. 34:23–30; 37:24–25; Zech. 12:7–10). It is nowhere suggested that this new David will be anything but human; he may have almost superhuman characteristics at times, but the original story of David has elements of this.

One of the areas often debated in the past was that of the "Servant Songs" (Isa. 42:1–4; 49:1–6; 50:4–9; 52:13–53:12). The figure in these passages suffers and is thought by many eventually to be killed (especially Isa. 52:13–53:12); he also seems to be suffering for the sins of others ("vicarious suffering"). This has naturally led to a messianic interpretation being given to this figure, especially in Christian circles where he could be compared with Jesus (e.g. Luke 24:44–47; cf. Bellinger/Farmer 1998). There are two problems with this interpretation. The first relates to the proper understanding of the figure in its original context: Is the figure anything more than Israel personified (cf. Isa. 44:1; 49:3)? Does the figure really suffer vicariously and die? (cf. Whybray 1978 who argues against both). The second problem is whether the figure is presented as messianic. Some of the later Jewish texts do see a messianic figure in the passage, though sometimes a conquering messiah (Neubauer/Driver 1876); however, none of these texts is likely to be pre-70. Brownlee (1953, 1954) had argued that the long Isaiah scroll (1QIs^a) read "anointed" in Isaiah 52:14–15 instead of "marred". Most recently Hengel has thought that a messianic interpretation could be found in some early Jewish texts (mainly 1QIs^a and 4Q541); however, he can point to no evidence for a "suffering messiah" interpretation in pre-Christian texts. Although he still wishes to allow that such may have existed, there is so far no clear evidence for such an interpretation before 70 CE (cf. Collins 1995: 123–26). On Daniel, see below.

Ben Sira

Caquot, A. (1966) "Ben Sira et le messianisme", *Semitica* 16: 43–68.

Horbury, W. (1998) "Messianism in the Old Testament Apocrypha", in J. Day (ed.) *King and Messiah in Israel and the Ancient Near East*: 402–33, especially 413–19.

Jacob, E. (1958) "L'histoire d'Israël vue par Ben Sira", in *Mélanges bibliques rédigés en l'honneur de André Robert*: 288–94.

Martin, J. D. (1986) "Ben Sira's Hymn to the Fathers: a Messianic Perspective", *OTS* 24: 107–23.

Smend, R. (1906–7) *Weisheit des Jesus Sirach*.

With his emphasis on the priesthood and little in the way of eschatological speculation, Ben Sira might be thought to have had no interest in a messiah. Yet several passages have excited conjecture on the subject, primarily 49:16 and 45:25. Already Smend (1906–7: 476) had seen the exaltation of Adam, in 49:16, as being rooted in a messianic hope. Similarly, Jacob (1958) argued that 49:16 and other passages (e.g. 17:1–2; cf. Job 15:7) showed an original Adam glorified and perfected as wisdom itself; Ben Sira was seen as having abandoned a national escatology for an "adamic" one in a sapiential context. The other verse, 45:25, refers to the covenant with David, then states, "the inheritance of *'š* is to his son alone". The word can be read as *'ēš*, the normal Hebrew word for "fire", and has been taken to refer to the priestly inheritance of service at the altar; however, some scholars take the word as a defective spelling of *'yš*, to be read as *'îš* "man", perhaps even equivalent to king (cf. Martin 1986: 112–16). Caquot (1966) and others are skeptical that such a view is found in Ben Sira, but Martin compares the *Animal Apocalypse* (*1 En.* 89–90) in which the white bull imagery applied to Adam ceases with Isaac but is then resumed at the end of the apocalypse, apparently in a reference to the messiah. This might suggest that the adamic imagery is messianic (1986: 118–19).

Qumran scrolls

Atkinson, K. (1998) "On the Herodian Origin of Militant Davidic Messianism at Qumran: New Light from *Psalm of Solomon* 17", *JBL* 118: 435–60.

Brooke, G. J. (1998) "Kingship and Messianism in the Dead Sea Scrolls", in J. Day (ed.) *King and Messiah in Israel and the Ancient Near East*: 434–55.

Charlesworth, J. H., H. Lichtenberger, and G. S. Oegema (eds) (1998) *Qumran-Messianism: Studies on the Messianic Expectations in the Dead Sea Scrolls*.

Collins, J. J. (1994) "The Works of the Messiah", *DSD* 1: 98–112.

—— (1995) *The Scepter and the Star: The Messiahs of the Dead Sea Scrolls and Other Ancient Literature.*

Eisenman, R. (1983) *Maccabees, Zadokites, Christians and Qumran.*

Eisenman, R., and M. O. Wise (1992) *The Dead Sea Scrolls Uncovered: The First Complete Translation and Interpretation of 50 Key Documents Withheld for Over 35 Years.*

Knibb, M. A. (1995) "Messianism in the Pseudepigrapha in the Light of the Scrolls", *DSD* 2: 165–84.

Puech, E. (1999) "Le 'Fils de Dieu' en 4Q246", *Eretz-Israel* 26: 143*–52*.

Starcky, J. (1963) "Les quatres étapes du messianisme à Qumrân", *RevB* 70: 481–505.

Tabor, J. D., and M. O. Wise (1994) "4Q521 'On Resurrection' and the Synoptic Gospel Tradition: A Preliminary Study", *JSP* 10: 149–62.

Vermes, G. (1992) "The Oxford Forum for Qumran Research: Seminar on the Rule of War from Cave 4 (4Q285)", *JJS* 43: 85–94.

Zimmermann, J. (1998) *Messianische Texte aus Qumran: Königliche, priesterliche und prophetische Messiasvorstellungen in den Schriftfunden von Qumran.*

A variety of eschatalogical figures occur in those Qumran texts that seem to be related to one another; however, the messianic expectations at Qumran appear not to have been a major part of their eschatological view. At least, the texts do not refer to them often, though they are there in the background. It has also been argued – not unreasonably – that their views developed and changed over time, perhaps moving from the expectation of only one messianic figure to a situation with several. For example, the *War Scroll* (1QM) describes a series of eschatological battles between the Sons of Light and the Sons of Darkness, yet this writing says nothing about a messianic figure. The *Damascus Document* speaks of "the anointed of Aaron and Israel" (CD 12:23–13:1). Is this meant to be one messiah or two? CD 19:10–11 seems to have one figure in mind when it refers to "the messiah of Aaron and Israel". On the other hand, the *Community Rule* speaks of "the prophet and the messiahs of Aaron and Israel" (1QS 9:11). In none of these passages is the function of the messiah described. The passages which refer explicitly to a messiah or messiahs are few and somewhat unspecific. Another important passage is found in the text sometimes referred to as the *Messianic Rule* (1QS^a 2:11). Here a messiah of Aaron (a priestly messiah) and a messiah of Israel seem to be distinctly envisaged.

One of the earliest texts with a heavenly messiah is 11QMelchizedek (perhaps from the first century BCE). In this text, the Melchizedek of Genesis 14:18–20 (cf. Psa. 110:4 and Hebrews 5 and 7) is a heavenly figure (identical with the archangel Michael) who opposes Satan. At one point we have the following statement about an "anointed one" (messiah): "it is the time for the 'year of grace' of Melchizedek, and of [his] arm[ies, the nat]ion of the holy ones of God, of the rule of judgment, as is written. . . . Its interpretation: The mountains [are] the prophet[s] . . . And the messenger i[s] the anointed one of the spir[it] as Dan[iel] said [about him: *(Dan 9:25]*" (2:9, 17–18). The fragmentary nature of the text makes it difficult to interpret, but the deliverance comes at the end of ten jubilees (490 years), just as with Daniel 9. Indeed, Daniel 9:25 seems to be cited, though whether "the anointed one" is identical with Melchizedek or is a separate figure is not clear.

Several recently published texts also have messianic overtones, or at least have been so interpreted. One of the main ones is the *Messianic Apocalypse* (4Q521) which describes the various marvelous things that "the Lord" will do, along with mention of "his messiah". In language borrowed from Isaiah 61:1, it is stated that the captives will be released, the blind given sight, the wounded healed, and the dead given life (4Q521 2.II:7–8, 12–13). This has been compared with a passage in the gospels (Matt. 11:2–5//Luke 7:19–22; Wise/Tabor 1994), though the text as read by most scholars seems to describe what "the Lord" does, and is not ascribing these actions to the messiah (cf. Collins 1995: 121; Zimmermann 1998: 347). Precisely what form of a messiah is being spoken of here is difficult to say, though possibly he is an eschatological prophet on the model of Elijah (Collins 1995: 120–22).

Another document is the *Son of God* text (4Q246). The term "messiah" is not used in the extant remains; however, the description of what the "son of God" does matches descriptions of messianic activities elsewhere. A variety of explanations have been given for this text (Brooke 1998: 445–49), but the messianic interpretation has been argued at some length by Collins (1995: 154–72). One of the main problems is whether the text is describing the activities of a historical figure or an eschatological one. As noted above (p. 272), some have seen 4Q541 as messianic. The text refers to the succession of high priests, including possibly the last one, but it does not clearly refer to an eschatological messiah (Brooke 1998: 449; Collins 1995: 124–26; contrast Zimmermann 1998: 275–77).

One text of considerable interest in recent years is 4Q285. Eisenman and Wise (1992) proposed that a slain messiah was depicted in the text. Because the idea of a suffering messiah seems to be post-Christian and not in any early texts, this interpretation could have been sensational, since many Christian scholars had long sought a Jewish predecessor to the image of Jesus as a suffering messiah. (However, it should be noted that Eisenman [1983] argues these texts are Christian, arising from the circle of James the Just and thus not evidence of a pre-Christian suffering messiah.) This interpretation, which depends on the interpretation of a rather fragmentary text, has been met with almost universal rejection (Vermes 1992; Collins 1995: 58–60; Zimmermann 1998: 86–87).

The Qumran messianic picture is not a simple one, therefore; quite some time ago Starcky (1963) had argued for a four-stage historical development of beliefs on the question. Although this is overly schematic, a chronological development is still probably a factor in the variety of messianic figures (Brooke 1998: 450–52). The Qumran texts in general tend to put the emphasis on the priestly and prophetic elements of leadership rather than the princely, which may explain why so little is said about the messiah from Judah.

Psalms of Solomon

Apart from the Qumran scrolls, which are not easy to date, the *Psalms of Solomon* (from about 40 BCE) are one of the earliest non-biblical texts to discuss the question, especially 17–18. The messianic figure is a king in the image of David (17:21), righteous and holy (17:35). He will smash the gentile oppesors of Jerusalem with a rod of iron (17:22–25). There is nothing about this figure that indicates a heavenly origin, however; he appears to be a human being with perhaps some larger-than-life characteristics. Nothing is said about how long he would reign, whether he would have successors, and the like; in short he is very much in the image of various OT passages giving a similar picture.

Similitudes of Enoch (1 Enoch 37–71)

Probably from the first century CE, the *Similitudes of Enoch* (*1 Enoch* 37–71) speak of a figure called the "Elect One" of righteousness (39:6; 45; 49:2; 50; 51; 52; 53:6; 55:4; 61; 62) who is also identified with one called the "Son of Man" (46; 48; 62; 63:11; 69:27–29). There are clear links between the Lord of Spirits and the Son of Man, on the one hand, and the Ancient of Days and "one like a son of man" in Daniel 7, on the other, suggesting that the *Similitudes* are evidence for a particular interpretation of the Daniel chapter. This same figure is later referred to as the "messiah" (48; 52). Eventually, he seems to be identified with Enoch himself, but that is thought by many to be a secondary development (71:14–17). Thus, the messiah here is a heavenly figure. (On the question of the "Son of Man", see pp. 282–83 below.)

Philo

Borgen, P. (1997) *Philo of Alexandria: An Exegete for his Time*.
Fischer, U. (1978) *Eschatologie und Jenseitserwartung im hellenistischen Diaspora-judentum*.
Goodenough, E. R. (1938) *The Politics of Philo Judaeus, Practice and Theory*.
Grabbe, L. L. (1988a) *Etymology in Early Jewish Interpretation: The Hebrew Names in Philo*.
—— (1999c) "Eschatology in Philo and Josephus", in A. Avery-Peck and J. Neusner (eds) *Judaism in Late Antiquity: Part 4 Death, Life-after-Death, Resurrection and the World-to-Come in the Judaisms of Antiquity*: 163–85.

Hecht, R. D. (1987) "Philo and Messiah", in J. Neusner, W. S. Green, E. S. Frerichs (eds) *Judaisms and Their Messiahs at the Turn of the Christian Era*: 139–68.

Mack, B. L. (1991) "Wisdom and Apocalyptic in Philo", in D. T. Runia, D. M. Hay, and D. Winston (eds) *Heirs of the Septuagint: Philo, Hellenistic Judaism and Early Christianity: Festschrift for Earle Hilgert*: 21–39.

Tobin, T. H. (1997) "Philo and the Sibyl: Interpreting Philo's Eschatology", in D. T. Runia and G. E. Sterling (eds) *Wisdom and Logos: Studies in Jewish Thought in Honor of David Winston*: 84–103.

Wolfson, H. A. (1947) *Philo: Foundations of Religious Philosophy in Judaism, Christianity, and Islam*.

The following discussion is an abbreviated form of my more detailed treatment elsewhere (Grabbe 1999c). A number of scholars have argued that Philo held a type of messianic belief (Goodenough 1938: 115–19; Wolfson 1947: 2.395–426; for a detailed critique of their views, see Hecht 1987: 140–48). The most recent defence of this interpretation has been given by Borgen (1992; 1997: 261–81). The main appeal is to Philo's treatise *Rewards and Punishments* (*De Praemiis et Poenis*). The question here is whether the future hope envisaged a messianic figure or leader as an individual as normally understood. One passage might imply some sort of messianic figure and has certainly been interpreted in this way. In discussing the triumph of the righteous over their enemies, Philo states that if some have the temerity to attack them, "'there shall come forth a man', say the oracles, and leading his host to war he will subdue great and populous nations" (*Praem.* 94–95). Philo's comments in this passage appear to be based on the LXX text of Num. 24:7a which states, "There will come forth a man from his seed and will rule over many nations" (though the MT reads rather differently: "Water shall flow from his waterskins, and his/its seed in many waters"). The passage is also quoted in *Vita Mosis* 1.288–91 where Philo is expounding the whole of Balaam's oracle in Num. 24.

Since Philo read the LXX text carefully and literally but did not know the Hebrew (cf. Grabbe 1988: 63, 233–35), he had to interpret Num. 24:7 as a reference to a particular man. In *Vita Mosis* 1.289–91 Philo has simply interpreted the passage to mean a ruler of some sort (perhaps Moses), but in this case he makes nothing further of it. Similarly, he introduces Num. 24:7 into *Praem.* 95 to make a point about a military leader, but again he does not take the issue further. If he took the "man" of LXX Num. 24:7 as a messianic figure, why does he give no hint that this is his interpretation? In fact, a number of rather different suggestions have been made as to whom "man" in this passage refers in Philo's thinking: as a reference to God himself (Oegema 1994: 118–19; cf. Fischer 1978: 201) or to Israel (Mack 1991: 35). The important point is that, having introduced the subject, he drops it even though he did not need to.

Tobin (1997) has argued that Philo is deliberately opposing much more radical eschatological views which foresaw the overthrow of the Romans by a savior figure, as exemplified in such writings as *Sibylline Oracles* 3 and 5 (cf. also Hecht 1987: 160–61). A messianic savior figure does not fit easily into Philo's theological system (as also argued by Fischer, Hecht, and Mack; cf. also Oegema 1994: 118, 122).

Josephus

Fischer, U. (1978) *Eschatologie und Jenseitserwartung im hellenistischen Diaspora-judentum*.

Grabbe, L. L. (1997d) "The 70-Weeks Prophecy (Daniel 9:24–27) in Early Jewish Interpretation", in C. A. Evans and S. Talmon (eds) *The Quest for Context and Meaning*: 595–611.

—— (1999c) "Eschatology in Philo and Josephus", in A. Avery-Peck and J. Neusner (eds) *Judaism in Late Antiquity: Part 4 Death, Life-after-Death, Resurrection and the World-to-Come in the Judaisms of Antiquity*: 163–85.

This section is only a summary of more detailed studies (Grabbe 1997d; 1999c). To describe Josephus's views is difficult: on the one hand, he discusses a series of oracles that he associates with the Roman conquest of Jerusalem and hints at some anti-Roman interpretations of Daniel; on the other hand, he clearly writes with the possibility of a Roman readership and seems to be rather cagey about explicit references to messianic expectations. For example, he explicitly denies that the war with Rome had anything to do with an eschatological war in which the Jewish nation would be delivered. This is hardly surprising since, writing sometime after the events, he knew that there had been no divine or messianic intervention to save the Jews and destroy the Romans. Instead, he interprets the alleged prophecies as having been misunderstood or even as prophesying disaster.

Josephus quotes an oracle that speaks of a "ruler from the East" (*War* 6.5.4 §§311–13; cf. Tacitus, *Histories* 5.13.2; Suetonius, *Vespasian* 4.5; 5.6; Grabbe 1997d). He makes no stated association between it and his prediction that Vespasian would become emperor, which he claims came to him in a dream (*War* 3.8.3 §§351–53), but one suspects a connection (cf. Fischer 1978: 168–74). The central question is, did Josephus genuinely believe that Vespasian was the intended fulfilment of these prophetic interpretations? One is left with the strong impression that Josephus himself *once* believed in various oracles thought to predict a coming messianic deliverer. A number of such oracles were evidently taken by many Jews as predictions of ultimate deliverance. Even in the very last days of the siege of Jerusalem, as the Romans were breaching the walls, a large number of those in the city were still expecting to be delivered, against all appearances (*War* 6.5.2 §§283–87). By the final days of the siege, Josephus probably did not believe such views, but his ready participation in the revolt hints that the oracles later applied so readily to Vespasian were originally seen by Josephus himself as providing hope of a Jewish victory.

We have a strong indication that Josephus's beliefs about prophecy were more complex than his explicit statements might lead us to believe. For example, he mentions a couple of other oracles (*War* 4.6.3 §388; 6.2.1 §109) which he does not refer to Vespasian, though he interprets them to fit with that view. The situation is best explained if Josephus changed his interpretation of those oracles which he had originally understood as prophesying a messianic victory over the Romans.

The crux of Josephus's personal beliefs is probably found in his discussion of the book of Daniel, in particular Daniel 2 (*Ant.* 10.10.3–4 §§195–210). He applies the head of gold to Nebuchadnezzar (*Ant.* 10.10.4 §§208–10, as Dan. 2:38 itself does). The hands and shoulders represent the two kings who bring the Babylonian empire to an end, later interpreted as Cyrus the Persian and Darius the Mede (*Ant.* 10.11.4 §§247–48). They are in turn defeated by a king from the West who can only be Alexander; his empire is subsequently brought down by a power like iron which, though not explicitly identified, must be Rome. The last is destroyed by a "stone made without hands", whose meaning was revealed to Alexander; Josephus says that he is not going to say what this was but anyone interested can read Daniel to find out (*Ant.* 10.10.4 §210). Josephus was writing these words about Daniel at the end of the first century CE, at approximately the same time as the authors of 4 Ezra and Revelation. Did he also apply the prophecy of Daniel to Rome, expecting its destruction by supernatural means? It seems likely. He does not write as one who expected it to fall shortly, unlike some of his contemporary apocalypticists; nevertheless, he gives strong hints that his messianic interpretations of prophecy, though postponed to a more distant future, had not changed.

4 Ezra/2 Baruch

Hayman, A. P. (1998) "The 'Man from the Sea' in 4 Ezra 13", *JJS* 49: 1–16.

From toward the end of the first century CE, we have two main apocalypses, both of which have messianic figures though with some slight differences. 4 Ezra 7:28–35 speaks of "my son the messiah" who will be revealed in the endtime and reign for 400 years. The messianic age is not described in detail, but it is followed by the death of all human beings and then the general resurrection and final judgment. *2 Baruch* is similar but does not envisage the death of the messiah, only his gradual revelation and a smooth transition from the Messianic Kingdom into the final Kingdom of God (29–30). A golden age of peace and prosperity will dawn as the messiah begins to be revealed, with feasting on Leviathan and Behemoth and also the treasures of manna. After the full revelation of the messiah, the souls of the righteous are to be raised from their storehouses to enjoy all this, while the wicked will be punished.

4 Ezra 13 is another significant text. Although the term "messiah" is not used, a heavenly "man from the sea", who is also referred to as "God's son" (13:32), has characteristics to take into account. The messiah is also mentioned in the eagle vision of 4 Ezra 11–12. Here he appears in the form of a lion from the forest who rebukes Rome for its sins and its pride (11:37–12:3). He is of the stock of David but has been kept back until the endtime. The pre-existence of the messiah seems to be a theme in both 4 Ezra and *2 Baruch*.

Sibylline Oracles

O'Neill, J. C. (1991) "The Man from Heaven: *SibOr* 5.256–259", *JSP* 9: 87–102.

The *Sibylline Oracles* contain material covering a period of about 300 years. *Sib. Or.* 3:489–829 has various eschatological passages. There are references to the "king from the sun" (3.652) who is also said to be the "seventh" (3.193, 3.318, 3.608). It is generally agreed that the reference is to one of the Ptolemaic rulers, perhaps the most likely being Ptolemy VI Philometor who had good relations with the Jews. *Sib. Or.* 3:702–31 describes the "sons of the great God" living in peace around the temple, while 3:741–95 pictures a renewed form of life on earth, a type of golden age or millennium. A messianic figure in the form of the Egyptian king and a messianic age were thus expected in the second century BCE. Some passages seem to relate to Cleopatra VII and perhaps an expectation that she would fill the role of messiah. A reference to a "mistress" (*despoina*) seems to have her in mind and to predict the subjugation of Rome to Asia (3:350–80). Several other prophecies relating to the endtime (3:46–63 and 3:75–92) indicate a period after the disappointment of Actium, when hope in Cleopatra had failed. In *Sib. Or.* 5 the attitude is openly hostile to Egypt (5:179–99), and hope is now placed in a messianic figure who comes from heaven (5:108–9, 155–61, 414–28). Even after the revolts under Trajan and Hadrian, at least in Egypt Jews still hoped for deliverance by a messiah of some sort in the not–too–distant future.

New Testament

The NT has its own perspective on messianism, especially determined by its view of Jesus. This aspect of NT teachings will not be discussed further; nevertheless, some passages seem to imply that some Jews expected a conquering messiah who would free Israel from her oppressors. For example, Jesus is asked by the disciples in Acts 1:6–7 whether it was the time when "the kingdom of Israel" would be restored, but he gives an evasive reply.

Rabbinic literature

Collins, J. J. (1995) *The Scepter and the Star: The Messiahs of the Dead Sea Scrolls and Other Ancient Literature*.

Dix, G. H. (1926) "The Messiah ben Joseph", *JTS* 27: 130–43.

Heinemann, J. (1975) "The Messiah of Ephraim and the Premature Exodus of the Tribe of Ephraim", *HTR* 68: 1–15.

Neusner, J. (1984) *Messiah in Context: Israel's History and Destiny in Formative Judaism*.

—— (1987b) "Mishnah and Messiah", in J. Neusner; W. S. Green; and E. S. Frerichs (eds) *Judaisms and Their Messiahs at the Turn of the Christian Era*: 265–82.

Pearson, B. W. R. (1998) "Dry Bones in the Judean Desert: The Messiah of Ephraim, Ezekiel 37, and the Post-Revolutionary Followers of Bar Kokhba", *JSJ* 29: 192–201.

Torrey, C. C. (1947) "The Messiah son of Ephraim", *JBL* 66: 253–77.

It has long been taken for granted that Judaism of the rabbinic period had a strongly developed concept of "the messiah" and, indeed, that was often drawn upon to elucidate the situation in early Christianity. Neusner's study (1984) has now shown that the situation is more complex than previously recognized. The earliest rabbinic documents (the Mishnah, Tosefta, Tannaitic Midrashim) actually avoid the concept, and "messiah" means only the properly designated and consecrated high priest. Neusner argues that this is not accidental (because, as might be argued, the concern of the Mishnah was mainly legal) but was organic to the Judaism of the Mishnah. That Judaism rooted itself in a timeless and ahistorical view of the world in which sanctification was the primary concern; eschatology as such had little place in this system. With the developments in the Amoraic period, messianism could be introduced (or reintroduced since it was definitely a part of Judaism before 135 CE). Nevertheless, the sort of messiah envisaged by the Amoraic and later texts was thoroughly rabbinized. The documents were now very much concerned with historical salvation.

Of particular concern over the years has been the concept of a "messiah ben Joseph" who was slain in battle (*b. Sukkah* 52a–52b). Several attempts have been made to trace this concept earlier but cannot be said to make a convincing case (Torrey 1947; Dix 1926). Heinemann (1975) has argued that the idea was developed following the Bar Kokhba revolt to explain how Bar Kokhba was correctly identified as the messiah but was also slain. In sum, no evidence has been found for belief in the death of a messiah in battle for the pre-70 period.

THE "SON OF MAN"

Casey, M. (1979) *Son of Man: The Interpretation and Influence of Daniel 7*.
Charles, R. H. (1913) *The Book of Enoch*.
Collins, J. J. (1977) *The Apocalyptic Vision of the Book of Daniel*.
—— (1993) *A Commentary on the Book of Daniel*.
—— (1995) *The Scepter and the Star: The Messiahs of the Dead Sea Scrolls and Other Ancient Literature*.
Davies, P. R. (1985) *Daniel*.

One of the most intriguing figures is the "son of man" known from Daniel 7 and especially from the *Similitudes of Enoch* (*1 En.* 37–71), though it must be admitted that much of the interest has been stimulated by use of the title in reference to Jesus in the NT. A fierce debate in recent years has centered on its origins and implications for the NT. Several issues are involved:

- the meaning of the figure of the "son of man" in its original context in Daniel 7
- the dating and significance of the term "son of man" in *1 Enoch* (whether it is pre-Christian or perhaps has been influenced by Christian interpretations)
- the significance of Jesus's statements about the "son of man" in the Gospels

The last point is beyond our purposes, but the first two need to be addressed.

It is almost universally agreed among scholars that "one like a son of man" in Daniel 7 represents "the people of the holy ones of the Most High", as Dan. 7:27 states. This may originally have been the community or group responsible for Daniel, the *maskilim* of other parts of the book (see pp. 60–61 above). In later interpretation, these people are taken to be the Jewish people. It has been argued that the figure is specifically the archangel Michael, so prominent elsewhere in the book, though Michael would still be functioning as a representative of the Jewish people (Collins 1977: 144–46; opposed by Davies 1985: 105–6). Thus, in Daniel itself the term "son of man" (*bar 'ĕnāš*) simply means "human being", as it commonly does in Hebrew and Aramaic; however, in context the "one like a son of man" may be a heavenly figure.

The *Similitudes of Enoch* were once drawn on to demonstrate how the term "son of man" had become a messianic title in Judaism long before Jesus (e.g. Charles 1913). This depended on a dating of the *Similitudes* to pre-Christian times; however, with the publication of the Aramaic fragments of *1 Enoch*, it was argued that the *Similitudes* were a Christian work of the third or fourth century CE (see p. 97 above). This dating has not generally been accepted, but a dating to the first century, either before or after 70, is now common. There is a clear connection with Daniel 7, since the Ethiopic reference to the "chief of days" (*'ĕzi' mawā'ĕlāt*) seems to be a rendering of the Aramaic "ancient of days" (*'attîq yômîn*). As in Daniel 7, there is also a figure called the "son of man" (*walda sab'*: 46; 48; 62; 63:11; 69:27–29) who is identified with the "elect one of righteousness" (39:6; 45; 49:2; 50; 51; 52; 53:6; 55:4; 61; 62), as well as with the "messiah" (48; 52).

The extent to which these data are relevant for the NT and the correct understanding of Jesus's sayings and/or self-understanding can be debated (cf. Casey 1979 versus Collins 1993:), but this question is beyond our purposes here. What can be said is that the term "son of man" in the *Similitudes* is a messianic title, and there is not a trace of Christian interpretation here. It seems very unlikely that, if these chapters had been written by a Christian scribe, he would have been able to avoid any reference to Jesus or the NT. With the significant consensus that the *Similitudes* are first century, it seems likely that a messianic title "son of man" had developed in Judaism by this time and may have been available either to Jesus or to the writers of the Gospels.

SICARII, ZEALOTS, AND OTHER "REVOLUTIONARY" GROUPS

Applebaum, S. (1971) "The Zealots: The Case for Revaluation", *JRS* 61: 155–70.

Black, M. (1974) "Judas of Galilee and Josephus's 'Fourth Philosophy'", in O. Betz, *et al.* (eds) *Josephus-Studien*: 45–54.

Borg, M. (1971) "The Currency of the Term 'Zealot'", *JTS* 22: 504–12.

Dyson, S. L. (1971) "Native Revolts in the Roman Empire", *Historia* 20: 239–74.

—— (1975) "Native Revolt Patterns in the Roman Empire", *ANRW II*: 3.138–75.

Grünewald, T. (1999) *Räuber, Rebellen, Rivalen, Rächer: Studien zu* Latrones *im Römischen Reich*.

Hengel, M. (1989) *The Zealots: Investigations into the Jewish Freedom Movement in the Period from Herod I until 70 AD*.

Horsley, R. A. (1979a) "Josephus and the Bandits", *JSJ* 10: 37–63.

—— (1979b) "The Sicarii: Ancient Jewish 'Terrorists'", *JR* 59: 435–58.

—— (1981) "Ancient Jewish Banditry and the Revolt against Rome, A.D. 66–70", *CBQ* 43: 409–32.

—— (1984) "Popular Messianic Movements around the Time of Jesus", *CBQ* 46: 471–95.

—— (1985a) "Menahem in Jerusalem: A Brief Messianic Episode among the Sicarii – Not 'Zealot Messianism'", *NT* 27: 334–48.

—— (1985b) "'Like One of the Prophets of Old': Two Types of Popular Prophets at the Time of Jesus", *CBQ* 47: 435–63.

—— (1986a) "Popular Prophetic Movements at the Time of Jesus: Their Principal Features and Social Origins", *JSNT* 26: 3–27.

—— (1986b) "The Zealots: their Origin, Relationships and Importance in the Jewish Revolt", *NT* 28: 159–92.

—— (1987) *Jesus and the Spiral of Violence: Popular Jewish Resistance in Roman Palestine.*

Horsley, R. A., and J. S. Hanson (1999) *Bandits, Prophets, and Messiahs: Popular Movements in the Time of Jesus.*

Isaac, B. (1984) "Bandits in Judaea and Arabia", *HSCP* 88: 171–203.

McClaren, J. S. (1998) *Turbulent Times? Josephus and Scholarship on Judaea in the First Century CE.*

Macmullen, R. (1967) *Enemies of the Roman Order: Treason, Unrest, and Alienation in the Empire.*

Michel, Otto (1967–68) "Studien zu Josephus: Simon bar Giora", *NTS* 14: 402–8.

Nikiprowetzky, V. (1973) "Sicaires et Zélotes – une Reconsidération", *Semitica* 23: 51–64.

Rhoads, D. M. (1976) *Israel in Revolution: 6–74 C.E.: A Political History Based on the Writings of Josephus.*

Shaw, B. D. (1984) "Bandits in the Roman Empire", *Past and Present* 105: 3–52.

Smith, M. (1971b) "Zealots and Sicarii, their Origins and Relation", *HTR* 64: 1–19.

Yadin, Y. (1966) *Masada: Herod's Fortress and the Zealots' Last Stand.*

Zerbe, G. M. (1993) *Non-Retaliation in Early Jewish and New Testament Texts: Ethical Themes in Social Contexts.*

General comments

According to the extant sources (primarily Josephus), there were a number of movements among the Jews in the Roman period. Some of these were evidently short-lived, especially where they caused concern on the part of the Roman military authorities. To what extent these were only the "tip of the iceberg" can be debated, but what little is known is sufficient to indicate that the "philosophies" of Josephus were hardly a summary of all the religious groups at the time. Recent attempts to apply sociological analysis to these various groups are helpful, but one must keep in mind that a rigid distinction cannot easily be made between a social and a religious movement at this time. There may have been religious overtones even when the movement in question could be described in the sociological terms applied to secular movements in modern times. Also, models from modern sociological movements do not always fit very well, and too rigid an application can be distorting.

What may appear to us as a social or political movement, from our distance in time and worldview, may have been intensely religious to insiders. Trying to determine the exact nature of a movement is not easy, however. One of the problems is that the sources are often hostile to these movements and make little attempt to give a full or fair description. Many are lumped together as "bandits" (*lēistēs*), but this term was used indiscrimately to refer both to the straightforward criminal or thief and to what might be called in modern terms "revolutionaries" or "social bandits" (but see now the criticisms of Grünewald [1999] who argues that "social bandits" did not exist in Roman times). Those ancient writers mentioning them, though, may not have seen any difference. Many who were called "bandits" were indeed genuine bandits who had become such because of the oppressive and troubled circumstances (Horsley 1979a). There are instances in which banditry among the peasant population developed into a popular revolt, which appears to be what happened in first-century Judea. Under Roman rule, there were times when people took to banditry as a means of survival (Macmullen 1967; Dyson 1971, 1975; Shaw 1984).

According to Josephus, in the late 40s and 50s this practice rapidly escalated. To use his own words, "the country was overrun with bandits" (*Ant.* 20.9.5 §215). This "spiral of violence" has been seen as an important cause of the war itself. McClaren (1998) has recently challenged this point of view, arguing that it is Josephus's own creation. McClaren's main criticism – that scholars may have depended too much on Josephus's own interpetation here – is correct, but it does not address an important issue: that Jewish dissatisfaction with Roman rule increased as time went on. The restoration of the native monarchy in the person of Agrippa I was probably helpful, but his early death and the rapid return to direct Roman rule would have made the frustration even more acute. For these reasons, I am less quick to dismiss Josephus's picture than McClaren, though he is right about the need for careful reading (see also pp. 108–9 above).

Although it is not always possible to be sure, there are hints that a number of these movements were messianic in character. They generally looked to a particular leader, and in some cases the leader was proclaimed (or proclaimed himself) king (Horsley 1984). Thus, the leader became God's anointed (even if the exact definition of "anointed" varied somewhat), that is, a messianic figure.

The "Fourth Philosophy" and the Sicarii

In addition to the three main sects (Sadducees, Pharisees, and Essenes), Josephus describes another group which he refers to as the "Fourth Philosophy" (*Ant.* 18.1.1 §§4–10; 18.1.6 §23). He states that it was essentially the same as the Pharisees except for its belief that only God should be recognized as king and ruler, the founders being Judas the Galilean and Zadok (Saddokos) the Pharisee. He goes on to say that in the latter part of the 40s the movement gave rise to the Sicarii, a group which specialized in assassinations of Jewish officials (the name apparently comes from *sica*, the name of a type of dagger [*Ant.* 20.8.8 §§186–87]). There is good reason to question Josephus's statement about Judas the Galilean as the founder of the Sicarii, however, because it was probably based partly on his own deductions and partly on his own bias toward blaming the "insurgents" for the war (Rhoads 1976: 52–60).

The Sicarii were quite active during the two decades after Agrippa I's death in 44 CE (*War* 2.13.3 §§254–57). In addition to killing Jewish officials, they took to kidnapping important officials (e.g. members of the high priest's family) and holding them for ransom (*Ant.* 20.9.3 §§208–10). Despite suffering from these crimes, some of the high priests were also alleged to have hired the Sicarii to do some of their own dirty work. Even certain of the Roman governors reportedly availed themselves of the Sicarii talents! (*Ant.* 20.8.5 §§162–66). The Sicarii generally avoided clashes with the Romans, preferring to assassinate Jews who were seen as collaborators rather than make attempts on Roman officials. There is something of a problem in that *sicarii* could be used as a common noun to mean "assassins". Thus, we cannot be sure that all the groups in the 40s, 50s, and early 60s referred to by this term were part of a single organization.

The activities of the Sicarii were very important in the events leading up to the revolt, by destablilizing Roman rule and discouraging Jews from serving in the administration. On the other hand, once the fight against Rome began they played only a brief part. One of their leaders, Menahem, grandson of Judas the Galilean, led a group in Jerusalem for a period of time in 66; however, he and many of his followers were killed by the those under Eleazar (*War* 2.17.6–9 §§425–48). The survivors fled to Masada where they remained aloof from the war until besieged by the Romans after the fall of Jerusalem (*War* 7.8.1–9.2 §§252–406). Some of the Sicarii escaped the destruction and caused difficulties in Egypt and Cyrene in the early 70s (*War* 7.10.1 §§410–19, 437–50). This is the last we hear of the group.

The Sicarii have been compared to the modern "urban terrorist" (Horsley 1984) in the use of both assassination and kidnapping to further their political goals. Apart from the question of whether "urban" is a useful term in this context, the Sicarii should not be seen as solely political since there are some indications that they were in part motivated by eschatological and messianic expectations. For example, Menahem took on royal trappings and evidently even set himself up as a messianic figure, which was one of the reasons for his assassination by the Zealots (*War* 2.17.8–9 §§433–34, 443–46). The Sicarii should not be confused with the Zealots, though they often are, but form a distinct group with a different history and goals.

Zealots

It was during the 66–70 revolt that the group called the Zealots first becomes apparent in Josephus's story. This group was particularly active in Jerusalem before and during the siege. Josephus says about them (*War* 4.3.3–9 §§135–61):

> [135] In the end, satiated with their pillage of the country, the brigand chiefs of all these scattered bands joined forces and, now merged into one pack of villainy, stole into poor Jerusalem. . . . [138] Fresh brigands from the country entering the city and joining the yet more formidable gang within, abstained henceforth from no enormities. . . . [158] This latest outrage was more than the people could stand, and as if for the overthrow of a despotism one and all were now roused. . . . [160] Their efforts were supported by the most eminent of the high priests, Jesus, son of Gamalas, and Ananus, son of Ananus, who at their meetings vehemently upbraided the people for their apathy and incited them against the Zealots; for so these miscreants called themselves, as though they were zealous in the cause of virtue and not for vice in its basest and most extravagant form.

There is a debate on the use of the term "zealot" (from Greek *zēlotēs*). The term may be used generically for anyone who displayed zeal in devotion to God like that of Phineas (Numbers 25), and for this reason some have used it indiscriminately to refer to any revolutionary group (e.g. Hengel 1989). However, Josephus clearly uses the term primarily in reference to a particular group who had themselves taken this name. It is therefore unhelpful to lump all these various groups together as Zealots (with a capital letter), even if they tended to have certain characteristics in common.

The earlier history of the Zealots is unknown. Some have argued that they first formed about 68 CE from a coalition of resistance groups who withdrew to Jerusalem, as noted in the quotation just given. On the other hand, there may be a reference to their existence already as early as the beginning of the war in late 66 or early 67 (*War* 2.22.1 §651):

> Ananus, nevertheless, cherished the thought of gradually abandoning these warlike preparations and bending the malcontents and the infatuated so-called zealots to a more salutary policy; but he succumbed to their violence, and the sequel of our narrative will show the fate which befell him.

The question is whether "zealot" here is a proper name or only an epithet. The context suggests a name; if so, there is nothing to rule out a longer history.

What is clear is that they should not be confused with the Sicarii whose history is better known (see above); even if the Zealots may have had some organic connection with the Fourth Philosophy/Sicarii at some point, they are kept separate by Josephus. The Zealots fought bravely and fanatically in the final siege of Jerusalem, and most of them perished in the battle. The Sicarii had left Jerusalem long before. It was they, not the Zealots, who held out at Masada, despite Yadin's confusing reference to that last holdout against Rome as Zealot (Yadin 1966).

One of the reasons that the Zealots should not be used confusedly of all groups is that a number of these parties fought one another before the Romans finally tightened the siege. There were several factional leaders rivaling one another in the final months of the war. The result was that even while Titus was preparing the final siege of Jerusalem, three separate groups controlled different portions of the city and fought each other ferociously. Josephus summarizes the situation at the beginning of his Book 5 (*War* 5.1.1–3 §§1–20).

SYNTHESIS

Charlesworth, J. H. (ed.) (1992) *The Messiah: Developments in Earliest Judaism and Christianity.*

Charlesworth, J. H., H. Lichtenberger, and G. S. Oegema (eds) (1998) *Qumran-Messianism: Studies on the Messianic Expections in the Dead Sea Scrolls.*

Collins, J. J. (1995) *The Scepter and the Star: The Messiahs of the Dead Sea Scrolls and Other Ancient Literature.*

Day, J. (ed.) (1998) *King and Messiah in Israel and the Ancient Near East: Proceedings of the Oxford Old Testament Seminar.*

Grabbe, L. L. (2000a) "Eschatology in Philo and Josephus", in A. Avery-Peck and J. Neusner (eds) *Judaism in Late Antiquity: Part 4 Death, Life-after-Death, Resurrection and the World-to-Come in the Judaisms of Antiquity*: 163–85.

Laato, A. (1997) *A Star Is Rising: The Historical Development of the Old Testament Royal Ideology and the Rise of the Jewish Messianic Expectations.*

Neusner, J. (1984) *Messiah in Context: Israel's History and Destiny in Formative Judaism.*

Neusner, J., W. S. Green, and E. S. Frerichs (eds) (1987) *Judaisms and Their Messiahs at the Turn of the Christian Era.*

Oegema, G. S. (1998) *The Anointed and his People: Messianic Expectations from the Maccabees to Bar Kochba.*

Zerbe, G. M. (1993) *Non-Retaliation in Early Jewish and New Testament Texts: Ethical Themes in Social Contexts.*

Zimmerman, J. (1998) *Messianische Texte aus Qumran: Königliche, priesterliche und prophetische Messiasvorstellungen in den Schriftfunden von Qumran.*

Several recent studies have attempted to survey the general question of messiahs and messianic figures during the Second Temple period (Oegema 1998; Collins 1995; Day 1998; Charlesworth 1992; Neusner/Green/Frerichs 1987). Other specialized studies have focused on particular texts or figures (Zimmerman 1998; Charlesworth/Lichtenberger/Oegema 1998; Grabbe 2000a). These now supersede many of the older works which have serious methodological flaws, or which drew on defective editions of sources or lacked sources now available today. As will be clear from the survey of sources given above, there was not a uniform belief or a unilinear development of beliefs, though the main source of such beliefs in all their variety appears to have been the anointed ruler and the anointed priest of pre-exilic times.

First, the question raised by the Jesus and the NT view of him must be confronted. The Greek title *christos* "anointed" evidently became applied to Jesus within the decades after his death. Some Gospel passages also picture him as being asked whether he was "the Christ" – evidently a reference to a Jewish belief in the coming of a messiah. The problem for the scholar of early Judaism is that the Gospels have their own agenda, centering on Jesus and the development of Christology. The NT gives us some glimpse into messianic expectations, but to use it alone is to gain a very distorted view of the true situation and to overlook the genuine complexity of the subject among the various Jewish groups and communities.

Having objected to the gross simplification found in so many treatments of the subject, I am well aware of the dangers of trying to synthesize the diversity of views and texts, especially since some texts are still not clear about the views. Nevertheless, it is necessary to try to bring some order into the quite multifarious situation. Any synthesis is to some extent a distortion, but if it is realized that what follows is dealing with the question at a broad level and that a full understanding requires an engagement with the sources in all their individuality, such an exercise can be useful. Five strands of thought on the messiah can be identified:

1. The pre-exilic roots (cf. Day 1998; Laato 1999) of the "messiah" lay in the main "anointed" figure (Hebrew *māšîăḥ*; Aramaic *měšîḥā'*), who was the king (e. g., 1 Sam. 10:1; 16:1, 13; 24:7; Psalm 2). The term could be used not only of a native king but also of a foreign king such as Cyrus who was seen as a deliverer (Isa. 45:1–6). However, the high priest was also anointed and could be called by that title (Lev. 7–8; 10:7; Ps. 133:2). These two concepts appear to inform and channel all the speculations on the subject in the Second Temple period.

2. The idea of a future earthly king also had its OT roots since a number of passages refer to David *redivivus*, an ideal king on the model of David who would rule a restored Israel. It is the picture that probably appealed to many Jews throughout the Second Temple period, though the actual attestation in extant texts is somewhat skimpy: the *Psalms of Solomon* 17–18, various hints in Josephus about different revolutionary movements, and perhaps

4 Ezra 7. Bar Kokhba may have seen himself or been seen as an earthly messiah, though interpretation of the full data is difficult (*JCH*: 579–81).

3. A priestly figure seems to be the concept embodied in the Qumran "messiah of Aaron". If Ben Sira had expectations of a messianic figure (a disputed question), it was probably in this mold.

4. A number of passages picture a heavenly messiah, including 11QMelchizedek, 4 Ezra 13, and the *Similitudes of Enoch*. The messiah of 2 Baruch is revealed from heaven, though whether he is a heavenly figure is uncertain.

5. No messianic figure is evident in several texts, such as the Wisdom of Solomon, Philo, and the *Testament of Abraham*. These stress individual eschatology and the immediate judgment of the individual after death, the soul being the essence of the person. Such texts seem to sublimate national eschatology to wider concerns about the Jewish people. Although it is possible that messianic views were extant but were suppressed for fear of persecution, the overall theology of these writers does not require a messianic figure. Neither does the world view found in the Mishnah (Neusner 1984); even though a messiah appears in the Amoraic literature, it is very much a tamed and future figure, and does not correspond to the strong apocalyptic view found in some pre-70 texts.

One of the topics that arises perennially is the question of whether there was a "suffering messiah" concept in pre-70 Judaism. Again, this is usually raised in a NT context and concerns the question of whether the idea of Jesus's suffering had precedents in Judaism. The question was answered in the negative in recent times, with no pre-70 sources indicating such an idea. The death of the messiah in 4 Ezra 7:29 has no redemptive significance – he is not a "suffering messiah"; rather, he dies along with all humans alive at the time in order to set the stage for the general resurrection and judgment. The one figure produced frequently in the past to justify the concept of a messiah who suffers and dies is the "messiah ben Joseph" of some rabbinic writings, but this concept is presently known only from late texts and may well be a construct developed to counter Christian ideas about Jesus or to justify the acclaim of Bar Kokhba as the messiah after he had been killed by the Romans.

Now, some of the Qumran scrolls have caused the question to be reopened (p. 275 above). There are several issues here (though each has been considered above under the appropriate set of texts). The first concerns the "suffering servant" of Deutero-Isaiah. The concept has been of great interest to both OT and NT scholars and has produced an enormous amount of scholarly literature, but most of it is irrelevant to our question. As far as we can tell, the servant of Isaiah 40–55 was not a messianic figure in its original context; on the other hand, one or two people have thought they could find a messianic interpretation (or hints of it) in some of the Qumran scrolls. So far this has not produced good evidence for a "suffering messiah". Another issue concerns the attempt to find a "pierced messiah" in 4Q285; this has been more or less resolved in a consensus among Qumran scholars that no such figure in fact exists in this text (p. 275 above). As far as can be determined from present textual evidence, the NT view of Jesus as both a messiah and one who suffered and died for the sins of his people was developed from the experience of the early church and has no precedent as such in Judaism.

Oegema's study (1998) attempts to relate the messianic expectations at different times to the historical circumstances in Palestine. This is to some extent successful. There are two factors complicating the issue, however. The first is the variety of expectations that existed at the same time in different parts of Judaism. The second is the fact that messianic beliefs, like many others, can take on an intellectual and emotional life of their own once they become a part of a widespread worldview. This development cannot always be related to the social situation in a simple way, and it would be a mistake to see the different views as simply a reflection of, and determined by, social developments.

14

JEWS AND JUDAISM IN THE HELLENISTIC WORLD

This chapter mainly concentrates on how the Jews and Judaism were looked at in the wider context of the Hellenistic and Roman ancient Near East (we have no real information from the Persian period). Although including Palestine, it especially focuses on the Diaspora. The chapter brings together several disparate topics, but they all relate to two basic questions: How did the Jews see themselves? How were the Jews and Judaism perceived by non-Jews? Two issues of importance for the inside view are those of the land of Israel and attitudes toward it, both in Palestine and in the Diaspora, and the question of gender and sexuality which affected how many individual Jews saw their own identity.

HOW THEY SAW THEMSELVES

Jewish identity and conversion

Binder, D. D. (1999) *Into the Temple Courts: The Place of the Synagogues in the Second Temple Period.*

Carleton Paget, J. (1996) "Jewish Proselytism at the Time of Christan Origins: Chimera or Reality?" *JSNT* 62:65–103.

Cohen, S. J. D. (1999) *The Beginnings of Jewishness: Boundaries, Varieties, Uncertainties.*

Feldman, L. H. (1993) *Jew and Gentile in the Ancient World: Attitudes and Interactions from Alexander to Justinian.*

Goodman, M. (1992) "Jewish Proselytising in the First Century", in Judith Lieu, J. L. North, and Tessa Rajak (eds) *Jews among Pagans and Christians in the Roman Empire*: 53–78.

—— (1994) *Mission and Conversion: Proselytizing in the Religious History of the Roman Empire.*

Grabbe, L. L. (2000h) "Hat die Bibel doch recht? A Review of T. L. Thompson's *The Bible in History*", *Scandinavian Journal of the Old Testament* 14: 114–38.

—— (forthcoming b) Review of S. J. D. Cohen, *The Beginnings of Jewishness*, *JNES*.

Jones, S., and S. Pearce (eds) (1998) *Jewish Local Patriotism and Self-Identification in the Graeco-Roman Period*.

Kraabel, A. T. (1981) "The Disappearance of the 'God-fearers'", *Numen* 28: 113–26.

Levinskaya, I. (ed.) (1996) *The Book of Acts in Its Diaspora Setting*.

McKnight, S. (1991) *A Light among the Gentiles: Jewish Missionary Activity in the Second Temple Period*.

Murphy-O'Connor, J. (1992) "Lots of God-Fearers? 'Theosebeis' in the Aphrodisias Inscription", *RB* 99: 418–24.

Nolland, J. (1981) "Uncircumcised Proselytes?" *JSJ* 12: 173–94.

Reynolds, J., and R. Tannenbaum (1987) *Jews and Godfearers at Aphrodisias*.

Rutgers, L. V. (1998) "Roman Policy towards the Jews: Expulsions from the City of Rome during the First Century C.E.", *The Hidden Heritage of Diaspora Judaism*: 171–97

Smith, J. Z. (1980) "Fences and Neighbors: Some Contours of Early Judaism", in W. S. Green (ed.) *Approaches to Ancient Judaism, Volume II*: 1–25.

Thompson, T. L. (1999) *The Bible in History: How Writers Create a Past* (UK title); *The Mythic Past: Biblical Archaeology and the Myth of Israel* (USA title).

Wander, B. (1998) *Gottesfürchtige und Sympathisanten: Studien zum heidnischen Umfeld von Diasporasynagogen*.

Will, E., and C. Orrieux (1992) *Prosélytisme juif? Histoire d'une erreur*.

On the question of Jewish identity, there are a number of issues to be dealt with here:

- Who was a Jew? How did one become a Jew in the first place?
- Could a non-Jew convert to Judaism?
- What was the process of conversion?
- Was there a Jewish "mission" to seek converts?
- Could one cease to be a Jew?
- Who are the "God-fearers" found in a number of ancient sources?

Like most religions at this time, Judaism was primarily an ethnic religion. You were a Jew because you were born a Jew, and if you were born a Jew, you lived by the Jewish religious law. This view has recently been challenged (Thompson 1999: 254–66), but the alternative opinion is not likely to be embraced by scholars of Second Temple Judaism (Grabbe 2000h; for a full investigation of the question, see Cohen 1999). It may be that at certain points in some documents "Jew/Jewish" had a purely religious content, such as embracing the Jewish religion, though perhaps even then there may always have been ethnic overtones.

Personal Jewish identity was usually bound up with certain specific items, particularly:

- the central institution was the temple and its cult, most important in Palestine itself but also a spiritual center for Jews in the Diaspora
- the concept of the land, as a possession and home for individuals but also as the place which God had chosen and where he had made his own abode in some sense – the land as a divine inheritance had been a part of Israelite thinking from an early period
- belief in one God
- the concept of being a part of the "chosen people"
- the rejection of images in worship
- the "Torah" (i.e. those traditions and interpretations of the OT seen as important for religious identity and religious observance)
- circumcision

Most of these characteristics are straightforward; they seem to occur in almost all groups as far as we can determine, and Greco-Roman writers often remark on them. It is difficult to find persons identifying themselves as Jews who lack one or more of these, yet we can find an exception to almost every one if we look hard enough. What about the the Leontopolis temple which lasted until 70 CE? How did the Samaritans fit in with their temple on Gerizim? The land was a rather distant ideal for many Diaspora Jews: how many regarded it as high in importance to their identity? The question of belief in one God is not as straightforward as one would like (see pp. 210–19 above). Some of the iconography found in synagogues (admittedly these are all post-70) and in coins press hard on the aniconic concept. On circumcision, see the discussion below. The most problematic item is possibly "Torah" since there is evidence that different Jews had different ideas about what should be included in the concept (canon), the interpretation of that which was included (exegesis), and the relative importance of the accepted traditions (authority).

Therefore, defining a core of beliefs which were a *sine qua non* for being a Jew is difficult. Yet the basic religious heritage was the same for Jews of every stripe: that legacy was essentially the story of Israel. God had been involved in the life of the people since Creation. A line connected each Jew/Israelite back to the first man Adam and the first woman Eve, but it was Abraham who had been the one chosen from all the other nations and peoples to be the father of God's people. A special covenant had been made with Abraham, and a special covenant had been made with his descendants, the people of Israel. "We are Abraham's seed and heirs according to the promise" is a claim which every Jew could and most would make (cf. Gal. 3:29). The Torah told them about the promise, and circumcision was the sign in the flesh confirming it. Certain practices also marked them off from the surrounding peoples: refusal to eat particular meats, observance of the sabbath or other festivals, and perhaps some purity regulations. These points were universal. Yet there were some interesting distinctions between the natives of Judea and those living in the Diaspora.

Jewish identity was usually a matter of birth. Problems arose only if one

- had one Jewish and one non-Jewish parent
- was a Gentile but wanted to become a Jew
- had been a Jew but renounced the ancestral religion.

Various passages in the OT indicate that outsiders could become part of the community and take on its religious identity (cf. Exod. 12:43–49; Deut. 23:4–9; Ruth 1:16–17). Sojourners among the people were also expected to conform to Jewish religious practices even while remaining outsiders (Num. 15:15). How early these passages are to be dated is a question, and one can query whether any are earlier than the Second Temple period. In any case, the question of conversion seems to have become an issue mainly in the Greek and Roman periods. We know of a number of specific examples in antiquity in which gentiles were converted to Judaism, as well as a general attitude which allowed conversion. The whole royal house of Adiabene was apparently converted around the turn of the era, and Queen Helena was instrumental in helping to avert a famine in Judea (*Ant.* 20.2.3–5 §§41–53). The NT mentions examples of conversion (Acts 6:5), as does rabbinic literature.

The process of conversion is nowhere described in pre-70 sources. One apparently just began to live by Jewish religious practices. We have no indication of a formalized ceremony, involving a priest or any other figure. For men circumcision was clearly the main formal step (cf. Smith 1980: 10–15). In an anecdote told by Josephus (*Ant.* 20.2.3–4 §§41–43), the king of Adiabene was advised by one Jewish merchant that he could convert without circumcision because of his special status as king, but another Jew convinced him that circumcision was necessary. It was the latter advice that the king followed. This is the only example to suggest that circumcision was not a necessity for full entry into the Jewish community. If the story is read in context, there seems no reason to think of a general practice of conversion without circumcision; rather, this was a special case involving a king with potentially hostile subjects (cf. Nolland 1981: 192–94). Thus, circumcision seems to be a universal practice for male proselytes. We have no information with regard to women. It is frequently asserted in handbooks and commentaries that both males and females had to undergo a ritual bath ("proselyte baptism"), as well as circumcision for males (Schürer: 3.173–74). Although this is a practice referred to in rabbinic literature (e. g., *B. Yeb.* 46a), we have no evidence for it before 70 (Cohen 1999: 168–70, 222–23). Indeed, the silence of Josephus and other sources suggests that such was not the practice. It may well be that the baptism ritual developed under the influence of Christianity.

With mixed marriages, it probably depended on how the offspring was brought up. One who was circumcized and brought up as a Jew was not likely to have had his Jewishness called into question. But if not, could one claim to be a Jew by having a Jewish mother? This matrilinear transfer of Jewishness is well known from later Judaism until the present day and seems to go back as far as the Amoraic period, but there is no evidence of such a practice operating before 70. On the contrary, both rabbinic evidence and such examples as Acts 16:1–3 indicate that ethnic identity tended to be passed on from the father (Cohen 1999: 263–73, 363–77).

The main obstacle to conversion was the requirement of circumcision, which is why converts were more often women than men. This is also why there developed a group of adherents to the community, often men, who took on Jewish observances without making the full step of circumcision and complete conversion. These were frequently designated by the term "God-fearer" (*theosebēs* in Greek, cf. the terms *seboumenoi, phoboumenoi* in Acts; Wander 1998). The existence of these individuals has been disputed, partly because many of the references to "God-fearers" in the early sources are simply to pious Jews (Feldman 1993: 342–43). More recently, Kraabel has argued that the term "God-fearer" and "semi-proselyte" should be dropped as non-existent entities (e.g. 1981). However, the discovery of the Aphrodisias inscription (Reynolds/Tannenbaum 1987) has convinced most scholars that "God-fearer" did often have the technical meaning of one who adhered to Judaism, even being a member of a synagogue, without having undergone circumcision (Levinskaya 1996: 51–126; Binder 1999: 380–89; Schürer: 3.1.150–76; cf. Murphy-O'Connor 1992).

It was once proposed that there was an extensive Jewish "mission" to seek converts, parallel to the Christian mission that developed in the early church (see the list of scholars putting forward this thesis in Feldman 1993: 555–56). As discussed in the previous paragraphs, we know that some gentiles converted to Judaism, and no doubt Jews were instrumental in this, by teaching Judaism or at least by providing information and answering questions. We cannot assume that Jews were always just passive instruments in the process; it is likely that some Jews took a more active role. There are some episodes where our sources assert that certain Jews were seeking converts (e.g. in Rome in 19 CE; see the discussion in *JCH*: 398; Carleton Paget 1996: 88–90; Rutgers 1998: 171–97). The question is whether such scattered episodes, even if interpreted as positive evidence of active proselytizing, amount to more than the initiative of a few individual Jews. A number of recent studies have argued against any widespread conversion activity (McKnight 1991; Goodman 1992; 1994). Their evidence is well presented; however, Carleton Paget (1996) has rightly noted that we cannot necessarily lump all Jews together. It seems to me that one can accept some missionary activity on the part of some Jews without assuming a wholesale or organized mission as such. The question of whether Judaism was perceived as a Hellenistic mystery cult may also bear on this issue (*JCH*: 533).

The question of those who abandoned Judaism is more difficult than it might seem on the surface. For example, Josephus says that Philo's nephew Tiberius Julius Alexander had abandoned his ancestral religion (*War* 2.5.2 §100); however, we are given insufficient data to make sense of this. Is this a judgment of Josephus which Tiberius Alexander would have hotly disputed? Did Tiberius Alexander renounce his Judaism? Or did he quietly ignore Jewish practices when not in the Jewish community? Was he never circumcized, or did he submit to epispasm, or was the circumcision simply ignored as if it were a physical blemish? Similarly, those judged to be evildoers by the authors of 1 and 2 Maccabees would probably have considered themselves fully Jewish (e.g. Jason; see *JCH*: 256–58, 277–81). Even those (few!) who disguised their circumcision may have regarded themselves as practitioners of an enlightened Judaism). We can only guess because we do not have their side of the story. 3 Macc. 1:3 similarly mentions a Jew named Dositheus who had "abandoned the law and left the customs of his fathers", but no details are given and precise interpretation is impossible.

Ideology of the land and the concept of exile

Barstad, H. M. (1996) *The Myth of the Empty Land: A Study in the History and Archaeology of Judah During the "Exilic" Period*.

Becking, B. (1992) *The Fall of Samaria: An Historical and Archaeological Study*.

Carroll, R. P. (1992) "The Myth of the Empty Land", in D. Jobling and T. Pippin (eds) *Ideological Criticism of Biblical Texts*: 79–93.

Davies, W. D. (1974) *The Gospel and the Land: Early Christianity and Jewish Territorial Doctrine*.

—— (1982) *The Territorial Dimensions of Judaism*.

Gafni, I. M. (1997) *Land, Center and Diaspora: Jewish Constructs in Late Antiquity*.

Grabbe, L. L. (ed.) (1998b) *Leading Captivity Captive: "The Exile" as History and Ideology*.

Hasel, G. F. (1972) *The Remnant: The History and Theology of the Remnant Idea from Genesis to Isaiah*.

—— (1976) "Remnant", *IDBSup*: 735–36.

Hausmann, J. (1987) *Israels Rest: Studien zum Selbstverständnis der nachexilischen Gemeinde*.

Mendels, D. (1987) *The Land of Israel as a Political Concept in Hasmonean Literature*.

—— (1992) *The Rise and Fall of Jewish Nationalism: The History of Jewish and Christian Ethnicity in Palestine within the Greco-Roman Period (200 B.C.E.– 135 C.E.)*.

Oded, B. (1979) *Mass Deportations and Deportees in the Neo-Assyrian Empire.*

Roberts, J. J. M. (1973) "The Davidic Origin of the Zion Tradition", *JBL* 92: 329–44.

—— (1982) "Zion in the Theology of the Davidic-Solomonic Empire", in T. Ishida, *Studies in the Period of David and Solomon and Other Essays: Papers Read at the International Symposium for Biblical Studies, Tokyo, 5–7 December, 1979*: 93–108.

Scott, J. M. (1997) (ed.) *Exile: Old Testament, Jewish, and Christian Conceptions.*

Unnik, W. C. van (1993) *Das Selbstverständnis der jüdischen Diaspora in der hellenistisch-römischen Zeit.*

It seems evident that there was a Diaspora from an early time. The deportation policy of the Assyrians, and later the Babylonians and Persians, caused many thousands, or even millions, of people to be shifted around the ancient Near East after defeat (Oded 1979). First, Samaria fell to the Assyrians about 722 BCE (cf. Becking 1992); then more than a century later in 587 the Southern Kingdom fell to Nebuchadnezzar. It seems likely that quite a few of the people were left in the land, but clearly there was a large population exchange, even if the precise number deported and imported can only be guessed at. To the best of our knowledge, the descendants of those taken from the Samarian region never returned and became lost to history (hence, the legend of the "Ten Lost Tribes"), but a return of the Judeans is described in the early chapters of Ezra.

A theology of the land is attested in literature no later than the Persian period and may have already developed during the period of the Israelite monarchy. A number of elements contributed to such a view, including belief in "the inviolability of Zion" that we find in several biblical passages (cf. Roberts 1973; 1982). Central to the belief was that God had promised the land to Abraham and his descendants: the "promised land" was Israel's by right and any other inhabitants were interlopers. The independence of the Jewish state made Jews aware of the importance of their own land, and this in turn led to further theological reflection when Judah came under foreign domination again. Many biblical passages focus on the importance of the land and how Israel/Judah might lose it, with exile from the land one of the worst punishments (e.g. Lev. 26; Deut. 28; 1 Kings 8:34, 46–43; Isa. 40:1–11; 51:9–23). Whether any of these passages is earlier than 587 BCE might be debated, but they and statements in post-exilic literature (e.g. Ezra–Nehemiah) show that a strong theology of the land had developed by the Persian period at the latest.

This theology dominates the present text which often carries the pattern of sin–punishment–exile–repentance–return (see the essays in Scott 1997; Grabbe 1998b). A good many of the passages on this theme have been dated by scholars to the Persian period. Judah had been punished for her sins by being removed from the land, but the punishment was now complete, and

Yhwh had intervened to cause her to return. Another theme also appears: the concept of the purified remnant. The remnant idea can be found in a variety of texts in the ancient Near East (cf. Hasel 1972; 1976), but the idea of a remnant which had been purified by the "fire" of exile became especially important in some OT texts (e.g. Isa. 6:11–13; see Hausman 1987). The returnees were this remnant (Zech. 8:6, 11, 12) but also the nucleus of a new "holy" community (Isa. 6:13), while the peoples living in the land were foreigners usurping what God had given to his people. The fact that the majority of the population had not been taken from the land (Carroll 1992; Barstad 1996), with their descendants making up the bulk of the population, was ignored. The main theme in Ezra is this conflict between those living in the land and those returning from exile, whether hindering the building of the temple or creating problems by intermarriage. Ezra's prayer emphasizes that, as a "surviving remnant", the community of the newly returned must not become entangled in the "uncleanness" of the people around them (Ezra 9:8–15).

We do not have much information on the subject from the first part of the Greek period. A book such as Tobit (pp. 44–45 above), which is likely to be from this time, suggests how those in the Diaspora lived and thought, including how they continued to look toward Jerusalem where the surviving Israelites would return to rebuild the temple (Tobit 14:4–7). Whether the doctrine of the land was used as an excuse for Hasmonean expansion is a question, though *Jubilees* and the fragments of Eupolemus might suggest this. Through the second and first centuries – moving from Seleucid rule to the Hasmonean "greater Israel" to subordination by Rome – we see a range of attitudes (see Mendels 1988 for a survey). Alongside the belief that the land belongs to Israel and all others should be eliminated (the view well known from many biblical texts) appear other beliefs. For example, *Jubilees* distinguishes between the "Canaanites" who should be eliminated and the Edomites who are kin to Israel and, despite friction, can be accommodated by being brought under Israelite rule (*Jub.* 35–38); the same contrast applies to the Ishmaelites with whom they should also live in peace (*Jub.* 22:1–4).

Once Judah had lost its independence again, we see reactions to this, with both attempts to justify this loss of independence and the continuing exile, and also a desire to regain lost territories. The sins of the Jews are seen as the cause of the new domination by foreigners (*Ps. Sol.* 2:1–14; 8:1–22; 17:5–18). A spiritualization of the concept of the land and exile is found in some literature (e.g. Philo, *Spec. Leg.* 4.178; *Somn.* 2.250). Others saw possession of the land in eschatological terms (e.g. *Ps. Sol.* 17–18; *Ant.* 18.1.1 §§4–8). It is likely that this strong theology of the land was a factor in the various revolts through the first century, culminating in the 66–70 revolt.

The view of the land of Israel did not all go in one direction, however (Gafni 1996: 27–40). Perhaps as a reaction to the terra-centric view of many Jews in Palestine, some of those in the Diaspora came up with counterproposals that helped to neutralize the land ideology by taking away any stigma of living outside the land. This is not surprising since the majority of Jews were living in the Diaspora by the turn of the era. One justification was that living abroad as "colonists" was an honorable state, indicating God's blessings on Israel by widening its habitation (cf. *Ant.* 4.6.4 §115). Another was the Jewish witness or mission to Gentiles by living among them (cf. Tob. 13:6, though the evidence for this is mainly from later rabbinic statements). Although the evidence is not always straightforward, some data point to Jews who maintained their Jewish identity but also regarded their local region as their "fatherland" (*patris* [Gafni 1996: 41–57), a form of what might be called "local patriotism". There is even evidence that in the talmudic period, the Babylonian Jews developed a pro-Babylonian stance in which Babylonia was seen as Abraham's original home which had some of the same qualities as the land of Israel, though this was in part a response to a strong land ideology being developed among Palestinian rabbis (Gafni 1996: 58–78).

It is known that the practice of interment in the land of Israel of the bodies of those died abroad was an indication of the land ideology; however, it seems that this did not develop until the third century CE, long after the Second Temple period (Gafni 1996: 79–95).

Gender and sexuality

Archer, L. J. (1990) *Her Price Is Beyond Rubies: The Jewish Woman in Graeco-Roman Palestine.*

Arjava, A. (1996) *Women and Law in Late Antiquity.*

Bar-Ilan, M. (1998) *Some Jewish Women in Antiquity.*

Brenner, A. (ed.) (1995) *A Feminist Companion to Esther, Judith and Susanna.*

Brody, R. (1999) "Evidence for Divorce by Jewish Women?" *JJS* 50: 230–34.

Brooten, B. J. (1982) *Women Leaders in the Ancient Synagogue.*

—— (1991) "Iael προστάτης in the Jewish Donative Inscription from Aphrodisias", in B. A. Pearson (ed.) *The Future of Early Christianity: Essays in Honor of Helmut Koester*: 149–62.

—— (1996) *Love between Women: Early Christian Responses to Female Homoeroticism.*

Brosius, M. (1996) *Women in Ancient Persia (559–331 BC).*

Brown, C. A. (1992) *No Longer be Silent: First Century Jewish Portraits of Biblical Women: Studies in Pseudo-Philo's* Biblical Antiquities *and Josephus's* Jewish Antiquities.

Camp, C. V. (1991) "Understanding a Patriarchy: Women in Second Century Jerusalem Through the Eyes of Ben Sira", in A.-J. Levine (ed.) *"Women Like This": New Perspectives on Jewish Women in the Greco-Roman World*: 1–39.

Cotton, H. M. (1995) "The Archive of Salome Komaïse Daughter of Levi: Another Archive from the 'Cave of Letters'", *ZPE* 105: 171–208.

Douglas, M. (1966) *Purity and Danger: An Analysis of the Concepts of Pollution and Taboo.*

Fitzmyer, J. A., SJ (1999) "The So-Called Aramaic Divorce Text from Wadi Seiyal", *Eretz-Israel* 26: 16*–22*.

Goodman, M. (1991) "Babatha's Story", *JRS* 81:169–75.

Horst, P. W. van der (1995) "Images of Women in Ancient Judaism", in R. Kloppenborg and W. J. Hanegraaff (eds) *Female Stereotypes in Religious Traditions*: 43–60.

Ilan, T. (1995) *Jewish Women in Greco-Roman Palestine: An Inquiry into Image and Status.*

—— (1999) *Integrating Women into Second Temple History.*

Isaac, B. (1992) "The Babatha Archive", *IEJ* 42: 62–75.

Kraemer, R. S. (1992) *Her Share of the Blessings: Women's Religions among Pagans, Jews and Christians in the Greco-Roman World.*

Levine, A.-J. (ed.) (1991) *"Women Like This": New Perspectives on Jewish Women in the Greco-Roman World.*

Lewis, N. (1994) "The Babatha Archive: A Response", *IEJ* 44: 243–46.

McKeating, H. (1979) "Sanctions against Adultery in Ancient Israelite Society, With Some Reflections on Methodology in the Study of Old Testament Ethics", *JSOT* 11: 57–72.

Muffs, Y. (1969) *Studies in the Aramaic Legal Papyri from Elephantine.*

Neusner, J. (1973b) *The Idea of Purity in Ancient Judaism: The Haskell Lectures, 1972–1973.*

—— (1981) *Judaism: The Evidence of the Mishnah.*

Newsom, C. A., and S. H. Ringe (eds) (1998) *Women's Bible Commentary: Expanded Edition.*

Nissinen, M. (1998) *Homoeroticism in the Biblical World: A Historical Perspective.*

Rajak, T. (1992) "The Jewish Community and its Boundaries", in J. Lieu, J. L. North, and T. Rajak (eds) *Jews among Pagans and Christians in the Roman Empire*: 9–28.

Rajak, T., and D. Noy (1993) *"Archisynagogoi*: Office, Title and Social Status in the Greco-Jewish Synagogue", *JRS* 83: 75–93.

Schottroff, L., S. Schroer, and M.-T. Wacker (1998) *Feminist Interpretation: The Bible in Women's Perspective.*

Szesnat, H. (1999) "Philo and Female Homoeroticism: Philo's Use of γύνανδρος and Recent Work on *Tribades*", *JSJ* 30: 140–47.

One of the aims of recent history writing has been to include ordinary men and women in its purview. This is often easier said than done because literary sources tend to focus on the upper classes and the wealthy. Yet archaeology and some other sources may give us a surprising glimpse into the lives of ordinary people, such as the women Babatha (Isaac 1992; Lewis 1994; Goodman 1991) and Salome Komaïse (Cotton 1995). Ilan (1999) has recently suggested ways in which women may be made a part of Second Temple Judaism, and a number of studies have attempted to dig out information on women that had previously been overlooked (e.g. Brooten 1982; Kraemer

1992). The subject is a large one and can only briefly be addressed here because of limitations of space. Four general points can be made, and then selected illustrations follow:

1. We can begin by recognizing that the various Jewish communities of this period existed in a patriarchal society. The paterfamilias – the head of the household – was usually the eldest man, and he wielded considerable authority in the eyes of both law and society. Legally, women were usually considered to be under the authority of either their father or their husband (or sometimes other male family members such as a brother).

2. Within this given, however, the relationships between the sexes were often very complex, and one's status and position was determined not only by gender but also by social class, wealth, and societal attitudes and expectations. Just acknowledging the patriarchal nature of Jewish society does not take our analysis very far (cf. Camp 1991). The "oppressor/oppressed" model is a caricature and fails to bring any subtlety or nuance to the actual situation.

3. Neither legally nor socially were women and children "mere chattels", in spite of restrictions placed on their activities (cf. Muffs 1969: 54–56). Legally, women were restricted in matters of inheritance, ownership, custody of children, and power to act as a free citizen. Socially, women were confined to a clearly defined sphere of activity which tended to center around the home and family. The fact that the legal position of women and children was often unacceptable from a modern point of view (though that can be said of the position of women and children in many modern societies) should not allow us to assume that the complex relationships within a family that we know today were any different in antiquity. The love of a husband for his wife and a father for his daughters is not a twentieth-century invention. Families are and have always been complex entities, varying greatly from family to family, and intra-family relations do not necessarily conform to their position from a legal point of view. But the legal and social position of Jewish women seems also to have varied considerably between communities, depending on the wider society in which they were situated.

4. Some of the religious regulations, especially those relating to purity rules, are understood by anthropologists as a means of social control and assigning women to a particular sphere of life (see pp. 140–41 above).

On the question of marriage, it is not always possible to speak generally since customs varied from place to place and over time. Also, there is often a question of how far one can generalize from specific examples, and when the examples come from literature (as is frequently the case) there is always a question of whether they are descriptive of actual practice in society or only literary devices. With these caveats, some general comments can be made with caution, though they naturally risk oversimplification.

As was common in the ancient Near East, marriage was normally arranged between the husband (or his family) and the father or nearest male relative of the woman (e.g. Gen. 24:50–57; 2 Sam. 13:1–13), though at least in theory the woman had some say in the matter (cf. Gen. 24:57). This arrangement with a male relative was apparently not invariable, especially in the case of a widow or unmarried woman without close male relatives. Widows and divorced women (if not living in the parental home) seem to have had considerable autonomy to act independently (cf. Judith). As usual, independence for both men and women depended greatly on wealth: only those with sufficient wealth could hope to maintain an independent lifestyle, but a wealthy woman without close male relatives could apparently have done so. On the other hand, even a woman of the rank of Salome the sister of Herod had to bow to his decisions about such things as marriage (cf. *Ant.* 16.7.6 §§221–25), though it must be said that this applied equally to Herod's sons and the other men in his household.

In the home itself the wife and older females seem to have had a good deal of autonomy. Women were usually in charge of activities in the home. Judging from modern societies in the Middle East, which are still often patriarchal legally and socially, women had a great deal of freedom of action in the home and in female society, and the interference of men was greatly restricted. The place of women in public roles is more difficult to ascertain since some of the stories of such are clearly fiction. For example, what should we glean about women from the story of the extraordinary exploits of Judith? (cf. the essays in Brenner 1995). What about the figure of Wisdom who is represented as a woman but also in some cases as a goddess? Some of the women we know about were high in society, such as Queen Helena of the royal house of Adiabene which converted to Judaism (cf. Brosius 1996 on what we know of Persian women). Queen Helena did a number of good deeds for the Jews in Palestine (*Ant.* 20.2.5 §§49–53). We also know of Berenice the sister of Agrippa II who was supposedly admired by Titus at one point as a potential wife. She was a queen in her own right and bore this title (*JCH*: 436; cf. Acts 25:24, 26; 26:2, 19, 27 where the author shows his ignorance by not having Festus and Paul address her as queen along with her brother as king). It has been argued that women could be heads of synagogues and hold other offices (Brooten 1982; 1991; van der Horst 1995: 58–60; but see the criticisms of Rajak [1992: 22–24] and Rajak/Noy [1993: 83–87]).

Women could own property at all times, from all that we know, though the exact situation is best attested in legal documents known from Elephantine in the Persian period and from the Judean desert papyri from the 1st century CE. According to several first-century marriage contracts, any property brought into the marriage by a woman continued to belong to her and would pass on to her children in the event of her death. The income from the property of married women could be used by their husbands, but the property remained theirs and would be taken with them if they divorced or would be passed to their children if they died (cf. the marriage contracts from Murabba'at and Naḥal Ḥever). Although it has usually been assumed that women could not initiate divorce in Palestine, they certainly could in the Elephantine community in Egypt (*AP* 15 = *TAD* B2.6; *TAD* B3.8; Muffs 1969: 3, 55). Josephus says that Salome, Herod's sister, divorced her husband (*Ant.* 15.7.10 §259), though this has usually been explained as invoking Greco-Roman custom; also her royal status marked her off from other Jewish women. However, Ilan has recently argued that XHev/Ṣe ar 13 shows evidence that an ordinary Jewish woman sent her husband a bill of divorcement (1999: 253–62). Ilan's argument that this interpretation should not be rejected out of hand is valid, but the question of whether it is still the most likely interpretation has not been settled (Brody 1999; Fitzmyer 1999).

The purity regulations of Jewish law would have affected the daily lives of all Jews, men and women, but they especially impinged on the lives of Jewish women (Neusner 1971; 1981). Pre-menopausal adults would have had a significant portion of each month during which they would have had to restrict their contact with others because the impurity would otherwise be passed on. As discussed in a previous chapter (pp. 140–41), purity regulations are strictest in those societies where a great deal of control is placed on the freedom of women. One of the questions one must ask is to what extent the various purity regulations would have been observed by ordinary Jews. All indications are that the basic regulations were heeded and acted on by most people; however, sectarian literature suggests that many people did not pay attention to the special taboos developed by the different sects.

A brief final word about same-sex relations. Wherever homosexuality is discussed, it is always with disgust and condemnation (Lev. 18:22; Romans 1:26–27). Homosexual rape was a way of humiliating prisoners of war (though such rape is usually carried out by heterosexuals). In the Pentateuch the punishment is said to be stoning; however, many other breaches of the law supposedly entailing the death penalty (e.g. adultery) were evidently not so treated in actual practice (cf. McKeating 1979). But whatever the actual penalty in society we have no instances in which homoeroticism is treated positively. Lesbianism is seldom discussed and appears not to have been envisaged by the biblical writers (but see Brooten 1996 who finds such in Rom. 1:26-27). Whether this is because the legislators were unaware that such existed or whether it was simply not condemned is difficult to say. The former seems more likely since the relations between the sexes in a patriarchal society would serve to keep men ignorant of same-sex relations between women. However, the subject is not absent from some other Jewish sources such as Pseudo-Phocylides (192) and Philo (Szesnat 1999).

HOW OTHERS SAW THEM

Philo-Judaism and anti-Judaism

Cohen, S. J. D. (1999) *The Beginnings of Jewishness: Boundaries, Varieties, Uncertainties.*

CPJ: 2.25–107.

Daniel, J. L. "Anti-Semitism in the Hellenistic-Roman Period", *JBL* 98 (1979) 45–65.

Farmer, W. R. (ed.) (1999) *Anti-Judaism and the Gospels.*

Feldman, L. H. (1993) *Jew and Gentile in the Ancient World: Attitudes and Interactions from Alexander to Justinian.*

—— (1995) "Reflections on Rutger's "Attitudes to Judaism in the Greco-Roman Period", *JQR* 86: 153–70.

Gager, J. G. (1972) *Moses in Greco-Roman Paganism.*

Goodman, M. (1987) *The Ruling Class of Judaea: The Origins of the Jewish Revolt against Rome A.D. 66–70.*

Guterman, S. L. *Religious Toleration and Persecution in Ancient Rome* (1951).

Horsley, R. A. (1995) *Galilee: History, Politics, People.*

Kasher, A. *Jews and Hellenistic Cities in Eretz-Israel* (1990).

Musurillo, H. A. (ed.) (1954) *The Acts of the Pagan Martyrs: Acta Alexandrinorum.*

Neusner, J., and E. S. Frerichs (ed.) (1985) *"To See Ourselves as Others See Us".*

Rabello, A. M. "The Legal Condition of the Jews in the Roman Empire", *ANRW II* (1980) 13.662–762.

Rutgers, L. V. (1998) "Attitudes to Judaism in the Greco-Roman Period: Reflections on Feldman's *Jew and Gentile in the Ancient World"*, *The Hidden Heritage of Diaspora Judaism*: 199–234

Schäfer, P. (1997) *Judeophobia: Attitudes toward the Jews in the Ancient World.*

Sevenster, J. N. (1975) *The Roots of Pagan Anti-Semitism in the Ancient World.*

Slingerland, H. D. (1998) *Claudian Policymaking and the Early Imperial Repression of Judaism at Rome.*

Yavetz, Z. (1993) "Judeophobia in Classical Antiquity: A Different Approach", *JJS* 44: 1–22.

We have little if any reference to the Jews in non-Jewish sources dating from the Persian period; as far as we know the Jews were regarded by the Persians much as any other minority group in their empire. One of the first references to the Jews by a non-Jewish writer is from Hecateus of Abdera (quoted on pp. 37–38 above). His account looks to be favorable on the whole (though Schäfer [1997: 16–17] strangely sees it as negative). Other early writers are also positive, recognizing the Jews as having strange customs in some cases, but sometimes admiring them as one of the exotic groups of eastern philosophers (e.g. Megasthenes [*GLAJJ* #14]; Clearchus of Soli [*GLAJJ* #15]; see further examples in Gager 1972; Feldman 1993). The first writer who seems to be negative is the Egyptian priest Manetho (*GLAJJ* ## 19–21) who wrote a history of Egypt in Greek about 300 BCE; however, a number of scholars believe that the anti-Jewish passages are not part of the original writer (cf. *GLAJJ*: 1.64). Thus, it becomes a matter of opinion when anti-Jewish writing had its origin.

Terms such as "anti-Semitic", "anti-Jewish", "philo-Jewish", "Judeophobia", and the like have been used in discussions about the attitudes of Greeks and others to the Jews. A term such as "anti-Semitic" carries connotations of modern racist propaganda and attitudes which may be questionable when applied to the Greco-Roman world (Sevenster 1975: 1–6). Some consider it a misnomer and would prefer some other term (Feldman 1993: 84), such as "anti-Jewish", though there are problems even with this term (Daniel 1979: 45–56). It has also been argued that, in any case, "anti-Semitism" as thought of today did not exist in the Greco-Roman period.

The Greeks in antiquity were often contemptuous of non-Greeks, applying the name "barbarian" to them (though this seems to have originated in reference to their unintelligible languages). This is a universal attitude toward outsiders and hardly surprising. More interesting are those Greeks who wrote approvingly and even in admiration of certain non-Greek peoples, holding them up as models to their own people, especially in the early Hellenistic period following Alexander's conquests (much as some Enlightenment writers extolled the recently discovered "primitive" peoples as welcome contrasts to their own decadent society). Considering the positive comments of some earlier writers, when, where, and how did the anti-Jewish expressions originate? While there are several possible answers, and the situation is complex and cannot be summarized in any simple fashion, five factors are recognized:

1. The Maccabean conquests may have created resentment among the local peoples of the Palestinian region, though we have little direct evidence of this. Whether the Idumeans and Itureans were converted by force (Horsley 1995: 42–45), as alleged by Josephus, or by agreement is a matter of debate (*JCH*: 329–31; Cohen 1999: 110–19), but the Idumeans generally seemed to have remained faithful to Judaism. Conquest of a people by their neighbors was not a new idea, and the Jews were not unique, but the Maccabean conquests displaced a significant population of non-Jews, including many of those descended from the original Macedonian conquerors. This built resentments that were felt locally for a very long time, which may be one of the factors in the slaughter of Jewish populations in Greek cities at various times (cf. Kasher 1990).

2. There are indications that it was in Egypt – where the Jews had a long history of settlement, at least from Ptolemaic times (cf. *Aristeas* 4) – that the real problems began. Although the statement of Josephus that Jewish settlement had already begun at the time of Alexander's conquest is unlikely, it may well have had its origins as early as the period of Ptolemy I (cf. *JCH*:

211–12). Except possibly for 3 Maccabees (*JCH*: 177–78), we have no indication of any major difficulties between the Jewish community and the Greek inhabitants of the city until Roman times, though the presence of Jews high up in the Egyptian army could have created some resentments (*Ant.* 13.10.4 §§284–87). A sea-change in attitude seems to have taken place with the Roman conquest of Egypt.

The Greek citizens of Alexandria had an enormous pride in their ancestry and tradition, and the Roman takeover was a great blow to their prestige and self-esteem. Further, the leaders of Judea (Hyrcanus II and Antipater) had contributed a good deal to the conquest of Egypt and had gained Roman goodwill as a result (*JCH*: 343). While most of the Jews were not citizens of the city (*JCH*: 405–9), they nevertheless enjoyed special privileges which citizens also possessed but which the native Egyptians did not. Thus, the Jews were seen – rightly or wrongly – by the Greek citizens of Alexandria and elsewhere in Egypt to be on the side of the Romans and, conversely, enemies of the Greek community. Then, when Jews began to agitate for Alexandrian citizenship or similar rights (*JCH*: 405-9), smoldering resentment and hatred burst into full flame. This seems to have been the foundation of anti-Judaism in Egypt, which increased as time went by.

The earliest indications of this anti-Jewish attitude are literary (e.g. Manetho [*GLAJJ* ##19–21], if the anti-Jewish passages are authentic), but no concerted action seems to have been taken until the reign of Caligula. Things came to a head in 38 CE, probably in large part because of Jewish agitation for citizenship or at least special privileges for their community, and riots broke out against the Jewish community (*JCH*: 399–401). Eventually, Claudius affirmed Jewish rights regarding religion but warned them about agitating for citizenship or special privileges. Peace was restored but much of the bitterness remained and was passed on to future generations until it culminated in the revolt under Trajan (*JCH*: 596–99). It seems that two of the Alexandrian delegation were tried before Claudius and perhaps even executed by him. A legendary memory of these Alexandrian "martyrs" was preserved in the *Acta Alexandrinorum* (Musurillo 1954; *CJP*: 2.66–81).

3. The customs and religious practices of the Jews may have played a role. The Jews were reputed to have odd customs, but other local peoples had peculiar customs as well, some no less laughable to the educated Greco-Roman. Circumcision, for example, was practiced by a whole range of Oriental peoples. Thus, this does not seem to be the primary cause; nevertheless, Greco-Roman writers often comment on Jewish customs, usually negatively: people who worship the sky without images (Hecateus of Abdera, *apud* Diodorus Siculus 40.3.4; Strabo, *Geographica* 16.2.35 [p. 761]), who keep the sabbath (e.g. Agatharchides of Cnidus, *apud* Josephus, *Contra Apionem* 1.22 §§209–11; Horace, *Sermones* 1.9.68–70; Ovid, *Ars Amatoria* 1.75–76), who do not eat pork (Philo, *De Legatione ad Gaium* 361), or who are misanthropic (this is found especially in several writers associated with Egypt, e.g. Apion,

apud Josephus, *Contra Apionem* 2.8 §§91–95, but occurs even among writers otherwise sympathetic to the Jews [e.g. Hecateus of Abdera, *apud* Diodorus Siculus 40.3.4]).

4. As will be discussed in the next section, a more general reason for anti-Semitism was that the Jews were themselves seen as intolerant and misanthropes (cf. Goodman 1987: 97–99). As noted above, this attitude may have been fostered by events under Hasmonean rule. After fighting and winning a bitter battle against religious persecution, the Maccabees then proceeded to eliminate all other forms of worship in the territories under their control. The Idumeans and Itureans were converted to Judaism (see the first point above). Non-Jewish cults and cult places were destroyed. Even later under Roman rule, there were occasional acts of aggression against non-Jewish cults which were completely illegal under Roman law, such as the destruction of Roman altars that preceded Caligula's attempt to place a statue in the temple (*JCH*: 401–5). The various lies about Jewish origins and worship (especially that of human sacrifice) were symbolic of this perception of the Jews as haters of all other peoples.

5. The question of citizenship was a source of irritation on both sides. It is clear that most Jews were not citizens, either of Rome or of the Greek cities where they presided (*JCH*: 405–9). Only a few wealthy, upper-class individuals (e.g. the family of Philo) were citizens; however, there were Jews in Alexandria, for example, who wanted to become citizens and caused ill feeling among the Greek population by their efforts to achieve this. This was one of the causes of the riots in 38 CE and following, and apparently remained a bone of contention after Claudius issued his decree about the situation in 41 CE (*JCH*: 408).

Religious tolerance

Cogan, M. (1993) "Judah Under Assyrian Hegemony: A Re-examination of Imperialism and Religion", *JBL* 112: 403–14.

Noethlichs, K. L. (1996) *Das Judentum und der römische Staat: Minderheitenpolitik im antiken Rom*.

Pucci Ben Zeev, M. (1998) *Jewish Rights in the Roman World: The Greek and Roman Documents Quoted by Josephus Flavius*.

Rajak, T. (1984) "Was There a Roman Charter for the Jews?" *JRS* 74: 107–23.

Stanton, G. N., and G. G. Stroumsa (eds) (1998) *Tolerance and Intolerance in Early Judaism and Christianity*.

Zerbe, G. M. (1993) *Non-Retaliation in Early Jewish and New Testament Texts: Ethical Themes in Social Contexts*.

The basic stance of the ruling empires in the ancient Near East was that of religious tolerance. Although some sort of participation in certain cultic rites may have been required to demonstrate submission (see Cogan 1993 for the latest discussion), not just the Persians but also the Assyrians and Babylonians allowed their subject peoples to worship as they chose. The only breach we have of this principle is the decrees of Antiochus IV, but otherwise Judaism was a tolerated religion throughout the Second Temple period. The Persians had allowed (and, according to biblical statements, even encouraged) the Jewish cult and traditional customs. There is no indication that anything changed with the Greek conquest; similarly, under Roman rule the Jews enjoyed religious rights.

These religious rights were sometimes represented as being unique to the Jews, even over against their Gentile neighbors. Although some of the alleged decrees granting the Jews special privileges are suspect, there were also unquestioned decrees permitting the free exercise of their traditional customs and way of life (cf. Pucci Ben Zeev 1998). For example, when the *collegia* (associations, usually political in nature) were periodically banned, the Jewish synagogues were specifically exempted most of the time (*Ant.* 14.10.8 §§213–16). Even during and after the 66–70 war, there is no indication of official persecution or restriction on Judaism as such (despite riots and mob action against the Jews in various of the Greek cities in the Syro-Palestinian region [*JCH*: 449]). Thus, the anti-Semitic attitudes and actions clearly attested must be weighed against this official recognition and tolerance.

However, on the whole the Romans treated all religious minorities alike, with a policy somewhere between tolerance and suppression (Noethlichs 1996; cf. Rajak 1984). That is, state security came first, and any perceived threat to Rome was dealt with ruthlessly, but unless a religion was seen as a threat it was allowed (see Noethlichs for the sources). Thus, in 41 CE in response to riots against the Jewish community in Alexandria, Claudius affirmed Jewish rights regarding religion, yet he also warned the Jews about agitating for citizenship or other special privileges. The decrees quoted by Josephus allegedly granting privileges were in most cases an example of this basic tolerance of native worship and customs and nothing more (Pucci Ben Zeev 1998); Josephus is wrong in implying that they went beyond this, and his claim for citizenship of the Jewish communities in various Greek cities is only propaganda (*JCH*: 405–9).

Thus, the Jewish refusal to worship other gods was the occasion for astonishment and resentment among pagans, and perhaps even an excuse to suspect subversive attitudes toward the state, but this by itself might have been accepted. It certainly became the object not just of suspicion but of fear and even hatred, however, when it was combined with an active attempt to suppress other forms of worship. To the Greeks and Romans, the Jews demanded religious tolerance, then in some cases turned round to deny it to others. The frequent assertion that Jews were exempted from the state or emperor cult is incorrect (Pucci Ben Zeev 1998). This cult was seen by the

Romans as a symbol of submission to Roman rule, and no one was exempt; however, the Jewish sacrifices for the Roman ruler in Jerusalem and the dedications in local synagogues were seen as fulfilling the requirement. (This is why the termination of these sacrifices in 66 CE was a clear indication of rebellion [*War* 2.17.2–4 §§409–17].) For practical purposes, the Jews did not have to take part in the actual state cult, but there was no official exemption as such.

SYNTHESIS

We can summarize much of the content of this chapter by focusing, first, on how Jews were perceived within their own community and, secondly, how they were viewed by the other inhabitants of the Mediterranean world. Jewish identity was mainly a matter of birth; one was a Jew because one's parents were Jewish. A question arose in three situations: if both parents were not Jewish, if a non-Jew wished to become one, or if a Jew abandoned his ancestral religion. Unlike later practice, ethnic identity generally followed that of the father, so that a Jewish father meant a Jewish son or daughter. Because of the few examples of those who allegedly left their faith, it is difficult to say much about what this meant.

Conversion, although apparently envisaged in some manner in some OT texts, became a practical issue only in the Greek and Roman periods, as far as we know. There is evidence of Gentiles who were interested in Judaism and converted completely; in addition, another group of people (mostly men) did not go as far as circumcision but were interested in Judaism and took on at least some of its religious observances. These "God-fearers" are referred to in a number of texts, as most scholars now accept. Becoming Jewish was straightforward enough. There is no evidence of a formalized procedure (whether involving priests or anyone else). One adopted Jewish beliefs and practices including, for men, circumcision. The "proselyte baptism" known from rabbinic literature is not attested for pre-70 times. A systematic or extensive Jewish "mission" of seeking converts is unlikely, though there is evidence that individual Jews may have actively proselytized.

The Greco-Roman sources showed a wide range of attitude toward the Jews. There were those who admired them as philosophers (Clearchus [*apud* Josephus, *Contra Apionem* 1.22 §§176–83] who is supposedly quoting Aristotle, though scholars tend to be skeptical of this last point) and in other ways (Hecateus of Abdera; see pp. 37–39 above). They are often derided for their strange customs, though it must be said that this attitude of Greeks and Romans applied indiscriminantly to most of the "barbaric" peoples of the East. Genuine anti-Jewish feelings become evident mainly in the aftermath of the Hasmonean conquests. These are most strongly represented by Greek writers from Alexandria and reflect the help given by Hyrcanus II and

Antipater to the Romans in the conquest of Egypt and to the agitation of some Alexandrian Jews for citizenship. Jewish intolerance for other religions and especially for divine statues was probably a factor as well (especially in Caligula's attempt to set up a statue in the Jerusalem temple). Judaism may have been evaluated as another Hellenistic mystery cult, such as Isis worship (*JCH*: 533). The view of these was ambivalent: they were very popular among certain segments of the population but were viewed with suspicion by many in the ruling classes.

The ideology of the land was a significant force in Jewish thinking and also seems to have been behind certain actions as well. On the one hand, the land ideology was a source of strength to those Jews who lived in Palestine, especially when they were under foreign rule. They could always hope that in time they would once again gain control of their own destiny, as long as they retained their attachment to the land. On the other hand, the idea that Palestine was the "promised land" for the Jews could be used to justify hostility toward other inhabitants, territorial expansion, opposition to foreign rule, and even eschatologically inspired revolts to return to an ideal territory in which all Jews lived. Yet the majority of Jews lived in the Diaspora, and however much Judah, Jerusalem, and the temple were a symbol of their identity and religion, most found ways to accommodate themselves to their surroundings, and there is little sign of of mass immigration to the land of Israel. Some of them wished to better their position and gain citizenship of the Greek cities in which they lived. On the whole, this was not successful, but the understandable desire of Jews to join the ranks of Greek citizens created problems in Alexandria and elsewhere.

Most of the information we have about women relates to the upper classes or to fictional ideals such as Judith, and we know little of ordinary people, whether men or women. Recent archaeological finds have helped to redress the balance, with insight into the lives of a few ordinary women such as Babatha and Salome Komaïse. In general a patriarchal society can be taken for granted, but within that framework the situation of woman was often more complex, with more freedoms and autonomy, than sometimes admitted. The situation also varied from community to community, with the Diaspora communities sometimes showing women as being more equal or independent than those in Palestine itself.

Overall, the position of Jews in the Hellenistic and Roman world still needs a great deal of exploration, with many of the old assumptions brought into question.

III

CONCLUSION

15

JUDAISM IN THE SECOND TEMPLE PERIOD: A HOLISTIC PERSPECTIVE

Judaic religion in the Second Temple period needs to be considered as a unit. There were many continuities from First Temple times, and many aspects continued into the rabbinic period; nevertheless, the period marked off in its beginning by the exilic period and at its end by Yavneh contains within its great variety a conceptual, ideological, thematic, and developmental unity that should be recognized and characterized. The Second Temple period is a coherent period of Jewish history and needs to be treated as such. While any boundaries one draws are to some extent artificial and certainly do not mark off watertight, hermetically sealed entities, nevertheless, the destruction of Jerusalem and the temple in 587/586 BCE and the deportation of some Judeans marks an important break in history, as does the destruction of Jerusalem and the temple in 70 CE. The religion(s) of the Jewish people were greatly shaped by both events. To begin the study of Judaism of this time with the coming of Alexander both misses the many innovations of the Persian period and overly emphasizes the changes brought about by Hellenistic culture; it also overlooks the broader congruence of religion from the exile to Yavneh. The real watershed was not the coming of Alexander but the exilic period.

To understand religion in the Second Temple period one must understand the movements of history. Judaism began as one particular variety of Northwest Semitic religion. Recent study has come more and more to the conclusion that Israelites were Canaanites (cf. the survey in Grabbe 2000c). Israel arose in Canaan from the native peoples; the Israelite religion was a Canaanite religion, and the Hebrew Bible is the best preserved example of Canaanite literature (Grabbe 1994b). Only later did the biblical writers invent their own version of the Canaanites as a literary construct, creating from fantasy a demonic people with a perverted religion that deserved destruction (Lemche 1991), though in some cases making use of old legends and even names from mythology (e.g. the Rephaim). The national god of the Israelites was Yhwh, but he had a female consort and other gods were also worshiped. The polemics against Baal worship in the time of Ahab and Jezebel may have represented genuine concerns over an imported cult from the Phoenician area, because the data indicate that Baal was one of the deities uncontroversially honored on Israelite soil. This plurality of belief and practice did not completely cease with the Neo-Babylonian conquest of Judah or the change to Persian rule, but we find a strong monotheistic trend beginning about that time.

Despite some recent skepticism, there was an entity called Israel and a related entity called Judah in the First Temple period, and there is evidence of a continuity from First Temple to Second Temple times, whether from an ethnic, a religious, or a cultural perspective (Grabbe 1999a), even if many of the old certainties can no longer be maintained. The end of the First Temple period and the destruction of the Jewish monarchical state brought many changes, though some of these are clearer in retrospect than they probably were at the time. The religious picture attested in the time of Cyrus has much in common with that known from the time of Vespasian, and for convenience we can call the whole religious complex "Second Temple Judaism". Yet during the seven centuries of the Second Temple period, there were major changes and developments, and the variety found at the end was at least as great as at the beginning. For this reason, we can also speak of "Judaisms", indicating the fact that each individual Judaic system can be called a Judaism. "Judaic religion" is the container which holds all the different and diverse Judaisms of the time.

Two main forces shaped and characterized the Jewish religion through these centuries. The centripetal force was the temple, the center for all Jews, drawing them together toward a single ethnic deity and a single place of worship, a priesthood that interpreted and taught the traditional laws, as well as carrying out the cult, and a land believed to be given to the Jewish people as a divine gift. The centrifugal force first came to the fore in the Diaspora, removed as it was from the temple and land. The condition of living in the Diaspora, away from the temple and land, was itself a major centrifugal force, but there was more. The main force was a bundle of innovations that moved Jewish religion away from the necessity of the temple and priesthood, and consisted of the development of sacred scripture, the importance of biblical reading and interpretation, the rise of the synagogue, and the emphasis on prayer and non-sacrificial worship. These innovations arose in the Diaspora but came to exercise a considerable influence on the Judaism practised in Palestine itself. They were not exclusive to the Diaspora, in that much textual development seems to have taken place on Palestinian soil, though their significance was much greater abroad; however, others originated in the Diaspora (e.g. the synagogue) and only latterly found a place in Palestinian Judaism.

The description just given of the two main forces cannot avoid a certain oversimplification, partly because a strict Palestine/Diaspora dichotomy did not obtain and partly because these various trends were not always interrelated but, rather, developed at their own rate in their own environment.

As already noted, the growth of scripture, canon, and standardized text owed much to work done in Palestine, probably even by the priesthood itself. The emphasis placed on scripture as the source of religious authority seems to have been characteristic of certain sects in the homeland itself and not just Diaspora communities; on the other hand, the symbolic importance of the temple for Diaspora Jews was great, even if they never laid eyes on it during their entire lifetime.

The significance of the Persian period for the succeeding centuries cannot be overemphasized. Its importance is often overlooked for two reasons: a recognition that we know little about it in any detail and the misplaced assumption that the real break in Jewish history came with the Greek conquest. Our ignorance of specific events in the Persian period is a major problem, but this is no reason to throw up our hands and declare that the period is a "black hole" and we can say nothing about it. On the contrary, there is much that can be assigned to the time of Persian rule with reasonable (or even a good deal of) confidence.

The first and one of the most important events after the end of Neo-Babylonian rule was the reestablishment of the temple. We do not know exactly when this took place (since the date in Ezra 6:15 cannot be relied on), but it was not only a reaffirmation of the traditional cult and worship of Yhwh but also the beginning of priestly governance of the Judean community, a major innovation. Whatever the expectations, the monarchy had come to an end for the time being and this was realized. The temple establishment in general and the high priest in particular stepped in to fill the gap left by the loss of the monarchy and nationhood. The Jerusalem nobility was also included in the broader decision-making process, as one might expect, but some of the powerful noble families during the entire Second Temple period were of priestly origin. The priestly and noble advisers to the high priest may already have made up a formal council under Persian rule, though definitive evidence is lacking. The Persians appointed a governor some or even all the time. This individual was sometimes Jewish (to infer that he always was Jewish goes well beyond the evidence). Examples of both close cooperation and considerable friction between the governor and the high priest are given in the biblical text (e.g. Joshua and Zerubbabel, Eliashib and Nehemiah). Such political maneuverings for advantage are what we would expect in any human organization.

Religious teaching was done either through the family, by the parents and grandparents, or through the priesthood. Judah itself was only a small province, and all Jews could go up periodically to the temple to participate in the cult. Illiteracy was no problem since all that one needed to know was taught by the priests, whether of the proper cultic practices or the religious tradition and "sacred history" of the Jewish people. Whatever the problems with extracting historical data from the books of Ezra and Nehemiah and the post-exilic prophets, they illustrate the centrality of the temple to religious practice and worship.

It was also probably in the Persian period that much of the Hebrew scriptures took shape. We know that some data in the biblical text show a relatively accurate knowledge of the Israelite and Judean kings, at least as far as their sequence, general chronological placement, and some of the major events of their reigns are concerned (Grabbe 1997g: 24–26; 1998c: 84–90). To what extent these data confirm the representation of history in the contexts in which they occur is currently a debated point, as is the question of how much crystalization of tradition had taken place before the fall of Jerusalem to Nebuchadnezzar. Yet the testimony of Ben Sira (44–49) indicates that large sections of the biblical text (Genesis to 2 Kings, the Major and Minor Prophets, 1 and 2 Chronicles) were already in much their present shape. Not only were they in existence but also they were considered authoritative, suggesting the passage of some amount of time. This itself suggests an origin in the Persian period, but there are also other arguments for this dating; e.g. the destruction of Jerusalem and the temple would have created an impetus to put the traditions in order lest they be lost.

Thus, probably by the Ptolemaic period, certain books were widely accepted as sacred in some sense and were being taught as a part of the Judaic religious tradition. However, it is anachronistic to assume that the formulation of a body of sacred scripture would suddenly transform the religion. The temple was still the focus not only of worship but also of teaching and ruling. One should also be cautious about speaking of much interpretative activity in the Persian and Ptolemaic periods, at least in the conventional sense of the term. The biblical books were still firmly in the hands of the priests who were responsible for their teaching and exposition. Only a small portion of the population was sufficiently literate to read such books with facility, and the number of copies available would have been very few. Only the priesthood and those of wealth and privilege would have had direct access to these books. The seed of scriptural authority was only sown in the Persian period, while the harvest of biblical interpretation and independent sects did not reach maturity until much later.

There were other major developments in the area of religion. The monotheistic trends seen in Deuteronomy and other biblical passages, and its full expression in Second Isaiah, appear to have triumphed in the Persian period. At no time after the end of the Persian period do we find blatant polytheism in any Jewish texts or other sources. Where some have questioned the use of the term "monotheism", they have really been questioning other aspects of Judaism, especially angelology. The angelic world was probably derived ultimately from the old pantheon, but it quickly took on a life of its own. However much angels were heavenly beings, no Jewish text of this time suggests that they in any way compromised the divinity of the one true God. On the contrary, the activities of the myriads of angels found in some writings were the means by which God's uniqueness was maintained; they were merely vehicles for his divine rule. Although Persian-period texts say little of this developing angelology, the full-blown manifestation in the early Ptolemaic period shows the extent to which it had grown during the Persian period.

The complex phenomenon of prophecy also developed in new ways. We do not hear too much of the social phenomenon (i.e., a description of prophets in action) except for Haggai and Zechariah, yet a number of the prophetic books were evidently written under Persian rule (e.g. Third Isaiah) while others were edited or expanded during this period. Prophetic writing also began to move in new directions. Some of the prophetic books of this period have some or many characteristics in common with apocalyptic writings. Apocalyptic is a scholarly construct made on the basis of extrapolating from the contents of apocalyptic and other writings. Although it contains elements known from both prophecy and mantic wisdom, this does not make it something different from prophecy. Rather, it seems to be prophetic writing which has gone in a new direction and developed or absorbed new characteristics. We should not disassociate it from prophecy and the prophetic tradition but see it as just a form or sub-genre of prophecy. Some would classify a book like Zechariah as apocalyptic (as well as prophecy), in which case the phenomenon is already attested in the Persian period. But even if not, the emergence of fully developed apocalyptic in the early Greek period shows that it had evolved during the Persian period.

Some have wanted to see considerable Persian influence, especially from the Zoroastrian religion (cf. *JCH*: 100–2). There is a good deal in common, especially in the eschatological area but not only there. For example, the developing Jewish belief in a resurrection has its best parallel in Zoroastrian worship, while the last judgment and the punishment of the wicked in fire match later views in Judaism. The complex angelology that had developed in Judaism by the end of the Persian period also has its counterpart in Zoroastrianism. Two questions remain, however: the first is whether we have borrowings or only parallel developments that arose from the internal logic within Judaism itself. The second question concerns the lateness of much Zoroastrian literature which is a millennium or more after Achaemenid times. The argument is that in the *Gathas* we have early poetry from Zarathushtra himself, but not everyone accepts this, nor is there agreement on when he lived. At this stage of study much is uncertain and a decisive judgment is hard to make. The question must remain open for the time being.

We do not know much about the first part of the Persian period, while the latter half is more or less a blank for Judah (except where recent archaeological study has started to give some information on it). Yet when we see what was already in existence by the Ptolemaic period, we can judge some of the major developments during those two enigmatic centuries. The scene was well set for the way Judaism would move in the next several centuries while the temple was standing. The Persian period was seminal and must be reckoned with in any account of Second Temple Judaism.

We now come to the arrival of the Greeks, about which so much has been made in past treatments of Jewish history. The conquest of Alexander did not have the immediate impact that Nebuchadnezzar's did; indeed, the beginning of many histories with Alexander is based in part on a misunderstanding of the significance of Hellenization on the ancient Near East. The assumption that the Greeks brought something completely new and radically challenging to Judaism simply follows the prejudice of some Jewish sources and especially of their modern interpreters. We know that Greek influence had already begun long before Alexander, primarily through two media: coastal trading (the Phoenician cities were especially affected) and Greek mercenary troops (possibly used even in the Israelite and Judean courts). We should not exaggerate the pre-Alexander inroads of Greek culture into Palestine, but the point is that things Greek were not new.

It often seems to be assumed that what the Greeks did was replace the native culture or customs, either by cultural superiority or by force, with the Jews being the sole exception to this tide of Hellenization. In fact, the Greeks only brought a new element to the venerable and deeply entrenched cultures of the ancient Near East, nor did they seem to have much interest in having their ways of doing things adopted by the native peoples; on the contrary, their belief in Greek culture as superior made them want to keep it as a privilege for themselves alone. It was the natives who wanted to share in this new entity in their midst because they saw it as a stepping stone to achieving success, as a symbol of status, and as desirable for a better and happier life. The upper classes quickly acted to gain for themselves and/or their children a Greek education, and some did give up their traditional lifestyle for one modeled completely on the Greek. Most did not go so far, however, but adopted those aspects of Greek culture that seemed useful while not abandoning their own.

As for the rest of the people, the non-aristocrats who made up the vast bulk of the population, their lives changed little. They had new rulers and paid taxes to a different regime. The language of the higher levels of bureaucracy was in Greek, but much of the work of administration, especially that which came in contact with most people, was carried out in the local language; for Palestine and much of the Seleucid empire this was Aramaic. The local agents for the Greek government were often natives, anyway. People were aware of the many new Greek cities, either new foundations or old Oriental cities with a new charter, and many natives lived in them. Thus, most people became aware of new cultural elements in their midst, but they did not usually affect the average person all that much.

This Hellenistic world was not, therefore, just the Greek world plunked down in Asia – it was something new: a synthesis of the Greek and the native; however, there was no blending (*Verschmelzung*) of the two in most cases. As time went on, the mixture changed and eventually some actually blending of styles developed, but this took centuries. The main characteristic of the Hellenistic culture was the existence of the various cultural elements side by side. The primary attributes of the Greek empires were not actually taken over from the old Greek city-states of the Greek mainland but were, on the contrary, a direct appropriation from the old Oriental empires. Rulership by a king; the elaborate bureaucracies of administration; the royal courts which attracted philosophers, literati, physicians, and other intellectuals, along with the extensive entourage of friends of the king; the waging of war with mercenary armies or military colonists – these were all taken over from the Egyptian and Asian empires which the Greeks replaced. In many ways, the new rulers went native.

Most importantly, we have no evidence that the Jews reacted any differently from other aboriginal peoples. The Greeks were conquerors and to be feared and obeyed, not loved, but so had been the Assyrians, Egyptians, Babylonians, and Persians. There was nothing more insidious about Greek culture than that of their long-term neighbors in the Near East. Some Jews, such as the aristocratic Tobiads, seem to have quickly recognized where their advantage lay and moved to embrace the new rulers and their culture. Most Jews were poor agrarian workers and could only view all this from afar. Some elements of Greek culture may have been seen as symbolic of the conquerors and thus despised or eschewed for that reason, but for the most part it was a matter of giving a shrug and getting on with life as had happened under new conquerors for thousands of years. Soon many aspects of Greek culture had become so familiar that they would not have been recognized as foreign. The Greeks did not try to impose their religion, any more than had the previous empire builders, and the Jews would not have been under any threat from Greek culture in the religious sphere. When resistance came to Greek rule, it was not from the Jews but elsewhere (e.g. Egypt) and took the form not of cultural resistance but of literary opposition (certain prophetic tracts such as the *Demotic Chronicle* and the *Potter's Oracle*) and even actual popular revolts.

For Jewish history the first part of the Greek period has perhaps as many gaps as the first part of the Persian period. We know hardly any events concerning the Jews during the years from Alexander's march through Asia until Zenon's journey through Palestine in 259 BCE, a period of almost three quarters of a century. What we do have is a description of the Jews in Palestine, along with an odd but fascinating historical sketch, by Hecateus of Abdera about 300 BCE. The few legendary sources, such as of Alexander coming to Jerusalem or the migration of Ezekias the high priest to Egypt, are highly suspect and the extraction of any historical data is very difficult (pp. 73–74 above; *JCH*: 174, 181–83). But with the Zenon papyri arising from Zenon's tour through Palestine and southern Syria, we have invaluable contemporary information that can be put together with other later and less reliable material to reconstruct something of the history of this period.

It appears that little had changed from the last days of Persian rule to the time when we next see Judah in the middle of the third century. The high priest was still the main representative of the Jewish people to the overlord (now the Greeks instead of the Persians). He was also advised by a council of some sort (though we have no reference to this until the end of the Ptolemaic period). Politics were still dominated by a few powerful families, in this case being the high priestly family of the Oniads and the Tobiads with their home territory across the Jordan. No simple Tobiad/Oniad dichotomy should be advanced, however, for the two families were intermarried. For example, Joseph Tobiad was the nephew of the high priest Onias II, and we later know that Hyrcanus Tobiad had connections with the temple and the high priest Onias III (2 Macc. 3:10–11). The one thing that had changed from the Persian period, evidently, was that there was no governor for the province of Judah. The Ptolemies seem to have governed by treating Coele-Syria (Palestine and southern Syria) as a part of Egypt and not an entity with its own separate governor.

The Tobiad romance (as told by Josephus) fills in some aspects of history in the latter part of the third century, but little relating directly to religion. Other sources do provide some data on religion but, interestingly, they relate mainly to the situation outside Palestine. Although there was a Diaspora already in Persian times, especially in Mesopotamia, we know little about it, apart from the Elephantine community in Egypt. But we start to hear of further settlements in Egypt during the Ptolemaic period. The information comes in bits and pieces, mainly in passing references (e.g. *Aristeas* 12–13), meaning that the details are skimpy but the fact of settlement reasonably well established. One of the most important events was the translation of the Pentateuch into Greek, apparently during the reign of Ptolemy II (282–246 BCE). It is significant for several reasons: first, it shows that the Pentateuch was not only written by this time but was also seen as authoritative scripture vital to the community; second, the teachings of the law needed to be accessible to those who did not know the original language, suggesting that those other than priests had an interest in reading it. The event of translation was itself unusual since translation of literature was not a common practice at this time, but it had far-reaching consequences because it made the Bible available to any Jew who read Greek, which was probably the majority of Jews in the Mediterranean world by 70 CE.

Another source of information about religion is certain sections of the book of *1 Enoch* and related literature. The *Book of Watchers* (*1 En.* 1–36) and the *Astronomical Book* (reflected in *1 En.* 72–82, though probably more extensive than this) appear to have been written in the early part of the Ptolemaic period, as was possibly the *Book of Giants* (known from Qumran but not in *1 Enoch*). These tell a remarkable story. They show an interest in one of the antediluvian patriarchs, though this may be more because of his astrological connections than because of his position in sacred history. The ascription of evil to the fall of angels who sinned through intercourse with human women is not found anywhere explicitly in the Hebrew Bible, and the origin of demons as the spirits of the giant mixed offspring of the angels and women is also unique to *1 Enoch* (unless the fragmentary *Book of Giants* once contained the story). The elaborate angelology and the heavenly journeys undertaken by Enoch show concerns only hinted at in Jewish literature previously known. Some of the prophets had visions of heaven or of God (Isaiah, Ezekiel, Amos), but no detailed description of the workings of the divine world had been given before.

1 Enoch is often judged to be sectarian in origin. This may be the case, but there are a lot of questions to be answered, including the one of whether sects already existed in this period. The main reason for identifying it as being from a breakaway sect is the solar calendar in 72–82. From all the information we have, a solar–lunar calendar was observed in the temple as far back as we can go. The festivals had to fit the solar year, but the months were calculated by the phases of the moon. On the other hand, the solar calendar may have been an old priestly one (as suggested by the dates in Gen. 6–9); if so, it was not used – or at least not used for official festivals. In its present form *1 Enoch* 72–82 promotes the solar calendar; however, if Milik is right, the original *Astronomical Book* reconciled the solar and lunar cycles which might suggest a more complex situation. Also, it seems that the information in the book was probably a body of priestly knowledge. We cannot disassociate priests from esoteric knowledge nor from apocalyptic speculation (Grabbe 1989; 1995a: 65, 176–78). The book could be the product of priests who had severed their connections with the temple establishment, but we do not know that for certain. Also, those who preserved the book and perhaps engaged in editing it may not have been those who originally wrote. The sections of *1 Enoch* that arose in the early Greek period show surprising developments that could only have taken place through the Persian period.

Something else new emerged with little fanfare during the third century but with far-reaching consequences: the synagogue. On this see below.

The Seleucid conquest in 200 BCE began one of the most paradoxical periods in Jewish history, a period of a century and a half filled with contradictions. A rule which was welcomed by most Jews, and began with the affirmation of Jewish rights, had declared the Jewish religion illegal within a few decades. A group of Jewish people who only asserted the logic of almost 150 years of cultural accommodation were blamed as apostates. A group of patriots who banded together to defend their temple and religion also adopted what many regarded as illegitimate goals and established an illegitimate priesthood and dynasty, ending with a deeply divided people and delivering the nation once again into the hands of foreign rulers. Both the Hellenistic reformers and the Maccabean movement initially had popular support, and both brought the nation into chaos – no doubt unintentionally in both cases.

In order to understand this period, the simplistic dichotomies have to be avoided and the aspirations of all participants understood (*JCH*, ch. 5; Grabbe 2000b). The black-and-white picture of "Hellenists" versus "Orthodox" is still too influential, grossly distorting the proper understanding of this era in Jewish history. Not least is a misunderstanding of the actions and intentions of the new Seleucid rulers. When Antiochus III conquered Coele-Syria (Syro-Palestine), in his eyes he was simply returning to Seleucid rule what was rightfully theirs, granted to them by an act of settlement in 301. There is no evidence that either he or the two sons (Seleucus IV and Antiochus IV) who succeeded him in turn had a particular interest in the Jews or in any "Hellenistic mission". Antiochus III continued to try to expand his empire until stopped by the Romans in 190 BCE. When Antiochus IV took the throne in 175, he took up where his father left off, though just like his father he was ultimately to be thwarted by the Romans and to be killed while robbing a temple. Again, the Jews as such were only one of many peoples in his realm and hardly of major interest. It was the Jews themselves who turned to Antiochus for patronage.

Shortly after Antiochus came to the throne, he was approached by Jason, the brother of the high priest Onias III, who offered money to be given the priesthood. The matter was no doubt of small significance to Antiochus except that the money brought by Jason would be a welcome addition to the war chest he was building up to support his plans for expansion. In addition he granted another of Jason's requests: to turn Jerusalem into a Greek foundation or *polis*. This was not because Antiochus was a cultural imperialist but because Jason paid for the privilege, probably in the form of an annual tribute. Antiochus had no interest in changing the Jewish religion; for his part neither did Jason. What he wanted was a city organized along Greek lines which allowed the new citizens of Jerusalem to enjoy the best of Hellenistic culture but without changing the traditional temple cult. Despite the best efforts of its author, 2 Maccabees 4 cannot point to any breach of the traditional Jewish law or violation of the temple establishment and worship. Jason's power base remained the temple, whatever changes he was able to make in the city government. There is also no evidence that any Jews were less than happy with the new arrangement. If some were not pleased (and the law of averages says that some must not have liked the idea), they have left no mark in the sources; on the contrary, most of the inhabitants of Jerusalem seem to have welcomed the new arrangements.

Yet Jason had set a dangerous precedent in buying the high priestly office, because what he had done could be done by others. In this case, Menelaus (not a member of the Oniad high priestly family but probably a priest nonetheless) went to Antiochus and offered him an even higher sum to be made high priest. Antiochus accepted and Jason was driven from Jerusalem.

Menelaus had no reason to keep the "Hellenistic reform" going, and there is no indication that he did, though our sources are mainly silent on the question. What is clear is that, by alleged breaches of Jewish law (contrast his behavior with that of Jason), he alienated the people of Jerusalem, who rioted and killed Menelaus's brother. This was about 170 BCE, at which time Antiochus invaded Egypt. Menelaus remained in office but a second invasion of Egypt was stopped by the Romans, following which Jason tried unsuccessfully to retake the temple from Menelaus by force. Events after this become confused but culminated in Antiochus's taking the unprecedented step of outlawing the practice of Judaism (in Judah, at least) and polluting the temple with a pagan sacrifice. The problem is that our sources do not give a clear reason why Antiochus did this. There are even hints that Menelaus may have been partly responsible, but it is unlikely that he bears the entire blame.

The resistance movement that developed against this gross violation of Jewish worship was probably not initiated by the Maccabean family (despite 1 and 2 Maccabees), but the father and brothers managed to assume leadership. As far as we can tell, the original goal was simply to drive out the Syrian troops in control of the temple area and to purify and restore the cult. This was done in a remarkable period of three years, probably in December 165 BCE (Grabbe 1992a); not long after this Antiochus himself issued a decree tacitly recognizing the new situation and withdrawing the measures against the practice of Judaism (cf. 2 Macc. 11:27–33; cf. 2 Macc. 9:19–27; *JCH*: 259–63), though he was himself killed in December 164 BCE, only a year after the temple came back into Jewish hands.

One might have expected the resistance to stop, having accomplished its purpose, but the goals had evidently changed. Now the fighters were working to eject the foreign troops from Jerusalem. There was a certain logic to this. However, the new Seleucid king Antiochus V was willing to make concessions: Menelaus was executed and a new high priest Alcimus installed. A number of Jews wanted to end the conflict, but the Maccabees insisted on continuing with the war. This prolonging of the conflict led to the death of Judas about 162 BCE, at which point the Maccabees seem to have been abandoned by all but their most loyal supporters. However, Jonathan went on with the resistance, though without much success until the emergence of rival dynasties for the Seleucid throne allowed him to play off one against the other for concessions. By the time Jonathan was killed by one of the pretenders to the Seleucid throne (*c.*143 BCE), the Maccabees had become a major force both as leaders of the Jewish nation and as players in imperial politics. They founded what became known as the Hasmonean dynasty of priests and an independent Jewish state (officially from about 140 BCE but in reality rather later, perhaps from about 125 BCE). Later rulers were even to adopt the title "king".

One might have expected the Hasmoneans to be popular with the people, having restored first the temple and then national independence after so many centuries. The people were divided, however, with many disenchanted with Hasmonean rule, especially as time went on. Eventually, some Jews were so disaffected toward Alexander Janneus's rule (103–76 BCE) that they actually helped Demetrius III, one of the rival Seleucid rulers, to invade the country. The Hasmonean kingdom ended when Aristobulus II and Hyrcanus II, the two brothers vying for the throne, brought in the Romans who promptly established Roman control of the country. A dynasty which should have brought the people together in a feeling of community and a unity of purpose seems to have done just the opposite.

We can summarize what happened through this period by noting the unplanned and unforeseen consequences following from the actions of both the Hellenistic reformers and the Maccabees. The supporters of the Hellenistic reform had not caused the suppression of Judaism; on the contrary, they had sent a delegation to Antiochus some years earlier complaining of Menelaus's alleged violation of temple sanctity. Nevertheless, their actions were seen by later writers (especially the books of Maccabees) as the cause of all the problems and, it must be admitted, Jason's illegitimate appropriation of the high priesthood started a chain of events that ended in an "abomination of desolation" being set up in the temple. The Maccabees had started with the noble aim of freeing the temple from its pollution, which they accomplished. But their goals changed, and they helped to bring about an independent state. One would think that they would be popular with the people, yet a significant portion of the population opposed them at various times, and some regarded their priesthood as unlawful. Instead of unifying, they divided.

One of the stranger byproducts of this period was the founding of a rival temple to Jerusalem (p. 82 above). According to one account in Josephus, it was the son of the deposed high priest Onias III who moved to Egypt after his father's death and built the temple; however, Josephus gives another account in which it is Onias III himself (who was not killed) who fled to Egypt and founded the temple. This is a surprising twist to events, that the son of the high priest or even the high priest himself should violate the long-held command of worshiping only in Jerusalem. The time of the multiple high places had passed centuries before, and the only other temple was the Samaritan one on Gerizim, but the Samaritans were separate from the Jews (whatever their common beliefs and perhaps common origins). However, the Leontopolis temple seems to have been run along the same lines as the temple in Jerusalem. If nothing else, it illustrates the complexities of Judaic religion.

It was probably during this period that the major sects originated or at least became significant. Sectarian movements may have begun as early as the Persian period (cf. p. 184 above), but being under foreign rule would have kept them small and suppressed (cf. Baumgarten 1997: 188–92). Josephus first mentions the sects during the governorship of Jonathan Maccabee, but there is no reason to think this is the definitive time when they arose. What does seem clear is that the Sadducees, Pharisees, and Essenes were all in existence and flourishing by about 100 BCE (see Chapter 9 above). We know a certain amount about the activities of the Sadducees and Pharisees but little about their beliefs; conversely, we know a fair amount about Essene beliefs but only come across a few individuals identified as Essenes.

The Sadducees and Pharisees first appear in the reign of either John Hyrcanus or Alexander Janneus as rivals for political power with the Hasmoneans; however, the Pharisees became opponents to the regime (though hardly the only ones) and evidently suffered as a result. Yet under Alexandra Salome they became the power behind the throne and were able to promulgate their particular teachings (whatever these were – we are not told). During the next half century, our sources mention neither the Sadducees nor the Pharisees, until the reign of Herod when the Pharisees (or some Pharisees, at least) attempted to gain influence with members of his household. He quickly nipped this in the bud. He also fined Pharisees (who were said to number about 6,000) for refusing to take an oath of loyalty; on the other hand, he granted favors to two individual Pharisees because they had made correct predictions about him. (Herod also exempted the Essenes from punishment even though they refused to swear the loyalty oath.)

The Sadducees were said to be small in number but to include some of the most important and influential figures among their ranks. Only a few individuals are identified as Sadducees, though this includes one or two high priests. The Pharisees seem to have included a broader base, but our sources mention some priests who were Pharisees, and the Pharisee Gamaliel I was evidently a member of the Sanhedrin. His son Simon was one of the leaders of the 66–70 revolt, though no connection is made between this position and his being a Pharisee. But on the whole there is no evidence that the Pharisees controlled the priesthood or religious teaching or even the synagogues (whether in Palestine or elsewhere). The only time we have evidence that the Pharisees did have major control in society was during the nine years under Alexandra Salome.

The Pharisees – like the Essenes and other religious types – may well have been looked up to by the ordinary people, and as a result they may have had influence beyond their number. But such general respect is quite different from saying that many people followed Pharisaic regulations in their ordinary life. What most of the people followed were the teachings of the temple priests. But most Jews were poor and had to work for a living. The did not have the luxury of replicating the temple and its purity in the home and eating food in the same ritual that was followed by priests in the temple. Getting enough to eat and sufficient to clothe themselves and raise their families was itself a full-time preoccupation. The minimal purity regulations, known from the Pentateuch, were probably observed, especially when planning to visit the temple, but the average Jew is not likely to have gone beyond this.

As already noted, we have some evidence of Diaspora communities in Mesopotamia and Egypt (Elephantine) in the Persian period. With the coming of the Greeks, there was further expansion: into Egypt, Cyrenaica, and Syria. During the Roman period Jewish settlement seems to have expanded considerably to the westward, with communities in Asia Minor, Greece, and Italy. We know only a little about the Jewish populations in those areas and not usually the history of when they first came and what happened over time. Probably the best recorded are the Jewish inhabitants of Egypt, but there are many gaps. Around the turn of the era there is some evidence of movement between Babylonia and Palestine.

The data are not abundant, but what emerges is a different lifestyle and practice of religion outside Palestine. This was to be expected. Many Jews did undoubtedly come from a great distance in the Diaspora to worship at the Jerusalem temple, but the expense meant that only a few could afford to do it often and many probably never made the journey during their lifetime. The temple was an ideal, but this was insufficient to retain the focus of their worship. A book like Tobit suggests that the home and family were initially the place where one exercised religion through prayer, festival and sabbath observance, and acts of charity. But that was eventually found to be insufficient; hence, the rise of the synagogue. From the information we have, the first synagogues originated in Egypt during the reign of Ptolemy II, perhaps contemporaneously with the LXX translation. By this time the Jews in Egypt evidently found their remoteness from the temple a problem (though, within a century, a local temple had also been built). The *proseuchē* ("prayer house") or *sunagogē* ("gathering, meeting"/synagogue) became quite popular in the Diaspora in the next century or so. Unfortunately, we have little information until quite late. The Theodotus inscription (which most date to the turn of the era but others put well after 70 CE) mentions study and hospitality for strangers; however, the name "prayer house" suggests prayer was conducted there, and Agatharchides mentions the Jews worshiping in their "temples" with outstretched hands. It seems unlikely, prime facie, that such a gathering in the absence of the temple would not have developed some sort of communal worship at an early stage.

What is clear is that the need for the synagogue was felt primarily away from the Jerusalem temple, and the institution spread to the fringes of Palestine and then to Judah itself only at a late stage, at least after the Maccabean revolt and perhaps even in the first century BCE or possibly as late as the first century CE. This is very much in keeping with the centrality of the temple cult to Judaism. The synagogue was initially only an inferior substitute. However, despite the ambiguity of the evidence, the balance of probability is that synagogues existed in Judah and even Jerusalem sometime before the 66–70 war with Rome. This arrival of a new and different institution was symbolic of how practices in the Diaspora were starting to affect the homeland. Although originally a surrogate for the temple, synagogue services were of a different nature – with a different theological conceptualization – from participation in the cult. Even though prayer and the law were not absent from the temple itself, the centrality of prayer and the written word involved quite a different religious mythology; indeed, it was now possible for some Jews to make use of both institutions.

Sacred scripture had been increasing in importance with the passage of time. The concept of authoritative holy writings already existed, along with a substantial core collection, at least as early as the Persian period, but it is difficult to see very much emphasis being put on it. The number of copies available and the number of people with the competence and time to read them was extremely small. These books were initially in the hands of the priesthood, as was their interpretation and the promulgation of their contents. But an individual like Ben Sira had some access to these writings, even if he seldom quotes them. A number of the writings of this time could have drawn on the written word, but they could equally have been inspired by oral teachings since the letter of the Bible is not cited or dealt with. (It is not even clear whether a writing such as *1 Enoch* 1–36 has a direct connection with the Bible.) However, late in the second century the biblical text became the subject of extensive commentary, as we know from the Qumran texts. Clearly some copies had begun to circulate outside the temple precincts. We also know that the Diaspora communities were interested in having copies of the law, which they gained by the LXX translation about the mid-third century. It is possible that Hebrew manscripts on which the translation was based had been supplied officially by the Judean authorities.

This does not mean that either the text or canon were settled. As far as we can tell both processes continued up to about the end of the first century CE. The text circulated in a variety of forms, not only in Hebrew but also in its Greek form which seems to have been revised several times to try to bring it closer in line with the developing Hebrew text. The question of textual variety is not a simple one (see pp. 158–65 above), but part of it is no doubt due to continuing growth, both at the textual and sometimes even at the literary level throughout this period. Further books appear to have become regarded as sacred and authoritative during the Greek and Roman periods, including Qohelet (Ecclesiastes) and Daniel. Unfortunately, when, how, and why certain books were admitted to the canon is unknown to us, though the present Hebrew canon seems to have been more or less established by 100 CE.

The process of Judaism becoming a "religion of the book" was under way by the Greek period, but it had its impact first in the Diaspora and in those groups that had shut themselves off from the temple establishment. If the high priest is God's representative on earth, but you have no access to him because of living a long way away or because you consider the current office holder as disqualified, you have to find a substitute. The natural substitute was a body of writings that could be approached independently of priestly authority. Those who participated regularly in the temple cult could also have benefited from the written word, but they would probably have done so through priestly mediation (public readings, teaching of morality, exposition involving biblical contents, instruction in correct matters of legal and ritual observance). The collection of writings would have been seen as the source of divine knowledge, even if in practice that information came only via the priesthood.

The coming of the Romans changed things greatly for those living in Judea. Not only had they exchanged independence for life under a conqueror once more, but Roman rule was different. Judah was ruled more or less directly as a Roman province, though Hyrcanus II and his ally Antipater had prominent places in the rule. Hyrcanus was still high priest but with severely restricted powers. The few years after Jerusalem was taken in 63 BCE were harsh ones. Judah was unavoidably caught up in the Roman civil war and suffered heavy taxation. However, Antipater's sons Herod and Phasael developed rapidly into efficient administrators during this period, Herod especially showing great promise even though he was the younger brother. The Parthian invasion of 40 BCE provided the opportunity for Herod, though he could easily have lost his life, like his brother. Proclaimed king over Judah, Herod had to defeat Aristobulus's son Antigonas, then walk a knife-edge between Mark Antony, Cleopatra, and Octavian, not to mention that Antigonas's sons several times raised revolts against him. Herod showed himself to be a remarkable individual.

Evaluation of Herod is difficult, not least because almost all sources are heavily prejudiced against him. The story of Herod and the wise men has especially colored how he is seen today. If one wanted to add up the negative qualities of Herod's rule, there would be quite a sum. Yet a lot of the negative aspects were those common to rulers of his age, including the Hasmoneans. The positive elements make a startling contrast and a necessary corrective for a proper evaluation. The fact is that, overall, Herod's reign was good for the Jews, not only for those in Judea but for the Jewish communities in the Diaspora. All rulers collected taxes, but Herod's were no higher than others, and he had the sensibility to provide some relief during times of famine. Through his contact with Augustus and his family, Herod championed Diaspora communities on more than one occasion when they were under local pressure. He renovated the temple and made it one of the most magnificent structures of the East. However, his greatest contribution was the peace that he brought to the region so that people's lives ceased to be disrupted by the wars that had gone on since the time of Antiochus IV.

Herod not only respected Jewish religious sensibilities but was also a practicing Jew himself. His own ancestry is difficult, but it is clear that he saw himself as Jewish. As a ruler and one well educated in Greco-Roman culture, his observance of the law was more liberal than that approved of by some groups. It brings us back to the issue debated since the time of Nehemiah: to what extent are Jews allowed to accommodate to the non-Jewish culture around them? The answer given by Eleazar, Jason, and Herod may not have been acceptable to some Jewish groups at the time, but the approach seems to be parallel to the views that have led to Liberal Judaism today. Although too liberal for some, especially when outside Judea, Herod did not allow pictorial images in his private chambers and baths in the home and fortress he constructed at Masada.

Where Herod created some serious problems is not primarily in his personal religion but in other actions. As a young governor of Galilee he had been called before the Sanhedrin to account for his actions. He did not forget this insult and reportedly decimated its membership through execution once he became king, leaving it little more than a body in name only. He also began the practice of frequently changing the high priest. Under Herod's rule the high priest, of course, had little actual power. This might have been good or bad, but it all meant that the office lost credibility in the eyes of many Jews. Although there are no suggestions that Herod interfered with the temple duties of the high priest, there may have been those who suspected this of being the case. Finally, he locked up the high priestly garments and would not allow them out except just before a major festival. From Herod's point of view, it was a way of controlling his subjects, but it was another insult to the prestige and authority of the high priestly office.

Whatever Herod's faults the loss of Herodian rule exposed the people to the insensitive and sometimes even brutal realities of direct Roman rule. Provincial governors were not known for their enlightened administration, and it had been a tradition that a provincial governorship allowed one to amass a fortune. Judaism was allowed to be practiced but only if due respect was paid to the state, including a version of the state cult, since the Jews were not excused this. They were allowed to omit the traditional altars and sacrifices only because sacrifices for the emperor and his family were offered in the Jerusalem temple and many synagogues had inscriptions dedicated to the ruler. Anything hinting at rebellion received immediate and often violent attention.

People coped with Roman rule, as they had Greek rule and Near Eastern rule before that, in various ways. One way of dealing with all life's vicissitudes was through religion, sometimes in a more demotic form than that found formally in the temple. "Popular religion" is a term sometimes used to describe the beliefs and practices among the people that differ from the official cult. Strictly, there is no distinction, of course, since religion is religion, whether it is that of the priests or the lay people. However, it is useful to recognize that the common people at times did what was not officially sanctioned by the written law, the priestly teachings, or perhaps even the main sects. With the pluralistic nature of Judaism in this period, deciding what to put under the label "popular religion" is difficult. However, we might especially put the practice of the various esoteric arts in this category (divination, magic, astrology, and other means of discerning the future), as well as the veneration of "saints" and the cult of the dead. We might include the mystical tradition here since there was more than one opinion of its legitimacy. Some of these forms are clearly the survival of the old polytheistic religion or other practices once current among the Israelites when Yhwh was only one God among many. The honoring of the tombs of dead "saints" probably has its roots in the cult of the dead, a practice becoming better known with new archaeological finds. Doubtless some of the traditional burial rites (e.g. embalming) had their roots in the cult of the dead.

The evidence for the esoteric arts is always going to be paltry because by their nature these skills were kept secret. We know something about them from a few texts written by insiders (or former insiders), from certain magical texts left behind to continue their work, from symbols left on buildings or elsewhere, or passing hints in literature. The astrological symbols left on later synagogue floors show that astrology was widespread, a fact that we probably would not be aware of from most of our sources; however, our texts do indicate a certain ambivalence toward astrology. Later mystical texts hint at what was going on before 70, especially if combined with a study of the early apocalyptic literature. Certain gnostic trends and speculation seem also to have had their place in the Judaism of this time (*JCH*: 514–19; Grabbe 1996a: 94–110), though Gnosticism is anti-Judaic in many ways. Some interpretations in Gnostic literature could have come only from Jewish insiders knowledgeable in certain interpretations of Jewish traditions. It also seems to be the case that some prominent figures practiced some of the esoteric arts privately. This was not hypocrisy since they saw no conflict between their secret and their open religious rites, though esoteric knowledge was often thought to be legitimate only if confined to the initiates or those considered "mature".

Sometimes these matters presented a problem and caused friction between the Jews and their Roman overlords. Charismatic individuals, and eschatological and messianic movements, had become an established part of both the social and religious scene. Ideas of an afterlife seem to have started developing during the Persian period and continued to do so during Greek and Roman rule. Often this involved only personal afterlife, but many Jews looked forward to a climax to history, a great cosmic cataclysm in which God would intervene to save his people and destroy their enemies. In some cases, this involved a messianic figure of one sort or another (and there were many different variations on the theme) but not always. Now and then our sources tell us about a particular individual who was seen as having special powers, perhaps of healing, casting out demons, foreseeing the future and even bringing about specific events through prayer or magical knowledge. Such individuals did not always acquire a following, but they often did. The result was that many Jews were expecting imminent divine intervention to break the Roman yoke; more problematically, some individuals saw themselves as God's instrument in getting the process started by one means or another.

It usually did not matter if a revolt was intended; a group of potentially unruly individuals, especially if obedient to a leader whose objectives were not at all clear, would be pounced on immediately. There had been periodic revolts since Roman rule was established over the region, and, if anything, they appear to have increased through the first century under Roman rule. Agrippa I may have exacerbated the situation, since his reign was too short to take on many negative aspects, but it served to remind the people how much better off they were with a Herodian ruler than under direct Roman rule. Some movements may not have intended any direct challenge to Roman rule, but their very existence was seen as a threat. Other groups with a plainly revolutionary aim, such as the Sicarii, may have been motivated by religious ideals. Sadly, we know too little in most cases to characterize or make judgments about the movements that flit across the pages of Josephus.

When the revolt against Rome came in 66 CE, however, it had the support of many younger members of the high priestly and Herodian families (Price 1992). It was a popular revolt which caught the Romans off guard. It was a hopeless cause, despite the initial successes, because the Romans were able to concentrate a large portion of their military resources on the region. A major puzzle remains as to why, after driving out the Romans in the first round, the revolutionary government did not make proper preparation for the concerted Roman offensive which would unquestionably come. Instead, the different groups fought among themselves, dividing Jerusalem up among the factions and making common cause only when the Romans had invested the city. Our main source, Josephus, does not tell us because he tries to hide the popular nature of the revolt and the extent to which the upper classes were the driving force behind it. There are hints, however, that many had eschatological expectations, believing that they would be saved by divine intervention, and human military preparations were ultimately of no value. Otherwise, it is very difficult to explain the events that took place between 66 when Cestius was defeated and the final assault on Jerusalem in 70.

The destruction of Jerusalem and the temple in 70 was a traumatic event, yet there were evidently many who expected them to be rebuilt – as they had been after the exile. Some saw the very fact of what had happened as a sign of the eschaton and looked for the imminent intervention of God to destroy Rome and exalt the Jews. Their hopes were ultimately and finally dashed in the disastrous Bar Kokhba revolt of 132–35 CE. Much more significant in retrospect was the small gathering at Yavneh. To what extent it was known about and given weight is difficult to say, though some outsiders (Josephus?) apparently realized its potential.

With hindsight we can see how certain pre-70 trends were highly important in meeting the post-70 situation without temple or priestly leadership. The Pharisaic emphasis on creating a model of the temple in one's own home and seeing eternal values in the daily routine was probably very important, and much Pharisaic tradition appears to have found its place in rabbinic Judaism (albeit in developed and edited form). But other elements giving direction to the new situation were those aspects of Judaism that had evolved to meet the Diaspora situation: the synagogue, prayer, and the study of written scriptures. These had already started to have an effect on Palestinian Judaism even before 70. The seeds were sown for a Judaism *sine templo*; even if the temple had not been destroyed, Judaism might well have developed in new directions anyway. This does not mean that the sacrificial cult would have been abandoned. There would have been economic questions about the operation of the cult, but it must be remembered that most sacrifices had only token portions burned on the altar (as well as certain parts going to the priests) while most of the meat went to the offerer and his family. Even without the Roman destruction, Judaism was likely to have developed a new shape which placed more emphasis on these "para-temple" practices. The events of 66–70 hastened this process, and from the ashes a new Jewish phoenix took flight.

BIBLIOGRAPHY

Abegg, Martin, Jr, Peter Flint, and Eugene Ulrich (eds) (1999) *The Dead Sea Scrolls Bible*, Edinburgh: T. & T. Clark.

Ackroyd, P. R. (1970) *The Age of the Chronicler*, Supplement to Colloquium – The Australian and New Zealand Theological Review.

Aharoni, Yohanan (1981) *Arad Inscriptions*, in cooperation with Joseph Naveh; Jerusalem: Israel Exploration Society.

Albertz, Rainer (1978) *Persönliche Frömmigkeit und offizielle Religion: Religionsinterner Pluralismus in Israel und Babylon*, Calwer Theologische Monographien A 9; Stuttgart: Calwer.

—— (1994) *A History of Israelite Religion in the Old Testament Period*, 2 vols; London: SCM; ET of *Geschichte der israelitischen Religion*, 2 vols; Das Alte Testament Deutsch Ergänzungsreihe 8; Göttingen: Vandenhoeck & Ruprecht, 1992.

Aleksandrov, G. S. (1973) "The Role of Aqiba in the Bar Kokhba Rebellion", in J. Neusner, *Eliezar ben Hyrcanus*, 2 vols; SJLA 4; Leiden: Brill: 2.428–42 (= *REJ* 132 [1973] 65–77).

Alexander, Philip S. (1984) "Comparing Merkavah Mysticism and Gnosticism: An Essay in Method", *JJS* 35: 1–18.

—— (1986) "VII. Incantations and Books of Magic", in Emil Schürer, *The History of the Jewish People in the Age of Jesus Christ (175 B.C.–A.D. 135)*, Eng. version revised and ed. G. Vermes, F. Millar, and M. Goodman; Edinburgh: T. & T. Clark: 3.342–79.

—— (1996) "Physiognonomy, Initiation and Rank in the Qumran Community", in Hubert Cancik, Hermann Lichtenberger, and Peter Schäfer (eds) *Geschichte–Tradition–Reflexion: Festschrift für Martin Hengel zum 70. Geburtstag: Band I Judentum*, ed. Peter Schäfer; Tübingen: Mohr (Siebeck): 385–94.

Anderson, Gary A. (1987) *Sacrifices and Offerings in Ancient Israel: Studies in their Social and Political Importance*, HSM 41; Atlanta: Scholars Press.

Anderson, Gary A., and Saul M. Olyan (eds) (1991) *Priesthood and Cult in Ancient Israel*, JSOTSup 125; Sheffield Academic Press.

Anderson, Gary A., and Michael E. Stone (eds) (1999) *A Synopsis of the Books of Adam and Eve*, 2nd revised edn; SBLEJL 5; Atlanta: Scholars Press.

Andreasen, N.-E. A. (1972) *The Old Testament Sabbath*, SBL Dissertation 7, Missoula: Scholars Press.

Applebaum, S. (1971) "The Zealots: The Case for Revaluation", *JRS* 61: 155–70.

—— (1979) *Jews and Greeks in Ancient Cyrene*, SJLA 28; Leiden: Brill.

Archer, L. J. (1990) *Her Price Is Beyond Rubies: The Jewish Woman in Graeco-Roman Palestine*, JSOTSup 60; Sheffield Academic Press.

Argall, Randal A. (1995) *1 Enoch and Sirach: A Comparative Literary and Conceptual Analysis of the Themes of Revelation, Creation and Judgment*, SBLEJL 8; Atlanta: Scholars Press.

Arjava, Antti (1996) *Women and Law in Late Antiquity*, Oxford: Clarendon Press.

Athanassiadi, Polymnia and Michael Frede (eds) (1999) *Pagan Monotheism in Late Antiquity*, Oxford: Clarendon Press.

Atkinson, Kenneth (1998a) "Towards a Redating of the Psalms of Solomon: Implications for Understanding the *Sitz im Leben* of an Unknown Jewish Sect", *JSP* 17: 95–112.

—— (1998b) "On the Herodian Origin of Militant Davidic Messianism at Qumran: New Light from *Psalm of Solomon* 17", *JBL* 118: 435–60.

Auld, A. Graeme (1994) *Kings Without Privilege: David and Moses in the Story of the Bible's Kings*, Edinburgh: T. & T. Clark.

Aune, David E. (1980) "Magic in Early Christianity", *ANRW II*: 23.2: 1507–57.

—— (1983) *Prophecy in Early Christianity and the Ancient Mediterranean World*, Grand Rapids, MI: Eerdmans.

Avigad, Nahman (1976) *Bullae and Seals from a Post-Exilic Judean Archive*, Qedem 4; Jerusalem: Hebrew University.

Bamberger, B. J. (1977) "Philo and the Aggadah", *HUCA* 48: 153–85.

Barag, Dan, *et al.* (eds) (1994) *Masada IV: The Yigael Yadin Excavations 1963–1965, Final Reports*, Masada Reports; Jerusalem: Israel Exploration Society.

Barclay, John M. G. (1996) *Jews in the Mediterranean Diaspora from Alexander to Trajan (323 BCE–117 CE)*, Edinburgh: T. & T. Clark.

Bar-Ilan, Meir (1998) *Some Jewish Women in Antiquity*, BJS 317; Atlanta: Scholars Press.

Barker, Margaret (1992) *The Great Angel: A Study of Israel's Second God*, London: SPCK.

Bar-Kochva, Bezalel (1996) *Pseudo-Hecataeus*, On the Jews: *Legitimizing the Jewish Diaspora*, Hellenistic Culture and Society 21; Berkeley/Los Angeles/London: University of California.

Barnett, P. W. (1980–81) "The Jewish Sign Prophets – A.D. 40–70: Their Intentions and Origin", *NTS* 27: 679–97.

Barr, James (1979) "The Typology of Literalism in Ancient Biblical Translations", *Mitteilungen des Septuaginta-Unternehmens* 15 (= *Nachrichten der Akademie der Wissenschaften in Göttingen*, Phil.-hist. klasse, Nr. 11): 275–325.

Barstad, Hans M. (1996) *The Myth of the Empty Land: A Study in the History and Archaeology of Judah During the "Exilic" Period*, Symbolae Osloenses 28; Oslo/Cambridge MA: Scandinavian University Press.

—— (1997) "History and the Hebrew Bible", in Lester L. Grabbe (ed.) *Can a "History of Israel" Be Written?*, European Seminar in Historical Methodology 1 = JSOTSup 245; Sheffield Academic Press: 37–64.

Barthélemy, D. (1963) *Les devanciers d'Aquila*, VTSup 10; Leiden: Brill.

Bartholomew, Craig G. (1998) *Reading Ecclesiastes: Old Testament Exegesis and Hermeneutical Theory*, AnBib 139; Rome: Pontifical Biblical Institute.

Bartlett, John R. (1998) *1 Maccabees*, Guides to Apocrypha and Pseudepigrapha; Sheffield Academic Press.

Barton, John (1997a) *The Spirit and the Letter: Studies in the Biblical Canon*, London: SPCK (= *Holy Writings, Sacred Text: The Canon in Early Christianity*, Louisville, KY: Westminster John Knox).

—— (1997b) *Making the Christian Bible*, London: Darton, Longman, and Todd (= *How the Bible Came to Be*, Louisville, KY: Westminster John Knox).

Bauckham, Richard (1993) *The Climax of Prophecy: Studies on the Book of Revelation*, Edinburgh: T. & T. Clark.

—— (1998) *The Fate of the Dead: Studies on the Jewish and Christian Apocalypses*, NovTSup 93; Leiden: Brill.

Bauer, Walter (1971) *Orthodoxy and Heresy in Earliest Christianity*, eds Robert A. Kraft and Gerhard Krodel; Philadelphia: Fortress; ET and supplementation of *Rechtgläubigkeit und Ketzerei im ältesten Christentum*, Beiträge zur historischen Theologie 10; Tübingen: Mohr (Siebeck), 1934.

Baumgarten, Albert I. (1984–85) "*Korban* and the Pharisaic *Paradosis*", *JANES* 16–17: 5–17.

—— (1987) "The Pharisaic *Paradosis*", *HTR* 80: 63–77.

—— (1997) *The Flourishing of Jewish Sects in the Maccabean Era: An Interpretation*, JSJSup 55; Leiden: Brill.

Baumgarten, Joseph M., Esther G. Chazon, and Avital Pinnick (eds) (2000) *The Damascus Document: A Centennial of Discovery: Proceedings of the Third International Symposium of the Orion Center for the Study of the Dead Sea Scrolls and Associated Literature, 4–8 February, 1998*, STDJ 34; Leiden: Brill.

Becker, Joachim (1980) *Messianic Expectation in the Old Testament*, transl. D. E. Green; Edinburgh: T. & T. Clark; Philadelphia: Fortress; ET of *Messiaserwartung im Alten Testament*, Stuttgart: Katholisches Bibelwerk, 1977.

Becking, Bob (1992) *The Fall of Samaria: An Historical and Archaeological Study*, Studies in the History of the Ancient Near East 2; Leiden: Brill.

—— (1998) "Ezra's Re-enactment of the Exile", in Lester L. Grabbe (ed.) "*The Exile" as History and Ideology*, JSOTSup 278 = European Seminar in Historical Methodology 2; Sheffield Academic Press: 40–61.

Becking, Bob, and Meindert Dijkstra (eds) (1998) *Één God aleen . . .? Over monotheïsme in Oud-Israël en de verering van de godin Asjera*, Kampen: Kok Pharos.

Beckwith, Roger (1985) *The Old Testament Canon of the New Testament Church and its Background in Early Judaism*, London: SPCK.

Beentjes, Pancratius C. (1997a) *The Book of Ben Sira in Hebrew: A Text Edition of all Extant Hebrew Manuscripts and a Synopsis of all Parallel Hebrew Ben Sira Texts*, VTSup 68; Leiden: Brill.

—— (ed.) (1997b) *The Book of Ben Sira in Modern Research*, BZAW 255; Berlin/New York: de Gruyter.

Bellinger, William H., Jr, and William R. Farmer (eds) (1998) *Jesus and the Suffering Servant: Isaiah 53 and Christian Origins*, Harrisburg, PA: Trinity Press International.

Ben-Dov, Meir (1985) *In the Shadow of the Temple: The Discovery of Ancient Jerusalem*, transl. I. Friedman; Jerusalem: Keter; ET of חפירות הר הבית, Jerusalem: Keter, 1982.

—— (1986) "Herod's Mighty Temple Mount", *BAR* 12/6: 40–49.

Berchman, Robert M. (ed.) (1998) *Mediators of the Divine: Horizons of Prophecy, Divination, Dreams and Theurgy in Mediterranean Antiquity*, SFSJH 163; Atlanta: Scholars Press.

337

Bergren, Theodore A. (1997) "Nehemiah in 2 Maccabees 1:10–2:18", *JSJ* 28: 249–70.

Berlinerblau, Jacques (1996) *The Vow and the "Popular Religious Groups" of Ancient Israel: A Philological and Sociological Inquiry*, JSOTSup 210; Sheffield Academic Press.

Berman, D. (1979) "Hasidim in Rabbinic Traditions", in P. J. Achtemeier (ed.) *Society of Biblical Literature 1979 Seminar Papers*, Missoula, MT: Scholars Press: 2.15–33.

Bernstein, Moshe, Florentino García Martínez, and John Kampen (eds) (1997) *Legal Texts and Legal Issues: Proceedings of the Second Meeting of the International Organization for Qumran Studies, Cambridge 1995, Published in Honour of Joseph M. Baumgarten*, STDJ 23; Leiden: Brill.

Berquist, Jon L. (1995) *Judaism in Persia's Shadow: A Social and Historical Approach*, Minneapolis: Fortress.

Bertrand, J. M. (1982) "Sur l'inscription d'Hefzibah", *ZPE* 46: 167–74.

Bickerman, E. J. (1967) "Koheleth (Ecclesiastes) or The Philosophy of an Acquisitive Society", *Four Strange Books of the Bible: Jonah/Daniel/Koheleth/Esther*, New York: Schocken: 139–67.

—— (1976) "The Date of Fourth Maccabees", *Studies in Jewish and Christian History*, AGAJU 9/1; Leiden: Brill: 1.275–81.

—— (1980a) "Une question d'authenticite: les privilèges juifs", *Studies in Jewish and Christian History*, AGAJU 9/2; Leiden: Brill: 2.24–43.

—— (1980b) "La charte séleucide de Jérusalem", *Studies in Jewish and Christian History*, AGAJU 9/2; Leiden: Brill: 2.44–85 (orig. *REJ* 100 [1935]).

—— (1980c) "Une proclamation séleucide relative au temple de Jérusalem", *Studies in Jewish and Christian History*, AGAJU 9/2; Leiden: Brill: 2.86-104 (orig. *Syria* 25 [1946–48]).

Binder, Donald D. (1999) *Into the Temple Courts: The Place of the Synagogues in the Second Temple Period*, SBLDS 169; Atlanta: Scholars Press.

Birnbaum, Ellen (1996) *The Place of Judaism in Philo's Thought. Israel, Jews, and Proselytes*, BJS 290; Studia Philonica Monographs 2; Atlanta: Scholars Press.

Black, Matthew (1970) *Apocalypsis Henochi Graece*, Pseudepigrapha Veteris Testamenti Graece 3; Leiden: Brill.

—— (1974) "Judas of Galilee and Josephus's 'Fourth Philosophy'", in O. Betz, *et al.* (ed.) *Josephus-Studien*, O. Michel FS; Göttingen: Vandenhoeck & Ruprecht: 45–54.

—— (1985) *The Book of Enoch or I Enoch: A New English Edition with Commentary and Textual Notes*, SVTP 7; Leiden: Brill, 1985.

Blackburn, Barry Lee (1991) *Theios Aner and the Markan Miracle Traditions: A Critique of the Theos Aner Concept as an Interpretative Background of the Miracle Traditions Used by Mark*, WUNT 2/40; Tübingen: Mohr (Siebeck).

Blenkinsopp, Joseph (1981) "Interpretation and the Tendency to Sectarianism: An Aspect of Second Temple History", in E. P. Sanders, *et al.* (eds) *Jewish and Christian Self-Definition 2*, Aspects of Judaism in the Graeco-Roman Period; London: SCM: 2.1–26.

—— (1990) "A Jewish Sect of the Persian Period", *CBQ* 52: 5–20.

—— (1991) *The Pentateuch: An Introduction to the First Five Books of the Bible*, London: SCM.

—— (1995) *Sage, Priest, Prophet: Religious and Intellectual Leadership in Ancient Israel*, Library of Ancient Israel; Louisville, KY: Westminster John Knox.

—— (1996a) *A History of Prophecy in Israel*, 2nd edn; Louisville, KY: Westminster John Knox.

—— (1996b) "An Assessment of the Alleged Pre-Exilic Date of the Priestly Material in the Pentateuch", *ZAW* 108: 495–578.

—— (1998) "The Judaean Priesthood during the Neo-Babylonian and Achaemenid Periods: A Hypothetical Reconstruction", *CBQ* 60: 25–43.

Boccaccini, Gabriele (1991) *Middle Judaism: Jewish Thought, 300 B.C.E. to 200 C.E.*, Minneapolis: Fortress.

—— (1998) *Beyond the Essene Hypothesis: The Parting of the Ways between Qumran and Enochic Judaism*, Grand Rapids, MI: Eerdmans.

Bohak, Gideon (1995) "CPJ III, 520: The Egyptian Reaction to Onias' Temple", *JSJ* 26: 32–41.

—— (1996) *Joseph and Aseneth and the Jewish Temple in Heliopolis*, SBLEJL 10; Atlanta: Scholars Press.

Böhler, Dieter (1997) *Die heilige Stadt in Esdras α und Esra-Nehemia: Zwei Konzeptionen der Wiederherstellung Israels*, OBO 158; Freiburg (Schweiz): Universitätsverlag; Göttingen: Vandenhoeck & Ruprecht.

Bokser, Baruch M. (1985) "Wonder-Working and the Rabbinic Tradition: The Case of Hanina ben Dosa", *JSJ* 16: 42–92.

—— (1992) "Unleavened Bread and Passover, Feasts of", *ABD*: 6.755–65.

Bolin, Thomas M. (1996) "When the End Is the Beginning: The Persian Period and the Origins of the Biblical Tradition", *SJOT* 10: 3–15.

—— (1997) *Freedom Beyond Forgiveness: The Book of Jonah Re-Examined*, JSOTSup 236 = Copenhagen International Seminar 3; Sheffield Academic Press.

Borg, M. (1971) "The Currency of the Term 'Zealot'", *JTS* 22: 504–12.

Borgen, Peder (1997) *Philo of Alexandria: An Exegete for his Time*, NovTSup 86; Leiden: Brill.

Borgen, Peder, Kåre Fuglseth, and Roald Skarsten (2000) *The Philo Index: A Complete Greek Word Index to the Writings of Philo of Alexandria*, Leiden: Brill; Grand Rapids, MI: Eerdmans.

Böttrich, Christfried (1991) "Recent Studies in the *Slavonic Book of Enoch*", *JSP* 9: 35–42.

—— (1992) *Weltweisheit, Menschheitsethik, Urkult: Studien zum slavischen Henochbuch*, WUNT 2. Reihe 50; Tübingen: Mohr.

—— (1996) *Das slavische Henochbuch*, JSHRZ, Band 5 Apokalypsen, Liefergung 7; Gütersloh: Gütersloher Verlagshaus.

Bourdillon, M. F. C., and M. Fortes (eds) (1980) *Sacrifice*, London: Academic Press.

Bowman, Alan K., and Greg Woolf (eds) (1994) *Literacy and Power in the Ancient World*, Cambridge University Press.

Braun, Joachim (1999) *Die Musikkultur Altisraels/Palästinas: Studien zu archäologischen, schriftlichen und vergleichenden Quellen*, OBO 164; Freiburg (Schweiz): Universitätsverlag; Göttingen: Vandenhoeck & Ruprecht.

Breitenstein, U. (1976) *Beobachtungen zu Sprache, Stil und Gedankengut des Vierten Maccabäerbuchs*, Basel/Stuttgart: Schwabe.

Brenner, Athalya (1989) *The Song of Songs*, Old Testament Guides; Sheffield Academic Press.

—— (ed.) (1993a) *A Feminist Companion to Song of Songs*, The Feminist Companion to the Bible 1; Sheffield Academic Press.

—— (ed.) (1993b) *A Feminist Companion to Ruth*, The Feminist Companion to the Bible 3; Sheffield Academic Press.

—— (ed.) (1995) *A Feminist Companion to Esther, Judith and Susanna*, The Feminist Companion to the Bible 7; Sheffield Academic Press.

Brewer, David Instone (1992) *Techniques and Assumptions in Jewish Exegesis before 70 CE*, TSAJ 30; Tübingen: Mohr (Siebeck).

Brock, Sebastian P. (1974) *Testamentum Iobi*, PVTG 2; Leiden: Brill.

—— (1979) "Aspects of Translation Technique in Antiquity", *Greek, Roman, and Byzantine Studies* 20: 69–87.

—— (1984) "The Psalms of Solomon", in H. F. D. Sparks (ed.) *The Apocryphal Old Testament*, Oxford: Clarendon: 649–82.

—— (1996) *The Recensions of the Septuagint Version of I Samuel* (with a foreword by Natalio Fernández Marcos; Quaderni di Henoch 9; Torino: Silvio Zamorani Editore.

Brock, Sebastian P., *et al.* (1973) *A Classified Bibliography of the Septuagint*, ALGHJ 6; Leiden: Brill.

Brody, Robert (1999) "Evidence for Divorce by Jewish Women?" *JJS* 50: 230–34.

Brooke, George J. (1985) *Exegesis at Qumran: 4Q Florilegium in its Jewish Context*, JSOTSup 29; Sheffield Academic Press.

—— (1998) "Kingship and Messianism in the Dead Sea Scrolls", in John Day (ed.) *King and Messiah in Israel and the Ancient Near East: Proceedings of the Oxford Old Testament Seminar*, JSOTSup 270; Sheffield Academic Press: 434–55.

Brooke, George J., with Florentino García Martínez (eds) (1994) *New Qumran Texts and Studies: Proceedings of the First Meeting of the International Organization for Qumran Studies, Paris 1992*, STDJ 15; Leiden: Brill.

Brooke, George J., Lawrence H. Schiffman, and James C. VanderKam (eds) (1994–) *Dead Sea Discoveries* 1– .

Brooten, Bernadette J. (1982) *Women Leaders in the Ancient Synagogue*, BJS 36; Atlanta: Scholars Press.

—— (1991) "Iael προστάτης in the Jewish Donative Inscription from Aphrodisias", in Birger A. Pearson (ed.) *The Future of Early Christianity: Essays in Honor of Helmut Koester*, Minneapolis: Fortress: 149–62.

—— (1996) *Love between Women: Early Christian Responses to Female Homoeroticism*; University of Chicago.

Brosius, Maria (1996) *Women in Ancient Persia (559–331 BC)*, Oxford Classical Monographs; Oxford: Clarendon Press.

Brown, C. A. (1992) *No Longer Be Silent: First Century Jewish Portraits of Biblical Women: Studies in Pseudo-Philo's* Biblical Antiquities *and Josephus's* Jewish Antiquities, Gender and the Biblical Tradition; Louisville, KY: Westminster John Knox.

Brownlee, William H. (1953) "The Servant of the Lord in the Qumran Scrolls I", *BASOR* 132: 8–15.

—— (1954) "The Servant of the Lord in the Qumran Scrolls II", *BASOR* 135: 33–38.

Budd, Philip J. (1996) *Leviticus* (New Century Bible Commentary; Grand Rapids, MI: Eerdmans; London: Marshall Pickering, 1996).

Burkes, Shannon (1999) *Death in Qoheleth and Egyptian Biographies of the Late Period*, SBLDS 170; Atlanta: Scholars Press.

Bush, Frederic (1996) *Ruth/Esther*, WBC 9; Dallas: Word Books.

Busink, T. A. (1980) *Der Tempel von Jerusalem von Salomo bis Herodes: Eine archäologisch-historische Studie unter Berücksichtigung des westsemitischen Tempelbaus: 2. Von Ezechiel bis Middot*, Leiden: Brill.

Butterworth, M. (1992) *Structure and the Book of Zechariah*, JSOTSup 130; Sheffield Academic Press.

Calabi, Francesca (1998) *The Language and the Law of God: Interpretation and Politics in Philo of Alexandria*, transl. M. Leone; SFSHJ 188; Atlanta: Scholars Press.

Calduch-Benages, N., and J. Vermeylen (eds) (1999) *Treasures of Wisdom: Studies in Ben Sira and the Book of Wisdom: Festschrift M. Gilbert*, BETL 143; Leuven: Peeters/University Press.

Cameron, Averil, and Amélie Kuhrt (eds) (1993) *Images of Women in Antiquity*, 2nd edn; London: Routledge.

Camp, Claudia V. (1991) "Understanding a Patriarchy: Women in Second Century Jerusalem Through the Eyes of Ben Sira", in Amy-Jill Levine (ed.) *"Women Like This": New Perspectives on Jewish Women in the Greco-Roman World*, SBLEJL 1; Atlanta: Scholars Press: 1–39.

Caquot, André (1966) "Ben Sira et le messianisme", *Semitica* 16: 43–68.

Carleton Paget, James (1996) "Jewish Proselytism at the Time of Christian Origins: Chimera or Reality?" *JSNT* 62: 65–103.

Carroll, Robert P. (1992) "The Myth of the Empty Land", in David Jobling and T. Pippin (eds) *Ideological Criticism of Biblical Texts*, Semeia 59; Atlanta: Scholars Press: 79–93.

Carter, Charles E. (1999) *The Emergence of Yehud in the Persian Period: A Social and Demographic Study*, JSOTSup 294; Sheffield Academic Press.

Casey, Maurice (1979) *Son of Man: The Interpretation and Influence of Daniel 7*, London: SPCK.

Cavallin, H. C. C. (1974) *Life after Death: Paul's Argument for the Resurrection of the Dead in I Cor 15, Part I: An Enquiry into the Jewish Background*, ConB, NT Series 7:1; Lund: Gleerup.

Charles, R. H. (1908) *The Testaments of the Twelve Patriarchs, Translated . . . with Notes*, Oxford: Clarendon.

—— (ed.) (1913a) *Apocrypha and Pseudepigrapha of the Old Testament*, 2 vols; Oxford: Clarendon.

—— (1913b) *The Book of Enoch*, Oxford: Clarendon.

—— (1920) *A Critical and Exegetical Commentary on the Revelation of St. John*, 2 vols; ICC; Edinburgh: T. & T. Clark.

Charles, R. H., and W. R. Morfill (1896) *The Book of the Secrets of Enoch*, Oxford: Clarendon.

Charlesworth, James H. (1980) "The Portrayal of the Righteous as an Angel", in J. J. Collins and G. W. E. Nickelsburg (eds) *Ideal Figures in Ancient Judaism: Profiles and Paradigms*, SBLSCS 12; Atlanta: Scholars: 135–51.

—— (ed.) (1983–85) *Old Testament Pseudepigrapha*, 2 vols; Garden City, NY: Doubleday.

—— (1987) "Jewish Interest in Astrology during the Hellenistic and Roman Period", *ANRW II: Principate*: 20.2.926–50.

—— (ed.) (1992) *The Messiah: Developments in Earliest Judaism and Christianity*, with

J. Brownson, M. T. Davis, S. J. Kraftchick, and A. F. Segal; The First Princeton Symposium on Judaism and Christian Origins; Minneapolis: Fortress.

—— (ed.) (1994) *The Lord's Prayer and Other Prayer Texts from the Greco-Roman Era*, with M. Harding and M. Kiley; Valley Forge, PA: Trinity Press International.

Charlesworth, James H., Hermann Lichtenberger, and Gerbern S. Oegema (eds) (1998) *Qumran-Messianism: Studies on the Messianic Expections in the Dead Sea Scrolls*, Tübingen: Mohr (Siebeck).

Charlesworth, James H., *et al.* (eds) (1994–) *The Dead Sea Scrolls: Hebrew, Aramaic, and Greek Texts with English Translations. I– ,* The Princeton Theological Seminary Dead Sea Scrolls Project; Tübingen: Mohr; Louisville, KY: Westminster John Knox.

Chazon, Esther G. (1992) "Is *Divrei ha-me'orot* a Sectarian Prayer?" in Devorah Dimant and Uriel Rappaport (eds) *The Dead Sea Scrolls: Forty Years of Research*, STDJ 10; Jerusalem: Magnes Press: 3–17.

—— (1994) "Prayers from Qumran and Their Historical Implications", *DSD* 1: 265–84.

Chazon, Esther G. and Michael E. Stone (eds) (1999), with the collaboration of Avital Pinnick, *Pseudepigraphic Perspectives: The Apocrypha and Pseudepigrapha in Light of the Dead Sea Scrolls: Proceedings of the International Symposium of the Orion Center for the Study of the Dead Sea Scrolls and Associated LIterature, 12–14 January, 1997*, STDJ 31; Leiden: Brill.

Cheon, Samuel (1997) *The Exodus Story in the Wisdom of Solomon: A Study in Biblical Interpretation*, JSPSup 23; Sheffield Academic Press.

Chesnutt, Randall D. (1995) *From Death to Life: Conversion in Joseph and Aseneth*, JSPSup 16; Sheffield Academic Press.

Chiat, M. J. S. (1981) "First-Century Synagogue Architecture: Methodological Problems", in L. I. Levine (ed.) *Ancient Synagogues Revealed*, Jerusalem: Israel Exploration Society: 49–60.

—— (1982) *Handbook of Synagogue Architecture*, BJS 29; Atlanta: Scholars Press.

Childs, Brevard S. (1959) "The Enemy from the North and the Chaos Tradition", *JBL* 78: 187–98.

Chyutin, Michael (1997) *The New Jerusalem Scroll from Qumran: A Comprehensive Reconstruction*, JSPSup 25; Sheffield Academic Press.

Clifford, Richard J. (1999) *Proverbs*, OTL; London: SCM; Louisville, KY: Westminster John Knox.

Clines, David J. A. (1974) "The Evidence for an Autumnal New Year in Pre-exilic Israel Reconsidered", *JBL* 93: 22–40.

—— (1976) "New Year", *IDBSup*: 625–29.

—— (1984a) *Ezra, Nehemiah, Esther*, Century Bible Commentary; London: Marshall, Morgan & Scott; Grand Rapids, MI: Eerdmans.

—— (1984b) *The Esther Scroll: The Story of the Story*, JSOTSup 30; Sheffield Academic Press.

—— (1989) *Job 1–20*, WBC 17; Dallas: Word.

—— (1990) "The Nehemiah Memoir: The Perils of Autobiography", *What Does Eve Do to Help? and Other Readerly Questions to the Old Testament*, JSOTSup 94; Sheffield Academic Press: 124–64.

Cody, A. (1969) *A History of Old Testament Priesthood*, AnBib 35; Rome: Pontifical Biblical Institute.

Cogan, Mordechai (1993) "Judah under Assyrian Hegemony: A Re-examination of Imperialism and Religion", *JBL* 112: 403–14.

Coggins, Richard J. (1987) *Haggai, Zechariah, Malachi*, OT Guides; Sheffield: JSOT Press.

—— (1998) *Sirach*, Guides to Apocrypha and Pseudepigrapha; Sheffield Academic Press.

Cohen, Shaye J. D. (1984) "The Significance of Yavneh: Pharisees, Rabbis, and the End of Jewish Sectarianism", *HUCA* 55: 27–53.

—— (1987) *From the Maccabees to the Mishnah*, Library of Early Christianity; Philadelphia: Westminster.

—— (1999) *The Beginnings of Jewishness: Boundaries, Varieties, Uncertainties*, Hellenistic Culture and Society 31; Berkeley/Los Angeles/London: University of California.

Collins, John J. (1977) *The Apocalyptic Vision of the Book of Daniel*, HSM 16; Atlanta: Scholars Press.

—— (1979) (ed.) *Apocalypse: The Morphology of a Genre*, Semeia 14; Atlanta: Scholars Press.

—— (1980) "The Epic of Theodotus and the Hellenism of the Hasmoneans", *HTR* 73: 91–104.

—— (1993) *A Commentary on the Book of Daniel*, Hermeneia; Minneapolis: Fortress.

—— (1994) "The Works of the Messiah", *DSD* 1: 98–112.

—— (1995) *The Scepter and the Star: The Messiahs of the Dead Sea Scrolls and Other Ancient Literature*, Anchor Bible Reference Library; New York: Doubleday.

—— (1997a) *Apocalypticism in the Dead Sea Scrolls*, Literature of the Dead Sea Scrolls; London/New York: Routledge.

—— (1997b) *Jewish Wisdom in the Hellenistic Age*, OTL; Edinburgh: T. & T. Clark; Louisville, KY: Westminster/John Knox.

—— (1998) *The Apocalyptic Imagination: An Introduction to Jewish Apocalyptic Literature*, 2nd edn, Grand Rapids, MI: Eerdmans.

—— (ed.) (1999) *The Encyclopedia of Apocalypticism: Volume 1: The Origins of Apocalypticism in Judaism and Christianity*, New York: Continuum.

—— (2000) *Between Athens and Jerusalem: Jewish Identity in the Hellenistic Diaspora*, 2nd edn; Grand Rapids, MI: Eerdmans; Livonia, MI: Dove.

Collins, John. J., and James H. Charlesworth (eds) (1991) *Mysteries and Revelations: Apocalyptic Studies since the Uppsala Colloquium*, JSPSup 9; Sheffield Academic Press.

Collins, John J., and Peter W. Flint (eds) (2000) *The Book of Daniel: Composition and Reception*, The Formation and Interpretation of Old Testament Literature = VTSup; Leiden: Brill.

Collins, Nina L. (1991) "Ezekiel, the Author of the *Exagoge*: His Calendar and Home", *JSJ* 22: 201–11.

Cook, Johann (1997) *The Septuagint of Proverbs: Jewish and/or Hellenistic Proverbs?: Concerning the Hellenistic Colouring of LXX Proverbs*, VTSup 69; Leiden: Brill.

Cook, Stephen L. (1995) *Prophecy and Apocalypticism: The Postexilic Social Setting*, Minneapolis: Fortress.

Cotter, Wendy, CSJ (1999) *Miracles in Greco-Roman Antiquity: A Sourcebook*, The Context of Early Christianity; London/New York: Routledge.

Cotton, Hannah M. (1995) "The Archive of Salome Komaœse Daughter of Levi: Another Archive from the 'Cave of Letters'", *ZPE* 105: 171–208.

Cotton, Hannah M., and J. Geiger (1989) *Masada II: The Yigael Yadin Excavations 1963–1965, Final Reports: The Latin and Greek Documents*, with a contribution by J. D. Thomas; Jerusalem: Israel Exploration Society.

Cotton, Hannah M., and Ada Yardeni (eds) (1997) *Aramaic, Hebrew and Greek Documentary Texts from Naḥal Ḥever and Other Sites, with an Appendix Containing Alleged Qumran Texts (The Seiyâl Collection II)*, DJD 27; Oxford: Clarendon Press.

Cowley, A. (1923) *Aramaic Papyri of the Fifth Century B.C.*, Oxford: Clarendon; reprinted Osnabruck: Otto Zeller, 1967.

Craig, Kenneth M., Jr (1999) "Jonah in Recent Research", *CR: BS* 7: 97–118.

Craigie, Peter C. (1973) "Helel, Athtar and Phaethon (Jes 14$_{12-15}$)", *ZAW* 85: 223–25.

Crawford, Sidnie White (1998) "Lady Wisdom and Dame Folly at Qumran", *DSD* 5: 355–66.

Crenshaw, James (1988) *Ecclesiastes*, OTL; London: SCM.

—— (1998) *Education in Ancient Israel: Across the Deadening Silence*, Anchor Bible Reference Library; New York: Doubleday.

Cribiore, Raffaella (1996) *Writing, Teachers, and Students in Graeco-Roman Egypt*, American Studies in Papyrology 36; Atlanta: Scholars Press.

Cross, Frank M., and Esther Eshel (1997) "Ostraca from Khirbet Qumran", *IEJ* 47: 17–29.

Cross, Frank M., and Shemaryahu Talmon (eds) (1975) *Qumran and the History of the Biblical Text*, Cambridge, MA: Harvard.

Cryer, Frederick H. (1987) "The 360-Day Calendar Year and Early Judaic Sectarianism", *SJOT* 1: 116–22.

—— (1994) *Divination in Ancient Israel and its Near Eastern Environment: A Socio-Historical Investigation*, JSOTSup 142; Sheffield Academic Press.

—— (1997) "The Qumran Conveyance: A Reply to F. M. Cross and E. Eshel", *SJOT* 11: 232–40.

Cryer, Frederick H., and Thomas L. Thompson (eds) (1998) *Qumran Between the Old and New Testaments*, JSOTSup 290 = Copenhagen International Seminar 6; Sheffield Academic Press.

Daube, David (1990) "On Acts 23: Sadducees and Angels", *JBL* 109: 493–97.

Davenport, Gene L. (1971) *The Eschatology of the Book of Jubilees*, SPB 20; Leiden: Brill.

Davidson, Maxwell J. (1992) *Angels at Qumran: A Comparative Study of 1 Enoch 1–36, 72–108 and Sectarian Writings from Qumran*, JSPSup 11; Sheffield Academic Press.

Davies, Graham I. (1991) *Ancient Hebrew Inscriptions: Corpus and Concordance*, Cambridge University Press.

Davies, Philip R. (1977) "*Ḥasîdîm* in the Maccabean Period", *JJS* 28: 127–40.

—— (1982a) *Qumran*, Cities of the Biblical World; Guildford, Surrey: Lutterworth.

—— (1982b) "The Ideology of the Temple in the Damascus Document", *JJS* 33: 287–301.

—— (1983) *The Damascus Covenant: An Interpretation of the "Damascus Document"*, JSOTSup 25; Sheffield Academic Press.

—— (1985) "Eschatology at Qumran", *JBL* 104: 39-55.

—— (1987) *Behind the Essenes: History and Ideology in the Dead Sea Scrolls*, BJS 94; Atlanta: Scholars Press.

—— (1989) "The Social World of the Apocalyptic Writings", in Ronald E. Clements (ed.) *The World of Ancient Israel: Sociological, Anthropological and Political Perspectives, Essays by Members of the Society for Old Testament Study*, Cambridge University Press: 251–71.

—— (1995a) "Was There Really a Qumran Community?" *CR: BS* 3: 9–36.

—— (1995b) "God of Cyrus, God of Israel: Some Religio-Historical Reflections on Isaiah 40–55", in Jon Davies, Graham Harvey, and Wilfred G. E. Watson (eds) *Words Remembered, Texts Renewed: Essays in Honour of John F. A. Sawyer*, JSOTSup 195; Sheffield Acadmic Press: 207–25.

—— (1998) *Scribes and Schools: The Canonization of the Hebrew Scriptures*, Library of Ancient Israel; Louisville, KY: Westminster John Knox; London: SPCK.

Davies, W. D. (1974) *The Gospel and the Land: Early Christianity and Jewish Territorial Doctrine*, Berkeley/Los Angeles: University of California.

—— (1982) *The Territorial Dimensions of Judaism*, Berkeley/Los Angeles: University of California.

Davila, James R. (1998) "4QMess ar (4Q534) and Merkavah Mysticism", *DSD* 5: 367–381.

Day, John (1985) *God's Conflict with the Dragon and the Sea*, Cambridge University Press.

—— (ed.) (1998) *King and Messiah in Israel and the Ancient Near East: Proceedings of the Oxford Old Testament Seminar*, JSOTSup 270; Sheffield Academic Press.

Day, Linda (1995) *Three Faces of a Queen: Characterization in the Books of Esther*, JSOTSup 186; Sheffield Academic Press.

Day, Peggy L. (1988) *An Adversary in Heaven: śāṭān in the Hebrew Bible*, HSM 43; Atlanta: Scholars Press.

Deines, Roland (1997) *Die Pharisäer: Ihr Verständnis im Spiegel der christlichen und jüdischen Forschung seit Wellhausen und Graetz*, WUNT 101; Tübingen: Mohr (Siebeck).

Delcor, M. (1973) *Le Testament d'Abraham: Introduction, traduction du texte grec et commentaire de la recension grecque longue, suivie de la traduction des Testaments d'Abraham, d'Isaac et de Jacob d'après les versions orientales*, SVTP 2; Leiden: Brill.

Dell, Katharine J. (1991) *The Book of Job as Sceptical Literature*, BZAW 197: Berlin/New York: de Gruyter.

deSilva, David A. (1998) *4 Maccabees*, Guides to Apocrypha and Pseudepigrapha, Sheffield Academic Press.

De Troyer, Kristin (1997) *Het einde van de Alpha-tekst van Ester: Vertaal- en verhaaltechniek van MT 8,1–17, LXX 8,1–17 en AT 7,14–41*, Leuven: Peeters.

Deutsch, Nathaniel (1999) *Guardians of the Gate: Angelic Vice Regency in Late Antiquity*, Brill's Series in Jewish Studies 22; Leiden: Brill.

Dexinger, Ferdinand (1977) *Henochs Zehnwochenapokalypse und offene Probleme der Apokalyptikforschung*, SPB 29; Leiden: Brill.

Dietrich, Manfried, Oswald Loretz, and Joaquín Sanmartín (eds) (1995) *The Cuneiform Alphabetic Texts from Ugarit, Ras Ibn Hani and Other Places* (KTU: 2nd, enlarged edn), Abhandlungen zur Literatur Alt-Syrien-Palästinas und Mesopotamiens 8; Münster: Ugarit-Verlag = KTU.

Dietrich, Walter, and Martin A. Klopfenstein (eds) (1994) *Ein Gott allein? JHWH-Verehrung und biblischer Monotheismus im Kontext der israelitischen und altorientalischen Religionsgeschichte*, Orbis Biblicus et Orientalis 139; Freiburg [Schweiz]: Universitätsverlag; Göttingen: Vandenhoeck & Ruprecht.

Díez Macho, Alejandro (1960) "The Recently Discovered Palestinian Targum: Its Antiquity and Relationship with the Other Targums", in *Congress Volume Oxford 1959*, VTSup 7; Leiden: Brill: 222–45.

Dihle, Albert (1974) "ψυχή", sections "A. ψυχή in the Greek World" and "C. Judaism: I, Hellenistic Judaism", in Gerhard Friedrich (ed.) *TDNT* 9: 608–17, 632–35.

DiLella, Alexander (1996) "The Wisdom of Ben Sira: Resources and Recent Research", *CR: BS* 4: 161–81.

Dillon, John (1977) *The Middle Platonists: A Study of Platonism 80 B.C. to A.D. 220*, Classical Life and Letters; London: Duckworth.

Dimant, Devorah, and Uriel Rappaport (eds) (1992) *The Dead Sea Scrolls: Forty Years of Research*, STDJ 10; Jerusalem: Magnes Press.

DiTommaso, Lorenzo (1998) "A Note on Demetrius the Chronographer, Fr. 2.11 (= Eusebius, *PrEv* 9.21.11)", *JSJ* 29: 81–91.

Dix, G. H. (1926) "The Messiah ben Joseph", *JTS* 27: 130–43.

Dogniez, Cécile (1995) *Bibliography of the Septuagint/Bibliographie de la Septante (1970–1993)*, with a Preface by P.-M. Bogaert; VTSup 60; Leiden: Brill.

Donner, Herbert, and W. Röllig (1962–64) *Kanaanäische und aramäische Inscriften, Mit einem Beitrag von O. Rössler*, vols 1–3; Wiesbaden: Harrassowitz.

Dorothy, Charles V. (1997) *The Books of Esther: Structure, Genre and Textual Integrity*, JSOTSup 187; Sheffield Academic Press.

Douglas, Mary (1966) *Purity and Danger: An Analysis of the Concepts of Pollution and Taboo*, London: Routledge & Kegan Paul.

—— (1999) *Leviticus as Literature*, Oxford University Press.

Dupont-Sommer, A. (1949) "De l'immortalité astrale dans la 'Sagesse de Salomon' (III 7)", *Revue des Études Grecques* 62: 80–87.

Durand, Xavier (1997) *Des Grecs en Palestine au III$_e$ siècle avant Jésus-Christ: Le dossier syrien des archives de Zénon de Caunos (261–252)*, Cahiers de la Revue Biblique 38; Paris: Gabalda.

Dyck, Jonathan E. (1998) *The Theocratic Ideology of the Chronicler*, Biblical Interpretation Series 33; Leiden: Brill.

Dyson, S. L. (1971) "Native Revolts in the Roman Empire", *Historia* 20: 239–74.

—— (1975) "Native Revolt Patterns in the Roman Empire", *ANRW II*: 3.138–75.

Edelman, Diana V. (ed.) (1995) *The Triumph of Elohim: From Yahwisms to Judaisms*, Contributions to Biblical Exegesis and Theology 13; Kampen: Kok Pharos; Grand Rapids, MI: Eerdmans.

Edwards, Douglas R., and C. Thomas McCollough (eds) (1997) *Archaeology and the Galilee: Texts and Contexts in the Graeco-Roman and Byzantine Periods*, SFSHJ 143; Atlanta: Scholars Press.

Eisenman, Robert (1983) *Maccabees, Zadokites, Christians and Qumran: A New Hypothesis of Qumran Origins*, SPB 34; Leiden: Brill.

Eisenman, Robert, and Michael O. Wise (1992) *The Dead Sea Scrolls Uncovered: The First Complete Translation and Interpretation of 50 Key Documents Withheld for Over 35 Years*, Shaftesbury, Dorset/Rockport, MA: Element.

Eissfeldt, Otto (1917) *Erstlinge und Zehnten im Alten Testament: Ein Beitrag zur Geschichte des israelitisch-jüdischen Kultus*, Beiträge zur Wissenschaft vom Alten Testament 22, Leipzig: J. C. Hinrichs.

Emmerson, Grace I. (1992) *Isaiah 56–66*, Old Testament Guides; Sheffield Academic Press.

Engbert-Pedersen, Troels (1999) "Philo's *De Vita Contemplativa* as a Philosopher's Dream", *JSJ* 30: 40–64.

Engel, Helmut (1998) *Das Buch der Weisheit*, Neuer Stuttgarter Kommentar: Altes Testament 16; Stuttgart: Katholisches Bibelwerk.

Evans, Craig A. (1993) "A Note on the 'First-Born Son' of 4Q369", *DSD* 2: 185–201.

Evans, Richard J. (1997) *In Defence of History*, London: Granta Books.

Evans-Pritchard, E. (1956) *Nuer Religion*, Oxford University Press.

Everson, A. J. (1974) "The Days of Yahweh", *JBL* 93: 329–37.

Falk, Daniel K. (1998) *Daily, Sabbath, and Festival Prayers in the Dead Sea Scrolls*, STDJ 27; Leiden: Brill.

Farmer, William R. (ed.) (1999) *Anti-Judaism and the Gospels*, Harrisburg, PA: Trinity Press International.

Feldman, Louis H. (1993) *Jew and Gentile in the Ancient World: Attitudes and Interactions from Alexander to Justinian*, Princeton, NJ: Princeton University Press.

—— (1995) "Reflections on Rutgers' 'Attitudes to Judaism in the Greco-Roman Period'", *JQR* 86: 153–70.

—— (1998a) *Studies in Josephus' Rewritten Bible*, JSJSup 58; Leiden: Brill.

—— (1998b) *Josephus's Interpretation of the Bible*, Hellenistic Culture and Society 27; Berkeley/Los Angeles/London: University of California.

Feldman, Louis H., and John R. Levison (eds) (1996) *Josephus' Contra Apionem: Studies in its Character and Context with a Latin Concordance to the Portion Missing in Greek*, AGAJU 34; Leiden: Brill.

Fine, Steven (ed.) (1996) *Sacred Realm: The Emergence of the Synagogue in the Ancient World*, Oxford University Press; New York: Yeshiva University Museum.

—— (1997) *This Holy Place: On the Sanctity of the Synagogue during the Greco-Roman Period*, Christianity and Judaism in Antiquity 11; Notre Dame, IN: University of Notre Dame.

—— (ed.) (1999) *Jews, Christians, and Polytheists in the Ancient Synagogue: Cultural Interaction during the Greco-Roman Period*, Baltimore Studies in the History of Judaism; London/New York: Routledge.

Finkelstein, J. J. (1961) "Amisaduqa's Edict and the Babylonian 'Law Codes'", *JCS* 15: 91–104.

Finkelstein, Louis (1936) *Akiba: Scholar, Saint and Martyr*, New York: Jewish Theological Society.

Finnegan, Ruth (1988) *Literacy and Orality: Studies in the Technology of Communication*, Oxford: Blackwell.

Fischer, Alexander A. (1997) *Skepsis oder Furcht Gottes? Studien zur Komposition und Theologie des Buches Kohelet*, BZAW 247; Berlin/New York: de Gruyter.

Fischer, T. (1979) "Zur Seleukideninschrift von Hefzibah", *ZPE* 33: 131–38.

Fischer, Ulrich (1978) *Eschatologie und Jenseitserwartung im hellenistischen Diasporajudentum*, BZNW 44; Berlin/New York: de Gruyter.

Fishbane, Michael (1985) *Biblical Interpretation in Ancient Israel*, Oxford: Clarendon; reprinted with addenda 1989.

Fittschen, Klaus, and Gideon Foerster (eds) (1996) *Judaea and the Greco-Roman World in the Time of Herod in the Light of Archaeological Evidence: Acts of a Symposium Organized by the Institute of Archaeology, the Hebrew University of Jerusalem and the Archaeological Institute, Georg-August-University of Göttingen at Jerusalem, November 3rd–4th 1988*, Abhandlungen der Akademie der Wissenschaften in Göttingen, Philologisch-Historische Klasse, 3te Folge, Nr 215; Göttingen: Vandenhoeck & Ruprecht.

Fitzmyer, Joseph A., SJ (1995a) "The Aramaic and Hebrew Fragments of Tobit from Cave 4", *CBQ* 57: 655–75.

—— (1995b) "Tobit", in James VanderKam (ed.) *Qumran Cave 4: XIV Parabiblical Texts, Part 2*, DJD 19; Oxford: Clarendon: 1–84.

—— (1998) *The Acts of the Apostles: A New Translation with Introduction and Commentary*, AB 31; New York: Doubleday.

—— (1999) "The So-Called Aramaic Divorce Text from Wadi Seiyal", in Baruch A. Levine, Philip J. King, Joseph Naveh, and Ephraim Stern (eds) *Frank Moore Cross Volume = Eretz-Israel* 26; Jerusalem: Israel Exploration Society: 16*–22*.

Fitzpatrick-McKinley, Anne (1999) *The Transformation of Torah from Scribal Advice to Law*, JSOTSup 287; Sheffield Academic Press.

Flesher, Paul V. M. (1989) "Palestinian Synagogues before 70 CE: A Review of the Evidence", in J. Neusner (ed.) *Approaches to Ancient Judaism VI: Studies in the Ethnography and Literature of Judaism*, BJS 192; Atlanta: Scholars Press: 68–81; reprinted in Urman, Dan, and Paul V. M. Flesher (eds) (1995) *Ancient Synagogues: Historical Analysis and Archaeological Discovery*, vols 1–2; SPB 47; Leiden: Brill: 27–39.

Flint, Peter W. and James C. VanderKam (eds) (1998), with the assistance of Andrea E. Alvarez, *The Dead Sea Scrolls after Fifty Years: A Comprehensive Assessment, vol. 1*, Leiden: Brill.

—— (1999), with the assistance of Andrea E. Alvarez, *The Dead Sea Scrolls after Fifty Years: A Comprehensive Assessment, vol. 2*, Leiden: Brill.

Focke, Friedrich (1913) *Die Entstehung der Weisheit Salomos: Ein Beitrag zur Geschichte des jüdischen Hellenismus*, FRLANT 22; Göttingen: Vandenhoeck & Ruprecht.

Foerster, Gideon (1981) "The Synagogues at Masada and Herodium", in Lee I. Levine (ed.) *Ancient Synagogues Revealed*, Jerusalem: Israel Exploration Society: 24–29.

—— (1995) *Masada V: The Yigael Yadin Excavations 1963-1965, Final Reports: Art and Architecture*, with a contribution by Naomi Porat; The Masada Reports; Jerusalem: Israel Exploration Society.

Fohrer, Georg (1982) "Der Tag Jhwhs", *Eretz-Israel* 16: 43*–50*.

Fossum, Jarl E. (1985) *The Name of God and the Angel of the Lord: Samaritan and Jewish Concepts of Intermediation and the Origin of Gnosticism*, WUNT 36; Tübingen: Mohr (Siebeck).

Fox, Michael V. (1999) *A Time to Tear Down and a Time to Build Up: A Rereading of Ecclesiastes*, Grand Rapids, MI: Eerdmans.

Freedman, David Noel (ed.) (1992) *Anchor Bible Dictionary*, 6 vols; Garden City, NY: Doubleday.

Frerichs, Ernest S., and J. Neusner (eds) (1986) *Goodenough on the History of Religion and on Judaism*, BJS 121; Atlanta: Scholars Press.

Freyne, Seán (1980) "The Charismatic", in G. W. E. Nickelsburg and J. J. Collins (eds) *Ideal Figures in Ancient Judaism*, SBLSCS 12; Atlanta: Scholars Press, 1980: 223–58.

Funck, Bernd (ed.) (1996) *Hellenismus: Beiträge zur Erforschung von Akkulturation und poli-*

tischer Ordnung in den Staaten des hellenistischen Zeitalters, Akten des Internationalen Hellenismus-Kolloquiums 9.–14. März 1994 in Berlin, Tübingen: Mohr (Siebeck).

Gafni, Isaiah M. (1997) *Land, Center and Diaspora: Jewish Constructs in Late Antiquity*, JSPSupp 21; Sheffield Academic Press.

Gager, J. G. (1972) *Moses in Greco-Roman Paganism*, SBLMS 16; Nashville: Abingdon.

Gamberoni, Johann (1997) "Das 'Gesetz des Mose' im Buch Tobias", in Georg Braulik (ed.) *Studien zu Pentateuch: Walter Kornfeld zum 60 Geburtstag*, Vienna: Herder: 227–42.

García Martínez, Florentino (1988) "Qumran Origins and Early History: A Groningen Hypothesis", *Folio Orientalia* 25: 113–36.

—— (1992) *Qumran and Apocalyptic: Studies on the Aramaic Texts from Qumran*, STDJ 9; Leiden: Brill.

—— (1996) *The Dead Sea Scrolls Translated: The Qumran Texts in English*, 2nd edn; trans. W. G. E. Watson; Leiden: Brill; Grand Rapids, MI: Eerdmans.

García Martínez, Florentino, and Ed Noort (eds) (1998) *Perspectives in the Study of the Old Testament and Early Judaism: A Symposium in Honour of Adam S. van der Woude on the Occasion of his 70th Birthday*, VTSup 73; Leiden: Brill.

García Martínez, Florentino, and Eibert J. C. Tigchelaar (eds and trans.) (1997–98) *The Dead Sea Scrolls Study Edition: Volume One, 1Q1–4Q273; Volume Two, 4Q274– 11Q31*, Leiden: Brill.

Gauger, Jörg-Dieter (1977) *Beiträge zur jüdischen Apologetik: Untersuchungen zur Authentizität von Urkunden bei Flavius Josephus und im I. Makkabäerbuch*, Bonner Biblische Beiträge 49; Cologne/Bonn: Peter Hanstein.

Gennep, A. van (1960) *The Rites of Passage*, London: Routledge & Kegan Paul.

Georgi, Dieter (1980) *Weisheit Salomos*, Jüdische Schriften aus hellenistisch-römischer Zeit III/4; Gütersloh: Mohn: 391–478.

Gera, Dov (1998) *Judaea and Mediterranean Politics 219 to 161 B.C.E.*, Brill's Series in Jewish Studies 8; Leiden: Brill.

Gereboff, J. (1979) *Rabbi Tarfon*, BJS 6; Atlanta: Scholars Press.

Gerstenberger, Erhard S. (1996) *Leviticus: A Commentary*, OTL; Louisville, KY: Westminster John Knox; ET of *Das dritte Buch Mose: Leviticus*, Das Alte Testament Deutsch 6; Göttingen: Vandenhoeck & Ruprecht, 1993.

Gibson, John C. L. (1975–82) *Textbook of Syrian Semitic Inscriptions*, vols 1–3; Oxford: Clarendon.

Gilbert, M., SJ (1973) *La critique des dieux dans le Livre de la Sagesse (Sg 13–15)*, AnBib 53; Rome: Pontifical Biblical Institute.

—— (1984) "Wisdom of Solomon", in M. E. Stone (ed.) *Jewish Writings of the Second Temple Period: Apocrypha, Pseudepigrapha, Qumran Sectarian Writings, Philo, Josephus*, Compendia Rerum Iudaicarum ad Novum Testamentum 2/2; Assen: Van Gorcum; Minneapolis: Fortress: 301–13.

—— (1986) "Sagesse de Salomon (ou Livre de la Sagesse)", in J. Briend and E. Cothenet (eds) *Supplément au Dictionnaire de la Bible*, Paris: Letouzey & Ané: 11.58– 119.

Gnuse, Robert Karl (1982) "A Reconsideration of the Form-Critical Structure in I Samuel 3: An Ancient Near Eastern Dream Theophany", *ZAW* 94: 379–90.

—— (1996) *Dreams and Dream Reports in the Writings of Josephus: A Traditio-Historical Analysis*, AGAJU 36; Leiden: Brill.

—— (1997) *No Other Gods: Emergent Monotheism in Israel*, JSOTSup 241; Sheffield Academic Press.

Golb, Norman (1995) *Who Wrote the Dead Sea Scrolls?* New York/London: Scribner.

Goldenberg, Robert (1997) *The Nations that Know Thee Not: Ancient Jewish Attitudes towards Other Religions*, The Biblical Seminar 52; Sheffield Academic Press.

Goldstein, Bernard R., and David Pingree (1977) "Horoscopes from the Cairo Geniza", *JNES* 36: 113–44.

Golka, Friedemann W. (1993) *The Leopard's Spots: Biblical and African Wisdom in Proverbs*, Edinburgh: T. & T. Clark.

Goodblatt, David (1980) "Towards the Rehabilitation of Talmudic History", in Baruch Bokser (ed.) *History of Judaism: The Next Ten Years*, BJS 21; Atlanta: Scholars Press: 31–44.

—— (1987) "Sanhedrin", *Encyclopedia of Religion*, New York/London: Macmillan: 13.60–63.

—— (1994) *The Monarchic Principle: Studies in Jewish Self-Government in Antiquity*, TSAJ 38; Tübingen: Mohr (Siebeck).

Goodenough, Erwin R. (1935) *By Light, Light: The Mystic Gospel of Hellenistic Judaism*, New Haven, CT: Yale.

—— (1938) *The Politics of Philo Judaeus, Practice and Theory: with a General Bibliography of Philo*, with H. L. Goodhart; New Haven, CT: Yale.

—— (1953–65) *Jewish Symbols in the Greco-Roman Period*, vols 1–13; Bollingen Series 37; New York: Pantheon.

—— (1962) *An Introduction to Philo Judaeus*, revised edn; Oxford: Clarendon.

—— (1988) *Jewish Symbols in the Greco-Roman Period*, abridged edn, with Introduction by J. Neusner; Bollingen Series; Princeton, NJ: Princeton University Press.

Goodman, Martin (1983) *State and Society in Roman Galilee, A.D. 132–212*, Oxford Centre for Postgraduate Hebrew Studies; Totowa, NJ: Rowman & Allanheld.

—— (1987) *The Ruling Class of Judaea: The Origins of the Jewish Revolt against Rome A.D. 66–70*, Cambridge University Press.

—— (1991) "Babatha's Story", *JRS* 81: 169–75.

—— (1992) "Jewish Proselytising in the First Century", in Judith Lieu, J. L. North, and Tessa Rajak (eds) *Jews among Pagans and Christians in the Roman Empire*, London: Routledge: 53–78.

—— (1994a) *Mission and Conversion: Proselytizing in the Religious History of the Roman Empire*, Oxford University Press.

—— (1994b) "Texts, Scribes and Power in Roman Judaea", in Alan. K. Bowman and Greg Woolf (eds) *Literacy and Power in the Ancient World*, Cambridge University Press: 99–108.

—— (1995) "A Note on the Qumran Sectarians, the Essenes and Josephus", *JJS* 46: 161–66.

—— (1997) *The Roman World 44 BC–AD 180*, with the assistance of Jane Sherwood; Routledge History of the Ancient World; London/New York: Routledge.

—— (ed.) (1998a) *Jews in a Graeco-Roman World*, Oxford: Clarendon Press.

—— (1998b) "Jews, Greeks, and Romans", in Martin Goodman (ed.) (1998a) *Jews in a Graeco-Roman World*, Oxford: Clarendon Press: 3–14.

—— (1999) "A Note on Josephus, the Pharisees and Ancestral Tradition", *JJS* 50: 17–20.

Gordis, Robert (1978) *The Book of Job: Commentary, New Translation, and Special Studies*, Morshet Series 2; New York: Jewish Theological Seminary.

Gorman, F. H., Jr (1990) *The Ideology of Ritual: Space, Time and Status in the Priestly Theology*, JSOTSup 91; Sheffield Academic Press.

Goudoever, J. van (1961) *Biblical Calendars*, Leiden: Brill.

Gowan, Donald E. (1986) *Eschatology in the Old Testament*, Philadelphia: Fortress.

Grabbe, Lester L. (1977) *Comparative Philology and the Text of Job: A Study in Methodology*, SBLDS 34; Chico, CA: Scholars Press.

—— (1979a) "The Jannes/Jambres Tradition in Targum Pseudo-Jonathan and its Date", *JBL* 98: 393–401.

—— (1979b) "Chronography in Hellenistic Jewish Historiography", in P. J. Achtemeier (ed.) *Society of Biblical Literature 1979 Seminar Papers*, SBLSPS 17; Missoula, MT: Scholars Press: 2.43–68.

—— (1981) "Chronography in 4 Ezra and 2 Baruch", *Society of Biblical Literature 1981 Seminar Papers*, SBLASP, Chico, CA: Scholars Press: 49–63.

—— (1982a) "The End of the World in Early Jewish and Christian Calculations", *RevQ* 41: 107–108.

—— (1982b) "Aquila's Translation and Rabbinic Exegesis", *Essays in Honour of Yigael Yadin* (= *JJS* 33): 527–36.

—— (1987a) "Josephus and the Reconstruction of the Judaean Restoration", *JBL* 106: 231–46.

—— (1987b) "Fundamentalism and Scholarship: The Case of Daniel", in B. P. Thompson (ed.) *Scripture: Method and Meaning: Essays Presented to Anthony Tyrrell Hanson for his Seventieth Birthday*, Hull: University Press: 133-52.

—— (1987c) "The Scapegoat Ritual: A Study in Early Jewish Interpretation", *JSJ* 18: 152–67.

—— (1988a) *Etymology in Early Jewish Interpretation: The Hebrew Names in Philo*, BJS 115; Atlanta: Scholars Press.

—— (1988b) "Synagogues in Pre-70 Palestine: A Re-assessment", *JTS* 39: 401–10; reprinted in Urman, Dan, and Paul V. M. Flesher (eds) *Ancient Synagogues: Historical Analysis and Archaeological Discovery* (vols 1–2; SPB 47; Leiden: Brill, 1995): 17–26.

—— (1989) "The Social Setting of Early Jewish Apocalypticism", *JSP* 4: 27–47.

—— (1991a) "Maccabean Chronology: 167–164 or 168–165 BCE?" *JBL* 110: 59–74.

—— (1991b) "Reconstructing History from the Book of Ezra", in P. R. Davies (ed.) *Second Temple Studies: The Persian Period*, JSOTSup 117, Sheffield: JSOT: 98–107.

—— (1991c) "Philo and Aggada: A Response to B. J. Bamberger", in David T. Runia, David M. Hay, and David Winston (eds) *Heirs of the Septuagint: Philo, Hellenistic Judaism and Early Christianity: Festschrift for Earle Hilgert = SPA* 3; Atlanta: Scholars Press: 153–66.

—— (1992a) *Judaism from Cyrus to Hadrian: Vol. 1: Persian and Greek Periods; Vol. 2: Roman Period*, Minneapolis: Fortress Press; reprinted London: SCM, 1994.

—— (1992b) "The Translation Technique of the Greek Minor Versions: Translations or Revisions?" in George J. Brooke and Barnabas Lindars (eds) *Septuagint, Scrolls and Cognate Writings: Papers Presented to the International Symposium on the Septuagint and Its Relations to the Dead Sea Scrolls and Other Writings (Manchester, 1990)* (SBLSCS 33; Atlanta: Scholars Press, 1992): 505–56.

—— (1992c) "The Authenticity of the Persian 'Documents' in Ezra", read to the Aramaic Section of the Society of Biblical Literature annual meeting, San Francisco, November 1992, publication forthcoming.

—— (1993a) *Leviticus*, Society for Old Testament Study, Old Testament Guides; Sheffield: JSOT.

—— (1993b) 'Betwixt and Between: The Samaritans in the Hasmonean Period', in E. H. Lovering, Jr (ed.) *Society of Biblical Literature 1993 Seminar Papers*, SBL SSP 32; Atlanta: Scholars Press: 334–47.

—— (1994a) 'What Was Ezra's Mission?' in T. C. Eskenazi and K. H. Richards (eds) *Second Temple Studies: 2. Temple Community in the Persian Period*, JSOTSup 175, Sheffield: JSOT: 286–99.

—— (1994b) "'Canaanite': Some Methodological Observations in Relation to Biblical Study", in G. J. Brooke, *et al.* (ed.) *Ugarit and the Bible: Proceedings of the International Symposium on Ugarit and the Bible, Manchester, September 1992*, Ugaritisch-Biblische Literatur 11; Münster: Ugarit-Verlag: 113–22.

—— (1994c) Review of S. Mason, *Flavius Josephus on the Pharisees*, *JJS* 45: 134–36.

—— (1995a) *Priests, Prophets, Diviners, Sages: A Socio-historical Study of Religious Specialists in Ancient Israel*, Valley Forge, PA: Trinity Press International.

—— (1995b) "Hellenistic Judaism", in Jacob Neusner (ed.) *Judaism in Late Antiquity: Part 2 Historical Syntheses*, HdO: Erste Abteilung, der Nahe und Mittlere Osten 17; Leiden: Brill: 2.53–83.

—— (1996) *An Introduction to First Century Judaism: Jewish Religion and History in the Second Temple Period*, Edinburgh: T. & T. Clark.

—— (1997a) *Wisdom of Solomon*, Guides to Apocrypha and Pseudepigrapha; Sheffield Academic Press.

—— (1997b) "The Current State of the Dead Sea Scrolls: Are There More Answers than Questions?" in S. E. Porter and C. A. Evans (eds) *The Scrolls and the Scriptures: Qumran Fifty Years After*, Roehampton Institute London Papers 3 = JSPSup 26; Sheffield Academic Press: 54–67.

—— (1997c) "4QMMT and Second Temple Jewish Society", in M. Bernstein, F. García Martínez, and J. Kampen (eds) *Legal Texts and Legal Issues: Proceedings of the Second Meeting of the International Organization for Qumran Studies, Cambridge 1995, Published in Honour of Joseph M. Baumgarten* (STDJ 23; Leiden: Brill, 1997) 89–108.

—— (1997d) "The 70-Weeks Prophecy (Daniel 9:24-27) in Early Jewish Interpretation", in Craig A. Evans and Shemaryahu Talmon (eds) *The Quest for Context and Meaning: Studies in Biblical Intertextuality in Honor of James A. Sanders*, Biblical Interpretation Series 28; Leiden: Brill: 595–611.

—— (1997e) "The Book of Leviticus", *Currents in Research: Biblical Studies* 5: 91–110.

—— (ed.) (1997f) *Can a "History of Israel" Be Written?* European Seminar in Historical Methodology 1 = JSOTSup 245; Sheffield: Sheffield Academic Press.

—— (1997g) "Are Historians of Ancient Palestine Fellow Creatures – Or Different Animals?" in Lester L. Grabbe (ed.) *Can a "History of Israel" Be Written?* JSOTSup 245 = ESHM 1; Sheffield Academic Press: 19–36.

—— (1997h) Book review: N. Golb, *Who Wrote the Dead Sea Scrolls?*, *DSD* 4: 124–28.

—— (1998a) *Ezra and Nehemiah*, Readings; London: Routledge.

—— (ed.) (1998b) *Leading Captivity Captive: "The Exile" as History and Ideology*,

JSOTSupp 278 = European Seminar in Historical Methodology 2; Sheffield Academic Press.

—— (1998c) "'The Exile' under the Theodolite: Historiography as Triangulation", in Lester L. Grabbe (ed.) *Leading Captivity Captive: "The Exile" as History and Ideology*, JSOTSup 278 = European Seminar in Historical Methodology 2; Sheffield Academic Press: 80-100.

—— (1998d) "Triumph of the Pious or Failure of the Xenophobes? The Ezra/Nehemiah Reforms and their *Nachgeschichte*", in Siân Jones and Sarah Pearce (eds) *Studies in Jewish Local Patriotism and Self-Identification in the Graeco-Roman Period*, JSPSup 31; Sheffield: Sheffield Academic Press: 50–65.

—— (1998e) "Poets, Scribes, or Preachers? The Reality of Prophecy in the Second Temple Period", in *Society of Biblical Literature 1998 Seminar Papers*, SBLSPS; Atlanta: Scholars Press: 2.524–45.

—— (1999a) "Israel's Historical Reality after the Exile", in Bob Becking and Marjo Korpel (eds) *The Crisis of Israelite Religion: Transformation of Religious Tradition in Exilic and Post-Exilic Times*, OTS 42; Leiden: Brill: 9–32.

—— (1999b) "Sadducees and Pharisees", in Jacob Neusner and Alan J. Avery-Peck (eds) *Judaism in Late Antiquity: Part Three. Where We Stand: Issues and Debates in Ancient Judaism: Volume 1*, HdO: Erste Abteilung, der Nahe und Mittlere Osten 40; Leiden: Brill: 35–62.

—— (1999c) Review article: A. I. Baumgarten, *The Flourishing of Jewish Sects in the Maccabean Era*, *JSJ* 30: 89–94.

—— (1999d) Review of K. De Troyer, *Het einde van de Alpha-tekst van Ester: Vertaal-en verhaaltechniek van MT 8,1–17, LXX 8,1–17 en AT 7,14–41*, *CBQ* 61: 331–32.

—— (2000a) "Eschatology in Philo and Josephus", in Alan Avery-Peck and Jacob Neusner (eds) *Judaism in Late Antiquity: Part 4 Death, Life-after-Death, Resurrection and the World-to-Come in the Judaisms of Antiquity*, HdO: Erste Abteilung, Der Nahe und Mittlere Osten, Bd. 49; Leiden: Brill: 163–85.

—— (2000b) "The Hellenistic City of Jerusalem", in John Bartlett and Sean Freyne (eds) *Jews in the Hellenistic and Roman Cities* (Dublin: Royal Irish Academy; London: Routledge) in the press.

—— (2000c) "Writing Israel's History at the End of the Twentieth Century", in André Lemaire (ed.) *Congress Volume Oslo 1998*, VTSup 80; Leiden: Brill: 203–18.

—— (ed.) (2000d) *Did Moses Speak Attic? Jewish Historiography and Scripture in the Hellenistic Period*, JSOTSup = European Seminar in Historical Methodology 3; Sheffield Academic Press, forthcoming

—— (2000e) "The Pharisees – A Response to Steve Mason", in Jacob Neusner and Alan Avery-Peck (eds) *Where We Stand: Issues and Debates in Ancient Judaism, Volume 3*, HdO: Erste Abteilung, Der Nahe und Mittlere Osten, Bd.; Leiden: Brill: 35–47.

—— (2000f) "A Dan(iel) for All Seasons: For Whom Was Daniel Important?", in J. J. Collins and P. W. Flint (eds) *The Book of Daniel: Composition and Reception* (The Formation and Interpretation of Old Testament Literature = VTSup; Leiden: Brill, forthcoming).

—— (2000g) "Jewish Historiography and Scripture in the Hellenistic Period", in L. L. Grabbe (ed.) *Did Moses Speak Attic? Jewish Historiography and Scripture in the Hellenistic Period* (JSOTSup = European Seminar in Historical Methodology 3; Sheffield Academic Press, 2000).

—— (2000h) "Hat die Bibel doch recht? A Review of T. L. Thompson's *The Bible in History*", *Scandinavian Journal of the Old Testament* 14: 114–38.

—— (forthcoming a) "Tobit", in James D. G. Dunn and John W. Rogerson (eds) *Commentary 2000*, Grand Rapids, MI: Eerdmans.

—— (forthcoming b) Review of S. J. D. Cohen, *The Beginnings of Jewishness*, *JNES*.

Graf, Fritz (1997) *Magic in the Ancient World*, transl. F. Philip; Revealing Antiquity 10; Cambridge, MA and London: Harvard University Press.

Graham, M. Patrick, and Steven L. McKenzie (eds) (1999) *The Chronicler as Author: Studies in Text and Texture*, JSOTSup 263; Sheffield Academic Press.

Gray, John (1970) "The Book of Job in the Context of Near Eastern Literature", *ZAW* 82: 251–69.

Gray, Rebecca (1993) *Prophetic Figures in Late Second Temple Jewish Palestine: The Evidence from Josephus*, Oxford: Clarendon.

Green, William Scott (ed.) (1977) *Persons and Institutions in Early Rabbinic Judaism*, BJS 3; Atlanta: Scholars Press.

—— (1978) "What's in a Name? – The Problematic of Rabbinic 'Biography'", in William Scott Green (ed.) *Approaches to Ancient Judaism: Theory and Practice*, BJS 1; Atlanta: Scholars Press: 77–96.

—— (1979) "Palestinian Holy Men: Charismatic Leadership and Rabbinic Tradition", *ANRW II*: 19.2: 619–47.

—— (1980) "Context and Meaning in Rabbinic 'Biography'", in William Scott Green (ed.) *Approaches to Ancient Judaism, Volume II*, BJS 9; Atlanta: Scholars Press: 97–111.

Greenspoon, Leonard (1997) "'It's All Greek to Me': Septuagint Studies Since 1968", *CR: BS* 5: 147–74.

Grelot, Pierre (1956) "Isaie xxiv 12–15 et son arrière-plan mythologique", *Revue de l'Histoire des Religions* 149: 18–48.

Griffiths, J. Gwyn (1987) "Egypt and the Rise of the Synagogue", *JTS* 38: 1–15; reprinted in Dan Urman and Paul V. M. Flesher (eds) *Ancient Synagogues: Historical Analysis and Archaeological Discovery*, vols 1–2; SPB 47; Leiden: Brill, 1995: 1.3–16.

Gruenwald, Ithamar (1970–71) "Further Jewish Physiognomic and Chiromantic Fragments", *Tarbiz* 40: 301–19 (in Hebrew).

—— (1980) *Apocalyptic and Merkavah Mysticism*, AGAJU 14; Leiden: Brill.

—— (1995) "Major Issues in the Study and Understanding of Jewish Mysticism", in Jacob Neusner (ed.) *Judaism in Late Antiquity: Part 2 Historical Syntheses*, HdO: Erste Abteilung, der Nahe und Mittlere Osten 17; Leiden: Brill: 2.1–49.

Grünewald, Thomas (1999) *Räuber, Rebellen, Rivalen, Rächer: Studien zu Latrones im Römischen Reich*, Forschungen zur antiken Skläverei 31; Stuttgart: Franz Steiner.

Grünwaldt, Klaus (1999) *Das Heiligkeitsgesetz Leviticus 17–26: Ursprüngliche Gestalt, Tradition und Theologie*, BZAW 271; Berlin/New York: de Gruyter.

Gunneweg, A. H. J. (1965) *Leviten und Priester: Hauptlinien der Traditionsbildung und Geschichte des israelitisch-jüdischen Kultpersonals*, FRLANT 89; Göttingen: Vandenhoeck & Ruprecht.

—— (1987) *Nehemiah*, KAT 19.2; Gütersloh: Mohn.

Habas, Ephrat (Rubin) (1999) "Rabban Gamaliel of Yavneh and his Sons: The Patriarchate before and after the Bar Kokhva Revolt", *JJS* 50: 21–37.

Habel, Norman C. (1985) *The Book of Job: A Commentary*, OTL; Philadelphia: Westminster; London: SCM.

Hachlili, Rachel (1997) "The Origin of the Synagogue: A Re-assessment", *JSJ* 28: 34–47.

Halperin, David J. (1988) *The Faces of the Chariot: Early Jewish Responses to Ezekiel's Vision*, TSAJ 16; Tübingen: Mohr (Siebeck).

Halpern-Amaru, Betsy (1999) *The Empowerment of Women in the* Book of Jubilees, JSJSup 60; Leiden: Brill.

Hamerton-Kelly, Robert G. (ed.) (1987) *Violent Origins: Ritual Killing and Cultural Formation*, Stanford University Press, CA.

Hamilton, Gordon J. (1998) "New Evidence for the Authenticity of *bšt* in Hebrew Personal Names and for Its Use as a Divine Epithet in Biblical Texts", *CBQ* 60: 228–50.

Handy, Lowell K. (1994) *Among the Host of Heaven: The Syro-Palestinian Pantheon as Bureaucracy*, Winona Lake, IN: Eisenbrauns.

Hanhart, Robert (1983) *Tobit*, Septuaginta 8/5; Göttingen: Vandenhoeck & Ruprecht.

—— (1999) *Studien zur Septuaginta und zum hellenistischen Judentum*, ed. Reinhard Gregor Kratz, FAT 24; Tübingen: Mohr (Siebeck).

Hann, R. R. (1982) *The Manuscript History of the Psalms of Solomon*, SBLSCS 13; Chico, CA: Scholars Press.

—— (1988) "The Community of the Pious: The Social Setting of the Psalms of Solomon", *SR* 17: 169–89.

Hanson, Paul D. (1973) *The Dawn of Apocalyptic*, Philadelphia: Westminster.

—— (1980) "From Prophecy to Apocalyptic: Unresolved Issues", *JSOT* 15: 3–6.

Haran, Menahem (1978) *Temples and Temple-Service in Ancient Israel*, Oxford: Clarendon.

Harrington, Daniel J., SJ (1971) "The Biblical Text of Pseudo-Philo's *Liber Antiquitatum Biblicarum*", *CBQ* 33: 1–17.

—— (1974) *The Hebrew Fragments of Pseudo-Philo's* Liber Antiquitatum Biblicarum *Preserved in the* Chronicles of Jerahmeel, SBLTT 3; Pseudepigrapha Series 3; Missoula, MT: Scholars Press.

—— (1986) "The Bible Rewritten (Narratives)", in Robert A. Kraft and George W. E. Nickelsburg (eds) *Early Judaism and its Modern Interpreters*, SBLBMI 2; Atlanta: Scholars Press; Philadelphia: Fortress: 239–47.

—— (1992) "Philo, Pseudo-", *ABD* 5: 344–45.

—— (1997) *Wisdom Texts from Qumran*, Literature of the Dead Sea Scrolls; London/New York: Routledge.

Harrington, Daniel J., Jacques Cazeaux, Charles Perrot, and Pierre-Maurice Bogaert (eds) (1976) *Pseudo-Philon, Les Antiquités Bibliques*, vols 1–2; Source Chrétiennes 229–30; Paris: Cerf.

Harrington, Hannah K. (1995) "Did the Pharisees Eat Ordinary Food in a State of Ritual Purity?" *JSJ* 26: 42–54.

Harris, William V. (1989) *Ancient Literacy*, Cambridge, MA: Harvard.

Hartley, John E. *Leviticus* (WBC 4; Dallas: Word Books, 1992).

Harvey, Graham (1996) *The True Israel: Uses of the Names Jew, Hebrew and Israel in Ancient Jewish and Early Christian Literature*, AGAJU 35; Leiden: Brill.

355

Hasel, Gerhard F. (1972) *The Remnant: The History and Theology of the Remnant Idea from Genesis to Isaiah*, Monographs 5; Berrien Springs, MI: Andrews University.

—— (1976) "Remnant", *IDBSup*: 735–36.

Hausmann, Jutta (1987) *Israels Rest: Studien zum Selbstverständnis der nachexilischen Gemeinde*, Beiträge zur Wissenschaft vom Alten und Neuen Testament 124: Stuttgart: Kohlhammer.

Hay, David M. (1979–80) "Philo's References to Other Allegorists", *Studia Philonica* 6: 41–75.

—— (1991a) "Philo's View of Himself as an Exegete: Inspired, but not Authoritative", *Heirs of the Septuagint: Philo, Hellenistic Judaism and Early Christianity. Festschrift for Earle Hilgert = SPA* 3: 40–52.

—— (ed.) (1991b) *Both Literal and Allegorical: Studies in Philo of Alexandria's* Questions and Answers on Genesis and Exodus, BJS 232; Atlanta: Scholars Press.

Hayes, John H., and Sara R. Mandell (1998) *The Jewish People in Classical Antiquity: From Alexander to Bar Kochba*, Louisville, KY: Westminster John Knox, 1998.

Hayman, A. Peter (1991) "Monotheism – A Misused Word in Jewish Studies?" *JJS* 42: 1–15.

—— (1998) "The 'Man from the Sea' in 4 Ezra 13", *JJS* 49: 1–16.

—— (1999) "The Survival of Mythology in the Wisdom of Solomon", *JSJ* 30: 125–39.

Hayward, C. T. Robert (1992) "The New Jerusalem in the Wisdom of Jesus ben Sira", *SJOT* 6: 123–38.

—— (1994) "Major Aspects of Targumic Studies 1983–1993: A Survey", *CR: BS* 2: 107–22.

—— (1996) *The Jewish Temple: A Non-Biblical Sourcebook*, New York/London: Routledge.

Hecht, Richard D. (1987) "Philo and Messiah", in Jacob Neusner, W. S. Green, and E. S. Frerichs (eds), *Judaisms and Their Messiahs at the Turn of the Christian Era*, Cambridge University Press: 139–68.

Hedrick, Charles W. (1980) *The Apocalypse of Adam: A Literary and Source Analysis*, SBLDS 46; Chico, CA: Scholars Press.

Heger, Paul (1999) *The Three Biblical Altar Laws: Developments in the Sacrificial Cult in Practice and Theology, Political and Economic Background*, BZAW 279; Berlin/New York: de Gruyter.

Heinemann, Joseph (1968) "The Triennial Lectionary Cycle", *JJS* 19: 41–48.

—— (1975) "The Messiah of Ephraim and the Premature Exodus of the Tribe of Ephraim", *HTR* 68: 1–15 (orig. *Tarbiz* 40 [1970–71]: 450–61).

—— (1977) *Prayer in the Talmud: Forms and Patterns*, Studia Judaica 9; Berlin/New York: de Gruyter.

Hemer, Colin J. (1989) *The Book of Acts in the Setting of Hellenistic History*, ed. C. H. Gempf; WUNT 49; Tübingen: Mohr (Siebeck).

Hengel, Martin (1971) "Proseuche und Synagoge: Jüdische Gemeinde, Gotteshaus und Gottesdienst in der Diaspora und in Palästina", *Tradition und Glaube: Festgabe für K. G. Kuhn* (ed. G. Jeremias, et al.; Göttingen: 1971): 157–84; reprinted in J. Gutmann (ed.) *The Synagogue: Studies in Origins, Archaeology, and Architecture* (New York: Ktav, 1975): 27–54.

—— (1974) *Judaism and Hellenism*, 2 vols; London: SCM; Philadelphia: Fortress; ET of *Judentum und Hellenismus: Studien zu ihrer Begegnung unter besonderer Berücksichtigung Palästinas bis zur Mitte des 2 Jh.s v. Chr*, 2nd edn; WUNT 10; Tübingen: Mohr (Siebeck), 1973.

—— (1989) *The Zealots: Investigations into the Jewish Freedom Movement in the Period from Herod I until 70 AD*, Edinburgh: T. & T. Clark; ET of *Die Zeloten: Untersuchungen zur jüdischen Freiheitsbewegung in der Zeit von Herodes I. bis 70 n. Chr.*, 2nd edn; AGAJU 1; Leiden: Brill, 1976.

—— (1996) "Zur Wirkungsgeschichte von Jes 53 in vorchristlicher Zeit", in Janowski, Bernd, and Peter Stuhlmacher (eds) (1996) *Der leidende Gottesknecht: Jesaja 53 und seine Wirkungsgeschichte, mit einer Bibliographie zu Jes 53*, FAT 14; Tübingen: Mohr (Siebeck): 49–91; reprinted in Martin Hengel (1999) *Kleine Schriften II: Judaica, Hellenistica et Christiana*, eds J. Frey and D. Betz; Tübingen: Mohr (Siebeck): 72–114.

Henten, Jan Willem van (ed.) (1986) "Datierung und Herkunft des Vierten Makkabäerbuches", in J. W. van Henten, *et al.* (eds) *Tradition and Re-interpretation in Jewish and Early Christian Literature: Essays in Honour of Jürgen C. H. Lebram*, SPB 36; Leiden: Brill: 136–49.

—— (1989) *Die Entstehung der jüdischen Martyrologie*, SPB 38; Leiden: Brill.

—— (1997) *The Maccabean Martyrs as Saviours of the Jewish People: A Study of 2 and 4 Maccabees*, JSJSup 57; Leiden: Brill.

Heusch, L. de (1985) *Sacrifice in Africa: A Structuralist Approach*, Manchester University Press.

Hezser, Catherine (1998) *The Social Structure of the Rabbinic Movement in Roman Palestine*, TSAJ 66; Tübingen: Mohr (Siebeck).

Hill, Andrew E. (1998) *Malachi: A New Translation with Introduction and Commentary*, AB 25D; New York: Doubleday.

Himmelfarb, Martha (1983) *Tours of Hell*, Philadelphia: University of Pennsylvania.

—— (1993) *Ascents into Heaven in Jewish and Christian Apocalypses*; Oxford University Press.

Hoffman, Lawrence A. (1995) "Jewish Liturgy and Jewish Scholarship", in Jacob Neusner (ed.) *Judaism in Late Antiquity: Part 1, The Literary and Archaeological Sources*, HdO: Erste Abteilung, der Nahe und Mittlere Osten 17/1; Leiden: Brill: 239–66.

Hoffmann, Y. (1981) "The Day of the Lord as a Concept and a Term in the Prophetic Literature", *ZAW* 93: 37–50.

Hogan, Karina Martin (1999) "The Exegetical Background of the 'Ambiguity of Death' in the Wisdom of Solomon", *JSJ* 30: 1–24.

Hoglund, Kenneth G. (1992) *Achaemenid Imperial Administration in Syria–Palestine and the Missions of Ezra and Nehemiah*, SBL DS 125; Atlanta: Scholars Press.

Holladay, Carl R. (1977) *Theios Aner in Hellenistic-Judaism: A Critique of the Use of this Category in New Testament Christology*, SBLDS 40; Atlanta: Scholars Press.

—— (1983) *Fragments from Hellenistic Jewish Authors, Volume I: Historians*, SBLTT 20, Pseudepigrapha Series 10; Atlanta: Scholars Press.

—— (1989) *Fragments from Hellenistic Jewish Authors, Volume II: Poets: The Epic Poets Theodotus and Philo and Ezekiel the Tragedian*, SBLTT 30, Pseudepigrapha Series 12; Atlanta: Scholars Press.

—— (1995) *Fragments from Hellenistic Jewish Authors, Volume III: Aristobulus*, SBLTT 39, Pseudepigrapha Series 13; Atlanta: Scholars Press.

—— (1996) *Volume IV: Orphica*, SBLTT 40; Pseudepigrapha Series 14; Atlanta: Scholars Press.

Horbury, William (1982) "The Benediction of the *Minim* and Early Jewish–Christian Controversy", *JTS* 33: 19–61; revised in (1998a).

—— (1998a) *Jews and Christians in Contact and Controversy*, Edinburgh: T. & T. Clark: 67–110.

—— (1998b) *Jewish Messianism and the Cult of Christ*, London: SCM.

—— (1998c) "Messianism in the Old Testament Apocrypha", in J. Day (ed.) *King and Messiah in Israel and the Ancient Near East: Proceedings of the Oxford Old Testament Seminar*, JSOTSup 270; Sheffield Academic Press: 402–33.

Horbury, William, and David Noy (eds) (1992) *Jewish Inscriptions of Graeco-Roman Egypt, with an Index of the Jewish Inscriptions of Egypt and Cyrenaica*, Cambridge University Press.

Horgan, M. P. (1979) *Pesharim: Qumran Interpretations of Biblical Books*, CBQMS 8; Washington, DC: Catholic Biblical Association.

Horsley, Richard A. (1979a) "Josephus and the Bandits", *JSJ* 10: 37–63.

—— (1979b) "The Sicarii: Ancient Jewish 'Terrorists'", *JR* 59: 435–58.

—— (1981) "Ancient Jewish Banditry and the Revolt against Rome, A.D. 66–70", *CBQ* 43: 409–32.

—— (1984) "Popular Messianic Movements around the Time of Jesus", *CBQ* 46: 471–95.

—— (1985a) "Menahem in Jerusalem: A Brief Messianic Episode among the Sicarii – Not 'Zealot Messianism'", *NovT* 27: 334–48.

—— (1985b) "'Like One of the Prophets of Old': Two Types of Popular Prophets at the Time of Jesus", *CBQ* 47: 435–63.

—— (1986a) "Popular Prophetic Movements at the Time of Jesus: Their Princpial Features and Social Origins", *JSNT* 26: 3–27.

—— (1986b) "The Zealots: their Origin, Relationships and Importance in the Jewish Revolt", *NovT* 28: 159–92.

—— (1987) *Jesus and the Spiral of Violence: Popular Jewish Resistance in Roman Palestine*, San Francisco: Harper.

—— (1995) *Galilee: History, Politics, People*, Valley Forge, PA: Trinity Press International.

Horsley, Richard A., with John S. Hanson (1999) *Bandits, Prophets, and Messiahs: Popular Movements at the Time of Jesus*, 1985 edn with new preface; Harrisburg, PA: Trinity Press International.

Horst, Pieter W. van der (1978) *The Sentences of Pseudo-Phocylides: Introduction, Translation and Commentary*, SVTP 4; Leiden: Brill.

—— (1988) "Pseudo-Phocylides Revisited", *JSP* 3: 3–30.

—— (1994a) "The Birkat ha-Minim in Recent Research", *Hellenism–Judaism– Christianity: Essays on Their Interaction*, Contributions to Biblical Exegesis and Theology 8; Kampen: Kok: 99–111; original publication in *Expository Times* 105 (1993–94).

—— (1994b) "Silent Prayer", *Hellenism–Judaism–Christianity: Essays on Their Interaction*, Contributions to Biblical Exegesis and Theology 8; Kampen: Kok: 252–77; original publication in *Numen* 41 (1994).

—— (1995) "Images of Women in Ancient Judaism", in Ria Kloppenborg and Wouter J. Hanegraaff (eds) *Female Stereotypes in Religious Traditions*, Studies in the History of Religions (*Numen* Book Series) 66; Leiden: Brill: 43–60.

—— (1998a) "Sortes: Sacred Books as Instant Oracles in Late Antiquity", in L. V. Rutgers, et al., *The Use of Sacred Books in the Ancient World*, Contributions to Biblical Exegesis and Theology 22; Leuven: Peeters: 143–73.

—— (1998b) "Neglected Greek Evidence for Early Jewish Liturgical Prayer", *JSJ* 29: 278–96.

—— (1999) "Was the Synagogue a Place of Sabbath Worship before 70 CE?" in Steven Fine (ed.) *Jews, Christians, and Polytheists in the Ancient Synagogue: Cultural Interaction during the Greco-Roman Period*, Baltimore Studies in the History of Judaism; London/New York: Routledge: 18–43.

Horst, Pieter W. van der, and Gregory E. Sterling (2000) *Prayers from the Ancient World: Greco-Roman, Jewish and Christian Prayers*, Christianity and Judaism in Antiquity 13; South Bend, IN: Notre Dame.

Houston, Walter (1993) *Purity and Monotheism: Clean and Unclean Animals in Biblical Law*, JSOTSup 140; Sheffield Academic Press.

Hübner, Hans (1999) *Die Weisheit Salomons: Liber Sapientiae Salomonis*, Das Alte Testament Deutsch, Apokryphen Band 4; Göttingen: Vandenhoeck & Ruprecht.

Hurtado, Larry W. (1993) "What Do We Mean by 'First-Century Jewish Monotheism'?", in Eugene J. Lovering, Jr (ed.), *Society of Biblical Literature 1993 Seminar Papers*, SBLSPS 32; Atlanta: Scholars Press: 348–68.

—— (1998a) *One God, One Lord: Early Christian Devotion and Ancient Jewish Monotheism*, 2nd edn; Edinburgh: T. & T. Clark.

—— (1998b) "First-Century Jewish Monotheism", *JSNT* 7: 3–26.

Hurvitz, Avi (1974) "The Date of the Prose-Tale of Job Linguistically Reconsidered", *HTR* 67: 17–34.

Husser, Jean-Marie (1994) *Le songe et la parole: Etude sur le rêve et sa fonction dans l'ancien Israël*, BZAW 210; Berlin/New York: de Gruyter.

—— (1999) *Dreams and Dream Narratives in the Biblical World*, transl. Jill M. Munro; The Biblical Seminar 63; Sheffield Academic Press.

Hüttenmeister, F., and G. Reeg (1977) *Die antiken Synagogen in Israel*, 2 vols; Beihefte zum Tübinger Atlas des Vorderen Orients, Reihe B, Nr 12; Wiesbaden: Reichert.

Idinopulos, Thomas A. and Brian C. Wilson (eds) (1998) *What Is Religion? Origins, Definitions, and Explanations*, Studies in the History of Religions (*Numen* Book Series) 81; Leiden: Brill.

Ilan, Tal (1995) *Jewish Women in Greco-Roman Palestine: An Inquiry into Image and Status*, TSAJ 44; Tübingen: Mohr (Siebeck).

—— (1999) *Integrating Women into Second Temple History*, TSAJ 76; Tübingen: Mohr (Siebeck).

Isaac, B. (1984) "Bandits in Judaea and Arabia", *HSCP* 88: 171–203.

—— (1992) "The Babatha Archive", *IEJ* 42: 62–75.

Jackson, H. M. (1996) "Echoes and Demons in the Pseudo-Philonic *Liber Antiquitatum Biblicarum*", *JSJ* 27: 1–20.

Jacob, Edmond (1958) "L'histoire d'Israël vue par Ben Sira", in *Mélanges bibliques rédigés en l'honneur de André Robert*, Travaux de l'Institut Catholique de Paris 4; Paris: Bloud & Gay: 288–94.

Jacobs, Martin (1995) *Die Institution des jüdischen Patriarchen: Eine quellen- und traditions-kritische Studie zur Geschichte der Juden in der Spätantike*, TSAJ 52; Tübingen: Mohr (Siebeck).

Jacobson, Howard (1996) *A Commentary on Pseudo-Philo's* Liber Antiquitatum Biblicarum, *with Latin Text and English Translation*, vols 1–2; AGAJU 31; Leiden: Brill.

James, M. R. (1917) *The Biblical Antiquities of Philo*, Translations of Early Documents 1: Palestinian Jewish Texts; reprinted London/New York: 1971.

Jamieson-Drake, D. W. (1991) *Scribes and Schools in Monarchic Judah: A Socio-Archaeological Approach*, JSOTSup 109; Social World of Biblical Antiquity 9; Sheffield: Almond Press.

Janowski, Bernd, and Peter Stuhlmacher (eds) (1996) *Der leidende Gottesknecht: Jesaja 53 und seine Wirkungsgeschichte, mit einer Bibliographie zu Jes 53*, FAT 14; Tübingen: Mohr (Siebeck).

Japhet, Sara (1983) "People and Land in the Restoration Period'', in Georg Strecker (ed.) *Das Land Israel in biblischer Zeit: Jerusalem-Symposium 1981 der Hebräischen Univer-sität und der Georg-August-Universität*, Göttinger Theologische Arbeiten 25; Göttingen: Vandenhoeck & Ruprecht: 103–25.

—— (1993) *I & II Chronicles: A Commentary*, OTL; London: SCM; Louisville, KY: Westminster John Knox.

—— (1997) *The Ideology of the Book of Chronicles and its Place in Biblical Thought*, Beiträge zur Erforschung des Alten Testaments und des Antiken Judentums 9; Frankfurt/Bern/New York: Lang (corrected reprint of 1989 edn).

Jeansonne, S. P. (1988) *The Old Greek Translation of Daniel 7–12*, Washington, DC: Catholic Biblical Association.

Jeffers, Ann (1996) *Magic and Divination in Ancient Palestine and Syria*, Studies in the History and Culture of the Ancient Near East 8; Leiden: Brill.

Jellicoe, Sydney (1968) *The Septuagint and Modern Study*, Oxford: Clarendon.

Jenkins, Keith (1991) *Re-Thinking History*, London/New York: Routledge.

—— (ed.) (1997) *The Postmodern History Reader*, London/New York: Routledge.

Jenson, Philip P. (1992) *Graded Holiness: A Key to the Priestly Conception of the World*, JSOTSup 106, Sheffield Academic Press.

Jervell, Jacob (1998) *Die Apostelgeschichte*, 17. Auflage, 1. Auflage dieser Auslegung; Meyers kritisch-exegetischer Kommentar über das Neue Testament 3; Göttingen: Vandenhoeck & Ruprecht.

Jobes, Karen H. (1996) *The Alpha-Text of Esther: Its Character and Relationship to the Masoretic Text*, SBLDS 153; Atlanta: Scholars Press.

Johnstone, William (1997) *1 and 2 Chronicles: Vol. 1, 1 Chronicles 1–2 Chronicles 9: Israel's Place among the Nations; Vol. 2, 2 Chronicles 10–36: Guilt and Atonement*, JSOTSup 253–54; Sheffield Academic Press.

Jones, Gwilym H. (1993) *1 & 2 Chronicles*, Old Testament Guides; Sheffield Academic Press.

Jones, Siân, and Sarah Pearce (eds) (1998) *Jewish Local Patriotism and Self-Identification in the Graeco-Roman Period*, JSPSup 31; Sheffield Academic Press.

Jonge, Marinus de (1978) *The Testaments of the Twelve Patriarchs: A Critical Edition of the Greek Text*, with H. W. Hollander, H. J. de Jonge, and T. Korteweg; PVTG 1.2; Leiden: Brill.

—— (1992) "Patriarchs, Testaments of the Twelve", *ABD*: 5.181–86.

Kabasele Mukenge, André (1998) *L'unité littéraire du livre de Baruch*, Études bibliques, nouvelle série no. 38; Paris: Librairie Lecoffre, Gabalda.

Kalimi, Isaac (1995) *Zur Geschichtsschreibung des Chronisten: Literarisch-historiographische Abweichungen der Chronik von ihren Paralleltexten in den Samuel- und Königsbüchern*, BZAW 226; Berlin/New York: de Gruyter.

Kalmin, Richard (1999) *The Sage in Jewish Society of Late Antiquity*, London/New York: Routledge.

Kampen, John (1986) "A Reconsideration of the Name 'Essene' in Greco-Jewish Literature in Light of Recent Perceptions of the Qumran Sect", *HUCA* 57: 61–81.

—— (1988) *The Hasideans and the Origins of Pharisaism: A Study in 1 and 2 Maccabees*, SBLSCS 24; Atlanta: Scholars Press.

Kanter, S. (1979) *Rabban Gamaliel II*, BJS 8; Atlanta: Scholars Press.

Kapera, Zdzisław Jan (ed.) (1990–) *The Qumran Chronicle* vol. 1– .

—— (1996) *Mogilany 1993: Papers on the Dead Sea Scrolls Offered in Memory of Hans Burgmann*, Qumranica Mogilanesia 13; Cracow: Enigma Press.

—— (ed.) (1998) *Mogilany 1995: Papers on the Dead Sea Scrolls Offered in Memory of Aleksy Klawek*, Qumranica Mogilanensia 15; Cracow: Enigma Press.

Kayatz, Christa (1966) *Studien zu Proverbien 1-9: Eine form- und motivgeschichtliche Untersuchung unter Einbeziehung ägyptischen Vergleichsmaterials*, WMANT 22; Neukirchen-Vluyn, Germany: Neukirchen Verlag.

Kee, Howard Clark (1990) "The Transformation of the Synagogue after 70 C.E.: Its Import for Early Christianity", *NTS* 36: 1–24.

Keel, Othmar (1977) *Jahwe-Visionen und Siegelkunst: Eine neue Deutung der Majestäts-schilderungen in Jes 6, Ez 1 und 10 und Sach 4*, Stuttgarter Bibelstudien 84/85; Stuttgart: Verlag Katholisches Bibelwerk.

—— (1994) *The Song of Songs*, transl. F. J. Gaiser; Continental Commentary; Minneapolis: Fortress; ET of *Das Hohelied*, Züricher Bibelkommentare; Zurich: Theologischer Verlag, 1986.

Keel, Othmar, and Christoph Uehlinger (1998) *Gods, Goddesses, and Images of God in Ancient Israel*, transl. Thomas H. Trapp; Minneapolis: Fortress; Edinburgh: T. & T. Clark; ET of *Göttinnen, Götter und Gottessymbole: Neue Erkenntnisse zur Religionsgeschichte Kanaans und Israels aufgrund bislang unerschlossener ikonographischer Quellen*, 4th expanded edn; Quaestiones Disputatae 134; Freiburg: Herder, 1998.

Kelly, Brian E. (1996) *Retribution and Eschatology in Chronicles*, JSOTSup 211; Sheffield Academic Press.

Kenney, John Peter (ed.) (1995) *The School of Moses: Studies in Philo and Hellenistic Religions in Memory of Horst R. Moehring*, BJS 304; Studia Philonica Monographs 1; Atlanta: Scholars Press.

Kerkeslager, Allen (1997) "Maintaining Jewish Identity in the Greek Gymnasium: A 'Jewish Load' in *CPJ* 3.519 (= P. Schub. 37 = P. Berol. 13406)", *JSJ* 28: 12–33.

Kiley, Mark, *et al.* (1997) *Prayer from Alexander to Constantine: A Critical Anthology*, London/New York: Routledge.

Kiuchi, N. (1987) *The Purification Offering in the Priestly Literature: Its Meaning and Function*, JSOTSup 56, Sheffield: JSOT Press.

Klein, Lillian R. (1997) "Esther's Lot", *CR: BS* 5: 111–45.

Kleinig, John W. (1993) *The Lord's Song: The Basis, Function and Significance of Choral Music in Chronicles*, JSOTSup 156; Sheffield Academic Press.

Kloppenborg, John S. (1982) "Isis and Sophia in the Book of Wisdom", *HTR* 75: 57–84.

Knibb, Michael A. (1995) "Messianism in the Pseudepigrapha in the Light of the Scrolls", *DSD* 2: 165–84.

Knibb, Michael A., and Pieter W. van der Horst (eds) (1990) *Studies on the Testament of Job*, SNTSMS 66; Cambridge University Press.

Knohl, Israel (1987) "The Priestly Torah Versus the Holiness School: Sabbath and the Festivals", *HUCA* 58: 65–117.

—— (1995) *The Sanctuary of Silence: The Priestly Torah and the Holiness School*, Minneapolis: Fortress.

Kobelski, P. J. (1981) *Melchizedek and Melchireša'*, CBQMS 10; Washington, DC: Catholic Biblical Association.

Koch, Klaus (1995) *Die Reiche der Welt und der kommende Menschensohn: Studien zum Danielbuch (Gesammelte Aufsätze 2)*, edited by Martin Rösel; Neukirchen-Vluyn, Germany: Neukirchener Verlag.

—— (1997) *Europa, Rom und der Kaiser vor dem Hintergrund von zwei Jahrtausenden Rezeption des Buches Daniel*, Berichte aus den Sitzungen der Joachim Jungius-Gesellschafter der Wissenschaften E. V. Hamburg, Jahrgang 15, Heft 1; Göttingen: Vandenhoeck & Ruprecht.

Koester, Helmut (1985) "The Divine Human Being", *HTR* 78: 243–52.

Kolarcik, Michael (1991) *The Ambiguity of Death in the Book of Wisdom 1–6: A Study of Literary Structure and Interpretation*, AnBib 127; Rome: Pontifical Biblical Institute.

Kooij, Arie van der, and Karel van der Toorn (eds) (1998) *Canonization and Decanonization: Papers Presented to the International Conference of the Leiden Institute for the Study of Religions (Lisor) held at Leiden 9–10 January 1997*, Studies in the History of Religions [*Numen* Book Series] 82; Leiden: Brill.

Körting, Corinna (1999) *Der Schall des Schofar: Israels Feste im Herbst*, BZAW 285; Berlin/New York: de Gruyter.

Koskeniemi, Erkki (1994) *Apollonios von Tyana in der neutestamentlichen Exegese: Forschungsbericht und Weiterführung der Diskussion*, WUNT 2/61: Tübingen: Mohr (Siebeck).

Kossmann, Ruth (1999) *Die Esthernovelle – Vom Erzählten zur Erzählung: Studien zur Traditions- und Redaktionsgeschichte des Estherbuches*, VTSup 79; Leiden: Brill.

Kottek, Samuel S. (1995) *Medicine and Hygiene in the Works of Flavius Josephus*, Studies in Ancient Medicine 9; Leiden: Brill.

Kraabel, A. T. (1981) "The Disappearance of the 'God-fearers'", *Numen* 28: 113–26.

Kraemer, Ross Shepard (1992) *Her Share of the Blessings: Women's Religions among Pagans, Jews and Christians in the Greco-Roman World*, Oxford University Press.

—— (1998) *When Aseneth Met Joseph: A Late Antique Tale of the Biblical Patriarch and his Egyptian Wife, Reconsidered*, Oxford University Press.

Kraft, Robert A. (1974) *The Testament of Job according to the SV Text*, with Harold Attridge, Russell P. Spittler, and J. Timbie; SBLTT 5, Pseudepigrapha Series 4; Missoula, MT: Scholars Press.

Kramer, Samuel Noel (1969) *The Sacred Marriage Rite: Aspects of Faith, Myth, and Ritual in Ancient Sumer*, Bloomington: Indiana University Press.

Kraus, F. R. (1939) *Texte zur babylonischen Physiognomatik*, AfO Beiheft 3.

—— (1947) "Weitere texte zur babylonischen Physiognomatik", *Orientalia* 16: 172–206.

Kraus, Hans-Joachim (1966) *Worship in Israel: A Cultic History of the Old Testament*, Oxford: Blackwell.

—— (1988) *Psalms 1-59: A Continental Commentary*, transl. H. C. Oswald; Minneapolis: Augsburg; ET of *Psalmen*, 1. Teilband, *Psalmen 1–59*, Neukirchen-Vluyn, Germany: Neukirchener Verlag, 1978.

Kugel, James (1994) "The Jubilees Apocalypse", *DSD* 1: 322–37.

Kugler, Robert A. (1996) *From Patriarch to Priest: The Levi-Priestly Tradition from Aramaic Levi to* Testament of Levi, SBLEJL 9; Atlanta: Scholars Press.

Kugler, Robert A., and Eileen M. Schuller (eds) (1999) *The Dead Sea Scrolls at Fifty: Proceedings of the 1997 Society of Biblical Literature Qumran Section Meetings*, SBLEJL 15; Atlanta: Scholars Press.

Kuhrt, Amélie (1983) "The Cyrus Cylinder and Achaemenid Imperial Policy", *JSOT* 25: 83–97.

Kunin, Seth D. (1998) *God's Place in the World: Sacred Space and Sacred Place in Judaism*, London/New York: Cassell.

Laato, Antti (1997) *A Star Is Rising: The Historical Development of the Old Testament Royal Ideology and the Rise of the Jewish Messianic Expectations*, University of South Florida International Studies in Formative Christianity and Judaism; Atlanta: Scholars Press.

—— (1998) "The Apocalypse of the Syriac Baruch and the Date of the End", *JSP* 18: 39–46.

Lacocque, André (1999) "The Different Versions of Esther", *Biblical Interpretation* 7: 301–22.

Landau, Y. H. (1966) "A Greek Inscription Found Near Hefzibah", *IEJ* 16: 54–70.

Lang, Bernhard (1986) *Wisdom and the Book of Proverbs: An Israelite Goddess Redefined*, New York: Pilgrim Press; ET of *Frau Weisheit: Deutung einer biblischen Gestalt*, Düsseldorf: Patmos, 1975.

Laniak, Timothy S. (1998) *Shame and Honor in the Book of Esther*, SBLDS 165; Atlanta: Scholars Press.

Lapin, Hayim (1995) *Early Rabbinic Civil Law and the Social History of Roman Galilee. A Study of Mishnah Tractate* Baba' Meṣi'a', BJS 307; Atlanta: Scholars Press.

LaPorte, Jean (1983) *Eucharistia in Philo*, Studies in the Bible and Early Christianity 3; Lewiston, NY; Queenston, Ontario; Lampeter, Wales: Edwin Mellen.

Lapp, Paul, and Nancy Lapp (1992) "'Iraq el-Emir'", in E. Stern (ed.) *The New Encyclopedia of Archaeological Excavations in the Holy Land* (4 vols; New York: Simon & Schuster; Jerusalem: Israel Exploration Society, 1992): 2.646–49.

Larcher, C., OP (1969) *Études sur le Livre de la Sagesse*, Études Bibliques; Paris: J. Gabalda.

—— (1983–85) *Le Livre de la Sagesse ou la Sagesse de Salomon*, 3 vols; Études Bibliques, nouvelle série 1; Paris: Gabalda.

Larkin, Katrina J. A. (1994) *The Eschatology of Second Zechariah: A Study of the Formation of a Mantological Wisdom Anthology*, Contributions to Biblical Exegesis and Theology 6; Kampen: Kok Pharos.

—— (1995) *Ruth and Esther*, Old Testament Guides; Sheffield Academic Press.

Lease, G. (1987) "Jewish Mystery Cults since Goodenough", *ANRW II*: 20.2.858–80.

Lee, J. A. L. (1983) *A Lexical Study of the Septuagint Version of the Pentateuch*, SBLSCS 14; Chico, CA: Scholars Press.

Lefkovits, Judah K. (2000) *The Copper Scroll (3Q15): A Reevaluation: A New Reading, Translation, and Commentary*, STDJ 25; Leiden: Brill.

Leith, Mary Joan Winn (ed.) (1997) *Discoveries in the Judaean Desert, XXIV: Wadi Daliyeh, Vol. I, The Wadi Daliyeh Seal Impressions*, Oxford: Clarendon Press.

Lemche, Niels Peter (1976) "The Manumission of Slaves–the Fallow Year–the Sabbatical Year–the Jobel Year", *VT* 26: 38–59.

—— (1979) "*Andurārum* and *Mīšarum*: Comments on the Problem of Social Edicts and their Application in the Ancient Near East", *JNES* 38: 11–22.

—— (1991) *The Canaanites and Their Land: The Tradition of the Canaanites*, JSOTSup 110; Sheffield Academic Press.

—— (1993) "The Old Testament – a Hellenistic Book?" *SJOT* 7: 163–93.

LeMoyne, J. (1972) *Les Sadducéens*, Études Bibliques; Paris: Lecoffre.

Lenger, M.-T. (1964) *Corpus des Ordonnances des Ptolémées*, Académie Royale de Belgique, Classe des Lettres, Mémoires, t. 56/5; Brussels: Palais des Académies.

Leon, Harry J. (1995) *The Jews of Ancient Rome*, updated edn with new introduction by Carolyn A. Osiek: Peabody, MA: Hendrickson.

Levenson, Jon D. (1997) *Esther: A Commentary*, OTL; London: SCM; Louisville, KY: Westminster/John Knox.

Levine, Amy-Jill (ed.) (1991) *"Women Like This": New Perspectives on Jewish Women in the Greco-Roman World*, SBLEJL 1; Atlanta: Scholars Press.

Levine, Baruch A. (1974) *In the Presence of the Lord: A Study of Cult and Some Cultic Terms in Ancient Israel*, SJLA 5, Leiden: Brill.

—— (1989) *Leviticus*, Torah Commentary; Philadelphia: Jewish Publication Society.

Levine, Lee I. (ed.) (1981) *Ancient Synagogues Revealed*, Jerusalem: Israel Exploration Society.

—— (1996) "The Nature and Origin of the Palestinian Synagogue Reconsidered", *JBL* 115: 425–48.

—— (1998) *Judaism and Hellenism in Antiquity: Conflict or Confluence?* The Samuel and Althea Stroum Lectures; Seattle/London: University of Washington Press.

—— (2000) *The Ancient Synagoge: The First Thousand Years*, New Haven, CT: Yale.

Levinskaya, Irina (ed.) (1996) *The Book of Acts in Its Diaspora Setting*, The Book of Acts in Its First Century Setting 5; Carlisle: Paternoster; Grand Rapids, MI: Eerdmans.

Levinson, Bernard M. (1997) *Deuteronomy and the Hermeneutics of Legal Innovation*, Oxford University Press.

Levison, John R. (1988) *Portraits of Adam in Early Judaism, from Sirach to 2 Baruch*, JSPSup 1; Sheffield Academic Press.

—— (1994) "Two Types of Ecstatic Prophecy according to Philo", *SPA* 6: 83–89.

—— (1995) "Inspiration and the Divine Sprit in the Writings of Philo Judaeus", *JSJ* 26: 271–323.

Lewis, Jack P. (1964) "What Do We Mean by Jabneh?" *Journal of the Bible and Religion* 32: 125–32.

Lewis, Naphthali (ed.) (1976) *The Interpretation of Dreams and Portents*, Aspects of Antiquity; Toronto/Sarasota, FL: Samuel, Stevens, Hakkert.

—— (1989) *The Documents from the Bar Kokhba Period in the Cave of Letters: Greek Papyri*, with Yigael Yadin and Jonas C. Greenfield (eds) *Aramaic and Nabatean Signatures and Subscriptions*, Jerusalem: Israel Exploration Society.

—— (1994) "The Babatha Archive: A Response", *IEJ* 44: 243–46.

Lewy, H. (1958) "The Biblical Institution of *D⁽ʳôr* in the Light of Akkadian Documents", *Eretz-Israel* 5: 21*–31*.

Liesen, Jan (2000) *Full of Praise: An Exegetical Study of Sir 39, 12–35*, JSJSup 64; Leiden: Brill.

Lightstone, Jack N. (1983) "Judaism of the Second Commonwealth: Toward a Reform of the Scholarly Tradition", in H. Joseph, *et al.* (eds) *Truth and Compassion: Essays on Judaism and Religion in Memory of Rabbi Dr. Solomon Frank*, Ontario: Wilfrid Laurier University: 31–40.

—— (1984) *The Commerce of the Sacred: Mediation of the Divine among Jews in the Graeco-Roman Diaspora*, BJS 59; Atlanta: Scholars Press.

—— (1988) *Society, the Sacred, and Scripture in Ancient Judaism*, Studies in Christianity and Judaism 3; Waterloo, Ontario: Wilfrid Laurier University.

Lim, Timothy H. (1992) "The Chronology of the Flood Story in a Qumran Text (4Q252)", *JJS* 43: 288–98.

—— (1993) "The Wicked Priests of the Groningen Hypothesis", *JBL* 112: 415–25.

Lim, Timothy H., in consultation with Philip S. Alexander (1997) *The Dead Sea Scrolls Electronic Reference Library, vol. 1*, DSS Electronic Reference Library 1; Leiden: Brill; Oxford University Press.

[no ed.] (1999) *The Dead Sea Scrolls Electronic Reference Library, 2, including the Dead Sea Scrolls Database (Non-Biblical Texts) Edited by Emanuel Tov*, prepared by the Foundation for Ancient Research and Mormon Studies and its Center for the Preservation of Ancient Religious Texts at Brigham Young University, Provo, Utah; Leiden: Brill; Oxford University Press.

Limburg, James (1993) *Jonah: A Commentary*, OTL; Louisville, KY: Westminster John Knox; London: SCM.

Lindsay, Dennis R. (1993) *Josephus and Faith: Pistis and Pisteuein as Faith Terminology in the Writings of Flavius Josephus and in the New Testament*, AGAJU 19; Leiden: Brill.

Lipscomb, W. Lowndes (1990) *The Armenian Apocryphal Adam Literature*, University of Pennsylvania Armenian Texts and Studies 8; Atlanta: Scholars Press.

Loader, J. A. (1979) *Polar Structures in the Book of Kohelet*, BZAW 152; Berlin: de Gruyter.

Lohfink, Norbert (1998) *Studien zu Kohelet*, Stuttgarter Biblische Aufsatzbände (SBAB) 26; Stuttgart: Katholisches Bibelwerk.

Longenecker, Bruce W. (1997) "Locating 4 Ezra: A Consideration of its Social Setting and Functions", *JSJ* 28: 271–93.

Longenecker, Richard N. (1999) *Biblical Exegesis in the Apostolic Period*, 2nd edn; Grand Rapids, MI, and Cambridge: Eerdmans; Vancouver: Regent College Publishing.

Loretz, Otto (1993) "Nekromantie und Totenevokation in Mesopotamien, Ugarit und Israel", in B. Janowski, *et al.* (eds) *Religionsgeschichtliche Beziehungen zwischen Kleinasien, Nordsyrien und dem Alten Testament: Internationales Symposion Hamburg 17.–21.März 1990*, OBO 129; Göttingen: Vandenhoeck & Ruprecht: 285–315.

Lyons, E. L. (1987) "A Note on Proverbs 31.10–31", in K. G. Hoglund, *et al.* (eds) *The Listening Heart: Essays in Wisdom and the Psalms in Honor of Roland E. Murphy, OCarm*, JSOTSup 58; Sheffield: JSOT: 237–45.

Maccoby, Hyam (1989) *Judaism in the First Century*, Issues in Religious Studies; London: Sheldon Press.

McClaren, James S. (1998) *Turbulent Times? Josephus and Scholarship on Judaea in the First Century CE*, JSPSup 29; Sheffield Academic Press.

McCreesh, T. P. (1985) "Wisdom as Wife: Proverbs 31:10–31", *RB* 92: 25–46.

McCullagh, C. Behan (1998) *The Truth of History*, London/New York: Routledge.

Macdonald, John (1971) "Samaritans", *Encyclopaedia Judaica* 14.728–32.

Mach, Michael (1992) *Entwicklungsstadien des jüdischen Engelglaubens in vorrabbinischer Zeit*, TSAJ 34; Tübingen: Mohr (Siebeck).

Mack, Burton L. (1973) *Logos und Sophia: Untersuchungen zur Weisheitstheologie im hellenistischen Judentum*, Studien zur Umwelt des Neuen Testaments 10; Göttingen: Vandenhoeck & Ruprecht.

—— (1974–75) "Exegetical Traditions in Alexandrian Judaism: A Program for the Analysis of the Philonic Corpus", *Studia Philonica* 3: 71–112.

—— (1985) *Wisdom and the Hebrew Epic: Ben Sira's Hymn in Praise of the Fathers*, Chicago Studies in the History of Judaism; Chicago/London: University of Chicago.

—— (1991) "Wisdom and Apocalyptic in Philo", in David T. Runia, David M. Hay, and David Winston (eds), *Heirs of the Septuagint: Philo, Hellenistic Judaism and Early Christianity: Festschrift for Earle Hilgert*, SPA 3; BJS 230; Atlanta: Scholars Press: 21–39.

Mackay, E. Anne (ed.) (1999) *Signs of Orality: The Oral Tradition and its Influence in the Greek and Roman World*, Mnemosyne Supplement 188; Leiden: Brill.

McKay, Heather A. (1994) *Sabbath and Synagogue: The Question of Sabbath Worship in Ancient Judaism*, Religions in the Graeco-Roman World 122; Leiden: Brill.

—— (1998) "Ancient Synagogues: The Continuing Dialectic Between Two Major Views", *CR: BS* 6: 103–42.

McKay, John (1970) "Helel and the Dawn-Goddess", *VT* 20: 451–64.

McKeating, Henry (1979) "Sanctions against Adultery in Ancient Israelite Society, With Some Reflections on Methodology in the Study of Old Testament Ethics", *JSOT* 11: 57–72.

McKenzie, John L. (1956) "Mythological Allusions in Ezek 28$_{12-18}$", *JBL* 75: 322–27.

McKnight, Scott (1991) *A Light among the Gentiles: Jewish Missionary Activity in the Second Temple Period*, Minneapolis: Fortress.

McLay, Tim (1996) *The OG and Th Versions of Daniel*, SBLSCS 43; Atlanta: Scholars Press.

Macmullen, Ramsey (1967) *Enemies of the Roman Order: Treason, Unrest, and Alienation in the Empire*, Cambridge, MA: Harvard; reprinted London: Routledge, 1993.

McNamara, Martin, MSC (1966) *The New Testament and the Palestinian Targum to the Pentateuch*, AnBib 27; Rome: Pontifical Biblical Institute.

—— (1972) *Targum and Testament: Aramaic Paraphrases of the Hebrew Bible: A Light on the New Testament*, Grand Rapids, MI: Eerdmans.

Magness, Jodi (1995) "The Chronology of the Settlement at Qumran in the Herodian Period", *DSD* 2: 58–65.

Mahé, Jean-Pierre (1981) "Le livre d'Adam georgien", in R. van den Broek and M. J. Vermaseren (eds) *Studies in Gnosticism and Hellenistic Religons Presented to Gilles Quispel on the Occasion of his 65th Birthday*, Leiden: Brill: 227–60.

Maier, Christl (1995) *Die "fremde Frau" in Proverbien 1–9: Eine exegetische und sozial-geschichtliche Studie*, OBO 144; Freiburg (Schweiz): Universitätsverlag; Göttingen: Vandenhoeck & Ruprecht.

Maier, Johann (1990) *Zwischen den Testamenten: Geschichte und Religion in der Zeit des zweiten Tempels*, Die Neue Echter Bibel Ergänzungsband zum Alten Testament 3; Würzburg: Echter Verlag.

Main, Emmanuelle (1990) "Les Sadducéens vus par Flavius Josèphe", *RB* 97: 161–206.

Mandell, Sara R. (1991) "Did the Maccabees Believe that They Had a Valid Treaty with Rome?" *CBQ* 53: 202–20.

Mantel, H. (1961) *Studies in the History of the Sanhedrin*, Cambridge University Press.

—— (1976) "Sanhedrin", *IDBSup*: 784–86.

Marcus, Ralph (1943) "Appendix D. Antiochus III and the Jews (*Ant.* xii. 129–153)", in H. S. J. Thackery (ed.) *Josephus*, LCL; London: Heinemann; Cambridge, MA: Harvard: 7.743–66.

Margalioth, Mordecai (1966) *Sepher Ha-Razim: A Newly Discovered Book of Magic from the Talmudic Period*, Jerusalem: Yediot Achronot.

Martin, James D. (1986) "Ben Sira's Hymn to the Fathers: a Messianic Perspective", in A. S. van der Woude (ed.) *Crises and Perspectives*, OTS 24; Leiden: Brill: 107–23.

Marx, A. (1989) "Sacrifice pour les péchés ou rites de passage? Quelques réflexions sur la fonction du *hattā't*", *RB* 96: 27–48.

—— (1994) *Les offrandes végétales dans l'Ancien Testament: Du tribut d'hommage au repas eschatologique*, VTSup 57; Leiden: Brill.

Mason, Rex (1994) *Zephaniah, Habakkuk, Joel*, Old Testament Guides; Sheffield Academic Press.

Mason, Steve (1989) "Was Josephus a Pharisee? A Re-Examination of *Life* 10–12", *JJS* 40: 31–45.

—— (1991) *Flavius Josephus on the Pharisees: A Composition-Critical Study*, SPB 39; Brill, Leiden.

—— (1992) *Josephus and the New Testament*, Peabody, MA: Hendrickson.

—— (1994) "Method in the Study of Early Judaism: A Dialogue with Lester Grabbe", *JAOS* 115: 463–72.

—— (ed.) (1998) *Understanding Josephus: Seven Perspectives*, JSPSup 32; Sheffield Academic Press.

—— (1999) "Revisiting Josephus's Pharisees", in Jacob Neusner and Alan Avery-Peck (eds) *Where We Stand: Issues and Debates in Ancient Judaism, Volume 2*, HdO: Erste Abteilung, Der Nahe und Mittlere Osten, Bd.; Leiden: Brill: 23–56.

Mattill, A. J., Jr (1978) "The Value of Acts as a Source for the Study of Paul", in C. H. Talbert (ed.) *Perspectives on Luke–Acts*, Edinburgh: T. & T. Clark: 76–98.

May, Herbert G. (1962) "The King in the Garden of Eden: A Study of Ezekiel 28:12–19", in B. W. Anderson and W. Harrelson (eds) *Israel's Prophetic Heritage: Essays in Honor of James Muilenburg*, New York: Harper: 166–76.

Meadowcroft, T. J. (1995) *Aramaic Daniel and Greek Daniel: A Literary Comparision*, JSOTSup 198; Sheffield Academic Press.

Meigs, A. S. (1978) "A Papuan Perspective on Pollution", *Man* 13: 304–18.

Mendels, Doron (1987) *The Land of Israel as a Political Concept in Hasmonean Literature*, TSAJ 15; Tübingen: Mohr (Siebeck).

—— (1992) *The Rise and Fall of Jewish Nationalism: The History of Jewish and Christian Ethnicity in Palestine within the Greco-Roman Period (200 B.C.E.–135 C.E.)*, The Anchor Bible Reference Library, New York/London: Doubleday.

Mendelson, Alan (1988) *Philo's Jewish Identity*, BJS 161; Atlanta: Scholars Press.

Metso, Sarianna (1997) *The Textual Development of the Qumran Community Rule*, STDJ 21; Leiden: Brill.

Mettinger, T. N. D. (1995) *No Graven Image? Israelite Aniconism in Its Ancient Near Eastern Context*, ConB, Old Testament Series 42; Stockholm: Almqvist & Wiksell.

Meyer, Marvin, and Paul Mirecki (eds) (1995) *Ancient Magic and Ritual Power*, Religions in the Graeco-Roman World 129; Leiden: Brill.

Meyers, Carol L., and Eric M. (1987) *Haggai, Zechariah 1–8*, AB 25B; Garden City, NY: Doubleday.

—— (1993) *Zechariah 9-14*, AB 25C; Garden City, NY: Doubleday.

Meyers, Eric M. (1971) *Jewish Ossuaries: Reburial and Rebirth: Secondary Burials in Their Ancient Near Eastern Setting*, BiOr 24; Rome: Pontifical Biblical Institute.

—— (1976) "Galilean Regionalism as a Factor in Historical Reconstruction", *BASOR* 221: 93–101.

—— (1985) "Galilean Regionalism: A Reappraisal", in W. Scott Green (ed.) *Approaches to Ancient Judaism, Volume V: Studies in Judaism and Its Greco-Roman Context*, BJS 32; Atlanta: Scholars Press, 1985: 5.115–31.

—— (1994) "Second Temple Studies in the Light of Recent Archaeology: Part I: The Persian and Hellenistic Periods", *CR: BS* 2: 25–42.

Meyers, Eric M., Adam Lynd-Porter, Melissa Aubin, and Mark Chancey (1995) "Second Temple Studies in the Light of Recent Archaeology: Part II: The Roman Period, A Bibliography", *CR: BS* 3: 129–54.

Meyers, Eric M., and J. F. Strange (1981) *Archaeology, the Rabbis and Early Christianity*, Nashville: Abingdon.

Michel, Otto (1967–68) "Studien zu Josephus: Simon bar Giora", *NTS* 14: 402–08.

Mildenberg, Leo (1996) "*yěhūd* und *šmryn*: Über das Geld der persischen Provinzen Juda und Samaria im 4. Jahrhundert", in Hubert Cancik, Hermann Lichtenberger, and Peter Schäfer (eds) *Geschichte–Tradition–Reflexion: Festschrift für Martin Hengel zum 70. Geburtstag: Band I Judentum*, ed. Peter Schäfer, Tübingen: Mohr (Siebeck): 119–46.

—— (1998) *Vestigia Leonis: Studien zur antiken Numismatik Israels, Palästinas und der östlichen Mittelmeerwelt*, Ulrich Hübner and Ernst Axel Knauf (eds); Novum Testamentum et Orbis Antiquus 36; Freiburg [Schweiz]: Universitätsverlag; Göttingen: Vandenhoeck & Ruprecht.

Milgrom, J. (1976) *Cult and Conscience: The ASHAM and the Priestly Doctrine of Repentance*, Leiden: Brill.

—— (1991) *Leviticus 1–16*, AB 3, Garden City, NY: Doubleday.

—— (1992) "Priestly ('P') Source", *ABD* 5.454–61.

—— (1993) "Response to Rolf Rendtorff", *JSOT* 60: 83-85.

Milik, J. T. (1976) *The Books of Enoch: Aramaic Fragments of Qumran Cave 4*, Oxford: Clarendon.

Miller, James E. (1990) "Dreams and Prophetic Visions", *Biblica* 71: 401–4.

Miller, Patricia Cox (1994) *Dreams in Late Antiquity: Studies in the Imagination of a Culture*, Princeton, NJ: Princeton University Press.

Moor, Johannes C. de (1997) *The Rise of Yahwism: The Roots of Israelite Monotheism*, 2nd edn; Bibliotheca Ephemeridum Theologicarum Lovaniensium 91; Leuven: Peeters/University Press.

Moore, Carey A. (1992) "Tobit, Book of", *ABD* 6.585–94.

—— (1996) *Tobit: A New Translation with Introduction and Commentary*, AB 40a; New York: Doubleday.

Morgan, M. A. (1983) *Sepher Ha-Razim: The Book of Mysteries*, SBLTT 25, Pseudepigrapha Series 11; Chico, CA: Scholars Press.

Mowinckel, Sigmund (1956) *He That Cometh*, transl. G. W. Anderson; Oxford: Blackwell; ET of *Han som kommer*, Copenhagen: Gad, 1951.

Muffs, Yochanan (1969) *Studies in the Aramaic Legal Papyri from Elephantine*, Studia et Documenta 8; Leiden: Brill.

Mulder, Martin Jan, and Harry Sysling (eds) (1988) *Mikra: Text, Translation, Reading and Interpretation of the Hebrew Bible in Ancient Judaism and Early Christianity*, CRINT 2/1; Assen/Maastricht: Van Gorcum; Minneapolis: Fortress.

Mullen, E. Theodore, Jr (1980) *The Assembly of the Gods: The Divine Council in Canaanite and Early Hebrew Literature*, HSM 24; Chico, CA: Scholars Press.

Munoa, Phillip B., III (1998) *Four Powers in Heaven: The Interpretation of Daniel 7 in the Testament of Abraham*, JSPSup 28; Sheffield Academic Press.

Muraoka, T., and John F. Elwolde (eds) (1997) *The Hebrew of the Dead Sea Scrolls and Ben Sira: Proceedings of a Symposium Held at Leiden University, 11–14 December 1995*, STDJ 26; Leiden: Brill.

Murphy, Frederick J. (1993) *Pseudo-Philo: Rewriting the Bible*, Oxford University Press.

Murphy, Roland E., and Elizabeth Huwiler (1999) *Proverbs, Ecclesiastes, Song of Songs*, New International Biblical Commentary, Old Testament Series 12; Peabody, MA: Hendrickson; Carlisle: Paternoster.

Murphy-O'Connor, Jerome (1974) "The Essenes and their History", *RB* 81: 215–44.

—— (1985) "The *Damascus Document* Revisited", *RB* 92: 223–46 (= K. H. Richards [ed.], *Society of Biblical Literature 1986 Seminar Papers Series*, SBLASP 25; Atlanta: Scholars Press: 369–83).

—— (1992) "Lots of God-Fearers? 'Theosebeis' in the Aphrodisias Inscription", *RB* 99: 418–24.

Musurillo, H. A. (ed.) (1954) *The Acts of the Pagan Martyrs: Acta Alexandrinorum*, Oxford: Clarendon.

Naveh, Joseph, and Shaul Shaked (1985) *Amulets and Magic Bowls: Aramaic Incantations of Late Antiquity*, Jerusalem: Magnes; Leiden: Brill.

—— (1993) *Magic Spells and Formulae: Aramaic Incantations of Late Antiquity*, Jerusalem: Magnes.

Netzer, Ehud (1982) "Ancient Ritual Baths (*Miqvaot*) in Jericho", *Jerusalem Cathedra* 2: 106–19.

—— (ed.) (1991) *Masada III: The Yigael Yadin Excavations 1963–1965, Final Reports: The Buildings: Stratigraphy and Architecture*, Masada Reports; Jerusalem: Israel Exploration Society.

Neubauer, Adolf, and S. R. Driver (1876) *The Fifty-Third Chapter of Isaiah according to the Jewish Interpreters: I. Texts; II. Translations*, with an Introduction by E. B. Pusey; 2 vols; reprinted with Prolegomenon by R. Loewe, New York: Ktav, 1969.

Neusner, Jacob (1965–70) *A History of the Jews in Babylonia*, vols 1–5; Leiden: Brill.

—— (1970) *Development of a Legend: Studies on the Traditions Concerning Yohanan ben Zakkai*, SPB 16; Leiden: Brill.

—— (1971) *The Rabbinic Traditions about the Pharisees before 70*, 3 vols; Leiden: Brill.

—— (1972) "Emergent Rabbinic Judaism in a Time of Crisis: Four Responses to the Destruction of the Second Temple", *Judaism* 21: 313–27.

—— (1973a) *From Politics to Piety*, Englewood Cliffs, NJ: Prentice-Hall.

—— (1973b) *The Idea of Purity in Ancient Judaism: The Haskell Lectures, 1972–1973*, with a critique and commentary by M. Douglas, SJLA 1; Leiden: Brill.

—— (1973c) *Eliezer ben Hyrcanus*, 2 vols; SJLA 4; Leiden: Brill.

—— (1979) "The Formation of Rabbinic Judaism: Yavneh (Jamnia) from A.D. 70 to 100", *ANRW II*: 19.2.3–42.

—— (1980) "The Present State of Rabbinic Biography", in G. Nahon and C. Touati (eds) *Hommage à Georges Vajda: Études d'histoire et de pensée juive*, Louvain: Peeters: 85–91.

—— (1981) *Judaism: The Evidence of the Mishnah*, Chicago University Press.

—— (1983) "Varieties of Judaism in the Formative Age", *Formative Judaism II: Religious, Historical, and Literary Studies*, BJS 41; Atlanta: Scholars Press: 59–89.

—— (1984) *Messiah in Context: Israel's History and Destiny in Formative Judaism*, Philadelphia: Fortress.

—— (1986) "Preface", in E. S. Frerichs and J. Neusner (eds) *Goodenough on the History of Religion and on Judaism* (BJS 121; Atlanta: Scholars Press, 1986): ix–xix [= "Introduction" to E. R. Goodenough, *Jewish Symbols in the Greco-Roman Period* (abridged edn, 1988] ix–xxxvii).

—— (1987a) *The Wonder-Working Lawyers of Talmudic Babylonia: The Theory and Practice of Judaism in its Formative Age*, Studies in Judaism; Lanham, MD: University Press of America (= [1966] *A History of the Jews in Babylonia II*: 251–87; [1968] *A History of the Jews in Babylonia III*: 95–194; [1969] *A History of the Jews in Babylonia IV*: 179–402; [1970] *A History of the Jews in Babylonia V*: 244–342).

—— (1987b) "Mishnah and Messiah", in Jacob Neusner, W. S. Green, and Ernest S. Frerichs (eds) *Judaisms and Their Messiahs at the Turn of the Christian Era*, Cambridge University Press: 265–82.

—— (1988a) *Invitation to the Talmud: A Teaching Book*, revised and expanded edn, including Hebrew texts; reprinted in SFSJH 169; Atlanta: Scholars Press, 1998.

—— (1988b) *Invitation to Midrash: The Workings of Rabbinic Bible Interpretation: A Teaching Book*, revised and expanded edn, including Hebrew texts; reprinted in SFSJH 170; Atlanta: Scholars Press, 1998.

—— (1989) "Science and Magic, Miracle and Magic in Formative Judaism: The System and the Difference", in Jacob Neusner, Ernest S. Frerichs, and Paul V. M. Flesher (eds) *Religion, Science, and Magic: In Concert and Conflict*, Oxford University Press: 61–81.

—— (1991) *Judaism as Philosophy: The Method and Message of Mishnah*, Charleston, SC: University of South Carolina Press.

—— (1992) *The Transformation of Judaism: From Philosophy to Religion*, Champaign, IL: University of Illinois Press.

—— (1994) *Introduction to Rabbinic Literature*, Anchor Bible Reference Library; New York: Doubleday.

—— (ed.) (1995a) *Judaism in Late Antiquity: Part 1, The Literary and Archaeological Sources;*

Part 2, Historical Syntheses, 2 vols; HdO: Erste Abteilung, der Nahe und Mittlere Osten 17; Leiden: Brill.

—— (1995b) "Evaluating the Attributions of Sayings to Named Sages in the Rabbinic Literature", *JSJ* 26: 93–111.

—— (1996) Review of G. Boccaccini, *Middle Judaism, JSJ* 27: 334–38.

Neusner, Jacob, and Ernest S. Frerichs (eds) (1985) *"To See Ourselves as Others See Us": Christians, Jews, "Others" in Late Antiquity*, SPSH; Atlanta: Scholars.

Neusner, Jacob, Alan J. Avery-Peck, and William Scott Green (eds) (2000) *The Encyclopaedia of Judaism*, Leiden: Brill.

Neusner, Jacob; W. S. Green; and Ernest S. Frerichs (eds) (1987) *Judaisms and Their Messiahs at the Turn of the Christian Era*, Cambridge University Press.

Neusner, Jacob, and Clemens Thoma (1995) "Die Pharisäer vor und nach der Tempelzerstörung des Jahres 70 n. Chr.", in Simon Lauer and Hanspeter Ernst (ed.) *Tempelkult und Tempelzerstörung (70 n. Chr.): Festschrift für Clemens Thoma zum 60. Geburtstag*, Judaica et Christiana 15; Bern: Lang: 189–230.

Newman, Judith H. (1999) *Praying by the Book: The Scripturalization of Prayer in Second Temple Judaism*, SBLEJL 14; Atlanta: Scholars Press.

Newsom, Carol A. (1985) *Songs of the Sabbath Sacrifice: A Critical Edition*, HSS 27; Atlanta: Scholars Press.

Newsom, Carol A., and Sharon H. Ringe (eds) (1998) *Women's Bible Commentary: Expanded Edition*, Louisville, KY: Westminster John Knox; London: SPCK.

Nicholson, Ernest (1998) *The Pentateuch in the Twentieth Century: The Legacy of Julius Wellhausen*, Oxford: Clarendon.

Nickelsburg, George W. E. (1972) *Resurrection, Immortality, and Eternal Life in Inter-testamental Judaism*, Harvard Theological Studies 26; Cambridge, MA: Harvard.

—— (ed.) (1976) *Studies on the Testament of Abraham*, SBLSCS 6; Missoula, MT: Scholars Press.

—— (1981) "Some Related Traditions in the Apocalypse of Adam, the Books of Adam and Eve, and 1 Enoch", in Bentley Layton (ed.) *Rediscovery of Gnosticism: Proceedings of the International Conference on Gnosticism at Yale, 1978, Vol. 2: Sethian Gnosticism*, Studies in the History of Religions 41; Leiden: Brill: 515–39.

Niditch, Susan (1980) *The Symbolic Vision in Biblical Tradition*, HSM 30; Atlanta: Scholars Press.

Niehr, Herbert (1990) *Der höchste Gott: Alttestamentlicher JHWH-Glaube im Kontext syrisch-kanaanäischer Religion des 1. Jahrtausends v. Chr.*, BZAW 190; Berlin/New York: de Gruyter.

—— (1998) *Religionen in Israels Umwelt: Einführung in die nordwestsemitischen Religionen Syrien-Palästinas*, Neue Echter Bible: Ergänzungsband zum Alten Testament 5; Würzburg: Echter Verlage.

Nikiprowetzky, Valentin (1973) "Sicaires et Zélotes – une Reconsidération", *Semitica* 23: 51–64.

—— (1996) *Études philoniennes*, Patrimoines judaïsme; Paris: Cerf.

Nissinen, Martti (1998) *Homoeroticism in the Biblical World: A Historical Perspective*, Minneapolis: Fortress.

Nodet, Étienne (1997) *A Search for the Origins of Judaism: From Joshua to the Mishnah*, JSOTSup 248; Sheffield Academic Press; ET of *Essai sur les Origines du Judaïsme: De Josué aux Pharisiens*, Paris: Cerf, 1992.

Noethlichs, Karl Leo (1996) *Das Judentum und der römische Staat: Minderheitenpolitik im antiken Rom*, Darmstadt: Wissenschaftliche Buchgesellschaft.

Nolland, J. (1981) "Uncircumcised Proselytes?" *JSJ* 12: 173–94.

Noy, David (ed.) (1993) *Jewish Inscriptions of Western Europe: Volume 1, Italy (excluding the City of Rome), Spain and Gaul*, Cambridge University Press.

—— (1995) *Jewish Inscriptions of Western Europe: Volume 2, The City of Rome*, Cambridge University Press.

Nurmela, Risto (1998) *The Levites: Their Emergence as a Second-Class Priesthood*, SFSHJ 193; Atlanta: Scholars Press.

O'Brien, Julia M. (1990) *Priest and Levite in Malachi*, SBLDS 121; Atlanta: Scholars Press.

—— (1995) "Malachi in Recent Research", *CR: BS* 3: 81–94.

Oded, Bustenay (1979) *Mass Deportations and Deportees in the Neo-Assyrian Empire*, Wiesbaden: Reichert.

Oegema, Gerbern S. (1998) *The Anointed and his People: Messianic Expectations from the Maccabees to Bar Kochba*, JSPSup 27; Sheffield Academic Press; ET of *Der Gesalbte und sein Volk: Untersuchungen zum Konzeptualisierungsprozeß der messianischen Erwartungen von den Makkabäern bis Bar Koziba*, Schriften des Institutum Judaicum Delitzschianum 2; Göttingen: Vandenhoeck & Ruprecht, 1994.

Olyan, Saul M. (1993) *A Thousand Thousands Served Him: Exegesis and the Naming of Angels in Ancient Judaism*, TSAJ 36; Tübingen: Mohr(Siebeck).

O'Neill, J. C. (1991) "The Man from Heaven: *SibOr* 5.256–259", *JSP* 9: 87–102.

Ong, Walter J. (1982) *Orality and Literacy: The Technologizing of the Word*, London/New York: Methuen.

Oppenheim, A. Leo (1956) "The Interpretation of Dreams in the Ancient Near East, With a Translation of an Assyrian Dream-Book", *Transactions of the American Philosophical Society* 46: 179–354.

Orlinsky, Harry M. (1975) "The Septuagint as Holy Writ and the Philosophy of the Translators", *HUCA* 46: 89–114.

—— (1991) "Some Terms in the Prologue to Ben Sira and the Hebrew Canon", *JBL* 110: 483–90.

Orlov, Andrei A. (1998) "Titles of Enoch–Metatron in *2 Enoch*", *JSP* 18: 71–86.

Overman, J. Andrew (1993) "Recent Advances in the Archaeology of the Galilee in the Roman Period", *CR: BS* 1: 35–58.

Parente, Fausto, and Joseph Sievers (eds) (1994) *Josephus and the History of the Greco-Roman Period: Essays in Memory of Morton Smith*, SPB 41; Leiden: Brill.

Parry, Donald W. and Eugene Ulrich (eds) (1999) *The Provo International Conference on the Dead Sea Scrolls: Technological Innovations, New Texts, and Reformulated Issues*, STDJ 30; Leiden: Brill.

Pearson, Brook W. R. (1998) "Dry Bones in the Judean Desert: The Messiah of Ephraim, Ezekiel 37, and the Post-Revolutionary Followers of Bar Kokhba", *JSJ* 29: 192–201.

Peltonen, Kai (1996) *History Debated: The Historical Reliability of Chronicles in Pre-Critical and Critical Research*, Publications of the Finnish Exegetical Society 64; Helsinki: The Finnish Exegetical Society; Göttingen: Vandenhoeck & Ruprecht.

—— (2000) "A Jigsaw without a Model?: The Dating of Chronicles", in L. L. Grabbe (ed.) *Did Moses Speak Attic? Jewish Historiography and Scripture in the Hellenistic Period*,

JSOTSup = European Seminar in Historical Methodology 3; Sheffield Academic Press.

Perkins, Pheme (1977) "Apocalypse of Adam: The Genre and Function of a Gnostic Apocalypse", *CBQ* 39: 382–95.

Person, Raymond F., Jr (1993) *Second Zechariah and the Deuteronomic School*, JSOTSup 167; Sheffield Academic Press.

—— (1996) *In Conversation with Jonah: Conversation Analysis, Literary Criticism, and the Book of Jonah*, JSOTSup 220; Sheffield Academic Press.

Petersen, David L. (1984) *Haggai and Zechariah 1–8: A Commentary*, OTL; Louisville, KY: Westminster John Knox; London: SCM.

—— (1995) *Zechariah 9–14 and Malachi: A Commentary*, OTL; Louisville, KY: Westminster John Knox; London: SCM.

Pietersma, Albert (1984) "Kyrios or Tetragram: A Renewed Quest for the Original Septuagint", in Albert Pietersma and Claude Cox (eds) *De Septuaginta: Studies in Honour of John William Wevers on his Sixty-Fifth Birthday*, Mississauga, Ontario: Benben Publications: 85–101.

Piñero, A. (1993) "Angels and Demons in the Greek *Life of Adam and Eve*", *JSJ* 24: 191–214.

Poehlmann, William (1992) "The Sadducees as Josephus Presents Them, or The Curious Case of Ananus", in A. J. Hultgren, D. H. Juel, and J. D. Kingsbury (eds) *All Things New: Essays in Honor of Roy A. Harrisville*, Word and World Supplement Series 1; St Paul, MN: Luther Northwestern Theological Seminary: 87–100.

Poirier, John C. (1996) "Why Did the Pharisees Wash their Hands?" *JJS* 47: 217–33.

Pomykala, Kenneth E. (1995) *The Davidic Dynasty Tradition in Early Judaism: Its History and Significance for Messianism*, SBLEJL 7; Atlanta: Scholars Press.

Poorthuis, M. J. H. M., and J. Schwartz (eds) (2000) *Purity and Holiness: The Heritage of Leviticus*, Jewish and Christian Perspectives 2; Leiden: Brill.

Pope, Marvin H. (1973) *Job*, 3rd edn; AB 15; Garden City, NY: Doubleday.

Porten, Bezalel (1968) *Archives from Elephantine: The Life of an Ancient Jewish Military Colony*, Berkeley/Los Angeles: University of California.

—— (1996) *The Elephantine Papyri in English: Three Millennia of Cross-Cultural Continuity and Change*, Documenta et Monumenta Orientis Antiqui 22; Leiden: Brill.

Porten, Bezalel, and Ada Yardeni (1986–) *Textbook of Aramaic Documents from Ancient Egypt: 1–* , Hebrew University, Department of the History of the Jewish People, Texts and Studies for Students; Jerusalem: Hebrew University.

—— (1993) "Ostracon Clermont-Ganneau 125(?): A Case of Ritual Purity", *JAOS* 113: 451–56.

Porton, Gary G. (1976–82) *The Traditions of Rabbi Ishmael*, SJLA 19; Parts 1–4; Leiden: Brill.

—— (1981) "Defining Midrash", in Jacob Neusner (ed.) *The Ancient Study of Judaism*, New York: Ktav: 1.55–92; revision of G. G. Porton (1979) "Midrash: Palestinian Jews and the Hebrew Bible in the Greco-Roman Period", *ANRW: II Principiat*: 19.2.103–38.

—— (1986) "Diversity in Postbiblical Judaism", in Robert A. Kraft and George W. E. Nickelsburg (eds) *Early Judaism and its Modern Interpreters*, SBLBMI 2; Atlanta: Scholars Press; Philadelphia: Fortress: 57–80.

—— (1992) "Midrash", *ABD*: 4.818–22.

Potter, David (1994) *Prophets and Emperors: Human and Divine Authority from Augustus to Theodosius*, Revealing Antiquity 7; Cambridge, MA and London: Harvard University Press.

Price, Jonathan J. (1992) *Jerusalem Under Siege: The Collapse of the Jewish State 66–70 CE*, Brill's Series in Jewish Studies 3; Leiden: Brill.

Prosic, Tamara (1999) "Origin of Passover", *SJOT* 13: 78–94.

Pucci Ben Zeev, Miriam (1993) "The Reliability of Josephus Flavius: The Case of Hecataeus' and Manetho's Accounts of Jews and Judaism: Fifteen Years of Contemporary Research (1974–1990)", *JSJ* 24: 215–34.

—— (1998) *Jewish Rights in the Roman World: The Greek and Roman Documents Quoted by Josephus Flavius*, TSAJ 74; Tübingen: Mohr (Siebeck).

Puech, Emile (1993) *La croyance des Esséniens en la vie future: Immortalité, résurrection, vie éternelle? Histoire d'une croyance dans le Judaïsme Ancien*: vol. I: *La résurrection des morts et le contexte scripturaire*; vol. II: *Le données qumraniennes et classiques*, with an introduction by André Caquot; Études bibliques, nouvelle série nos. 21–22; Paris: Gabalda.

—— (1999) "Le 'Fils de Dieu' en 4Q246", in Baruch A. Levine, Philip J. King, Joseph Naveh, and Ephraim Stern (eds) *Frank Moore Cross Volume* = *Eretz-Israel* 26; Jerusalem: Israel Exploration Society: 143*–52*.

Pulikottil, Paulson U. (2000) *Transmission of the Biblical Text in the Qumran Scrolls: The Case of the Large Isaiah Scroll (1QIs^a)*, JSOTSup; Sheffield Academic Press.

Qimron, E., and John Strugnell (eds) (1994) *Qumran Cave 4: V, Miqsat Ma'ase ha-Torah*, DJD 10; Oxford: Clarendon Press.

Rabenau, Merten (1994) *Studien zum Buch Tobit*, BZAW 220; Berlin/New York: de Gruyter.

Rad, Gerhard von (1959) "The Origin of the Concept of the Day of Yahweh", *JSS* 4: 97–108.

Rajak, Tessa (1984) "Was There a Roman Charter for the Jews?" *JRS* 74: 107–23.

—— (1992) "The Jewish Community and its Boundaries", in Judith Lieu, J. L. North, and Tessa Rajak (eds) *Jews among Pagans and Christians in the Roman Empire*, London: Routledge: 9–28.

Rajak, Tessa, and David Noy (1993) "*Archisynagogoi*: Office, Title and Social Status in the Greco-Jewish Synagogue", *JRS* 83: 75–93.

Redditt, Paul L. (1986a) "The Book of Joel and Peripheral Prophecy", *CBQ* 48: 225–40.

—— (1986b) "Once Again, the City in Isaiah 24–27", *Hebrew Annual Review* 10: 317–35.

—— (1989) "Israel's Shepherds: Hope and Pessimism in Zechariah 9–14", *CBQ* 51: 632–42.

—— (1992) "Zerubbabel, Joshua, and the Night Visions of Zechariah", *CBQ* 54: 249–59.

—— (1994a) "The Book of Malachi in its Social Setting", *CBQ* 56: 240–55.

—— (1994b) "Nehemiah's First Mission and the Date of Zechariah 9–14", *CBQ* 56: 664–78.

—— (1995) *Haggai, Zechariah and Malachi*, New Century Bible Commentary; London: Harper Collins; Grand Rapids, MI: Eerdmans.

—— (1999) *Daniel, Based on the New Revised Standard Version*, New Century Bible Commentary; Sheffield Academic Press.

Reese, James M. (1970) *Hellenistic Influence on the Book of Wisdom and Its Consequences*, AnBib 41; Rome: Pontifical Biblical Institute.

Reeves, John C. (1992) *Jewish Lore in Manichaean Cosmogony: Studies in the* Book of Giants *Traditions*, Monographs of the Hebrew Union College 14; Cincinnati: Hebrew Union College Press.

Reider, Joseph (1957) *The Book of Wisdom*, Jewish Apocryphal Literature; New York: Dropsie College.

Reif, Stefan (1993) *Judaism and Hebrew Prayer: New Perspectives on Jewish Liturgical History*, Cambridge University Press.

Rendtorff, Rolf (1993) "Two Kinds of P? Some Reflections on the Occasion of the Publishing of Jacob Milgrom's Commentary on Leviticus 1–16", *JSOT* 60: 75–81.

Reynolds, Joyce, and Robert Tannenbaum (1987) *Jews and Godfearers at Aphrodisias: Greek Inscriptions with Commentary*, Cambridge Philological Society, Suppl. 12; Cambridge: Cambridge Philological Society.

Rhoads, D. M. (1976) *Israel in Revolution: 6–74 C.E.: A Political History Based on the Writings of Josephus*, Philadelphia: Fortress.

Richardson, Peter (1996) *Herod: King of the Jews and Friend of the Romans*, Studies on Personalities of the New Testament; Columbia, SC: University of South Carolina.

Ritmyer, Leen, and Kathleen Ritmyer (1998) *Secrets of Jerusalem's Temple Mount*, Washington, DC: Biblical Archaeology Society.

Rivkin, Ellis (1972) "Defining the Pharisees: The Tannaitic Sources", *HUCA* 43: 205–40.

Roberts, J. J. M. (1973) "The Davidic Origin of the Zion Tradition", *JBL* 92: 329–44.

—— (1982) "Zion in the Theology of the Davidic-Solomonic Empire", in T. Ishida, *Studies in the Period of David and Solomon and Other Essays: Papers Read at the International Symposium for Biblical Studies, Tokyo, 5-7 December, 1979*, Winona Lake, IN: Eisenbrauns: 93–108.

Robertson, David A. (1972) *Linguistic Evidence in Dating Early Hebrew Poetry*, SBLDS 3; Missoula, MT: Society of Biblical Literature.

Roddy, Nicolae (1996) "'Two Parts: Weeks of Seven Weeks': The End of the Age as *Terminus ad Quem* for *2 Baruch*", *JSP* 14: 3–14.

Rofé, Alexander (1985) "Isaiah 66:1–4: Judean Sects in the Persian Period as Viewed by Trito-Isaiah", in A. Kort and S. Morschauser (eds) *Biblical and Related Studies Presented to Samuel Iwry*, Winona Lake, IN: Eisenbrauns: 205–17.

—— (1999) *Introduction to the Composition of the Pentateuch*, The Biblical Seminar 58; Sheffield Academic Press.

Royse, James R. (1991a) *The Spurious Texts of Philo of Alexandria: A Study of Textual Transmission and Corruption with Indexes to the Major Collections of Greek Fragments*, ALGHJ 22; Leiden: Brill.

—— (1991b) "Philo, Κύριος, and the Tetragrammaton", in David T. Runia, David M. Hay, and David Winston (eds) *Heirs of the Septuagint: Philo, Hellenistic Judaism and Early Christianity: Festschrift for Earle Hilgert* = *SPA* 3; Atlanta: Scholars Press: 167–83.

Rubenstein, Jeffrey L. (1995) *The History of Sukkot in the Second Temple and Rabbinic Periods*, BJS 302; Atlanta: Scholars Press.

Rubinkiewicz, Ryszard (1992) "Abraham, Apocalypse of", *ABD*: 1.41–43.

Runia, David T. (1986) *Philo of Alexandria and the* Timaeus *of Plato*, Philosophia Antiqua 44; Leiden: Brill.

—— (1993) *Philo in Early Christian Literature. A Survey*, Compendia Rerum Iudaicarum ad Novum Testamentum III/3; Assen: Van Gorcum.

—— (1995) *Philo and the Church Fathers: A Collection of Papers*, Supplements to Vigiliae Christianae 32; Leiden: Brill.

Rutgers, Leonard Victor (1995) *The Jews in Late Ancient Rome: Evidence of Cultural Interaction in the Roman Diaspora*, Religions in the Graeco-Roman World 126; Leiden: Brill.

—— (1998) *The Hidden Heritage of Diaspora Judaism*, Contributions to Biblical Exegesis and Theology 20; Leuven: Peeters.

Sacchi, Paolo (1996) *Jewish Apocalyptic and its History*, transl. W. J. Short; JSPSup 20; Sheffield Academic Press; ET of *L'apocalittica giudaica e la sua storia*, Brescia: Paideia Editrice, 1990.

Sæbø, Magne (ed.) (1996) *Hebrew Bible/Old Testament: The History of its Interpretation, Volume I: From the Beginnings to the Middle Ages (Until 1300), Part 1: Antiquity*, in cooperation with Chris Brekelmans and Menahem Haran; Göttingen: Vandenhoeck & Ruprecht.

Saldarini, Anthony J. (1975) "Johanan ben Zakkai's Escape from Jerusalem: Origin and Development of a Rabbinic Story", *JSJ* 6:189–204.

—— (1988) *Pharisees, Scribes and Sadducees in Palestinian Society: A Sociological Approach*, Wilmington, DE: Glazier; Edinburgh: T. & T. Clark.

Salters, Robin B. (1994) *Jonah & Lamentations*, Old Testament Guides; Sheffield Academic Press.

Sanders, Edward P. (1992) *Judaism: Practice and Belief 63 BCE–66 CE*, London: SCM; Philadelphia: Trinity Press International.

Sanders, James A. (1967) *The Dead Sea Psalms Scroll*, Ithaca, NY: Cornell University.

Sanderson, Julia (1986) *An Exodus Scroll from Qumran: 4QpaleoExod^m and the Samaritan Tradition*, HSS 30; Atlanta: Scholars Press.

Sasson, Jack (1982) "An Apocalyptic Vision from Mari?: Speculations on *ARM* X: 9", *MARI* 1: 151–67.

—— (1983) "Mari Dreams", *JAOS* 103: 283–93.

—— (1990) *Jonah: A New Translation with Introduction, Commentary, and Interpretations*, AB 24b; New York: Doubleday.

Sasson, Victor (1986) "The Book of Oracular Visions of Balaam from Deir 'Alla", *Ugarit-Forschungen* 17: 283–309.

Sawyer, John F. A. (ed.) (1996) *Reading Leviticus: A Conversation with Mary Douglas*, JSOTSup 227; Sheffield Academic Press.

Schäfer, Peter (1978) "R. Aqiva und Bar Kokhba", *Studien zur Geschichte und Theologie des rabbinischen Judentums*, AGAJU 15; Leiden: Brill: 65–121.

—— (1980) "Aqiva and Bar Kokhba", William Scott Green (ed.) *Approaches to Ancient Judaism II*, BJS 9; Atlanta: Scholars Press: 113–30.

—— (1992) *The Hidden and Manifest God. Some Major Themes in Early Jewish Mysticism*, transl. A. Pomerance; SUNY Series in Judaica: Hermeneutics, Mysticism, and Religion; Albany: State University of New York Press; ET of *Der verborgene und offenbare Gott: Hauptthemen der frühen jüdischen Mystik*, Tübingen: Mohr (Siebeck), 1991.

—— (1997) *Judeophobia: Attitudes toward the Jews in the Ancient World*, Cambridge, MA, and London: Harvard University Press.

Schäfer, Peter, and Joseph Dan (eds) (1993) *Gershom Scholem's* Major Trends in Jewish Mysticism *50 Years After: Proceedings of the Sixth International Conference on the History of Jewish Mysticism*, Tübingen: Mohr (Siebeck).

Schäfer, Peter, and Hans G. Kippenberg (eds) (1997) *Envisioning Magic: A Princeton Seminar and Symposium*, Studies in the History of Religions [*Numen* Book Series] 75; Leiden: Brill.

Schäfer, Peter, and Shaul Shaked (eds) (1994–99) *Magische Texte aus der Kairoer Geniza I–III*, 3 vols; TSAJ 42, 64, 72; Tübingen: Mohr (Siebeck).

Schams, Christine (1998) *Jewish Scribes in the Second-Temple Period*, JSOTSup 291; Sheffield Academic Press.

Schaper, Joachim (1995) "The Jerusalem Temple as an Instrument of the Achaemenid Fiscal Administration", *VT* 45: 428–39.

Schiffman, Lawrence H. (1991) *From Text to Tradition: A History of Second Temple and Rabbinic Judaism*, Hoboken, NJ: Ktav.

Schmid, Konrad (1998) "Esras Begegnung mit Zion: Die Deutung der Zerstörung Jerusalems im 4. Esrabuch und das Problem des 'bösen Herzens'", *JSJ* 29: 261–77.

Schoors, A. (1992) *The Preacher Sought to Find Pleasing Words: A Study of the Language of Qoheleth*, Orientalia Lovaniensia Analecta 41; Leuven: Peeters/Departement Orientalistiek, Leuven.

—— (ed.) (1998) *Qohelet in the Context of Wisdom*, BETL 136; Leuven: Peeters/University Press.

Schottroff, Luise, Silvia Schroer, and Marie-Theres Wacker (1998) *Feminist Interpretation: The Bible in Women's Perspective*, trans. M. and B. Rumscheidt; Minneapolis: Fortress; ET of *Feministische Exegese: Forschungerträge zur Bibel aus der Perspektive von Frauen*, Darmstadt: Wissenschaftliche Buchgesellschaft, 1995.

Schramm, Brooks (1995) *The Opponents of Third Isaiah: Reconstructing the Cultic History of the Restoration*, JSOTSup 193; Sheffield Academic Press.

Schremer, Adiel (1997) "The Name of the Boethusians: A Reconsideration of Suggested Explanations and Another One", *JJS* 48: 290–99.

Schröder, Bernd (1996) *Die "väterlichen Gesetze": Flavius Josephus als Vermittler von Halachah an Griechen und Römer*, TSAJ 53; Tübingen: Mohr (Siebeck).

Schultz, Richard L. (1999) *The Search for Quotation: Verbal Parallels in the Prophets*, JSOTSup 180; Sheffield Academic Press.

Schüpphaus, J. (1977) *Die Psalmen Salomos: Ein Zeugnis Jerusalemer Theologie und Frömmigkeit in der Mitte des vorchristlichen Jahrhunderts*, ALGHJ 7; Leiden: Brill.

Schürer, Emil (1973–87) *The Jewish People in the Age of Jesus Christ*, revised and ed. G. Vermes, et al.; 3 vols in 4; Edinburgh: T. & T. Clark.

Schüssler Fiorenze, Elizabeth (ed.) with the assistance of S. Matthews (1994) *Searching the Scriptures: Volume 1. A Feminist Introduction*, London: SCM.

—— (1994) *Searching the Scriptures: Volume 2. A Feminist Commentary*, with the assistance of Ann Brock and Shelly Matthews; London: SCM.

Schwartz, Daniel R. (1990) *Agrippa I: The Last King of Judaea*, TSAJ 23; Tübingen: Mohr (Siebeck).

—— (1992) *Studies in the Jewish Background of Christianity*, WUNT 60; Tübingen: Mohr (Siebeck).

Schwartz, Seth (1990) *Josephus and Judaean Politics*, CSCT 18; Leiden: Brill.

—— (1994) "On the Autonomy of Judaea in the Fourth and Third Centuries B.C.E.", *JJS* 45: 157–68.

—— (1999) "The Patriarchs and the Diaspora", *JJS* 50: 208–22.

Schwenk-Bressler, Udo (1993) *Sapientia Salomonis als ein Beispiel frühjüdischer Textauslegung: Die Auslegung des Buches Genesis, Exodus 1–15 und Teilen der Wüstentradition in Sap 10–19*, Beiträge zur Erforschung des Alten Testaments und des antiken Judentums 32; Frankfurt am Main: Lang.

Schwienhorst-Schönberger, Ludger (ed.) (1997) *Das Buch Kohelet: Studien zur Struktur, Geschichte, Rezeption und Theologie*, BZAW 254; Berlin/New York: de Gruyter.

Scott, James M. (ed.) (1997) *Exile: Old Testament, Jewish, and Christian Conceptions*, JSJSup 56; Leiden: Brill.

Segal, Alan F. (1977) *Two Powers in Heaven*, SJLA 25; Leiden: Brill.

—— (1981) "Hellenistic Magic: Some Questions of Definition", in R. van den Broek and M. J. Vermaseren (eds) *Studies in Gnosticism and Hellenistic Religions Presented to Gilles Quispel on the Occasion of his 65th Birthday*, Leiden: Brill: 349–75.

Segal, Judah Ben-Zion (1963) *The Hebrew Passover from the Earliest Times to A.D. 70*, London Oriental Series 12; Oxford University Press.

Seland, Torrey (1995) *Establishment Violence in Philo and Luke. A Study of Non-Conformity to the Torah and Jewish Vigilante Reactions*, Biblical Interpretation Series 15; Leiden: Brill.

Seow, Choon-Leong (1997) *Ecclesiastes: A New Translation with Introduction and Commentary*, AB 18C; New York: Doubleday.

—— (1999) "Qohelet's Eschatological Poem", *JBL* : 209–34.

Shaw, B. D. (1984) "Bandits in the Roman Empire", *Past and Present* 105: 3–52.

Skehan, Patrick W., and Alexander DiLella (1987) *The Wisdom of Ben Sira*, AB 39; Garden City: Doubleday.

Slingerland, H. Dixon (1977) *The Testaments of the Twelve Patriarchs: A Critical History of Research*, SBLMS; Missoula, MT: Scholars Press.

—— (1998) *Claudian Policymaking and the Early Imperial Repression of Judaism at Rome*, SFSHJ 160; Atlanta: Scholars Press.

Sly, Dorothy I. (1996) *Philo's Alexandria*, London/New York: Routledge.

Small, Jocelyn Penny (1997) *Wax Tablets of the Mind: Cognitive Studies of Memory and Literacy in Classical Antiquity*, London/New York: Routledge.

Smend, Rudolph (1906–7) *Weisheit des Jesus Sirach*, 3 vols; Berlin: de Gruyter.

Smith, Jonathan Z. (1978) "Sacred Persistence: Towards a Redescription of Canon", in William Scott Green (ed.) *Approaches to Ancient Judaism: Theory and Practice*, BJS 1; Atlanta: Scholars Press: 11–28.

—— (1980) "Fences and Neighbors: Some Contours of Early Judaism", in William Scott Green (ed.) *Approaches to Ancient Judaism, Volume II*, BJS 9; Atlanta: Scholars Press: 1–25.

Smith, Mark S. (1990) *The Early History of God: Yahweh and the Other Deities in Ancient Israel*, San Francisco: Harper.

Smith, Morton (1967) "Goodenough's *Jewish Symbols* in Retrospect", *JBL* 86: 53–68.

—— (1971a) *Palestinian Parties and Politics That Shaped the Old Testament*, New York: Columbia.

—— (1971b) "Zealots and Sicarii, their Origins and Relation", *HTR* 64: 1–19.

—— (1978) *Jesus the Magician*, San Francisco: Harper and Row.

—— (1983) "On the Lack of a History of Greco-Roman Magic", in H. Heinen, *et al.* (eds) *Althistorische Studien: Hermann Bengtson zum 70. Geburtstag dargebracht von Kollegen und Schülern*, Historia Einzelschriften 40; Wiesbaden: Steiner: 251–57.

Snaith, John G. (1967) "Biblical Quotations in the Hebrew of Ecclesiasticus", *JTS* 18: 1–12.

Soden, Wolfram von (1965) "Das Fragen nach der Gerechtigkeit Gottes im Alten Orient", *Mitteilungen der Deutschen Orient-Gesellschaft* 96: 41–59 (= *Bibel und Alter Orient*, Berlin/New York: de Gruyter, 1985: 57–75).

Soll, William (1988) "Tobit and Folklore Studies, with Emphasis on Propp's Morphology", in David J. Lull (ed.) *Society of Biblical Literature 1988 Seminar Papers*, SBLSPS 27; Atlanta: Scholars Press: 39–53.

Sommer, Benjamin D. (1996) "Did Prophecy Cease? Evaluating a Reevaluation", *JBL* 115: 31–47.

Spencer, Richard A. (1999) "The Book of Tobit in Recent Research", *CR: BS* 7: 147–80.

Spilsbury, Paul (1998) *The Image of the Jew in Flavius Josephus' Paraphrase of the Bible*, TSAJ 69; Tübingen: Mohr (Siebeck).

Stadelmann, H. (1980) *Ben Sira also Schriftgelehrter: einer Untersuchung zum Berufsbild des vor-makkabäischen Sofer unter Berücksichtigung seines Verhältnisses zu Priester-, Propheten- und Weisheitslehrertum*, WUNT 2. Reihe, Nr 6; Tübingen: Mohr (Siebeck).

Stanton, Graham N., and Guy G. Stroumsa (eds) (1998) *Tolerance and Intolerance in Early Judaism and Christianity*, Cambridge University Press.

Starcky, Jean (1963) "Les quatres étapes du messianisme à Qumrân", *RB* 70: 481–505.

Steck, Odil Hannes (1993) *Das apokryphe Baruchbuch: Studien zu Rezeption und Konzentration "kanonischer" Überlieferung*, FRLANT 160; Göttingen: Vandenhoeck & Ruprecht.

Steck, Odil Hannes, Reinhard G. Kratz, and Ingo Kottsieper (eds) (1998) *Das Buch Baruch; Der Brief des Jeremia; Zusätze zu Ester und Daniel*, Das Alte Testament Deutsch, Apokryphen 5; Göttingen: Vandenhoeck & Ruprecht.

Stegemann, Hartmut (1998) *The Library of Qumran: On the Essenes, Qumran, John the Baptist, and Jesus*, Kampen: Kok Pharos; Grand Rapids, MI: Eerdmans; ET of *Die Essener, Qumran, Johannes der Taüfer und Jesus: Ein Sachbuch*, Freiburg: Herder, 1993.

Stein, Edmund (1957) "The Influence of Symposia Literature on the Literary Form of the Pesaḥ Haggadah", *JJS* 8: 13–44; reprinted in Henry A. Fischel (ed.) *Essays in Greco-Roman and Related Talmudic Literature*, Library of Biblical Studies; New York: Ktav, 1977: 198–229.

Steins, Georg (1995) *Die Chronik als kanonisches Abschlussphänomen: Studien zur Entstehung und Theologie von 1/2 Chronik*, Bonner biblische Beiträge 93; Weinheim, Germany: Beltz Athenäum.

Stemberger, Günter (1995) *Jewish Contemporaries of Jesus: Pharisees, Sadducees, Essenes*, trans. Allan W. Mahnke; Minneapolis: Fortress; ET of *Pharisäer, Sadduzäer, Essener*, Stuttgart: Katholisches Bibelwerk, 1991.

—— (1996) *Introduction to the Talmud and Midrash*, 2nd edn., transl. and ed. M. Bockmuehl, with a foreword by J. Neusner; Edinburgh: T. & T. Clark; Minneapolis: Fortress Press; ET (and revision) of *Einleitung in Talmud und Midrasch*, 8., neubearbeitete Auflage; Munich: Beck, 1992.

Stern, Menahem (1974–84) *Greek and Latin Authors on Jews and Judaism*, 3 vols; Jerusalem: Israel Academy of Arts and Sciences.

Steudel, Annette (1994) *Der Midrasch zur Eschatologie aus der Qumrangemeinde (4QMidrEschat^{a,b}): Materielle Rekonstruktion, Textbestand, Gattung und traditionsgeschichtliche Einordnung des durch 4Q174 ('Florilegium') und 4Q177 ('Catena A') repräsentierten Werkes aus den Qumranfunden*, STDJ 13; Leiden: Brill.

Stocker, Margarita (1998) *Judith: Sexual Warrior, Women and Power in Western Culture*, New Haven, CT, and London: Yale University Press.

Stone, Michael E. (1972) *The Testament of Abraham: The Greek Recensions*, SBLTT; Missoula, MT: Scholars Press.

—— (1978) "The Book of Enoch and Judaism in the Third Century B.C.E.", *CBQ* 40: 479–92.

—— (1982) "Reactions to the Destructions of the Second Temple", *JSJ* 13: 195–204.

—— (ed.) (1984) *Jewish Writings of the Second Temple Period: Apocrypha, Pseudepigrapha, Qumran Sectarian Writings, Philo, Josephus*, CRINT 2/2; Assen: Van Gorcum; Philadelphia: Fortress.

—— (1988) "Enoch, Aramaic Levi and Sectarian Origins", *JSJ* 19: 159–70.

—— (1992) *A History of the Literature of Adam and Eve*, SBLEJL 3; Atlanta: Scholars Press.

—— (1996a) *Texts and Concordances of the Armenian Adam Literature: Volume I: Genesis 1–4, Penitence of Adam, Book of Adam*, SBLEJL 12; Atlanta: Scholars Press.

—— (1996b) *Armenian Apocrypha Relating to Adam and Eve*, SVTP 14; Leiden: Brill.

—— (1996c) "B. Testament of Naphtali", in J. VanderKam (ed.) *Qumran Cave 4: XVII, Parabiblical Texts, Part 3*, DJD 22; Oxford: Clarendon: 73–82.

Stone, Michael E. and Esther G. Chazon (eds) (1998) *Biblical Perspectives: Early Use and Interpretation of the Bible in Light of the Dead Sea Scrolls: Proceedings of the First International Symposium of the Orion Center for the Study of the Dead Sea Scrolls and Associated Literature, 12–14 May, 1996*, STDJ 28; Leiden/New York/Köln: Brill.

Stone, Michael E., and Jonas C. Greenfield (1979) "Remarks on the Aramaic Testament of Levi from the Geniza", *RB* 86: 214–30.

—— (1996) "A Aramaic Levi Document", J. VanderKam (ed.) *Qumran Cave 4: XVII, Parabiblical Texts, Part 3*, DJD 22; Oxford: Clarendon: 1–72.

Strange, James F. (1979) "Archaeology and the Religion of Judaism in Palestine", *ANRW II Principiat*: 19.1.646–85.

Street, Brian V. (1984) *Literacy in Theory and Practice*, Cambridge Studies in Oral and Literate Culture; Cambridge University Press.

Stuckenbruck, Loren T. (1995) *Angel Veneration and Christology: A Study in Early Judaism and in the Christology of the Apocalypse of John*, WUNT 2/70; Tübingen: Mohr (Siebeck).

—— (1997) *The Book of Giants from Qumran: Texts, Translation, and Commentary*, TSAJ 63; Tübingen: Mohr (Siebeck).

Sussmann, Y. (1989–90) "The History of *Halakha* and the Dead Sea Scrolls: A Preliminary to the Publication of 4QMMT", *Tarbiz* 59: 11–76 (Heb.); partial ET in Qimron, E., and John Strugnell (eds) (1994) *Qumran Cave 4: V Miqṣat Maʿaśe ha-Torah*, DJD 10; Oxford: Clarendon Press: 179–200.

Suter, David W. (1979) *Tradition and Composition in the Parables of Enoch*, Missoula, MT: Scholars Press.

Swanson, Dwight D. (1995) *The Temple Scroll and the Bible: The Methodology of 11QT*, STDJ 14; Leiden: Brill.

Swartz, Michael D. (1996) *Scholastic Magic: Ritual and Revelation in Early Jewish Mysticism*, Princeton, NJ: Princeton University Press.

Szesnat, Holger (1999) "Philo and Female Homoeroticism: Philo's Use of γύνανδρος and Recent Work on *Tribades*", *JSJ* 30: 140–47.

Tabor, James D. (1986) *Things Unutterable: Paul's Ascent to Paradise in its Greco-Roman, Judaic, and Early Christian Contexts*, Lanham, MD: University Press of America.

Tabor, James D., and Michael O. Wise (1994) "4Q521 'On Resurrection' and the Synoptic Gospel Tradition: A Preliminary Study", *JSP* 10: 149–62.

Talmon, Shemaryahu (1958) "The Calendar Reckoning of the Sect from the Judaean Desert", in Chaim Rabin and Yigael Yadin (eds) *Aspects of the Dead Sea Scrolls*, Scripta Hierosolymitana 4; Jerusalem: Magnes: 162–99; German translation: "Kalender und Kalenderstreit in der Gemeinde von Qumran", in Shemaryahu Talmon (1988) *Gesellschaft und Literatur in der Hebräischen Bibel: Gesammelte Aufsätze 1*, Information Judentum 8; Neukirchen-Vluyn, Germany: Neukirchener Verlag: 152–89.

—— (1986) "The Emergence of Jewish Sectarianism in the Early Second Temple Period", *King, Cult and Calendar in Ancient Israel*, Jerusalem: Magnes, 1986: 165–201 (= slightly shortened translation of German version in E. Schluchter (ed.) *Max Webers Sicht des antiken Christentums*, Frankfurt: Suhrkamp, 1985: 233–80).

Talmon, Shemaryahu, and Yigael Yadin (eds) (1999) *Masada VI: Yigael Yadin Excavations 1963–1965, Final Reports: Hebrew Fragments; The Ben Sira Scroll*, Jerusalem: Israel Exploration Society.

Talshir, Zipora (1999) *I Esdras: From Origin to Translation*, SBLSCS 47; Atlanta: Scholars Press.

Taylor, Joan E. (1998) "A Second Temple in Egypt: The Evidence for the Zadokite Temple of Onias", *JSJ* 29: 297–321.

Tcherikover, V. A., A. Fuks, and M. Stern (1957–64) *Corpus Papyrorum Judaicarum*, 3 vols; Cambridge, MA: Harvard; Jerusalem: Magnes.

Terian, Abraham (ed.) (1992) *Quaestiones et solutiones in Exodum I et II, e versione armeniaca et fragmenta graeca: Introduction, traduction et notes*, Les Oeuvres de Philon d'Alexandrie 34c; Paris: Cerf.

Theissen, Gerd (1983) *The Miracle Stories of the Early Christian Tradition*, transl. F. McDonagh; ed. J. Riches; Philadelphia: Fortress.

Thomas, J. D. (1972) "The Greek Text of Tobit", *JBL* 91: 463–71.

Thompson, Thomas L. (1999) *The Bible in History: How Writers Create a Past* (UK title); *The Mythic Past: Biblical Archaeology and the Myth of Israel* (American title), London/New York: Random House Jonathan Cape.

Tiede, David L. (1972) *The Charismatic Figure as Miracle Worker*, SBLDS 1; Missoula, MT: Society of Biblical Literature.

Tigay, Jeffrey H. (1986) *You Shall Have No Other Gods: Israelite Religion in the Light of Hebrew Inscriptions*, HSS; Atlanta: Scholars Press.

Tigchelaar, Eibert J. C. (1996) *Prophets of Old and the Day of the End: Zechariah, the Book of Watchers and Apocalyptic*, OTS 35; Leiden: Brill.

Tiller, Patrick A. (1993) *A Commentary on the Animal Apocalypse of 1 Enoch*, SBLEJL 4; Atlanta: Scholars Press.

Tilly, Michael (1997) "Geographie und Weltordnung im Aristeasbrief", *JSJ* 28: 131–53.

Tobin, Thomas H., SJ (1997) "Philo and the Sibyl: Interpreting Philo's Eschatology", in David T. Runia and Gregory E. Sterling (eds) *Wisdom and Logos: Studies in Jewish Thought in Honor of David Winston*, SPA 9; BJS 312; Atlanta: Scholars Press: 84–103.

Toorn, Karel van der (1990) "The Nature of the Biblical Teraphim in the Light of the Cuneiform Evidence", *CBQ* 52: 203–22.

—— (1992) "Anat-Yahu, Some Other Deities, and the Jews of Elephantine", *Numen* 39: 80–101.

—— (1996) *Family Religion in Babylonia, Syria and Israel: Continuity and Change in the Forms of Religious Life*, Studies in the History and Culture of the Ancient Near East 7; Brill: Leiden.

—— (ed.) (1997) *The Image and the Book: Iconic Cults, Aniconism, and the Rise of Book Religion in Israel and the Ancient Near East*, Contributions to Biblical Exegesis and Theology 21; Leuven: Peeters.

Toorn, Karel van der, Bob Becking, and Pieter W. van der Horst (eds) (1999) *Dictionary of Deities and Demons in the Bible*, 2nd edn; Leiden: Brill; Grand Rapids, MI: Eerdmans ($= DDD^2$).

Torrey, Charles C. (1947) "The Messiah son of Ephraim", *JBL* 66: 253–77.

Tov, Emanuel (1976) *The Septuagint Translation of Jeremiah and Baruch: A Discussion of an Early Revision of the LXX of Jeremiah 29–52 and Baruch 1:1–38*, HSM 8; Missoula, MT: Scholars Press.

—— (1988) "The Septuagint", in M. J. Mulder and H. Sysling (eds) (1988) *Mikra: Text, Translation, Reading and Interpretation of the Hebrew Bible in Ancient Judaism and Early Christianity*, CRINT 2/1; Assen/Maastricht: Van Gorcum; Minneapolis: Fortress: 161–88.

—— (1992) *Textual Criticism of the Hebrew Bible*, Assen/Maastricht: Van Gorcum; Minneapolis: Fortress.

—— (1997a) *Der Text der Hebräischen Bibel: Handbuch der Textkritik*, Stuttgart/Berlin/Köln: Kohlhammer.

—— (1997b) *The Text-Critical Use of the Septuagint in Biblical Research*, 2nd revised edn; Jerusalem Biblical Studies 8; Jerusalem: Simor.

—— (1999a) *The Greek and Hebrew Bible: Collected Essays on the Septuagint*, VTSup 72; Leiden: Brill.

—— (1999b) "The Papyrus Fragments Found in the Judean Desert", in J.-M. Auwers and A. Wénin (eds), *Lectures et relectures de la Bible: Festschrift P.-M. Bogaert*, BETL 144; Leuven: Leuven University/Peeters: 247–55.

Tov, Emanuel, *et al.* (1990) *The Greek Minor Prophets Scroll from Nahal Hever (8HevXIIgr)*, DJD 8; Oxford: Clarendon.

Trafton, Joseph L. (1985) *The Syriac Version of the Psalms of Solomon: A Critical Evaluation*, SBLSCS 11; Atlanta: Scholars Press.

—— (1986) "The Psalms of Solomon: New Light from the Syriac Version?", *JBL* 105: 227–37.

—— (1992) "Solomon, Psalms of", *ABD*: 6.115–17.

—— (1994) "The *Psalms of Solomon* in Recent Research", *JSP* 12: 3–19.

Trebilco, Paul R. (1991) *Jewish Communities in Asia Minor*, SNTSMS 69; Cambridge University Press.

Trebolle Barrera, Julio (1998) *The Jewish Bible and the Christian Bible: An Introduction to the History of the Bible*, trans. W. G. E. Watson; Leiden: Brill; Grand Rapids, MI: Eerdmans.

Tromp, Johannes (1993) *The Assumption of Moses: A Critical Edition with Commentary*, SVTP 10; Leiden: Brill.

Tromp, N. (1969) *Primitive Conceptions of Death and the Nether World in the Old Testament*, BiOr 21; Rome: Pontifical Biblical Institute.

Turdeanu, Émile (1981) *Apocryphes slaves et roumains de l'Ancien Testament*, SVTP 5; Leiden: Brill.

Twelftree, Graham H. (1993) *Jesus the Exorcist: A Contribution to the Study of the Historical Jesus*, WUNT 2/54; Tübingen: Mohr (Siebeck).

Ulfgard, Håkan (1998) *The Story of Sukkot: The Setting, Shaping, and Sequel of the Biblical Feast of Tabernacles*, Beiträge zur Geschichte der Biblischen Theologie 34; Tübingen: Mohr (Siebeck).

Ulrich, Eugene C., Jr (1978) *The Qumran Text of Samuel and Josephus*, HSM 19: Missoula, MT: Scholars Press.

—— (1999) *The Dead Sea Scrolls and the Origins of the Bible*, Studies in the Dead Sea Scrolls and Related Literature; Grand Rapids, MI: Eerdmans.

Unnik, Willem Cornelis van (1993) *Das Selbstverständnis der jüdischen Diaspora in der hellenistisch-römischen Zeit*, AGAJU 17; Leiden: Brill.

Urman, Dan, and Paul V. M. Flesher (eds) (1995) *Ancient Synagogues: Historical Analysis and Archaeological Discovery*, vols 1–2; SPB 47; Leiden: Brill.

Vaillant, A. (1952) *Le livre des secrets d'Hénoch: Texte slave et traduction française*, Textes publiés par l'Institut d'Études slaves 4; Paris: Institut d'Études Slaves.

VanderKam, James C. (1984) *Enoch and the Growth of an Apocalyptic Tradition*, CBQMS 16; Washington, DC: Catholic Biblical Association.

—— (1986) "The Prophetic-Sapiential Origins of Apocalyptic Thought", in James D. Martin and Philip R. Davies (eds) *A Word in Season: Essays in Honour of William McKane*, JSOTSup 42; Sheffield Academic Press: 163–76.

—— (1994a) *The Dead Sea Scrolls Today*, Grand Rapids, MI: Eerdmans; London: SPCK.

—— (1994b) "Genesis 1 in Jubilees 2", *DSD* 1: 300–21.

—— (1997) "Mantic Wisdom in the Dead Sea Scrolls", *DSD* 4: 336–53.

—— (1998) *Calendars in the Dead Sea Scrolls: Measuring Time*, The Literature of the Dead Sea Scrolls; London/New York: Routledge.

Veltri, Giuseppe (1997) *Magie und Halakha: Ansätze zu einem empirischen Wissenschafts-begriff im spätantiken und frühmittelalterlichen Judentum*, TSAJ 62; Tübingen: Mohr (Siebeck).

Vermes, Geza (1972–73) "Hanina ben Dosa': A Controversial Galilean Saint from the First Century of the Christian Era", *JJS* 23: 28–50; 24: 51–64.

—— (1973) *Jesus the Jew: A Historian's Reading of the Gospels*, New York: Macmillan.

—— (1992) "The Oxford Forum for Qumran Research: Seminar on the Rule of War from Cave 4 (4Q285)", *JJS* 43: 85–94.

Viviano, Benedict T., OP, and Justin Taylor, SM (1992) "Sadducees, Angels, and Resurrection (Acts 23:8–9)", *JBL* 111: 496–98.

Waerden, B. L. van der (1952) "History of the Zodiac", *AfO* 16: 216–30.

Waltke, Bruce K. (1965) *Prolegomena to the Samaritan Pentateuch*, unpublished PhD thesis; Cambridge, MA: Harvard University.

—— (1970) "The Samaritan Pentateuch and the Text of the Old Testament, in J. B. Payne (ed.) *New Perspectives on the Old Testament*, Waco, TX: Word: 212–39.

Wan, Sze-kar (1994) "Charismatic Exegesis: Philo and Paul Compared", *SPA* 6: 54–82.

Wander, Bernd (1998) *Gottesfürchtige und Sympathisanten: Studien zum heidnischen Umfeld von Diasporasynagogen*, WUNT 104; Tübingen: Mohr (Siebeck).

Washington, Harold C. (1994) *Wealth and Poverty in the Instruction of Amenemope and the Hebrew Proverbs*, SBLDS 142; Atlanta: Scholars Press.

Waubke, Hans-Günther (1998) *Die Pharisäer in der protestantischen Bibelwissenschaft des 19. Jahrhunderts*, Beiträge zur historischen Theologie 107: Tübingen: Mohr (Siebeck).

Weber, Reinhard (1991) "Eusebeia und Logismos: Zum philosophischen Hintergrund von 4. Makkabäer", *JSJ* 22: 212–34.

Weeks, Stuart (1994) *Early Israelite Wisdom*, Oxford Theological Monographs; Oxford: Clarendon Press.

Wegner, Judith Romney (1992) "Leviticus", in Carol A. Newsom and Sharon H. Ringe (eds) *The Women's Bible Commentary*, Louisville, KY: Westminster John Knox; London: SPCK: 36–44.

Weiss, M. (1966) "The Origin of the 'Day of the Lord' – Reconsidered", *HUCA* 37: 29–60.

Weitzman, Michael P. (1999) *The Syriac Version of the Old Testament: An Introduction*, University of Cambridge Oriental Publications 56; Cambridge University Press.

Werline, Rodney Alan (1998) *Penitential Prayer in Second Temple Judaism: The Development of a Religious Institution*, SBLEJL 13; Atlanta: Scholars Press.

Werman, Cana (1997) "Levi and Levites in the Second Temple Period", *DSD* 4: 211–25.

Wernberg-Møller, P. (1961) "Some Observations on the Relationship of the Peshitta Version of the Book of Genesis to the Palestinian Targum Fragments", *Studia Theologica* 15: 128–80.

—— (1962) "Prolegomena to a Re-examination of the Palestinian Targum Fragments of the Book of Genesis Published by P. Kahle, and their Relationship to the Peshitta", *JSS* 7: 253–66.

Westermann, Claus (1995) *Roots of Wisdom: The Oldest Proverbs of Israel and Other Peoples*, Louisville, KY: Westminster John Knox; Edinburgh: T. & T. Clark; ET of *Wurzeln der Weisheit*, Göttingen: Vandenhoeck & Ruprecht, 1990.

Whedbee, J. William (1977) "The Comedy of Job", in Robert Polzin and David Robertson (eds) *Studies in the Book of Job*, Semeia 7; Missoula, MT: Scholars Press: 1–39.

White, Robert J. (ed.) (1975) *The Interpretation of Dreams:* Oneirocritica *by Artemidorus (Translation and Commentary)*, Noyes classical Studies; Park Ridge, NJ: Noyes.

Whybray, R. N. (1978) *Thanksgiving for a Liberated Prophet: An Interpretation of Isaiah Chapter 53*, JSOTSup 4; Sheffield Academic Press.

—— (1981) "The Identification and Use of Quotations in Ecclesiastes", *Congress Volume: Vienna 1980*, VTSup 32; Leiden: Brill: 435–51.

—— (1987) *The Making of the Pentateuch: A Methodological Study*, JSOTSup 53, Sheffield: JSOT Press.

—— (1989a) *Ecclesiastes*, New Century Bible; London: Marshall Morgan and Scott; Grand Rapids, MI: Eerdmans.

—— (1989b) *Ecclesiastes*, Old Testament Guides; Sheffield: JSOT Press.

—— (1994a) *The Composition of the Book of Proverbs*, JSOTSup 168; Sheffield Academic Press.

—— (1994b) *Proverbs*, New Century Bible; London: Marshall Morgan and Scott; Grand Rapids, MI: Eerdmans.

—— (1995a) *The Book of Proverbs: A Survey of Modern Study*, History of Biblical Interpretation Series 1; Leiden: Brill.

—— (1995b) *Introduction to the Pentateuch*, Grand Rapids, MI: Eerdmans.

Will, Édouard (1991) '*Iraq el-Amir: Le Chateau du Tobiade Hyrcan*, Texte et Album; Paris.

Will, Édouard, and C. Orrieux (1992) *Prosélytisme juif? Histoire d'une erreur*, Paris: Les Belles Lettres.

Willi, Thomas (1995) *Juda–Jehud–Israel: Studien zum Selbstverständnis des Judentums in persischer Zeit*, Forschungen zum Alten Testament 12; Tübingen: Mohr (Siebeck).

Williams, David S. (1999) *The Structure of 1 Maccabees*, CBQM 31; Washington, DC: Catholic Biblical Association.

Williams, Margaret H. (1994) "The Jews of Corycus – A Neglected Diasporan Community from Roman Times", *JSJ* 25: 274–86.

—— (1998) *The Jews among the Greeks and Romans: A Diaspora Handbook*, London: Duckworth.

Williamson, H. G. M. (1979) "The Origins of the Twenty-Four Priestly Courses: A Study of 1 Chronicles xxiii–xxvii", *Studies in the Historical Books of the Old Testament*, VTSup 30; Leiden: Brill: 251–68.

Wills, Lawrence M. (1995) *The Jewish Novel in the Ancient World*, Myth and Poetics; Ithaca, NY, and London: Cornell.

Wilson, Walter T. (1994) *The Mysteries of Righteousness: The Literary Composition and Genre of the Sentences of Pseudo-Phocylides*, TSAJ 40; Tübingen: Mohr (Siebeck).

Winston, David (1979) *The Wisdom of Solomon: A New Translation with Introduction and Commentary*, AB 43; Garden City, NJ: Doubleday.

—— (1989) "Two Types of Mosaic Prophecy according to Philo", *JSP* 2: 49–67.

Winter, Bruce W. (1997) *Philo and Paul among the Sophists*, SNTSMS 96; Cambridge University Press.

Wise, Michael Owen (1994a) "Thunder in Gemini: An Aramaic Brontologion (4Q318)", *Thunder in Gemini And Other Essays on the History, Language and Literature of Second Temple Palestine*, JSPSup 15; Sheffield Academic Press: 13–50.

—— (1994b) "By the Power of Beelzebub: An Aramaic Incantation Formula from Qumran (4Q560)", *JBL* 113: 627–50.

—— (1997) "To Know the Times and the Seasons: A Study of the Aramaic Chronograph 4Q559", *JSP* 15: 3–51.

Wolfson, Harry Austryn (1947) *Philo: Foundations of Religious Philosophy in Judaism, Christianity, and Islam*, 2 vols; Cambridge, MA: Harvard.

Woude, A. S. van der (1990) "A 'Groningen' Hypothesis of Qumran Origins and Early History", *RevQ* 14: 521–42.

Wright, Benjamin G. (1989) *No Small Difference: Sirach's Relationship to its Hebrew Parent Text*, SBLSCS 26; Atlanta: Scholars Press.

Wright, J. Edward (1997) "The Social Setting of the Syriac Apocalypse of Baruch", *JSP* 16: 81–96.

Wyatt, Nicolas (1973–74) "'Attar and the Devil", *Transactions of the Glasgow University Oriental Society* 25: (1976) 85–97.

—— (1996) *Myths of Power: A Study of Royal Myth and Ideology in Ugaritic and Biblical Traditions*, Ugaritisch-Biblische Literatur 13; Münster: Ugarit-Verlag.

Yadin, Yigael, and Y. Meshorer (1989) *Masada I: The Yigael Yadin Excavations 1963–1965, Final Reports: The Aramaic and Hebrew Ostraca and Jar Inscriptions; The Coins of Masada*, Jerusalem: Israel Exploration Society.

Yarbro Collins, Adele (1976) *The Combat Myth in the Book of Revelation*, Harvard Dissertations in Religion 9; Missoula, MT: Scholars Press.

Yavetz, Zvi (1993) "Judeophobia in Classical Antiquity: A Different Approach", *JJS* 44: 1–22.

York, Anthony D. (1974–75) "The Dating of Targumic Literature", *JSJ* 5: 49–62.

Zahavy, T. (1977) *The Traditions of Eleazar Ben Azariah*, BJS 2; Atlanta: Scholars Press.

Zakovitch, Yair (1999) *Das Buch Rut: Ein jüdischer Kommentar*, transl. Andreas Lehnardt, with an introduction by Erich Zenger; Stuttgarter Bibelstudien 177; Stuttgart: Katholisches Bibelwerk.

Zerbe, Gordon M. (1993) *Non-Retaliation in Early Jewish and New Testament Texts: Ethical Themes in Social Contexts*, JSPSup 13; Sheffield Academic Press.

Ziegler, Joseph (1980a) *Sapientia Salomonis*, 2nd edn; Septuaginta, Vetus Testamentum Graecum 12/1; Göttingen: Vandenhoeck & Ruprecht.

—— (1980b) *Sapientia Iesu Filii Sirach*, 2nd edn; Septuaginta, Vetus Testamentum Graecum 12/2; Göttingen: Vandenhoeck & Ruprecht.

—— (1999) *Susanna, Daniel, Bel et Draco*, 2nd edn, ed. Olivier Munnich; foreword by R. Smend; Septuaginta, Vetus Testamentum Graecum 16/2; Göttingen: Vandenhoeck & Ruprecht.

Zimmerman, Johannes (1998) *Messianische Texte aus Qumran: Königliche, priesterliche und prophetische Messiasvorstellungen in den Schriftfunden von Qumran*, WUNT: 2. Reihe 104; Tübingen: Mohr (Siebeck).

Zipor, Moshe A. (1997) "The Flood Chronology: Too Many an Accident", *DSD* 4: 207–10.

Zuckerman, Bruce (1991) *Job the Silent: A Study in Historical Counterpoint*, Oxford University Press.

Zuckermandel, M. S. (1881) *Tosephta: Based on the Erfurt and Vienna Codices with Parallels and Variants*, with *Supplement to the Tosephta* by Saul Libermann, new edn; Jerusalem: Wahrmann Books, 1970.

INDEX OF MODERN AUTHORS

NB: to avoid unnecessary duplication, the names in the Bibliography are not in this index.

Abegg, M. 67
Ackroyd, P. R. 13, 14
Aharoni, Y. 210, 212
Albertz, R. 1, 3, 19–20, 132, 135, 176
Aleksandrov, G. S. 120, 124
Alexander, P. S. xiv, 68, 241, 248, 251
Alexandre, M. 89
Anderson, G. A. 95, 96, 129
Andreasen, N.-E. A. 132
Applebaum, S. 106, 108, 283
Archer, L. J. 300
Argall, R. A. 41, 50
Arjava, A. 300
Athanassiadi, P. 210, 217
Atkinson, K. 84, 273
Aubin, M. 106, 108
Auld, A. G. 19–20, 165, 167
Aune, D. E. 236, 240, 248, 250–1, 253
Auwers, J.-M. 107
Avery-Peck, A. J. 1, 90, 116, 186, 206, 258, 276, 278
Avigad, N. 29, 33

Bamberger, B. J. 89, 92
Barag, D. 106, 107
Barclay, J. M. G. 1, 3
Bar-Ilan, M. 300
Barker, M. 210, 217
Bar-Kochva, B. 37, 73–4, 136
Barnett, P. W. 252
Barr, J. 49–50
Barstad, H. M. xv, 3, 6–7, 13, 15, 29, 31, 297, 299
Barthélemy, D. 158, 162

Bartholomew, C. G. 42
Bartlett, J. xv
Barton, J. 152
Bauckham, R. 117, 257
Bauer, W. 152, 156
Baumgarten, A. I. 52–3, 108, 111–12, 150, 152, 185–6, 192, 206–7, 326
Baumgarten, J. M. 67
Becker, J. 271
Becking, B. xvii, 3, 13, 15, 210, 212, 297–8
Beckwith, R. 152
Beentjes, P. C. 50
Bellinger, W. H., Jr 271–2
Ben-Dov, M. 132, 133, 135
Bengtson, H. 249
Benoit, P. 106–7
Berchman, R. M. 241
Bergren, T. A. 59–60
Berlinerblau, J. 175–6
Berman, D. 252–3
Bernstein, M. 67, 185
Berquist, J. L. 29
Bertrand, J. M. 46–7
Bickerman, E. J. xiv, 42–3, 46–7, 99
Binder, D. D. 170, 174, 292, 296
Birnbaum, E. 89
Black, M. 283
Blackburn, B. L. 252–3
Blenkinsopp, J. xv, 26–7, 133, 150, 183–4, 232
Boccaccini, G. 1–2, 5, 67, 69
Bogaert, P. 94
Bohak, G. 76, 82, 105–6

Böhler, D. 13–14
Bokser, B. M. 121, 133, 141, 252–3
Bolin, T. M. 17, 153
Borg, M. 283
Borgen, P. 89, 276–7
Böttrich, C. 98–9
Bourdillon, M. F. C. 129
Bowman, A. K. 150, 152
Braulik, G. 44
Braun, J. 133, 143
Breitenstein, U. 99
Brenner, A. 23, 25, 60, 65, 300, 303
Brewer, D. I. 165, 169
Briant, P. xiv
Briend, J. 86
Brock, S. P. xiv, 49–50, 85, 104, 158,
    162
Brody, R. 300, 304
Broek, R. van den 96, 249
Brooke, G. J. xiv, 67, 69, 158, 165, 273,
    275–6
Brooten, B. J. 300–1, 303–4
Brosius, M. 300, 303
Brown, C. A. 300
Brownlee, W. H. 271–2
Budd, P. J. 26
Burgmann, H. 68
Burkes, S. 42
Bush, F. 23, 25
Busink, T. A. 133, 135
Butterworth, M. 15
Buttrick, G. A. xvii

Calabi, F. 89, 91
Calduch-Benages, N. 50
Camp, C. V. 300, 302
Cancik, H. 241
Caquot, A. 273
Carleton Paget, J. 292, 296
Carroll, R. P. xiv, 29, 31, 297, 299
Carter, C. E. 29
Casey, M. 282–3
Cavallin, H. C. C. 257
Cazeaux, J. 94
Chancey, M. 106, 108
Charles, R. H. xvi, 98–9, 101–2, 117,
    282
Charlesworth, J. H. xviii, 67, 242, 273,
    288–9
Chazon, E. G. 67, 69, 170, 173
Cheon, S. 86–7
Chesnutt, R. D. 105

Chiat, M. J. S. 170, 174
Childs, B. S. 257
Chyutin, M. 68, 117, 119
Clifford, R. J. 21
Clines, D. J. A. 13, 14, 22–3, 133, 142,
    158, 163
Cody, A. 133
Cogan, M. 308–9
Coggins, R. J. 50
Cohen, S. J. D. xv, 1, 2, 5, 76, 79, 121,
    123, 185, 292–3, 296, 305–6
Collins, J. J. xv, 60, 67, 70, 73, 74–5,
    86, 88, 95, 98–101, 104–5, 183–4,
    232, 234–5, 252, 271, 273–5, 281–3,
    288–9
Collins, N. L. 70
Cook, J. 158, 161
Cook, S. L. 232
Cothenet, E. 86
Cotter, W. 248
Cotton, H. M. 106–7, 300–1
Cowley, A. xvi
Craig, K. M., Jr 17
Craigie, P. 219, 221
Crenshaw, J. L. 42, 44, 150–1
Cribiore, R. 150
Cross, F. M. 67, 70, 158, 163
Cryer, F. H. 67, 70, 133, 143, 248, 250

Dan, J. 249, 251
Daniel, J. L. 305–6
Daube, D. 185, 198
Davidson, M. J. 219
Davies, G. I. 210
Davies, P. R. xv, 13, 29, 68, 153, 183–4,
    199, 203, 205–6, 233, 257, 282
Davies, W. D. 297
Davila, J. R. 248
Day, J. 210, 215, 271, 273, 288, 289
Day, L. 24
Day, P. L. 219, 225
Deines, R. 185
Delcor, M. 101
Dell, K. J. 22–3
deSilva, D. A. 99
De Troyer, K. 24, 158, 163
Deutsch, N. 219
DeVaux, R. 203
Dexinger, F. 62
Dietrich, M. xviii
Dietrich, W. 210, 212
Díez Macho, A. 158, 164

Dihle, A. 257, 263
Dijkstra, M. 210, 212
DiLella, A. A. 50, 258, 260
Dillon, J. 89, 91, 210, 216, 217, 227, 228
Dimant, D. 68, 170
DiTommaso, L. 48
Dix, G. H. 281
Dogniez, C. 158
Donner, H. xviii
Dorothy, C. V. 24, 158, 163
Douglas, M. 129, 131, 133, 140, 300
Driver, S. R. 272
Dunn, J. D. G. 44
Dupont-Sommer, A. 266, 269
Durand, X. 39
Dyck, J. E. 19
Dyson, S. L. 283, 285

Edelman, D. V. 210, 212
Edwards, D. R. 106
Eisenman, R. 274–5
Eissfeldt, O. 133, 137
Elwolde, J. F. 50
Emmerson, G. I. 18
Engbert-Pedersen, T. 206
Engel, H. 86
Ernst, H. 186
Eshel, E. 67, 70
Evans, C. A. 68, 185, 199, 246, 278
Evans, R. J. 6–7
Evans-Pritchard, E. 129
Everson, A. J. 257

Falk, D. K. 68, 170, 172
Farmer, W. R. 271–2
Feldman, L. H. 92, 165, 168, 292, 296, 305–6
Fine, S. 170–1
Finkelstein, J. J. 133, 143
Finkelstein, L. 121, 124
Finnegan, R. 150, 152
Fischer, A. A. 42
Fischer, T. 46–7
Fischer, U. 98, 257, 276–8
Fishbane, M. 165–6
Fittschen, K. 106
Fitzmyer, J. A. 44–5, 185, 194, 301, 304
Flesher, P. V. M. 170, 172, 249
Flint, P. W. 60, 67–8
Focke, F. 86
Foerster, G. 106–7, 171, 174
Fohrer, G. 257

Fortes, M. 129
Fossum, J. E. 211, 217, 219
Fox, M. V. 42–3
Frank, S. 183
Frede, M. 210, 217
Freedman, D. N. xvi
Frerichs, E. S. 175, 249, 277, 281, 288–9, 305
Freyne, S. 252–3
Friedrich, G. xix
Fuglseth, K. 89
Funck, B. 52–3

Gafni, I. M. 297, 299–300
Gager, J. G. 305
Gamberoni, J. 44–5
García Martínez, F. 9, 67–9, 185
Gauger, J.-D. 46–8
Geiger, J. 106–7
Gennep, A. van 129, 132
Georgi, D. 86
Gera, D. 40
Gereboff, J. 121
Gerstenberger, E. S. 26–8
Gibson, J. C. L. xix
Gilbert, M. 86–7
Gnuse, R. K. 211–12, 217, 236, 243–5
Golb, N. 68–70, 199, 202
Goldstein, B. R. 242
Golka, F. W. 21
Goodblatt, D. 121–2, 144–5
Goodenough, E. R. 175–7, 276–7
Goodman, M. xiv, 108, 121, 124–5, 133, 140, 151, 178, 180, 185, 192, 199, 292, 296, 301, 305, 308
Gordis, R. 22
Gorman, F. H., Jr 129, 131
Goudoever, J. van 133, 141, 143
Gowan, D. E. 257
Grabbe, L. L. 219, 257
Graetz, H. 185
Graf, F. 248
Graham, M. P. 19
Gray, J. 22
Gray, R. 236, 243, 245
Green, W. S. 1, 116, 121–2, 178, 252–3, 277, 281, 288–9
Greenfield, J. C. 102–3, 106
Greenspoon, L. 158
Grelot, P. 219, 221
Griffiths, J. G. 171, 173
Gruenwald, I. 242–3, 248, 250–1

Grünewald, T. 283, 285
Grünwaldt, K. 26
Gunneweg, A. H. J. 13–14, 19, 21, 133, 135
Guterman, S. L. 305

Habas, E. (Rubin) 121
Habel, N. C. 22
Hachlili, R. 171, 173
Hall, R. G. 117, 118
Halperin, D. J. 248, 251
Halpern-Amaru, B. 63
Hamerton-Kelly, R. G. 129, 131
Hamilton, G. J. 211, 213
Handy, L. K. 219–20
Hanegraaff, W. J. 301
Hanhart, R. 44
Hann, R. R. 85
Hanson, J. S. 236, 284
Haran, M. 26–8, 133, 141
Harrington, D. J. 68, 94–5, 165, 168
Harrington, H. K. 186
Harris, W. V. 151–2
Hasel, G. F. 297, 299
Hausmann, J. 297, 299
Hay, D. M. 90–1, 165, 211, 236, 277
Hayes, J. H. 77, 79
Hayman, A. P. 117, 211, 217
Hayward, C. T. R. 50, 133
Hecht, R. D. 277–8
Hedrick, C. W. 95–6
Heger, P. 129, 132
Heinemann, J. 171, 173, 175, 281
Heinen, H. 249
Hemer, C. J. 186, 194
Hengel, M. 242, 271–2, 283, 287
Henten, J. W. van 59–60, 100, 175, 177
Heusch, L. de 129, 132
Hezser, C. 121, 124–5
Hilgert, E. 89, 211, 277
Hill, A. E. 15
Himmelfarb, M. 266, 268
Hoffman, L. A. 171
Hoffmann, Y. 258
Hogan, K. M. 86
Hoglund, K. G. 21, 30, 33
Holladay, C. R. xiv, 48–9, 70, 71, 73, 252–3
Horbury, W. 106, 108, 171, 173, 273
Horgan, M. P. 165, 167
Horsley, R. A. 236, 240–1, 283–6, 305–6

Horst, P. W. van der xvii, 88, 104, 165, 169, 171, 173–4, 301, 303
Houston, W. 130–1
Hübner, H. 86
Hultgren, A. J. 186
Hurtado, L. W. 211, 216–17, 219
Hurvitz, A. 22–3
Husser, J.-M. 243–4
Hüttenmeister, F. 171, 174
Huwiler, E. 21, 25, 42

Idinopulos, T. A. 3–4
Ilan, T. 301, 304
Isaac, B. 284, 301
Iwry, S. 183

Jackson, H. M. 219
Jacob, E. 273
Jacobs, M. 121
Jacobson, H. 94–5
James, M. R. 94
Jamieson-Drake, D. W. 26, 28
Janowski, B. 248, 272
Japhet, S. 14, 19, 20–1
Jeansonne, S. P. 158, 163
Jeffers, A. 248
Jellicoe, S. 158, 211, 215
Jenkins, K. 6–7
Jenson, P. P. 130–1
Jobes, K. H. 24, 158, 163
Jobling, D. 29, 297
Johnstone, W. 20
Jones, G. H. 20
Jones, S. 13, 17, 30, 293
Jonge, M. de 101
Joseph, H. 183

Kabasele Mukenge, A. 66
Kalimi, I. 20
Kalmin, R. 151
Kampen, J. 67, 183, 185, 199, 205
Kanter, S. 121, 123
Kapera, Z. J. 68
Kasher, A. 305–6
Kayatz, C. 21, 225, 228
Kee, H. C. 171, 174
Keel, O. 25, 211, 213–14, 220–1
Kelly, B. E. 20
Kenney, J. P. 90
Kerkeslager, A. 77
Kiley, M. 171
Kippenberg, H. G. 249

Kittel, G. xix
Kiuchi, N. 130, 132
Klawek, A. 68
Klein, L. R. 24
Kleinig, J. W. 133, 143
Klopfenstein, M. A. 210, 212
Kloppenborg, J. S. 225, 228
Kloppenborg, R. 301
Knibb, M. A. xiv, 104, 274
Knierim, R. P. 130, 132
Knohl, I. 26–7
Knoppers, G. N. 133
Kobelski, P. J. 220, 223
Koch, K. 60, 61
Koester, H. 252, 254, 300
Kolarcik, M. 86, 88, 258, 262
Kooij, A. van der 153
Korpel, M. 3
Kort, A. 183
Körting, C. 133, 141
Koskeniemi, E. 252–4
Kossmann, R. 24
Kottek, S. S. 92
Kottsieper, I. 61, 66
Kraabel, A. T. 293, 296
Kraemer, R. S. 105–6, 301
Kraft, R. A. 104, 165
Kramer, S. N. 25–6
Kratz, R. G. 61, 66
Kraus, F. R. 242, 243
Kraus, H.-J. 134, 144
Kugel, J. 63
Kugler, R. A. 68, 102
Kuhnen, H.-P. 106, 108
Kuhrt, A. xiv, 30–1
Kunin, S. D. 130

Laato, A. 246, 272, 288–9
Lacocque, A. 24, 163
Landau, Y. H. 46–7
Lang, B. 225, 228
Laniak, T. S. 24
Lapin, H. 121, 124–5
LaPorte, J. 90
Larcher, C. 86
Larkin, K. J. A. 15, 24, 25
Lauer, S. 186
Layton, B. 96
Lease, G. 175, 177
Lee, J. A. L. 49
Lefkovits, J. K. 68
Leith, M. J. W. 28

Lemche, N. P. 134, 143, 153, 157, 315
LeMoyne, J. 186, 197–8
Lenger, M.-T. 46–7
Leon, H. J. 106, 108
Levenson, J. D. 24
Levine, A.-J. 300–1
Levine, B. A. 130, 132
Levine, L. I. 170–1
Levinskaya, I. 293, 296
Levison, J. R. 92, 95, 236
Lewis, J. P. 153, 155
Lewis, N. 106–7, 243, 301
Lewis, T. J. 258
Lewy, H. 134, 143
Lichtenberger, H. 241, 273, 288–9
Liebesny, H. 46–7
Liesen, J. 50
Lieu, J. 292, 301
Lightstone, J. N. 178, 181, 183–4
Lim, T. H. 68–9, 134, 143
Limburg, J. 17
Lindars, B. 158
Lindsay, D. R. 92
Lipscomb, W. L. 95–6
Loader, J. A. 42–3
Lohfink, N. 42
Longenecker, B. W. 117, 121
Longenecker, R. N. 165–6
Loretz, O. xviii, 248, 250
Lovering, E. H., Jr 211
Lull, D. J. 44
Lynd-Porter, A. 106, 108
Lyons, E. L. 21–2

McClaren, J. S. 92, 108, 112, 284–5
Maccoby, H. 1, 2
McCollough, C. T. 106
McCreesh, T. P. 21–2
McCullagh, C. B. 7
Mach, M. 220
Mack, B. L. xv, 50, 86, 90–1, 220, 225, 228, 277–8
McKane, W. 233
Mackay, E. A. 151
McKay, H. A. 171, 174
McKay, J. 220, 221
McKeating, H. 301, 304
McKenzie, J. L. 220–1
McKenzie, S. L. 19
McKnight, S. 293, 196
McLay, T. 158, 163

Macmullen, R. 249–50, 284–5
McNamara, M. 158, 164, 225, 229
Magness, J. 68
Mahé, J.-P. 96
Maier, C. 21, 225–6
Maier, J. 1, 2
Main, E. 186, 188
Mandell, S. R. 77, 79
Mantel, H. 144, 145
Marcus, R. 46–7
Margalioth, M. 249–50
Martin, J. D. 233, 273
Marx, A. 130, 132
Mason, R. 17
Mason, S. xiv, 92–3, 185–6, 190
Mattill, A. J., Jr 186, 194
May, H. G. 220–1
Meadowcroft, T. J. 158, 163
Meeks, W. A. 237
Meigs, A. S. 130–1
Mendels, D. 297, 299
Mendelson, A. 90–1
Meshorer, Y. 107
Metso, S. 68
Mettinger, T. N. D. 211
Meyer, M. 249
Meyers, C. L. 15
Meyers, E. M. 15, 28, 106, 108,
   175–7
Michel, O. 284
Mildenberg, L. 106, 108
Milgrom, J. 27–8, 130, 132
Milik, J. T. 41, 97–9, 323
Miller, J. E. 243
Miller, P. C. 243
Mirecki, P. 249
Moor, J. C. de 211, 217
Moore, C. A. 44, 66
Morfill, W. R. 98–9
Morgan, M. A. 249–50
Morschauser, S. 183
Mowinckel, S. 258
Muffs, Y. 301–2, 304
Mulder, M. J. 165–6, 175
Mullen, E. T., Jr 220
Munoa, P. B. 101
Muraoka, T. 50
Murphy, F. J. 94, 95
Murphy, R. E. 21, 25, 42
Murphy-O'Connor, J. 199, 203, 206,
   293, 296
Musurillo, H. A. 305, 307

Naveh, J. 249
Netzer, E. 107, 134, 140
Neubauer, A. 272
Neusner, J. xv, 1, 3–4, 90, 108, 113,
   116–17, 120–6, 130–1, 165, 168,
   170–1, 175–8, 180–1, 186, 192–6,
   198–9, 206, 248–53, 258, 276–8, 281,
   288–90, 301, 304–5
Newman, J. H. 171
Newsom, C. A. 27, 171–2, 301
Nicholson, E. 26
Nickelsburg, G. W. E. xvii, 74–5, 252,
   258, 260, 266
Niditch, S. 244–5
Niehr, H. 1, 211–12
Nikiprowetzky, V. 284
Nissinen, M. 301
Noethlichs, K. L. 308–9
Nolland, J. 293, 295
North, J. L. 292, 301
Noy, D. 106–8, 171, 301, 303
Nurmela, R. 134–6

O'Brien, J. M. 15, 134–5
Oded, B. 298
Oegema, G. S. 273, 277–8, 288–9, 291
Olyan, S. M. 129, 220–1, 224
Ong, W. J. 151–2
Oppenheim, A. L. 244–5
Orlinsky, H. M. 49, 75, 153
Orlov, A. A. 98
Orrieux, C. 293
Overman, J. A. 107–8

Parente, F. 92
Parry, D. W. 69
Payne, J. B. 159
Pearce, S. 13, 17, 30, 293
Pearson, B. A. 300
Pearson, B. W. R. 281
Peltonen, K. 20
Perkins, P. 96
Perrot, C. 94, 175
Person, R. F., Jr 15, 17
Petersen, D. L. 15
Pietersma, A. 211, 215
Piñero, A. 220
Pingree, D. 242
Pinnick, A. 67
Pippin, T. 29, 297
Poehlmann, W. 186, 189
Poirier, J. C. 186

Polzin, R. 22
Poorthuis, M. J. H. M. 26
Pope, M. H. 22–3
Porten, B. xix, 28–9, 134, 141, 211, 214
Porter, S. E. 68, 185, 199
Porton, G. G. 121, 165, 167
Potter, D. 241, 249
Price, J. J. xiv, 108, 110, 112, 333
Pritchard, J. B. xvi
Propp, W. H. C. 44
Prosic, T. 134, 141
Pucci Ben Zeev, M. 37, 74, 92, 94, 308–9
Puech, E. 258, 274
Pulikottil, P. U. 165–6

Quispel, G. 96, 249

Rabello, A. M. 305
Rabenau, M. 44
Rad, G. von 258
Rajak, T. xiv, 92, 94, 171, 292, 301, 303, 308–9
Rappaport, U. 68, 170
Redditt, P. L. 15, 61, 183–4
Reeg, G. 171, 174
Reese, J. M. 86
Reeves, J. C. 41
Reider, J. 86
Reif, S. C. xv, 171, 173
Rendtorff, R. 26–7
Reynolds, J. 293, 296
Rhoads, D. M. 284, 286
Richardson, P. 108, 109
Ringe, S. H. 27, 301
Ritmyer, K. 134–5
Ritmyer, L. 134–5
Rivkin, E. 186, 194
Robert, A. 273
Roberts, J. J. M. 30–1, 298
Robertson, D. A. 22–3
Roddy, N. 246
Rofé, A. 27, 183–4
Rogerson, J. W. 44
Röllig, W. xviii
Royse, J. R. 90, 211, 215
Rubenstein, J. L. 134, 142
Rubinkiewicz, R. 118–19
Runia, D. T. 89–1, 211, 277
Rutgers, L. V. 107–8, 114, 165, 258, 293, 296, 305

Sæbø, M. 166
Sacchi, P. 233
Saldarini, A. J. xiv, 121–2, 184, 186, 192–4, 198
Salters, R. B. 17–18
Sanders, E. P. 1, 2, 147, 183
Sanders, J. A. 225, 226
Sanders, J. T. 258, 260
Sanderson, J. 161
Sanmartín, J. xviii
Sasson, J. 17, 18, 244
Sasson, V. 244
Schäfer, P. 122, 124, 241, 249–51, 305
Schams, C. 134, 151–2
Schaper, J. 30, 33
Schiffman, L. H. 1, 2, 67, 69
Schmid, K. 118
Scholem, G. 249, 251
Schoors, A. 42
Schottroff, L. 301
Schramm, B. 18
Schremer, A. 186, 199
Schröder, B. 93
Schroer, S. 301
Schuller, E. M. 68
Schultz, R. L. 166–7
Schüpphaus, J. 85
Schürer, E. xix, 66, 85–6, 88, 94, 96, 98, 100–2, 105, 118, 158, 205, 248, 250, 295–6
Schwartz, D. R. 134, 136, 151
Schwartz, J. 26
Schwartz, S. 52, 108, 110, 122, 125–6
Schwenk-Bressler, U. 86
Schwienhorst-Schönberger, L. 42
Scott, J. M. 3, 5, 7, 298
Segal, A. F. 211, 217–18, 249–50
Segal, J. 134, 141
Seland, T. 90
Seow, C.-L. 42–3
Sevenster, 305–6
Shaked, S. 249
Shaw, B. D. 284, 285
Shedl, C. 65
Sievers, J. 92
Skarsten, R. 89
Skehan, P. W. 258, 260
Slingerland, H. D. 102, 305
Sly, D. I. 90
Smend, R. 273
Smith, J. Z. 178, 180, 293, 295

Smith, Morton 176, 184, 211–13, 249–50, 252–3, 284
Smith, M. S. 211–12
Snaith, J. G. 166–7
Soden, W. von 22
Soll, W. 44–5
Sommer, B. D. 237
Spencer, R. A. 44
Spilsbury, P. 93
Stadelmann, H. 51
Stanton, G. N. 308
Starcky, J. 274–5
Steck, O. H. 61, 66
Stegemann, H. 69
Steins, G. 14, 20
Stemberger, G. 116–17, 186, 206
Sterling, G. E. 171, 277
Stern, M. xvii
Steudel, A. 69
Stocker, M. 65
Stone, M. E. xviii, 41, 67, 69, 95, 101–3, 125–6, 184
Strange, J. F. 175–7, 242
Street, B. V. 151–2
Stroumsa, G. G. 308
Stuckenbruck, L. T. 41, 216–17
Stuhlmacher, P. 272
Sukenik, E. 202
Sussmann, Y. 186, 199
Suter, D. W. 97
Swanson, D. D. 69
Swartz, M. D. 249
Swete, H. 158
Sysling, H. 165–6, 175
Szesnat, H. 301, 304

Tabor, J. D. 220, 266, 268, 274–5
Talbert, C. H. 186
Talmon, S. 51, 107, 134, 137, 143, 158–9, 161, 163, 184, 246, 278
Talshir, Z. 14
Tannenbaum, R. 293, 296
Taylor, J. 187, 198
Taylor, J. E. 77, 82
Tcherikover, V. A. xiv, xvii
Teeple, H. M. 237
Terian, A. 90
Theissen, G. 252, 254
Thoma, C. 186, 198
Thomas, J. D. 44–5
Thompson, T. L. 6–7, 68, 293
Tiede, D. L. 252–3

Tigchelaar, E. J. C. 9, 68–9, 233
Tiller, P. A. 62
Tilly, M. 75–6
Tobin, T. H. 277–8
Toorn, K. van der xvii, 153, 176, 211–14, 218
Torrey, C. C. 281
Tov, E. 66, 68, 107, 159–60, 163
Trafton, J. L. 85
Trebilco, P. 107–8
Trebolle Barrera, J. 166
Tromp, J. 74–5
Tromp, N. 258, 266, 268
Turdeanu, E. 96, 98
Twelftree, G. H. 249, 252–3

Uehlinger, C. 211, 213–14
Ulfgard, H. 134, 142
Ulrich, E. C. xv, 67, 69, 159, 162
Unnik, W. C. van 298
Urman, D. 172

Vaillant, A. 98
VanderKam, J. C. xiv, 44, 63, 67–8, 134, 143, 233, 236
Veltri, G. 249
Vermaseren, M. J. 96, 249
Vermes, G. xix, 200, 205, 252–3, 274–5
Vermeylen, J. 50, 86
Viviano, B. T. 187, 198

Wacker, M.-T. 301
Waerden, B. L. van der 242
Waltke, B. K. 159, 161
Wan, S. 237
Wander, B. 293, 296
Washington, H. C. 21
Waubke, H.-G. 187
Weber, M. 8
Weeks, S. 21–2
Wegner, J. R. 27, 134, 140
Weiss, M. 258
Weitzman, M. P. 159–60
Wellhausen, J. 185
Wénin, A. 107
Werline, R. A. 172
Werman, C. 134
Wernberg-Møller, P. 159, 160
Westermann, C. 21
Whedbee, J. W. 22–3
White, R. J. 244

Whybray, R. N. 21, 27, 42–4, 225–6, 272
Will, E. 40, 293
Willi, T. 20, 166–7
Williams, D. S. 59
Williams, M. H. 107–8
Williamson, H. G. M. 20–1, 134, 137
Wills, L. M. 44–5
Wilson, B. C. 3, 4
Wilson, W. T. 88
Winston, D. 86–7, 211, 237, 277
Winter, B. W. 90
Wise, M. O. 242, 246, 250, 274–5
Wolfson, H. A. 237, 277
Wolters, A. 21–2
Woolf, G. 150, 152
Woude, A. S. van der 69
Wright, B. G. 51

Wright, J. E. 118
Wright, J. W. xiv
Wyatt, N. 212, 215, 220–1

Yadin, Y. 51, 106–7, 134–5, 159, 161, 284, 288
Yarbro Collins, A. 118, 120
Yardeni, A. xix, 28–9, 106, 134, 141
Yavetz, Z. 305
York, A. D. 159, 164

Zahavy, T. 122
Zakovitch, Y. 25
Zerbe, G. M. 284, 288, 308
Ziegler, J. 51, 61, 86
Zimmermann, J. 274–5, 288–9
Zipor, M. A. 134, 143
Zuckerman, B. 22
Zuckermandel, M. 113

INDEX OF NAMES AND SUBJECTS

Aaron 274
Abaddon 260
Abel 263
Abiathar 144
"abomination of desolation" 78, 326
abortion 63
Abraham 63, 72–3, 118, 294, 298, 300;
    taught astrology to Phoenicians 242
Abraham, Testament of 100–1
Acta Alexandrinorum 305, 307
act–consequence relationship 23
Actium 98
Adam 41, 62, 118, 230, 273, 294
Adam and Eve literature 95, 168
Adam, Apocalypse of 96
Adiabene 114, 295
Adonai 215
adultery 304
afterlife 4, 41, 45, 51, 177, 197, 235,
    257–70, 332
Agatharchides of Cnidus 114, 174, 307,
    328
Agrippa I 109, 110, 163, 285–6, 333
Agrippa II 110, 126
Ahab 213, 315
Ahaz 132
Ahaziah 213
Ahiqar 24, 76
Alcimus 66, 79, 184, 325
Alexander the Great 6, 14, 52, 54, 74,
    242, 279, 306, 315, 320
Alexander Janneus 77, 79–80, 188, 191,
    205, 326–7
Alexandra Salome 81–2, 111, 187–9,
    191, 199, 208–9, 327
Alexandria 52, 72, 78, 90, 100, 168,
    174, 179, 261, 268, 308–9

allegorical interpretation/allegorists 25,
    72, 80, 90–1, 165, 168–9
almsgiving 45
alphabet, Moses as inventor of 71
alpha-text, of Esther 24, 163
Amidah: see Shimoneh Esreh
Anan 146
Ananus, high priest 189, 287
Anat 213
Anat-Bethel 214
Anat-Yahu 214
Anatolia 54
Ancient of Days 97
angels/angelology 34, 36, 41, 96–7, 119,
    185, 187, 194, 198, 201, 217, 219,
    230, 261, 264, 318–19, 323;
    of destruction/punishment 260–1;
    myth of fallen angels 41, 58, 97, 103,
    323; names of angels in magic 251
aniconic worship 39, 58, 218, 294
animals, worship of 88
anthropomorphisms 72
anti-Judaism 305–8
Antiochus III 46–8, 71, 146, 177,
    324–6, 330; edicts of 46
Antiochus IV 34, 64, 66, 77–80, 110,
    269, 309, 324–6, 330
Antiochus V 325
Antipater 109, 307, 311, 330
anti-semitic 305–9
Aphrodisias 293, 296
Apion 307
apocalyptic/apocalypses 9, 36, 41, 58,
    61–2, 75, 103–4, 110, 112, 124–6,
    319, 323, 332; definition of
    apocalypse 234; different from
    prophets/prophecy? 240

apologetic, Jewish 76, 81
apostates 88, 323
Aqiva 124, 125–6
Aquila 160–3, 165
Arad, ostraca from 212
Aramaic, as lingua franca 54
Araq el-Emir 148
archaeological finds 28–9
archangels 97, 222, 230–1
Archelaus 74, 109, 201
archisynagogoi 171
Aristeas, Letter of 75–6
Aristobulus I 80, 168
Aristobulus II 80
Aristobulus, philosopher 72–3, 80, 91
aristocracy/aristocrats 111, 149
Aristotle 310
Artapanus 71–2, 76, 80
Artaxerxes II 240
Artaxerxes III 65
Artemidorus 244
Artemis 205
Asael 222
Asaph, Psalms of 144
asceticism 45, 194
Asherah/Asherim 212–14
Asia Minor 100, 179
Asidaioi 60, 184
Asmodaeus 221
assassins 286
Assyria/Assyrians 57, 64–5, 179,
    218–19, 242, 298, 309, 321
Astarte 219
astral immortality 63, 88, 264, 269
astrology 65, 72, 113, 177, 241–3, 322,
    331–2
Athalia 81
Athirat 214
Athtar 219, 220
Atonement, Day of 104, 131, 142, 225
auditions 234
Augustus 89, 110
Aviv, Hebrew month 142
Azazel 118, 120, 224–5, 231, 265,
    268

Baal 213–15, 315
Babatha 107, 112, 126, 301, 311
Babylon/Babylonia/Babylonians 34, 65,
    113, 173, 178, 242, 252, 298, 300,
    309, 321; Babylonian creation myth
    215; Babylonian Jews 300

Bagohi 29, 32, 146
bandits 146, 283–8
baptism, alleged for proselytes 295–6
barbarian 306
Bar Kokhba 107, 124–6, 290; Bar
    Kokhba revolt 100, 117, 122, 281,
    290, 333
Baruch, Apocalypse of (2 Baruch) 117–20
Baruch, Jeremiah's scribe 66
bathing, ritual 97, 201, 202
Bathsheba 172
Beelzebub 250
Behemoth 120, 280
Belial 120, 223, 225, 231; "streams of"
    260
Beliar 225
Ben Sira 50–2, 152, 154, 178, 329;
    biblical quotations in 166; when
    written 157
Berenice, the sister of Agrippa II 303
Berossus 242
Bethel 213
Bethulia 65
betrothal 195
Birkat ha-minim 171, 173
Boethus 199
Boethusians 141, 186, 195–7, 199
Bogomils 99
Booths, Feast of 63
brigands *see* bandits
Buddhism 4
burial 112, 203, 332

Caesar 85
Caesarea 113, 173
calendar 41, 53, 63, 103–4, 141, 143,
    149, 323
Caligula 87, 110, 307, 308, 311
Canaanites 299, 315
canon 18, 25, 55, 91, 94, 114, 152–57,
    170, 179–80, 197–8, 316, 329
celebacy 203–4, 208
Cenaz 239
Cestius 333
Chaldean science, astrology as 242
Chaoskampf 120, 215
charismatic(s) 113, 332
cherubim 221–2, 265
Chnum 29
Christianity/Christians 175, 177, 193,
    251–2
christology 289

Chronicles, 1 and 2 19–21, 157, 160, 167
chronography 75, 101, 119, 246–8
circumcision 81, 103, 180, 294–7, 307, 310
citizenship 307–9, 311
Claudius 307–9
Clavicula Solomonis 250
Clearchus of Soli 305, 310
Cleopatra VII 97, 280, 330
Coele-Syria 322, 324
coinage 28–9, 80
collegia 309
comedy 23
commentaries, biblical 90; as form of biblical interpretation 167; from Qumran 80
Communism 4
conflagration, universal (*ekpyrosis*) 98, 120, 265, 268
Confucianism 4
conversion 105, 292–7, 310
cosmic secrets 41
council: *see* Sanhedrin
Council, Divine 220–1, 224, 227
Covenant Code 25
creation 99
crisis literature 256
cult 4, 16–17, 19, 21, 27, 31–2, 39, 40, 51, 58, 62, 66, 77, 93, 95, 99, 109, 114, 119, 122, 170, 178–9, 181–2, 195, 203, 294, 309, 315–17, 325, 331, 334; anthropological and theological basis of 129–32; different for different groups 207; official Roman 331; prophets 28
cult of the dead: *see* dead, cult of
Cyrenaica/Cyrene 286, 327
Cyrus xiv, 31, 33, 272, 279, 289, 316

Dagan 245
Damascus 70, 202
Dan, cult place 213, 250
Daniel 60–1, 157, 160, 163, 244; compiled by someone like Eupolemus 71; Josephus on 279; as a prophet 239
Darius the Mede 279
"darkness, sons of" 223
David 25, 30–1, 85, 144, 154, 172, 213, 273; David *redivivus* 272, 289
Day, Last Great, of Sukkot 142

dead, cult of 250, 258, 267, 331–2
dead, spirits of 63
death 88–9, 100–1, 119
Decalogue 161
Demetrius the Chronographer 48–9, 56, 58, 168
Demetrius III 80, 188, 326
demons/demonology 34, 42, 45, 96–7, 219–25, 253, 323, 332
Demotic Chronicle 321
deportations 31, 156
Deuteronomy, priests in 135; Deuteronomic School 35; Deuteronomic tradition 51; Deuteronomists 216; and *Temple Scroll* 154
Deuteronomistic History 35; Deuteronomistic School 208; historical data in 157, 166
devil 105, 220, 221, 225, 231; *see also* demons
diarchy 16, 32
Diasporanovelle 24
diatribe 100
Dinah 73, 105
Dionysus 218
divination/diviners 4, 51, 58, 65, 74, 177–8, 234, 236, 241, 331; Jewish views on 241
divorce 29, 112, 195, 304
Documentary Hypothesis 27
Domesday Book 7
Dositheus, alleged apostate 297
dreams 51, 201, 243–5

earthquake 206
Ebionite 162
ecstasy 105
Eden 118
Edom/Edomites 105, 299
education, Greek 40, 54, 55, 73, 78, 87–8, 320
Egypt/Egyptians 23, 29, 38–9, 54, 56–7, 64, 71–2, 74, 79, 82, 88, 100, 104, 120, 151, 212, 242, 258, 266, 280, 286, 307, 321, 325–7
Eighteen Benedictions 173
ekpyrosis: *see* conflagration, universal
El 214, 216
elders, in rabbinic literature 195
Eleazar, rebel leader in war 286
Eleazer, high priest 330

"Elect One of righteousness", in *1 Enoch* 97, 276, 283
Elephantine 28, 214, 303, 327
Eliashib 317
Elijah 213, 275
Eloah 23
Elohim 215, 222, 229
Elyon 214–15
empire, last before the eschaton 61, 64, 118
encomium 87
Endor, woman of 250
Engedi 200
Enoch 41, 62, 103, 184, 263; *1 Enoch* 41–2, 58, 62-3, 97, 157, 167–8, 222, 224; *1 Enoch* in Ethiopic canon 156; when *1 Enoch* written 157
Enoch, Slavonic (*2 Enoch*) 98–9
Enuma Elish 215
ephod 239
epispasm 297
ʿ*ērûv* 197
eschatology 4, 16–17, 19, 36, 41, 51, 61, 81–2, 88–9, 95, 99, 103–4, 110, 120, 125, 257–70, 319, 332–3
1 Esdras 13–15, 163; when written 157
Eshbaal 213
Eshem-Bethel 214
esoteric arts 4, 58, 149, 176, 241–51, 255, 331–2
Essenes 82, 111–12, 184–5, 198–9, 203, 260, 263, 285, 326–7; Essene hypothesis of Qumran 69; etymology of name 200, 205; as prophets 239
Esther 142, 154–6, 163; in canon 157
Ethiopians 72, 266
etymologies, of Hebrew names 91, 169
Euphrates 264
Eupolemus, son of John 47, 61, 71, 78, 80
Eupolemus, Pseudo- 242
Eve 41, 62, 118, 294
exile 5, 6, 31, 82, 297–300, 315, 333
exodus from Egypt 29, 63, 72
exorcism 251, 253–4, 332
Ezekias, high priest 74, 321
Ezekiel, book of in canon 155
Ezekiel the Dramatist 55, 72, 168
Ezra 13–15, 31, 57, 154–5, 160, 247, 299; Apocalypse of Ezra (*4 Ezra*) 117–20; in canon 157

famine 17
fasting 66
fathers, traditions of 197
fertility cult 26
festivals 45, 138, 141–3, 170, 181–2, 195, 208, 295
Festus 303
final judgment: *see* judgment, final
first-fruits 137
Firstfruits, Feast of 63
First Fruits of Oil, Festival of 142
First Fruits of Wine, Festival 142
firstlings 137, 138
flood 62, 99
Florus 146
Folly, Dame 226
foundation legends, of post-exilic Jerusalem 14, 31
Fourth Philosophy 189, 208, 285–6, 288

Gabriel, archangel 222–3
Galilee/Galilean 79, 80, 175, 252, 331
Gamaliel: family of 208; Gamaliel I 111, 123, 194–6, 198, 327; Gamaliel II 123; house of 198
Gamla 140, 174
garments, of high priest 109–10
Gehenna 120, 264–5
gender xiii, 140–1, 300–4
Genizah 243
Gentiles, court of 135
Gerizim 148, 161, 294, 326
gerousia 48, 66; *see also* Sanhedrin
Gethsemene 172
giants 58, 222, 323; *Giants, Book of* 322
Gnostic/Gnosticism xiii, 99, 113, 176, 218, 251, 332
God, son(s) of 216, 221, 224, 229
goddess 214, 227–8, 303
God-fearers 89, 114, 292–7, 310
"Golden Rule", negative formulation 45
governor, of Judah 16, 29, 32–3, 52, 144, 146, 286, 317, 322, 331
Graf-Wellhausen hypothesis 27
Greek thought, and Qohelet 43
Groningen hypothesis about Qumran 69

Hades 89, 262, 265, 268
Hadrian xiv, 120, 280
halakha/halakot 186, 196, 198

Hanina ben Dosa 253
Hannah 172
Hanukkah 60
ḥărēdîm 184
Hasideans/Hasidim 60, 82, 183–5, 205
Hasmoneans 71, 135–6, 176, 191, 205, 208, 299, 308, 330
healing 254, 332
"heave offering" 137
heaven 19, 38, 75, 97, 99, 119–20, 280, 323; host of 212, 220, 222; queen of 213; surrogate for "God" 216
Heaven, God of (title) 215
Hebrew language, and Qohelet 44; Philo's knowledge of 277
Hebron 214
Hecateus of Abdera 37–9, 218, 307–8
Hecateus, Pseudo- 73–4
Hefzibah inscription 46–7
Helel 219, 220–1
Helena, queen of Adiabene 114, 295, 303
Hellenization/Hellenistics 53–5, 59–60, 320–1, 324; Hellenistic Jerusalem 71; Hellenistic reform 77; and the Jews 53–5
hermeneutical rules 256
Herod 8, 74, 108–11, 134, 141, 146–7, 149, 189, 191, 201, 252, 303, 327, 330
Herod Antipas 74
Herodians 126, 149, 176, 183, 191–3, 333
Herodium 113, 174
Herodotus 269
ḥevel (Qohelet) 43
ḥever of Jews 80
Hezekiah, the Persian governor 74
hierocracy 52
Hillel 45, 111, 113, 123, 195–6, 198–9, 208; Hillel, house of 194–6, 198
historiography 6–8, 58
Holiness Code (H) 27
Holophernes 65
holy day 24; see also festivals
Holy of Holies 142
holy men 113; see also charismatic
Homer 81, 91, 258, 267; Homeric poetic language 73
homosexuality 65, 304
Honi the Circle-drawer 253
horoscopes 242
Hyperberetaios 47

hypostasis 217, 224, 227, 229
Hyrcanus II 80
Hyrcanus Tobiad 54

Iaoel, angel 119, 224
idols/idolatry/images 38, 88, 105, 118, 294; see also aniconic worship
Idumeans 79, 306, 308
immortality, of soul 201, 257–70
infernus 264
intermediaries 234
interpretation, inspired 255; rules of 169
Ionic Enlightenment 43
Isaac 63, 73
Isaiah 18, 31; Isaiah scroll (1QIsᵃ) 160; Second Isaiah on monotheism 217
Ishbosheth 213
Ishmaelites 121, 299
Isis 87, 228, 311
Israelites, Court of 141
Itureans 79, 306, 308

Jacob 63, 105
Jael 24
James the Just 275
"Jamnia, Synod of" 121, 155; see also Yavneh
Jason, high priest 71, 77–8, 82, 146, 297, 324–6, 330
Jeddous 39
Jehoida 144
Jehoram 213
Jericho 140
Jerome 156, 160
Jerusalem 172
Jesus 45, 119, 193, 216, 236, 247, 250, 252–4, 271–2, 282, 289
Jesus, son of Gamalas, high priest 287
Jezebel 213, 315
Job 43, 161, 164; Testament of Job 104–5
Jobab 105
Johanan, name on coins 80
John, apostle 194
John the Baptist 192
John the Essene 201
John, father of Eupolemus 47, 71
John Hyrcanus I 77, 79–80, 188, 191, 197, 205, 327
Jonathan Maccabee 146, 205, 325–6
Jonathan, name on coins 80
Jonathan, son of Saul 213
Jordan 97

Joseph 244
Joseph Tobiad 40, 52–4
Joseph and Asenath 105–6
Josephus passim, 92–4, 186, 216, 278–9;
Antiquities as example of "rewritten
Bible" 168; on the canon 155; as
prophet 239; version of biblical text
162
Joshua, book of among Samaritans
179
Joshua, high priest 14, 16, 31–2, 317
Joshua, as prophet 239
Josiah 148
Jotapata 245
Jove 218
Jubilees 63–4; in Ethiopic canon 156;
used a solar calendar 143; when
written 157
Jubilee year 142
Judah ha-Nasi 117
Judas, executed by Herod 252
Judas Maccabeus 60, 62, 78, 146, 154,
184, 325
Judas the Essene 201
Judas the Galilean 286
Judeophobia 305–8
judgment, final 101, 119, 257–70
Judith 24, 65–6, 81–2, 303, 311; when
written, 157

kaige, version of text 162
Kenaz, judge 95
Khirbet Beit Lei inscriptions 212
Khirbet el-Qom inscription 214
Khirbet Qumran 70, 114, 200, 205
king 27–8, 30–1, 35, 38, 79–80, 104–5,
110, 126, 136, 144, 149, 154, 199,
216, 235, 272–3, 289, 318, 321, 325
Kuntillet Ajrud inscription 214
kurios 215

Lachish ostraca 212
Lamentations 155, 156
land 294; ideology of 15, 34, 82, 294,
297–300, 311; priestly ownership of
38, 39
land, people(s) of 15–16, 32–4
Latin, Old, version 160
law 31, 61, 63, 76–7, 82, 93–4, 122–3,
322, 324–5, 330–1; ascribed to Moses
38; in hands of priests 57; public
reading of 180; scrolls of 60

Lazarus 266
Lebanon 47
lectionary cycle 174, 175
legal sections of OT 25
Leontopolis 65, 82, 294
lesbianism 89, 304
lēistēs 285
Levi 16, 63
Levi, Aramaic 184
Leviathan 120, 280
Levites 21, 57, 135–8, 143, 148,
151–2
Leviticus 129–43, 164; as a source of
temple ritual 139
Liber Antiquitatum Biblicarum 94–5
"Light, Sons of" 223
literacy 57, 151, 318
liturgy 139
Logos 181, 216–17, 225, 227–30
logos protrepiticus (Greek *logos protreptikos*)
87
"Lord of Spirits" 276
Lucian, textual revision 24, 162–3
Lucifer 221, 225, 231

Maat, Egyptian goddess 228
Maccabees/Maccabean revolt 20, 146,
177, 184–6, 247, 306, 308;
Maccabees, Books of 59–60, 157; 3
Maccabees 307; 4 Maccabees
99–100
magic 4, 45, 113, 177, 181, 248–51,
331–2
Malachi, priests in 135
mal'ak Yhwh 220
Mamre 177
"Man of Lies" 205
"man, son of" 222
Manaemus the Essene 201
Manetho 74, 306–7
mantic wisdom 61, 319
Marduk 215
Mari 244–5
Mark Antony 330
marriage 34, 66, 112, 195, 200–1, 203,
302–3; sacred 26
martyrdom 61, 75, 81–2, 260, 262;
"Alexandrian martyrs" 307
Masada 107, 125, 161, 174, 200, 286,
288, 331
maśkîlîm 71, 260, 282
Masoretic text 24, 50, 71, 159–65

Mastema 222, 225, 231
Matthias, disciple of Judas 252
Media 64
Megasthenes 305
Melchireša 223
Melchizedek 99, 223, 274
Melito of Sardis 156
memrā' 229
Menahem, the Sicarii leader 190, 286
Menelaus 78–79, 324–6
menorah 195
menstruation 139–40, 304
Mephibosheth 213
Meribaal 213
merits of the fathers 101
Mesopotamia 23, 26, 54, 57, 151, 327
Messiah/messianism 4, 64–5, 85, 97,
 111, 119–20, 124–5, 193, 198, 208,
 236, 241, 247, 271–91, 332; Messiah
 ben Joseph 281, 290; messianic Age
 247; messianic woes 269; suffering
 272, 290
metempsychosis 262–3
Methusalah 99
Micaiah 244
Michael 274
Michael, archangel 75, 96, 119–20,
 222–4, 274, 282
midrash 104, 167; Hellenistic midrash in
 Wisdom of Solomon 167
millennium 65, 119, 246
minim 195
Minor Prophets, scroll of (8HevXIIgr)
 107
miqve' 140
Mishnah 116–17, 121–3, 125, 181, 195,
 198
mission, by Jews to convert 104, 114,
 292–7, 310
monotheism 34, 39, 58, 89, 207, 215–19,
 224, 230, 294, 316, 318
Montanism 105
moon, new 141–3
Moses 27, 38–9, 49, 63, 71–2, 75,
 218–20, 230; books of 45, 208;
 prophet like 240; *Testament of Moses*
 (Assumption of) 74–5
Murabba'at 107, 304
music 143
mystery cults, Hellenistic 297, 311
mystical Hellenistic Judaism,
 Goodenough thesis 177

mysticism 4, 113, 248–51; merkavah
 mysticism 105

Nabonidus 251
Naḥal Ḥever 107, 304
names, surrogate 213; theophoric 213
Naomi 25
nb'/nāvi' 233
Near East, Hellenistic 179
Nebuchadnezzar 6, 15, 66, 279, 298,
 318
necromancy 19, 58, 250; *see also* dead,
 cult of
Negev 214
Nehemiah 8, 13–15, 31, 33–5, 60, 154,
 160, 317, 330; book of, in canon 157;
 Nehemiah Memorial 14; on Persian
 governor 144
Neofiti, Targum 160, 164
Nero *redivivus* 98, 120, 265
Netinim 136
Nicolaus of Damascus 79
Nineveh 18
Nisan, Babylonian month 142
Noah 99; *Noah, Book of* 62, 97
nobles of the Jews 29, 146
novel, Jewish 45

Octavian 330
offering, cereal 138; guilt (*'āšām*) 139;
 sin (*ḥaṭṭā't*) 139; *tāmîd* 139; wine 138
oil defiling 201
Olivet prophecy of the Gospels 264
Olympus 261
Oniads 40, 53, 322, 324; Onias II 145,
 322; Onias III 82, 247, 322, 324, 326;
 Onias IV 82
Onias the Rainmaker 252, 253
oracles 120, 278–9; Hellenistic 64
oral culture 152
Orphica, pseudo- 73
Orphics 81, 261
Ostan, brother of Anan in the
 Elephantine texts 29, 146
Othniel 239

pantheon, Northwest Semitic 220–1,
 224
papyri 28
para-biblical scriptural interpretation
 72, 168; para-biblical writing 56
paradise 96, 101, 222

paradosis 185
Passover 29, 64, 141; Passover Papyrus from Elephantine 29, 141
Patriarchs, Testaments of the Twelve 5, 101–4
Paul, apostle 181, 194, 266, 303
P document 26–8
Pentateuch 35, 39, 63, 76, 90, 114, 166, 168, 179, 197–8, 322, 327; Tobit shows knowledge of 45; when written 157
Pentecost 63, 199
periodization of history 119
persecution 75, 78
Persia, prince of 223
Pĕrûšîm 194
pesharim 169, 180, 245; Pesher exegesis 167
Peshitta 160
Peter, apostle 194
Phaethon 219
Phanuel, archangel 222
Pharisees (*Pĕrûšîm?*) 80–2, 93, 95, 111–12, 115, 121–4, 148, 152, 180, 185–96, 205, 252, 262–3, 266, 285–6, 326–7, 333
Phasael 330
Philip, son of Herod 74
Philo 9, 50, 72, 86–7, 89–92, 94, 100, 104, 110, 157, 165, 168–70, 179, 181, 200–1, 215, 216–17, 223–4, 227–8, 276–8, 297, 304, 308; on the canon 154
Philo the Epic Poet 73
Philo-Judaism 305
philosophy, Greek 57, 181
Phineas 287
Phocylides, Pseudo- 88
Phoenicia/Phoenicians 54, 213, 242, 315, 320
physicians 51
physiognomy 243
Plato/Platonism 72, 89, 91, 216–17, 223, 228
Pliny the Elder 200, 202, 204
polis 54, 77–8, 324
Pollion, the Pharisee 189
polytheism 88, 206, 212, 215, 228, 230, 318, 331
Pompey 79, 85, 114
popular religion 58, 175, 331
population, of Palestine 113

pork 307
Potter's Oracle 321
powers, in Philo's system 216–17, 229; two in heaven 217
prayer 4, 5, 65–7, 139, 148, 170, 178–9, 182, 201, 316, 328, 332, 334
prayers 201
preparation day ("eve") before each festival 66
priest, high 15, 30, 32, 38–40, 48, 52, 66, 74, 79, 80, 82, 109, 110–11, 135, 138, 144–6, 194, 196, 199, 205, 239, 272, 275, 286, 317, 322, 324–6, 329, 331; on the Day of Atonement 142; priest-kings 77
"Priest, Wicked" 80, 205–6
priests/priesthood 15, 17, 32, 35, 38–9, 47, 51, 53, 57–8, 60, 66, 63, 74, 78, 81, 99, 103, 105, 111, 126, 148, 151–2, 176, 178, 184, 191, 195, 197, 199, 208, 223, 272–3, 295, 310, 316–17, 322–5, 327, 329, 331, 333–4; chief priests (*archiereis*) 149, 188, 194, 199; priestly school 35
"Prince of Lights" 223
prodigies 269
prophet/prophecies 51, 58, 61, 98, 179, 181, 198, 213, 236–7, 252, 274, 319; cultic prophets 21; definition of 232–6; failure of 18; false, according to Josephus 239; Former, when written 157; Latter, when written 157, 179; Major 166; methodological points for social analysis 241; prophetic figures 178; in the Second Temple period 236–41, 248; sources of in Second Temple period 240
prophētēs, Greek word for "prophet" 233
prophets of Asherah 214
proselytes/proselytizing 105, 114; alleged baptism 310
proseuchē 56, 113, 173, 328; *see also* synagogues
prostasis 52
prostatēs 40
prostitute 226
Proverbs 21–2, 161
Psalms, question of connection with cult 144; Psalms Scroll (11QPsalms[a]) 154
Pseudo-Hecateus 136
Pseudo-Phocylides 304

P-source, and women 140; as a source of temple ritual 139
Ptolemy I 55, 74, 306
Ptolemy II 47, 49, 76, 322, 328
Ptolemy V 46
Ptolemy VI 65, 280
Ptolemy VII 65
Ptolemy VIII 65
Ptolemy, minister of Antiochus III 46
Purim 24, 142
purity 4, 16, 112, 122, 131, 139, 170, 181–2, 186, 195, 198, 208, 295, 304, 327; *thr* 139; *ṭm'* 139; women and 140
Pythagoreanism 4,72

Q-source 192, 193, 197
Qohelet 42–4, 155, 157, 161
Qumran 50, 56, 112, 114, 148, 152, 160–1, 163, 165, 169, 179, 180–1, 185, 187, 322; canon at 154; para-biblical texts at 168; used solar calendar 143

Rainer papyrus 47
Ramael, angel 119
Raphael, archangel 221–2
religion, family 176; "popular" 175
religious tolerance 308–10
remnant 34, 299
Rephaim 315
resistance, to Greeks and Romans 61, 64
resurrection 36, 45, 61, 81, 85, 88–9, 96, 100–1, 119–20, 177, 187, 194, 198, 257–70, 319; of the spirit 64
reward in paradise/heaven or punishment in hell 257–70
"rewritten Bible" 56, 63, 71–3, 80, 94–5, 104, 168
Ruth 24–5, 155; in canon 157

Sabaoth 216
sabbath 64, 66, 72, 89, 103, 114, 141, 180, 193, 197–8, 201, 203, 208, 295, 307, 328
sabbath, millennial 246
sabbatical year 142
sacrifice 5, 46, 48, 51, 75, 99, 120, 148, 195, 334; in Jerusalem for the Roman ruler 310; theories of 129–32

Sadducees (*Ṣaddûqîm?*) 82, 111, 148, 194, 263, 266, 267, 285, 326–7
sage, Hellenistic 76
saints, veneration of 331
Salome, Herod's sister 303–4
Salome Komaïse 107, 112, 126, 301, 311
salvation 4, 257–70
Samais, the Pharisee 189
Samaria 29, 218, 298; Samaria ostraca 213, 214; Samarian gods 219
Samaritans xiii, 20, 73, 157, 294, 326; Samaritan Pentateuch 159, 179; Samaritan text 161
Sanballat 33
Sanhedrin 32, 47–8, 52, 109, 144–7, 149, 194, 199, 317, 322, 327, 331
Sarah, daughter-in-law of Tobit 172, 221
Sargon II 218
Sariel, archangel 222
Satan 75, 97, 105, 119, 221, 223–5, 231, 274
satraps 33
Saul 31, 213, 250
schools 151
Scopas 46
scribes/scribalism 35, 47, 51, 57, 102, 122, 146, 150–2, 192–3, 235, 263
scriptural interpretation 152, 165–70, 181
scripture 4, 45, 63, 114, 123, 126, 152, 180, 182, 316, 318, 329, 334
seals, Israelite 213
sect/sectarianism 4, 9, 53, 82, 91, 93, 95, 111, 122, 124, 126, 176, 317–18, 326; baptismal sect 120
"Seekers after Smooth Things" 205
Seleucus IV 77, 324
"semi-proselyte" 296
Semitisms 101
senate: *see* Sanhedrin
Sefer ha-Razim 250
Septuagint translation 9, 24, 49–50, 56, 67, 71–2, 75–6, 104, 153, 155, 157–65, 169, 179, 181, 322, 328–9
seraphim 221–2, 265
sexuality xiii, 45, 65, 89; *see also* gender
Shaddai 23, 215
shades, of the dead in Homer 258
shame, concept in Ben Sira 260
Shammai 111, 123, 195–6, 198, 208; house of 194–6, 198

Shavuot 141
Shechem 73
Shema 217
Shemihazah 222
Sheol 226, 258, 261, 267, 268
Sheshbazzar 15, 32
Shiloh 172
Shimoneh Esreh 173
Sibyl 277
Sibylline Oracles 64–5, 73, 81, 97–8, 120, 125
Sicarii 111, 206, 208, 283–6, 333
Simon II, high priest 48, 145
Simon the Essene 201
Simon Maccabee 205
Simon son of Gamaliel I 190–1, 194–6, 198, 327
Sinai 72
Sinaiticus 44–5
singers, in temple 136, 146, 148
slaves 201
Socrates 72
solar symbols 213
Solomon 25, 71, 85, 251, 262; *Psalms of Solomon* 84–5
"Son of God" 275, 279, 280
"Son of Man" 97, 276, 282–3
Song of Songs 25–6, 155, 168; canon in 157
soul 41–2, 75, 85, 88–9, 95–6, 100–1, 181, 197, 201, 223
spirit(s) 194, 198
spirit, holy 239
"Spirits, Lord of" 97
statues, divine 311
Stoicism/Stoics 4, 228
suffering, messiah 272; "suffering servant" of Deutero-Isaiah 290; vicarious? 272
Sukkot 104, 142
Sumer 54
Sunday, Shavuot on 141
Sunday, Wave Sheaf Day on 141
sun, king from 64
Symmachus 160, 162, 163
synagogues 8, 60, 170–5, 296; women as head of 303
Syria 100, 179, 328

tabernacle 135
Tabernacles, Festival of 197
tamid 78

Tannaitic literature 116–17, 199; *Tannaitic Midrashim* 181; Tannaitic sources 194, 197
Targums 160, 164, 174–5, 229; Targum Pseudo-Jonathan, as "rewritten Bible" 168
Tartarus 120, 261–2, 265
Taurus 243
taxes 33, 46–8
Taxo 178
Teacher of Righteousness 181, 204–6, 247
teachers, priests as 136
temple 4, 6, 15, 17, 19, 21, 27, 30–3, 35, 40, 45–6, 53, 58, 60, 62, 66, 75, 77–8, 93, 95, 109, 113–14, 119–20, 126, 132–43, 176, 178–9, 180, 182, 195, 203, 205, 208, 214, 218–19, 230, 265, 280, 294, 299, 308, 315, 317–18, 323, 325–8, 331, 333–4; prayer at 172; singers 21
Temple Scroll (11QT) 135
teraphim 213
tĕrûmāh 137
tetragrammaton 215
tĕvûl yôm 196
text 55, 56, 94, 180, 182, 316; development of 158; "Old Palestinian" 95
theios anēr 253
theocracy 52
theodicy 23, 45, 118
Theodotion 161–3
Theodotus 73
Theodotus inscription 174, 328
theos 215
Therapeutae 104
Tiamat 215
Tiberias 89
Tiberius Alexander, Julius 87, 297
Tigris 97
Tishri, Hebrew month 142
Titans 261
tithe 4, 45, 137, 198; cattle 138; Poor 137, 138; Second 137–8
Titus 288, 303
tĕnûfāh 137
Tobiads 15, 29, 40, 53, 321–2; story of 40; Tobiad romance 54
Tobias 39, 40, 54, 55, 221
Tobit 24, 44–5, 328; when written 157
tolerance 123, 308–10

tombs, of holy men places of worship 177
to ōn/ho ōn, Philo's terms for God 216, 228
torah, oral 193
tradition, ancestral 192
tradition, oral 166
traditions of the fathers 208
Trajan 120, 280, 307
transmigration of souls 262–3
Trumpets, Day of 104, 142
Tun-Ergehen-Zusammenhang 23
Tyre 71

Ugarit 214; Ugaritic texts 215
underworld 42, 258
universalism 18–19
uraeus 221
urban terrorist 286
Uriel, archangel 119, 222
Urim and Thumim 136
Ushan period 126, 199

Vaticanus 44
Vespasian 122, 239, 245, 278–9
Vesuvius 120
violence, "spiral of" 108–9
visions 52, 63, 234, 235, 243–5; compared with dreams 244–5
vows 137
Vrevoil, angel 222
Vulgate, Latin translation 160

Wadi ed-Daliyeh papyri 28
Watchers, fall of 41
Wave Offering 137
Wave Sheaf day 141
Weeks, Feast of 197
widow 137
wisdom 51, 61, 260; "crisis" in 43, 57; Egyptian wisdom tradition 21; figure of wisdom 22, 225–8; Hellenistic 76; Hellenistic midrash in Wisdom 167; mantic 236; wise in Daniel 208
Wisdom, Book of (Wisdom of Solomon) 86–8, 156

women 25–6, 29, 65, 81, 95, 105, 122, 135, 148, 195, 200, 203, 207, 296; and the cult 140–1
Women, Court of 135, 141
wonderworkers 254
Woodgathering, Festival of (or Festival of Wood Offering) 142
world, age of 75

Xenophon 24

Yaḥad ostracon 70
Yahwism 18; Yahweh-alone movement 184, 213; see also Yhwh
Yamm 215
Yavneh 120–4, 155, 185, 198, 208, 315, 333
yeṣer 41
Yehohanan 29
Yehud/Yehudi/Yehudim 5, 28, 31, 32, 33
Yhwh 5, 9, 19, 23, 31, 34, 172, 179, 212–15, 217–18, 222, 225–6, 228–30, 235, 299, 315, 317, 332; day of 17; house of 212
Yohanan ben Zakkai 116, 122–3, 196, 198
Yom ha-Kippurim 104

Zadok 144–5, 199
Zadok the Pharisee 286
Zarathushtra 319
Zealots 111, 206, 208–9, 286–8
Zechariah 15–17, 32, 33, 319; on relation of Persian governor and high priest 144; visions of 245
Zenon 321; papyri 39–40
Zerubbabel 14, 16, 31–3, 317
Zeus 261
Zimri-Lim 244
Zion 17, 31, 66; tradition of inviolability 31, 298
Zipporah 49
Zodiac 242
Zoroastrianism 34, 36, 319

INDEX OF CITATIONS

Hebrew Bible

NB: the Hebrew order of the books is followed here.

Genesis 1–Exodus 12 63
Genesis 96
  1–3 95
  1 63, 94, 215
  3 221
  6–9 143
  6.1–4 168
  14 99
  14.18–20 274
  24.50–57 303
  24.57 303
  32.23–33 220
  34 73, 105
  36.33–34 105
  46.2 244
Exodus 3.2–5 220
  12.43–49 295
  13.11–15 137
  19.6 34
  20–23 25
  20.3 217
  20.4 218
  23.3 89
  23.10–11 142
  29.38–42 139
  32.10–11 161
  34.19–20 137
Leviticus 95, 164
  1–16 136
  1–15 195
  1–7 138
  1.1–9 130
  2.14–16 137
  4.20 130

4.26 130
4.31 130
4.35 130
5.10 130
5.13 130
5.16 130
5.18 130
5.26 (Eng. 6:7) 130
6.12–16 139
7–8 289
7.19–21 139
7.29–36 137
8.10–12 272
10.7 289
11–15 136, 139
12 140
12.6 140
12–15 140
14.50–51 139
15.19–24 140
16 131, 224
18.22 304
19.22 130
23.9–14 141
23.15 141
23.36 142
23.40 142
25 63
25.8–17 142
25.10–11 143
25.19–22 142
25.23–34 142
26 298
27 137

27.16–24 142
27.26–27 137
27.32–33 138
27.34 39
Numbers 3 135
4 135
8 135
9.6–7 139
12.1 72
15.15 295
15.25 130
15.26 131
15.28 131
16 136
17.5 135
17.18–21 136
18 135
18.12–18 137
18.21–32 137
18.24 39
19.17 139
24.4 244
24.7 277
25 287
28.3–8 139
35.1–8 137
36.4 142
36.13 39
Deuteronomy 34
5.7 217
5.8 218
6.4 217
7.1–5 34
9.20 161
10.9 39
12.4–14 213
12.11 131
12.12 39
13.17–19 137
13.18 137
14.22–29 137
14.28–29 138
15.1–3 142
15.12–15 142
17.8–13 136
18.1–2 137
18.4 137
18.9–14 19
19.17 136
21.5 136
22.6–7 89
23.4–9 295

24.8 136
25.5–10 25
26.1–11 137
28 298
28.1 39
31.9–13 136
31.24–26 136
32.8 214
33.8 136
33.10 136
Joshua 24 212
Judges 155
6.11–22 220
13.2–23 220
1 Samuel 179
1.9–13 172
1.28 154
2.5 154
3.1–15 244
4.4 221
6.8 244
9.9 154
10.1 289
15.22–23 213
16.1 289
16.13 289
18.29 139
19.12 144
20.25 144
24.7 289
28 250
2 Samuel 2.8 213
6.2 221
12.20 172, 173
13.1–13 303
17.15 144
21.7 213
22.11 221
24.1 221
24.15–17 220
28 94
1 Kings 71
6.23–28 221
6.29 221
6.32 221
6.35 221
8 172
8.34 298
8.46–43 298
12–13 213
14.15 212
15.13 214

16.31–32 213
18–19 213, 214
18.3 213
18.30–32 213
22.5–28 213
22.13–28 244
22.19–22 220
2 Kings 8.15–53 212
10.18–28 213
11–12 144
11 146
12.8–11 146
16.15 139
17.16 213
21.3 213
21.7 214
22.8–14 146
23.4 146
23.7 214
23.24 213
Isaiah 18
6.1–2 221
6.11–13 299
6.13 299
8.19–22 250
9.5–6 (Eng. 9.6–7) 272
13 19
14 97, 225
14.9–15 258
14.12–15 219
14.12 221
16.5 272
24–27 183, 259
26.19–21 259
27.1 215
27.19 267
40–55 34, 290
40.1–11 298
40.18–20 218
41.8–20 19
41.21–29 217
42.1–4 272
43.10–13 217
44.1 272
44.6–8 217
44.9–20 218
45 217
45.1–6 289
46.1–2 218
45.1 272
46.9 212
48.12–13 212

49.1–6 272
49.3 272
50.4–9 272
51.9–23 298
51.9–11 217
51.9–10 215
51.10–11 67
52.13–53.12 272
52.14–15 272
56–66 18–19
56 18, 66
56.2–6 141
56.3–7 19
56.7 173
57.3–13 250
57.13–19 19
58.12 19
60.7 19
60.17 19
60 19
61.1 275
62.6–9 19
62.8–9 19
63.1–6 19
64.9–10 19
65.1–7 250
65.11–12 19
65.17–26 258
65.17–25 119
66.1–4 183
66.3–4 19
66.15–16 19
66.17 19
66.18–24 19
Jeremiah 155, 161, 179
2 212
10.2–10 218
17.24–25 272
18 18
23.5–6 272
24 67, 245
25.11–12 247
29–52 66
29 67
29.10 247
30.8–9 272
32.6–15 137
33.12–26 272
34.8–16 142
41.4–5 30
44.17–19 213
44.25 213

Ezekiel 1 221
  1.1 244
  4.4–5 247
  4.5 206
  6.11 119
  8.3 244
  10 221
  16 168
  21.26–27 213
  23 168
  23.40 220
  28 221, 225
  28.12–18 220
  33 18
  34.23–30 272
  37 259, 281
  37.11–14 259
  37.24–25 272
  40–44 119
  40.45–46 135
  43.15–16 145
  44.10–15 135
  44.10–14 136
  44.13 136
  44.15–16 135
  44.23–24 136
  44.24 136
  46.13–15 139
Hosea 3.4 213
  14.9 154
  14.10 154
Joel 17, 183
  1.9 17
  1.13 17
  1.16 17
  2.12–14 18
  2.13–14 17
  2.14 17
  2.17 17
  2.18–27 17
  3.5 (Eng. 2.32) 17
  4.1 (Eng. 3.1) 17
  4.2–14 (Eng. 3.2–14) 17
  4.2 (Eng. 3.2) 17
  4.12–14 (Eng. 3.12–14) 17
  4.16–18 (Eng. 3.16–18) 17
  4.19 (Eng. 3.19) 17
  4.21 (Eng. 3.21) 17
Amos 7.7–9 245
  8.1–3 245
Obadiah 213
Jonah 17–18, 25

Habakkuk 245
Haggai 15–17, 32, 33, 319
  1.1 32
  1.2–11 16
  1.4–11 33
  1.8 16
  2.2 32
  2.4–9 16
  2.4 16
  2.11–13 136
  2.20–23 16
  2.21 32
Zechariah 15–17, 32, 33, 319
  1–8 235
  2.11–17 17
  3 16, 32
  3–4 33
  4 16, 32
  5 16
  6 16
  6.9–15 32
  6.9–13 17
  6.9–8.17 33
  8 17
  8.6 299
  8.11 299
  8.12 299
  9–14 183
  10.2 213
  12.7–10 272
  14 17
Malachi 15
  1.11 18
  1.12 16
  2.4–7 16
  3.1–5 17
  3.19–24 (Eng. 4.1–6) 17
Psalms 173
  2 289
  2.2 272
  2.7 216
  18.11 221
  23.1 154
  37.4 154
  50 144
  73–83 144
  74.8 173
  74.13–14 215
  82.1 214
  82.6 216
  89.7–8 214
  89.9–10 215

90.4 246
110.4 274
128 258
133.2 289
Proverbs 21–2, 51, 57, 161
1–9 88
1 226
1.8 22
1.20–33 226
6.20 22
8 226, 228
8.1–11 226
8.12–21 226
8.22–34 226
8.22 154
8.30 226
9 226
30–31 22
31.1–9 22
31.10–31 21, 22
31.27 21
Job 22–3, 51, 57, 105
1.6–12 221
2.1–7 221
4.13 244
7.14 244
15.7 273
20.8 244
28.12–28 67
26.12–13 215
28 23, 226
28.20–24 226
33.15 244
40–41 120
Song of Songs 25–6, 155, 216
Ruth 18, 24–5, 155, 157
1.16–17 295
Qohelet 42–4, 51, 55, 57, 61, 105, 329
1.2 43
1.14 43
2.13–14 43, 57
2.14–16 44
2.16 44
2.17 43
2.19 43
2.21 43
2.23 43
2.26 43
3.18–21 44
4.4 43
4.8 43
4.16 43

6.9 43
7.23–24 43, 57
8.5–8 44
8.16–17 43, 57
11.8 43
12.8 43
12.9–14 43
Esther 23–4, 179
Daniel 75, 183, 184, 198, 329
1–6 61
2 279
2.38 279
2.44 260
3 86
6 86
6.11 172, 173
7–12 61, 78, 81
7 97, 244, 276, 282
7.9 216
7.19–27 269
7.23–27 260
7.24–27 78
7.27 282
8.11–14 139
8.16 223
8.23–26 78
8.23–25 269
9 246, 247, 248
9.4–19 67
9.21 223
9.24–27 78
9.25 275
10 244
10.13 223
10.20–21 223
10.21 223
11 269
11.25–12.3 78
11.33–35 78
11.40–12.3 260
12.1–3 61, 81
12.1 223
12.2–3 260
12.2 177
Prayer of Azariah 172
Prayer of Manasseh 172
Song of the Three Young Men 172
Ezra 13–15, 32–4, 317
1–6 31, 32
1 32
1.8–11 32
2.36–63 136

2.41 143
2.60 15
2.63 136
3 32, 143
3.10–13 143
4–6 33
5.13–16 33
5.14–16 32
5.14 32
6.13–22 33
6.15 317
7–10 15
8.26–27 48
9–10 34
9 172
9.6–15 212
9.8–15 299
Nehemiah 13–15, 32–4, 317
1.1–7.4 (Eng. 1.1–7.5) 14
5.15–18 32
6.3 220
7.39–60 136
7.44 143
7.62 15
7.72 (Eng. 7:73)–8.12 15
7.72 (Eng. 7:73) 136
8–9 142
8 166
8.14–17 142
8.18 142
9–10 34
10.35 142
10.37–39 137
11.1–2 14
11.22–23 143
12.24 143
12.27–47 143
12.31–43 14
13.4–31 14
13.4–9 144
13.10 137
13.15–22 141
13.28 144
1 Chronicles 19–21
1–9 167
2.55 151
8.33 213
8.34 213
9.39 213
9.40 213
21.1 221
21.16–20 220

23–27 20
23.4 136
24 137
24.6 151
25 143, 144
2 Chronicles 19–21, 71
6.40 173
7.15 173
15.3 136
19.5–11 136
19.11 136
20.14–17 143
23–24 145
23 146
24.4–11 146
26.16–20 145, 146
31.6 138
34.9–18 145
34.13 151
34.14–22 146

Apocrypha, Pseudepigrapha, and other early Jewish writings

Abraham, Apocalypse of 117–20, 125
1–8 118, 218
9–32 118
10.3 118, 224
13 118, 224
14.5 118, 224
15–29 265
18 265
19 265
21–29 265
21.3 265, 268
22.5–23.13 118, 224
25 118
27 265
27.1–5 118
28–30 265
29.2 119
29.5–7 118, 224
29.14–21 265
29.15 119
29.17–18 118
30.2–8 119
31.1–4 119
31.1 119, 265
31.2–7 118, 224
31.2 119

Abraham, Testament of 100–1, 168
  A 1 263
  A 7 263
  A 11–14 263
  A 11–13 101
  A 12.16–18 101
  A 13.12 268
  A 14.1–11 101
  A 14.8 268
  A 19.7 101
  B 4 263
  B 7.15–16 101
  B 7.16 263
  B 8–11 101
  B 9–11 263
  B 9.9 268
  B 11.3–10 97
  B 13 263
Aristeas, Letter of (Pseudo-) 49, 56, 75–6
  4 306
  9–40 76
  12–13 322
  83–120 76
  95 143
  128–71 76
  134–43 76
1 Baruch 1.1–14 66–7
  1.15–3.8 172
  3.9–4.4 66, 67
  3.15–4.4 226
  3.20–23 226
  3.31–32 226
  3.36–4.1 226
  4.1 67
  4.5–5.9 66
2 Baruch 117–20, 125
  21.23 119
  27 119
  29–30 279
  29.4 120
  30 265
  30.2 119
  39–40 119
  39.7–40.3 119
  44.15 265, 268
  49–51 265
  50–51 119
  50 267
  53–74 264, 269
  53.6 119
  55.3 119
  59.2 265, 268

  64.7 265, 268
  69–70 270
  70 119
  70.9 119
  72–74 119
Ben Sira 22, 50–2, 57, 105, 167
  Prologue 153, 178
  7.29–31 51
  17.1–2 273
  17.7 222
  17.32 222
  24 67, 226
  24.2 222
  24.6–12 226
  24.23 226
  34.1–7 51
  34.6 52
  34.18–35.16 51
  36.20–21 51
  38.9–11 51
  38.24–39.11 51, 57
  39.1–3 51
  42.17 222
  44–50 153, 157, 178
  44–49 167
  45.2 222
  45.25 273
  46.1 237
  48.24–25 237
  49.16 273
  50.1–21 145
  51.13–30 226
1 Enoch 41–2, 58, 62–3, 97, 157, 167–8,
  222, 224
  1–36 41
  1.9 42
  3.2 216
  6 222
  7 222
  8 222
  9.7–10 222
  10.6 259
  14.8–25 42
  15.8–12 222
  17–19 42
  19.1 222
  20 222
  21 42
  22 42, 259, 268
  23–25 42
  26–27 42
  28–36 42

37.4 216
37–71 62, 97
38.2 216
38.4 216
38.6 216
39.6 276, 283
40 97
40.10 222
42.1–3 227
45 276, 283
46 276, 283
46.1 216
46.6 259
47.3 216
48 276, 283
48.2 216
49.2 276, 283
50 276, 283
51 276, 283
51.1 259
52 276, 283
53.6 276, 283
54 97
54.6 97
55.4 276, 283
56 97
56.1 222
60.2 216
61 276, 283
61.5 259
61.10 222
62 276, 283
63.11 276, 283
65–68 97
66.1 222
69 97
69.1–15 222
69.27–29 276, 283
71 97
71.1 222
71.10 216
71.14–17 276
72–82 41, 53, 58
82.13–20 222
83–85 62
83–90 62
83–105 62
85–90 78
86–89 62
89.73–90.5 62
89–90 273
90–105 62

90 81
90.6–15 62
90.33 259
91.10 259
91.12–17 62
92.3–4 259
93 62
93.2–9 269
98.2 63
99.5 63
102.3–104.6 259
102.5–11 63
103–104 63
104.2 63
104.5 259
104.10–12 63
105–7 62
106–7 97
108 62
108.11–12 63
2 Enoch 98–9, 216
 1–38 265
 1.3–5 222
 4–6 222
 7 222
 8–10 265
 8.8 222
 10 222
 10.1–3 268
 11–17 99
 11–12 222
 14 222
 18 222
 19 222
 20–21 222
 22.10–11 222
 24–32 99
 38–67 99
 41–42 265
 52.15 265
 59.3 99
 61.2–5 265
 65.6–11 265
 69–70 99
 69.12 99
 71–72 99
1 Esdras 14, 16, 157, 163
4 Ezra 117–20, 125, 168
 4.40–42 264
 5.1–13 264
 6.18–28 264, 270
 6.49–52 120

7 290
7.26–30 119
7.28–35 279
7.28 247
7.29 290
7.31–36 264
7.78–101 264
8.52–54 264
11–13 264
11–12 280
11.33–12.3 264
11.37–12.3 280
12.31–34 264
13 279, 280, 290
13.32 280
13.38 264, 268
13.39–50 264
14.10–12 119
14.35 264
14.44–46 155
14.48 246
Job, Testament of 23, 104–5, 224
1.6 105
2–5 105, 218
2.2 105
4.1 262
20.9 105
38.8–40.3 262
48.3 105
52.6–10 105
52.10 262
Joseph and Asenath 105–6
14–17 106
Jubilees 63–4, 216
1.29 260
2 63
2.25–33 64
4.30 246
5.1–11 222
6.17–31 63
6.32–38 63
10.1–14 222
15.1–4 63
16.30–31 142
17.15–18 223
17.20–31 63
22.1–9 63
22.1–4 299
23.20–22 260, 267
23.22–31 260
23.31 64
30.18–20 63

31.8–15 138
31.11–17 63
32.27–29 63
34.17–19 63
35–38 299
44.1–4 63
48.9–19 223
49 64, 141
49.17–21 141
49.6 141
50 64, 141
Judith 65–6, 167
4.2–3 66
4.6–8 66
4.11–15 66
4.12 66
4.14–15 66
8.4–6 172
8.6 66
8.21 66
8.24 66
8.36–10.2 173
9 65, 172
9.8 66
9.13 66
11.12–15 66
11.13 138
11.14 146
12.1–4 66
12.6–8 172
12.17–19 66
16.16–20 66
16.22 66
Levi, Testament of 101–4
16–18 (Greek) 103–4
Bodleian col. c, 9–21 (Cairo) 103
Liber Antiquitatum Biblicarum (Pseudo-
Philo) 94–95, 216
3.10 95
8.7–8 105
16.3 95
22.8–9 95
25–28 95
28.6–10 239
32.3 95
32.13 95, 264
33.3–5 95
33.3 264
33.5 264
44.10 95, 264
44 218
62.9 95

1 Maccabees 59–60
  1.56–57 60
  1.60–61 81
  2.21 216
  2.29–38 78
  2.39–42 184
  3.18 216
  4.44–46 237
  7.12–16 184
  8.17 71
  9.27 237, 239
  13.41–42 79
  14.41 237
2 Maccabees 59–60, 100, 177
  1–2 60
  1.10–2.18 59
  1.10 146
  2.13–15 154
  3 77
  3.10–11 53
  4 135
  4.11 47
  4.32–34 247
  4.39–50 78
  4.43–50 146
  6.10 81
  7 81
  7.9 261
  7.11 261
  7.14 261
  7.23 261
  9.19–27 325
  11.27–33 325
  11.27 146
  12.43–45 261
  14.6 184
  14.46 261
3 Maccabees 86, 177, 307
  1.3 297
4 Maccabees 99–100, 177
  1.1 100
  1.11 100
  6.29 100
  7.18–19 262
  9.7–9 262
  9.9 262, 268
  10.4 262
  13.17 100
  14.5–6 262
  15.3 100
  16.25 262
  17.4–6 262

  17.5 100
  17.18 100
  17.21 100
  18.23 100
Moses, Apocalypse of 95–7, 216
  13.3–5 96
  13.3–6 96, 264
  15–30 96
  22.3 97
  29 97
  32.4 96, 264
  33 97
  37.3 97
  37.5 96
  40.1–2 96
  40.2 97
  43.1–3 264
Moses, Testament of 61, 74–5, 81, 168
  5.1–6.1 75
  6.2–9 74
  9 75, 178
Naphthali, Testament of 102, 103
Pseudo-Phocylides 88–9
  8 89
  54 89
  84–85 89
  102–15 89, 262
  102 89
  147–48 89
  175–206 89
Sibylline Oracles 64–5, 73, 81, 97–8, 120,
  125
  3 81, 278
  3.1–96 120
  3.46–63 98
  3.63–74 120
  3.75–92 98
  3.84–92 268
  3.97–349 64
  3.185–86 65
  3.193 64
  3.213–64 65
  3.286–94 65
  3.318 64
  3.319–20 65
  3.350–80 97
  3.350–64 269
  3.489–829 64, 65
  3.520–72 269
  3.564–67 65
  3.595–607 65
  3.601–18 64

3.608 64
3.624–34 120
3.635–56 265
3.652 64
3.657–68 265
3.669–701 265
3.702–95 265
3.702–31 280
3.715–19 65
3.741–95 65
3.762–66 65
3.772–73 65
4 120
4.4–30 120
4.40–114 64
4.102–29 265
4.102–14 64
4.115–36 120
4.130–78 270
4.130–51 265
4.130–48 269
4.152–78 265
4.159–61 268
4.165 120
4.171–78 268
4.179–92 265
5 120, 278
5.1–13 270
5.93–110 265
5.108–9 280
5.137–154 120
5.137–54 265
5.155–61 280
5.162–78 269
5.179–99 280
5.214–27 265
5.256–59 265, 280
5.361–85 265
5.361–80 120
5.397–413 120
5.414–25 265
5.414–28 280
5.420–24 266
5.447–530 270
5.447–83 266
5.484–511 266
5.501–3 65
5.512–31 266
5.527–31 268
Solomon, Psalms of 84–5
1.4–8 85
2.1–14 85

2.2–5 85
2.15–31 85
2.31 85
3.10–12 261
3.11–12 85
4 85
8.1–22 85
8.11–22 85
13.11 261
14.1–5 261
14.3–5 85
14.6–9 261
14.9–10 85
15.12–13 261
17–18 85
17.5–18 299
17.5–15 85
17.21 276
17.22–25 276
17.22 85
17 273
17.35 276
Solomon, Testament of 84, 250–1
Tobit 24, 44–5, 157, 167, 221, 328
1.4–6 45
1.6–8 45
1.8 45
1.11 45
1.16–17 45
1.17–19 45
2.1–3 173
2.1–5 45
2.3–8 45
2.6 45
2.14 45
3 172
3.7–9 45
3.8 221
3.17 45
4.3–4 45
4.8–11 45
4.15 45
5.4–5 45
6.13 45
6.15 45
7.11–13 45
8.1–3 45
8.7 45
12.6–21 45
12.8–9 45
13.6 300
14.3 45

14.4–7 299
14.10–11 45
14.11–13 45
Vita Adae et Euae 95–7, 216
1.1–22.2 96
6–10 97
12–16 97, 223
25–29 96
49.1–50.2 96
51.1–2 264
Wisdom, Book of (Wisdom of Solomon)
86–8, 100, 110, 156, 217
1.13–15 262
2.23 262
3.4 262
3.7–9 88
4.1 262
6–12 227
6–7 227
6.17–18 227
7.12 227
7.15–20 227
7.22–23 227
7.22 227
7.25–26 227
8.2–3 227
8.5–8 227
8.13 262
8.17 262
8.19–20 88
10 227
11–19 88
11 227
12.24–13.19 88
13–19 227
13–15 218
15.3 262
15.18–19 88

6.11–20 203
7.6–7//19.2–3 203
7.6 202
9.10–16 202
10.10–13 202
10.14–11.18 203
11.18–21 203
12.1–2 203
12.19–14.16 202
12.23–13.1 274
14.12–16 202
15.5 203
16.10–12 203
16.13 203
19.2 202
19.10–11 274
20.14–15 247
1Q21 103
1Q32 119
1Q33 223
1Q34 172
1Q34^{bis} 172
1QH 172, 202
1QH 11.19–22 260
1QH 11.27–36 260
1QH 14.29 260
1QH 14.34 260
1QH 19.3–14 260
1QH 19.12 260
1QIs^{a} 160, 272
1QIs^{b} 160
1QM 202, 223, 274
1QM 1 223
1QM 1.10–11 223
1QM 7.3 203
1QpHab 167
1QpHab 7.1–5 181
1QpHab 7.3–5 238
1QS 202, 203
1QS 1.11–12 202
1QS 3.4–5 202
1QS 3.13–4.26 223
1QS 4.11–14 260, 268
1QS 4.12 223
1QS 5.1–22 202
1QS 5.13–14 202
1QS 6.2 202
1QS 6.6–8 180
1QS 6.8–10 202
1QS 6.10–13 202
1QS 6.13–23 202
1QS 6.16–23 202

Dead Sea Scrolls

Damascus Document (CD) 199, 202
1.1–11 206
1.4–9 53
1.5–11 247
1.5–6 206
1.11–12 260
2.18–21 223
4.10–5.2 203
4.12–21 223
5.17–19 223

1QS 6.25 202
1QS 7.2–3 202
1QS 7.13 202
1QS 9.9–11 238
1QS 9.11 274
1QSa 1.1 260
1QSa 1.4 203
1QSa 1.9–11 203
1QSa 2.11 274
1QSa 202
2Q24 119
4Q22 = 4QpaleoExod^m 161
4Q37 = 4Q^j 214
4Q119–22 = 4QLXX ^{a,b}, 4QLXXNum,
    4Q 161
4Q156–57 = 4QtgJob 164, 230
4Q174 = 4QFlorilegium 69
4Q177 69
4Q186 243
4Q213–14b = 4Q TLevi^{a–f} ar 103
4Q213 = 4Q TLevi^a ar, frag. 5 103
4Q214b, frags 2–6, 1:2–6 103
4Q245 290
4Q246 274, 275
4Q266–73 202
4Q266 2.1–11 206
4Q285 274, 275
4Q318 242
4Q385 260
4Q397 frags 14–21.10 = 4Q398 frags
    14–17.2–3 154
4Q400–7 = 4QShirShabb^{a–h} 172, 223
4Q491–496 = 4QM1–6 223
4Q503 172
4Q504–6 = 4QDibHam^{a–c} 173
4Q507–9 172
4Q521 274, 275
4Q521 2.II.7–8 275
4Q521 2.II.12–13 275
4Q534 248
4Q541 272, 275
4Q544 = 4QVisions of Amram^b 223
4Q554–55 119
4Q559 246
4Q560 250
4QEn^c 62
4QFlor frag. 1, II, 3, 24, 5:3 238
4QFlorilegium 165
4QJer^a (4Q70) 161
4QMidrEschat^{a,b} 69
4QMMT 69, 156, 185, 186, 196
4QMMT frags 14–17:2–3 154

4QpHab 7.1–6 245
4QpHab 202
4QpPs^a 2.6–8 247
4QprNab 251
4QTNaph (4Q215) 103
5Q12 202
5Q15 119
6Q15 202
5/6HevEp15 142
8HevXIIgr 162
11Q13 223
11Q17 = 11QShirShabb 172, 223
11Q18 119
11QMelchizedek 99
11QMelchizekek 2.9 275
11QMelchizedek 2.17–18 275
11QPs^a 154, 226
11QT 196
11QT 19–25 142
11Q10 = 11QtgJob 164, 230
XHev/Se ar 13 304
Yahad ostracon 70
MasShirShabb 223
Mur 88 160
Giants, Book of 41

Philo

Abr. 62–84 242
    120–31 229
Agr. 50 154
    51 229
Cher. 27–30 229
    27 238
Conf. 146 229
    176–82 261
    177 224
Congr. 57 262
    97 261
Ebr. 31 154
Flaccus 47–49 173
    53 173
Fug. 66 261, 224
    68–71 261
    94–118 229
    97 229
    108–9 229
    109 227
Gig. 6–16 223
    12–16 261

Hyp. 11.1–17 200
  11.1 200, 202
  11.4–5 200
  11.4 202
  11.5 202
  11.6 201
  11.8–9 201
  11.11 202
  11.12 201
  11.14–17 200
Leg. ad Gaium 6 229
  132–134 173
  361 307
Leg. Alleg. 2.3 216
  1.31–42 261
  2.77 261
  3.96 229
Migr. Abr. 34–35 238
  38 154
Mut. 115 154
  139 154
  143 154
  223 261
Plant. 14 223
  39 154
  138 154
Post. 39 262
Praem. 40 216
  94–95 277
Probus 75–87 200
  75 200, 203
  76 200, 201–2
  79 201
  81 202
  84 201
  85–86 200, 202
  86 202
Quaes. Exod. 2.68 229
Quaes. Gen. 1.4 229
  2.62 229
  3.11 261
  4.74 261
Quis Heres 78 154
  259–66 238
Quod Det. 81–85 261
Quod Deus 6 154
  10 154
  11 228
  139 154
Somn. 1.34 261
  1.67 229
  1.151 261

  1.215 229
  1.229–30 229
  1.254 154
  2.164–65 238
  2.242 154
  2.250 299
Spec. Leg. 1.156 138
  4.178 299
  67–70 148
Virt. 62 154
  95 138
Vita Contemp. 2 229
Vita Mosis 1.263–99 238

Josephus

War 1.2.8 §§67–69 188
  1.5.1–4 §§107–19 81
  1.5.2–3 §§110–14 187
  1.8.5 §170 145
  1.13.9 §270 109
  1.22.1 §433–34 109
  1.27.1 §537 145
  1.28.3 §559 145
  1.29.2 §§571 187
  1.33.2–4 §§648–55 252
  2.5.2 §100 297
  2.6.1–2 §§80–91 110
  2.8.2–13 §§120–61 200
  2.8.2 §§120–21 200
  2.8.3 §122 200, 202
  2.8.4 §124 200, 202
  2.8.5 §128 201
  2.8.6 §135 201
  2.8.7 §§137–42 201, 202
  2.8.8 §§143–44 201
  2.8.9 §147 203
  2.8.10 §150 201
  2.8.11 §§154–58 201
  2.8.12 §159 201
  2.8.13 §160 201
  2.8.14 §§162–66 187
  2.13.3 §§254–57 286
  2.13.4–5 §§258–64 252
  2.13.5 §§261–63 239
  2.14.4 §285 173
  2.15.6 §331 146
  2.16.2 §336 146
  2.17.2–3 §§410–11 188
  2.17.6–9 §§425–48 286
  2.17.6 §425 142

2.17.8–9 §§433–34 286
2.20.4 §567 201
2.22.1 §651 287
3.2.1 §11 201
3.8.1–7 §§340–91 263
3.8.3 §§351–52 245
3.8.9 §§399–407 245
4.3.3–9 §§135–61 287
4.4.3 §236 70
4.6.3 §388 279
5.1.1–3 §§1–20 288
6.2.1 §109 279
6.5.2 §285–87 239
6.5.4 §311 247
7 125
7.8.1–9.2 §§252–406 286
7.10.1 §§410–19 286
7.10.2 §423 82
7.11.1–3 §§437–50 239
Ant. Proem. 3 §13 246
1.7.2 §158 242
1.8.2 §§166–68 242
4.4.3 §68 138
4.6.4 §115 300
4.7.2 §165 239
4.8.1–46 §§176–314 93
4.8.8 §205 138
4.8.22 §240 138
6.5.6 §359 239
6.6.3 §115 239
6.12.4–5 §§254 239
7.4.1 §76 239
7.14.7 §§365–67 137
8.2.5 §§45–49 251
8.15.6 §418 238
10.10.3–4 §§195–210 279
10.10.4 §§208–10 279
10.11.4 §§245–49 239
10.11.7 §§267–69 239
11.7.1 §§297–301 135
11.7.6 §322 239
12.1.1 §8 55
12.3.3–4 §§138–46 46
12.3.3 §141 48
12.3.3 §143 48
12.3.4 §§145–46 47
12.4.1–11 §§154–236 40
12.4.1 §§158–59 40
12.4.2 §§160-66 145
12.9.7 §387 82
13.5.8 §166 146
13.5.9 §171–72 188

13.6.1–6 §§407–32 81
13.10.5–7 §§288–99 188
13.10.6 §§293–300 80
13.10.7 §299 239
13.11.2 §311 201
13.15.5–16.1 §§401–8 188
13.16.1–5 §§408–23 189
14.2.1 §§22–24 253
14.5.4 §91 145
14.9.3 §167 146
14.9.4–5 §§168–80 146
14.9.4 §175 146
14.10.8 §§213–16 309
15.1.1 §3 189
15.7.10 §259 304
15.10.4 §§365–71 109
15.10.5 §373 201
15.11.3–5 §§391–20 135
16.2.3–5 §§27–65 109
16.7.6 §§221–25 303
16.11.1–3 §§357–67 145
17.2.4–3.1 §§41–47 189
17.6.2–4 §§149–67 252
17.13.3 §§347–48 201
18.1.1 §§4–10 285
18.1.3 §§4–23 189
18.1.5 §18 201
18.1.6 §23 285
18.4.3 §§92–95 110
19.6.3 §§300–5 173
20.2.1–5 §§17–53 114
20.1.1–2 §6–13 110
20.2.3–4 §§41–43 295
20.2.5 §§49–53 303
20.5.1 §§97–99 111
20.5.2 §100 87
20.8.5 §§162–66 286
20.8.6 §§167–72 111
20.8.8 §181 138
20.8.10 §188 239
20.9.1 §§199–200 149
20.9.2 §206 138
20.9.3 §§208–10 286
20.9.5 §215 285
20.9.6 §§216–18 143
Life 1 §2 137
2 §9 93
2 §§10–12 189
2 §§10–11 200
2 §12 93
5 §§21 190
10–12 186

12 §63 138
12 §64 145
13 §69 145
15 §80 138
34 §169 145
38 §§190–91 194
39 §197 190
54 §277 173
66 §368 145
76 §422 137
76 §§424–25 239
Ag. Apion 74
 1.1 §1 246
 1.8 §§37–43 94
 1.22 §§176–83 310
 1.22 §§192 55
 1.22 §§201–4 241
 2.8 §§91–95 308
 2.8 §§102–4 135, 141
 2.30 263

**New Testament and early
Christian writings**

Matthew 1 245
 3.7–10 193
 4.17 216
 5.3 216
 9.10–13 193
 11.2–5 275
 12.1–8 193
 12.9–14 193
 12.27–28 250
 12.38 193
 15.1–20 193
 16.1 193
 19.3–12 193
 21.45 193
 22.15–22 193
 22.15–16 193
 22.41–46 193
 23.2 193
 24 266, 270
 26.35 172
Mark 192, 197
 2.6 193
 2.15–17 193
 2.23–28 193
 3.1–6 193
 7.1–23 193
 7.5 193

8.11 193
10.2–12 193
12.13–17 193
12.13 193
12.35–37 193
12.38 193
13 266, 270
14.12–25 141
14.32 172
Luke 3.7–9 193
 5.21 193
 5.29–32 193
 6.1–5 193
 6.6–11 193
 7.1–5 174
 7.19–22 275
 11.37–41 193
 11.39–52 192
 16.18 193
 16.19–31 266
 20.20–26 193
 20.41–44 193
 21 266, 270
 22.39 172
 23.43 266
 24.44–47 272
 24.44 156
John 197, 199
 1.1–5 229
 7.37 142
 9.13–34 180
 9.22–35 193
 12.42 193
Acts 197, 199
 1.6–7 281
 1.13–14 173
 2.46–3.1 173
 2.46 172
 3.1 172
 4.1–2 194
 5.17–39 194
 5.21–41 146
 5.34 194
 5:36 111
 5.42 172
 6.5 295
 16.1–3 296
 16.9–10 245
 17.32 263
 18.9 245
 21.37–38 252
 21.38 111

22–23 194
22.3 194
23 185
23.6–9 266
23.8–9 187
23.8 194
25.24 303
25.26 303
26.2 303
26.19 303
26.27 303
Romans 1.26–27 304
1 Corinthians 181
2 Corinthians 12.1–4 245
Galatians 3.29 294
Philippians 3.4–6 192
Hebrews 99, 195
  5 274
  7 274
  10.4 130
2 Peter 3.8 246
Jude 9 75
  14–16 156
  14–15 42
Revelation 6 119
  6.1–8 119
  6.9–11 119
  8–9 119
  12 120
  13 269
  13.1–8 118
  15–16 119
  17 118, 269
  18 119
  20 266
  20.1–6 119
  20.4–15 119
  20.4 246
  21 119
Barnabas 15.4 246
Origen, *De Princ.* 3.2.1 75
Eusebius, *His. Eccl.* 4.26.13–14 156
  Praep. Evang. 9.17.3–4 242
  Praep. Evang. 9.29.1–3 49

Rabbinic writings

Mishnah 116, 122, 125, 181, 195, 198
  Avot 2.8 123
  Bekorot 9.1–8 138

Ḥag. 2.4 141
Maʿaser Sheni 138
Menaḥ. 5.6 137
Menaḥ. 10.3 141
Miq. 4.5 196
Neziqin 122, 195
Parah 3.7 195
Peʾah 8.2 138
Qodašim 195
Rosh ha-Sh. 1.1 142
Rosh ha-Sh. 1.7 143
Shab. 1:4 196
Sukk. 2.7 196
Sukk. 4.1–6 142
Taan. 3.8 253
Yad. 3.5 155
Yad. 4.6–8 196
Tosefta 117, 198
  Hag. 3.35 195
  Negaʿim 1:16 = Zuckermandel 619
  113
  Parah 3.8 195
  Yad. 2.20 196
Avot de Rabbi Natan 4 122
Jerusalem Talmud
  Ned. 5.6 196
Babylonian Talmud
  B. Batra 134a 196
  Hag. 13a 155
  Meg. 7a 155
  Men. 45a 155
  Qidd. 66a 188
  Shab. 13b 155
  Sukk. 28a 196
  Sukk. 52a–52b 281
  Taʿanit 23a 81
  Yeb. 46a 295

Inscriptions and ancient Near Eastern writings

ANET 321 213
AP 15 29, 304
  21 29, 141
  22.124–25 214
  30–32 28, 29
  30–31 32
  30.18–19 28, 146
  31 28
  44.3 214

Arad 16.3 212
  18.2 212
  18.9 212
  21.2 212
  21.4 212
  40.3 212
CPJ 1 39
  1.11–15 55
  1.118–21 55
  1.118–30, texts ##1–6 39
  1.147–78 55
  2.25–107 305
  3.519 77
  4 39, 40
  6 39
Cyrus Cylinder (ANET 315–16) 31
  Davies 1991 #8.017 214
  1991 #15.005 212
  1991 #25.003 214
KAI #181.14–18 212
  ##183–88 213
  #192.2 212
  #192.5 212
  #193.3 212
  #194.3 212
  #194.9 212
  #195.1 212
  #195.7–8 212
  #196.1 212
  #196.12 212
  #197.1 212
KTU 1.3.3.37–42 215
  1.5.1.1–3 215
  1.6.1.39–63 221
  1.23 221
  2 215
Nimrud Prism 4.29–33 218
TAD A4.1 29, 141
  A4.7–9 28, 29
  A4.7–8 32
  A4.7.18–19 28, 146
  A4.8 28
  B2.6 304
  B3.8 304

B7.3.3 214
C3.15.127–8 214
TSSI #2 213
  #12 ii.2 212
  #12 ii.5 212
  #12 iii.3 212
  #12 iii.9 212
  #12 iv.1 212
  #12 v.7–8 212
  #12 vi.1 212
  #12 vi.12 212
  #12 ix.1 212
  #16.14–18 212
Theodotus inscription 328

Greek and Roman writings

Agatharchides of Cnidus (*GLAJJ*
  ##301a) 114, 141
Apion (*GLAJJ* #170) 219
Artemidorus, *Oneirocritica* 1.1–3 244
Cassius Dio 37.17.2–3 218
Damocritus (*GLAJJ* #247) 219
Diodorus Siculus 34–35.1.3 219
  40.3.1–7 37
  40.3.4 218, 307–8
Frontinus (*GLAJJ* #229) 141
Horace, *Sermones* 1.9.68–70 307
Juvenal, *Satires* 6.542–47 245
Livy, apud *Scholia in Lucanum* 2.593 218
Meleager (*GLAJJ* #43) 141
Mnaseas of Patara (*GLAJJ* 1.97–100)
  219
Ovid, *Ars Amatoria* 1.75–76 307
  (*GLAJJ* ##141–43) 141
Pliny, *Nat. His.* 5.73 70, 200
Plutarch, *Ques. conviv.* 6.2 218
Strabo 16.2.35 218, 307
Suetonius, *Vesp.* 4.5 278
Tacitus, *Hist.* 5.5 218
  5.13.2 278
Varro, apud Augustine, *De civ. Dei* 4.31
  218

424